LIVE AID

LIVE AID

THE DEFINITIVE 40-YEAR STORY

PAUL VALLELY

new modern

new modern

First published in the UK in 2025 by New Modern
An imprint of Putman Publishing
Mermaid House, Puddle Dock, Blackfriars, London, EC4V 3DB

@newmodernbooks
@newmodernbooks

Hardback ISBN: 978-1-917923-38-5
Trade paperback ISBN: 978-1-917923-41-5
eBook ISBN: 978-1-917923-40-8
Audio ISBN: 978-1-917923-39-2

A CIP catalogue record for this book is available in the British Library.

Publishing and editorial: Pete Selby and James Lilford
Typesetting: Marie Doherty

1 3 5 7 9 10 8 6 4 2

New Modern is an imprint of Putman Publishing
www.newmodernbooks.co.uk
www.putmanpublishing.co.uk

MIX
Paper | Supporting
responsible forestry
FSC
www.fsc.org   FSC® C018072

Printed and bound in Great Britain by Clays Ltd, Elcograf S.p.A.

for Christine
always

ABOUT THE AUTHOR

Paul Vallely was covering the 1984–85 famine in Ethiopia for *The Times* when he and Bob Geldof first met. Inspired by his on-the-ground reporting, Geldof asked him to travel across Africa with him in 1985 to decide how to spend the £140 million raised by Live Aid.

He co-wrote Bob's bestselling autobiography *Is That It?* and wrote a number of publications on Live Aid and Live 8 for the Band Aid Trust. In 1990, he wrote a pioneering study, *Bad Samaritans: First World Ethics and Third World Debt*, which set Geldof and Bono on the charity-to-justice journey from Live Aid to Live 8.

He also worked as Geldof's adviser on the Commission for Africa, which laid the groundwork for the Gleneagles G8 pressurising world leaders to double aid to Africa and cancel its debts. He wrote the Penguin edition of the *Commission for Africa* report and was a co-author of its full report, *Our Common Interest*. He was chair of two international development agencies, Traidcraft and the Catholic Institute for International Relations and is a senior research fellow at the Global Development Institute, University of Manchester.

CONTENTS

FOREWORD

Forty years ago, I wrote a book called *Is That It?*. I needed to make some money after spending two years working on Band Aid and Live Aid and their consequences – one of which was that I was broke and the bills needed paying. The other was that the fame that I was familiar with from being in a big rock 'n' roll band had metastasised into a vast universal glow of approbation, ranging from reluctantly admitted admiration to a sort of semi-religious hysteria. It was unnerving. People projected upon me all the qualities they wished that they possessed or all the goodness and selflessness they wished could govern the sad Hobbesian human condition. Wrong guy.

Walking into a restaurant or onto an aeroplane, the entire room or fuselage would rise and erupt into applause. Normally, people who see a famous face become skittish if encountered on a street or otherwise going about the necessities of the everyday. Now, old ladies, seeing me, would stand rooted to the spot, their hands to their mouths, before hesitantly approaching, reaching out a tentative, trembling hand to touch me. Upon contact, they would begin to sob. Some would collapse into my arms or hug me. It was unbearable. I just wanted to go back to work, to play rock 'n' roll. Brother Teresa I ain't!

I wrote my autobiography to make some cash and tell the actuality of my life hitherto, and in so doing hopefully dispel the awful cult of personality that had suddenly, bewilderingly, sprung up around some imaginary character conjured in the public mind by the massive movement engendered by Live Aid. Foolishly, naïvely but perhaps understandably, while the populist hoopla swirled about me, I thought, *Now what…?*

This book by Paul Vallely is the answer. I've known Vallely for, oh, for ever. We're mates. It was his writing in *The Times* that I followed. The clarity of the prose. The way he could tell the story of a vast famine by focusing on a specific person whom he would allow to tell their story. In so doing, the awful pity of the people caught in this maelstrom of suffering bore through you to the pit of your soul and stirred a profound rage at the terrible unfairness, the injustice of it all. When he got thrown out and banned by the thugs running Ethiopia in 1985, I knew I could trust him. That's not something I would admit to for any other journalist! I called him and he spoke with knowledge and understanding of the reality of the situation he had reported on – stuff that couldn't be told then or there simply wasn't enough space. He informed me. When I went to Africa to look at how to spend the Live Aid millions, I asked him to come with me. He's been on the long journey with me ever since, offering advice, thoughts, information and friendship. He knows the story backwards because he's part of it. He writes so much I've forgotten, or actually didn't know was happening in the first place, within what someone called 'arguably the greatest mass civil rights movement in history'.

So this is not the continuation of the autobiography, which Paul had helped me write. It's not *Is That It?* part 2. It's not 'What Bob Did Next', except partially – because Band Aid simply couldn't go away. It was too huge. It had touched all corners of the world and seemingly all corners of the human heart, imagination and mind. I'm aware of how corny that sounds, but how else does one explain the extraordinary outpouring of celebratory memory engendered this fortieth anniversary year by television documentaries, theatrical productions, re-releases or new interpretations of the original records? Or this book?

Of course, for me – floundering in the wake of Live Aid's enormity – there could be no going back, although I didn't understand that then and would certainly have rejected the notion that, forty years later, I would wake every morning with ten or twelve Band Aid emails detailing today's awfulness from the Horrorlands. I just wanted to get back to my job of being a rock 'n' roll singer in a rock 'n' roll band. But I kind of wasn't allowed to. I was now, whether I wanted to be or not, canonised St Bob! And saints don't write rock songs.

But haloes are heavy things. So, of course, I continued making and escaping into music anyway. Albums, songs, tours and – unbelievably, wonderfully, amazingly – the Boomtown Rats celebrate our fiftieth year this year. Who'd have thought? Who'd have thought any of it, in fact?! It's been a year of anniversaries. Not just Live Aid; it's also twenty years since we organised the Live 8 concerts in the home countries of the eight world leaders who could do something about the unbearable yoke of debt which hung around the necks of the people of Africa.

That began with a challenge from Vallely. He wrote somewhere: 'For all his skill as a populist, Bob Geldof could not shift the agenda from one of charity to one of justice.' That stung! But it set me on an extraordinary adventure just as improbable, just as thrilling, just as profound and, without any shadow of doubt, just as impactful and bonkers as all the records, concerts, bands, performances, trucks, ships, food aid and all the other stuff. It took me from pop and poverty through the practicalities of politics to learn how to pull on the levers of power.

But whatever my desire and need to return to the music which came naturally to me, I was also obliged to continue with Band Aid and what flowed from it. It had become simply too big. The responsibility was, at least it seemed to me, to take this thing we had conjured out of the flimsiest soil to its ultimate logical political/economic conclusion. But obviously not by myself. I understood this at the absolute very beginning of all of it when I made that phone call to Midge Ure, my fellow writer/singer/musician. I made many calls like that. Always the same. 'Will you help?' The answer was always the same: 'Yes.'

Band Aid had worked. For once in our bloody lives, something had actually worked exactly as we had imagined, but on a vastly different scale to anything any of us had anticipated. The people who, for whatever personal and or professional reason, had gathered about me to enable the realisation of this absurdly normal and originally pedestrian idea of using your ability – in my case, writing tunes – to stop others starving, were, as you will read, extraordinarily gifted individuals, each to their own professions but equally as personalities and as thinking, adventurous, daring compassionate human beings. They were a bunch of rebels or outlaws by inclination and by any standard, but so very good at their jobs; whatever their chosen profession, they had made it to the top. Others gave up everything, tossing up their lives to gather round this struggling Irishman to make his mad, blustering convictions a brilliant reality. No one got paid. Ever. They just ... did it. 'Cos they could. And they wanted to. And it was working. So why stop?

Millions of lives were saved in those terrible years of the Great African Famine of 1984–87. And then – down the years, daily, indeed to the very second that I am writing this – Band Aid continues to administer vast monies gathered still from individuals, record royalties, YouTube Live Aid channels etc., and directed immediately to the poorest, most wounded, hurt and hungry of those most politically benighted war-torn, climate-ravaged parts of northern Ethiopia, Sudan, Somalia and elsewhere. Millions of people had been wantonly slaughtered, raped and dispossessed by whichever thug can gather a bunch of killers around them and rain mayhem, chaos and ruin down upon the innocent.

Through the years, the logic of what we were doing became evident. We could – and would – continue as we had always done, distributing monies to the affected peoples and regions, but we could also 'weaponise' Live Aid's vast audience and turn it into the biggest political lobby for change the world had ever seen. Yes, certainly keep as many people alive as possible and then help provide education, housing, sanitation, healthcare, farming implements, etc. Band Aid did, and does, all of that. But if this misery was ever to stop, then the root causes of this condition needed to be addressed, attacked and, as much as possible, rectified and altered. That was the journey from Band Aid to Live Aid to Live 8 and beyond. This book tells that story.

Poverty is an economic condition. It is empirical. It is not always natural and it is unnecessary. Indeed, its continuation is very much against anyone's interests. It is at the root of almost all human conflicts. Scarcity of any kind of resource will push individuals and whole peoples to extreme behaviour in a desperate endeavour to alter their situation. It pushes them to leave their homes and head into mass migration on small boats.

A generation of young people grew up deeply affected by their personal experience of that glorious day in July 1985. Many became politicians, or changed their career ambitions and decided to study what had been exposed to them by Live Aid and the vast human outpouring of compassion. We were an often tragic and awful species, but we were also a brilliant and loving one. There was hope. But hope is not a plan. And if Live Aid had shown us anything, it had clearly demonstrated that, by perhaps working outside of or around the normal channels of change, things could be different, that the world isn't immutable. Change can happen. Change is necessary, it is desirable, it is inevitable and, should you want to – and as Live Aid proved – the individual is not powerless in a world of seemingly vast indifference to you or, well, anything! You could be a cog, however small, in tilting the world towards justice. You yourself could actually change things.

In 1985, after Live Aid, I was seized by an intuition. The concert, and the improbably vast audience of shared sentiment, and the torrent of cash that poured in, was not only what had made it rock 'n' roll's most glorious day. There was also a sort of collective shift or shudder of some common knowledge. An unspoken conscious realisation had emerged – no matter how fleetingly – that we were better than we thought. We were alright. Not everything was hopeless. Not every effort a waste. That there was other stuff just as important and possible as simply living, doing the job, raising the kids. Back in 1985, I wrote – and I'm quite amazed now writing this that I understood the significance of that momentary societal flicker – 'the avenues of possibility have been opened up. Walk down them.'

Many, many did. And a different bunch of smart, young economists, developmental wonks, political strategists and others gathered about the Band Aid axis and began the journey of which most of you are unaware but which is described in this book. On this extraordinary adventure, together, we ultimately altered the economic, political, structural and, crucially, conversational dynamic between the North and South, between rich and poor, between 'us' and 'them'.

But now we are living through an age characterised by the death of kindness, by the deliberate conscious denial of empathy and by a great applauded uncaring, where unfeasibly wealthy men and women cackle their articulated scorn of the poor, the ill, the damaged or the weakened. Apparently, these people they verbally bully and demean and dismiss are all 'losers'. Apparently, the 'winners' can only be the blustering lords of silly, preposterous wealth or those with armies and the apparatus of repression.

But this too will pass; 'What of the night ... The morning comes.' And when that newer morning does come, memory will provide antidote to this new cruelty. There will be many who will recall those blistering hot days in the summer of '85 when a great universal kindness, the empathy that is the glue of humanity, enveloped the globe and made a shared, utterly good, unsullied 'humanness' a possibility. The time when an outrageous bunch of outlaws, rebels, naysayers and free-thinkers took a small Christmas song and rode it all the way to the very heart of the global political and economic structures of the world. And they really, actually, did change laws, implement economic justice and alter consciousness within the cloistered classes of political and economic leaders and of society itself.

It's extraordinary what three chords and a good tune can do.

Bob Geldof
London, September 2025

MAP OF ETHIOPIA

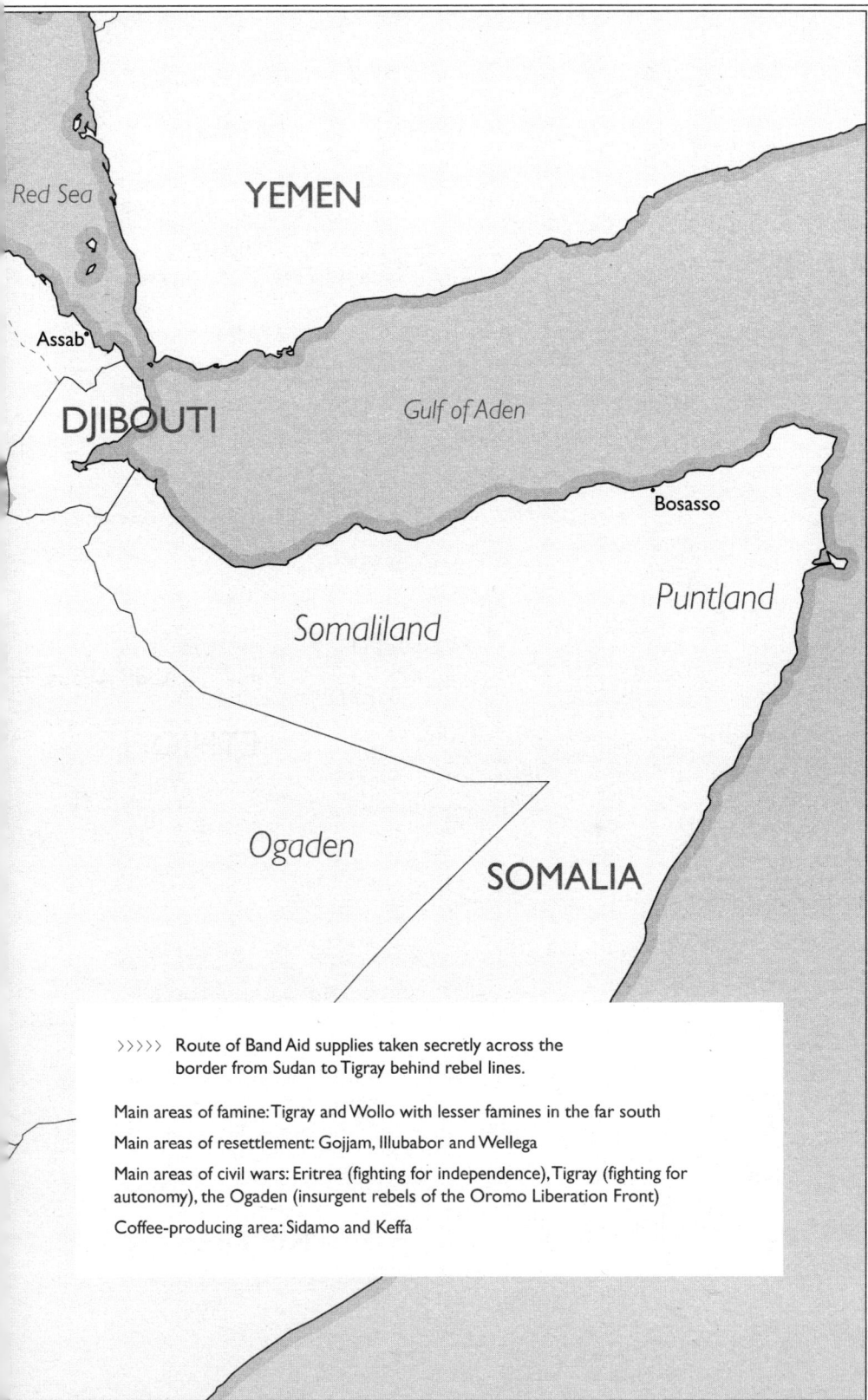

Red Sea

YEMEN

Assab

DJIBOUTI

Gulf of Aden

Bosasso

Somaliland

Puntland

Ogaden

SOMALIA

>>>>> Route of Band Aid supplies taken secretly across the
border from Sudan to Tigray behind rebel lines.

Main areas of famine: Tigray and Wollo with lesser famines in the far south

Main areas of resettlement: Gojjam, Illubabor and Wellega

Main areas of civil wars: Eritrea (fighting for independence), Tigray (fighting for
autonomy), the Ogaden (insurgent rebels of the Oromo Liberation Front)

Coffee-producing area: Sidamo and Keffa

CHAPTER 1

SIX CHARACTERS IN SEARCH OF A STORY

Claire's story

It would soon be Christmas. There was only one guest in the hotel. It was the finest building in town, but that was not saying much. The Castle Hotel had been designed to reflect the historic architecture of the palace of Emperor Yohannes IV with its stone facades, castle-like turrets and arched windows – a blend of Ethiopian and European influences. But, by 1984, it had seen better days. It stood on a mound above Mekele, which felt like a ghost town with its dusty dirt roads. Once there had been trees and grass, but no more. The hotel stood like a decrepit sentinel above the drought-parched settlement.

In her first-floor bedroom, with its peeling walls once a shocking pink and a gaudy yellow, the young Red Cross nurse had done her best to brighten up the place. As an antidote to the grim clinic where she worked seven days a week, from sunrise to sunset, feeding high-energy milk drinks to malnourished skeletal children, she had put two posters on the wall. One was a picture of a cake oozing cream and jam with the caption: 'Already she was more deeply involved than she cared to admit'. The other was of a jammy doughnut beneath which were with the words: 'After this, she could never go back to muesli'. Years later, Claire Bertschinger would look back on the posters as tasteless, but at the time they did something to relieve the horror of her situation.

It was nearly dark. The military curfew had required her to be back in the hotel by 6 p.m. The town of Mekele was still under government control and heavily garrisoned. But the surrounding countryside was increasingly dominated by the rebel Tigray People's Liberation Front (TPLF). The war was intensifying, with the Ethiopian army's military operations harassing the local population, and the guerrillas of the TPLF launching hit-and-run attacks on military convoys and bases.

The room had an en suite, but there was no running water. There was a bucket of water which had to last two days. So she sat in the bath and sloshed water sparingly over herself with a plastic cup, wiping the dirt of the refugee camp from her body with a flannel. She had to keep the rest of the bucket to flush the toilet later.

The hotel had only a couple of hours of electricity a day and they were over. As the dusk faded, Claire lit two candles by her bed and wrote a letter home. The bed was plagued with bedbugs. At night, they would march defiantly across the sheets, indifferent to any insecticide. She whipped back the sheet and, before the beasts could scuttle away from the flickering light, she smashed a bar of soap down on them – bang, bang, bang, bang, bang – managing to squash a couple. She was covered in fleabites from the camp, which caused allergic reactions, which ulcerated on her legs. She could do without any more nasty bites from the bugs. As it was, she would lie in bed, furiously resisting the urge to scratch the bites, which she knew would bring more infection.

She blew out the candles. She had one solace – her little shortwave radio which could intermittently pick up the BBC World Service. The letters she received from her mother and sister back in England were weeks out of date by the time they arrived, so the radio was her one link with the rest of the world in these days before the internet or mobile phones. Most nights, she listened to it in bed in the dark.

The night air was cool. December is the coldest month in the Tigray highlands. The sky was dark; the new moon gave minimal light. Outside, she could hear the howls of the hyenas. She switched on the radio. She had broken off the aerial once, when she was closing her suitcase, so she now had a wire hanging down from the wall to the little shortwave radio to try to improve the reception. But the sound faded in and out, as though it was being blown by the wind, so she could not hear everything clearly. They were playing a song. 'Feed the world,' it said. The radio presenter said something about a character called Bob Geldof and something about Ethiopia.

'But it wasn't quite clear because, you know, the sound came and went.

"Do they know it's Christmas?", they sang. And the radio said something about Geldof raising money and I became incandescent with rage. Who was this Geldof guy making money for himself, capitalising on the misery of the people of Ethiopia? It was criminal. How could someone jump on the bandwagon of a famine in Ethiopia to make money for themselves? I had got hold of the wrong end of the stick entirely.'

Bob's story

Bob Geldof sat alone in the evening gloom in his Victorian townhouse in Chelsea. He was exhausted. The past few weeks had been a blur as he whipped the British music industry into line to produce a record which became the fastest-selling pop single in UK chart history. He had corralled the leading pop stars of the day, a raft of top music executives, the record manufacturers and the high-street retailers, and so many others, to all give their services for free to produce a charity record to raise funds for the starving of Ethiopia. Then he had persuaded TV and radio broadcasters to play it. It was mid-December and he had just flown back across the Atlantic after promoting 'Do They Know It's Christmas?' in the United States.

The process felt natural to him. It was what he'd done for the past ten years with his band, the Boomtown Rats – the music, the writing, the recording, the video, hustling the record company and the media to promote it. But this was something different. It wasn't just that the scale of things had now become colossal. It was that he had been thrust into becoming a figurehead for something in the popular imagination, something huge and hard to comprehend. And now here he was, at home, alone.

His partner Paula Yates was off working in Newcastle on *The Tube*, a showcase for emerging bands and those of a more alternative bent. She had taken their baby Fifi and their nanny Anita, whom the toddler called Nee-Naw. The house was empty. As Geldof sat there, he heard voices outside in the street, the voices of children, moving from door to door. Carol singers. As they drew near, he could hear the familiar words of the Christmas story. A mother and a baby, innocent, vulnerable.

> *All is calm, all is bright*
> *Round yon Virgin, Mother and Child*
> *Holy Infant so tender and mild*

As they finished the carol they paused, but only briefly, before singing again:

> *It's Christmas time*
> *And there's no need to be afraid.*

By himself, in the dark, Bob Geldof cried.

Woldu's story

It was a miracle – of that Woldu Menameno had no doubt. His daughter had been dead; they all told him so. But now he was walking home with the living, breathing child in his arms.

It was barely a month since the family had left their home in the village of Lahama in the Ethiopian central highlands. People had begun dying there. 'Falling like leaves,' Woldu said, after drought had dropped like a curse on their once-fertile valley. 'It wasn't just hunger and hardship, it was the time, as we say, of the apocalypse.' The entire village had taken the decision to leave together. Everyone was terrified that if they stayed behind there would be no one to bury them.

Woldu packed some pots and pans and blankets on the family donkey. He lifted his little son Silas onto one shoulder and his daughter Birhan on the other. Their older sisters, Lemlem and Azmera, could walk the seven-hour trek to the feeding centre. Woldu had heard that one had been set up outside Mekele. But when they arrived at the edge of the hills and looked down on the town in the windswept plain below, they heard blast after blast of the Tigrayan conch that announces a death in the family.

Rather than going down to the plain, they turned towards a smaller feeding centre in the town of Kwiha. There, beneath the shadow of St Mary's Church, they huddled together under a blanket, by a wall, in the open air. The night was freezing cold. By day, the sun was pitiless. As the days passed, three-year-old Birhan grew slowly weaker. Soon she was too feeble to stand. She developed a rasping cough, which Woldu feared was a death rattle. Having heard of a clinic with Western medicine, Woldu gently lifted the bundle of bones that was his precious child and carried her for ten miles – to the grey stone clinic of St Vincent de Paul, run by Irish nuns in the dusty hamlet of Latchi on the far side of Mekele.

They arrived too late in the day to be seen and Woldu was told they would have to wait until the next day. 'My heart sank. We slept out in the open under my shawl. I held her close,' he said. A kind stranger gave them a handful of wheat, but Birhan was too weak to eat. Her father knew he was losing her. The night was impenetrably dark and cold. As dawn came, he could see that there were ten families ahead of them in the queue for the clinic. But when he tried to get the child to stand, she collapsed next to the wall. She did not move. Her eyes rolled back. There was no heartbeat.

Woldu was too distraught to notice that a foreign TV crew were there, moving down the line of people waiting with desperate hope to be admitted to the clinic. The Canadian reporter, Brian Stewart from CBC News, called one of the nuns. His camera crew filmed the Irish nurse taking the pulse in Birhan's neck and pronouncing that it was too late: 'There isn't anything we can do really for this child at all. The child is too far gone. The child will die very soon.' The sisters had seen so many cases like this before. Stewart, shaking with shock, withdrew – 'to at least allow her dignity in death,' he later said.

'Many others had died and now it was her turn,' Woldu said. 'What worried me was where to find a spade to dig a grave.' But the foreign nuns had spades and people to dig the graves. They dug a cold grave for Birhan. Yet when her father lifted her to take her there, his daughter was still warm. Woldu could feel the faintest of heartbeats: 'I then touched her heart and felt warmth.' He shouted to the nurse, who came over. 'I grabbed the white woman's hand and made her touch her too.' The nun was shocked to feel a pulse. She gave the child a rehydration injection. When the Canadian crew returned to film the little girl's funeral, for which a ragged shroud had already been laid out, they were astonished to find Birhan had pulled through.

'My joy had no limit. The sun shone on me,' Woldu said. 'I saw so many people die, but she survived. God allowed her to live for a reason.'

Brian Stewart later recalled his last sight of her in the famine: 'Still weak, frightened, carried by her father out of the relief centre, back into the chaos outside. The nurses thought she'd be now safe and we had to move on.' But the encounter would not leave him. He played it over and over in his mind. 'I was overwhelmed with emotion. I'd expected the worst and, for the first time in days, I saw this burst of hope.' He could not have appreciated how, twenty years later, Birhan Woldu would bring hope to a billion people and more.

It was not the end of the story. Later in the week, back in the Hilton Hotel in Addis Ababa, the CBC film editor Colin Dean was splicing together the horrendous footage that Stewart's crew had shot in the famine zone. It was made even more awful by the incongruity of Dean editing them in the luxurious confines of the Hilton. But he had to work long hours to get the sequence back to CBC in Toronto. To soften the horror, Dean put on a music tape. It was only later that he realised he was subconsciously fitting the images to the rhythms of the music. The track was 'Drive', a melancholy ballad by the American new-wave band, the Cars. Its lyrics offered an elusive haunting counterpoint to the harrowing images:

> *Who's gonna tell you when it's too late?*
> *Who's gonna tell you things aren't so great?*
> *You can't go on, thinking nothing's wrong, but now*
> *Who's gonna drive you home tonight?*

It was a love song about a dysfunctional relationship, but it somehow made emotional sense heard beneath the terrible footage from the camps. As he finished his work, Colin Dean found himself sitting in front of the edit machine, crying. Towards the end of the film, which the whole world would later see, is the agonised face of a girl with swollen lips and half-closed eyelids. It is Birhan Woldu. The girl who had turned back on the doors of death.

Dawit's story

It was 7 p.m. on a Saturday evening when the man in charge of administering the delivery of food aid in Ethiopia stepped off the plane at Heathrow. He did not expect what was about to happen.

Every time Dawit Wolde Giorgis had been here before over the previous year and a half, it had been to ask for food aid for his starving people. Every time, he had been turned away virtually empty-handed. It was not just that people didn't believe him. Their minds were closed to listening, because he was from a Marxist government which was an ally of Soviet Russia. 'I couldn't understand the indifference of the international community,' he said. 'Every day, over one thousand people were dying. Every day for over a year. How much lead time does the world need to respond?'

This time it was different. On previous trips, Ethiopia's Commissioner for Relief and Rehabilitation had been forced to fight for the ear of the press. This time, there was a bustling crowd of reporters waiting for him at the airport. Even the bumptious chairman of the *Daily Mirror*, Robert

Maxwell, was there to shake his hand in front of the TV cameras. The British government minister responsible for the aid budget, Timothy Raison, had gone into his office on his day off specially to meet Dawit. 'A year ago, it was I who had come begging to him. Now he was waiting for me in his office on a Saturday night.'

A barrage of questions were flung at Dawit at a furious pace by reporters:

'Commissioner, is it true that your government spent £100 million for your anniversary celebrations at a time when every pound meant life and death to your people?'

'Commissioner, do you have anything to say about the 400,000 bottles of whisky that were recently shipped to your country at a cost of millions?'

'Are your allies, the Soviet Union and the Eastern European nations, helping you in your effort to save lives?'

'How many millions of dollars do you spend on your military, Commissioner? Why haven't you diverted this money to emergency relief in order to save lives?'

Dawit knew the answers to these questions. But he couldn't tell the truth.

For more than a year, he had toured the famine regions in the north of his country, watching the situation slowly deteriorate. His own government did not want to receive his reports; they felt it would tarnish the forthcoming celebrations of the tenth anniversary of the overthrow of the feudal emperor Haile Selassie and the arrival of their glorious Marxist revolution. The international community turned a blind eye for different reasons; Ethiopia was on the wrong side in the Cold War, the four decades of open hostility between the West and the Soviet Union. Yet, even though Dawit knew better than most what was happening on the ground, there was something disturbing about the film footage he was shown at the airport. It was the report which the BBC reporter Michael Buerk and his cameraman Mohamed Amin had sent from Korem a few weeks earlier. It showed the destitution and degradation of Dawit's own people in Ethiopia.

'It had a chilling effect even on me, who had been there,' Dawit later said. 'But the way it was shown – the graphic exposition, the details and the words of Michael Buerk – sent a shock into my heart, my conscience. I was deeply disturbed and I cried at the airport. I really cried.' Years later, Dawit could still repeat Buerk's commentary, word for word, so deeply was the film burned into his heart.

He was a good deal less impressed with the other great influence which was forcing British politicians to make an about-turn on aid for Ethiopia. Dawit now heard the Band Aid record which had shot to No 1 in the charts. "'Do they know it's Christmas?" was an insulting question to ask,' he thundered. 'It's offensive. It just assumes that Ethiopians don't know Christmas, that Ethiopians are not Christians. It is so untrue and so distorted. Ethiopia was a Christian country before England… We knew Christmas before your ancestors.'

Dawit was grateful for the money Band Aid was raising, and for the political pressure it was exerting, but when Bob Geldof – 'a smart city boy full of arrogance and vulgar language' – arrived in Ethiopia a month later, 'I didn't like him,' Dawit said. The first thing Dawit did was to send him not to a feeding camp, but to Lalibela, one of Christianity's most ancient centres in the heart of the massive Abyssinian plateau. The churches there were not built from the ground up; they were chiselled, down, so that the ground level has become the top of the church and the building is hewn from the solid rock below. Yet even these do not go back to the start of Ethiopian Christianity, which became the state religion in 330 AD. Its illuminated gospel manuscripts are the oldest in existence. It was important, said Dawit, that Bob Geldof should see 'that he was not coming to a desolate country full of African savages'.

Harry's story

In New York, just before Christmas, Harry Belafonte was watching television when on the screen appeared the dishevelled figure of Bob Geldof. The Irish pop star had paid a quick trip to the United States to promote the record made by the British supergroup that he had pulled together to raise funds for Ethiopia. Belafonte knew about the famine. In the US, the news on the major networks had been filled with reports for weeks. But watching TV that night, he learned that 'Do They Know It's Christmas?' had already raised $8 million for Ethiopia.

Belafonte was discomfited.

'We have white folks saving black folks. We don't have black folks saving black folks,' he said to himself. 'That's a problem. We need to save our own people from hunger.'

Belafonte, who had stormed the pop charts and smashed racial barriers in the 1950s, was more than a popular singer and entertainer. Such was his commitment to the civil rights movement that he was blacklisted in Hollywood during the McCarthy era. In the 1960s, he had marched alongside Martin Luther King and had become his close confidant. He had taken Frank Sinatra to the southern states, where Sinatra then refused to play to segregated audiences – and proudly told how, when the black members of Sinatra's band were abused, Frank solved the problem by asking the mafia to assign a mobster to each of the black musicians. Watching Geldof on the television, Belafonte felt 'ashamed and embarrassed at seeing a bunch of white English kids doing what black Americans ought to have been doing'. He picked up the phone.

'When Belafonte called me, it was just two days before Christmas,' recalled Ken Kragen, who was manager of many of the highest-charting US artists in the early 1980s.

'We should do a big benefit concert,' Belafonte said.

Kragen had a better idea. 'Harry, let's just take the idea Bob already gave us. Let's make a record. We've got bigger artists, a bigger market, the biggest artist in the world... Let me see if we can put that together.'

Kragen had a meeting coming up with his client Lionel Richie, who had just been asked to host the American Music Awards in a month's time. The Los Angeles event would bring together the biggest names in music. After the ceremony would be the ideal time to do the recording. Instead of being driven to the after-show party, the stars could all be taken to the recording studio.

Lionel Richie said yes straight away and wanted the great producer and arranger Quincy Jones involved. Kragen caught Quincy Jones as he was about to board a plane to Hawaii for Christmas. Quincy also said yes, adding: 'I'm seeing Michael tomorrow. I'll run it by him. See what he thinks.' Michael Jackson was in too. From Lionel's limo, they put in a call to Stevie Wonder. The only question now was who was going to write the song ...

Belafonte rang Kragen to check how it was all going.

'So, Ken, have you been thinking about what we talked about?'

'Well, I've got a song written by Michael Jackson, Lionel Richie and Stevie Wonder. Quincy Jones is producing ...'

'Happy Christmas, Ken.'

'Happy Christmas, Harry.'

My story

To these five characters in search of a story at Christmas 1984, we may add a sixth. At my home to the west of London, I was packing my bag to travel to Ethiopia to report on the famine for *The Times*. I had had my jabs – yellow fever, typhoid, hepatitis, cholera and the rest – and had packed my malaria pills. I was only waiting for the Ethiopian Embassy in London to clear my visa and then I would be off to RAF Lyneham in Wiltshire to travel to Addis on a lumbering Hercules C-130 cargo plane filled with supplies for the famine region. The journey would be so long – and slow, thanks to the prop-driven engines – that a refuelling stopover would be needed at RAF Akrotiri in Cyprus.

The journey which followed was even longer. Indeed, it has lasted forty years.

When I arrived in Ethiopia, I spent two months reporting on the famine. Many of the stories I sent back were heart-breaking accounts of how ordinary people were being crushed by the merciless hunger. But one touched me to the core.

'Go to Bati,' someone told me. 'Things are better there.' I had returned to Addis after reporting from the epicentre of the famine in the northern highlands. It had been a shattering experience. But food aid was apparently arriving in Bati. That would make a more uplifting piece for the paper.

Bati was a market town on the edge of the Rift Valley, halfway between the highlands and the desert lowland plains. It was the fastest-growing refugee camp in Ethiopia. Distressed peasants were arriving at the rate of 1,000 a day, so the camp soon became the second-biggest city in the country. At one point, so many people were dying every day that the camp employed 128 full-time grave diggers. But it was far from the area of fighting between the Ethiopian army and the insurgent rebels, so the government had sent food there and the Red Cross had put in a comprehensive medical programme.

The people were in better health. Surprisingly, the effect was unnerving. In Korem and Mekele, the people in the camps seemed to have gone beyond despair; they sat like breathing statues, drained of everything except the mechanics of being alive. In Bati, the response was more devastatingly human. People smiled, cursed, begged, laughed, held out their hands or stared in silent accusation.

Between the tents, a happy little boy played with a toy made from a stick and the empty box of an anti-diarrhoea medicine. In the yard of the feeding centre, the men sat on their haunches in a semi-circle; some stared pointedly at the ground, others looked with pleading expectation, others yet with forthright curiosity, and others with glaring hostility. I found it hard not to avert my gaze. It did not feel right that an outsider should witness their shame. These people were robbed of independence, initiative and privacy. They were a proud people and they resented it.

In the hospital tent, the canvas walls had Christmas pictures fastened above the beds. They had been sent by children in Scandinavia, reminders of a world far away from this reality. In one corner, under a picture of a snowman, sat Fatima Muhammed. She was a beautiful woman with the fine features of the Afar nomads. She smiled as I approached, and yet before her was the most horrifying sight I had ever seen.

On the bed was her eighteen-month-old child, Hadra. She lay like a grotesque puppet, her head huge, her limbs like insensible twigs. Her enormous eyes stared with such ferocity as if they had an independent life and were straining to move back inside her head, away from the world outside which had brought her to this. Her mouth was open and a fly ran around her little lips. Fatima brushed it away.

I asked the list of questions which had by now become a practised routine to me – about life back home, the failed harvest and its impact on her family. The interpreter translated the replies.

It seemed an inanity to ask, but I did: 'How is the child?'

'She is dying,' Fatima said. 'After she dies, I will go back to my village to see my son. He is four years old.'

I told her I was sorry and I hoped that the boy was well. She smiled and said something else.

'What was that?' I asked the interpreter.

'She says, "Thank you". She says, "How are you? How is your family? Are they well?"'

I answered with empty platitudes, then smiled and nodded, with no real answer to give. She smiled too. We smiled at each other over the emaciated body of her dying child. I had treated her as a victim. She had treated me as her equal. The contrast was unbearable.

Things were far more complicated in Ethiopia than they had appeared from watching the news back home. The famine was getting worse, not better. It hadn't just been caused by drought, though the rains had failed for three years and the farming topsoil was all blowing away. The Ethiopian government was fighting a war against three different sets of rebels and was spending almost half the country's annual income on arms. The starving people behind the rebel lines were allowed no food aid. The country's Marxist dictator was imposing policies upon the farmers which had been tried by Stalin in Russia in the 1930s, where they had produced an earlier famine. I wrote about all this.

What I could not know was that, back in London, Bob Geldof was eagerly reading my reports on all this in *The Times*.

After two months, I was thrown out of the country by the regime's secret police and branded 'an enemy of the revolution' after revealing that there were deadly outbreaks of cholera in a number of refugee camps. The government was refusing to acknowledge this – and therefore refusing doctors the medical equipment to treat it – for fear it would jeopardise the $20 million a year it was making exporting cattle to the Middle East.

After the Live Aid concert in July 1985, Bob Geldof contacted me and asked to join him on a trip across the Sahel – from Mali through Burkina Faso, Niger, Chad, and Sudan to Ethiopia – to help him decide how to spend the millions raised by the concert. It was the starting point for a relationship that has lasted four decades, during which I have been an adviser to Geldof on international development, co-written his autobiography and stood alongside him throughout his campaigning ever since. That relationship has given me an inside view of the years which have spanned Band Aid – through Live Aid, Jubilee 2000, Drop the Debt, the Commission for Africa, Make Poverty History, Live 8 and the Gleneagles G8 summit – to the West End musical *Just For One Day* and the various television and radio documentaries to mark forty years of Live Aid.

It has been a curious amalgam of pop, poverty, politics, power, pain and passion – a combination at which these first pages have tried to hint. And it has thrown up a host of fascinating behind-the-scenes stories and insights which this book uncovers. But let us now begin at the beginning.

CHAPTER 2

A TERRIBLE FAMINE

Dinner at the imperial palace was an ostentatious affair with flaming torches and plates of solid gold. The cups, too, were of pure gold, beaten to the thickness of a cigarette paper. Behind each guest's chair stood their own personal liveried butler. Every high-backed chair was upholstered in red Morocco leather with a crown and a lion of Judah embossed in gold at the top in acknowledgement of the emperor's full title: 'Conquering Lion of the Tribe of Judah, His Imperial Majesty Haile Selassie, King of Kings of Ethiopia, Lord of Lords, Elect of God', a dynasty which he traced back to the legendary King Solomon and the Queen of Sheba in the tenth century BCE.

From the high ceilings hung magnificent chandeliers. On the floor were thick carpets on which the emperor's white poodles, Lulu and Rosa, played by the feet of their imperial master while senior members of his court prostrated themselves flat on the floor before him. The menu for the nine-course meal was in French as well as Amharic; the wines had all been imported from France and were of the finest vintages. After the cream of asparagus soup, the palace chef served filets de poisson d'akaki à la duglêré, fish caught in central Ethiopia's great Akaki River – a river in which the fish are now filled with heavy metals after the Akaki became a toxic drain for sewage, industrial waste and storm water from the capital, Addis Ababa.

First crowned as regent in 1916 – alongside his aunt, the Empress Zaouditou – the man then known as Ras Tafari took the throne of Abyssinia in 1930. As emperor, he took the name Haile Selassie, which means 'Power of the Trinity'. It was a genuflection to the ancient Christian heritage of a country which embraced that faith in the fourth century, long before most of Europe did. In the early days, this feudal overlord was something of a reformer, much praised for his role in abolishing slavery. He founded a university from his own pocket. But, as the years passed, encompassed on all sides by fabulous wealth and privilege, the nation's benevolent patriarch grew out of touch with his people and developed an unbending antipathy to further reform. As both his physical and mental powers weakened, he could no longer juggle the hundreds of tasks through which he had previously micro-managed his kingdom. He had lived too long. He had been in power for forty-four years.

In 1973, a severe drought gripped the north of the country, centred on the regions of Wollo and Tigray – the exact same regions it was to bedevil in 1984–85. It brought widespread famine. Discontent grew against the emperor, fed by images of famine victims from the north. A British television crew arrived in Ethiopia led by the journalist, Jonathan Dimbleby. His ITV programme, *The Unknown Famine*, suggested that 200,000 people had died. The broadcast shocked the Western world into acting and brought a massive influx of aid from rich countries. But it also fed the growing unrest in Ethiopia's capital, particularly within the middle classes, along with the young intellectuals at the university among whom Marxist–Leninist ideas had spread. Anger focused on the government's failure to recognise the seriousness of the famine. By February 1974, mass demonstrations were taking place across the country and a wave of strikes and army mutinies followed. Military units across the country sent representatives to the capital to present their grievances to the government. The most vocal, and most radical, was a group of junior and mid-level officers who called themselves the Committee – or, in Amharic, the Derg. The revolution, initially led by left-wing students, was now taken over by the army.

The driving force behind the Derg was Major Mengistu Haile Mariam. He soon came to dominate the group by a variety of methods, not least murdering his rivals. One of his more ingenious machinations was to instruct Ethiopian television to run Dimbleby's harrowing film intercut with footage of the luxurious indulgences of the imperial court, including footage of a cake that had been specially flown from Italy. Army officers ordered the eighty-two-year-old emperor to watch it and arrived at the palace next morning to read him an act of dethronement. Mengistu imprisoned the emperor on 12 September 1974. Three days later, it renamed itself the Provisional Military Administrative Council. Not long after, Mengistu ordered the murder of its moderate chairman and took over as strongman leader. A year later, Hailie Selassie was murdered by the Derg. But it would be twenty years before an Ethiopian court, in 1994, revealed that several former army officers had strangled the 225th descendant of the dynasty of King Solomon and the Queen of Sheba in his bed.

In the spring of 1975, a group of Marxist students entered a sociology class at the university that was taught by the wife of a US diplomat and declared: 'We can't have the imperialists teaching here. This class is over. The university is closed down. We are taking over.' The government, over a period of months, shut down the entire university, took out all the students and sent them out to collective farms. '[They] destroyed the university, destroyed the farming, closed down the medical school, everything,' the American diplomat said. 'Our relationships with Ethiopia went down to zero.'

But the revolutionaries soon split into different factions with different brands of Marxist ideology. Mengistu, who had by now made himself a colonel, launched a wave of violence that he openly called the Red Terror, in which anyone the Derg deemed a counter-revolutionary was eliminated. To be educated and young was enough to make someone a target. At least 10,000 people were killed and many more viciously tortured to spread terror in the population and repress dissent. Every night, corpses were shown on national television as a warning to the public. The following day, the bloodied bodies were left on the roadside, with denunciatory placards on them, to advertise the killings of the previous night. Anyone who inspected the bodies, searching for friends or relatives, was targeted for detention or execution themselves. Relatives had to pay one Ethiopian dollar for each 'wasted bullet' in order to have the body returned.

Mengistu took Soviet Russia as his model for the Ethiopian Revolution. This was the height of the Cold War when the United States and the Soviet Union used proxy nations like Ethiopia as stages on which to act out their intense ideological power struggle. Mengistu mirrored the tactics of Stalin – not just in his brutal repression, but also in heavily centralised control. He nationalised land, banks and industries, and pursued Stalinist collectivisation policies that forced farmers into government-controlled villages and compelled them to sell their crops to the state at below-market prices. He even created one-party state – the Workers' Party of Ethiopia – modelled on the Communist Party of the Soviet Union. But his unrealistic policies, mismanagement and corruption – combined with the cost of his constant warfare with armed rebels in Eritrea, Tigray and Oromo – led to a drastic fall in food production. The man who came to power on the back of Haile Selassie's mismanagement of famine in 1973 was about to cause a far more deadly famine in which more than a million people were to die.

⁙

Warning signs that another famine in Ethiopia was looming were there from 1982 when a drought wiped out harvests in Tigray, Wollo and Eritrea. But it was not until 1983 that news reached the charity Save the Children of the continuing drought. They heard of great food losses in the north, particularly in Wollo and Tigray. Mark Bowden, the organisation's East African regional director, set out from his base in Kenya for Ethiopia to see for himself. He took with him the BBC's East Africa correspondent Mike Wooldridge. On the road, they were struck by the number of people on the move from their homesteads in the hills down to the plains and along the main roads, 'people who'd come to places on the road where they hoped that food would be delivered where they could get some help'.

'People were looking pretty thin,' Wooldridge said. By measuring the diameter of children's upper arms, aid workers could tell that malnutrition was setting in. 'It was very evident in 1983, after just one failed harvest, that famine was looming.'

The Ethiopian government knew what was happening. Its relief commissioner was Major Dawit Wolde Giorgis, a young Marxist army officer, who had made his name fighting against insurgent rebels in Eritrea. In the summer of 1983, Dawit toured Tigray and Wollo, and reported back to Mengistu that a terrible famine was on the way.

Mengistu dismissed his report: 'Don't let these petty human problems that always exist in transition periods consume you. There was famine in Ethiopia for years before we took power – it was the way nature kept the balance.' The Ethiopian dictator was more concerned with implementing his Stalinist plans for agriculture and fighting his civil war against Tigrayan and Eritrean insurgents. Above all, he was focused on planning the celebrations for the tenth anniversary of his glorious revolution in September of the following year.

By August 1983, hundreds were dying daily. Dawit summoned all the foreign aid agencies in the country to a meeting. The following month, he gathered the ambassadors of all the Western nations to appeal for donations of grain from abroad. He then flew to Rome to brief the United Nations Food and Agriculture Organization, then to Geneva to other UN agencies and the Red Cross. In November, he held another donors' conference in Addis to appeal for food aid, before flying to New York to inform the UN General Assembly of the urgent need for help.

'Unless the situation is salvaged immediately,' he told the meeting, 'the death toll may rise to truly catastrophic proportions.'

No one responded with anything like the urgency that was required. Western governments regarded Ethiopia's Marxist regime with suspicion. 'They wanted us to pay a price for the ideology that we have taken,' Dawit later said. Ethiopia's socialist friends in Eastern Europe also completely ignored Dawit. Aid agencies increased supplies of food and medicine, but nowhere near the scale that was required. Later, some governments claimed that they had not heard there was a famine until late 1984.

'If that was so,' said Dawit, 'it was because they chose not to listen.'

❋

In February 1984, Dawit began getting reports from his staff that 10,000 deaths a week were now being recorded in Ethiopia's 240 shelters and food distribution centres. The town of Korem (population 3,000) was swamped by 100,000 desperate people who gathered at the relief centre which Save the Children had opened there. On 30 March, Dawit called a meeting of the representatives of foreign governments, UN agencies and voluntary aid agencies at the government-owned Ghion Hotel in Addis. There, the relief commissioner presented shocking data on food shortages and rising deaths in famine-stricken areas. He showed Relief and Rehabilitation Commission (RRC) films from the affected areas and warned the international community that 5 million Ethiopians were at risk of starvation. Immediate food aid was needed. A million tonnes of it. It was a figure, history was to show, that was remarkably accurate.

But Western donors were hesitant. Why should we provide large-scale assistance, they said, when the Ethiopian government is squandering more than half its annual budget on the largest army in Black Africa – with more than 250,000 full-time soldiers – fighting wars in Eritrea and Tigray? Won't food aid just be diverted to the army instead of reaching famine victims?

What made things worse for Dawit was that some senior officials at the conference, under Mengistu Haile Mariam's influence, downplayed the severity of the famine. They avoided calling it a national emergency for fear that the need for Western aid might be seen as a sign of the weakness of its Marxist ideology and might undermine the regime's control over the distribution of resources. While some donor countries pledged small amounts of aid, there was no major breakthrough at the conference.

Dawit decided to appeal direct to donor governments, flying all round Europe and the US to meet with top officials. Given the reluctant response of donors, he reduced his ask from 950,000 tonnes to just 450,000. But in the UK, the main aid minister was too busy to see him and a junior politician just quizzed Dawit on Ethiopia's alignment to the Soviet Union, its civil wars and its Marxist economics. In the end, the UK promised just £30,000. 'The British government was damned if it was going to give anything more than the most minimal gesture of aid,' recalled Paddy Coulter, then head of communications for Oxfam. Dawit's trips to Brussels, Geneva, New York and Rome proved equally fruitless. Indeed, in Rome, the UN Food and Agriculture Organization declared Ethiopia could only transport 125,000 tonnes – and cut the official ask to that figure. And none of that had been delivered when Michael Buerk arrived in Korem in October and filed the news report which shocked the whole world.

Buerk had paid an earlier visit to Ethiopia in July 1984. He had been sent by his BBC bosses to find a famine story because ITV were about to broadcast an hour-long documentary called *Seeds of Despair*. Ironically, the team who made the documentary had originally travelled to Ethiopia to make a film about soil erosion, but when they arrived, they realised there was something more important to record; after three consecutive years of drought the rural population of thousands of elderly people and children were dying from starvation and famine-related diseases. When the British broadcasting authorities saw a preview of *Seeds of Despair*, they gave permission for a money-raising appeal to be made by UK aid agencies under the banner of the Disaster Emergencies Committee (DEC). The BBC bosses told Buerk to find a famine story, quickly, to jump on the DEC bandwagon.

The best place would be Mozambique, Buerk thought. It was not too far since he was based in South Africa. But it had taken him a month-long battle with 'mind-numbing bureaucracy' to get a visa the last time he'd applied for one to go there.

Buerk wired Paddy Coulter at Oxfam: 'Need urgent advice on where I can leap in and out quickly with harrowing pictures of drought victims. ... presumably at a cost that would keep Upper Volta in asparagus for years.'

'Ethiopia is the place we are most worried about,' replied Coulter. But there was a similar problem there. When Dawit had returned from his tour of Western capitals in his unsuccessful search for food aid, he had been summoned to see Mengistu. The Ethiopian dictator was not best pleased. Indeed, his cheekbones were trembling with rage. Western imperialists, he said, would exploit the famine to undermine the Derg's proletarian revolution. Dawit was falling into their trap, Mengistu said menacingly. He was to hold no more donor meetings, go on no more fundraising tours of Europe or the US, and he was to restrict the movement of foreigners in the countryside. No more travel permits were to be issued for the famine areas in the north.

But Coulter – who Buerk described as 'a wickedly amusing Irishman with a conscience, the most worldly and effective of do-gooders' – had a way round this. Before joining Oxfam, he had worked as a volunteer for two years with a wily old Catholic nun who was now in the far south of Ethiopia. He knew from her that the food situation there was very bad too. Since there was no fighting there, Coulter was able to pull strings in Addis to get Buerk permission to travel south.

It had been raining when Buerk arrived in Wolaita. The landscape looked deceptively green and lush, and the BBC man was temporarily fazed. But the rains had come too late. There had been no harvest. In one village, a woman was dying in her hut after just burying her two sons outside its door. All around, gaunt and hungry babies were sucking fruitlessly on the empty breasts of their listless mothers. A funeral passed by with the body of a child suspended from two poles. Seven thousand people were dying here every month. Buerk's report made the lead on the *Nine O'Clock News* and was inserted into a disaster appeal. More than £9 million poured in from the British public, but still Western governments declined to act.

Mengistu's ban on journalists travelling north from Addis kept the worsening famine hidden from the world's eyes. But at the start of September, the Ethiopian government allowed 200 reporters into the country to witness four days of pageantry and parades, banquets and celebrations, to mark the tenth anniversary of the Marxist revolution, which were to be attended by the Derg's friends and allies in the Soviet bloc. The event, which cost more than $50 million, was an extraordinary extravaganza for a nation where, the reporters suspected, millions were starving somewhere in the north, out of sight of the world. Even aid workers were now being refused permits to travel north.

Hundreds of Soviet-made tanks, armoured personnel carriers, rocket launchers and artillery worth $200 million rumbled through Revolution Square past gigantic portraits posters of Marx, Engels and Lenin. Some 70,000 students, peasants and troops marched or goosestepped through triumphal arches provided by North Korea and bearing legends such as 'Long Live Proletarian Internationalism'. As they passed the reviewing stand where Mengistu and guests of honour from the Soviet Politburo and East Germany stood to attention, the crowd shouted, 'Long live the revolution', 'Down with imperialism' and 'Revolutionary motherland or death' – seemingly heedless of the fact that death was indeed the lot of thousands of their countrymen and women a day's drive from the capital.

Mengistu addressed the nation in a televised broadcast which lasted more than five hours. His boastful, repetitive, boring speech – as one observer put it – devoted just a minute and a half to the 'recurring droughts' which plagued his country, describing them as a 'constraint on the successful implementation of agricultural policies'. It was just another reason to implement his glorious ten-year plan. Not one word about starvation.

'Mengistu was detached from reality, living in a world created by his own illusions,' relief commissioner Dawit later wrote after he defected to the United States. 'There was no place in his world for famine.'

The only shortage Mengistu complained of was of Scotch whisky. He had ordered 40,000 cases – nearly half a million bottles – for the celebrations, but it had been held up in the UK because of a strike by dockers.

✽

Five hundred miles away, they were deeply unimpressed by all this. Television sets had been delivered to towns all across Ethiopia so that the open-mouthed peasants could gawp in awe at the power and magnificence of the Derg. In Mekele, the capital of drought-stricken Tigray, a TV had been delivered to the Castle Hotel, one of the few places which had electricity, even if it only came on for an hour or two a day. The hotel only had one resident, that Red Cross nurse from Hertfordshire, Claire Bertschinger – the woman who was to inspire Bob Geldof to launch Band Aid.

'No one came to watch it,' she recalls. 'Everyone had been instructed to gather at the local stadium – which was really just a dusty bare field – for the town's own celebrations.' That meant that the feeding centre where she worked from sunrise to sunset, seven days a week, had been closed by order of the local party officials. 'I just stayed in my room and washed my hair and wrote a letter home.' The next day, a few old men gathered in the lobby to watch the TV. It was playing an old black-and-white Robin Hood film on an unending loop.

The young nurse had arrived in Ethiopia just four months before, after spending a year with the International Committee of the Red Cross in the war zones of Lebanon. As she alighted from the Ethiopian Airlines propeller-driven DC3 Dakota, her nostrils had been assaulted by the smell of dust, sweat, human and animal excrement, all mingled with the fragile scent of eucalyptus. 'I'd never been to Africa before,' she said. 'I'd no idea what was going to hit me, what I was going to find.'

What she found was a feeding centre that had space for 500 children but with a thousand or more waiting outside in the hope of being admitted. They sat with their parents on the flat, parched earth, in tunics so torn they afforded the wearer no modesty. The children were, she said, just skin and bones, with no fat or muscle on their arms and legs.

Claire had been sent by the Red Cross in Geneva to increase the number of calories the children received in the hope that they would recover faster. She decided to change the way children were chosen to be fed. The old system was that the children nearest the gate of the feeding centre gate were taken in first. She wanted to find those most in need yet who were still fit enough to survive if fed. Some were too far gone to be helped.

Claire briefed the local staff on how the children were to be selected from now on. All those seeking admittance were to line up in rows outside the wall of the centre. She taught the Ethiopian staff how to place their fingers around the upper arm of each child to gauge how malnourished the child was. But the locals refused.

'They're our brothers, our sisters, our cousins. How can we?' the Ethiopian staff told the British nurse. 'You must do it, Claire. We can't.'

The pressure was agonising. As she walked up and down between the ten rows, each of more than 100 children, she was careful never to stop in case someone thrust a baby into her arms. Even so, parents tugged at her clothes, calling, 'Mamma, mamma. Come, come, come.' They pleaded with her to lift up their child.

'I couldn't just take the children of those who were the strongest and could shout out. To be fair, I would have to pick the right ones. The right ones weren't the most malnourished, because we knew that they would be dead within twenty-four or forty-eight hours anyway. We didn't have sufficient food for more than a fraction of the sick children, so I had to select those I knew would have the best chance of survival if they were helped now, but who would die without emergency feeding.'

The people had arrived in the cold mist before dawn and sat patiently while the cooks in the feeding centre prepared a high-energy milk drink made from butter oil, dried skimmed milk, sugar and boiling water. Several sittings were required for the children who had already been admitted. By the time it came to select more children to admit, it was midday and those waiting were sitting under the beating sun with little protection from their tatters of clothes.

The selection took two hours.

Most of the children in the long lines had had their heads shaved, a traditional response to illness or suffering to guard against lice infestations and skin infections. A tuft of hair, or *quntcho*, had been left on the heads of some of the younger children in the belief that the angels would use it to pull a mischievous toddler out of trouble. Now, Claire was told, it was there so that if they died, God could grab it and pull them up to heaven. Many of those she could not admit would die within the next week to ten days.

It was around this time that she wrote a letter to the British Red Cross in which she said: 'They must think that I am like a god who, with a nod of the head, can decide if they are in or out ... The pressure is unbearable.'

Early every morning, as she lay in bed in her room in the Castle Hotel, three miles from the feeding centre, she would hear the haunting blast from an ancient conch with which the local people announced that a death had occurred in the night. As she made her way to the feeding centre, she would see the parade of people carrying the dead to be buried.

But no food aid came.

In desperation, on 30 September 1984, more than forty aid agencies working throughout Ethiopia issued an appeal to the rest of the world. Dramatically it began:

> Ethiopia has not experienced a food shortage of this magnitude within living memory. More than 6 million people are estimated to be affected by food shortage. The number of people arriving at feeding centres far exceeds the supplies of available food. There is no doubt that if substantial quantities of food are not forthcoming immediately, hundreds of thousands of people will die.

Europe and the United States, which had had a bumper harvest, ignored the appeal.

And still no food aid came.

CHAPTER 3

DEATH IN THE LIVING ROOM

This is how things changed. At the end of September 1984, the Ethiopian relief commissioner was called to the office of the Ethiopian dictator. Mengistu was now finally worried about the famine – but only because the journalists he had invited to commemorate the tenth anniversary of the overthrow of Haile Selassie had spoken to diplomats and aid workers while they were in Addis Ababa. Their stories had drawn unfavourable comparisons between Mengistu's lavish jamboree and the reports of a hidden famine in the north that had dramatically worsened over the summer. It was, he felt, tarnishing his image before the international community.

Worse than that, the beggars who had been removed from the streets of the capital ahead of the anniversary had returned – and in greater numbers. Refugees from the countryside were swelling Addis. There was open talk of famine and how the government was doing nothing. Mengistu sensed he was in deep trouble. He wanted a briefing.

The disconcerted dictator listened to the head of his relief commission as though it were the first time that Dawit had spoken about malnutrition among millions of the population. The 6 million starving had now escalated to 7 million. Dawit spoke again of the need for an international appeal for assistance. But this time, Mengistu approved the idea. And when the relief commissioner asked him to meet key foreign donors personally, to Dawit's surprise, Mengistu agreed at once.

Dawit invited the ambassadors of Western nations to a meeting at the beginning of October in Addis. Harvests had been bountiful in Western nations. Moreover, thanks to the subsidies paid to its farmers, Europe was already sitting on mountainous wheat surpluses, grain which in some cases they were planning to store for the next ten years. In 1984–85, these were reaching their peak. That year, Europe had bumper harvests. Member states also had millions of tonnes of excess butter and unwanted beef, along with surplus milk stored in powdered form that was in addition to its 'milk lake'. Surely some of that could come the way of starving Ethiopians? Yet, at the end of the meeting, there was no indication that the donor governments were in a more giving mood.

But then came a move which broke the logjam. The British television journalist Peter Gill had been lobbying for some time for permission to travel to the famine region. He didn't just want news pictures of starving people, he told Dawit. He was making a documentary which planned to contrast the plight of Ethiopia's rural poor with Europe's bumper harvests – and to point out that Brussels was refusing to ship any of its surplus grain to the Horn of Africa. He had already filmed warehouses in East Anglia that were full of grain, he told the relief commissioner.

Dawit gave Gill permission to travel north. In early October, Gill and his Thames Television crew reached the town of Korem, the location of Ethiopia's single-largest feeding centre and the epicentre of the famine. Gill was the first foreign journalist to get there in three months.

He arrived just as the death toll in Korem for the first time reached 100 a day. And that was only one camp. By any reckoning, this was the measure of an appalling famine.

'The food which would save them is already in store in Britain and Europe,' Gill declared, before asking: 'Why don't we give our unwanted food to save the lives of those who need it?'

Yet, when Gill returned to base, there was no one to edit the film he had shot because the technicians at ITV were on strike. The unions refused to make an exception, even for such shocking subject matter. Eventually, unpaid volunteers were allowed to edit an emergency version, but the documentary's transmission date had been missed.

Dawit had been so keen on Gill's idea of trying to shame the European community into releasing a fraction of its grain mountain to feed the poor of Ethiopia that they had given him the only travel permit to travel north.

But Mike Wooldridge and Michael Buerk had now arrived back in Addis and were lobbying for permission to travel to Korem and Mekele with the VisNews cameraman, Mohamed Amin. They had been granted travel permits before they entered the country, but when they arrived in Addis, they found that Dawit had abruptly withdrawn their documentation.

The BBC team shuttled back and forth between the Relief Commission and the Ministry of Information without success. Meanwhile, Gill, now back from Korem, was asked by Ethiopian officials when he thought Michael Buerk's team should be allowed to travel. Gill, nobly indifferent to being beaten to the story by the BBC, replied that it was the Ethiopians' decision, not his. On 18 October, Michael Buerk, for BBC Television, and Mike Wooldridge, for BBC Radio, set out north with Mo Amin in a twin-engine Otter belonging to the US charity, World Vision.

❊

Buerk, Wooldridge and Amin did not go straight to Korem, but flew first to Mekele, the capital of Tigray province. Wooldridge says of the sight that greeted them: 'Although we had all worked on famine stories before, nothing had quite prepared us for what we found. The sheer scale of the famine was unbelievable, and the fact that people of all ages, not just the young and old, were starving was new to us.'

Buerk's coverage of southern Ethiopia in the summer hadn't prepared him for the apocalyptic sights that greeted him in Tigray. 'The speed of the deterioration of the people was so rapid that it had overtaken everyone. The roads were just littered with dying people. It was extraordinary. People suddenly realised they were going to die and a huge mass migration started. It tipped very quickly. In a wide swathe around Mekele, some 85,000 lay about without any food, without water and without hope. They'd walked there from all over the province and just sank down where they had come to a stop. And there was this feeling that, apart from the few agencies working there, no one knew about this thing.'

But it was down the road in Korem where they encountered the scenes which were to shake the world. They arrived at night and checked into the impressively named National Hotel, a shack with mud floors and a filthy bed with a scorpion in the soiled sheets. They set an early alarm so that they arrived at Ethiopia's largest refugee camp before dawn. In the pearly half-light of dawn, they gradually made out around them the biggest human tragedy of the late twentieth century.

Buerk was shocked by the sheer numbers, but he focused on individuals. One boy, he recalled, got shakily to his feet:

> His head looked much too big for his trunk and body. His knees seem to bulge between matchstick thighs and toothpick shins. It was his eyes, though, that I will never forget. They began tight shut but opened, wider and wider, as he took in the dying world around him. You could see it all in those eyes. Confusion. Loss. Fear. There was nobody left to comfort him. His lower lip trembled as he slowly turned his head. He began to wail, the high quavering sound of the truly terrified.

They found one of the camp's European aid workers, Dr Brigitte Vasset, a medic with the French medical agency Médecins Sans Frontières. She seemed near breaking point and, Buerk observed, was full of rhetorical questions to which there was no answer. Why was she there? What could you do, in the face of all that mass suffering? What was the point of being a doctor, of dispensing medicine and drugs, when there was no food?

The BBC man asked her what she thought of how little the rich countries had done to help.

'I don't know anything about politics,' she said. 'I only know I'm a witness of Korem and if something isn't done, thousands of people will die.'

She swiftly corrected herself. 'No, already thousands of people are dying. Hundreds of thousands of people will die.'

An old man in the crowd pressing around them suddenly collapsed and fell to his bony knees. Dr Brigitte turned around to help him. Buerk said she wore a look of such distracted hopelessness that he can still see it today: 'The sights, the smells, the despair – you never get them out of your head.'

There were sheds in Korem that had been put up by the government to shelter the hungry. Now they were simply places to go to die. Among the 7,000 people packed into them, Buerk and his cameraman saw a naked three-year-old girl under a drip. She had been admitted to the medical centre far too late. As they filmed, a worker came up, shook his head and took the drip away to someone else. The little girl shivered, coughed as if she was just clearing her throat and died on camera. Tears rolled down through the dust on her mother's cheeks. This was the last of her four children. Her husband had died the previous day. She had nobody left in the world, thought Buerk. Everything she had had, everyone she had loved, had gone.

By 9 a.m., the wailing – which had been a background noise in the camp ever since the sun rose – grew to a crescendo. In the shelter of a small ridge, grieving relatives were bringing the bodies of those who had died during the night. Each corpse was bound in sackcloth and tied tightly round the neck and waist and legs so the shape of the body inside could clearly be seen. Mo Amin's camera lingered upon the bodies of a mother and child, wrapped together in death. Two pairs of feet, mother and baby, protruded from the bottom of the grubby grey shroud.

The bodies kept coming for nearly two hours.

⁂

Further north, in Mekele, the BBC team were confronted not simply with the horror of starvation, but with the moral dilemma of how to respond to it. At the feeding centre, they met Claire Bertschinger. Buerk and Amin followed her as she was trying to feed the children.

'He followed me as I was trying to feed the kids,' she said. 'While I was surrounded by desperate skeletal and malnourished children, screaming and shouting, and pulling at my hands, Michael tried to ask me questions and get me to stand where they would get the best shot.'

'Can you pick up a really sick one for the camera?' she recalled him saying. Then he asked me if making those life-and-death decisions did anything to me. What a question! I was indignant. What on earth did you think it did to me? For a moment, I didn't know whether to take him seriously or not, but in the end, there was only one reply I could give: 'Yes, of course it does. What do you expect? It breaks my heart.'

The nurse later said of the BBC team that she 'couldn't get rid of them fast enough'. When they had gone, she took a baby with a dangerously low haemoglobin count to hospital. Finding that the laboratory technician had gone home, and discovering that she had the same blood group as the baby, she gave a unit of her own blood to save the baby's life. 'I thought she was a saint,' Buerk later said. 'She thought I was a prat.'

The truth was that, though Claire Bertschinger certainly thought very little of the BBC journalist, she also had a low view of herself. When she returned to England to be told by people that she'd done a marvellous job, she resisted the idea. 'I tried to explain to them that most of the people I was trying to help actually died. So, within a week or so, I stopped talking about my experiences because people weren't listening. I didn't talk about it for over twenty years. I didn't feel that I was doing good here. I felt like a Nazi sending people to the death camps because that's what I was doing – and that's lived with me. I thought I'd be hated by the Ethiopian people for not helping everybody.' Yet, when she finally faced up to those demons and returned to Ethiopia with Michael Buerk to make a film twenty years later, she discovered, of course, that she was welcomed back with open arms.

The BBC crew were now faced with the conundrum of how to get their shocking footage back to London. News films were usually sent via satellite, but the link from Nairobi to London was notoriously unreliable. The pictures or the sound often became distorted. But since the ITN technicians were still on strike, there was none of the urgency which competition routinely brings. The BBC in London decided to cancel the Nairobi feed and booked Buerk on the overnight British Airways flight to Heathrow.

This was to have a profound impact on the way the report was received by an unsuspecting world.

Buerk and his film editor, Mac Maclean, ran and re-ran the Korem tapes, putting the story together entirely in pictures – without any words. London had asked for a three- or four-minute report; Buerk cut the tape so it ran at eight and a half minutes. Some of Mo Amin's cinematic tracking shots across the wide Korem plain laid bare the massive scale of the human misery there. Then, with a detailed list in his hand that described and timed every shot, Buerk climbed on board the 747 for London.

He began writing the commentary as the plane trundled down the long Nairobi runway just after midnight. It was an eight-hour flight, which gave him the luxury of time. Most television news reports, he later said, were just written on the back of an envelope. But now he had time to hone his script. He dashed off a first draft and then went back over it, removing all unnecessary adjectives. People did not need to be told how to feel, he thought to himself. They just needed to be told what the pictures showed.

'I thought if they can't work out what to feel with these pictures, then we're all lost,' he said later. In his mind's eye, he was back in Korem and Mekele. But he knew he was writing for people watching a TV set in the corner of their comfortable living rooms.

What reference point could he use for people in the UK? He remembered the picture plates in his school bible – the figures in robes and cloaks, the donkeys – and the word 'biblical' came to mind. It took half a continent to get the opening right, flying over pitch-black land, working and reworking the sentences with the short shot list in front of him. Cocooned in the half-empty cabin, he had time not just to distil his disturbing experiences but to examine his own responses.

'I wanted to give the reports an emotional dimension, in an unemotional way, for no human being could be dispassionate in the face of such individual and collective suffering.'

For eight hours, completely cut off in the aeroplane, he wrote and rewrote, paring it down to plain, unadorned, often monosyllabic prose.

Back in London, he didn't show his editors the pictures until he had put the commentary on them and the report was complete. By the time he had finished, one of the technicians in the dubbing theatre was crying. When he showed it to his programme editors after the film ended, there was a silence. People stood looking at the empty screen. They coughed, cleared their throats, blew their noses. A voice at the back said, 'Fucking hell'. Another said, 'God Almighty'. Buerk was not the only one struggling to find the words to do justice to what had been filmed.

On 23 October 1984, the report went out on all BBC television bulletins. Over the ghastly footage, Buerk addressed the viewers in a voice which was deliberate and seemingly stripped of emotion:

Dawn, and as the sun breaks through the piercing chill of night on the plain outside Korem it lights up a biblical famine, now, in the twentieth century. This place, say workers here, is the closest thing to hell on earth.

Thousands of wasted people are coming here for help. Many find only death. They flood in every day from villages hundreds of miles away, dulled by hunger, driven beyond the point of desperation … 15,000 children here now – suffering, confused, lost…

Death is all around. A child or an adult dies every twenty minutes. Korem, an insignificant town, has become a place of grief...

There is not enough food for half these people ... People scrabble in the dirt as they go for each grain of wheat: for some, it might be the only food they have had for a fortnight or more...

Those who die in the night are brought at dawn to be laid at the edge of the plain, dozens of them, men, women, and children, under blankets or bound in sackcloth for burial ... A tragedy bigger than anybody seems to realise, getting worse every day...

The words were calm, sparse and dignified. Yet the images which went with them were stark and shocking. Together, they conveyed a barely concealed anger and disgust for what the world was allowing to happen here. Viewers saw agonisingly thin children staggering on shrivelled limbs, huddled starved figures hunched against the cold, Brigitte Vasset, the MSF doctor in Korem, with medicines but no food. And, a second report, the following day, showed the Red Cross nurse, Claire Bertschinger, the woman with the impossible task of choosing who would live and who would die.

The graphic package sent shockwaves through the British nation – and wider. The report was picked up by 425 television stations across the world and the landmark footage was seen by more than a billion people. Michael Buerk's journalistic masterpiece was one of the single most important pieces of journalism in broadcast history. Ronald Reagan saw it and, visibly moved, declared 'a hungry child knows no politics' and promised an immediate $50 million of emergency aid to the communist regime. The Australian prime minister Bob Hawke watched and wept in public. It prompted an explosion of private giving – and an unprecedented wave of global activism.

❖

Television viewers all around the world sat frozen with horror at the scenes that unfolded before them. But one of those watching, sitting comfortably at home in his Chelsea townhouse, was seized with the determination that he must do something. Bob Geldof had come home early that night. Most of his fellow rock stars were out gigging or partying in the evenings. But Geldof had spent the day in the offices of his London record company,

Phonogram, trying in vain to publicise the latest single by the Boomtown Rats. And no one was interested.

It was five years since the band's song 'I Don't Like Mondays' had been an international hit. Geldof had written it in response to a Californian school shooting in which a sixteen-year-old said she'd opened fire because 'I don't like Mondays. This livens up the day.' The US was the only major market in which the single wasn't a massive hit after fear of lawsuits and charges of bad taste kept the song from getting extensive radio play. Five years later, the Rats had just finished a new album, *In the Long Grass*, which they believed had three hit tracks on it. But the first single, 'Dave', had flopped, hitting Geldof hard because it was a deeply personal song about the band's saxophone player who had suffered a breakdown after his girlfriend was found dead in a public toilet next to an empty £5 bag of heroin. They had a sell-out tour booked for the New Year, but they would be playing only to diehard fans. 'Punk was over,' says the music PR Bernard Doherty. 'They weren't washed up, but they were certainly fading.' The Boomtown Rats had given way to a new generation of bands. Geldof felt he had lost his way. He was undergoing a crisis of confidence.

At 6 p.m., he turned on the TV news and saw something which put all his troubles in perspective. The BBC's *Six O'Clock News* began with Michael Buerk's report from Korem and then devoted half the programme to the situation in Ethiopia. At the end, the newscasters remained silent. Geldof sat struck with horror. His partner Paula Yates burst into tears and rushed upstairs to check on their nineteen-month-old baby, Fifi. Geldof remained transfixed to the television screen.

Millions of TV viewers watched that news report with the same sense of terrified impotence. What singled out Bob Geldof and gave him the conviction that he must act?

A journalist from *Life* magazine writing at the end of the year tried to answer that question with a line that was repeated endlessly by the media in the years that followed: 'When you meet this man you wonder: Did God knock at the wrong door by mistake and when it was opened by this scruffy Irishman, think, "Oh, what the hell – he'll do"?'

But the knock came at the right door. Bob Geldof was someone who had made things happen all his life. After his mother died when he was just six, he had had to learn to fend for himself since his father was a travelling salesman who was only home at weekends. He had to learn to organise. There had to be food in the house. There had to be coal to light a fire when he got in from school. Washing had to be taken to the launderette. Organising became second nature. It was something he transferred from the private to the public sphere in his teenage years in Dublin, working with homeless people and campaigning against apartheid – where he learned that activism could change things and anger became his animus. Perhaps the birth of his first daughter had increased his sensitivity to the suffering of children. Perhaps it was because of all this. Watching that television, he was filled with rage and shame.

That night he had promised to go to a party at the Chelsea Arts Club to mark the launch of a volume of essays by Peter York, the great style guru of the 1980s. Champagne was flowing so freely that some people had a glass in each hand. Waiters were carrying round trays of canapés. The cornucopia seemed to Geldof in ghastly contrast to what he had just witnessed on television.

'Yes, it's terrible,' agreed one partygoer, stuffing cocktail sausages into his mouth, as Geldof grew increasingly angry, turning away the champagne. All this for a style guide about manners and etiquette; it seemed utterly shallow in the face of what was happening just a few hours away by plane.

That night, Geldof went up to bed but couldn't sleep. The images of Korem ran through his mind like an unending horror movie. 'The pictures were of people so shrunken they seemed to be from another planet,' he later said. 'The camera wandered amongst them like a mesmerised observer, occasionally dwelling on one so long that it looked like he was looking at me sitting in my comfortable living room...' The reports on the screen were harrowing in the extreme. He felt complicit in the evil. People were, in effect, dying in his own home. He had to do something to purge his sense of guilt.

But what? He could write a cheque and send it off to one of the charities working in the field. Charity, he felt, was the most profound of human emotional responses. Without it, something inside will wither and die. But writing a cheque wasn't enough. It required, he said later, giving something of the self.

'What could I do? All I can do is write songs and make records. And a song by the Boomtown Rats wouldn't have made enough. Millions of people were at risk of dying. What was required was an act of compassion on an unprecedented scale.'

One picture haunted him. It was the image of the young Red Cross nurse – younger than he was – choosing which child could be saved and which left to die.

'In her was vested the power of life and death,' he said. 'She had become like God. That is unbearable to put upon anyone, at any point, but certainly on someone so young in such devastating circumstances.

'The thing I remember most was the picture of the wall. Outside were thousands of starving people. And there was this young woman who had to pick a handful of children that she could feed. Those who were chosen were led behind a waist-high stone wall. And the ones who hadn't been picked stood in front of this wall and looked at the chosen few on the other side, without any rancour or envy but with an intense stoic dignity.

'That waist-high wall was the difference between life and death. And I remember seeing one child just lay her exhausted head on her arm in resignation, her arm laid along the top of that wall, the flies buzzing around her eyes. She had been chosen to die. That's what made me do it. That one image is what made me do the whole thing.'

CHAPTER 4

REELING IN THE STARS

Paula Yates was up in Newcastle filming *The Tube*. Before she left London, she had put a green bowl on the pine table in the kitchen. In it, she had placed a note which said: 'Anyone who comes to this house must put £5 in here for Ethiopia.' Bob saw it and picked up the phone. He rang the Tyne Tees television studio in Newcastle.

Paula answered it in the green room.

'Who's on the show this week?' asked Bob.

'Midge. He's here with me now.'

'Put him on, will you?'

Paula passed the phone to Midge Ure, the lead singer of Ultravox. This was who Bob needed. Ure was something of a musical veteran – his first number-one single had been with Slik eight years earlier – and yet Ultravox were still at the forefront of the New Pop trend which had dominated the first half of the decade. Their latest album had sold almost a million copies.

'Did you see that horrendous footage from Ethiopia the other night? We've got to do something.'

Midge had not seen it. But he was convinced by the urgency in his friend's voice.

'Have you got a song?'

'No, I've got a bit of a … thing. But if you've got something…'

'I'll ring you tomorrow when I'm back in London.'

Geldof could not then quite put it into words. But he later he realised that everything he was about to do would swim against the current of the times.

Four years in and the 1980s was a decade of tumultuous change. It had seen the arrival of the first mass-market personal computer, the first Space Shuttle and the groundwork had been laid for the invention of the World Wide Web. In music, punk had long since transitioned to new wave and indie, with synthesisers and drum machines challenging the guitar for pop primacy. Bands like Duran Duran, one of the biggest groups of the decade, were beginning to be superseded by individual artists like Michael Jackson, Madonna and Prince. In 1984, two years after its release, Jackson's *Thriller* became the best-selling album of all time.

There was change in politics, abroad and at home. Dictatorships gave way to democracy across Europe and the Americas – in Argentina, Uruguay, Brazil and Chile. Trade unionists in Poland, under the banner of Solidarity, led a campaign of civil resistance which proved to be the beginning of the end of sixty years of European communism and the fall of the Berlin Wall. The US president Ronald Reagan had cranked up the Cold War against the Soviet Union with his 'Star Wars' missile system and massive increase in US military spending. His matching rhetoric about the 'evil empire' framed the divide as a moral struggle between freedom and tyranny – in which the starving people of Ethiopia were on the wrong side. Abroad, Margaret Thatcher, the first female leader in the Western world, had just done battle with Argentina over the Falkland Islands. At home, the Iron Lady had provoked a stand-off with Britain's coal miners and was in the middle of perhaps the most bitter industrial dispute in British history. It ran for more than a year through 1984 and 1985, and was to break union power in UK, much as Ronald Reagan weakened the unions in the US by crushing the air traffic controllers' strike in the US in 1981.

There was change in the economy. The old post-war consensus on how the world should run was breaking apart. Reagan, for all his avuncular personality, cut funding for education, housing and welfare for the poor, while slashing taxes for the wealthy. Thatcher did the same. On both sides of the Atlantic, old manufacturing industries were allowed to decline. Unemployment rose, urban decay spread, and the gap between rich and poor grew. Thatcherism and Reaganomics split the peoples of both countries. In London, the removal of regulatory control over the finance sector saw young working-class kids, wearing red braces and driving Porsches, suddenly make it in the City. On Wall Street, traders in colourful jackets, shouting and waving order slips, became the iconic image of the financial boom – along with yuppies wearing designer suits and Rolex watches, and carrying Filofaxes and brick-sized mobile phones. But this same Big Bang also paved the way for the global financial crisis of 2007–08.

All this brought change in social attitudes too. The 1980s ushered in a more selfish worldview. It was the Me Decade. A new individualism was abroad. Thatcher went further. 'There is no such thing as society,' she said, only 'individual men and women' who 'look to themselves first'. She was, said Geldof, half-admiringly, 'a punk prime minister – Johnny Rotten in drag'. In the US, stock trader Ivan Boesky, later jailed for insider trading, told business school students: 'I think greed is healthy. You can be greedy and still feel good about yourself.' The speech, via the movie *Wall Street*, gave the decade its motto: 'greed is good'. Britain embraced the more low-grade slogan 'Loadsamoney', based on an avaricious grotesque invented by the comedian Harry Enfield.

As recently as 1980, the Brandt Report had been produced by a commission of global economists, policymakers and development experts chaired by Willy Brandt, the former chancellor of West Germany. Officially entitled *North–South: A Programme for Survival*, it focused on the global divide between rich and poor nations – and recommended a large transfer of resources from developed to developing countries. But even as it was asking the international community to think about interdependence and shared values, the world was hurtling off in the other direction under the influence of Reaganomics and Thatcherite monetarism. Aid budgets were being cut year in, year out. The idea that there was something deeper than self-interest was being forgotten.

Such was the hostile world into which Bob Geldof was launching his plea for a new generosity.

❊

After his conversation with Midge Ure, Bob began to ring around his fellow musicians. This was before the days of mobile phones, of course, but he'd still accumulated a good few landline numbers over the years, as had Paula from presenting *The Tube* and through her work as a rock journalist. Her signature work was a book called *Rock Stars in Their Underpants*, which featured cheeky photos of Paul McCartney, David Bowie, Debbie

Harry, Lemmy Kilmister, David Lee Roth, Rod Stewart and Elton John. Reflecting the spirit of the volume, Andy Warhol described it as 'the greatest work of art in the last decade'. Many of the emerging generation of New Romantic stars were friends of the couple, frequently staying over at the twelfth-century Benedictine priory which Bob and Paula bought in Kent.

Though the Boomtown Rats were now struggling for a hit, Geldof was still a significant figure. He had several top-ten records to his name and had recently played the lead in Alan Parker's movie version of Pink Floyd's *The Wall*. He and Paula were rarely out of the newspapers, who had turned the couple into a pop version of the Charles and Diana soap opera. When Geldof rang, his peers took the call.

Sting and Simon Le Bon were first to come on board. And Bob's instinct was that, once others knew Sting and Simon Le Bon were involved, more would quickly follow.

On his way home from the Phonogram office, he passed Pushkin's, an antique shop in the King's Road. Inside, he saw Gary Kemp of Spandau Ballet looking at a piece of Arts & Crafts furniture.

'I'm a working-class lad,' Kemp recalls. 'Everything we ever owned in our house was bought on hire-purchase. I think the only thing we owned outright was our cat. So here I am, I'm feeling a bit more successful. I've got my own property. I'm intrigued by antiques. And bang, bang, bang on the window. And I look out and it's Geldof. And he comes charging in, regardless of the antique dealer who was in there, just taking over the place. He's so tall, his head is banging on a chandelier that's hanging in the shop.'

In a torrent of words, Geldof outlined the harrowing TV report from Ethiopia and added: 'Midge is writing the song. I've just spoken to Le Bon. They're in. Sting's said yes.'

Now Gary Kemp agreed Spandau would join: 'I'm going to Japan on tour. If it's going to happen, call me in Japan …'

That night, at a party, Geldof bumped into Gary's brother, Martin Kemp, Spandau's bass player. He too was full of enthusiasm at the idea. The word was out. Soon the phone calls were coming the other way.

The next day, Bob was in a taxi on his way to visit a friend who was ill. In the back of the cab, he took out his diary and, to the tune of a song that had been rejected by the other Boomtown Rats, scribbled the words 'It's Christmas time, and there's no need to be afraid…'. The words poured out. When he got to his friend's house, he mentioned the idea of his song for Ethiopia.

'I wrote the words on the way over.'

His friend produced a battered old Spanish guitar.

'Play it for us.'

Unbeknownst to Geldof, his friend had switched on a little tape machine. The first rudimentary recording of what became 'Do They Know It's Christmas?' had been made.

Over the weekend, Midge made a point of watching the reports from Ethiopia. 'They were all over the box so I couldn't miss it. I found it horrific that we should be seeing images like that in this day and age, but I also couldn't escape the feeling that anything I did would be nothing more than an empty gesture.' On Monday 5 November, he and Bob met up for lunch at Langan's Brasserie. The irony of talking about famine in a fashionable showbiz restaurant in Mayfair was not lost on Geldof, but the pair swiftly got to work. 'The quickest option – covering somebody else's song, like "White Christmas" – was out of the question because almost half of the monies earned by a record go to the writer,' said Midge. 'If we wrote it, the royalties might raise £100,000. We realised that we had to write and record a new song, and that we only had a few weeks left before Christmas.'

Bob had the song in his back pocket, but at this point didn't mention it. 'This wasn't like Bob,' Midge said later. 'He was sounding a lot less self-confident than usual. When the Rats were in their heyday, he'd have written the song himself and harassed all his friends for money. But, in 1984, the guys having the hits were Sting, Duran Duran, Paul Young, Spandau … and me. Not Bob. Of course, I didn't know any of this for years. Artists don't confess weakness and self-doubt to other artists, even if they are mates. Once I'd agreed to write with him, he could tell people: "Midge and I are writing the song together."'

As Bob was broke, Midge paid for lunch.

When Midge got back home, he didn't go out to the 24-track studio he had built at the back of his house in Chiswick. Instead, he sat at the kitchen table with a little Casio keyboard, just messing around, thinking about Christmas. 'I came up with this bell sound, a little third harmony part that made it sound familiar and added a touch of "Jingle Bells".' It was the voluntary of notes which would eventually appear on the recording as the backing for the end chorus. He played it slowly on his little keyboard, recorded it and couriered the tape round to Bob.

Next morning, he rang to get a reaction.

'What do you think? I thought it sounded very jingly and Christmassy.'

'I think it sounds like fucking *Z Cars,*' said Geldof, sarcastically, referencing the theme tune of the British police TV drama from the 1960s and '70s.

'Well, what have you got?'

'I've got something. I'll come round and play it to you.'

Geldof was in Chiswick within the hour. He read out the lyrics of the opening verse.

'It's Christmas time, and there's no need to be afraid. At Christmas time, we let in light, and we banish shade.'

'Not bad.'

'It's a bit fucking corny,' their author conceded. 'You can change the words. Just do what you want, I'm really not sure.'

'Yes, it's corny, but it's meant to be an anthem. Anthems are all corny. Play me the tune.'

Geldof had brought his guitar, a twelve-string which only had seven strings on it. The song was in his head, but he couldn't quite remember how to play it. He started bashing away on the seven out-of-tune strings. Midge stared at him, half in amazement, half in horror.

'Bob, will you please tune that thing?'

'No, it's fine. This is just to give you an idea.'

Every time he sang it, Midge recalled, the melody changed. Eventually, he decided to tape Bob. After he'd recorded a few versions, Midge said: 'Okay, let me work with that. Just leave me to come up with the music. I'll do the arrangement.'

Originally, Geldof had wanted Trevor Horn to produce the record. Horn had just produced two massive singles and an album for Frankie Goes To Hollywood and, in 1984, was the hottest producer in the UK. But when he was asked, he told Geldof that he took at least six weeks to record and mix a single, by which time Christmas would be long gone. By way of compensation, Horn offered Geldof a day in his recording studio for free. With this news, Bob turned to Midge and said: 'We don't have Trevor Horn. We do have twenty-four hours in Sarm West. You're the producer.'

They had just five weeks to get the song written, recorded, mixed, pressed and into the shops. The two men took on their different roles without further discussion.

✂

The pop world was not the only section of society animated by the ghastly scenes depicted on the Michael Buerk broadcast. In the days before digital television arrived to fragment the nation's viewing habits, watching the television news was a shared experience. Almost half the population watched the BBC's initial report. The public, members of parliament and leading church officials were united in their determination that something must be done. But what? During a heated debate in parliament, David Penhaligon MP posed a cutting question to Margaret Thatcher:

'As the prime minister so magnificently organised the commandeering of enough ships to carry our navy, army, air force to the Falklands, will she explain why famine relief in Ethiopia presents such a problem?'

The government came under immense pressure, which created a great dilemma for Mrs Thatcher. Aid was not one of her top priorities. In theory, her government made a distinction between long-term development aid and short-term life-saving emergency aid. In practice, the Iron Lady was not keen to send either to a wasteful and bureaucratic socialist state in military alliance with the Soviet Union, which was how she saw Ethiopia.

It was not a stance she could now maintain. Church leaders, including the Archbishop of Canterbury, Robert Runcie, and the leader of Britain's Catholics, Cardinal Basil Hume, were publicly calling for the UK to join the rest of Europe in taking some immediate steps. They wanted the Thatcher government to cut the usual red tape and rush emergency food and medicines to Ethiopia. Together with the Moderator of the Free Churches Donald English, they wrote a joint letter to the prime minister, asking the government to send RAF Hercules transport planes to Ethiopia. The pressure was building.

While Midge worked on the music, Bob returned to the phone. He called Virgin Records to get the number for Boy George. He chased other big names of the day: Frankie Goes To Hollywood, Paul Young, Paul Weller, the Human League… He began to make notes in his diary. What is the British Phonographic Industry? Get each record company to donate

£20,000? Do we need a trust fund? How do we handle the publishing and the Performing Rights Society?

But he forgot about the Musicians' Union, which was to cause a problem.

The next day, Geldof went back to his record company, Phonogram, and asked for a meeting with its four top executives: the general manager, the legal adviser, the marketing director and the man responsible for the end-to-end manufacturing from packaging to pressing.

'What's the top priority if we're going to do this quick?'

The first job in making a record quickly was, bizarrely, not the music. What took longest in 1984 was the artwork for the record cover.

'We need Peter Blake,' Geldof decided. Blake, the leading member of the 1960s pop art movement in the UK, had done the cover for *Sgt. Pepper's Lonely Hearts Club Band*. He was one of Britain's most respected artists. How to contact him? Geldof picked up the phone book and chose an art gallery at random. He rang the number.

'We're Peter Blake's agent, as it happens,' said the voice at the other end. It was one of a number of serendipitous coincidences which were to occur throughout the production of the Band Aid single. 'One of the things I was half-aware of at the time, but which I only really registered fully later on, was how willing everyone was to help,' recalled Bob. 'Something was happening, this weirdness, this otherness, out there in the whole country. There was some emotional centre to all of this.' Others saw him at the centre of what was happening, but to Geldof it all felt like something else was driving it. 'I didn't feel I was making it happen. I felt like it was happening to me. It was really odd.'

Half an hour later, the phone rang in the fourth-floor office Bob had been allocated at Phonogram's office in Bond Street. It was Peter Blake. They arranged to meet the following day in the tearoom of Fortnum & Mason, grocer to Her Majesty the Queen. Blake turned up with a rough draft. It was a montage, like his iconic album cover for the Beatles. He had begun it as soon as he had put the phone down. Blake had juxtaposed starving African children with a cosy festive scene.

'Can you finish it in a couple of days?' Geldof asked.

The biggest duo of the 1980s was Wham!. The pair had sold more than 18 million records already in less than half a decade. That evening, there was a party for the launch of their new album, *Make It Big*. Geldof did not think they would be interested in Band Aid. 'They were too big, too poppy and probably too busy,' he thought. Undaunted, he collared the band's manager Simon Napier-Bell and asked if George Michael might be interested in singing on a charity record for Ethiopia. The manager said yes without even asking the singer: 'I knew George would. He was very into charity.' The pair then fell to talking through the whole project.

'How do I maximise the profit?' Geldof asked Napier-Bell.

'Well, if it sells half a million – and you'll be lucky to do that in three weeks – and if you get a good percentage from Phonogram, and you donate all your publishing rights as the composers, that would be £72,000. Can't you eliminate some of the percentages?'

The next day, Geldof went into Phonogram. 'Can't we eliminate some of the percentages?' he asked the legal adviser.

Phonogram agreed to waive their profit entirely. 'Now, if you can get the costs and the labour for nothing, and if you can get the distributors to do it for nothing, you're close to 100 per cent profit,' their lawyer said.

'Okay. Who makes the most profit?'

'The retailers. They get 30 per cent.'

Most records in the UK were sold through six big retailers – Woolworths, WHSmith, HMV, Virgin, Boots and Our Price. Geldof phoned them up, one at a time, and systematically lied to them.

'All the other major chains have agreed to do it for free,' he told each one. 'Everyone has agreed so far. You're actually the last one I'm calling.'

'Okay, if they're doing it for free, I think we ought to too.'

This was to become a classic Geldof *modus operandi* – the Bob Bluff. He was to employ it later to great effect to persuade the top acts to play at Live Aid. Band Aid's lawyer, John Kennedy, came to call this Geldof's 'hoodwink method' – but he also deployed what Kennedy calls the 'blackmail approach'. In addition to the big six record sellers, there were hundreds of independent retailers. Their trade body told Geldof that they couldn't relinquish their profit because Christmas was when they made the money which kept them going the rest of the year.

'Look, I hear you guys,' Geldof said to them. 'But your problems do not compete with the problems of the people I'm trying to help. So, I'm asking you, on this one record, do this for us. And maybe the people who come in to buy this record from you will buy more records and, overall, you'll be the same or better.

'But if you can't do it, I understand. It's your call. But then, I'm afraid, I'll have to tell all the fans to buy the record not from you, but from one of the big stores that are not taking a cut from the money being raised for the starving in Ethiopia. Then you will lose all that Christmas footfall. That's okay, but it's your loss. And you understand that all the stars will have to tell their fans to do the same.' Geldof was not taking no for an answer.

He kept ringing bands. After five days on the phone, he was getting no resistance. 'I was amazed that everyone was saying yes,' he said. He tracked down U2 on tour. It was 2 p.m. and Bono had just got up. 'He sounded like a truck had rolled over his throat, but he said he would do it.' As he was ringing round, Francis Rossi of Status Quo came into the Phonogram office. 'You can put us down too,' he said.

Geldof had never got on with Paul Weller, but he too agreed over the phone. 'Yeah, we'll do it, Bob. Have you got a song?'

'Well, Midge and I are working on something…'

'I'll be there.'

Interestingly, Geldof discovered that if he got through to the artists direct, the response was always positive. But if he got through to their managers, their first instinct was to put obstacles in the way. So he focused on the performers and, as more and more agreed, he decided to aim higher. Bob went to see Paul McCartney, whom he'd met now and again over the years, and David Bowie, with whom he had hung out at the Blitz club in Covent Garden. Both would be away, but both offered to send spoken messages for the B-side of the single. Peter Blake's artwork came in. It was a colourful montage of a Victorian children's nursery at Christmas – but at the front sat two skeletal Ethiopian children depicted in black and white. It was shockingly perfect.

⁂

The stars were lining up, but the song was not finished. In the week beginning Monday 8 November 1984, Midge Ure went into his home studio and started making backing tracks for the emerging single. He and his engineer, Rik Walton, took a sample of the drums from the title track of the 1983 Tears For Fears album *The Hurting* and slowed it down to create an eerie groaning drone, which set the ominous tone for the start of the song with its tolling bell. Then they spent three days gradually piecing together synth parts onto a multi-track tape with a bassline and drum machine to conjure a ghostly wintery feeling. Midge did a guide vocal on top of this sketchy backing track. But it still wasn't there. They had two verses, but they didn't have a chorus, or a middle eight. He called Geldof in.

They sat there, just looking at one another, both thinking, *Where are we going with this?*. Midge was playing the guitar, initially just three simple chords.

'It has to be classic pop,' said Bob, 'a hook riff, easy-to-understand lyrics, but with a turnaround at the top.'

Midge kept strumming away.

'What do you do at Christmas?' Bob said. 'To celebrate?'

'You make a toast … you know … Cheers. Here's to you. Then everyone raises their glasses. So what's our toast?'

'Here's to you. Raise a glass for everyone … that's us here in England.' Bob paused. 'But this toast has to be embittered … Here's to them … underneath that burning sun.'

'Good. What else?'

'At Christmas, we get together, we exchange gifts. But they won't have anything to give. In Africa, they won't even know, let alone care, that it's Christmas.'

Which of them came up with the line 'Do they know it's Christmas?' neither could later remember. 'By then,' said Midge, 'the song was a true collaboration', although he unilaterally changed one key line. Originally Bob had written 'and there won't be snow in Ethiopia this Christmas'. But Midge just couldn't make it scan. 'I changed "Ethiopia" to "Africa".' But both knew that, though the song had to start dark and moody, it had to finish big and bright and Christmassy.

'We need something for the ending, something that we can sing over and over and over,' said Bob. 'We've got to get that "Happy Xmas, War is Over"/"Give Peace a Chance" chant in at the end.' Between them, they came up with 'Feed the world'.

As Midge worked on the arrangement, Bob returned to his phone calls. 'I'd hear him on the phone while I was working on the track at the mixing desk,' recalls Midge. 'He was in my other ear, shouting at people down the line. It only worked because Bob got straight through to people. I don't know how he got their telephone numbers, but he did. With the few who tried to wriggle out of it, Bob had no conscience – he promptly resorted to intimidation and blackmail. "I'll tell the world that you've fucking turned it down, that you're not doing it because you can't be fucking arsed."'

✄

Pressure was being piled on elsewhere. In parliament, the ruling Conservative Party was desperately trying to find someone else to blame for its government's inaction over the past year. On 21 November 1984, the House of Commons Foreign Affairs Committee summoned representatives of Oxfam and Save the Children to Westminster to interview them on the famine in Ethiopia. The committee's chairman, Sir Anthony Kershaw, a leading Conservative, wanted to know why the British government had been kept in the dark about the impending famine.

The overseas director of Save the Children, an old soldier named Colonel Hugh Mackay, was placed in the witness box. He did not mince his words. Save the Children's office in Ethiopia had informed the British Embassy in Addis Ababa that a serious famine was coming but they were not believed. They reported it to the government in London who, again, did not believe it because of what Colonel Mackay called 'that rather curious phenomenon that people will not believe a famine until they see it'.

Sir Anthony became increasingly flustered and angry.

'The Ethiopian famine … in our reckoning started two years ago,' Colonel Mackay declared.

'Did you report it?' asked the politician.

'Yes.'

'Then?'

'They did fuck-all, sir.'

Hansard, the official record of the UK parliament, did not record the old soldier's salty remark.

The following day, in a full debate in the House of Commons, Sir Anthony tried to defend the near-total inactivity of his government. 'I do not accept the moral blame for that disaster, which many people appear to think we should shoulder. We did not cause the drought, cut down the trees, overcrop the land or start the civil war. Why should we be blamed?'

he asked rhetorically before claiming, totally incorrectly, that the Ethiopian government had not asked for help until very recently.

The Labour MP, Tom Clarke, replied: 'The British people are not interested in that sort of argument.' The public realised 'that people are suffering, starving and dying'. Voters had written to him to say that the British government should not be penalising hungry people because a Marxist regime happens to be in control of Ethiopia. Starving people, he said, did not care whether it was 'Karl Marx or Groucho Marx' who was in charge.

Back at Save the Children, Colonel Mackay fulminated: 'How much lead time does the world's conscience really need? Do they really want to see children die before they believe the predictions of people like us?'

✁

Geldof fixed a date for the recording – Sunday 25 November 1984. 'How soon can we get the record out after that?' he asked Phonogram's product manager, John Waller.

'If we pull out all the stops, we can do it in four days,' Waller replied.

Bob Geldof had eliminated the percentages.

He would get practically 100 per cent of the money from the sale of each record.

Now he had gained an extra two weeks on his three-week selling period.

The Band Aid record could make a million pounds.

Not that it was called Band Aid at that point. Geldof had had the idea of a logo for the record. It would be a round map of the world in white, like a plate, with Africa in black. Either side would be a knife and fork. But he couldn't think of a name for the collection of superstars he had brought together. He proposed 'Food for Thought', half-heartedly. The Phonogram press office was unenthusiastic. Next, more satirically, he suggested 'The Bloody Do-Gooders'. Then one member of the Phonogram press team, Linda Valentine, suggested Band Aid. Brilliant, Geldof said. 'Apart from the obvious pun, there was now an extra dimension. What we were doing and what we would raise would be so small in the context of the problem. You can't put a Band-Aid, a sticking plaster, on a gaping wound of poverty.'

Now they needed a big launch. Media interest in the project was enormous once it became apparent how many big names were involved. But when Geldof contacted Britain's biggest-selling newspaper, the *Sun*, its editor Kelvin MacKenzie refused the offer of a front-page story – because he'd been offered an exclusive of Princess Diana's new dress.

'Seriously?' Geldof exploded. 'Princess Diana has a new dress – as opposed to the greatest collection of British artists ever?'

'It's an exclusive,' replied MacKenzie.

So Geldof turned to the second best-seller, the *Daily Mirror*, which had been running a big campaign to raise money for Ethiopia under the headline '*Mirror* Mercy Mission'. He offered them exclusive pictures of the recording session if they promised Band Aid the entire front page.

'Sorry, Bob, we'll do the story, but it's just not front-page material,' said a *Mirror* executive. Geldof was outraged. That morning, the *Mirror*'s front page had been taken up with a picture of the back of the head of the Princess of Wales. Bob got hold of the private number of the owner of the *Mirror*, Robert Maxwell, and called him.

'Can you give me the front cover?'

'Well, what do I get?'

'You get a picture of the greatest collection of pop stars ever assembled. Every one of your readers will have bought a record by one of them, and that's a guarantee.'

Maxwell immediately agreed to give over the newspaper's front page. It was another lesson which Geldof applied throughout the forty years of Live Aid: in future, always go straight to the top.

Two days before the recording, Paul Weller rang and asked if he could come and play guitar. If there was any previous rivalry between him and Bob, it had been set aside given the gravity of the cause. Sting and John Taylor from Duran Duran both offered to play bass. Midge told them to come down to his studio in Chiswick. Simon Le Bon offered to come too. He recorded the vocals for the whole song. Sting arrived and added a sequence of harmonies to the middle eight which helped bind the song together. 'Weller came and did some nice guitar work,' said Geldof, 'though in the end we couldn't use it because Midge had done the rest of the backing with electronics, and they just didn't work together.' Taylor was sweating with nerves at playing in front of Sting. 'It was a good session,' said Bob.

It had been four weeks since Geldof had seen the news bulletin about the famine. 'For weeks, I had kept those images alive, so that when I spoke to people, I conveyed a genuine sense of conviction and urgency.' But there was something else. Geldof was not, he said, a great believer in fate or destiny. But everything had fallen so easily into place. Everyone wanted to do their bit. It felt providential.

The day before the recording, Geldof had promised to appear on BBC Radio 1 on Richard Skinner's show to promote the new Boomtown Rats album. He kept the appointment. But he sacrificed the chance to plug the Rats to announce to the nation that a firmament of stars, the biggest names in British pop music, were the next day recording a charity single to raise money for the famine-struck people of Ethiopia.

Band Aid had been born.

CHAPTER 5

'DO THEY KNOW IT'S CHRISTMAS?'

'Okay, who's first?' asked Midge Ure. There was a lot of shuffling. No one wanted to be the first to perform a solo in front of what Bob Geldof later called the greatest single collection of contemporary musicians in British history.

'Come on, Tony,' said Geldof. 'You go first.'

Tony Hadley, the lead singer of Spandau Ballet, stepped forward in his white embossed shirt and black leather trousers. He did not seemed unnerved at the idea of going first, yet afterwards admitted: 'I couldn't say no because I'd look like a right plonker.' It was, he said, 'pretty scary' to sing the first solo in front of some of the greatest pop voices of the 1980s.

'Can't we all sing the chorus first?' Hadley asked, having heard it on the guide tape Midge played.

'We'll do that once everybody's arrived,' replied Midge.

He and Geldof discussed who should sing which part. They had so many stars on hand that they hit upon what Midge later reckoned was a recording innovation – to get individual lines sung by different singers. Midge wanted to keep the opening lines of the song for George Michael or, perhaps, Paul Young: 'It's Paul Young's range, the opening lines.'

Hadley was given a page of lyrics and Midge pointed to lines from the middle of the song: 'There's a world outside your window / And it's a world of dread and fear / Where the only water flowing is / The bitter sting of tears…'

Tony headed out onto the lonely studio floor, which had been cleared of everyone apart from the video crew, who pushed their cameras into his face as he sang. He only had two lines to sing, but getting it right in so short a time only made him more nervous – even if he didn't show it. He did it in two takes. Even Bono nodded slowly in silent approval. Competition had been set aside. Everyone sensed it.

'It was a brave thing to stand up there in the firing line, with every nose pressed against the control-room window, staring at him,' Midge later recalled. 'He did very well. So well, in fact, that everybody clapped. That broke the ice.'

That morning Geldof and Ure had arrived at the studio at 8 a.m. Notting Hill was usually deserted that early on a Sunday morning, 'suffering from a Saturday-night hangover', as Midge put it. But that Sunday, the world's media had besieged Basing Street outside Sarm West Studios. Bob and Midge pushed their way gently through the crowds of TV crews, photographers and waving microphones. Once inside the studio, there was no one else there. Not a single star in sight. Bob looked at Midge. 'If it's only the Boomtown Rats and Ultravox, it's going to be a fucking dull record,' he said to cover their nerves. Would anyone show up? Bob fretted. How would he control them all if they *did?* worried Midge.

The Boomtown Rats bass player, Pete Briquette, was one of the first to arrive. Next came Sting, a copy of that day's *Observer* tucked under his arm. They sat together in the studio's coffee area.

'So what's happening?' asked Sting.

'I don't know,' said Pete. 'I haven't a clue.'

Slowly the place started to fill. They came in ones and twos and gaggles. The record companies hadn't paid for anything. There were no limos, no entourages, no bodyguards. There was no Band Aid budget to get people there. Everyone arrived under their own steam. Paul Weller stepped smartly down the street in a long coat and scarf, marking his stride with a walking stick, like an Edwardian undergraduate. But many of the musicians looked like they had just got out of bed, or hadn't been to bed at all. Spandau Ballet and Duran Duran, who *did* both arrive in a limo, had been up all night, drinking together in Germany and hadn't slept on the flight back so intent were they on racing one another to Heathrow in their private jets. Bananarama, by contrast, arrived in a battered two-door VW Golf and were shocked by how many stars had turned up. 'It would have been nice if someone had let us know how big the event was going to be,' said Keren Woodward, 'so I could have at least not had greasy hair and a ponytail.'

Simon Le Bon was also taken aback by how many big names were crowded into the studio. 'When I was on the phone with Bob, it sounded to me that it was going to be me, Sting and Midge and Bob making a record,' he said. 'I thought I was going to get half the song. For the demo, I sang the entire song. I was a bit pissed off because when I walked in, they were recording somebody else singing one of my lines! That took a while to get my head around. I had to really rein in my egotistical emotions. Of course, after a couple of minutes, I realised exactly what was going on.' Seeing George Michael, Paul Young and Bono sitting together on a long couch at the back of the room was all the corrective he needed.

Bono had flown in from Dublin with U2's bass player Adam Clayton. They had left it to the last minute after debating whether it might look too uncool to appear in the same room as the kind of pop stars who appeared on the front cover of *Smash Hits*. They had eventually concluded that their reputation could survive the close proximity.

Around 10.30 a.m., Culture Club arrived from New York – without Boy George. Geldof exploded and yelled at the band's drummer, Jon Moss.

'Where the fuck's George?'

'I don't know. I haven't seen him for a couple of days. Maybe he never left New York.'

'Where's he staying?'

Geldof grabbed the phone and dialled New York, where it was 6 a.m. A sleepy voice answered.

'What the fuck are you still doing in New York? Get up and get here.'

'Oh, is it today?' mumbled George. 'Who's there?'

'Every fucker except you,' Bob shouted, reeling off the names of every star who had turned up. 'There is a Concorde in two hours. Get on it. This is fucking important, so get here.'

'I'll try,' said the sleepy voice at the other end.

'Don't fucking try,' shouted Geldof. 'Get up now.'

The first few hours were a milling chaos. The assembled stars knew one another's work from recordings and had seen each other on television, but many had never previously met those they regarded as rivals. 'I think every-one was nervous walking in the room as to how we would react with each other,' said Gary Kemp. There were nervy conversations. Geldof made awkward introductions: 'George, do you know Bono, and Paul Young?'. 'I always get really shy when there's loads of other pop stars about,' said George Michael. 'I tend to clam up a bit … but no one's come up and attacked me verbally yet!' he joked to Paula Yates. Yates was filming interviews for *The Tube* and also acting as a mother figure to the entire assembly.

By mid-morning, the editor of the *Daily Mirror* called Bob and said he needed the front-page photo of the assembled stars by 3 p.m. Bob and Midge herded the musicians together. 'It was like the school photo,' said Midge. 'All these giant stars were shuffling along, being awkward around each other, or showbiz-hugging each other,' said Bob.

But the group was brought together when Midge called them up to record the end chorus of the song. 'To keep everybody occupied, we recorded the chorus first,' recalled Midge. Everyone was lined up with copies of the lyrics. In unison they all sang 'Feed the world' and then separately 'Let them know it's Christmas time again'. Midge had done a brilliant job on the backing track; Geldof declared: 'It was radically different from what I had originally played him.' Everyone sang it over and over again, before Midge double-tracked it so it sounded 'as if there were thousands of voices singing'. There were no fewer than seven video crews filming the event for different media outlets.

A buzz built around the studio. 'There was an electric atmosphere,' said Pete Briquette of the Boomtown Rats. 'Everybody knew it was something very special.' That feeling was enhanced when film of them singing the chorus session appeared on the ITV lunchtime television news. Everyone gathered round to watch. 'It was shown just ninety minutes after we'd actually recorded it,' said Nigel Dick, who was directing the official video for Phonogram. 'There was a very clear sense that if it's on TV, this must be real. The very fact that we were still in the same room, the same bunch of people, and we were already watching this happening on TV had a big effect on everybody.'

Perhaps not quite everybody. At lunchtime, one hapless pop star shouted out to Geldof: 'Is there any food, Bob?' A cloud passed across Geldof's face. 'You're a fucking millionaire and you want free food? There's a fucking chip shop on the corner. Go and buy your own lunch.' Not a penny was taken from the Band Aid fund to pay for anything. All the artists sang without payment. And neither Bob nor Midge received any royalties from the song, then or in the years that followed.

Midge returned to the trickier business of recording the verses. He had split the lyrics into individual lines to give as many people as possible a mini-solo. 'The hard part was trying to decide who was singing what, where the edits were going to be, where one person took over halfway through a line from another,' said Midge. There weren't enough lines in the song to allocate one to every star. 'So Bob and I were sitting there with little bits of paper, graphs, working out who was going to do what, and with people turning up all the time, we had to keep changing the order.'

There was no precedent to follow; the whole notion of multi-artist charity singles didn't explode until after Band Aid. 'I didn't know of any previous record doing that, so maybe it was unique,' said Midge. 'The allocation of lines for everyone to sing was organic.' To make the edit easier, he got each soloist to sing two or three lines which he could edit later. 'Start the line with one artist and finish it with another because, to begin with, I had no idea how to chop this thing up.'

The singers had not heard the track in advance. There was no internet then and no effective way of circulating the demo ahead of time. They all walked into the studio cold and learned their lines on the spot, although Midge later concluded that the fact the song had to be done in a day meant that all the singers were happy to take instruction. There was no time for arguments. 'Sometimes, that kind of pressure creates something magical. We just had to nail it and get on. As it turns out, a lot of the vocal tracks were exceptional.'

Video director Nigel Dick agreed. Modern recording studios could make the ordinary sound wonderful, with so many effects and techniques that could be applied to improve vocal performances. 'But sitting there, with the camera just feet from the singers, I heard their voices unadorned. Paul Young sounded strong, soulful and clear. Sting's voice seemed strangely out of tune on its own, but then incredibly right in context. Bono's voice was like a wild emotional howl, unique and distinctive. George Michael amazed me with his control.' George's vocals 'were just unbelievable,' said Gary Kemp. 'There was a sense of euphoria for all being together.'

But even great vocalists needed to be taught the tune. 'Ironically, Bob was supposed to know how it went,' complained Midge. 'But every time he sang it to them, he sang a different melody. George Michael, Simon Le Bon, Glenn Gregory... No matter who, he kept giving them his off-key Bob Dylan version.' Finally, after they had decided to give the opening lines of the song to Paul Young, Bob leaned across Midge, pressed the talkback button on the control panel and sang a completely different melody.

'For fuck's sake, Bob, you're confusing people,' snapped an exasperated Midge. Turning to Paul Young, he said: 'One singer, one song. Just do it the way you feel is best.'

That sentiment didn't apply, however, to the idea of getting Status Quo to use their trademark harmonies on the mid-section of the song. 'I had Francis Rossi and Rick Parfitt on the mic for an hour,' said Midge. 'Francis sang his bit fine, but we watched Rick squawk, trying to hit the high notes. Finally, I despaired and told them, "That's great, thanks", knowing we were not going to use any of it.' As Midge was organising the next line-up, Rossi came up and whispered in his ear: 'Next time you want us to do a harmony part, ask who does the harmony. Live, Rick may sing along, but in the studio, I do all the vocals.'

But the most problematic line was to do with words rather than music. Geldof had allocated to Bono the acidic phrase: 'Tonight, thank God, it's them instead of you.' The younger Irishman was not happy.

'I'll sing any line but this one,' Bono said. 'Why would I want somebody else to go through this?'

Geldof was forceful in his response. 'That's not what it means. I'm not saying I want somebody else to suffer. I'm saying "It's only an accident of geography that it's not you. There but for the grace of God... Be grateful it's not you – and do something in response." We should be aware of our good fortune. Your kids are safe, thank God, your kids are safe.'

Bono remained unconvinced, so Geldof explained what had most troubled him while watching the BBC footage of the degradation in Ethiopia – that it was made worse by the irony of viewing it from the comforts of an expensive townhouse in fashionable Chelsea.

'It's about the rage I felt at the inhumanity of a world in which some people are starving while others are worrying about small things. This is not soggy liberalism. It is coded anger, like in Michael Buerk's report. People will buy the record because they share the rage, but also share the shame, the shame of thinking, *Thank God, tonight, it's them, instead of me.*'

Despite his misgivings, Bono sang it. And where Midge Ure had sung the line much lower on the guide tape, Bono leapt an octave on the controversial line. 'This huge voice erupted out of this little guy,' said Midge. 'I was standing next to Bono and I jumped. It felt as if I was standing next to an opera singer. He had the same massive power. That was it, one take. He just let it rip and it was phenomenal. Electric. Just sensational.'

Years later, Bono came to understand what Geldof was trying to do. Twenty years after, he wrote: 'It's the most biting line, and actually reveals how selfish a mindset we all have underneath. I think Bob was trying to be honest and raw and self-accusatory. Rather than sing, "We're lucky it's not us", he was saying, "Well, when you say that, you mean 'Lucky it's them'. Now look at it. Now look at yourself."'

On the day of the recording, Geldof's fire was turned in another direction. Someone asked him whether he had got the permission of the Musicians' Union for all the singers to waive their broadcast fees. Ordinarily, under an agreement between the union and the BBC, a fee had to be paid to an artist when their record was played on air. With thirty-seven singers on the Band Aid record, the BBC would have had to pay thirty-seven fees every time the record was played. Obviously, this was ridiculous; it would not be in the BBC's interest to play it at all. The artists all agreed that they were happy to waive their fee, but the consent of the union was needed.

'I assumed this would be just a box-ticking exercise, as usual with these bureaucrats,' Geldof recalled. 'But because it was Sunday, I was told "Not so fast, my lad". I couldn't believe it. It was very real.' After several unsatisfactory phone calls, Geldof reported back to the others and suggested a solution.

'Let's all leave the Musicians' Union and set up a Pop Musicians' Union. Hands up anyone who disagrees.'

No hands went up. The union was not well-loved among rock bands and pop stars who felt it prioritised the interests of classical and session musicians.

So Geldof rang the assistant general secretary of the union, Stan Hibbert, again.

'Stan, if we do not get a sign-off paper on this record, by the end of the day, we're all leaving the MU and we're setting up the PMU – Pop

Musicians' Union. Which means Radio 1 and *Top of the Pops* cannot play George Michael, Culture Club, the Police, Spandau Ballet, Duran Duran, Ultravox, the Boomtown Rats, Bananarama, Status Quo or the Style Council because the PMU won't give permission. So that's the end of Radio 1 and the end of *Top of the Pops* unless we get this piece of paper.'

'Don't threaten me, Bob,' the assistant general secretary said.

'It's not a threat, Stan. I'm serious.'

Shortly afterwards, a note was delivered to the studio outlining the Musicians' Union's 'support for Band Aid and its hoped-for achievements' with the assurance that 'whatever requirements are legally necessary' were being dealt with and that there would be zero impediments for immediate broadcast of the record on radio or TV. Another example of the Bob Bluff? 'I never once considered that I couldn't do it,' Geldof later told me. But it was not just a capitulation to Bob. It was an acknowledgement of the extraordinary mood that was building right across the nation.

❧

Earlier in the day, Phil Collins had arrived with his entire drum kit, insisting he would record a live drum track on top of Midge's programmed drum machine. 'It will take me half an hour to set up while you go and get a sandwich,' he insisted. 'You have got to have some real drums on the record. I'll do fills, between the electronics.'

Midge was nervous, fearful that he'd run out of time. 'Recording drums can take forever so I was a bit pissed off … but hell, this was Phil Collins. I couldn't say no. He was a huge superstar.' Phil got the studio engineer to set up his kit with high compressed mics behind the drums to give it his trademark big ambient sound. He did his soundcheck, said, 'Let me know when you want me' and then sat at the back of the room and waited. He was in the middle of recording his next solo album, *No Jacket Required*, at Townhouse Studios in nearby Shepherd's Bush and Sunday was his one day off. 'He didn't have to be there, but he sat there nice as pie, waiting for his turn.' He knew so much about producing records that he understood the process Midge had to go through.

He just sat on the sofa behind the mixing desk. 'Every so often, Phil's head would pop up and say: "Are you ready for me yet, boss?" and I said,

"Well, not quite yet…"' The veteran drummer sat there for hours, by which point he knew the song inside out. By the time the lead vocals were all done and he came to play, most of the younger stars had finished. But they did not want to go home. Although they were of a generation who would have dismissed Phil Collins and Genesis as dinosaurs in interviews with the music press, when it came to it, they knew they were in the presence of a master. When Jon Moss, the drummer with Culture Club, was asked why he was hanging around so long in the afternoon, he replied: 'I can't go until I see Phil Collins play.'

After sitting around for six hours, Collins got the nod. 'Phil went out and played the first run-through brilliantly,' recalled Midge. 'Everyone was in awe, because you're watching brilliance… He came back into the control room and listened to it once. To my ears, there was nothing wrong with it, but Phil wasn't happy.'

'No, I've overplayed. I need one more take.'

He went back out and played it again, but simpler. That was it, two takes, job done in eight minutes. Then he went home.

✷

Finally, just before 7.30 p.m., Boy George arrived straight off Concorde from Heathrow, 'wandering into the studio like Joan Collins', as Bob put it.

'Hey, Simon,' he said, grabbing Le Bon, 'here's your chance to crush the rumours' – and then dragged him up to the open studio door. As a dozen press photographers crowded in, with cameras flashing, George put his arm around Simon in a way which was calculated to do anything but crush gossipy rumours.

Le Bon had already done his lines but, emboldened by the arrival of George, he insisted on re-recording them. They were better second time around.

Geldof, never doubting that George would get there in time, had kept a couple of lines back for him.

'Can somebody get me some brandy?' George shouted, adding that his throat was shot from the previous nights' shows in the US.

'No,' said Midge. The Culture Club diva looked surprised. Nobody said no to Boy George, in those days one of the biggest stars in the world.

'You'll have to get it yourself. There's no record label flunkies here,' said Midge.

'If you want one, go to the shop round the corner and hope it's open,' said Geldof.

'And anyway,' said Midge, 'there isn't time.'

George smacked Geldof's bum and made do with a custard cream and a sausage roll.

Once in the studio, after singing his allocated line a couple of times, George stopped and began to suggest new ideas to Midge.

'Get on with it, you fucking old queen,' laughed Bob helpfully from behind the control-room glass.

'Shut up, you Irish tart,' retorted George and began to sing.

'And in our world of plenty ... throw your arms around the world at Christmas time.'

'He has such a beautiful voice,' said Geldof beneath his breath. 'He sounds like a black female blues singer. Don't matter what you look like. You got it or you ain't.'

Boy George sang his lines perfectly, then swanned out into the studio to spread mayhem. It had been worth the wait.

❊

The recording was virtually over, but most people hung around until 6 p.m. to watch themselves on the BBC evening news – the same bulletin which, a month earlier, had carried the harrowing report that had brought this starry assembly together. For all the exhilaration of the day, said Geldof, always in the background were the haunting images they had all seen from Ethiopia.

Many in the group were aware of the paradox of the thrill of being together – and the sadness of what had brought them together. 'All these egos together in one room,' said Sting. Yet 'there hasn't been one individual who's had an ego problem,' observed Jill Sinclair, the studio's co-owner. 'Every band that's ever slagged each other off...' interjected Boy George. 'But we've all got on,' countered Gary Kemp. 'It just fell into place,' said John Taylor. 'This has brought us together,' added Kemp. 'It's like a celebration,' concluded Taylor.

'It was an amazing experience,' said Sara Dallin of Bananarama. There was 'something infinitely, much more deeply, emotional than just a piece of music,' suggested Midge. 'There was something in the air. It was unity.' Spandau Ballet's manager, Steve Dagger, reflected: 'I remember thinking at the time, this is a real moment of pop history and I'm here.' And Nigel Dick admitted, much later: 'This might sound ridiculous, but I swear to God it happened, I remember thinking at that moment: "This is my Woodstock. This may be the highlight of my entire career." And I was okay with that.'

But it was Bono who added a different perspective to the reflective mood. He and Geldof had for years conducted an animated debate about religion. Geldof, an atheist (or an agnostic at any rate), was intrigued by the roots of Bono's Christian beliefs. The younger man looked across at the older one, with the words of the Band Aid song in his hand.

'It's a hymn really, isn't it? Far out, Bob. You got there in the end.'

'Fuck off,' laughed Geldof.

The hardest part of the Band Aid recording was not getting people there but getting them to leave. By the evening, everybody was in congratulatory mood. 'Guys were popping down the offie to buy a few drinks – George got his brandy eventually – and they were having a ball,' recalled Midge. Status Quo kept those who were interested supplied with cocaine. 'It became a party,' said the *Daily Mirror* pop writer Robin Eggar, who brought six bottles of wine from his flat. Status Quo locked Spandau Ballet in the toilet; the Spandaus had to kick the door down to get out. People were getting high, in more ways than one. 'They were all celebrating. They'd done their job,' said Midge. 'Meanwhile, I was trying to get into mix mode. I tried to kick them out, but they wouldn't leave. It was coming on midnight before we managed to chuck everybody out. Mixing a record can be a long process, something best not done under pressure.' The video crew left for the *Daily Mirror* printing plant to shoot the Band Aid front-page story coming off the newspaper presses.

Fortified by the rest of Boy George's brandy – which he had kindly donated to Sarm studio engineer Stuart Bruce as he left – Midge and Bob got down to the task of mixing.

Midge, Bob, Rik Walton and Stuart Bruce worked through the night. Around 2 a.m., they finished the A-side of the record, before turning their attention to the track on the B-side. Over the backing music, they overlaid messages from the big-name stars who couldn't be there on the day – Paul McCartney, David Bowie and Frankie Goes To Hollywood. They added in messages from a sprinkling of the singers who had just left the studio. One they omitted. When Steve Norman, the Spandau sax-player, was asked to do a message, he misunderstood the purpose of the exercise; instead of appealing for funds for the starving, thinking it was the kind of fan-message that bands routinely do for far-off radio stations, he said cheerily: 'I'd like to say hi to all our friends in Ethiopia. We've got no plans to be coming over next year, but we're working on it for the year after. Have a Happy Christmas.'

At 3 a.m., the phone rang. It was Robert Maxwell.

'Did you like the front page?' he said to Geldof.

'Yes. Thanks very much.'

Band Aid had been given the whole of the front page under the headline 'BILLION DOLLAR BAND'. The centrespread was the picture of all the Band Aid singers.

'We'd like to use the group picture to do a poster and sell it for the Mirror Ethiopia Appeal. That'll be alright, won't it?'

Geldof was indignant. Maxwell seemed to be trying to turn the whole Band Aid enterprise into an adjunct of his newspaper. There was something grotesquely crass about Maxwell. He had hastily sent one of the first relief planes to Ethiopia, but inanely filled it with wildly inappropriate material including slimming tablets and huge amounts of Chocolate Horlicks, which the famine victims would not touch, the Ethiopian palate being uncorrupted by sweet chocolate.

After a long row, they agreed to split the poster money fifty-fifty.

'Minus costs,' said Maxwell. 'The costs of printing.'

In the course of the argument, Maxwell had said, 'After all, it's all for the same cause.' But Geldof was not so sure. As they had argued, a distinct concept of Band Aid had begun to form in his mind. One of the things he disliked about charities was that they deducted overheads and administration costs from the money donated by the public. Surely there was a better way – a way of getting *all* the money raised, out to Ethiopia?

When all else was done, Midge taped Bob saying: 'This record was recorded on the 25th of November 1984. It is now 8 a.m. on the 26th. We've been here twenty-four hours and I think it's time we went home.'

Stuart Bruce ran off a cassette and a stereo quarter-inch tape of 'Do They Know It's Christmas?' and Bob headed off. First, he went home and played it for Paula. 'She really liked it and was surprised it had turned out as well as it did, given what seemed the complete mayhem of the day,' Bob said. Reassured by Paula's judgement, he set off for the BBC. There the Radio 1 DJ, Simon Bates, gave the Band Aid record its first airplay. Among those listening were Stuart Bruce, stuck in traffic in a taxi with the master-tape on his way to the mastering studio, and Midge Ure, driving home exhausted after the marathon session.

Bob introduced the song with the words: 'This is the most important record ever made, the most important moment in British pop history.' As the last 'Feed the world' died away, Bates was left unusually speechless. Bob leapt in again with the sales pitch.

'Virtually one hundred per cent of the money from this record, apart from the VAT, goes straight to Band Aid.'

The DJ interrupted: 'The trouble with charity is that a big part of your donation goes in admin costs.'

'I swear every penny will get to Ethiopia,' Geldof riposted. It was only later that he thought through the implications of what he had said. But, for now, he continued: 'I want everyone listening to buy it. We've only got three weeks. Let's make it the biggest-selling record of all time. Paul McCartney's "Mull of Kintyre" sold about two and a half million and that's the biggest so far. But there's 56 million people in this country. So we can easily beat that. Even if you've never bought a record in your life before, get it. It's only £1.35. That's how cheap it is to give someone the ultimate Christmas gift – their life. It's pathetic, but the price of a life this year is a piece of plastic with a hole in the middle.'

Radio 1 never played tapes, Midge thought, only actual records. And Bruce didn't just play it once. He played it three times. After that, Radio 1, breaking normal programming rules, played it every hour. It was only then that Midge knew that this was something huge. They had finished making the record, but the Band Aid story had only just begun.

Midge went to bed and grabbed a couple of hours' sleep. 'When I woke up, everything had gone ballistic. The TV reports were being repeated every ten minutes. The record had been played on Radio 1 again and again. Everyone knew about it. We knew it would be big, but not how big.'

Geldof got no sleep at all. He went straight to the office of a freelance music lawyer, John Kennedy, who had previously been the in-house lawyer of Bob's record company, Phonogram. Kennedy was working quietly in his tiny office when the door burst open.

'Kennedy, I need you to do one hour's work and you can't charge for it.'

'Sure. How about 2 p.m. on Thursday?'

'Fuck Thursday. Come with me now,' Geldof insisted and led the lawyer to see the record label. They had previously agreed to waive their cut of the Band Aid single, but Geldof now wanted it all legally watertight. And he wanted to make sure that Band Aid would get the money from the overseas as well as domestic sales. Phonogram readily agreed. Kennedy said he'd draw up the contract.

'By the way, who is the money to be paid to?' Kennedy asked.

'Good question,' Geldof replied. This was how, a few days later, the showbiz lawyer found himself in his local library reading a legal textbook on charity law. The Band Aid Charitable Trust was the eventual out-come. And Kennedy's *pro bono* hour was to stretch to forty years of unpaid involvement.

Geldof now began a hectic round of TV, radio and newspaper inter-views. Everyone wanted a piece of the Band Aid action. Everyone except the BBC's leading pop music programme, *Top of the Pops*. It had an inflexible rule that only records which were in the charts could feature on the show. There were no special cases, the producer Michael Hurll said. Not even for 8 million people at risk of starving to death? Geldof decided, after his lesson with Robert Maxwell, to go straight to the top. He called the BBC reception desk and asked to be put through to the controller of BBC One, Michael Grade.

'I'd just started. I hadn't been there that long,' recalled Grade. 'And my PA buzzed me through one evening, about six o'clock, and said, "Bob Geldof's on the phone for you." I said, "Who's he?" because pop music's not my thing particularly. And she said, "Well, the Boomtown Rats... it's a pop band." And I said, "Oh God, what does he want?"'

Grade, who was just winding down for the day with a whisky at his desk, recalled that he 'was feeling a bit sporty, and I thought, *I'll have a bit of fun with this geezer*. So I said, "Put him through. I'll just tweak his tail and send him off. I'll enjoy that." I was feeling a bit mischievous. Anyway, he came on and explained that he'd made this video with all these stars and wanted to get it on *Top of the Pops*. And I said, "Well, I know why you are ringing, because you don't get on *Top of the Pops* unless you're in the charts. So the answer is no, Mr Geldof.'"

"'I've got David Bowie to introduce it. Does that make a difference?"

"'No, the rules are the rules.'"

But there was something about his approach and his earnestness, said Grade. 'He didn't sound like a pop star. He was so intense and so reasonable on the phone. There was something about him that was... I can't really describe. I just took it seriously.'

So Grade said to Geldof: 'Look, send me the video, let me look at it and I'll call you back.'

Within an hour, the video arrived. Grade watched it and within a minute, rang Geldof back.

'Good news and bad news. Bad news is you're not going on *Top of the Pops*. The good news is, I'm going to delay *Top of the Pops* by five minutes and put your video on at seven o'clock as a programme in its own right. So it'll find its audience.'

'Oh, that's brilliant. Thank you. Thank you. Thank you.'

Why did Grade agree? 'Well, the original report that inspired Bob was a BBC news report, so it was a BBC story in journalistic terms. And I just thought it was a good thing to do. Why not? Television was under attack in those days, getting blamed for everything from bedwetting and nail-biting to drugs and violence. And I thought, *This is television as a power for good. So why not? Let's go for it.*' A couple of nights later, David Bowie flew over from Switzerland to record an introduction for the five-minute slot. He looked too elegant to be talking about starvation, Bob decided, so he pulled off his 'Feed the World' T-shirt and Bowie put it on. Before too long, Michael Grade, now Lord Grade, became a Band Aid trustee.

⁂

'Do They Know It's Christmas?' was rush-released by Phonogram on 3 December 1984. Everyone did their bit to maximise the amount it raised in the short space of time before Christmas Day. Phonogram's factories pressed the record for free. ICI donated the vinyl. Woolworths ordered 250,000 copies upfront. Soon, Phonogram was pressing 320,000 copies a day and still it wasn't enough. Every record factory in Britain, Ireland and Europe was pressing it. The women who packaged the record sleeves agreed to work through the night, without pay, to get the first batch done. The delivery drivers who took the record to the shops worked unpaid.

Many opened hours earlier than usual to cope with queues of customers eager to buy the single. Shoppers were buying boxes of records to give away as Christmas cards. Others were buying fifty copies and giving forty-nine back to be resold. A butcher in Plymouth took the Christmas turkey and goose out of his shop window and put the records on display instead. The Queen's grocer, Fortnum & Mason, rang Geldof to ask, 'How exactly does one sell a pop record?'

At times, Geldof was bemused. 'I was in a fever of activity. Everything I did seemed to work. Hundreds of people dropping everything and concentrating on this one thing – all working for free. Everything seemed to fall into place too easily. Was it coincidence, serendipity, synchronicity?'

The truth was that the entire nation seemed to have been moved by the terrible footage from Ethiopia. Like Geldof, they had all been paralysed with impotent horror at what they saw. Now they seized upon any opportunity they could find to help in any way they could. Band Aid had become about more than raising money. It enabled ordinary people to contribute something of themselves – a phenomenon which Comic Relief would build on a few years later.

'Something was going on and everyone felt good about doing this thing,' said Bob.

It was as if Band Aid had tapped into an underlying stream of altruism, which surfaced in direct reaction to the self-obsession which was coming to define the decade. The British public were articulating a better view of themselves. 'I didn't think twice about it at the time,' said Bob. 'It never occurred to me that this was bonkers.'

Such was the general generosity of spirit that the singer Jim Diamond, who was top of the charts that week with his song 'I Should Have Known Better' – and who had never had a solo hit record before – said in an interview: 'I'm delighted to be number one, but next week I don't want people to buy my record. I want them to buy Band Aid instead.' Wham!, who had been hoping for a festive number one with their new single 'Last Christmas', donated all the money from its sales to Band Aid. Other artists who didn't appear on the single, from Queen to Thompson Twins, donated the royalties from their current hits to Band Aid.

'Do They Know It's Christmas?' went straight to number one, outselling all the other records in the chart put together. It sold a million copies in the first week alone and stayed at the top for five weeks, selling more than 3 million copies in total. It was easily the biggest-selling single of all time in the UK. It raised more than £1 million in the first week and £5 million within a month. By 2025, it has raised £26 million – every penny of it spent on projects in Ethiopia.

CHAPTER 6

GELDOF GOES TO ETHIOPIA

That was that, thought Bob Geldof. He and his fellow musicians had done more than they had imagined would be possible to raise money for Ethiopia. But now it was over. The Boomtown Rats had a tour booked to promote the album they had made before all this began. The band may not have produced any hits recently, but they still had a loyal fanbase. Many of the forty decent-sized venues they had booked around the UK were already sold out. Geldof was relieved to be getting back to his old job.

The media, however, had a very different idea. The music press, eager for a new story, began to attack Geldof, asserting that Band Aid was a publicity stunt to revive his flagging pop career. The national newspapers had a different agenda. They wanted to move the Band Aid story on – by persuading Geldof to go to Ethiopia to see the famine for himself. The press wanted to see the pop star and a starving child in the same photograph. It's the only way to keep the story alive, said the reporters and photographers he encountered when he was promoting the Rats' new album, *In the Long Grass*. There was an irony in the title. Bob told anyone who asked that it was from an old Irish saying meaning that you've been around and about only not too visible: 'Where have you been?' 'I've been lying in the long grass.' But 'the long grass', in the English metaphor, was the place where people kicked things that they wanted to be forgotten.

The press were not interested in parsing metaphors, however. The famine was a massive story. But they couldn't, they said, just keep on printing pictures and stories about ghastly skeletal children. 'Do They Know It's Christmas?' had enabled them to keep writing about the subject. Now, at the start of 1985, they needed a fresh angle, they told Geldof. Otherwise, they said, without seeing the insensitivity of their words, the story would die. What they needed now was for Bob to go to Ethiopia.

Geldof refused. 'It's not necessary,' he said. 'I don't need to go there to see it. I've seen it already on television. There are experts to help decide how best to spend the money. They don't need a half-assed pop singer. Can't you see how distasteful that would be?' But then taste, he noted, had never been the strong point of the British popular press. Geldof was adamant in that view for some considerable time. But there was something else. 'He was frightened,' another Rat recalled. He had this sense that he was just a punk musician, and this was just too big for him.

But pressure now came from a different quarter. Record sales had already put £5 million in Band Aid's bank account. What to do with the money? At one point, Geldof would have thought about handing it over to established aid agencies like Oxfam and Save the Children. But those agencies would take part of the money to cover their overheads and he had given his word to the public that every penny raised by the record would go to Africa.

John Kennedy, who had by now become Band Aid's unpaid lawyer, told Geldof that he had no choice but to go to Africa. Bob continued his resistance.

'I didn't have to go to Vietnam to know there was a war on and that I was against it. I've seen politicians go. They're not needed. And neither am I.'

Kennedy dismissed that argument. 'The media is going to be all over this. If anything goes astray, it'll be a terrible scandal. You have to go out there, with the first shipment, and make sure that you see that it gets to the camp, so you can come back and say "Job done". Bob, this really is non-negotiable.'

Geldof reluctantly capitulated. But, determined not to spend any Band Aid money on the trip, he got a TV station to pay for the flight, a newspaper to pay for the jet fuel and another to cover his hotel bills. Another Band Aid principle had been established: always get your overheads paid by someone else. The price was that the media would accompany him everywhere – and try constantly to trick him into letting them get the photo they wanted above all else: 'Bob with a black baby', as a photographer from the *Daily Star* put it. It was the one photograph Geldof was determined to avoid.

On 6 January 1985, Geldof flew into Addis Ababa. A nine-day whistle-stop tour of refugee camps, feeding stations, empty grain stores and endless meetings with aid officials was to follow. At Bole airport, he was greeted by Berhane Deressa, deputy director of the government's Relief and Rehabilitation Commission (RRC). The Ethiopian official was expecting a British diplomat, 'someone in a three-piece suit'. He was taken aback when Geldof appeared. 'His hair was not combed. He hadn't shaved. He looked awful,' Berhane later laughed. Ethiopia, Bob discovered, operates on a different calendar, the one which England had abandoned in 1752 when rioters supposedly protested 'Give us back our eleven days'. Ethiopia was still on the calendar devised by Julius Caesar. Under it, Geldof had arrived, ironically, on Christmas Eve. 'We wondered if you'd like to go up to Lalibela for the celebrations,' Berhane asked.

Bob had read about Lalibela on the plane and its extraordinary underground churches. He was tempted. But he didn't want to look touristy.

'I'm here to meet people to find out how best to spend the money,' Geldof said.

'There are feeding camps in the area you could visit,' said Berhane persuasively. 'It would give you a grounding for your conversation with the relief workers here in the capital when you get back.' What he didn't say was that he was under instructions from his boss, Dawit Wolde Giorgis, to illustrate to Geldof that the Ethiopians *did*, in fact, know it was Christmas, whatever the Band Aid record had said.

Dawit and Geldof were not well matched. Unlike his deputy, Dawit was a member of the central committee of the Derg, Ethiopia's military regime. He had risen through the party ranks and had been, successively, deputy foreign minister, governor of Eritrea, and finally now head of the RRC. For more than a decade, he had been an ideological ally of Ethiopia's dictator, Colonel Mengistu Haile Mariam. He had continued to support him even during the Red Terror when Mengistu loyalists drove jeeps around the cities, shooting at people and hanging their bodies from lamp-posts. Later, he was to defect to the United States, but when Geldof met him, Dawit was the presentable face of the Marxist junta that ruled Ethiopia.

For his part, Dawit could not fathom the Irish rock singer. 'Geldof was a very strange person for me,' Dawit later wrote. 'I didn't know what to make of him. He was not a politician. He was not what you could call a humanitarian. He was also by no means an ordinary person. He was a smart city boy, full of arrogance and vulgar language, questioning all values. It was very difficult to talk to him because he was so cynical. My deputy, Berhane, somehow managed to handle him.'

The pair first met at the airport. Dawit was there to say farewell to Mother Teresa. The Nobel Peace Prize-winning nun had been in Ethiopia to visit fellow nuns working in the famine areas and Geldof was waiting to take the plane to Lalibela. Dawit introduced them nervously 'because I knew every other word out of Geldof's mouth was usually an obscenity'. Mother Teresa, he added, 'saved me a great deal of embarrassment by exerting her usual humbling influence'.

It was a revealing encounter. Mother Teresa may have been the exemplar of humility, but there was no false modesty about her. Indeed, there was a certainty of purpose which she displayed by embarrassing Dawit, in front of the TV cameras, into giving her two empty buildings she had seen on the way to the airport which she wanted to turn into orphanages. This airport lounge encounter between the media saint – the newspapers were still calling him St Bob – and a real one was sobering to Geldof. He told her why he had come. She told him about her work in Ethiopia, where her nuns cared for the old, the blind, the disabled and the incurably ill – the people overlooked by other agencies who concentrated on trying to save children. There was a lesson for Geldof in that; Band Aid too could do what other aid agencies would not. At the end of their conversation, she took his hand, then said: 'Remember this. I can do something you can't do, and you can do something I can't do. But we both have to do it.'

�֍

When the old Dakota prop-plane landed in Lalibela, Geldof discovered there was another reason the Ethiopians were keen to take him there. The Derg were fighting two civil wars at the same time in the north, in Eritrea and Tigray, and another in the south. Until a few weeks earlier, the rebel guerrillas of the Tigray People's Liberation Front had controlled Lalibela. The government forces had now retaken the place and the town was full of soldiers. It was no coincidence, Geldof was later to learn, that the areas of starvation and the areas fighting were, to a large extent, the same. There was more to it than a famine caused by drought.

But for now, he and Berhane Deressa, and their media entourage, checked into a local hotel, which was basic but clean with a balcony overlooking the town. As dusk fell, Geldof looked out. The sky had a dull orange glow from the setting sun. Blue smoke rose from the hundreds of tiny fires lit around the outskirts of the town. Out onto the balcony, looking very pleased with himself, came Berhane, carrying a little cassette recorder. The tape he had inserted was playing 'Do They Know It's Christmas?'. Geldof was taken aback. Two worlds collided. The song made perfect sense at that moment, in that place. It filled him with enormous sadness. *Tonight, thank God, it's them instead of you.* 'And in that voice, all the rage, all the shame.' They set off for the underground churches, where a six-hour-long Christmas midnight Mass was just beginning. The prayer was somewhat different there.

There were no other Westerners present – only the people of that high plateau, who had walked long hours to reach this ancient fastness of Christianity, where worship was conducted long before there were cathedrals at Canterbury, Paris or Ravenna. The place conjured the words of the historian, Edward Gibbon, who in 1788 wrote: 'Encompassed on all sides by the enemies of their religion, the Æthiopians slept near a thousand years, forgetful of the world by whom they were forgotten.'

The next morning, Christmas Day, they all set out for the local feeding station. But before they left, Geldof called all the photographers and cameramen together.

'I do not want any pictures taken of me with starving children,' he said sternly. 'We've seen them before, visiting politicians looking fat and concerned as they hold a child in their arms who is near to the point of death.'

'Christ, Bob, you know that's the picture we've been sent to get, you with one of the children Band Aid is trying to help? That is the picture,' said Kenny Lennox of the *Daily Star*.

'I know it is. And it is the picture that I don't want. It's disgustingly sensational. It degrades the people involved. You can take pictures of me in the camp. You can take pictures of the kids. But not the two together. This is my trip and anyone who's not prepared to agree to my rules can fuck off back to the plane.'

Geldof did not trust him. He knew Kenny was one of the photographers who had taken pictures of Princess Diana in her bikini when she was pregnant. But Kenny had his own motivation. He had spent days taking heart-rending photographs in the camps the month before, only to learn that his paper was not printing them. 'We lose circulation every time we use them,' his editor had told him. 'People get turned off by it. Come home.' He did not need Bob's chastisement.

If there was any bad feeling as a result of these exchanges, it was forgotten when they arrived at the German Emergency Doctors feeding camp. By a gigantic Red Cross flag, lines of people were queuing. They did not look in bad shape. But in the shed round the back were children who looked like those in the original BBC film. Only this time their eyes were looking directly at Bob.

Geldof began to cry. The photographers could not speak. They drove back to the airport in silence.

From there, they flew on to one of the two biggest camps in Ethiopia, at Mekele – the place where, in the BBC film, Claire Bertschinger had made her daily decisions on who should live and who would die. Claire had gone, moved on to start another feeding centre in a more remote location. But, to Geldof, the children here looked as bad as they had on the film in October. As he was passing, a child grabbed at his hand, then another, then three or four. Out of the corner of his eye, he saw the man from the *Daily Star* taking a shot of him with a long lens. He said nothing.

There were 50,000 people at the camp in Mekele, and more arriving every day. Bob stopped by one child who looked about four months old. Malnutrition is deceptive, he was told; the boy was nearer two – the age of Bob's own child in England. In this camp, he saw scenes too grim to describe. One child who was clearly close to dying has haunted him ever since. 'There can be no doubt that the little boy is dead now,' Bob later recalled. 'But he will not die in my imagination. Nothing can free him from the agonising process of death, which is fixed in my mind.'

Back in Addis Ababa the next day, Geldof embarked on a series of meetings to take advice from the various aid agencies already at work in the country. The scenes in the famine fields the day before had brought home to him how much of a novice he was. The £5 million Band Aid had raised had seemed a large amount when he left England; now he realised how little it was, and how much there was to do. He needed those with expertise to tell him where best to spend the money.

In the Ethiopian capital, Bob bumped into a fellow Irishman, Gus O'Keefe, a religious brother with the Congregation of the Holy Ghost – the same order which had taught Geldof as a boy at Blackrock College in Dublin. The Holy Ghost Fathers were missionaries who focused on education and social justice. Brother Gus ran the Christian Relief and Development Association (CRDA), which had become the coordinating body of all the voluntary agencies working in Ethiopia. He soon became Band Aid's key go-between with both the Ethiopian relief ministry and aid agencies on the ground. More than $5 million of Band Aid money was eventually channelled through the CRDA. A modest and understated man who was respected by all, Gus had gathered together the aid agency field officers to meet Geldof. They had not all come with open minds.

'I think all of us on the ground were slightly sceptical,' recalled Hugh Goyder, who oversaw Oxfam's operations in Ethiopia. 'And there was a bit of tension between Geldof and the traditional aid agencies. He saw us as somewhat slow and bureaucratic. Bob came into Ethiopia thinking that, with lots of international pressure, the problem could be solved quite quickly. He was an immensely charismatic character and the moment he appeared, all our nurses in particular fell in love with him. But he was very, very critical of us – and, we thought, for no particular reason.'

That feeling lessened when Geldof made it clear that he was there to listen and learn. The agencies should put their heads together, he said, and agree among themselves the best ways of spending the Band Aid cash. He asked for a list of the most urgently needed supplies and where they should first be distributed.

Back at Oxfam, Paddy Coulter saw more of an upside. 'When Geldof first burst on the scene, let's be candid, there was quite a bit of resentment within the aid agencies,' Coulter said. 'Who is this Irish musician? What the hell does he know about it?' He just looked like a blundering amateur. 'But this quickly changed into admiration. He was faced with an astonishing learning curve and he really got up to speed very quickly.'

One example of this was the innovative suggestion Geldof made to overcome the block which the United States, the world's biggest provider of aid, had put on Ethiopia. Washington had a rule that it would give no aid to any country that had nationalised American assets without paying compensation. Ethiopia had done exactly this after its Marxist revolution in 1975. Some twenty-five US companies said they were still owed compensation amounting to $30 million and the Ethiopian government refused to pay it.

'Why don't all the aid agencies get together,' Geldof said, 'raise the $30 million and pay off the debt to the American firms? That will open the door to far, far larger amounts of US aid.'

The idea proved too bold and too maverick for the traditional agencies, but such unconventional approaches were to later become one of the hallmarks of the Band Aid method of operation.

Geldof took the list of aid agency priorities to the Ethiopian government's Relief and Rehabilitation Commission. Dawit was not impressed. 'He had simple solutions to complex problems,' he later recalled. 'He was a little bit unselective in his words, shall we say. And the way he wore his ragged jeans was, for our taste, not good to say the least.' That was not all. Dawit felt Geldof was too ready to hand out advice.

'It seems to me your basic problem is one of PR,' Geldof opined. Dawit bridled quietly. Geldof continued, 'I may not know much about famine but I do know about PR.'

Ethiopia would get more international aid, he told Dawit, if it only explained itself better to the international media. The presence of large numbers of Russian 'agricultural advisers' didn't go down well. 'Nor does the government's policy of forcing farmers onto Russian planes to resettle them away from the rebel areas.'

Dawit, still in those days a Marxist ideologue, was now seething. He forced a laugh and said: 'I think you should meet the minister for the interior.'

Still, he took Geldof's list of priorities, which had been suggested by the aid agencies, and agreed to set up a liaison committee with Brother Gus to bring the agencies and the government together.

'Whatever you all agree on,' Geldof said, 'Band Aid will supply.'

❖

The minister of the interior was called Berhane Biyuh. When Geldof arrived, he stood up and began what was quite clearly going to be a formal address: 'On behalf of the Revolutionary Committee of...'

'Please, let's cut the crap, Minister, and get down to business.'

Berhane Deressa looked at the minister and said, 'I warned you.' The minister laughed uneasily.

Geldof had been told that the television cameras accompanying him would have to leave after the opening formalities. But he asked if the TV crew could remain. The minister agreed, somewhat reluctantly. Then Geldof confronted the minister with a list of concerns the agencies had given him, including their disquiet about the government's resettlement policy. The minister embarked upon an ideological anti-Western harangue, complaining that Ethiopia was the subject of adverse propaganda.

'Yes, you are,' agreed Geldof. 'I think that there is a misinformation campaign there, but you are to blame for it too. Look, the first pictures we saw of resettlement were these ancient and beautiful people starving and in rags under armed guard going into these vast Russian planes. They probably have never seen a plane. They have nothing left – only their dignity. And, to the West, the immediate psychological reaction is Jews being led at gunpoint into cattle trucks by the Nazis.'

The minister was momentarily silenced. Geldof could feel the encouragement of the journalists behind him. It was good television. But it was more than that. It was in that meeting that he suddenly saw the distinct value of Band Aid. It gave him the ability to say the unsayable. He could speak truth to power without fear of the consequences. He could confront those in power with the problems that aid workers and diplomats did not dare raise for fear of jeopardising long-term relationships. Band Aid was not only short-term, it was also essentially one-way traffic. 'They had to listen,' he reflected later, 'because I had not only the money, but the constituency of support which that money represented. And it was a populist, non-governmental constituency … a constituency of compassion.' Geldof had developed a new style of advocacy – which he was to deploy throughout the next forty years – and which I christened 'punk diplomacy'.

The most graphic example of this occurred when, shortly after, Geldof was offered a brief meeting with the Ethiopian dictator himself, Colonel Mengistu. Soon after he had taken power in 1975, Mengistu had presided over the Red Terror, that purge of his enemies in which Amnesty International estimated half a million people were killed over two years. When he was charged with genocide years later, the indictment of his crimes ran to 8,000 pages. Geldof had read the Amnesty reports before arriving in Ethiopia and, just before meeting, the dictator had returned from Tigray and Wollo, where peasant farmers were being rounded up, beaten with sticks, and forced at gunpoint onto Soviet Antonovs to be flown out of the rebel areas and down to the south-west of the country. Geldof was indignant at the inhumanity of Mengistu's behaviour towards the people Band Aid had come to feed.

He was ushered into a large marble room in the presidential palace. Most of the officials who had taken him in suddenly melted away. The Ethiopian dictator entered, accompanied by an interpreter. Mengistu stood stiffly, out of uniform in a civilian suit. He was unsmiling. He clearly did not want to meet the Irish singer, but Geldof had millions of pounds in his back pocket.

It was not, however, a very long meeting.

Through the interpreter, Mengistu asked Geldof for £1 million.

'To Bob, that was lighting the fuse,' said Kenny Lennox, the *Daily Star* photographer who was present.

Geldof exploded. Pointing to the Amnesty International report on Ethiopia he had taken into the meeting, Bob said, 'It says here you torture people.' He then proceeded to harangue the Ethiopian leader over the inhumanity of the way resettlement was being conducted. Despite the vehemence of Bob's attack, the military dictator refused to engage – whereupon Geldof told Mengistu he was a 'murdering cunt'. The interpreter stopped interpreting. It did not matter. 'Even Mengistu understood the F word,' said Lennox, 'when you put fourteen of them in each paragraph.' In fact, Mengistu had spent nearly three years on military training in the United States. His English was fluent. He would have been quite familiar with the language of the barrack room.

But saying the unsayable had become key to Geldof's conception of the purpose of Band Aid. 'He was fearless and almost totally without restraint,' recalled Michael Buerk. 'He said exactly what he thought to people. It was a moment I cherished.'

As for Geldof, he just shrugged. 'I was stressed and overwrought,' he told me afterwards, 'but anyway, things are seriously wrong when a bunch of pop musicians have to raise these issues … the issues should be raised by the politicians.'

Perhaps so, but Bob Geldof now knew that the Band Aid millions some-how gave him the authority to intervene in politics. Not just the authority, but also the duty.

✸

Geldof left Ethiopia in the middle of January, but kept in touch with what was happening in Ethiopia by reading the reports I was having published almost daily in *The Times*. Over the next couple of months, it became clear to him that the causes of the Ethiopian famine were far more complex than he had realised on that first visit – and so was the way that the various organisations interacted in the conflicted country.

The first thing that became clear was that the famine was becoming more entrenched, with the lack of food made worse by the Marxist agricultural policies of the regime. Even where the drought was not so bad, crop yields were down because of the attempts to organise subsistence farmers into producer cooperatives, just as happened when Stalin collectivised Soviet agriculture. As much as 90 per cent of all investment went into state farms which produced only 4 per cent of the country's needs. There was virtually no investment in peasant agriculture. All this meant that agriculture was on a knife-edge even before the rains failed.

Band Aid was to respond by providing money for drought-resistant seeds and tools, and replacing livestock for farmers who had lost all their herd during the famine.

The role of war in the famine became increasingly apparent. The Ethiopian government was fighting three rebel groups at once – in Tigray, Eritrea and the Ogaden. When ships bringing arms and food came into Ethiopia's two ports, it was the tanks, artillery, small arms, ammunition and bombs that were offloaded first. The government of the world's poorest country was spending half a million dollars a day on its military.

But it was the war on Tigray that was having the most devastating effect on the starving people. No international food aid was being sent behind rebel lines, where two million were without aid. In February 1985, I made public a secret Ethiopian government report which confirmed that more than three-quarters of the people in the famine-stricken province of Tigray were receiving none of the food aid now being sent by Western donors.

Band Aid would soon support a secret back-door relief operation as a result.

But it was my reporting on the government's resettlement scheme which was to have the biggest impact on Band Aid operations. The situation on the ground was far more complicated than the simplistic account put out by those on both the left and right who were ideologically opposed to Mengistu's Stalinist regime. I was still picking up reports that force or coercion was being used to resettle farmers. But I also began to hear from European diplomats and senior aid workers who were, for the first time, allowed to roam freely in resettlement areas. Conditions were hard there, the Westerners found, but they were better for many than had been the case in the arid northern highlands.

Suspicion about resettlement began to soften. Aid workers who had originally opposed it detected a change. 'People are moving voluntarily. The government is moving whole families. The people seemed pleased with their new homes,' an aid worker from World Vision, the biggest agency in Ethiopia, told me. 'Often they re-thatch the houses which the local farmers' associations have built for them, which is a sure sign of commitment.' People had settled down to cultivate their land with enthusiasm, a regular visitor to the resettlement area told me.

The same mixed picture was being reported by the BBC's East Africa correspondent, Mike Wooldridge, a more regular visitor to Ethiopia than Michael Buerk. But if picture was not clear-cut, what *was* becoming clear was that there were practical steps which Band Aid could take to improve life for those who were resettled, forcibly or voluntarily.

It also became clear that the failed rains were a far bigger problem than many of the West's anti-Mengistu critics later made out. Shortly before I left Ethiopia, I flew over large tracts of the dust-bowl provinces of Tigray and Wollo. For hours, the picture below was unchanging. Plains once described as the breadbasket of the north were covered in a rolling mist of what was once fertile topsoil. Eddies of spiralling dust rose in whirlwinds, hundreds of feet into the air. Stony riverbeds at the bottom of gorges a thousand feet deep showed not a sign of water or new vegetation. And the grazing land at the top of the plateaus was as bald and brown as old felt.

'There is no way that land like this can be made fertile in times of drought,' said an irrigation expert from the UN Food and Agriculture

Organization, who was flying with me. 'If it does not rain, then crops cannot be made to grow economically. Even if there was water at the bottom of those gorges, it would cost a fortune to raise it. It would be cheaper just to buy grain for the people every year.'

Band Aid subsequently supported tree-planting and terracing projects to combat soil erosion in the highlands and provided help in resettlement areas for farmers whose original land was beyond recovery.

Bob Geldof was reading all this in my reports for *The Times*, week after week. More than food aid was needed to solve the problem, he now realised. 'I began to realise,' he later told me, 'famine is nothing to do with hunger. Famine is to do with economics.' He began to consider a range of strategies through which Band Aid could respond.

Ironically, it was none of these critical revelations that got me in trouble with the Mengistu regime. What made the secret police come knocking at my hotel door were the reports I was writing about the growing epidemic of cholera in several refugee camps.

Cholera spreads rapidly through contaminated water where people are forced to live in crowded conditions without adequate sanitation. It causes severe diarrhoea and dehydration. It is easily treated, with intravenous fluids, oral rehydration and antibiotics – once it is identified.

But left untreated, cholera can be fatal within hours, even in previously healthy people. It is also a notifiable disease – which means a government is obliged to inform the World Health Organization (WHO) as cholera is a global public health threat. That brings restrictions on the movement of people and products.

Mengistu and Dawit were refusing to admit there was cholera in the camps – and refusing to allow the necessary medicines to be dispatched to the infected camps. They knew that, if they publicly admitted this, they would have to stop selling Ethiopia's cattle to Yemen, Saudi Arabia and Egypt, which earned Mengistu $22 million a year.

After I had published several reports exposing all this, the secret police arrived and watched while I packed my case and took me to the airport. I decided to go to Sudan.

Geldof had heard in Addis Ababa that there was famine too in neighbouring Sudan. On the way back to London in January 1985, he had stopped over in the Sudanese capital, Khartoum, to get a briefing from the aid agencies there. Refugees from Ethiopia were crossing the border in the east of the country.

Geldof went out to the region to check for himself. At Tukalabab, he found 80,000 people sitting on the desert floor with just a few ragged bits of cloth, stretched between bushes, to shelter them from the sun. Most had come from Tigray. There were just two doctors there and the camp store contained just fifteen bags of flour. The place was so seared into his memory that it was what came to mind when he was asked to speak to an assembly of leading US rock stars a few weeks later.

But the real threat lay further west, in Darfur and Kordofan, where the harvest had failed for the seventh year in succession. Within a few months, several million Sudanese would be going hungry there, the field director of Save the Children explained. Band Aid could do nothing about that, Geldof knew, because the record had raised money for Ethiopia, not Sudan. He flew back to London knowing that the record had not been enough.

Before he boarded the plane home, he was cornered in the foyer of the Hilton Hotel by a group of aid workers. One of them, Gayle Smith, told him about a covert aid operation to send food aid illicitly across the border from Sudan, through Eritrea and into Tigray. A shadowy organisation called the Emergency Relief Desk had been formed with the support of a number of aid agencies who wanted their identity kept secret for fear of reprisals on their operations in Ethiopia.

'We heard that Bob Geldof was coming to town,' Smith recalled, 'so we decided that we should ambush him at the Hilton. He was definitely the rock star, splayed out on the sofa. Anyway, we did this impassioned, very intense pitch – about how the majority of the peasants were on the other side of the Ethiopian battlelines and were not getting enough food, how the Scandinavian churches and others were supplying the food but how we needed trucks to get it into Tigray because at present there was no means of getting it in except by donkey.'

Gayle Smith would later become a special adviser on Africa to two US presidents, Bill Clinton and Barack Obama, and eventually ran the whole of Washington's international aid operation, USAID.

But to Geldof in the lobby of the Khartoum Hilton, she just looked like a zealous young aid worker. 'He didn't reject our proposal,' Smith recalled. 'But he was non-committal.'

Geldof was thinking. He needed more information.

Then news came through of a Yorkshire Television crew who had just spent six weeks behind Ethiopia's enemy lines, having entered covertly across the border from Sudan, accompanied by an armed rebel escort.

In an extraordinarily brave and bold piece of journalism, they travelled by night to avoid being ambushed or bombed by Ethiopian MiGs during the day. The film's director, Grant McKee, recorded one of the biggest mass migrations of the twentieth century – an exodus of a quarter of a million refugees who had abandoned their homes out of hunger.

He filmed them as they neared the end of a trek of up to thirty days and thirty nights after realising that they would starve to death if they remained at home. He conducted heart-rending interviews with elderly people who were too weak for the journey and who had chosen to remain behind to die alone rather than be a burden to their children and grandchildren, who had registered for migration with the Relief Society of Tigray, the aid agency of the Tigray People's Liberation Front.

'These people live on the wrong side of a civil war,' McKee said. 'When civil war and famine coincide, the world's aid system breaks down. All the world's major relief agencies make it a rule to operate only through recognised governments. The government in Ethiopia has lost control of Tigray. The Derg can't or won't distribute food in rebel-held areas. So two million drought-afflicted Tigrayans go empty-handed, victims of the politics of starvation.'

A hundred thousand tons of food was now arriving every month into Ethiopia. Tigray was getting less than 1 per cent of that. The amount being smuggled across the border from Sudan was less than 5 per cent of Tigray's basic needs.

Already it was estimated that 90,000 Tigrayans had died in the famine. The toll was rising; it was already 5,000 a week. There were so many funerals, McKee's film recorded, that priests no longer attended them all. The rebels seemed to control almost the whole of Tigray apart from the government-held towns and feeding stations. Starving people behind the rebel lines could watch Western aeroplanes daily landing grain, but the food stayed in the towns, just out of reach. In six weeks of travelling in the rebel held areas of Eritrea, Tigray and Wollo, McKee's crew saw none of the aid the world was sending through the Ethiopian government.

The Band Aid cash had been raised only for Ethiopia. Geldof knew the lawyers would say it couldn't be spent in Sudan. But could it be spent on Ethiopia going through the back door, through Sudan? 'It took some time,' recalled Gayle Smith. 'They needed proof of concept on the Emergency Relief Desk. And was food really monitored? I was a monitor during part of that time and I knew it was monitored far better than the food on the other side.'

Within a few weeks, Band Aid was funding the clandestine food-smuggling operation. Over the next six years, Band Aid spent more than £7 million feeding those Ethiopians who the world's main aid agencies could not reach.

CHAPTER 7

'WE ARE THE WORLD'

Just before he had left London for Ethiopia, Bob Geldof had received a phone call which took his breath away. It was early evening. He was watching the television in his Chelsea townhouse.

'Is that Barb Gerdorrf?' said a husky, gravelly voice, speaking very slowly.

'Yes. Who's that?'

'Harry. Harry Belafonte.'

Geldof was, unusually, unable to speak – momentarily at any rate.

Harry Belafonte had been a hero of his since he was a boy in Dublin. Bob was only five when Belafonte turned a slave work chant, 'Banana Boat Song', into a hit all over the world. But, as the years passed, he learned that Belafonte was a veteran civil rights campaigner who had organised the march where Martin Luther King delivered his 'I Have a Dream' speech. He had bailed King out of jail multiple times. He had been a strong opponent of apartheid and an early supporter of Nelson Mandela.

Geldof too had been outraged by apartheid. At the age of thirteen, he and his friend Mick Foley had established the South Dublin branch of the Anti-Apartheid Movement. He and Foley had given out protest leaflets when the South African rugby team was visiting Dublin. To this day, he has a little scar on his forehead where he was hit by an overzealous police baton during an anti-apartheid demonstration. He had wiped the blood from his head with the protest poster he was carrying and then stuck the bloodied poster on his bedroom wall as a teenage mark of honour. Racism was personal to him; after he left Ireland and was looking for rooms in England, he became familiar with the 'No blacks. No dogs. No Irish' posters in the lodging-house windows.

Now, one of the great heroes of his youth was calling him.

'We are really ashamed of what you Brit kids did.'

'I'm Irish…'

'Same thing!' And then he told Geldof that some of the top musicians in the US wanted to do what he had done: make a record to raise money for Ethiopia.

When he said 'top musicians', he meant it. 'I got Michael here.' Geldof heard him pass the phone to someone.

'Hi Bob, it's Michael.' Geldof didn't need to ask, 'Michael who?'

'It was Michael fucking Jackson on the phone – to me!' he later recounted. Bob was uncharacteristically awestruck. Paula, who was sitting next to him, stood up and did a little silent dance in a circle round their living room.

'It's really great what you're doing. We want to do that over here. Will you come over?' Jackson said.

'Sure,' said Geldof, recovering his cool. 'Yeah, I'll come over.'

✳

The recording of the single by the forty-six stars who became known as USA for Africa was a study in contrasts with the recording of 'Do They Know It's Christmas?'. Where Geldof had begun by ringing his fellow musician Midge Ure, Harry Belafonte's first call had been to the ultimate fixer. Ken Kragen ran arguably the top talent management company in Los Angeles. In turn, Kragen rang Larry Klein, who was producing the 1985 American Music Awards at the end of January. Kragen told Klein about the charity record Harry Belafonte was planning.

'I wanna put together a group of superstars, as many people as I can get. But to get these people in a room, recording together, it has to be the night of the AMAs,' Kragen told Klein. That would be the night that the most top musicians would be together in one place. Kragen's client, Lionel Richie, was hosting the awards. Richie was already on board, and he had recruited Quincy Jones to arrange and produce it because, in Richie's words, 'he had the respect of every musician on the planet'. Jones had brought in Michael Jackson, who didn't just want to sing but also offered to help Richie write the song. Kragen had envisaged asking Stevie Wonder to write the song with Richie, but over a number of days, Stevie didn't answer the phone to him, and nor did he return Richie's calls.

The next day, the day before Christmas, Richie's wife Brenda was in a jewellery store when in walked Stevie Wonder.

'Will you help me pick out some gifts, Brenda?'

'I will if you call my husband back!'

But Stevie Wonder still didn't call.

Yet even without Stevie Wonder, Kragen was beginning to build an impressive line-up of top names. What he needed to make it absolutely stellar was Bruce Springsteen. Kragen called Springsteen's manager, Jon Landau.

'Can we get Bruce?'

'Oh my God, Bruce is finishing up two years on the road. He's been touring constantly.'

'Jon, you personally are going to be able to take credit for saving millions of lives if you get your client to do this.'

Two weeks later, Landau called Kragen. 'Bruce is in.'

From that day on, Ken Kragen never made another outgoing call.

'All I did was answer the phone. The floodgates opened and mostly I had to turn people down. I wanted about twenty people. We ended up with forty-six.'

'Well, you have Bruce Springsteen,' someone said to him. 'Why not call Bob Dylan?'

✳

Midge Ure had begun to write 'Do They Know It's Christmas?' at his kitchen table on a little Casio keyboard. Michael Jackson and Lionel Richie had altogether more exotic surroundings. They met in Jackson's home in Encino, California, a large property with lush gardens, a recording studio, a private movie theatre, a dance studio – and a zoo. Ignoring that, however, they worked in Jackson's bedroom. Both nocturnal in their habits, they wrote through the night.

They wanted something big and stately, so they listened to the national anthems of various countries before settling on, of all things, 'Rule Britannia' as a template. They messed around for a long time, but nothing stuck.

But then Richie got a call from Ken Kragen, who reeled off the list of stars who had signed up for the project. 'I think we have Billy Joel. And we got Willie Nelson. I think we have Tina Turner, Huey Lewis, Paul Simon, Diana Ross, Ray Charles... And we're gonna do this on the night of the American Music Awards.' That was just two weeks away. The two songwriters immediately refocused their efforts.

All the while, Quincy Jones was nervously waiting. There was nothing he could do until he had the song. Fortunately, when they eventually delivered it on 21 January, he knew it was perfect. But where Midge Ure and Bob Geldof were happy to fly by the seat of the pants and have the British musicians hear the song for the first time in the recording studio, Jones wanted to take no chances. Exactly a week before the music awards, he and the two composers got together with a band to lay down a guide track which could be sent out to those who would appear on the record. Right in the middle of the session, in walked Stevie Wonder, saying he was there to write the song.

'We've finished writing it,' said Quincy. 'We're already putting the demo down.'

'Stevie looked shocked,' Richie recalled.

'How come somebody didn't tell me?' Stevie said.

'Well, yeah, we did... three weeks ago.'

The song itself in the bag and, in Richie's words, 'the baby about to get born', the three of them set about recording the guide vocal.

With 'Do They Know It's Christmas?', Ure and Geldof had just decided on the day who would sing which line. 'It just emerged organically,' said Midge. But Quincy Jones had a very different view. 'At first, Michael was talking about him and Lionel singing the leads and all the other guys just singing backgrounds. But I said, "No, that ain't gonna work."' As with Band Aid, Quincy recognised the importance of having every line sung by a different singer – and he wanted it all decided before the stars all arrived in the studio. 'We didn't want to encourage decision-making during the session. Any decision. Where they would stand, what they would sing, when they sing it – we had to think it through and spell it all out,' he said afterwards. 'Over the years, I'd learned the hard way that once a group of this size and stature gets involved in making decisions, you're in trouble.'

So he called in a musicologist, Tom Bahler, who was given the song and a list of the forty-six musicians available. Bahler started listening to every artist who was going to sing a solo, studying their vocal ranges and listening for differences and contrasts in tone and style. Then he wrote the name of each singer on a separate card and laid them on the floor in a semi-circle and allocated to each a line he felt they would be really comfortable in singing. It would also forestall stars asking why other people had certain parts. The answer would be: it fits their range. Once in the studio, there would be no rehearsal and no time for negotiating lines or where people stood. Each singer's name would be written on tape stuck to the floor.

'You can't be democratic when you have that many stars working together,' said Quincy. 'If you try to be democratic, you're in for chaos. This has gotta be seamless.'

With just four days to the recording, Jones sent out cassette tapes to the superstars who had agreed to participate. As with the Band Aid recording, artists had been invited on the basis of who was selling the most records. But, unlike in London, there were some disputes about who should appear. The biggest row came over the decision *not* to invite Madonna. Ken Kragen's senior assistant thought the 'Material Girl' singer would bring in a really different audience. Her single 'Like a Virgin' was number one in the US at the time of the recording, but Kragen insisted that, since each singer was only going to get half a line, their voice had to be immediately recognisable, as Cyndi Lauper's was. Madonna's producer, Nile Rodgers, who was with her in Los Angeles the night of the recording, said: 'It was a slap in the face … I know she felt bad.' She was not wanted 'because they didn't think she could sing. It broke her heart.' Madonna was said to be still 'incandescent' about the snub when she performed at Live Aid six months later, so much so that she churlishly refused to join in for the singing of 'We Are the World' at the end.

⁂

One person Kragen *was* anxious should be present was Bob Geldof. But Geldof had no money for the plane ticket. The recent lack of success of the Boomtown Rats meant his bank account was bare and the band's UK tour was still a few weeks ago. He wouldn't take money from the Band Aid funds, so Kragen paid for Bob's ticket while Paula's was paid for by the *News of the World* in return for a diary article. There was certainly plenty to write about.

The contrast between the British and American recordings could not have been more stark. In London, everyone rolled up looking pretty much as though they would look at home on a Sunday morning. At A&M, Charlie Chaplin's old studio in Los Angeles, it was top glamour. Limos drove the stars from the American Music Awards ceremony to the studio and queued at the door to drop off their celebrity cargo. Only Bruce Springsteen broke the mould, driving himself in an old Pontiac.

In London, they had put two big blokes on the door when the word got out and fans started to arrive. In Los Angeles, the security was formidable from the outset. Bob and Paula were issued with passes. Bob's admitted him to the actual studio, as well as the dressing rooms, make-up rooms and photography rooms, while Paula's only allowed her access to what Bob called the 'friends, liggers and freeloaders' enclosure. On an adjoining sound stage, she joined hundreds of other guests, including Brooke Shields, Jane Fonda, Steve Martin and Billy Joel's fiancée, supermodel Christie Brinkley. There, in front of two 25-foot-high video screens, linked by closed-circuit TV to the studio, was an astounding cornucopia of Hollywood extravagance. Fish carved in ice had caviar pouring out of their mouths onto silver salvers below. Tables groaned with smoked salmon, meats and canapés of every description. Drink was stacked in limitless quantities.

It was too much for Geldof.

'The room was full of Hollywood fat cats and their wives eating and drinking effortlessly and talking smoothly about how wonderful it all was to be contributing to famine,' he later recalled. 'I knew the food had been given free, but it was too much.'

Michael Jackson had not bothered to go to the Shrine Auditorium for the American Music Awards. That was probably just as well; *Thriller* had been beaten by Prince's *Purple Rain* for the award of Best Pop/Rock Album. Instead, he had arrived two hours early to rehearse, record his solo and multitrack the chorus. When Geldof got there, just after 10 p.m., Jackson was improvising harmonies.

'Try a third, Smelly,' suggested Quincy, who for some reason called Jackson by this odd but clearly affectionate nickname. Geldof asked why and was told it was short for Smelly Socks, which left him none the wiser.

Michael Jackson sang a perfect third.

His practice take could have graced the finished product, thought Geldof. 'It was a preposterous level of professionalism and talent.'

Around 10.30 p.m., the door into the studio opened. Bob Dylan came in, sat down beside Geldof and said hi. He looked terrible, Geldof thought. His face was all puffed out and there were deep black bags under his eyes. He looked as if he had just got up – which he may well have just done since the music awards ceremony certainly wasn't his kind of thing. 'We started talking about his last tour of Ireland,' said Geldof. 'He began to laugh as I reminded him of things I had been told about him. I was sitting there, talking to Bob Dylan. It was like talking to a man in a pub, I thought.'

The door opened again, only this time it was Diana Ross. 'Hi Bob,' she said.

'She was talking to *me*, not him!' marvelled Geldof.

'It's great what you have been doing, we're really proud of you,' she said. They talked about children. She asked Geldof about his daughter Fifi and then got out the photos of her own little boy.

'Every time the door opened, it was like a bit of my youth walked into the room,' said an awestruck Geldof. 'Paul Simon, Dionne Warwick, Stevie Wonder, Tina Turner, Willie Nelson, Smokey Robinson, Ray Charles…. It was like my teenage bedroom wall come alive.'

'Bruce Springsteen's just parked his car on the other side of the road and walked across – by himself – to the studio,' announced Ken Kragen, breathlessly. 'Can you believe it? No, I mean, he drove himself – no chauffeur, no limo. Then The Boss walked across himself, no bodyguards and no security.' Paul Simon looked across at Geldof, sharing a half-smile at such West Coast veneration.

'That's like the Statue of Liberty walking in,' said Billy Joel when Ray Charles arrived. Joel had a few years earlier written the song 'New York State of Mind' as a homage to Ray Charles. When Quincy Jones pointed that out, as he introduced them, Joel was visibly shaking.

'We've hit a different echelon here,' exclaimed Kenny Loggins when he saw Diana Ross. 'The energy in the room was really high. But at the same time, under it was a low hum of competition. The egos were still there.'

Yet only the artists themselves were allowed in the studio. Agents, assistants, PR people and record label flunkies all had to stay on the adjoining sound stage. The stars, many of whom had never actually met before, were forced to interact directly with one another and found it exhilarating. Some seemed timid or nervous. Others were fluttering around the bigger stars like besotted fans. Others were actually star-struck into silence. 'I felt like I was in a dream,' recalled Prince's percussionist, Sheila E. 'Everyone was a legend to me. Bob Dylan? I mean, I think I just said "Hi" and walked away because I was scared.'

Even Bruce Springsteen was overwhelmed. 'It was intoxicating just to be around that group of people,' he said.

Some were intoxicated in another way. Al Jarreau had started on the post-show celebratory wine a little too early, as was clear when he approached Bob Dylan. 'Bobby, in my own stupid way, I just want to tell you I love you,' Jarreau told Dylan, who looked vaguely horrified and walked away, leaving Jarreau sobbing, 'My idol!'

It was like first day of kindergarten, Lionel Richie noted wryly.

With the room now filled with stars, Paul Simon took a look around and said, drily: 'If a bomb lands on this place, John Denver's back on top.' Ironically, Denver had asked to join the recording, but had been turned down because he was 'too uncool', Geldof said.

'Check your ego at the door' read the sign that Quincy Jones had scribbled on a sheet of paper and posted by the studio entrance before the first singers had arrived. Just in case anyone hadn't read it, he now invited Bob Geldof to speak to the all-star studio.

'Listen, guys, guys,' Quincy began. 'First, I'd like you to meet Bob Geldof, who is really the inspiration for this whole thing. This is the man who put Band Aid together. And he just came back from Ethiopia and he'd like to talk to you.'

'Oh, would I?' mumbled Geldof who was, in that room, embarrassed, thrilled and awestruck in equal measure. *There are gods present*, he thought to himself. *I am truly not worthy.*

'Well, maybe, to put you in the mood of the song you're about to sing, which hopefully will save millions of lives...' he began.

The chattering stars around the room fell silent. Geldof was suddenly conscious of the responsibility which had descended upon his shoulders. He had unwittingly become the spokesman for the shame and outrage the world now felt at the events unfolding in Ethiopia. The memory of the camp at Tukalabab in the east of Sudan was still vivid in his mind from only a few days before.

'I don't know if we can conceive of "nothing". But "nothing" is not having water. On some of the camps, you'll see fifteen bags of flour for 27,500 people. And you see meningitis and malaria and typhoid buzzing around in the air. And you see dead bodies, lying side by side with the live ones. And, on a good day, you only see 120 people die slowly in front of you.'

Grave expressions started to pass across the faces of the wealthy superstars.

'And I don't want to bring anybody down. But maybe it's the best way of making – why you're really here tonight – come out through this song. So thanks a lot, everybody, and let's hope it works.'

Mostly the singers applauded. Paul Simon fiddled with his hair awkwardly. Michael Jackson stood silent, with his eyes cast down to the ground.

As Geldof finished, Quincy Jones said: 'If you didn't before understand what we're doing tonight, now you do.'

What Midge Ure had done in London so Quincy Jones did in California: he began with the chorus. Partly, this was to get everyone in tune with the song and, partly, it was so that stars wouldn't just leave after punching their solo line.

Michael Jackson had pitched the song very high and, after a run of choruses in unison, Jones told those who were singing an octave below to drop out for the next take.

'All the fellows with high voices, please. Up in the same octave as Michael's singing it. Everybody that can't sing it that high, just lay out. I don't wanna get octaves on this part. We're gonna do low octaves later. So, if it's too high for anybody, they can just rest.'

They tried again. But Quincy had spotted something.

'Bruce, were you singing then? Okay, well just leave it out this time.'

Bob took that as his cue that he shouldn't join in with his 'Geldof croak'. Instead, he got out his little camera and started snapping pictures of the unique assembly.

All was going well until, sometime after 1 a.m., Stevie Wonder objected to some scat-singing phrases Michael Jackson wanted to include.

Geldof agreed that Jackson's 'sha-lum sha-lingay' could be misconstrued as mocking an African language – an ironic intervention considering the criticisms which would later be levelled at his own song, 'Do They Know It's Christmas?'.

Stevie Wonder then declared that they should be singing some of the song in Swahili instead.

At this point, Quincy Jones, fearing that events might take a controversial turn, ordered the crews filming the evening to turn off their cameras while Stevie called a Nigerian friend to get an appropriate Swahili phrase.

Geldof pointed out that in Ethiopia people don't speak Swahili. And anyway, he said, the song wasn't talking to the people who were starving. It was addressed to the people who had the money, not to poor Africans.

Heedless, Stevie began singing 'ulimwangu latoto willi moing-gu', which didn't go down well with sections of the cast.

'Say what!' yelled Ray Charles. 'Willi what! Willi moing-gu, my ass! It's three o'clock in the goddamn mornin' – I can't even sing in English no more. Ring the bell, Quincy. Ring the bell!'

At which point, the redneck rocker Waylon Jennings declared: 'Well, ain't no good ol' boy ever sung Swahili. Think I'm outta here.' He walked out of the studio.

By 3 a.m., the chorus was in the can and Quincy told the singers to take an hour's break. Ray Charles announced he needed to go to the bathroom, to which Stevie Wonder said, 'I'll show you where it is' and seized him by the arm.

'The blind really are leading the blind,' someone shouted. The room burst into laughter and any previous tension dissolved.

Diana Ross took the opportunity at this point to walk up to Daryl Hall with her sheet music in her hands. 'Daryl, I'm your biggest fan,' the great Motown singer said. 'Would you sign my music for me?'

Everyone looked around. And soon the whole room was asking each other to sign their own piece of paper.

Geldof took his to Springsteen and said: 'Come on, Bruce.'

'Seriously?' said Bruce.

'Yes,' said Bob.

'People were gracious and wonderful about that,' said Kim Carnes. 'Nobody held back. Everybody wanted to get everybody's signature. Everyone knew it was a really special night.'

Sheila E was so flattered when the veteran stars came to get her autograph that she called Prince, who had gone to a club after the awards ceremony, and said: 'I think maybe you should come… It's pretty cool, and, you know, everyone's hanging out… We're having a great time.'

At 4 a.m., Quincy Jones set about recording the solo lines. There had never been enough time for twenty-one soloists to go into a recording booth and record their lines one at a time. Instead, he had stuck the names of the singers on tape on the floor around microphones in a large semi-circle. But Jones had had another reason for choosing this set-up. It generated the atmosphere of a live performance. 'That circle was the intimidating circle of life,' recalled Lionel Richie. 'Quincy was right. When it's time for you to sing, you are going to give 200 per cent because the class is looking at you. And to see everyone's preparation and vulnerability was pretty amazing. You were on your game at that point.' Everybody hung around and watched, said Kim Carnes: 'It took the song to another level of "Just how cool is this?"'

To be watched was exactly what Prince didn't want. He had been invited and indeed was expected – to the point where his part was actually printed under his name on the music. Jones had had the idea of having the two great rivals of the moment, Michael Jackson and Prince, at the same microphone. But Prince didn't turn up, despite Sheila E doing her best to get him there – and despite Lionel Richie phoning him at Carlos'n Charlie's private disco on Sunset Strip.

'I wanna play a guitar solo,' Prince said. 'In another room.'

'No, no, no,' replied Richie. 'We're all in the same room. I need you to come and sing.' The song was about unity through vocals, Quincy told him.

But the idea of walking into a room full of superstars to sing while they all watched was too intimidating to Prince, who was used to going into a recording studio and playing all the parts himself. He stayed on Sunset Strip and, when he came out of the club, his bodyguards beat up some photographers and ended up in jail. The *LA Times*' report of it the next day was so embarrassing to Prince that he wrote a song about it, 'Hello', which claimed that paparazzi had prevented him from attending. The lines on the charity song reserved for him were given to Huey Lewis.

As dawn approached, Bob Dylan was finally called to sing. He had looked uneasy all evening. The anthemic melody just didn't suit his style of singing. 'He stepped up to the microphone … and sounded nothing like Bob Dylan,' said Ken Kragen. 'He was so nervous … Lionel, Quincy and

Stevie asked everybody else to leave, apart from Geldof. They then sat down one at a time at the piano.'

It was Stevie Wonder who was midwife to Dylan's contribution. Playing the section over and over, Stevie began to sing in a mischievous caricature of Dylan's style. Dylan laughed and began to imitate the imitation of himself. It took several takes, but eventually, as Dylan grew in confidence, his voiced relaxed into his distinctive nasal drawl as he sang: 'It's a choice we're making … we're saving our own lives.'

'That wasn't any good,' said Dylan.

'I'm telling you, we got it,' said Quincy. 'That was fantastic.'

'If you say so,' said Dylan, unconvinced.

'I swear it is, man. It's perfect.'

Springsteen came in and said simply, 'Nice, Dylan.' He then went over to the mic to record a final solo vocal to run over the last chorus of the song. He delivered it with such passion that he broke out in a sweat. 'Springsteen sings his part once, kills it, just nails it,' Kragen remembered. 'It's so good you get shivers.'

It was 8 a.m. With the liggers long since departed, the final contributors emerged into the LA sunshine. Only Diana Ross stayed behind. She was crying softly.

'Diana, are you okay?' asked Quincy Jones.

'I don't want this to be over,' she replied. 'I think every individual in the world wants to contribute and they don't know how. I got a feeling that we're creating a shift in what's going on in the world today.'

The long evening had given Bob Geldof more than a feeling. He had the idea that perhaps they could put the two songs together the following Christmas for a fund-raising broadcast. It wasn't to happen, but it sowed the seed of something even more momentous.

CHAPTER 8

ST BOB VERSUS THE IRON LADY

'Well, do you want to see the prime minister of the United Kingdom or not?'

Bob Geldof was sitting in front of the television thinking about going to bed when the phone rang. It was Charles Powell, private secretary to Margaret Thatcher.

'The prime minister would like to see you.'

'Okay.' Geldof was not entirely surprised. Thatcher had tapped him on the shoulder a few days earlier and told him to come and see her. 'What date?' Geldof asked Powell. 'Let me get my diary.'

'No, now.'

'Charles, it's nearly 11 p.m....'

Powell brushed that trifling consideration aside and asked: 'What is it that you want to discuss?'

'Well, you called me,' said Geldof, playing for time. 'What is it that the prime minister wants to discuss?'

Powell cut to the chase. 'Do you want to see the prime minister of the United Kingdom or not?'

Ten minutes later, Geldof was cycling from his home in Chelsea to 10 Downing Street. Two vital questions were forming in his mind.

Shortly after the release of 'Do They Know It's Christmas?', the Irish government announced it would waive the VAT sales tax on the single, a tax that applied to other records. But, in the UK, the Thatcher government adamantly refused to do that.

This infuriated Geldof. Everyone had worked without payment on the record: its manufacture, its distribution and its sale. Every penny, Bob had promised the public would get to Ethiopia. Every penny apart from the 15 per cent tax cut the British government took. Each record sold for £1.35, of which the government took 20 pence in tax, which should have been going to feed the starving in Ethiopia.

Requests from the Band Aid Trust to the Thatcher administration that it should follow the example of the Irish fell on deaf ears.

Geldof was fuming. 'Thatcher – the Milk Snatcher who had once taken free milk away from schoolchildren – was now taking food from the starving people of Ethiopia which had been so generously donated by the British public.'

In December 1984, Geldof received a letter from the leader of the opposition, Neil Kinnock, asking if Band Aid would like the issue raised in parliament. But Bob had said no. 'If it had become a party-political thing, that would have divided Band Aid's support,' Geldof explained.

So Kinnock had written privately to Thatcher instead, but without success. The Labour leader even wrote to every living former prime minister and persuaded them to sign a letter to Thatcher asking for an exception to be made, given the severity of the situation in Ethiopia. But still the answer was no. If we exempt one charity from VAT, Thatcher said in her reply to Kinnock, then we will have to exempt them all.

Five months later, Thatcher was still holding that line. It was one of the two issues Geldof knew he must raise as he cycled to Downing Street. He was expecting to get a hard time from her. It would cost the Exchequer a lot of money. But, on his second point, he hoped it would be easier to make progress.

One of the images still haunting from that first BBC famine film was the low stone wall which divided thousands of starving people from the 300 who had been chosen by a Red Cross nurse to be fed. 'The 300 behind the wall had been given a can of butter oil, because that's all there was to eat,' he remembered. The image of the cans, each marked with the symbol of the Red Cross, was at the front of his mind as he cycled. That year, Europe's butter mountain had reached 1.4 million tonnes, thanks to the EU's crazy policy of subsidising farmers to over-produce to keep them in business. That year, it cost Europe's taxpayers £945 million just to keep the butter refrigerated – or to dispose of it once it had gone rancid. Why couldn't the good butter be sent to Ethiopia?

Geldof had touched on both these issues the first time he had met Thatcher. Several weeks before, in February 1985, he had been invited to an awards ceremony hosted by the *Daily Star* to celebrate 'True Brits with True Grit'. Geldof, despite being Irish, had been included. He was not disposed to attend until he heard that the awards were being given out by the prime minister.

'I knew this was a great opportunity to confront her publicly, so I accepted,' he said.

Geldof planned the encounter very carefully. 'I gave a lot of thought to what I would wear. I needed to look like a pop star, but not to come over as too outlandish.' He chose a lambswool shirt under a suit with a sparkle in its pinstripe. 'I realised that I was going to be taller than her. I needed to be quite close to her, so she would have to look up to me. And I decided I was going to be quiet, to keep my voice low, even if she annoyed me. I was determined not to be Hectoring Bob. I wasn't going to be trapped into being rude to the prime minister.'

As she handed out prizes to 'the kind of people who put the great into Great Britain', the PM singled out Geldof, but added, in a typically Thatcherite manner: 'For a long time it has been fashionable to encourage the belief that governments could deliver everything, including greatness as a nation. The state will provide. It isn't true.'

This was a red rag to Geldof. He wasn't asking the state to provide. He was asking it not to steal money from the starving. Introduced to her in the line-up before the lunch, he went straight to it.

'We've had a bit of a problem with the VAT on the record.'

She gave him her petrifying Medusa stare. 'We were so close,' he said later. 'I could see the fluffy blonde hair all over her face, powdered out, so you don't see it. And it suddenly struck me, it's the prime minister but she's a woman… Her hair, her make-up, impeccable. And she goes into feminine mode…'

'I know, but don't forget,' Thatcher replied smoothly, 'we've used some of your VAT to give back and to plough back. We've given again and again, and government has to get taxation from somewhere…'

Geldof switched to a new line of attack, criticising the way that the

European Union, of which the UK was a prominent member, was subsidising its farmers to produce food that no one wanted and that was just put into store.

'At the moment you've got a problem with the butter mountain, and you don't know how to dispose of it,' Geldof began softly. 'You sell it to the Russians as the cheapest way.'

Her eyes went icy blue, Geldof recalled. 'But I stayed very soft, and she got more strident.'

'I'm sorry, but butter doesn't do very much good in Africa, as you know. It's grain.'

'Well, butter oil actually does. It's one of the major supplementary foods...'

'Butter oil, if you can get it.'

'Well, it is a by-product of butter...'

Surprisingly, for a former research chemist, Thatcher seemed not to know that butter oil was refined from butter. Geldof's quiet tone had done the job. Mrs Thatcher was a woman who did not shy away from confrontation, but this was not going as well as she had expected. She had met more than her equal in Geldof. The exchange continued, with pop star matching prime minister blow for blow.

'Well, look, a lot is going, a lot of surplus food is going, but don't forget...'

'But, Prime Minister, there are millions dying and that's a terrible thing.'

'It's not as simple as that, Mr Geldof.'

'No, Prime Minister, nothing is as simple as dying.'

Thatcher's minders were trying to move her on throughout this exchange. 'All the time she tried to move away from me,' Geldof recalled, 'but she could not stand to let me have the last word.'

The irresistible force had met the immovable object. But Bob Geldof had become – to the delight of the nation – the only person ever to contradict the Iron Lady twice, to her face, in public.

All this had been captured by the television cameras. But then something happened which wasn't. Geldof and Thatcher were seated at separate tables at the lunch which followed. They were sitting back-to-back, so Geldof had no idea who it was who tapped him on the shoulder just after they had finished the starter. He turned to see the prime minister.

'Come and see me at Number 10, Mr Geldof,' she said, taking an early departure from the lunch before the main course arrived.

Wow, thought Geldof. *I've really bugged her.* But he could not work out what it meant. Perhaps she wanted another chance to beat him in the argument. Perhaps she thought he could be an ally in her ongoing struggles to get the European farm subsidies abolished. Perhaps, as a very canny politician, she recognised that she had locked horns with a populist figure with a different kind of power base, but one that was in its own way as potent as hers.

That sense was reinforced, far more crudely, when Geldof got into a taxi shortly after his skirmish with the PM. 'Fucking hell, mate,' said the driver. 'That Thatcher, you fucking gave it to her. You told her to fuck right off. I was fucking yelling at the TV screen. Thanks, mate.' Bob realised this was no longer just about feeding the starving, or about a group of pop stars setting aside their egos to do something for the common good. The glee in the driver's voice made him see that he had tapped into a discontent with the way politics was working. It was not just about compassion, it was about anger.

But that was not what Geldof wanted. 'I needed to get her on side, to be her friend if I could be.' It was a strategy which he and Bono were to put in play over the following four decades 'with Tony Blair, George Bush, Jesse Helms or whomever'. But it started with Margaret Thatcher.

Geldof parked his bike at the end of Downing Street and made his way to the famous black door of No 10. It opened without him having to knock and he was shown in. The place was empty. All the grand rooms on the lower floor were dark. He was taken past them to the top of the building and the prime minister's private flat. It was a very modest affair, which surprised him; it was small, slightly down at heel, with chintzy chairs and sofas. Mrs Thatcher was alone. Her red box of confidential government papers was on the table. She had finished going through them for the night and seemed very relaxed. She was in an armchair. She gestured Geldof to sit on a sofa. There was no one else there.

'Would you like a whisky, Mr Geldof?' she asked.

'There was no, "What would you like to drink?". Just "Would you like a whisky?",' he recalled. There was no alternative. She poured two glasses.

'Could I have a splash of water in it?'

A look of mild distaste passed across Thatcher's features, but she took Geldof's glass to the kitchen. He heard a splash from the kitchen tap and she returned and opened the conversation.

'You know I think that what you are doing is wonderful,' she began.

'Thank you very much. It's very difficult, you know. Have you ever been to these famine areas? It's appalling, Prime Minister. The devastation is terrible.'

Geldof then appealed for the government to waive the VAT on the single, which would release millions into the Band Aid fund for the people of Ethiopia.

'I'm afraid that if we exempt one charity from VAT then we will have to exempt them all,' she replied, parroting the reply she had given to Neil Kinnock.

Geldof changed tack. He had heard, he said, that the government was thinking of recalling the RAF transport Hercules planes which were dropping food aid into the most remote part of Ethiopia. It was really important that this did not happen, he said.

'The Africans need to step up to do this themselves,' she said and moved on to talk about the politics of Ethiopia's Soviet-backed government.

'It's hard for them to step up when they're in the middle of a civil war.'

'Well, that's the problem.'

'It's one of the problems. But there is a terrible drought. And the country lacks infrastructure, which is why the RAF flights are so critical. The British public are really proud of what the RAF are doing out there.'

'Oh, yes, that's wonderful. But providing aid is giving succour to the Marxist regime of Colonel Mengistu.'

Geldof knew that he was not going to change her mind about that, though he only discovered just how vehement her views were thirty years later when top-secret government papers on the Mengistu regime were released. Some months after her late-night whisky with Geldof, Thatcher wrote to the Foreign Office suggesting it should find ways of supporting anti-government rebels to overthrow this 'particularly cruel and objectionable government' – though she did concede that humanitarian aid should be continued.

That night, Mrs Thatcher wanted an argument over the politics of Ethiopia, Geldof concluded. 'She wanted entertainment at the end of a long day, that's for sure.'

But Bob did not want to play that game. In part, it was because his political views were nowhere near as left-wing as she supposed. But Geldof was after a different outcome. 'So I told her it was obscene that people should die of want in a world of surplus. The EU should not be sitting on mountains of surplus food. The Common Agricultural Policy is intellectually absurd, economically illiterate and morally repulsive,' Geldof said, trotting out a line he was to use repeatedly to the press.

'Oh, the arguments I've had about the Common Agricultural Policy...' the prime minister said. The two were singing from the same hymn-sheet at last.

After forty-five minutes, Thatcher brought the conversation to a close and Geldof was ushered downstairs to get on his bike and pedal home. Cycling through the night, he thought to himself: 'How fucking mad is this? A Paddy pop star drinking late-night whisky alone with the prime minister of Great Britain!'

For Geldof, the incident reinforced something that he had learned in his face-off with the Ethiopian dictator. The Band Aid millions gave him the moral authority – and, he felt, the responsibility – to stand up to politicians on behalf of the huge constituency of ordinary people who had given so much. Band Aid was more than a money-raising exercise. It was a subversive phenomenon which could wrest the political initiative from the parliamentary process into the hands of ordinary people. As Midge Ure later put it, it touched the hearts of an entire generation of people who were probably not interested in politics – and it did so far more effectively than any government could. 'Suddenly, here was a group of musicians who would do something for the common good and they caught everybody's imagination... It was a period of change. Big change.'

On the refund of the VAT, Geldof refused to take no for an answer. He continued to campaign publicly on the issue, winning the backing of the tabloid press whose readers had bought 'Do They Know It's Christmas?' in massive numbers.

One newspaper cartoon showed rows of starving Africans with bowls in their hands marked VAT – and a grotesquely fat and sweaty chancellor of the exchequer running along, grabbing money from the bowls and stuffing it into a bulging sack.

An opinion poll in London's *Evening Standard* showed a drop in the Conservative Party's popularity. A third of voters said it was because Mrs Thatcher had insisted on taxing the Band Aid single.

At this point, Thatcher's political ideology came into conflict with her practical politics. She set aside her distaste for Ethiopia's Marxist regime, along with her embrace of right-wing intellectuals like Peter Bauer, who declared that hand-outs to the poor world merely encouraged dependency. Thatcher had been so impressed that, a year before Band Aid, she made Bauer a life peer. But now Band Aid forced her to shift her ground.

A few weeks after their late-night whisky, Geldof received another after-hours phone call.

'Mr Geldof, could you stand by for the chancellor of the exchequer?'

At the other end of the phone, Geldof heard the smooth tones of a politician.

'Mr Geldof, the government is prepared to make a donation to Band Aid at the exact level of the VAT paid on the Band Aid record.'

'Thank you very much, Chancellor.'

'There is, however, um, one caveat. We would rather you didn't issue any statements about this to the press, since we can't announce this. I hope you'll see this as a matter of mutual trust.'

'Yes, of course. Thank you very much, and please thank the prime minister. I won't say anything.' And for years he didn't.

It wasn't the only money which kept pouring into Band Aid. It was coming from all angles. The tide of goodwill around Geldof did not abate. The press continued to call him St Bob, often now without irony. Old ladies would approach him in the street, reach out and touch him, and burst into tears. The public adulation was both surreal and overwhelming. 'It was massively embarrassing,' Geldof said. He felt a significant amount of trust was placed in him, which was both flattering and intimidating. 'He was no longer just a musician,' said Midge Ure, 'but a new style of charity worker who had made compassion hip.'

People were even handing cash to Geldof as he walked down the street. It was not uncommon for him to come home with £500 in his pocket to pay into the Band Aid account.

Throughout February 1985, at every gig on the Boomtown Rats tour, there were buckets at the back for donations. 'We had to put them there.

People were leaving money for Band Aid on their seats, at the box office or throwing it on the stage,' Bob said. An additional £50,000 was raised for Band Aid that way. The more money came in, the more Geldof realised he needed a proper organisation to help work out how to spend it. Bob had the big shopping list of needs supplied by the aid agencies on his trip to Ethiopia. But he knew nothing about grain, supplementary foods, or medicines, and he did not have the faintest idea about how to organise shipping to Africa. 'I knew I could not just keep playing things by ear.'

Until this point, Geldof was still working out of his record company's press office, where he had commandeered a desk. The Phonogram staff there had grown used to coping simultaneously with calls about the new Tears For Fears tour and calls about the current market price of grain in Port Sudan. But the problems were getting way beyond him.

One day, a smartly dressed man with a trim beard walked into the office and offered to help. Kevin Jenden was an architect with a successful practice in designing modish things like record studios, restaurants and shops. But he had also worked in Ethiopia, designing disaster-preparedness warehouses for the Red Cross and laying out a camp for 4,000 orphans from the war zones. Out there in 1981, he already knew that a major famine was coming. He could speak some Amharic, the dominant language of Ethiopia. He and his anthropologist wife Penny had also lived for some time in India. When news of the terrible 1984 famine broke out, he had volunteered his services, for free, to Oxfam and Save the Children, but they had not taken him up on his offer. Frustrated, he walked into Geldof's office and offered to work for Band Aid.

Jenden and Geldof hit it off at once. Like him, they were both suspicious of the traditional aid agencies. Kevin offered to work for Band Aid every afternoon, without payment, after spending the morning in his architectural office. But he soon abandoned his business to his partner and found himself working, unpaid, every minute of every waking day. By March 1985, Jenden was addressing the challenges related to aid distribution and despatching the first plane containing Land Rovers, high-protein biscuits, tents and dried milk in bags marked 'Love from Band Aid'. That labelling was important to Geldof. 'I thought everything should be branded so that people could visibly see their cash made tangible,' he said. He rejected the usual aid agency wording 'a gift from'. He wanted to convey the sense of 'something freely given out of shared humanness and understanding', which Band Aid embodied. 'Love was the better word than charity, which is devalued term. The money given to Band Aid was given out of love – pure and simple.' Penny Jenden soon joined her husband, bringing her experience as an anthropologist to bear on selecting projects for Band Aid to fund.

More and more people approached Bob to offer Band Aid their services for free. In a London café, a businesswoman, Valerie Blondeau, passed Geldof a note on a paper napkin.

'Do you need help?' it said.

'Yes,' he wrote on the other side and passed it back.

Judy Anderson, a labour lawyer from the US who was taking a sabbatical in England after sailing across the Atlantic, was next to join.

Another central tenet of the Band Aid philosophy was taking shape: whatever needed doing, there was someone you could ask to do it for free. They set up an office in a disused bus garage in London. All of the equipment was donated by big corporate companies and volunteers came in from all over. Nothing was spent on administration in order to fulfil the pledge that every penny from the record would go to Ethiopia. No one took so much as the price of a cup of coffee from Band Aid funds.

But who was regulating all this? If any of the money went astray, Geldof was told by the pop industry lawyer John Kennedy, the press would have a field day. By this point, Kennedy was fast becoming Band Aid's unpaid full-time lawyer. Band Aid ought to set up a trust, he told Geldof. They would need a minimum of four to six trustees. At that point, the phone rang. It was Midge Ure's manager, Chris Morrison. Geldof hijacked the call.

'Tell Midge he's gonna be a trustee. And so are you,' Bob said, as though he were doing them a favour. 'I'll be the chairman.' As he put down the phone, he turned to Kennedy and said, 'You're on it too.' Soon, Michael Grade, the controller of BBC One, was a trustee. So was Lord Harlech, another TV studio boss. And so too was Maurice Oberstein, the chairman of the British Phonographic Institute and one of the most colourful people in the music business. (When agents and managers brought music in for him to hear, Obie – as he was universally known – played it to his dog, Charlie. If the dog barked enthusiastically, the artist would be signed up.)

It was a steep learning curve for everyone. None of them had experience in this area. 'For the first six months of 1985, I was swept along, embroiled in four-hour meetings every day,' Midge recalled. 'We had discussions about ships, jeeps, high-protein biscuits, medication, trucks, sorghum. All the time I was thinking: "What is sorghum? I don't know what we are talking about. How come I'm responsible for all this money and I can't walk away from it?" Bob was thinking the same thing, but we were all enveloped and overcome by the whole scenario.'

Michael Grade, whose background and expertise were vastly different from Midge's, felt this same. 'Should we buy these trucks? Should we rent them? Should we let one of the aid organisations take it over and run it? It just snowballed.'

'We had this gung-ho attitude which meant we suggested a lot of stuff that regular charities couldn't – or wouldn't – do,' said Midge. 'Let's charter a ship. Let's get it out there now. Why should we wait a month? Bob's big thing was cutting through the red tape. Or ignoring it. That is something we were used to in the rock business.'

But this wasn't the rock business. After Geldof appeared on Terry Wogan's BBC One chat show and complained about the huge fees shipping companies charged to get grain out to Africa, a shipping agent called Ken Martin contacted him. Why didn't Band Aid charter some ships on long leases and then offer space in them to other aid agencies?

It was the kind of maverick scheme that Band Aid prided itself on having the flexibility to do. In April 1985, Martin agreed to ship the charity's famine relief supplies to Ethiopia and Sudan on condition that he was indemnified against all his costs. Band Aid chartered nine vessels and created a new shipping system of regular sea shuttles from the UK to the Red Sea ports.

At one point, Band Aid's video editor Nigel Dick arrived back in his office at Phonogram to find Geldof already there using the phone. He was calling President Mubarak of Egypt and asking for the use of the Suez Canal, for free, to get food through to the famine – without having to pay the stiff canal duties. 'Bob was calm, persuasive, relaxed and got what he wanted. It was as if he was asking the local constable to help out with the school fete.'

Other aid agencies could now book free space at much shorter notice than that required to charter ships independently. Band Aid's fleet transported around 100,000 tonnes of food, vehicles, tents and medical equipment over the next eighteen months at a cost of £6 million. A range of other agencies, from Oxfam to small voluntary and church groups, benefitted from Band Aid's free shipping service.

It was only years later that the trust discovered that Ken Martin had been running a scam. The ships would have been empty on the return journey, so he was hiring them out to firms with goods to transport from Africa to Europe and then pocketing the money for himself.

'This was so alien to everything the Band Aid was about,' said John Kennedy. 'He was the only person we sued over the years.' In 1994, Martin was ordered by a court to pay Band Aid the £2.5 million he had illicitly made. But Martin went bankrupt, so the extra cash never materialised for the Band Aid Trust.

There was one other narrow escape. One of the trust's financial advisers recommended to John Kennedy that Band Aid should shift its money to a bank paying 4 per cent more interest than it was getting at present. The increased interest would have brought in millions more for Ethiopia, the adviser argued.

Kennedy was momentarily tempted, but suspicious. He said no.

Not long afterwards, the Bank of Credit and Commerce International (BCCI) went spectacularly bust, owing $20 billion, after it was found to have been handling the money of customers who dealt in arms, drugs and money-laundering. It was so bad that police nicknamed it the Bank of Crooks and Criminals International.

'If we'd transferred our money, the bank would've taken £40 million of Band Aid money with it,' reflected Kennedy. 'Imagine the front-page headlines if that had happened.'

Effective scrutiny of Band Aid's activities was of particular concern to Michael Grade, who freely admitted to knowing nothing about aid or logistics. Nor did anyone else on the Band Aid Trust. They were, Grade wrote to Geldof in frustration, 'lamentably short of regular and systematic financial information'.

Grade saw it as his job to ensure that the governance of the charity was always open to scrutiny. 'We must be transparent. We mustn't do anything that people haven't given us the money to do.'

The trust appointed top accountants Stoy Hayward to manage the Band Aid books. Accountancy and audit fees were the only money taken from the trust's funds for anything other than dispatch to Ethiopia. The fees, at Geldof's insistence, came from Band Aid's corporate sponsors, not from the donations of the public, Geldof insisted. The trustees themselves took no expenses.

Expertise in those early days was provided to the trust by Penny Jenden. Early on, she said, most of the money was used for immediate relief.

'We all started as volunteers and we had a very limited goal early on,' she said. 'We thought there were projects just sitting there, waiting for money, and so we would find the good ones and fund them. But it hasn't worked out that way. We've had to become more of a development organisation.'

Under Penny Jenden's influence, Band Aid decided to spend 20 per cent of its funds on emergency food and medicine, 20 per cent on logistics, and the remaining 60 per cent on longer-term development projects. She introduced stringent administrative structures to ensure that aid reached its intended recipients and to underscore Band Aid's commitment to transparency and accountability in its operations. And she appointed a committee of experts – which included six of the UK's leading development academics, chaired by the former director general of Oxfam, Brian Walker – to advise on where the money should be spent.

Geldof joked it was the most 'over-qualified' body ever assembled, but it marked the start of greater cooperation between Band Aid and certain other agencies.

By summer 1986, the advisory board had reviewed over 700 applications for funding. Many were weak proposals submitted by organisations which assumed that the Band Aid newcomers would be something of 'a soft touch', as Walker put it. Some 450 were rejected outright.

But grants were approved for small-scale wells, micro-dams, market gardens, grain banks, grinding mills and training programmes, along with support for village-level agriculture or industry, particularly for women. A significant proportion of the grants were awarded to Africa-based voluntary groups. After eighteen months, the trust had developed enough expertise, and a network of relationships with reliable aid agencies in the UK and in Africa, to no longer need its expert advisory board.

Those who had seen Geldof at work in public might expect that he would have been bulldozing and autocratic as chairman of the Band Aid Trust. Not so, insisted his fellow trustees.

'I sat in dozens of trust meetings where Bob was so passionate about everything, but he always listened to what others were saying,' said Midge. 'He respected everyone round the table and, if we said, "Bob, you've lost it, this idea doesn't make any sense", he'd be big enough to admit it.' Michael Grade agreed: 'If the trustees have got a worry about something, and he's passionate about it, we have a good debate, and he will always go with the majority in the end. But he's usually right.'

Early in March 1985, Geldof walked into a trustees' meeting with a new idea. For three months, Band Aid had been having problems with the trucking operations that were supposed to carry aid from Sudan and Djibouti into Ethiopia. 'If we had another £4 million, we could buy our own fleet of trucks,' he announced. But where were they going to get the extra cash?

Bob had remembered an idea that he had toyed with back in the US while recording 'We Are the World': that the stars from the UK and US records could be brought together to perform the two songs live, the following Christmas.

Only now he knew he couldn't wait until Christmas. News of how bad the famine was affecting the whole continent kept coming in. It was spreading right across Africa, east to west, through the line of countries south of the Sahara. More money was now needed, more than ever. Something had to be done much sooner. Not another record. A concert. Band Aid was legally constituted so that its fundraising was only for Ethiopia. Now what was needed was to raise funds which could be spent all across Africa.

The trustees looked at one another. Obie whispered into Kennedy's ear.

'He's mad. You have to stop him. We do not know anything about putting on concerts. I'm going to resign.'

'You can't resign, Obie,' said Kennedy. 'I forgot to put a resignation clause in the trust deed.'

Geldof, of course, already had a plan. Outside the room, Harvey Goldsmith was waiting – one of the most successful concert promoters of all time.

CHAPTER 9

CONSTRUCTING A GLOBAL JUKEBOX

Harvey Goldsmith didn't even have the chance to unpack before the phone rang.

Britain's top music promoter had just come back from an historic ten-day tour of China with the pop duo Wham!. It had been the first time that a Western pop act had visited the Communist People's Republic.

'It's Geldof. You told me to ring when you got back from China. We've got to meet today.'

'I'm just off the plane. Ring me tomorrow.'

The next day, Goldsmith had been in his office for only six minutes when Geldof rang again. He was already in full bulldozer mode over his idea of getting together all the stars who had appeared on the British and American charity records for Ethiopia. More money was needed. He wanted to put on the biggest rock concert the world had ever seen.

While Harvey had been away, Bob had been busy. He had already got Spandau Ballet, Paul Young and Paul Weller to agree that they would appear, along with Mark Knopfler of Dire Straits, who were just about to release the world's first-ever million-selling CD. At the Ivor Novello songwriting awards in March, where he and Midge Ure had been presented with an award for 'Do They Know It's Christmas?', he had also asked Elton John, who agreed there and then. 'You don't say no to Bob,' said Elton afterwards.

Geldof knew that the idea of a concert was really going to take off when, an hour later, Elton's manager, John Reid, rang. Bob's heart sank. A manager ringing usually meant they were trying to wriggle out of the commitment that their artist had made. But this time was different.

'Just ringing to say how keen we are on this concert. Is there anything else we can do to help? Do you need use of an office, phones or anything?'

'Thanks, John. There is one thing you can do. When you bump into the managers of other bands, just make sure you tell them Elton is doing this.'

The day before Harvey's return from Beijing, Geldof rang Eric Clapton, Rod Stewart and the manager of the Who, Bill Curbishley. *Might the Who re-form for the concert?*, he wondered. By the time Bob and Harvey met up on 18 April, Geldof was already assembling an impressive starting list of stars.

Even before the first meeting, Harvey knew this was going to be big. That was made clear when Bob invited another promoter, Maurice James, to help. 'We don't need him,' said Harvey, but Bob insisted. 'This was now the Band Aid thing,' he said later. 'Rival pop artists came together. Rival record companies and retailers. Rival sections of showbiz. It wasn't necessary, but the gesture was, in my mind, crucial.' It was agreed that Harvey would look after the acts and production, while Maurice would deal with the ticket sales, marketing and promotion.

But Geldof had even bigger ideas than they expected. He now sprang upon them the idea of two concerts – one in the UK and the other in the US – linked by transatlantic satellite technology.

'The idea is we start at noon here and go until 5 p.m.,' Geldof explained. 'Then we join with America on a live two-way satellite relay. We have five hours of relay – back and forth, every other act – and then at 10 p.m., we hand over to America and they run for another five hours. Throughout, we broadcast constant appeals and give people phone numbers pledging donations on their credit cards.'

Geldof sat back for a moment, looking pleased with himself.

'You must be fucking mad,' said Harvey.

'Is it even technically possible?' asked Maurice pragmatically. Satellite technology was still in its infancy.

'No one's going to clear a television network for fifteen hours of pop music,' said Harvey.

'They will if it's the best music in the world, Harvey, a global event. They won't be able to say no,' said Geldof. 'MTV will definitely take it in the US and I'll ask here. We can do it on July the 6th, which is Independence

Day weekend in the States. We'll have the most important rock artists of the last twenty-five years on one stage. We'll get the top fifty bands, give them eighteen minutes each, so they just play their hits, so the audience won't get bored, and raise loads of money.'

'This is getting worse. You're fucking mad,' said Harvey. 'How are we going to do that? How are you going to get bands on and off the stage every eighteen minutes? It's impossible. And, anyway, why?'

'Because people are dying, Harvey. That's why.'

Bob knew that he would come round. Harvey always reacted like this. 'First, he sees the problem. Then the beauty of the idea. Then the solution,' Geldof said later. Harvey saw a pattern in Bob's behaviour too: 'He would throw the challenge out and I'd do it, but I'd do it my way. And I'd come back at him. There was this constant tension, but it actually proved to be positive. We would be ribbing each other, but we were getting the job done.'

'What will we call it?' Harvey asked.

'Live Aid. Because it will be a live performance of the artists on the Band Aid and USA for Africa records.'

Wembley Stadium was the obvious British venue, but they needed to find a suitable equivalent in the States. But first, Geldof set about contacting television stations, while Harvey put together a production team.

There were just eleven weeks to the chosen date.

❊

Harvey Goldsmith called his staff together to brainstorm. Who were the best people in the music industry to handle the nuts and bolts of all this? They fixed upon Andrew Zweck, one of the most experienced tour managers and producers who had previously worked with Pink Floyd. He would look after the technical side – the stage, sound, lights and backstage arrangements. Liaison with the bands and their managers over logistics and equipment would be the responsibility of Pete Smith, who had made a top career in artist promotion and management after booking many of the biggest bands in the world for Leeds University in the days when universities were the largest rock venues in the UK.

But first they had to secure Wembley as the venue. It was not as easy as Geldof had supposed.

'There's a boardroom battle going on there,' Harvey told Bob on his return from the stadium. 'There are two consortiums on the board who each own 40 per cent of the equity. No one's quite sure who owns the place. One guy hinted we could have it for free, but the others said the opposite.'

There were other options. Aston Villa had said Live Aid could have their ground, Villa Park. Maurice reckoned they could get Milton Keynes Bowl for free. Geldof was unimpressed.

'Aston Villa are in fucking Birmingham. No one in the US has even heard of it. And Milton Keynes is not much more than a fucking field,' Bob expostulated. 'It's got to be London to command the world's attention. Let's try Wembley again. It's London and it's got four walls for security. What's happening with America?'

Harvey put in a call to Bill Graham, the legendary rock promoter. Graham was the only concert promoter with a recognised profile, coast to coast, in the US. He had fixed national tours for Bob Dylan and the Rolling Stones. He worked by sub-letting legs of the tour to regional promoters. 'Harvey knew this,' wrote Pete Smith in an unpublished memoir, which he completed just before his death in 2022. 'Bill was respected by the TV and radio networks.' He could persuade the artists he managed, like Santana, to perform. 'That would encourage other major artists to engage. Live Aid needed the credibility that only Bill Graham could deliver.'

Graham was immensely creative and extraordinarily driven, but he had an ego as big as some of the stars he represented. He was an irascible control freak who ruled by fear and intimidation. 'He's a bad motherfucker,' said Isaac Tigrett, founder of the Hard Rock Café, who was to have a major row with Graham in the middle of the Live Aid concert. More than that, Graham insisted that the US leg of the concert had to be in California, where he was based.

'That's no good,' Harvey told him. 'It's got to be on the East Coast. It will never work on the West Coast because the time difference with London is too great.'

'I could get you Stanford Stadium for free,' Bill said. 'You'll make more money at Stanford.'

'It's not just about raising money,' said Harvey. 'It's about creating a worldwide event.'

Bill was adamant: he wanted San Francisco. This was going to be tricky.

❧

Getting TV coverage was also going to be harder than Geldof had imagined. Channel 4 had been enthusiastic when he first approached them, but now they said they couldn't afford to do it. It would cost them £1 million in cancellation fees to clear their schedules for a whole day.

Bob hadn't considered this. 'I had thought I was giving them a day's free programming,' he later reflected. 'I had thought they would be grateful. They turned it down and I was worried.'

Through a mutual friend, Geldof approached Mike Appleton, the producer of the BBC TV's leading rock programme, *The Old Grey Whistle Test*. Appleton rang Bob and asked who was in the concert line-up. Geldof followed his tried-and-tested Band Aid tactic of naming every famous person he had asked – without revealing that most of them hadn't actually said yes. He even added in a few he hadn't got round to asking yet.

On 18 May, Appleton went to his boss, Roger Laughton, who had been planning an all-night rock show later in the year called *Rock Around the Clock*. He met Bob and Harvey. Every time Laughton responded enthusiastically, Geldof raised the stakes.

'"We wanna film the whole concert," Bob told him. "We wanna put it all out, and we're gonna play in America,"' recalled Harvey, pointing out, forty years later, that the US end hadn't even been firmed up yet.

Laughton raised it under the next routine meeting with *his* boss, the controller of BBC Two, Graeme MacDonald. The minutes of the meeting show it came up as Item 16, at the very bottom of the page. By the following week, the idea of a Band Aid rock marathon had risen to Item 1 on the agenda. The minutes read: 'We agreed Band Aid concert is something the BBC must be involved in.'

But there was a problem. BBC Two had a commitment to run Open University programmes in the hours when the US concert would be at its peak. The situation was rescued by Band Aid trustee Michael Grade who, as BBC One controller, suggested that at 10 p.m., the show should transfer to BBC One for the remaining five or six hours.

'No one had ever had sixteen hours of anything on television,' laughed Harvey Goldsmith. 'Even the Olympics weren't that long, and certainly there had never been any music for that long. This was perfect. When BBC One came, in so did Radio 1. We had blanket national coverage.'

It was a massive breakthrough. The BBC involvement opened the way to a deal with an American television network. And it made Live Aid far more attractive to the UK artists who had not yet committed to appear. 'No British artist was going to turn down the opportunity to perform live,' Harvey Goldsmith later reflected. 'Playing live was very important in those days.'

There were just eight weeks to the concert.

❖

There had been no word from Bill Graham in California. Geldof decided he had better start ringing American bands himself. He decided to start at the top. In 1985, Bruce Springsteen was rock's biggest star.

'We need him,' Geldof said. 'It will be easy to get everyone else if Bruce agrees.'

But Springsteen's manager said that he couldn't possibly do a concert on 6 July as he was flying from the US to the UK that day. He had a week's shows booked at Wembley that very week and they were being promoted by none other than Harvey Goldsmith. Bob tried to get Harvey to move Springsteen's dates at Wembley.

'I couldn't, even if I'd wanted to, because they were part of a European schedule,' said Harvey later. So, in a desperate attempt to get Springsteen on board, Geldof decided to move the date of the Live Aid concert to the following Saturday, 13 July.

Harvey got Bob backstage passes to all the Springsteen Wembley shows in the hope that Geldof could persuade him. Privately, Harvey thought Bob was wasting his time. 'I knew how Bruce worked. Springsteen was highly selective about the charitable gigs that he did. He supported the homeless in the US and he would do it his way.'

But the changed date stuck. Wembley Stadium was available on 13 July and the new date was booked for Live Aid.

Despite Geldof's rule that everyone involved in Band Aid should be working for free, the owners of Wembley Stadium proved inflexible. They wanted £150,000 for the stadium for the day. Harvey managed to knock them down to £100,000, but they would not budge below that. Bob was all for naming and shaming them in the press. Harvey said they hadn't got time for that. 'Harvey was frightened of pissing him off because they might refuse him the stadium in the future,' Bob said. But this time it was Geldof who capitulated.

'Pay them. It's got to be London,' he told Harvey, grudgingly, but he insisted that the money must come from corporate sponsorship, not the public's donations.

For all its prestige as a venue, Wembley Stadium was not an easy venue for a rock concert.

Andrew Zweck, the man charged with making it work, knew that. The national home of English football was built in 1923 and its backstage area was really small. For concerts, the stage was placed behind one goal in front of the terraces that held the standing football fans.

'It had only a circulating corridor behind, and that's it. There was no space in the wings, left and right. There was not enough space to properly put on one band there and we were planning for twenty-two,' he said. 'Every band has their intrinsic sound, so every band would need their own gear. That was a lot of gear to handle and everything had to be miked up, plugged in and working in the right channel.'

Geldof's original plan was to have three stages. A band would be setting up on one, while another band was performing on the second, and a third band was getting their gear off the other stage. Zweck couldn't see how three separate stages could be fitted into the stadium. There just wasn't room. There was no space in the wings, left and right.

'So I took the idea from the television programme, *Sunday Night at the London Palladium*,' Bob recalled, 'which had a revolving stage at the end with all the performers of that week waving goodbye. It had stuck in my rebel teen mind because the Rolling Stones had refused to get on it and wave, which caused a national furore.' He drew a rough design, which looked like the Mercedes logo, and passed it to the leading set designer, Jeremy Thom, to make it work. A band would set up at the side in one third; the stage would turn them to face the crowd; and the band who had just finished their set would be getting their gear off out of sight after the stage had revolved through 33 degrees.

'Someone had seen a revolving stage at a car show,' Zweck recalled, 'so we contacted the trade show and they donated it to Band Aid.' But the problem was not entirely solved, as Zweck found when the giant turntable arrived.

Meanwhile, Wembley threw up a different kind of problem. Geldof expected that ARA – the firm that held the contract to do all the catering at the stadium – would donate all their profits to Band Aid, but ARA said no. Geldof was outraged: 'We can't have the food company being the only one making a profit on the day when everyone else is working free to help the starving.' He did some quick arithmetic on the number of hot dogs and bottles of cola they could expect to sell to the 72,000 expected capacity crowd.

'I reckon they could make £750,000 in that one day,' Geldof told Harvey Goldsmith. 'I'd better go and see them.'

At a meeting with the head of the Wembley caterers, who turned out to be a large American company, Geldof insisted: 'Either you forgo your profit or give Live Aid a percentage of your takings for the day.'

'If you provide the staff for the aisles for the day, we'll give you 10 per cent of what they sell.'

'Fuck off. We give you free staff and you give us 10 per cent! How generous! That's less than the wages you'd have to pay anyway. You give us your profit or I'll ask everyone who buys a ticket to bring packed food with them.'

'I don't think you can do that.'

'I think I can do what I like, pal.'

❧

With the BBC now fully on board, Pete Smith had a much easier task in organising the bands for the Wembley half of the concerts. He was, by now, the only full-time paid employee Band Aid ever hired. He was paid just £250 a week. 'If it all goes well, no one will ever hear about you,' said Goldsmith, when he gave Smith the job. 'If it's a disaster, you'll be famous.'

Pete did the legwork to make all of Bob's and Harvey's ideas actually work. 'A lot of these were very challenging,' recalled Andy Zweck, 'and necessitated a great deal of explaining, cajoling and vast amounts of time helping people to understand what was needed from them... Pete's communication and organisational skills, and endurance, were paramount. Bob and Harvey were running at 100 miles an hour most days, with ideas and demands flying in all directions, and Pete did a superb job of managing, administering and bringing it all together. 'When we now look back and see the iconic status the 1985 Live Aid concert has achieved, it's easy to ask: How could anyone fail to support such a momentous and worthy event?' But, continued Zweck, 'my memory of the intense period prior to the show is just how tricky it was to get real commitments from artists, broadcasters and the organisers of the American show. It was a bold new concept. Bob and Harvey were making it up as they went along, and not everyone "got it" as quickly as they would have liked.'

Pete Smith's task was to persuade the world's biggest pop and rock stars to perform for free, in a fifteen-to-twenty-minute slot, with a maximum of just four songs.

The artists had given an outline agreement to Geldof, but it was Pete who had the delicate job of deciding how long each should play – something which required him to make a judgement on how 'big' each band was.

It was Pete who decided how many songs each band was allowed, with some artists downgraded to one or two songs, or encouraged to collaborate with another act to make sure everyone could be included.

And Pete was the one drawing up the initial running order for the acts.

It was a job requiring the tact of a high-level diplomat.

❊

Towards the end of April, Geldof had a visitor to his home in Chelsea. It was a Malaysian oil millionaire called Ananda Krishnan who had been paying all the Band Aid office expenses. He wanted to turn Band Aid into a permanent institution. Bob told him there was no point as the trustees intended to wind it up after the concert was over. Anyway, Geldof told the millionaire that he was too preoccupied with trying to orchestrate TV events on the other side of the Atlantic.

'You should meet a guy I know called Mike Mitchell,' the millionaire said. 'He part-organised the TV satellites and sponsorship for the Olympics.'

A week later, Geldof was in New York, having got British Caledonian to cover his flight. He met Mitchell in a smart New York hotel. The American was keen from the outset. He was in the business of event management, so handling a global affair like Live Aid would be good for the reputation of his company. But he had a personal commitment. He had been involved in the US End Hunger campaign. The pair 'talked concept' for an hour and a half, at the end of which Mitchell had agreed to come on board.

Fixing the TV coverage at the American end proved far more difficult than the UK side had been. Geldof had got the recently launched music channel MTV to agree to turn their whole day over to Live Aid. But when he asked them to pay, they said they hadn't any money. But they did agree to give Band Aid all the advertising revenues received that day – and provide free use of their satellite and a link-up with all their affiliated independent stations. Mitchell said he would open negotiations with the three big US TV networks.

NBC and CBS immediately said it could not be done. 'We were laughed out of the networks' offices,' Mitchell recalled. 'The Olympics had just one location and three satellites going to the world. This was going to have sixteen satellites and eight locations. It had never been done. I didn't know if it was possible. It was like saying today "Let's do a concert on the moon".'

But Mitchell knew the people who could actually make this work. The day after Geldof left, 1 May 1985, Mitchell put in a call to Hal Uplinger, a former professional basketball player turned television producer, with whom he had worked on the Los Angeles Olympics the year before. Uplinger brought in a specialist in directing massive live events, Tony Verna, who had come from CBS Sports. Verna was the man who invented the instant replay. 'He was excellent because he was creative, understood the live aspect *and* the remote aspect,' said Uplinger.

Verna told him: 'If we do a sixteen-hour show, we're going to get lost.' So what they did was to design sixteen one-hour shows. 'You can control a one-hour show, you can't control a sixteen-hour show.' They brought in the two musical directors who regularly did the Grammys and all the big network musical shows. To supervise the technical production, they enlisted the man responsible for that same job at the LA Olympics. 'We tried to get the top people in their field wherever we could,' Uplinger said.

Their ambition was vast. They were planning a sixteen-hour, worldwide television broadcast – with five hours from the UK, five hours of overlapping and alternating transmissions from two countries simultaneously, and then six hours from the US. 'No one has ever required such massive amounts of time,' said Jim Tuverson, head of Television Videotape Satellite

Communications Group's West Coast operation, at the time. They would need, Hal Uplinger estimated, thirteen satellites, twenty-two transponders and a whole field of satellite uplink and downlink dishes so that the two concerts could be shown, live, to a total of 110 countries. He even came up with an idea of how to reach another forty-five countries that lacked the technology to pick up Live Aid from the satellites; he would put a four-hour edited version in the diplomatic bag from the States to every country in the world that had a TV station.

He worked out how Live Aid could reach a total estimated audience of two billion viewers, plus a further one billion listeners on radio – a global audience of three billion. That was two-thirds of the people living on the planet.

✂

Back in England, Geldof contacted Bernard Doherty of the leading PR firm, Rogers & Cowan. Bob told him he was 'volunteering' to handle the Live Aid media. Doherty was the press agent for Paul McCartney and David Bowie.

'Try to persuade Paul, Bernard. I've already spoken to his office and they think he should do it. He's just a bit nervous because he hasn't played in so long. Try Bowie as well.'

Harvey was keen that Queen should play. Bob was dismissive. The bill was so full that the chart in Harvey's office had bits of paper taped to the bottom to accommodate the extra acts. Top British bands were now being told they would have to go to the States to get on the line-up. 'Bands and their managers and record companies had suddenly finally understood the significance of what was about to happen and clamoured to be there,' Bob recalled. So they did not need Queen. To Geldof, they felt like the past.

'Bob sort of came from the post-punk explosion,' said Queen's drummer, Roger Taylor, years later. 'So he had pretensions of being a bit of punk and he probably thought we were slightly dinosaurs or something.'

Years later, Geldof confessed, 'I just thought it was overblown. Operatic. Subsequently, of course, we all have to admit that we thought the songs were great. With age, we're allowed to admit it.'

But Harvey insisted that they should be included. 'I knew they were just what was needed to lift the show mid-afternoon,' he said. Bob suspected that there was some incident in the past between Harvey and Queen which the promoter was seeking to repair.

So Bob rang Spike Edney. 'Spike had played trombone with the Rats when we had a horn section and he was now the keyboard player for Queen on stage.'

The band were in Australia at the end of a long tour.

'They're really knackered,' said Spike. 'They don't want to do anything.'

'Yeah, but they know what's going on?'

'Yeah, they know what's going on. They think it's good, but it's the end of a world tour...'

Geldof got the impression that Queen didn't think it had gone very well. Lead singer Freddie Mercury kept talking about making a solo album next. 'That's never a good sign for a band,' Bob said.

But Geldof kept pressing. 'Speak to Roger,' said Spike. 'Speak to Jim,' said Roger. Jim Beach was the band's manager.

'Bob, what you're doing is amazing,' said Jim. 'But I don't think it's really our thing.'

In 1984, Queen had played a series of segregated concerts in Sun City, white South Africa's answer to Las Vegas, which had been placed on a blacklist by anti-apartheid activists. Most artists joined the boycott. Queen had not. Geldof knew that 'not really our thing' was a veiled reference to the way Queen had subsequently been cold-shouldered by other bands.

'Ask Freddie to call me, Jim – please.'

The two men knew each other only a little. Geldof had been to a party once at Mercury's house. 'Amazing place, full of Japanese stuff,' Bob recalled. A few days later, Geldof's home phone rang at 10.30 p.m. at night. It was Freddie.

'Darling, what can I help you with?'

Bob gave him his usual pitch.

'Oh, Bobsy, I'm not so sure. I just don't think it's the right thing for us.'

Geldof thought quickly. He could exert the usual moral blackmail, but he sensed that, with Freddie, there was a better option: flattery.

Queen had, only the month before, completed that exhausting tenth world tour culminating Japan and Australia. At the Rock in Rio festival, they had headlined before a total audience of half a million – one of the largest paying crowds ever assembled for a rock concert.

'But Freddie, how could you think this?' said Bob. 'This is absolutely the thing for you to do. Freddie, it's your audience. It's not just Rio, it's the *world*.'

It was his best shot.

⁜

By the middle of May, Harvey Goldsmith and his team were starting to liaise earnestly with the BBC. They quickly realised that they operated in different worlds. The BBC planners were into meticulous detail. The Live Aid team were still working with the more fluid whims of rock star egos. Andy Zweck recalled the BBC team saying things like: 'If we are going to integrate with the States, and alternate acts between the US and the UK, we will have to have sixteen satellites, here. And we will need to be exact on the timing, there. They were writing it, like Light Entertainment in Studio Three: "This band will go off at 7:13, and the next one will come on at 7:14." And we just laughed. We said, "This is not how rock 'n' roll works. This is never gonna happen."'

But, as they attended meeting after BBC meeting, Zweck and the others were forced to change their minds.

'Soon we realised, as more technicians started appearing at these meetings – more serious people, who knew a lot more than us – that these people knew exactly what they were doing. And it was very reassuring. As we got more out of our depth, more experienced BBC people continually turned up and gave us the faith that actually it could work.'

Zweck began to realise that two overlapping transatlantic concepts could only work with immense time discipline.

On top of that, there was the complexity of the satellite link-ups. Harvey was bowled over by the BBC's technical expertise. 'We got to know the transmissions people and they were geeks of the highest order,' he said, recalling a BBC operations room dominated by a map of the world. 'It had all these crosses on it and trajectory lines of where these satellites are gonna be. And they were using a pair of compasses to work it all out and doing all the necessary calculations – in their heads, no computers – to figure out if it was possible to get a network of satellites that could all send the pictures from England, in sequence, so that there could be a continuous world feed.

And then back again from America so that we could get a feed from America when we needed it.

'They sorted out things that we hadn't even conceived of. The BBC folk regularly worked Wembley Stadium for the Cup Final. They knew the place backwards. Someone at Wood Lane had even got on to Goodyear and booked their airship for overhead shots.'

But Goldsmith and Geldof were unbeatable in their own area of expertise. 'At that point,' said Harvey, 'I had virtually stopped work on anything other than this project. And the whole of my office became the Live Aid office.' Harvey now made direct contact with those artists for whom he was the regular promoter. Queen, David Bowie and the Who fell into place, in that order. These acts toured with Harvey Goldsmith Entertainment (HE), so he set it in stone with each of them personally.

When he rang Phil Collins in Japan, where Collins was touring, Phil said he'd do it but flippantly added that he couldn't decide whether he wanted to play in the UK or US; he'd be happy to do both.

'Great idea,' said Geldof when he heard. Harvey promptly rang British Airways and said, 'I've got the most fantastic idea for you to promote Concorde…' Geldof contacted Lord King, head of the airline, and persuaded him to offer free flights on the supersonic jetliner, which would allow the Genesis superstar to get from one venue to another in time. The airline even rescheduled the plane's departure time to fit the Live Aid timetable.

Harvey rang Phil Collins' manager to tell him.

'He can play early in London. We'll have a helicopter waiting to take him to Heathrow. He'll get on Concorde, which will fly him to JFK.' Phil's manager, Tony Smith, laughed. 'Oh fuck. I didn't think you could actually fix that!'

Geldof had gone into the Phonogram office to use the phone there. All the transatlantic calls had sent the bill on his home landline soaring into thousands of pounds. He was ringing Stevie Wonder when Francis Rossi, of Status Quo, came in. The band had not played together for some time, but he said they might re-form if Geldof would let them play. Bob snapped up the offer immediately. Status Quo could open the concerts with their classic 'Rockin' All Over the World', he thought to himself. It would be the perfect opener. He left it to Pete Smith to break the bad news to Paul Weller, who had originally been asked to open the show with the Style Council.

Calls were now incoming as well as outgoing. U2 rang from the US to say they would play the Live Aid concert in London. The band had been dithering. With their star in the ascendant, and Bono being such a memorable presence on the original Band Aid single, they were a good addition. But Bob still had to capture his two big fish. He rang Bernard Doherty.

'How's it going with Bowie and McCartney?'

'David has been asked to do another benefit for Africa. He asked, "Is Geldof involved? I'm only doing the Geldof thing." So that's positive. But he's filming at the time, and it'll be touch and go whether he can put a band together.'

'What about McCartney?'

'Paul's people all think it's a great idea. They're really trying to persuade him. Basically, he's nervous. He hasn't played live for eight years and you're asking him to play in front of half the world. But they're working on him.'

❖

It was midnight. The phone rang. It was Mike Mitchell in New York. He was playing a very risky game. Two of the big three networks had turned down the chance to broadcast Live Aid, dismissing it out of hand. The only one that was interested was ABC, which had slipped to second in the network ratings and had least to lose by doing something adventurous.

'They have offered half a million, which is not good, not good at all. So I have told them it's not enough because the other two have each offered a million.'

'Have they?'

'No, they haven't offered at all.'

Mitchell was obviously a seasoned exponent of the Bob Bluff.

'We have to have a network deal, Bob, to get sponsorship.'

Geldof briefed Mitchell on a meeting he and Harvey had attended with the European Broadcasting Union. Representatives from TV stations across Europe had attended, all except the French, who hadn't shown up because they objected to the fact that all the acts were English-speaking.

The Europeans had come up with all manner of technical objections but, Geldof told Mitchell, they seemed easy to overcome. Bob had told the

Europeans: 'It's simple enough. There's a feed out of England and feed from America. If you're a commercial station, as soon as you see the Live Aid logo spinning, it means you have a three-minute commercial break. At any point you can opt out of the international signals, and if you have a domestic band or commentator standing by, you can put them on your own national network. At specific times, you will have an up-line to the satellite so you can contribute to the international feed. Four shows will be coming from the United States: the English signal, the international signal, the American domestic signal and a network special signal. You take the BBC signal. You must organise your own fundraising, which is a prerequisite of the show. Our accountants will check with you. Any problems, call us.'

Simple enough? The European broadcasters could be forgiven for thinking otherwise.

The Australians wanted a feed. But the USSR would only come in if an American network did.

'The Russians won't take it unless it's safe enough for the American networks. Their TV values, oddly enough, coincide exactly with ours,' Mitchell told Geldof.

'I've given ABC to noon on Friday to come up with a better offer. I'll ring you then.'

But Mitchell rang before then.

'The good news is we've got a $1 million sponsorship deal from Pepsi on the basis of our network TV deal. The bad news is that we haven't got a network TV deal yet.'

'ABC haven't called back?'

'ABC haven't called back.'

'Shit.'

'Shit.'

The next morning, the phone rang: it was Mick Jagger. Geldof had only met him once before – after a Stones gig in Madrid – but his tone on the phone was very friendly. Bob told him about Ethiopia and asked him if he would do the concert. The two agreed to meet for breakfast at The Savoy to discuss the idea. Bob took his dog Growler with him, only for him to eat Jagger's bacon and eggs. By way of compensation, Geldof gave Jagger a copy of *The Emperor* by Ryszard Kapuściński, a book about the last days of Haile Selassie.

'I don't know if the Stones will do it,' Jagger said. 'We're in the middle of this album and things aren't great at the moment. But, yeah, I'm up for it. I'll do it, even if the others won't.'

Geldof was delighted. The more artists of the stature of Mick Jagger he could entice onto the bill, the more chance there was of the US network buying in.

'Is David doing it?' Jagger asked. Yes, Geldof told him, David Bowie had agreed to appear.

'The main problem now is with the American acts,' Geldof told Jagger. 'Michael Jackson just doesn't seem to want to do it. I rang Quincy Jones to talk to him. I rang his manager. I rang the chairman of his record company. I'm having real problems with all the black American acts, to be honest. Diana Ross's excuse is that she's in LA, whatever sort of excuse that is. Kragen says that Lionel Richie is "doing his album". Prince is shy or something. Tina Turner is on tour, and Stevie Wonder's weird.'

'Why?' Mick asked.

'He keeps changing his mind. Says he doesn't want to be the token black superstar artist. He was in. Then, two days ago, Ewart Abner, his manager, rang and said he wasn't. Most of the American bands just kept asking "Is Bruce doing it?"'

'*Is* Bruce doing it?'

'He's said he'll think about it, but I don't know. His manager says he's tired and he's just got married. Anyway, I'm seeing him in a couple of days and I'll ask him again. But you'll definitely do it?'

'Yeah, definitely. Even if the rest won't, I'll put a band together and rehearse something.'

It was just six weeks to Live Aid day.

�֍

The phone rang again. It was Mike Mitchell.

'ABC have come in for $1 million!'

'Fantastic.'

'They will take three hours of the concert and want all the top acts in that timeslot: David Bowie, Elton John, Wham!, Paul McCartney, Bob Dylan, Eric Clapton, Mick Jagger, Led Zeppelin... Their advertisers want the big names. They all have to go into the three hours at the end of the Philadelphia show. That is the stipulation.'

ABC's advertisers now compounded the problem of the lack of black acts on the Live Aid bill.

'They were laying out a WASP* platform,' said Pete Smith. 'Of course, there was an issue with black artists on this. *Thriller* was the biggest-selling album in living memory, yet Michael Jackson was still battling to get on the front page of *Newsweek*, *Time* and *Rolling Stone*. There was a changing of the guard, but things were in transit culturally.'

But there were to be other reasons why black artists were under-represented at Live Aid.

�֍

Bob Geldof had given ABC a Live Aid cast list which was actually a wish list. He now moved up a gear in his bid to secure the really big names.

Geldof rang Pete Townshend, who was refreshingly direct.

'Yes, of course I'll do it. But what you really want is for the Who to get together, isn't it?'

That was something Geldof had not dared ask. The final split of the Who, he had heard, was bitter and irrevocable.

'That would be unbelievable.'

'I'll see what I can do,' the guitarist said.

Next, Bob flew to Paris, where the Rolling Stones were laboriously recording the album that would become 1986's *Dirty Work*. It was Ronnie Wood's birthday and there was a party for the guitarist in a little club. There, Geldof spoke to the Stones' bassist Bill Wyman and asked him if the band would do Live Aid.

'You'll never get Keith to agree,' said Wyman.

'Why not?'

'Cos Keith doesn't give a fuck.'

Soon afterwards, a letter arrived from Prince Rupert Loewenstein, the Stones' business manager. It said the band wished Live Aid well, but felt unable to participate. It was written on behalf of all the Rolling Stones.

Geldof phoned Jagger. 'Mick, what's going on...?'

---

* White Anglo-Saxon Protestant.

'It's okay,' said Jagger. 'It's just hassle with the band. I have to say that at the moment. But I'll be there, I give you my word.'

The PR man Bernard Doherty told Geldof the inside story. 'The Stones were, at the time, basically not a band in the true sense. They'd had a bit of a disastrous album that had come out a few years earlier called *Undercover*, so whilst they were recording, they weren't talking.' Charlie Watts, the band's drummer, was, said Doherty, 'the cement that held them together. They'd all settle their arguments by going to him.' But Charlie was off doing his jazz orchestra stuff. 'Bob picked the wrong year, the wrong decade actually, to ask the Rolling Stones to do anything.'

Back in London, Pete Townshend rang. 'Look, it's no good. I'll do it. But Roger will only do it if Kenney doesn't play. And John will only do it if Kenney *does* play.'

Kenney Jones had replaced the inimitable Keith Moon following his death in 1978, but Daltrey was never happy with Jones's style. 'He's a great drummer. He's just not right for this band,' Daltrey complained.

Townshend disagreed. It was another source of contention in the singer and the songwriter's eternal love-hate relationship. Eventually, the band's bass player, John Entwistle, who generally preferred to stand on the sidelines, was dragged into the acrimony.

'Do you mind if I phone John?' asked Geldof. 'Will it do any good?'

'It won't do any harm.'

Geldof rang him, but Entwistle was unmoved.

Bob rang Daltrey, who was equally resistant. In the end, Geldof deployed his tried and tested moral armlock.

'If the Who appear, we know we will get an additional million pounds of revenue,' said Geldof. 'Every pound we make will save a life. Please, Roger, do the fucking show.'

❊

It was the beginning of June, just two weeks to the press conference that Bob Geldof and Harvey Goldsmith had arranged to announce Live Aid to the world's media. And still they had no venue fixed in the United States. Despite frequent phone calls to Bill Graham, nothing seemed to be happening. The obvious venue, from a logistical and a symbolic point of view, was New York. Geldof decided to get on a plane to sort out the US operation himself. He had in mind Shea Stadium, where the Beatles had performed their two landmark shows in the mid-'60s.

But Shea Stadium was a mess. It was being refurbished and a huge section of the seats were unsafe. Madison Square Garden was too small. There was a giant football stadium at Meadowlands in nearby New Jersey, but to get it on 13 July, Band Aid would have to buy 10,000 tickets at $25 each for the game scheduled for the day after the concert. He flew back to London in despair.

'Look, New York is out of the question,' said Harvey. 'We can't go with Bill Graham in California because of the time difference. Meadowlands has the problems with the football players. We can go for the RFK stadium in Washington, which has no local promoter I feel happy about and is in the middle of a freeway an hour from everywhere. Or we can go for Philadelphia, which is only an hour from New York, is served by four airports and, in Larry Magid, has one of the best promoters in the States.'

Geldof was having none of it. 'Philadelphia's crap. What symbolic significance does it have? It's like having the UK concert in Stoke-on-Trent.'

Harvey countered: 'Larry went to see the mayor of Philadelphia. The stadium is free, no charge whatsoever. Full cooperation of the mayor, police, everything.'

'Why would they do all that for free?' Geldof asked.

'They need some good PR. They've just had an incident where the police bombed a house full of black anarchists and set the whole block on fire, so the mayor is looking for a feel-good factor.'

'Jesus, Harvey, we can't have Philadelphia with all that going on!'

Years later, they discovered the full story of what had happened.

Less than a month earlier, the Philadelphia police had attempted to clear a house occupied by a black liberation group named MOVE. Its members, who all changed their surname to Africa, were ecological as well as political radicals. They had eccentric views on science, medicine and technology, even advocating a return to a hunter-gatherer society. They had fortified the house and set up a loudspeaker that sent a constant barrage of political slogans into the surrounding streets.

Their neighbours in the Osage district were predominantly black working-class families who took exception to the dreadlocked radicals with their long record of defying city sanitation codes, assaulting neighbours and resisting local officials and law enforcement officers. The Osage residents demanded action at City Hall, which was run by Philadelphia's first black mayor, W. Wilson Goode.

On 13 May, just a month before the press conference to announce the Live Aid concerts, a search warrant was issued for the MOVE house and police tried to oust its occupants with tear gas and water cannons. The MOVE members then fired on the police who – after a twelve-hour siege, which was watched on live television by the city's inhabitants – sent in a helicopter to drop improvised explosives on the rooftop bunker of the premises. The house caught fire.

A continuing gun battle prevented firefighters from swiftly extinguishing the blaze, which destroyed almost four blocks of the neighbourhood. More than sixty houses were razed, eleven people were killed and 240 left homeless. A subsequent inquiry found that the city officials had acted with 'reckless disregard' and concluded that the debacle would not have happened in a predominantly white neighbourhood.

But none of this detail was available to Geldof and Goldsmith at the time.

In the end, it was Pete Smith who clinched the venue argument: 'From a concert production point of view, Philadelphia was really the only option for Live Aid.' It had good road access. Its airport was not too big, but it connected everywhere, and it wasn't far from the venue. And the city *did* have international significance. The name Philadelphia literally meant the City of Brotherly Love, Pete said. It is home to the Liberty Bell, the iconic symbol of American independence. It is the city where the Declaration of Independence was written and signed. Plus, the venue had a great name: JFK Stadium.

'Bob went very quiet,' says Harvey. 'I could see him thinking.'

'Bob, it's got to be Philadelphia,' Harvey said. 'It works logistically. It's the home of freedom, it's gonna be brilliant.'

Geldof muttered reluctantly under his breath.

'Bob, it's 2 a.m. We have to announce it, live, at a press conference in London and New York tomorrow. We do not have a venue. It has to be Philadelphia. Trust me.'

CHAPTER 10

WHAT HAPPENED TO THE BLACK ACTS?

Harvey Goldsmith shot a swift glance at Bob Geldof. Then a warning look. Then he kicked him under the table.

It was the press conference to announce to 400 newspaper, radio and television journalists, in London and in New York, what Geldof called, without exaggeration, 'the largest pop concert ever, with the greatest audience, and the most important artists of the last twenty years'. Then he read them out in almost alphabetical order.

'Bryan Adams, Adam Ant, the Boomtown Rats, David Bowie, Eric Clapton, Phil Collins, Elvis Costello, Dire Straits, Duran Duran, Bryan Ferry...'

Harvey gave Bob the first look. He knew that Bryan Ferry had been asked, but hadn't said yes.

'...Hall and Oates, Hall and Oates with the Temptations, Waylon Jennings, Billy Joel, Elton John, Howard Jones, Judas Priest, Nik Kershaw, Kris Kristofferson, Huey Lewis & the News, Alison Moyet, Billy Ocean, Robert Plant, the Power Station, the Pretenders, Queen...'

Queen might have agreed in private, Harvey thought, but their manager hadn't.

'...Sade, Santana, Paul Simon, Simple Minds, Spandau Ballet, Status Quo, Style Council, Sting, Tears For Fears, Thompson Twins, U2, Ultravox, Paul Young, Neil Young, Wham!...'

Shit, thought Harvey, firing the warning look. Tears For Fears hadn't even been asked.

'And we also last night received confirmation from Mick Jagger, Stevie Wonder and, about five minutes ago, we heard some wonderful news and that is that the Who, one of the greatest bands ever in rock music, are re-forming specifically for this event...'

That was when Goldsmith, sat to Geldof's left, aimed a kick at Bob beneath the table. The message had been to confirm that Pete Townshend would play, he thought, not all of the Who. On Bob's right, Band Aid's accountant, Phil Rusted, nervously switched his gaze back and forth from Geldof's face to the list from which Bob was reading.

'And two seconds before I came on, we got a phone call from Paul McCartney, who said that he is at the moment clearing his diary to ensure that he will be with us on July 13th.'

That call did come. But not until several weeks after Bob Geldof had announced it.

Bits of paper started flying round the room as notes were passed by people alarmed at the announcement. 'He just rattled off names,' laughed an incredulous Harvey Goldsmith afterwards. 'He just bullshitted his way through it. A number of those he listed actually never did play or couldn't or didn't want to. Others had been asked but not replied.'

That was unsurprising, said Live Aid's stage manager, Andrew Zweck. 'At the start, many of the artists were told: "We're not sure of the date. We're not sure of the American venue. You're not getting a contract. You're not getting paid. You've gotta come rehearsed. There'll be no time for a soundcheck." It was very hard at the start, particularly America, so it was no wonder a whole lot of artists came back and said "We'll think about it."' Even those who had given outline permission were not braced for the detail to be announced publicly.

'Before the press conference actually finished, I got a phone call from Queen's manager, Jim Beach, who was in New Zealand,' said Harvey.

'What's going on?' Beach asked Goldsmith. 'I've not been told about this...'

'I was pissed off. Bob announced we were doing it without even asking us,' said Curt Smith of Tears For Fears.

Bryan Ferry rang Bob direct to complain that, though he had been asked, he hadn't ever agreed to do it. 'Well, pull out, dude,' Geldof replied. 'You announce it, though.' That would be too embarrassing. Ferry played.

From the States, an irate Ewart Abner rang Geldof: 'Who told you to announce Stevie Wonder?'

'Stevie.'

'No, he didn't. He really wants to do it. But he's months behind with his next album and Motown are going crazy.' Stevie's manager wanted Bob to issue a press release saying he would not be playing.

'Okay,' said Bob. But didn't do it. Abner rang back. Still Geldof didn't. *Do it yourself*, he thought truculently.

Most bewildered were the Who. Despite Geldof's personal strong-arm intervention, they still hadn't committed. On the morning of the press conference, Pete Townshend had sent a message to say he would play without the rest of the band. Whether Bob misunderstood or wilfully misconstrued was unclear. But Townshend was certain about one thing. 'No, we weren't getting back together. It was blackmail, really,' he said forty years later. 'He was bullying because he believed that it was something that he passionately felt needed to be done. I don't think he would deny that he bullied us into doing it.'

'I sort of winged it,' Geldof confessed years later, 'because of the Band Aid record and the USA for Africa record. So I was absolutely certain that, you know, a good 80 per cent of those guys would show up on the day, in which case we had got a serious concert going on.'

The artists and their managers weren't the only ones to complain. In New York, a section of the press attacked the line-up because it contained few black acts. Geldof was furious. He had gone out of his way to ask all the big-name black acts in the States and all had declined to join in. 'I have asked them all,' Geldof told the press. 'Perhaps you should address the question not to me, but to them.'

Young black activists in the UK made the same complaint: 'Why are there no black English or West Indian bands on the bill for Wembley?' It's not about race, said Geldof. It was about which bands would draw the biggest audience. 'If a band sells a million records, then more people will watch than if they only sold thousands.' The more people who watched, the more money would be given, and the more lives would be saved.

But black people needed representation, he was told. 'It's not about representation. Race is irrelevant. If Bob Marley were alive, I'd be on my knees begging him to play. But no one's heard of Aswad or Steel Pulse outside the universities. Put them on the telly and people will switch off. If the choice is Wham! or Steel Pulse, on this show I'll take Wham!.' The black community newspaper *The Voice* was unconvinced. It called Live Aid the racist event of the decade due to its exclusion of black artists and its focus upon images of white millionaire philanthropists rushing to 'save' Africa. Bob Geldof replied to the criticism impatiently. 'What have these complaining fuckers ever done for Ethiopia?' he asked rhetorically.

Yet Geldof knew he had a real problem with black acts from the US. Even those black artists who had appeared on the USA for Africa single and the subsequent album – Diana Ross, Lionel Richie, Michael Jackson, Prince – were fighting shy of appearing.

'We had this unbelievable discussion with Michael Jackson's people,' said Goldsmith. 'We were saying this is to help people in Africa and he just wasn't interested.'

Geldof asked Quincy Jones to approach them. Jones put two employees on the case full time, contacting managers, lawyers and artists. But eventually Quincy came back to Geldof to say: 'I keep pressing on, "Where were the black guys?".'

Forty years later, the last interview Quincy gave was to Geldof. Still stung by the absence of Michael Jackson and the others, Bob pressed him yet again.

'But why weren't they there?' Geldof asked.

Quincy continued to avoid the question, as he had all these years, but Geldof persisted and finally the great man muttered into the lapel of his Moschino track suit: 'They couldn't give a fuck, Bob.'

Geldof could not bring himself to believe this. He had been told something similar when travelling in Ethiopia with a friend of Jesse Jackson's, who ran an African American aid agency and had complained that black sportsmen and entertainment stars had 'little or no social responsibility or conscience' when it came to action – though 'they would readily mouth the rhetoric'. Yet that hadn't, at all, been the vibe Bob had picked up from the black artists during the recording of 'We Are the World'.

With four weeks to go until the day of Live Aid, Bill Graham echoed Geldof's bewilderment when at a press conference he was asked by an angry black broadcaster – Georgie Woods of Philadelphia radio station WDAS-AM – 'Are you saying black artists won't perform?' Graham replied that 'every major black artist on the Billboard 200 chart and R&B chart' had been approached. Almost all had simply declined to perform. Graham was not entirely correct – Dionne Warwick, Run-D.M.C. and Philip Bailey had not been invited – but what he said was broadly true. The black superstars had all said no.

Geldof rang Ken Kragen, who had been instrumental in recruiting Michael Jackson, Lionel Richie and Stevie Wonder for 'We Are the World'. Kragen was president of Band Aid's sister fund, USA for Africa. 'He started calling me regularly in May, when he was finding that there was difficulty getting the key black acts,' said Kragen. 'He was very frustrated. What I told him, which is the truth, is that everybody is kind of acting like they already gave.'

But the media continued to press the issue of the absence of black megastars. *Rolling Stone* sought out Richard Walters, of the Norby Walters Agency, whose clients included Marvin Gaye, Patti LaBelle, Rick James, Kool and the Gang, the Four Tops and, for a short time, Michael Jackson. Walters lived up to his motto 'Say it Straight, and Stay with It' by asking: 'Why are artists not supporting it? Any individual artist can get on a plane and put himself there. It's the easiest thing in the world. They don't have to bring their band if their band's not available. Just their presence is important. Aretha Franklin, Smokey Robinson, Stevie Wonder – why aren't they doing it?'

On the face of it, everyone had a good excuse. Stevie Wonder had an album to finish. Diana Ross was on tour, as were the Pointer Sisters. Donna Summer was in the studio. Michael Jackson had 'major commitments' that he couldn't get out of. But, as would emerge later, there was more to it than that.

Other stars in the US were more amenable. Paul Simon not only said he would play at the concert, but also said he'd be happy to try to persuade Bob Dylan to do so too. He'd even suggest to Dylan that they do a duet together. There was talk of the two of them singing each other's songs in the finale: Simon singing 'Blowin' in the Wind' and Dylan performing 'Bridge Over Troubled Water'.

※

In the middle of June, Bernard Doherty got a phone call from Geldof.

'Mick Jagger and David Bowie are coming to your office tomorrow.'

'Why?'

'Because David knows that you've got a speakerphone and we can't find one at Phonogram.'

The next evening, Bowie and Jagger, along with Geldof and Goldsmith, appeared in Doherty's office. They were given tea and biscuits, and sat around the speakerphone to talk to Tony Verna and three other tech experts in the US.

'We'd like to do a duet together,' Mick explained, 'except I'm gonna be in the States and David's gonna be in England. How do we get the technology going for that?'

'The problem is that there will be a time-gap while the messages bounce back and forth between the satellites. We can get it down to half a second, but there will be a gap.

'It won't work,' said Tony Verna, sadly, down the line, 'because Mick in Philly won't be able to hear David in Wembley and vice versa. Only the TV audience will hear both.'

The conversation took a fantastical turn. What if one of them was up among the satellites in the Space Shuttle?, asked Bowie.

'Call NASA, Harvey!' exclaimed Bob excitedly. Such was the euphoria of the moment that, the next day, Goldsmith *did* actually ring the Kennedy Space Center in Florida and asked: 'Have you got a spare rocket we could send Mick Jagger up in? And can you get one up in time?'

'When are you talking about?'

'July.'

'Sorry, sir,' said the man from NASA. 'It takes six months for us to plan to do something like that.'

'Would it have been possible if we'd given you more notice?'

'No, not really, no. But it's a great idea. We love it,' he laughed.

What they did later agree was that the captain of the Space Shuttle would announce one of the bands from Space as the spacecraft passed over Philadelphia, ending seconds later as it passed over Wembley. In the event, that didn't happen because bad weather delayed the launch of the rocket. It was just as well Mick Jagger was not on board.

❋

The Live Aid tickets on sale in London were all snapped up within twenty-four hours of going on sale. They were priced at £25 – which was £5 for the ticket and a £20 'compulsory donation' to get around Margaret Thatcher's refusal to waive VAT once again. Some tickets were allocated regionally, sold through local coach firms. Within three days, they had sold out everywhere.

As talk of money came to the fore, Geldof received an unexpected phone call. It was from Paul McCartney. 'I rang Bob and I said, "Look, you're going to make a lot of money there, but are you sure it's going to all the right places?"' the former Beatle said. He grilled Geldof on how exactly the money would be collected, where would it go, how was it secured, how would it be distributed, who would do the accounts and audits, and whether the artists could see those accounts, if requested. Geldof answered each question as precisely as he could. McCartney signed off with a warning about 'the days when George put together a similar concert and it was really hard to get the money to the people, to get it to work, to translate it into food instead of it just going into some corrupt government officials' pocket'. Geldof would do well to speak to George, he advised.

A year after the breakup of the Beatles, George Harrison had invented the first ever multi-artist charity with his Concert for Bangladesh featuring himself, Bob Dylan, Eric Clapton, Leon Russell and the legendary sitarist Ravi Shankar in Madison Square Garden. The concert was to raise money for the people of Bangladesh who had been devastated by a cyclone, which killed 500,000 people and was followed by a bloody civil war.

Geldof knew Harrison a little. The former Beatle had turned up backstage after a Boomtown Rats gig in Oxford in the late '70s. Still, he was surprised when George now rang out of the blue.

George told Bob how he had made the mistake of raising the money before allocating it to a charity that would distribute it. The US Inland Revenue Service declared that, because the charity was not involved in staging the event, the concert was a commercial rather than a charitable activity – and demanded a massive tax cut from it.

George was immensely distressed, all the more so because it took fourteen years of legal battles before UNICEF got its cash. Huge amounts of the money raised went in legal fees, expenses and overheads. Of the $17 million the concert raised, only $8 million reached the UN children's charity.

At the end of the call, he offered two warnings: 'Get a good lawyer. And a good accountant.'

Geldof was grateful for the advice. But even as he was processing it, he was handling something else: his sense of awe at the fact that two Beatles, heroes of his youth, the first band he had ever seen live with his sister, had picked up the phone to ring *him*.

Geldof's contact with Harrison and McCartney sparked weeks of rumours that Live Aid might see a much-vaunted Beatles reunion. There was gossip about Julian Lennon – John's son – joining the three surviving Beatles on stage. Indeed, there had been discussions in various production meetings about a Beatles-based collaboration.

'We did sit around a table philosophising about it,' said Andrew Zweck. 'But there was no substance in getting George Harrison or Ringo there that I can remember. There was even one piece of publicity, with Julian Lennon's name on it there, but it was quickly withdrawn.'

Still the rumours were rife, said Pete Smith, a reflection of the increasing power that Live Aid was taking on as the weeks passed.

In fact, Geldof never approached Julian Lennon or anyone else around the Beatles. 'I never tried to do a Beatles reunion. It would have been pathetic – a morbid notion. It never entered my head to even try. Paul was more than enough.'

Indeed, it dismayed Geldof that having assembled the greatest collection of rock 'n' roll artists ever to perform on a single stage, there was still a demand for more. He had zero interest in putting the Beatles back together. When asked, as he repeatedly was, he would simply say: 'The Beatles can't be reformed. John is dead.'

But the rumours were to persist right until Live Aid day itself. On one dressing room door, a sign listed the three acts scheduled to use it during the day. On the bottom line was a final enigmatise listing: 'Ensemble Male'. It could only be, enthusiasts were sure, reserved for the reuniting Beatles.

A draft running order was beginning to take shape on Pete Smith's desk. Status Quo would open the concert with 'Rockin' All Over the World', the tune that BBC was now using in the Live Aid trailer. Paul Weller and the Style Council had graciously accepted being bumped from the opening act to the second slot. Paul Young had reached number one in the US single charts earlier in the year, so he was the natural act to bridge the transition from Wembley to Philadelphia at 5 p.m. UK time. Elton John was provisionally down to top the bill at 9 p.m. Pete now had to place the other artists in the running order.

But how? There was no pecking order in the paperwork given to each artist. All had been given the same simple one-page contract in which they agreed to perform without any payment and gave permission for their performance to be broadcast and for the rights to any royalties to go to Band Aid. Most had signed without hesitation. But all this gave Pete Smith a completely free hand.

The key piece of the jigsaw lay with Dire Straits who, in Pete's estimation, were 'the hottest breaking band in the world'. The complicating factor was that they were playing all week at Wembley Arena, just across the road from Wembley Stadium. 'We had to have them as high up the bill, as late as possible, yet allowing time for them to get back to the Arena and their own show at 8 p.m.'

Pete rang their manager, Ed Bicknell. Live Aid would duplicate all the equipment Dire Straits needed, Pete said, so all they had to do was come across the car park with their crew and their instruments. As for timing, he said, 'It has to be 6 p.m. That will be 1 p.m. on the East Coast. You get twenty minutes at 6 p.m. You can be back at the Arena by 7 p.m., ready for your 8 p.m. show.'

'Twenty minutes. That's half a song. Thanks a lot, Pete,' came the sardonic reply from a band known for playing extremely extended versions of their songs in concert. But Bicknell was happy with the timing – so much so that he asked for it to be set in stone. Pete held his breath. He wasn't sure he had the authority to do that. But he said yes and there was no going back. He attempted one proviso: 'Ed, if we agree this, you must not tell anyone. No one else has had a time confirmed yet. No one.'

'I promise.'

The next morning, Bryan Ferry's manager, Mark Fenwick, rang. Bryan would play after all, he said. 'We'd like a show time around 7 p.m.'

No times were being confirmed yet, Pete replied. But he knew what was coming.

'Look, Pete,' Fenwick said, 'I had dinner with Ed Bicknell last night…'

The telephone calls were now all incoming. Pete fielded them with firm delicacy. 'All decisions are being made on one basis only – raising the maximum money,' he told them. 'We put artists on the bill according to their record sales. The bigger the act, the better the time slot.' On the occasions when a manager got difficult, Pete said: 'Or I can get Bob to call you.'

The reply was always the same: 'No, thanks.'

Harvey Goldsmith intervened over the place allocated to Queen. The band wanted a spot near the top of the bill, but Harvey had other ideas. 'I knew that, from experience, if you are doing an all-day concert that starts midday and ends past ten o'clock at night, there is gonna be a low period around 6 p.m. There always is,' he said. Harvey had been working with Queen as their promoter. 'I knew how special Freddie was and I couldn't think of a better band to give a kick to the show in that low period.' He was proved right. 'July 13 was a hot day in London and the crowd were getting a little weary and Freddie went out there and he smashed it. I knew that slot was the perfect time for them.'

❧

Every evening at around 6 p.m., Bob Geldof would leave his allocated desk on the fourth floor of the Phonogram building and descend to the second floor, where visiting television crews from different nations were each allocated a separate room in which to set up their cameras. Geldof would move from room to room, giving each crew a three-minute interview to update them on the day's developments. After France, Germany, Japan, Australia and the US, he got to Canada and repeated what he'd said to the other national crews.

'We'd like you to watch this video,' the Canadian director said as soon as Geldof had finished his spiel. 'It's only three minutes.'

'Sorry, I haven't time,' Bob said. 'I've got half a dozen other interviews to do.'

The Canadians gave him the tape and begged him to watch it.

When the round of interviews was over, he went back upstairs to hit the phones once more. The record company receptionist, Marsha Hunt, who was fast becoming his personal assistant, was still there. She handed him a coffee and a sandwich.

Bob slipped the videotape into a machine and started to watch. He didn't eat the sandwich.

Who's gonna tell you when it's too late?

It was the video that Colin Dean had made late at night in Ethiopia in the autumn of 1984, cutting in the footage the CBC film crew had shot in the famine zone. It was the place Michael Buerk had described as the closest thing to hell on earth. Dean had only later realised he had subliminally cut the images of the skeletal children to 'Drive' by the Cars, the song he had been listening to on his headphone. Now here they were together, the starving and the song, in a ghastly work of art.

A child with a bulbous head and shrunken limbs, weakened by starvation, tried and tried again to stand up.

The child's pitiful courage was charged with a profound sadness by the lyrics of the song about a lost love who had slipped beyond reach. It had become a song about our interdependence.

At the end of the film Bob saw for the first time – though he did not know it then – the face of a dying child whose life was to become entwined with his for decades.

It was Birhan Woldu. Geldof did not know then that her name in Amharic meant Light. What was inescapable was that her light was fading.

At 11 p.m., Geldof had a meeting with David Bowie in Harvey Goldsmith's office to discuss his slot. Bob took the tape with him.

'Before we begin. I've just been given this. You should watch it.' Harvey and David stared in disbelief as the film began.

As the film and song ended, tears were falling down Bowie's face.

Bowie had been allocated five songs in the tight running order. But he now offered to drop one to make time to show the video to the Live Aid crowd.

'I don't care how many songs you want me to do,' Bowie finally said, 'but I'm giving up one to introduce this on stage.'

Geldof was alarmed. 'David, you can't do that.'

'Bob thought it might drive the television audience away,' said Harvey, 'and once people went away, they might not come back.'

'I don't care. I'm introducing this or I'm not doing the show.'

Geldof glanced at Harvey, who glared at him to shut up.

There was silence.

'Okay,' said Bob, finally.

It was to prove the emotional turning point of both the Live Aid concert – and, twenty years later, the Live 8 concert too.

❧

Things were coming together in London, but progress in the US was worryingly slow. Bill Graham had hired Larry Magid in Philadelphia, but appeared not to have done much else. He had not put the tickets on sale. He did not have a final line-up of the acts for Philadelphia. And he had lost the plans for the circular stage he'd been sent three weeks before.

At first, Geldof and Goldsmith made allowances. Graham, who had escaped the Holocaust as a child, had become embroiled in organising a protest against President Reagan, who had laid a wreath in a German military cemetery to commemorate the fortieth anniversary of the end of World War II in Europe. But Bitburg Cemetery did not only contain the graves of fallen German soldiers. Also buried there were forty-nine officers of the Waffen-SS. When Reagan defended his visit, Bill Graham, whose Jewish mother died on the way to Auschwitz, was prominent among American Jews who demonstrated against Reagan's behaviour. He took out a full-page ad in the *San Francisco Chronicle* in protest. Shortly afterwards, Graham's San Francisco offices were firebombed. Bill Graham had a lot on his mind other than Live Aid.

But there was more to it than that. Bill Graham was a visionary who started in the 1960s and pretty much invented the model for concert promoting in North America. He was single-minded. He was also a control freak. 'He was a genuine music lover,' said the Live Aid production manager, Andrew Zweck. 'And the experience for the fans was great. And he did many, many good things. But he became an egomaniac and a power monger. He was used to getting his own way. He was the king of San Francisco. He controlled everything – the venue, the ticketing, he owned the catering company, the limo company, the stagehand company. You were in Bill Graham's world. And he charged double of any other promoter in North America. And you were told "Do it our way or get lost". There were lawsuits and even fisticuffs.'

Graham, who had never been happy with the decision to hold the US end of the concert in Philadelphia, began to sabotage the whole enterprise.

Harvey Goldsmith, realising very late what was happening, called Pete Smith into his office.

'I need you to go and see Larry Magid, and then meet with Bill in New York,' he said. Magid was the big promoter in the city of Philadelphia. Although he didn't have the same status as Bill Graham on the wider American music scene, he knew the city inside out. Moreover, he knew how to handle Bill in a way Harvey could not. Though Harvey had brought Graham on board, he could not impose himself on him. Harvey and Bill were implacable rivals who had sparred for years over bands such as the Rolling Stones.

'It would be pistols at dawn,' Pete recalled. 'I had worked with these people. Harvey could not tell Bill what to do. Nor could Larry. Pete Wilson went with me. He would be the Harvey Goldsmith Enterprises man while I represented the Band Aid Trust and the BBC. All of this made diplomatic sense. I knew and respected Larry. I had met Bill a couple of times. I could speak fluent American too.' Smith and Wilson flew into Philadelphia, taking with them the latest BBC schedules from Mike Appleton. Larry Magid was in the lobby of the Four Seasons Hotel at 8 a.m. the next morning. After a tour of the venue, the JFK Stadium, he put the two Brits on the train to New York with the BBC schedule. 'We'll let the BBC lead the way,' he said. 'Just go and convince Bill Graham. That's not my job.'

Graham had moved from California to his East Coast office on New York's Upper East Side. When Smith and Wilson arrived, he was doing a network TV interview. This Live Aid event was going to be the biggest thing ever, he told the interviewer. He would make sure of that. Everyone would see. Smith hoped that Graham's public enthusiasm augured well. 'I inspected the pile of papers on his coffee table, just for something to do. Each page had a different artist's name on it. Numbers for agents and managers. There was a lot of paperwork.'

'Here's the BBC schedule, Bill, all written up and ready to go,' Pete said, passing the document across. 'This whole thing is shaping up as a worldwide TV event, primarily. As such, it makes sense for the BBC to lead. They have the start on this and we just needed to fit everything into their plan. It'll save us all a lot of effort if we follow this route. Larry is happy with that.'

Bill looked straight at Smith. 'Look, Pete, this is never going to happen.'

'Why not?'

Bill shot back. 'See that pile of papers on the coffee table? That's all the artists that want to play in Philadelphia. I refuse to work with half of these people.'

'Bill, there's a lot of artists there,' Pete said. 'What about the other half?'

He leaned in to Pete and said, very slowly, 'They refuse to work with me.'

Graham roared with laughter. But it was to turn out not to be that funny.

The pair began to go through Mike Appleton's pages with Bill moaning about the line-up being overloaded with British talent. Then he said that he was having problems with the ABC TV Special people and their demands for specific artists.

'Look, Madonna's manager will not agree unless she's included in the ABC Special. But their advertisers want the established rock stars. They don't want Madonna.'

'Surely this can be talked through,' Smith said in a mollifying tone.

'You talk to him,' barked Bill and punched the number on his autodial for Madonna's manager, Freddy DeMann.

'Freddy, it's Bill. I've got Pete Smith from England here with me. He's doing the Live Aid show. He wants to talk to you.'

Bill passed the telephone to the slightly flustered Pete Smith, who introduced himself and then, thinking quickly on his feet, told Madonna's manager that it would be better for her if she was not included in the ABC special.

'Think about it. Four p.m. in Philly is ideal for Madonna.'

'How come?'

'Your client is breaking through at every level in the US. But your international market is just beginning to explode. Four p.m. in Philadelphia is 9 p.m. in London. It's 10 p.m. in Paris, Frankfurt and Rome. That's prime time and we have BBC TV guaranteed and worldwide TV in train. It's Saturday night. The kids can all stay up and see Madonna on TV. On Live Aid. There's no school in the morning. And it will be breakfast time in Australia and Japan. They'll all get up and tune in. And there will be Madonna. It's Sunday, a day off. Perfect. But you'll miss this pan-international prime time TV opportunity if you go later with ABC.'

There was a pause.

'Let me talk to Bill,' said Freddy.

Bill took the phone and then put it down.

'What did he say?' Pete asked.

'Freddy said that I have to guarantee that Madonna is on at 4 p.m. in Philly or she's not coming,' replied Bill. 'Leave this schedule with me. I will call Larry, we'll get on it right away.'

Smith and Wilson checked in for the flight back to Heathrow. Harvey had told them to call him before they took off. Pete made a collect call to Harvey's home in St John's Wood, where it was past midnight. Bob Geldof was with him.

'How did you get on?'

'Good,' Pete replied. 'Larry gets it, of course. The venue is pretty run down, but they'll sort it. Bill was Bill. But he agreed to everything in the end.'

'You have to call him before you leave,' said Harvey.

'Why?'

'Just call him now. He'll still be there.'

The call to Graham's office connected directly from the airport lounge.

'Bill,' Pete said, 'I just wanted to thank you for your time today. We're about to fly back to London and I wanted to check in with you one more time.'

'Listen,' Bill Graham bellowed down the phone. 'You come over here with your file and your schedule. I am inundated with your English artists. If it wasn't for me, there would be no Live Aid show in America.' He was getting into his stride. The tirade lasted another three minutes or so. Then he stopped.

'I hear what you say, Bill, but what does this mean?'

'We'll do it as laid out,' he said. 'I just needed you to hear what I think, that's all.'

Back in London, Goldsmith was satisfied. Bill had deferred. The focus for the American Live Aid production was now understood, by all concerned, to be Larry Magid's office in Philadelphia. Bill Graham could effectively be by-passed.

If only it were to be that simple.

Geldof was more worried about a raft of other issues at the American end. Philadelphia was to have only two stages, not three, so the turnaround there was going to be twice as long as Wembley. Many of the artists in the US were not happy with a simple one-page contract, similar to the one being signed by the performers at Wembley. Above all, he discovered, although almost everyone in the UK was donating their services to Live Aid for free, in the US people were expecting to be paid. Only the bands and the promoters and Mike Mitchell were working without payment. The technical people expected to be paid.

'No one in the UK is getting paid,' he thundered at Mitchell.

'If you insist on that in the US, there will be no show,' said Mitchell. 'The unions won't wear it.'

Geldof was eventually persuaded that this was something on which he would have to compromise. But he was furious when he discovered that the Philadelphia operation was going to cost $3.5 million, whereas the total expenses at Wembley would only be £250,000. In London, Harvey Goldsmith pointed out, nearly all goods and services had been donated, including the sound and lighting systems, the monitor system, the stage, the rehearsal rooms, a small fleet of helicopters and airline tickets. Mitchell placated Geldof and Goldsmith by pointing out that an event the size of Live Aid would normally cost about $20 million to produce. But the sponsorship and donations Mitchell had fixed had reduced that significantly – so much so that corporate giving would cover all the overheads, including the rental of the satellites, which was being borne by the Philadelphia end. Geldof would be able to continue to make the promise that every cent of money donated by the public would be spent in Africa.

Far more troubling, Geldof now began to get phone calls from big US stars pulling out of the show. Paul Simon called to tell him he was being messed about. 'He was upset,' Geldof recalled. 'Every time he phoned anyone to get things organised, he met a blank wall.' He felt people were being deliberately obstructive towards him.

'Bill Graham told me to fuck off because "nobody needs Paul Simon on this show".'

'That's not true, Paul,' said Geldof. 'I really need you on the show. The world really needs you.'

'I'm not going to have someone like Bill Graham talk to me in the way he's talking to me,' Simon said. 'I won't work with this guy. I'm sorry.'

This was the final straw for Geldof. He and Goldsmith had been so worried about the lack of acts on the US line-up that they were encouraging

British acts to go to Philadelphia. Discussing the dilemma with Graham, the irascible promoter started screaming at Geldof down the phone.

'I don't *want* British acts! I don't *need* any!'

'Well, what American acts have you got? Why are you being obstructive to Paul Simon?'

'We've got this kid anyway...' He was talking about Madonna, who, while currently one of the hottest new acts in the world, was nowhere near comparable in stature to Paul Simon. 'Fuck Paul Simon,' he screamed again.

Geldof rang off and called Harvey. 'This guy's out of control. Totally out of control. He's going to fucking pull the whole thing down.'

Then Willie Nelson withdrew. Another blow.

With just three weeks to go, Bill Graham had stopped returning Bob's calls. Geldof and Goldsmith decided they had better get on a plane to New York. When they arrived in Graham's office, 'it was utter chaos,' Geldof recalled. 'Bill Graham was rude, superior and very distracted.' He and Geldof starting shouting at one another; Harvey just went very quiet. 'Then a female member of staff came in and started screaming at Bill in the middle of our meeting,' said Bob. 'Bill just stares at her and then gets up and walks out. And I don't see Bill Graham again.'

Things were even worse than they appeared. Graham, never happy with the decision to choose Philadelphia, was telling American stars that it was really just going to be a British event. The US concert was going to be an embarrassing failure and that they should pull out. Taking part could damage their careers, he said.

'We found out that Bill Graham was warning people off, telling them what wasn't happening or that it was badly organised,' recalled Andrew Zweck. 'Stevie Wonder, Billy Joel, Huey Lewis & the News, Boy George, Kris Kristofferson, Waylon Jennings were all on the poster. They all pulled out.' Harvey Goldsmith now realised that 'Bill had got to the point where he became actually obstructive'.

Bill Graham had done one good thing: he'd hired one of the best stage managers in the world, Michael Ahern. But when Graham lost the stage design that he had been sent from Wembley, the new man had drawn up his own.

Ahern's design was good, but he had divided the stage in two instead of three. 'That will never give you enough time to turn the acts around when bands are doing just fifteen minutes each,' said Geldof. 'In any case, the stage ought to be identical in both places. This isn't two concerts, it's one.'

He was right, but there was no time to change it now. On the day, the turnaround in Philadelphia was twice as long as at Wembley. The stage looked constantly over-crowded.

Alarmed, Bob and Harvey went to Philadelphia. After Graham's headquarters, Larry Magid's office at Electric Factory Concerts was an oasis of calm.

'What I never told Bob or Bill or Harvey was that, when I agreed to do this show,' Larry later said, 'I didn't have the city's permission. So I went to see the mayor, who turned us down flat.'

Instead of panicking, the unflappable Magid went to see the city's chief executive, who saw at once that Live Aid could be the antidote the city needed after the calamity of the recent MOVE bombing. Larry got permission.

The next day, he called a meeting of all the city's relevant heads of department. 'There were fifty people sitting at this large desk, and I'm sitting at the head of it', when in walks Bob Geldof, blithely unaware of Larry Magid's last-minute gamble. 'It was the first constructive meeting of the visit,' Geldof said afterwards.

'Thank you for doing this,' Geldof told the deputy mayor.

'We need it,' he replied with appealing frankness.

'Live Aid helped restore the city's image,' Larry said years later. 'It made the city feel good about itself again. Forty years on, you don't hear much about the bombing, but people still talk about Live Aid.'

Bill Graham, who had also attended the meeting, made a persuasive speech to the city fathers. But relations between him and Mike Mitchell had clearly broken down. Mike was now contacting artists direct, which infuriated Graham. Things looked set to get worse, Geldof thought.

Larry Magid tried to reassure the two visitors from the UK. 'Bill needs, for whatever reason, to be the centre of attention, and if you know that, it is easy to work with him.' But Mike Mitchell and the television execs were not so accommodating. Larry knew exactly what the problem was. 'There was in Bill's mind, a conflict,' said Larry, looking back. 'Whose show was it? Was it a live show? Was it a TV show? I couldn't care less. We just had to do what was right for the show.'

Magid was a peacemaker. Where Graham saw the UK acts as an intrusion on his private turf, Larry argued that it not only filled a lot of spaces, but also gave the Philly show extra credibility to have big names from elsewhere. 'I knew Bill. I knew his moods and I knew what he needed,' Larry added. 'I didn't care about power. To pull something like this off, it needs teamwork.'

As they left Larry Magid's office in Philadelphia, Bob whispered to Harvey with relief: 'Fuck, this *is* going to get done.' But, to be safe, when the pair got back to London, Harvey sent two of his staff out to work in Larry's office to closely coordinate all the preparations in Wembley and Philadelphia.

But the chaos created by Bill Graham was not over. Ken Kragen rang Graham and was told that the whole concert was a mess, and it was never going to work. Artists closely associated with Ken Kragen – Lionel Richie, Michael Jackson and Stevie Wonder – now didn't want to know about Live Aid. 'Most of the artists who did "We Are the World" were kind of talked out of playing Live Aid in Philadelphia,' said Harvey Goldsmith. 'Part of this was all this angst with Bill Graham that was going on. And, in part, it was because Ken Kragen didn't want the artists that had played on his record to do Live Aid because he wanted to do his own show.'

There had been some tension between Kragen and the Band Aid team previously. After the two records were made, Goldsmith had suggested a cooperation, which Kragen, who was president of USA for Africa, had turned down. 'It was just a funny situation. We tried to say "Let's put all the funds together", but they didn't want to do that. So what started off as a bit of camaraderie ended up being a little bit of angst,' Goldsmith recalled. 'We weren't looking to have a competition. That wasn't the object of the exercise. We wanted to work together and they wanted to do it their way. And so it became quite a sticky issue.'

That earlier rivalry seemed to raise its head again now at Live Aid.

'It was painfully obvious that it wouldn't have made any sense for Ken to suddenly arrive and say, "No, we are gonna do our *own* show",' said Harvey. 'Ours was already announced. We were on sale in Philadelphia at that time. It didn't make any sense at all. But I think there was a bit of jealousy from the American end.'

Pete Smith agreed. The refusal of the black acts to play at Live Aid was rooted in a rivalry, he said, which dated back to the two original charity singles. A number of US artists felt that, with their single, they had done their bit. Now the Brits were taking over again by organising a live show. 'In America, there was an agenda, that was brought from their Band Aid record, of that community of black acts committing or not,' Pete said, just before he died in 2022. 'It was like a block vote and, unfortunately, the block vote went against the Philadelphia show from the black artist community.'

A year later, Ken Kragen did organise his own charity event, Hands Across America, an attempt to create a human chain across the US along a 3,980-mile route from the Statue of Liberty to Los Angeles. Kragen hoped it would raise as much as $100 million from participants, who would pay $10 to be assigned a place in the line. But, in the event, although 5 million people participated, the chain was not unbroken and raised a more modest $15 million after operating costs.

So, ultimately, the reason Live Aid failed to secure the services of the biggest black superstars of the '80s was down to a number of factors. ABC thought that its largely white middle-class audience would prefer to see white rather than black artists on their nationwide three-hour network special. Bill Graham's self-serving lies destabilised the motivation of many artists, black as well as white. And Ken Kragen's plans for his own event meant that he failed to use his considerable influence to push artists like Lionel Richie, Michael Jackson and Stevie Wonder to appear.

The black critics in the media knew none of this.

'We don't know the extent of all the acts Bill Graham put off,' said Harvey Goldsmith, 'but what I discovered was that, three days before the concert, he actually told everybody it wasn't going to happen.' At the end of the day, although Bill remained the nominal head of the Philadelphia concert, he wasn't allowed to do anything by way of putting the show together. Live Aid's US television supremo, Mike Mitchell, decided to cut Graham out of the loop and started to contact stars direct to get the definite confirmation from the acts he needed. Bill Graham was outraged and, once more, massive rows ensued.

Within forty-eight hours of stepping in, Larry Magrid had booked half a dozen black acts. Born and raised in Philadelphia, he had been listening to the city's black musicians since the age of eleven. 'I went to every show, R&B, blues, early rock 'n' roll,' he said. 'Everybody in the business knew that I had an affinity towards black music.'

'We had the Four Tops, Bo Diddley – which was great for early influence. We had Patti LaBelle, who was on fire at the time. Run-D.M.C., which was the first big rap group, and the great songwriters Ashford & Simpson, who came up with the idea that they would bring Teddy Pendergrass onto the show – his first live appearance since he was disabled in an automobile accident, three years before.' Kool and the Gang and Prince both contributed videos. Magid was, said Pete Smith, 'the promoter's promoter, a true professional'.

'I saved Bob Geldof's ass by putting black acts on the show,' Magid joked. The line-up should have been even more balanced. 'But we had a great show. And how we pulled this thing off – five weeks to do a show like this – is insane.'

'Because of the wrangling and the shenanigans of Bill Graham, Live Aid would not have happened without Larry,' Andy Zweck said. 'Larry Magid saved the day.'

For all that, said Band Aid trustee Midge Ure, 'after the concert we were lambasted for not having enough black artists on the bill. It became this anti-colonial diatribe – "You whites, telling us poor black guys what to do." It was unfair, but it happened.' A number of individuals were to blame for that, but Bob Geldof was not the guilty party.

CHAPTER 11

GLITCHES AND HITCHES

After NASA had confirmed that, sorry, they couldn't find a rocket to send Mick Jagger to the Space Shuttle, David Bowie had a more down-to-earth idea.

It was just two weeks to Live Aid day and, on 29 June, Bowie was winding up a day's recording at Westside Studios in Holland Park, where he had been working on the title song for the film *Absolute Beginners*. The band and the engineers thought that perhaps the day was coming to a close, when Bowie produced a cassette and handed it to one of the musicians.

'Here you go, lads, go and learn this,' he said. The cassette label read 'Dancing in the Streets'.

'Mick Jagger's coming down in about an hour and we're recording a song for Live Aid.'

The Bowie/Jagger duet was still on. As the studio began to fill up with executives and producers of the *Absolute Beginners* movie, who had previously shown no interest in proceedings until now, Bowie's band began to tentatively run through their parts. Then Jagger arrived, with his daughter, Jade.

Having left the rest of the Stones bickering in Paris, Jagger had flown to England especially to record with Bowie.

'Calling out around the world,' roared Jagger, turning the opening line from the Motown classic into what was to become a clarion call for Live Aid.

'It was great to hear the whole band and singers all performing at the same time,' said the sound engineer Mark Saunders. 'It wasn't something that happened much – especially in the '80s when recording got a lot more clinical. They played two great takes and came in to listen.' The legendary producer Alan Winstanley, who was producing the sessions alongside his partner Clive Langer, remembers a less auspicious start. 'The band rehearsed "Dancing in the Street" an hour before Mick arrived – and they were terrible. They were tired and it sounded like awful cabaret. But when Mick arrived, he immediately started doing the Jagger strut, which made him and the band suddenly launch straight into top gear.'

It was agreed that the vocals would need to be re-sung. 'Not because they weren't good enough, but because they were all singing in the same room and therefore all the singers' voices were bleeding onto everyone else's microphones,' said the engineer. 'This would have compromised the mixing of the song – although that was how records were made, back in the '60s.'

The backing singers went first and swiftly nailed their parts, followed by Jagger. Though he was now alone in the studio, the singer gyrated as if he were playing to a packed Madison Square Garden. It was, as the session's drummer Neil Conti put it, as if he was on 'an ego trip' to try to upstage Bowie. Sometimes he disappeared from view to strut around the studio but always leaping back into the microphone spotlight in time to deliver the next punchy line. By contrast, Bowie laid down his vocals one line at a time, then stopped and listened back to them before doing the next. Occasionally, he would check his lines from a demo version before recording the next one. The contrast between the performer and the perfectionist was striking, but the end result was the same immaculate result from both.

Four hours later that same day, the recording complete, cars arrived to take the duo across the city to London's Docklands, where Bowie's favoured director, David Mallet, was waiting with a film crew to shoot the video. After the inside shots at a deserted warehouse at three o'clock in the morning, Mallet moved the filming outside – and decided the lighting was a problem. He called the Live Aid PR, Bernard Doherty, and said he needed four cars with their headlights on, parked down the road. 'That was how my beat-up old Honda Civic came to star in an epic video,' said Doherty. 'It took so long that they all had flat batteries at the end. We had to call out the roadside rescue in the morning to get them started.' After the long video shoot, Jagger took the tapes to New York where, in early July, brass and guitar overdubs were added and Bowie's old collaborator Rick Wakeman added uncredited piano.

The big names were falling into place, but they still had to land the biggest of all, the one for whom all the others on the bill would happily stand aside, without quibble or demur: Paul McCartney. Harvey Goldsmith had tapped into his long-standing connections to try to entice the former Beatle to play. And Bernard Doherty, who was McCartney's personal PR as well as the Live Aid press manager, had leaned on his client. But the singer had still not committed to taking part.

Geldof decided to ring him. McCartney had not played in public since before John Lennon had been murdered. Bob knew that fact alone would weigh heavy. Reluctance and desire would battle mightily in McCartney's breast.

Bob had a hunch that, if he approached Paul with a general request, it could be turned down relatively easily. So he rang Paul and asked him if he would play just one song.

'No band, Paul. No need to panic, or try to put some guys together, rehearse a set, etc.,' Geldof said. 'Just the one song on a single piano.'

'What song were you thinking of?'

'"Let it Be",' Bob said.

'Why that one?'

Bob mumbled something about it being a kind of blessing, a benediction, a sign of wisdom and hope to vast millions of people.

'Yes, there is no complacency in saying "Let It Be",' said McCartney. 'It's a call to action. Let me have a think about it.'

Geldof put down the phone but was still unsure. Goldsmith and Andy Zweck had been listening. They knew McCartney was the only possible conclusion to the show. Bob decided to write Paul a letter to explain himself better.

He was writing to Paul the person not Paul the 'mirror of a million projections', he began, the Paul who had with Linda watched the horrible footage from Ethiopia with what she described as dismay and disgust.

Bob wrote how the Beatles' music was synonymous with joy and optimism in the darknesses of people's lives. People of every age and culture had thrilled to that happiness and overriding sense of shared hope.

'Let It Be' was a hymn, he went on. A prayer. And so was Live Aid.

It spoke to everyone. It addressed our darkness, but said there would be a light that shines. Geldof recalled a stained-glass window he had seen in a church which referred to the Book of Job saying 'What of the Night? The Morning comes'. There will be an answer. But Paul's imprimatur was needed if the whole mad, huge project was to work. Only the presence of a Beatle could do that.

Bob pushed the letter into a postbox knowing he could do no more.

❊

Pete Smith was sitting at his desk just after lunch on the Friday two weeks before Live Aid day when Harvey called him into his office. He was to go, with Pete Wilson, to Paul McCartney's office in Soho Square and finally try to persuade the great man to come on board. The two Petes were to take everything McCartney might ask to see: schedules, stage plans, production schemas, BBC pages, the lot. Paul was about to make a decision, one way or another, and he wanted the facts, not spin.

As they waited, Pete Smith studied the large Picasso on the wall behind Paul's desk. It was not a print. Pete sat there wondering if he dare touch it. He didn't. When McCartney came in, he was indeed interested in everything: the stage plans, BBC schedules, the American timings, running orders.

'What pianos do you have?' he asked.

Anything that he wanted, Pete said. Paul wanted a Steinway. There were two Steinways on Pete's lists: Elton John's nine-foot white Model D concert grand and Freddie Mercury's smaller black conservatoire model. McCartney liked the idea of Elton's piano. Did he want a few other artists to join him for the chorus of 'Let It Be'? 'I never heard another song title suggested during all of the discussions,' recalled Smith. It was the only song Geldof had requested. McCartney settled upon David Bowie, Alison Moyet, Pete Townshend and Bob Geldof as his backing singers.

They had talked for almost an hour but, Pete later noted, 'it was all still exploratory'.

One last thing. Paul asked about the BBC promo trailers that he had seen after the TV news each evening. Each artist had their current album artwork flagged, while a roster of confirmed performers ran across the bottom as a moving graphic. Over it all, Status Quo sang 'Rockin' All Over the World'.

'Put my new album on the trailer tonight after the *Nine O'clock News* and I'll do it. I'll be home by then.' Pete rang Michael Appleton at the BBC from McCartney's office and the deal was done there and then. The trailer would be updated: Paul McCartney would close the show.

'I was going to do it all along,' McCartney laughed as he showed Pete out. 'The management told me to do it weeks ago.'

'The management?'

'The real management – my kids. They've been doing Live Aid projects at school for a month or more. They told me that I had to do it, weeks ago.'

✳

But that was not the end of it. Paul McCartney also wanted to see the man in charge of the sound. If he was only to play one song, everything had to be just right. Full of trepidation, Andy Zweck went to meet the ex-Beatle in the boardroom at Soho Square. 'It was very specific in detail,' Zweck recalled. '"Who's doing my sound? How will I hear myself? What are my monitors? Where will my piano be?"' Zweck remembered that, in 1979, McCartney did one night of a charity series in Hammersmith called Concerts for Kampuchea. 'And it went wrong. The sound was terrible that night.' It was so bad that the sound company got fired.

Six years later, the singer remembered.

'Don't worry, Paul. We've got the best people in the world here now. It won't go wrong.'

But, of course, it did go wrong.

✳

The slots at Wembley were filling up – so much so that a logjam occurred. Elvis Costello, who had been promised four songs, now found his slot being whittled away until he eventually got only one. He was not alone. By the time Simple Minds, the Pretenders, Billy Ocean and Duran Duran came on board, there was no room for them on the Wembley line-up. They were asked to play Philadelphia instead.

Things got even more crowded after Geldof gatecrashed the celebrity line-up at a Dire Straits concert just a week before Live Aid. The event, on 4 July 1985, was a rock gala benefit for the Prince's Trust at Wembley Arena. The Prince and Princess of Wales were in attendance. Bob told the royal couple about the Live Aid concert the following Saturday and asked if they would come.

'Will Phil Collins be there?' asked Princess Diana.

Geldof told her about Collins taking Concorde to play both concerts.

'Oh good. I think he's great,' she said, blushing enthusiastically.

Later that night, the Prince's Trust phoned Harvey Goldsmith and said the royal couple would attend. That would mean the national anthem would have to be played, so Status Quo would have to lose five minutes from their act. They accepted without demur.

'We had this amazing galaxy of rock stars and yet Diana was the most famous woman on the planet,' Geldof said. 'As soon as I knew she was going to come, I knew the Americans would tune in.'

Pete Smith was moving into the final strait. In addition to all the artists, he had to organise crew catering, helicopters from Battersea to Wembley and back, buses for artist transport, somewhere for the backstage crew to sleep in the final week and a piano tuner. But the US was still playing catch-up. Mike Mitchell had put together an ad hoc network consisting of scores of independent TV stations who were going to take fifteen hours or more of the show. Between them, they covered 85 per cent of all the television sets in the US. When ABC realised this, they demanded that the independent stations go off air while the three-hour ABC network special was being broadcast – with all the biggest stars from both the UK and the US. ABC wanted David Bowie, Elton John, Paul McCartney, the Who and Wham! in Wembley, along with Eric Clapton, Mick Jagger, Tina Turner and Led Zeppelin in Philadelphia. And they wanted them exclusively.

'We have to do it,' Mitchell told Geldof. 'We've given them our word.'

'Have we fuck! They can shove off.'

'We have to have network.'

'No, we don't. You've got 85 per cent of all the independent TV stations in America. We don't need ABC.'

But they did. The sponsors demanded it. So, in the end, Geldof had to capitulate, though he increased the price to ABC to $1.5 million – and the network paid.

Events were snowballing. There was still no news from Ken Kragen about Lionel Richie, but Bob Dylan's manager rang Geldof to say Dylan would definitely play. Geldof was hugely relieved. Without Lionel Richie, they would not be able to close the concert in Philadelphia with 'We Are the World'. Now perhaps Dylan would end with 'The Times They Are A-Changin''. Eric Clapton cancelled three gigs in Caesars Palace in Las Vegas, without even being asked, to play. Black Sabbath were to re-form. Mick Jagger was rehearsing a duet with Tina Turner.

The Who had had a rehearsal. It was a shambles. There was an almighty row. Everyone walked out after half an hour. 'A pretty standard Who rehearsal,' laughed Pete Townshend afterwards. 'It was like getting one man's four ex-wives together,' Geldof responded. The band had not played for three years and were barely on speaking terms. The whole venture was on-off-on-off until the very day itself.

Eventually, when the momentum of Live Aid was clear on both sides of the Atlantic, Ken Kragen rang and said *maybe* Lionel Richie would do it, but it had to be kept secret.

'No,' said Geldof. 'He's either doing it or he's not. If he is, then we'll announce it.' He needed to know whether or not the Philadelphia concert could end with 'We Are the World'.

After a flurry of 4 a.m. calls to and from Australia, the Australian Broadcasting Corporation were on board and would do a telethon, which was against their usual broadcasting rules. Geldof and Goldsmith's phone were ringing day and night. 'From about a week before the concert, the phones never stopped,' said Harvey. 'I literally got in such a state from lack of sleep that I ripped the phones out of the wall at home.'

The last piece of the jigsaw was Bruce Springsteen. Geldof went to see him four times in his run of UK concerts. The two men had known each other since meeting at the celebrated West Hollywood rock hotel, the Sunset Marquis, some years before. But though they chatted easily backstage, each time Bob failed to pluck up the courage to ask him about Live Aid face to face.

Jon Landau, Bruce's manager, tried to put Bob out of his misery. It would not happen, he told Geldof. Bruce and his band had been on their Born in the USA tour for thirteen solid months. They had done 140 gigs. The band needed a rest. And Bruce had just got married and promised his wife, Julianne Phillips, a honeymoon.

'He's tired, Bob. He wants some time with his wife,' said Landau. 'They've had no time. You don't need us, you've got everyone else. You've sold out. You've got our stage there at Wembley.' They had given instructions that it be left up for Live Aid. 'You can use that. That's our present, yeah? We'll pay for it.'

Bob had one last try and asked Bruce directly. But Springsteen could not be swayed. 'I've been on tour forever. We've just got married and if I don't give her a honeymoon at the end of this tour, then it'll be a divorce,' he laughed.

It was, at least, a definitive answer. But Springsteen later said he wished he'd stuck his guitar in the back seat of the car and turned up. He didn't realise quite how big it was going to be.

�֍

On the Monday of Live Aid week, Andrew Zweck and his team, who had also been running the UK leg of the Springsteen tour, arrived at Wembley and surveyed the scene. 'We got back from Leeds, exhausted,' he remembered. 'Bruce had gone home, saying, "I'll leave you my stage. I'll leave you my Portakabin dressing rooms. I'll pay the rent on all that for another week. That's my contribution." And we looked around the empty Wembley and this shell of a stage, and we thought, *What do we do now?*' How could they fit twenty-two bands onto the stage where, the week before, there had been only one? 'It was sheer unadulterated panic. I thought, *I'm out of my depth. This is a worldwide TV broadcast coming in five days' time. How the hell are we gonna do it?*'

Zweck phoned every experienced production manager he knew. 'Where are you? Drop what you're doing. Get on a plane. I'll send you a ticket. Come to London. We need you, we need you.' The top six guys on the planet were in Philadelphia, working for Eric Clapton, Led Zeppelin or one of the other major artists. 'They had a surfeit of experienced guys there. Too many. We had none. So I phoned everybody I knew who had any kind of management experience in production in London – people who ran lighting companies and sound companies and trucking companies – and said, "Come to Wembley." Nobody refused. Soon, there were a dozen of us who spent the whole week there, day and night.'

Springsteen had left behind his sub-stage, the basic platform on which to build the top stage. This, for Live Aid, was to be the revolving turntable. It was a great idea, but when it arrived, it weighed a ton. 'Actually, it weighed sixteen tons,' said Zweck. 'It sank into the wood the minute it went on. We had to disassemble it and bolster the floor. And then it kept failing. It was so heavy. It had never been used before in music.'

'Frankly, until we were on site, we still didn't really get a clear understanding of how huge this whole thing would be,' said the designer, Jeremy Thom. First, the cabling was not working. Then the fuses kept blowing. The weight was just too much. 'So we just burned the phones and suddenly it was headline news. It was in all the media.' The upside of this was that the industry experts came forward to solve the problem. Bernard Doherty, who knew a good story when he saw one, told the newspapers that they had shire horses on standby to pull the stage round if the mechanism failed on the day. It wasn't true, but it was good publicity.

So were the statistics of what was involved. Scores of workers were now on site putting together a stage which was 140 feet across, with eight tons of scaffolding and five miles of cabling. In Philadelphia, they were constructing the biggest stage ever built for a rock concert: 100 feet high and 300 feet wide, the size of an American football field. It too had a revolve, though with only two rather than three sections. But it also had problems. 'The night before the show, the turntable motor broke,' said Dave Skaff, one of the Philadelphia sound engineers. 'It just burnt up and it was too late to take it out.' The stage designer, Michael Tait, came up with an ingenious solution. He cut twenty holes in the turntable and fitted a vertical metal pipe in each so the revolve could be turned manually. Then Bill Graham made a call to the city's football team. 'The Philadelphia Eagles' defensive line came in and turned the turntable all day. That was pretty wild,' said Skaff. 'That was one of the ones that impressed me the most, that we could get anything done that we needed.'

There was one big mistake which Bob Geldof had made. The Live Aid mastermind continued to push his line that Band Aid would pay for nothing. There was always a way to get everything for free. He and Andrew Zweck fell out about it. Geldof, of course, won – but at what cost? 'Bruce Springsteen had the world's best PA system set up for his gig in Wembley seven days before,' recalled Zweck, 'so we went to that company and we said, "Can you leave the PA behind? We really want to use it next Saturday for Live Aid."'

'"We can do that, but there's costs," the sound people said. "We've booked the boats to take it back. We've got crew that'd need to sit in London for a week in hotels. We need an amount of money."'

But the word came from upstairs: 'We are not spending a penny. If they won't do it for nothing, then we'll get someone else.'

So Zweck told Springsteen's sound system people: 'Sorry, we can't. We are not allowed to spend a penny.' Instead, he got a PA from another supplier. 'And it wasn't as good. The staff weren't as experienced. And we paid a price in the failure of Paul McCartney's Live Aid sound when his mic channel was incorrectly plugged in. Although Paul got on with it, and the audience sang with him, and he made the best of it, it was deeply embarrassing' – especially after all the reassurances Zweck had given him.

'I haven't worked for him since,' Zweck noted wryly.

⁂

The day before the Live Aid concert, Wembley's official caterers, ARA, were still refusing to donate their profits to the Band Aid Trust. Geldof and Goldsmith decided to go to Wembley in person, where they met the stadium's deputy chairman, Jarvis Astaire. Geldof, for once, had met his match. Jarvis Astaire was no ordinary opponent. Before becoming number two at Wembley, he had been, for thirty years, Britain's leading boxing promoter. He was also big in professional wrestling.

'It was the only situation where I saw someone say no to Bob and get away with it,' Zweck recalled. 'Jarvis was a heavyweight, and old school. He didn't take to Bob's belligerent bad language. Bob had got away with it throughout every level of society. But Jarvis was not going to put up with it.'

'Listen, you little shit,' countered Astaire. 'Don't you come into my boardroom and tell me how to do business. I'm going to have my people remove you from the premises. You're not welcome here.'

'It was the only occasion I saw that Bob didn't win,' said Zweck. 'Pretty well everything else that he set his sights on he was able to achieve. It was a remarkable experience.'

Geldof, however, had the last laugh. After he left the meeting, he made a public announcement that everyone in the audience should bring their own food and drink, and boycott the catering.

The evening before Live Aid, Harvey Goldsmith left his office late and exhausted, after fielding calls from various managers, topped by another blazing row with Bill Graham in New York. 'He phoned me up and he said, you've gotta put this act on, and that act, and the other act.'

'"Bill, we're full. We're not putting any more on."

'He said, "I need you to put Black Sabbath on because I'm doing their merchandise deal." I said no and tried to calm him down and be positive about the whole thing.' But Bill Graham was really not happy.

Almost as soon as Goldsmith was home, the phone rang again. This time it was Andrew Zweck at Wembley.

'We've got a problem. The crew are exhausted, they say they're going home, they've had enough…'

'What the hell's going on?'

'The stage has packed up. It's not turning.'

Harvey jumped into his car and got to the nearest off-licence just before it closed. He bought three crates of beer, put them in the boot and sped off to Wembley. 'As I walked in the door, everybody said, "We've had enough. We just can't handle it anymore. We're exhausted and the ruddy stage is not working."

'"Right, okay, let's just stop there. First of all, in the boot of my car, just bring in the crates, give everybody a beer." So everybody sat down and had a beer and started talking.

'"Guys, it's tomorrow. We've gotta make this work. We've gotta figure out how to do it. Let's just stop and think about what it is that could have stopped the stage from turning."'

The crew were clearly pleased to see Harvey – and perhaps more so the beer.

'Maybe a cog is jammed,' one stagehand said, pulling on his beer. The crew began to discuss the options. Eventually, they discovered that a scaffolding pole had fallen into the machinery. 'They pulled the bloody thing out and managed to get the stage turning again,' said Harvey. It was coming up to midnight before they got to bed, Harvey at his home in St John's Wood and the crew in the tour bus which Pete Smith had stationed for them behind the stage earlier in the week. It was too risky to let them go home to their own beds.

Harvey was hardly asleep when the phone rang again. 'It was Tommy Mottola [the head of Sony Records] to say he was pulling out Mick Jagger unless Hall and Oates got a better slot in the running order.

'If you want to pull out Mick Jagger, be my guest. I'd like to see you try.'

✄

Over in Chelsea, Bob Geldof wasn't asleep. He had a painful back, from a suspected trapped nerve, and he was seized with night sweats, so much so that Paula had put towels underneath him in their bed. He lay awake, seized with fear at the possibility of failure. 'Personal failure, public failure, global failure,' he later told me. 'Fear that people would say, if it didn't work: "Geldof – what a wanker." But a far greater fear was that I might let down the bands who had done so much on my personal say-so. Eric Clapton had given up three nights in Las Vegas without me even asking. The Who, Led Zeppelin, the Beach Boys and Black Sabbath – all global giants – had re-formed for the Live Aid concert. Duran Duran had flown to America because there was no room on the bill in London. People had gone to immense effort, but never went on about it and never charged a penny.'

And then to make matters worse, the phone rang. It was U2's management, threatening that the band would pull out if they didn't get a soundcheck.

'Well, fucking pull out. No one's getting a soundcheck,' said Bob. 'I'm going back to bed.'

Philadelphia was five hours behind so Geldof and Goldsmith were unaware that, on the very eve of the Live Aid concert, the police had arrived at the JFK Stadium to arrest Bill Graham.

For some time, Bob and Harvey had been telling Larry Magid they were going to fire Graham. 'They kept telling me we'd got to get rid of him,' Larry said. 'It seemed like our show was out of control to them and it really wasn't. We really had the pulse of this show. I said, "No, I'll cover this. Don't worry about it. You can't fire him."'

But Bill had broken someone else's patience.

'All of a sudden, the police show up,' said Larry, who was working in the trailer he shared at the stadium with Graham.

'Can I help you?' Larry, polite as ever, asked the cops.

'Yeah, we're here to arrest Bill Graham.'

Bill wasn't in the trailer. Larry didn't know where he was.

Then, behind the law enforcement officers, in came the two men at the sharp end of the Live Aid television broadcast and its satellite uploads, Mike Mitchell and Tony Verna. They wanted Graham arrested for trespass.

The conflict over the control of the show had got ridiculous, Magid said. Graham had been refusing to let the television people have passes to access the stage.

'Where is he?

'He's gone, but you can't fire him the night before the show. It's just too involved and it's going to cause you heartaches.'

'Well, you're in charge,' Mitchell told Magid. Larry was unflustered. He already knew he was in charge. He always had been. He had run the whole physical plant, the whole stadium, many times before. He had the running of the show worked out. Mike Ahern, the best stage manager in the business, would run the timing of the show, not Bill. Mike would bring the acts on and off. Bill would think he was doing that, but his role would be purely in name only .

'Finally, the police left, and I just said, "Mike, just leave it to me. I know what to do."'

Larry Magid had been managing Bill Graham for some considerable time. He knew how to massage Graham's ego and how to get around him. He also knew that a lot of Bill's behaviour was bluster. As Jan Simmons, Bill's long-time assistant, later said: 'I'll never forget the first time Bill screamed into the telephone. He had been on a minutes-long tirade and then literally threw the phone down onto its cradle. Without a beat, he looked up at me and winked. I don't think Bill's blood pressure had risen one iota, although I suspect the person on the other end of the line needed a cold drink when it was over.' Graham was a master of intimidation. 'He knew just how to slowly begin to remove his wristwatch in such a way that the person he was staring down would become very afraid of this madman and back off.'

Larry was one of the few people who knew how to handle that. 'With Bill, you have to learn how to work against him while working with him,' Magid said enigmatically. But Graham's behaviour had now entered a new dimension. 'All of a sudden, everybody was coming to me and I'd have to translate Bill's understanding of the problem to them and handle the meetings that Bill could never have.'

What Larry knew was that a lot was going wrong in Bill Graham's private life. He was suffering from chronic fatigue and was taking Halcion, a drug for insomnia, which made him put his head down in meetings and just go to sleep. 'The fatigue, or whatever it was, would hit him.' Larry and Bill's assistant, Jan, would talk all the time. 'What's wrong with Bill? What's going on with Bill? Is he okay?'. But Larry knew well enough that there were other issues in Bill's life. He was going through a breakup and, at the same time, was trying to make a decision between two women that he had been having affairs with. His longtime on-off lover, Regina Cartwright, had asked him to marry her. He had said no, but was then cut up when she began another relationship.

After Bill had finished shouting and railing, Larry would meet separately with Jan to sort out pragmatic solutions. 'We got a lot of stuff done while he was asleep. I don't know if it would have worked without Jan. We had five really top-notch stage managers, who worked as a team, and I'd have meetings with them after Bill talked. We'd talk openly about what our problems were – with the acts and the managers – and how to resolve them.' All the progress was being made when Bill wasn't there.

Added to all that, Graham was under pressure, as the Live Aid date approached, from more and more artists asking to be put on the Philadelphia line-up. In the final week, close to 100 recording artists had asked to participate in the American show – obviously far more than could possibly perform. Graham started ringing Harvey's office in London, pushing acts that Geldof and Goldsmith did not want. Many were performers with whom Graham had long-standing relationships or merchandising deals. Saying no to top-flight artists 'could end the relationship', said the New York promoter John Scher, sympathising with Graham.

Artists and managers were jockeying for position. It was nightmarish, said Scher.

In the end, Graham was forced to turn down several big-name bands, despite starting the US show three hours early and shortening some sets to squeeze additional performers on to the bill. On the day, there were thirty-nine acts in Philadelphia compared with just twenty-two at Wembley.

Why did Bill Graham behave in such a way? There is a clue in his auto-biography – *Bill Graham Presents: My Life Inside Rock and Out*. One chapter deals with this period in which he lost the Rolling Stones as a client; his office was firebombed; he struggled with Live Aid; the longest relationship he'd ever had with a woman broke up; he discovered that the drug Halcion could change your personality; and he began thrice-weekly sessions with a psychiatrist. The chapter is entitled 'Breakdown'. 'He was losing the plot,' said Andrew Zweck. 'If you read his book, it's clear that he was having addiction problems, relationship problems, he was in mental decline, he was lost.' If the most famous rock 'n' roll promoter in the world was not having a breakdown, he was on the brink of one.

Larry Magid thought he could handle him. But the top television producers Mitchell and Verna had been pushed beyond breaking point – which was why they arrived with the police.

After hearing them air their grievances, Larry calmly took control. 'This isn't going to do this show any good. You don't want this type of notoriety,' he told Mike Mitchell. 'And as I said, we're covered. We're good. Five great stage managers. Michael Ahern is calling the show. We can rustle these acts on and off the stage.' He knew that the feeling from Harvey in London was that Philadelphia wasn't going to pull this show off at all. 'But I never lost confidence that this was going to happen.' And he knew that, from the global Live Aid point of view, the television was not incidental but fundamental to the success of the enterprise.

The wildman Graham had to be kept away from it.

Larry tracked down Bill, who had been taken aback by the appearance of the police. Larry had a plan: he would put Bill in the wings of the stage, where he knew Graham would feel in the centre of the action. But he would use Mike Ahern and the four other stage managers as a buffer to keep Graham away from the rest of the operation. 'So I said, "Bill, you stay on stage. We're gonna take care of everything else in running the show. Do not come off of the stage. Okay?" And whatever crisis he was going through, a breakdown or whatever, he knew that at the end, I saved his ass from getting arrested.'

It was a massive risk, but Larry was sanguine. 'We knew what to do. We knew the stadium. We knew all the city people. We had everything tied up. We knew that this was going to be a moment in history … and I thought that I could handle Bill Graham.'

What if the gamble failed? Larry shrugged. 'We were all going to bask in the sunlight of this show. Or we were going to look fucking stupid and it would mark us forever.'

CHAPTER 12

THE DAY THAT ROCKED THE WORLD

There was no helicopter landing spot at Wembley Stadium. This was a problem. The roads would be too crowded on the morning of the Live Aid concert, so all the stars were supposed to be arriving by air. The nearest landing space was a cricket pitch behind Wembley Park tube. Unfortunately, 13 July 1985 was – in addition to being the day of the biggest concert in the history of the planet – also the climax of the British Transport Sports Club cricket tournament. And, no, Noel Edmonds was told, the match couldn't be postponed.

The British TV presenter, as a sideline to his broadcasting work, owned a helicopter company based across the river in Battersea. Flying was a hobby. But, on Live Aid day, he was responsible for what was the largest civil helicopter airlift ever conducted. 'Somewhere along the line,' Edmonds recalled, 'someone had realised that if all the stars and hangers-on arrived at the same time, there could be 3,000 people backstage all at once. So the arrival and departure of these people throughout the entire day had to be staggered and a helicopter airlift was the easiest way to do that.'

The Civil Aviation Authority gave the Live Aid helicopters priority on London flight paths, but the Wembley cricketers were reluctant to do the same. Eventually, a good old British compromise was negotiated. The cricket match would continue, but whenever a helicopter was to about to land, the umpire would blow a whistle, lift the bails and the players would move to the boundary while the aircraft landed and discharged its cargo of rock superstars.

It was a day of jolly japes. Someone from David Bowie's management team had told the helicopter company that Bowie would only fly in a helicopter with a blue interior. 'We managed to find one,' said Edmonds, and when Bowie arrived, the pilot proudly showed him the inside of the aircraft. 'He looked at me as if I were mad,' Edmonds said. 'He didn't give a shit what colour the helicopter was.' But, by the afternoon, the cricket pavilion was hosting a wedding reception. As yet another helicopter landed, the wedding guests protested at the noise and demanded an end to the landings. 'Leave this to me,' said Bowie. He walked into the wedding reception, shouted, 'Sorry to interrupt, but we just want to say we're sorry about the noise' and had his photograph taken with the bride and groom, after which there were no more complaints.

For others, like Gary Kemp of Spandau Ballet, it was a more overwhelming experience. 'I flew in with the rest of the band and Kenney Jones, the drummer with the Who. It hit us then, flying over the stadium and seeing the thousands of people coming into the stadium. There was this sense of a grand event going on that could equal England winning the World Cup in 1966 or the Coronation in 1953. It was a day when, no matter how young you were, you'd remember where you were.'

Harvey Goldsmith had woken early and looked out of his bedroom window. The sun was shining. The air was crystal-clear. It was going to be a hot day. But the sun prompted him to think of something else. As soon as he arrived at Wembley, he sent one of the crew out to buy forty clocks. 'I want a clock in every dressing room, every entrance on stage, the green room, the catering room, anywhere you can think of,' he told one of his staff. By each clock, a notice was fixed, which said: 'I don't care what time you go on, but I do care what time you come off. Please stick to the time.' The precise dovetailing of two shows, on opposite sides of the Atlantic, was his primary preoccupation. And it was to remain so throughout the day.

'Every running order,' recalled Andy Zweck, 'had on it in big, bold letters: "KILL TIME AND YOU MURDER SUCCESS".' Messages were posted on hundreds of scraps of paper on a noticeboard. Harvey became an absolute stickler for punctuality.

'I told every band, every production manager, every manager, that if they went on five minutes late, they lost a number. And if they overran, the power would be turn off midstream.' He erected a traffic light system just off stage: green meant five minutes to go, yellow two minutes left and red meant 'get off the stage now'.

Goldsmith also made it clear that no one at all was allowed at the side of the stage and put heavy security guards on either side to enforce it. 'The only people I want on that stage are the artists playing and the next band ready to go on,' Harvey said. 'It worked,' he said, looking back forty years later. 'If you look at the TV pictures, you'll see that in Philadelphia there's people all over the bloody place. But in London there was no one: everybody played the game.' Apart from, he omitted to mention the Who. Pete Townshend rebelliously kicked the traffic lights and smashed one of them towards the end of the day. 'Because of the way the satellites travelled, we could lose contact with one before the next clicked in. I didn't want any gaps. I wanted everything to flow perfectly. I'd worked out my timings to the minute with the production crew. It was nerve-wracking because no one had ever done a show with this many major acts ever before.'

Half an hour before Live Aid began, at 11.30 a.m., the Prince and Princess of Wales arrived in the Wembley stadium banqueting hall to meet the stars. Almost everyone invited to join the line-up to meet the royals turned up – even those who would not be playing for another nine hours.

The usual rock cool was set aside, observed Andrew Zweck, and the star-struck stars came early to meet Princess Diana, who was at the peak of her popularity: 'Everyone wanted to have a photograph taken with her.'

As she came down the line, said John Kennedy, the Band Aid lawyer, 'Bob's flirting with her. She's flirting with Bob.' Paula Yates curtsied and gently pushed forward their daughter Fifi to present the princess with a slender bunch of flowers.

'She had to stop at a petrol station on the way to Wembley because she remembered she hadn't got any flowers for Princess Diana,' remembered Paula's TV producer, Jill S. Sinclair. Only at the last minute did Paula realise that the cheap garage-bought pink and white roses still had the price sticker on them.

'Fifi hadn't wanted to present the flowers, so Paula had bribed her with the promise of some more smoked salmon. When Fifi handed over the flowers, she said to the princess, "More fish, please".'

Pete Smith had made sure that Status Quo were at the front of the line-up. As soon as they had shaken hands with the royal couple, Pete rushed them off to the stage to start the show. It was a tricky passage to negotiate. The ancient stadium had only one small crowded corridor, so Pete took the opening band out of the protected backstage area and through a turnstile area filled with concert-goers, who immediately parted to let the musicians through.

The show began bang on time.

'It's 12 noon in London, 7 a.m. in Philadelphia, and around the world it's time for Live Aid,' boomed the voice of DJ Richard Skinner. 'Sixteen hours of live music, in aid of famine relief in Africa.' The Coldstream Guards sounded a royal fanfare as the prince and princess, followed by Bob Geldof, entered the royal box.

As Status Quo struck up 'Rockin' All Over the World', Prince Charles leaned over to Geldof and asked in clipped tones: 'Why did you pick these chaps to start?' Bob replied: 'Well, Sir, with the denim, the telecasters, the twelve-bar blues and the long hair, they are archetypal rock 'n' roll.'

'Theirs was,' wrote Pete Smith, 'the last word in first sets.' The band's lead singer, Francis Rossi, had a similar reaction: 'With a large audience like that, you do usually get a good vibe, but there was something totally unique and I'm not sure I've ever felt it since. It went in such a flash. We came off stage and got pissed real quick. I just hung about for the rest of the day. I think we'd been off a while when Bob came up and said, "Fucking hell – apparently there are two billion people watching." I thought, *I'm glad you didn't tell me that before.*'

During the next set, by the Style Council, Geldof slipped away from his place next to Charles and Diana in the royal box. In the wings, he lay down on a flight case. 'My back is killing me,' he declared.

'Turn over,' said David Bowie and one of his childhood heroes proceeded to give him a back massage. 'That's a great rock 'n' roll moment,' Bob later said – 'one of the most amazing moments in an amazing day.'

'Geldof, come on, we're on,' a Boomtown Rat called out and suddenly he was on the stage, the crowd having reserved their wildest cheers of the day for his arrival. 'The size of it, the enormity of this, hadn't struck me 'til then. It was like everyone I've ever said hello to in my life was conceivably watching this.' Officially, the crowd before him numbered 72,000, but there were a lot more packed in. Andrew Zweck later discovered that some of the turnstiles had been taking money to allow people in without tickets. But all Geldof knew was that this crowd was unlike anything he had seen before.

It was a moment which was originally not meant to be. Harvey Goldsmith had been adamant that Geldof should not play. 'We didn't have time, I knew we were gonna overrun. We had so many great acts on the show and he was stuffing more and more acts into it. I just felt that we've gotta draw the line somewhere.'

But the line was not to be drawn there. The Rats did three numbers, beginning with their biggest hit, 'I Don't Like Mondays'. But today the song about a US school shooting took on an entirely different meeting.

They can see no reasons, 'cos there are no reasons.

Forty years on, Geldof reflected that 'there is literally no reason why human beings should need to die when we live in a world of surplus food. That was in my mind that day.'

Tell me why…

'And I became aware of the build-up to the line I was going to sing next, and I knew it was fucking mad.'

The lesson today is how to die.

He paused, seized with a sudden clarity of purpose. The crowd screamed but Geldof stood stock-still and silent. This, he thought, is what I was put on this earth to do. He looked at the crowd, his hand held aloft, and then let it fall. He felt no sadness that the moment could not be prolonged. It was enough – this clear instant of absolute certainty.

The song continued. The crowd roared. 'Thank you very much,' said the singer. 'I just realised today is the best day of my life.'

Shortly afterwards, the Prince and Princess of Wales slipped away. 'He had to go to his mother's for lunch,' quipped Geldof afterwards. After lunch with the Queen, the Prince went off to play polo, where he reportedly said to a friend as he arrived: 'It was brilliantly organised. That Bob Geldof chap should have been a general.'

The royal couple's early departure meant that they missed the performance by Geldof's fellow Band Aid trustee, Midge Ure, though he was unaware of it until after he came off stage.

'My overriding emotion was terror,' Midge said. 'This was the biggest show I was ever going to do.' He hadn't slept much the night before, worrying about what could go wrong. But when he walked on stage, wearing the long grey silk coat he'd bought in Los Angeles two days before, his sunglasses disguised any nerves. The front page of the *Sunday Times* the next day was a close-up of those mirrored glasses, with the massive Wembley crowd reflected in them.

As he began to sing, the fear dropped away, replaced by a huge wave of excitement. 'When we started the intro to "Vienna", the crowd went ballistic,' he said. 'The atmosphere was electric, buzzing, the same buzz as I'd had when I had my first hit. Live Aid was that moment magnified a million times. A perfect moment.'

But as soon as he came off stage, he was surrounded by paparazzi.

'How do you feel about being shafted by Bob?'

'What do you mean?'

'You were swapped round with the Boomtown Rats so that he could perform for the royals.'

'Naw,' said Midge, determined not to sully the day by giving the tabloids a headline. But privately he was shocked at the idea. Shocked, but not surprised. 'In the weeks leading up to Live Aid, I had felt increasingly sidelined,' he said later. 'For the six months since Band Aid, it had been the two of us – Bob Geldof and Midge Ure. All of a sudden, it was Bob everywhere, while I had been relegated to the same stature as every other artist.'

That was not how Geldof saw it. He had needed Midge to make the record; now he needed Harvey to do the concerts. 'I invited him to jump into the front seat of the car I was driving, then when we stopped to pick up Harvey, I asked him to move to the back seat while Harvey took his place,' said Bob. Then the car stopped to pick up John Kennedy to set up the Band Aid Trust. 'When we stopped for Kennedy, Harvey moved back with Midge. The car has kept driving for forty years and everyone's still there in the car.'

Who changed the Wembley running order? Harvey Goldsmith was anxious that the finger of blame should not be pointed in his direction. 'It actually wasn't my decision. Probably Bob's decision, really.' But Geldof denied it. 'I didn't even know we'd been swapped,' he later said. 'I certainly wouldn't have requested that. I couldn't give a toss, just so long as we were on.'

Whoever took the decision, Midge felt slighted. 'It didn't spoil the day for me. Nothing could have done that. But I did feel dreadfully let down.'

Time salved the hurt. In 2013, Midge wrote that 'my negative feelings passed long, long ago. I never mentioned it to Bob because Bob, more than anyone, has always known what I contributed. At a Capital Awards Ceremony for Band Aid last year, Bob stood up and said: "I will start straight off by saying this would never have happened without Midge Ure." The entire audience stood up. I got a standing ovation – and I wasn't even there.'

Forty years on, Midge Ure is still a Band Aid trustee.

⁂

To Pete Smith, it was day full of unsung acts of heroism. Hero of the day, for him, was Elvis Costello. Originally, Pete had agreed that Elvis would play four songs, with his band, but as the running order came under increased pressure, Pete had whittled that down to three songs, and then two. Finally, he had rung Elvis on tour in Melbourne and said there would be time for only one song, without his band – solo, out in front, as the revolving platform turned to replace Spandau Ballet with Nik Kershaw. He half-expected Costello's manager, Jake Riviera, to declare that his client would not come for just a single song.

But, on the day, Costello turned up and, instead of singing 'Oliver's Army', as Pete Smith expected, he took to the stage and sang another man's song. 'I want you to help me sing this old northern English folk song,' he told the crowd before breaking into the Beatles' 'All You Need is Love'.

It was the very song that Geldof had taken as his template for the Band Aid single. It wasn't part of Costello's his usual repertoire; he had lines from the song scribbled on the back of his hand. But he did not need them. The delighted crowd sang them back to him as loudly as he sang to them, crystalising how the phenomenon of Live Aid was as much about the audience as the performers.

As Pete Smith later wrote, 'the line of the day was his and John Lennon's: "There's nothing you can do that can't be done."' Costello was suggesting that Live Aid was about 'how far there still was to go, rather than how far we'd come', as one pop critic put it. When Pete thanked him as he left the stage, Elvis shrugged a little smile and simply said, 'Pleased to do my bit.'

Among those watching was Paul McCartney at his home in Surrey.

Rather than putting him in the mood, the television was making him ever more nervous. Having not played in public for so long, the roar of the massive televised crowd only added to his anxiety.

In the car up to London, listening to the concert on the car radio, he became even more anxious.

'I don't think I can do this. It's been six years since I've played anything,' he told his wife, Linda, who told Geldof she had replied to her husband: 'Shut up. You're doing it.'

By the time his Mercedes got to the stadium and he changed ready for his appearance later in the day, he had donned a carapace of cool. Artists like Dylan and the Beatles had long been doing 'save-the-world kind of songs' like 'All You Need is Love', he said, expertly fielding a series of sceptical questions from a television interviewer. Despite the selfish materialism of the age, the ordinary British public were no less charitable than in previous eras. 'Whenever television comes over with those kind of pictures, you'll find people responding' in an outpouring of hope and idealism, he said. 'It's all there. It just needs to be awoken … and it needs people like Bob to organise it.'

Backstage, the artists were given a dressing room to use for half an hour before their performance to fix hair, make-up and wardrobe – and then another half an hour after they came off stage. Space was extremely limited. 'There was one little corridor and one dressing-room area, where there were four Portakabins left by Bruce Springsteen,' said Andrew Zweck. 'There was no space for anything more. There were six artists per Portakabin.' When their time was up, they had to remove everything and vacate. 'There was a man on the gate, but the rule was respected automatically,' said Pete Smith.

'Every artist that came to play at Wembley knew why they were there,' said Harvey Goldsmith. 'They were totally open to being pushed around like they'd never been pushed around before.' Once their time in the dressing-room plaza was up, they all migrated to the ad hoc café which had been built for them backstage.

The Mayfair restaurant owner, Isaac Tigrett, had offered free food and drink to the artists all day. 'Build me something and I'll make it into the Hard Rock Café,' he told Andy Zweck, who found a little bit of space on the edge of the Wembley car park area and built a plywood replica of the original. Tigrett dressed it with artefacts from his Hyde Park Corner venue: guitars, costumes, albums and gold discs. It was the same menu, same furniture, same tablecloths and same waiting staff outfits. The food the café provided was of the same standard as the West End restaurant, but everyone worked for free.

'Tigrett was a kind of mystical, spiritual character,' recalled Zweck. At the start of the day, while everyone was busy, he brought the whole café to a standstill.

'Stop everything. Everybody, come, form a circle. Hold hands,' Tigrett shouted.

A slightly mystified Zweck joined in.

'No matter who you are, no matter how small your role is today, you are important. This is one of the most significant things you've ever done. This is gonna be a day that you remember for the rest of your life.'

And he was right, said Zweck. 'I'm telling you, everybody who was in that circle with him will tell you the same. It *was* one of the greatest experiences we ever had.' And that moment of inspiration and dedication was a key part of it.

It was a hot day, and a confined space, but Tigrett's Hard Rock Café was packed all day with a firmament of stars. The food and drink was served for twelve hours on a complimentary basis, but the big jars along the bar, with signs asking for donations, were so full that they had to be emptied regularly.

'We all ended up paying fifty quid for a burger,' laughed Midge Ure afterwards. 'It was a stroke of genius.'

The staff at Wembley noted with pride that their jars contained three times the amount in cash donations compared to the Hard Rock Café in Philadelphia. That may have had something to do with Bill Graham. On his way to the stage in the JFK Stadium, the impresario spotted the US version backstage. Inevitably, he started to rant.

'Who gave permission for this to be here?' he railed.

'You did, Bill.'

'Oh, did I? Okay, then.'

And the day had only just begun for him.

❖

◀ 8 a.m. on Sunday 25 November 1984: Bob Geldof and Midge Ure anxiously wait outside Sarm West Studios in London to see if anyone will turn up to record the Band Aid single.'If it's only the Boomtown Rats and Ultravox, it'll be a fucking dull record,' Bob says. (Getty)

▶ Paul Weller and Bob Geldof set aside their old musical rivalry to rehearse 'Do They Know It's Christmas?' as the stars assemble. (Getty)

◀ Bob Geldof talks to Jill Sinclair, co-owner of Sarm West Studios, who donated the recording time to make the charity single. Stars nervously introducing themselves to one another in the control room include Paul Young, Bono and Simon Le Bon. Engineer Stuart Bruce, who looks on, didn't remove his flat cap all day. (Getty)

BAND AID are

1 Adam Clayton	15 Jody Watley	29 Francis Rossi
2 Phil Collins	16 Bono	30 Robert 'Kool' B
3 Bob Geldof	17 Paul Weller	31 Dennis Thomas
4 Steve Norman	18 James Taylor	32 Andy Taylor
5 Chris Cross	19 Peter Blake (sleeve artist)	33 Jon Moss
6 John Taylor	20 George Michael	34 Sting
7 Paul Young	21 Midge Ure	35 Rick Parfitt
8 Tony Hadley	22 Martin Ware	36 Nick Rhodes
9 Glenn Gregory	23 John Keeble	37 Johnny Fingers
10 Simon Le Bon	24 Gary Kemp	ALSO FEATURING:
11 Simon Crowe	25 Roger Taylor	David Bowie
12 Marilyn	26 Sarah	Boy George
13 Keren	27 Siobhan	Holly
14 Martin Kemp	28 Peter Briquette	Paul McCartney

▲ The assembled stars of Band Aid 1984. 'It was like the school photo,' said Midge. 'All these giant stars were shuffling along, being awkward around each other.' Key to the photo taken from the *Daily Mirror*. (Getty)

▲ Prime Minister Margaret Thatcher's eyes turn icy-blue as an unusually quietly spoken Bob Geldof confronts her over her decision to tax Band Aid's single for Ethopia. 'It's not as simple as that, Mr Geldof.' 'No, Prime Minister, nothing is as simple as dying.' (Getty)

◀ Dazed and bewildered, Bob Geldof looks around the refugee camp at Mekele, in the heart of Ethiopia's famine zone in January 1985. One dying child has haunted him ever since. 'He will not die in my imagination. Nothing can free him from the agonising process of death, which is fixed in my mind.' (Getty)

▲ Inspired by the Band Aid record, a host of top US stars made their own charity single, 'We Are the World'. Among them: Al Jarreau, Dionne Warwick, Lionel Richie, Kenny Rogers, Cindy Lauper, Bruce Springsteen, James Ingram, Bob Dylan, Diana Ross and Ray Charles. (Getty)

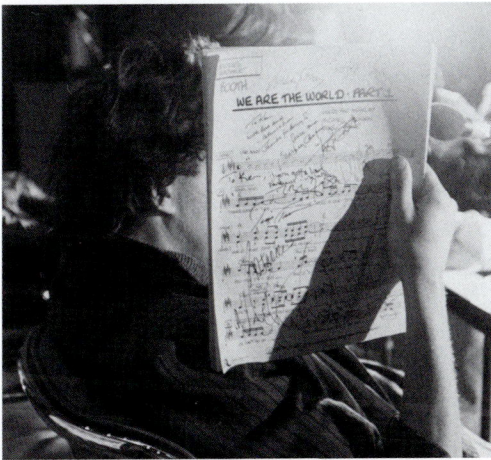

◀ Many of the top US music stars at the USA for Africa recording were so exhilarated at meeting one another, often for the first time, that they all autographed each other's sheet music. Here Bob Geldof holds up his copy at A&M Recording Studios in Los Angeles. (Getty)

▶ Bob Geldof tells the US media they have a moral responsibility to promote 'We Are the World' to save people in Africa. The 'USA for Africa' press conference in Los Angeles was also addressed by singer Harry Belafonte, music manager Ken Kragen and producer Quincy Jones – the team behind the US single. (Getty)

FEED THE WORLD

PHIL RUSHTED   BOB GELDOF   HARVEY GOLDSMITH   KEVIN JENDEN

Dom Fiorovanti   Bill Graham   Hal Uplinger   Harvey Schiller   Tony Verna

WEMBLEY STADIUM
Harvey Goldsmith, Maurice Jones & Bob Geldof present for
BAND AID
LIVE AID
[See Press for details]   TURNSTILES F
SAT., 13 JULY, 1985
GATES OPEN 10.00 a.m.
No ticket genuine unless it carries the
Wembley Lion superimposed on the Towers
Ticket £5 incl. VAT plus £20 donation
All proceeds to BAND AID
TO BE RETAINED   ISSUED SUBJECT TO THE CONDITIONS ON BACK

▼ 10 June 1985: Bob Geldof announces Live Aid to the media. He reels off a fantastic list of stars who will be appearing – though lots of them haven't yet agreed to perform. Bob is flanked by Band Aid accountant Phil Rushted, concert promoter Harvey Goldsmith and the director of the Band Aid Trust, Kevin Jenden. (Getty)

▲ Smiles all round at the US launch of Live Aid. From the left: Alan Hunter and Dom Fiorovanti from MTV, promoter Bill Graham, producer Hal Uplinger, marketer Harvey Schiller and TV director Tony Verna. What the others don't know is that soon Graham will be working to sabotage the event. (Getty)

◀ Ticket for the Live Aid Wembley concert. The government insisted on imposing VAT on the ticket price. So Geldof fixed it at just £5 – and asked everyone to add a £20 donation that Margaret Thatcher could not tax. (Getty)

▼ In the royal box, Bob Geldof 'explains' Status Quo to Prince Charles, while David Bowie chats with Roger Taylor and Brian May of Queen. Princess Diana is hoping Phil Collins will come on before they have to leave for lunch with the Queen. Sadly he didn't. (Getty)

▲ There were supposed to be 72,000 in the crowd for Live Aid at Wembley Stadium but entries beyond the originally proposed limit brought the total to nearer 80,000. (Getty)

▼ Bob Geldof raises his hand as he sings 'The lesson today is how to die'. The line takes on a new meaning – in the context of a famine in which a million people are thought to have perished. (Getty)

▲ Bono is held back by security after jumping from the stage and beckoning to a woman he said was in danger of being crushed in the crowd. It took so long that U2 ran out of time to play their current hit 'Pride (In the Name of Love)'. (Getty)

◄ Bono is comforted by Bob while leaving the stage – thinking he has blown U2's big moment. (Getty)

▼ Queen wave to the Wembley crowd at the end of a magical set that steals the show at Live Aid. Twenty years later it was voted the greatest rock gig in history. (Getty)

◤ Paul McCartney and David Bowie lark about for the cameras backstage ahead of their Live Aid appearances. Beneath his outward high spirits the former Beatles was very nervous. He hadn't played in public since before the death of John Lennon in 1980.

▲ Geldof passes the mic around a stage full of stars to take individual lines in a joyous chaotic version 'Do They Know It's Christmas?' After the Wembley finale, London handed over to Philadelphia for another five hours of music. Almost 2 billion people watched all round the world.

▶ An exhausted Bob Geldof and his partner Paula Yates backstage at Wembley Stadium after Live Aid.

(All images: Getty)

▲ An aerial view of the packed JFK Stadium in Philadelphia for the US leg of the Live Aid concert. As many as 100,000 people crammed in before a stage that was 'nine storeys high and as wide as a football field' – said to be the biggest stage ever built for a rock concert. (Getty)

▶ It ought to have been one of the greatest moments of Live Aid – Bob Dylan backed by Keith Richards and Ronnie Wood. In the event the final act in Philadelphia was catastrophic. The expression on Dylan's face says it all. (Getty)

◀ Lionel Richie and Harry Belafonte in an exuberant rendition of 'We Are the World' – bringing to an end sixteen hours of music in the biggest fundraising event the world had ever seen. (Getty)

▶ Reality check: after the exhilaration of the Live Aid concerts, Bob Geldof is once more confronted by the scale of Africa's need. Surrounded by refugees fleeing famine and war in Sudan and Chad in December 1985, he knows Live Aid is only a beginning, not an end. (Getty)

One of the unheralded innovations of the day was the number of stars who teamed up with others to perform. Geldof had wanted the Police to perform, but the band had just unofficially broken up. 'I wasn't gonna be with the Police, but I said I'll do it on my own,' said Sting. 'And then Bob teamed me and Phil Collins up together because he was on his own too. Johnny No Mates,' he laughed. 'Because Bob had been so successful with his first project, hugely successful, we thought: *Okay, he thought that would work. Let's see if this does.*'

Phil Collins felt the same. Genesis were off the road, songwriting, and Collins had been out promoting his successful solo albums. Bob and Harvey decided to put the two men together. It would save time for the running order and produce an interesting chemistry. And so it proved as they each sang a couple of their own songs and then joined together for two more.

❖

The partnerships of Phil Collins then became transatlantic. Immediately leaving Sting at the side of the stage, Collins was greeted by Pete Smith bearing a ticket for Concorde. It had arrived shortly before, courtesy of a representative of British Airways. The BA man had three tickets, one for Collins and his wife Jill, and one for Pete Smith.

'I'm not going,' said Pete. 'I'm staying here to see Paul McCartney.' Then he shouted around the room. 'Anybody want to go to New York and has their passport with them?'

'I'll go,' said one of the barmen from the Hard Rock Café. 'I always carry my passport – along with a banana, in case I get hungry.'

'Well, just make sure you eat it on the flight,' the barman was told, 'because US Customs won't let you take fruit into America.'

Minutes later, the barman, along with Phil and Jill Collins, climbed aboard a helicopter, piloted by Noel Edmonds, who flew them to Heathrow. There they boarded the supersonic jet to New York. 'All the baggage handlers came out to wave goodbye,' Collins recalled. After the plane took off, it made a short detour from the New York flight path to make a deliberate pass and aerial salute over Wembley Stadium. The crowd cheered wildly at the interconnected madness of it all.

There was, coincidentally, another singer on board. 'Cher was on the flight, just heading back to the States,' Collins recalled. 'I'd never met her before, so I went over and said hi. She asked what was going on. I told her about Live Aid.' Somehow, news of the whole Live Aid enterprise had escaped Cher, who was on her way back from the Cannes Film Festival. 'She asked whether I could get her on. I told her to just turn up.' And she did, joining in the Philadelphia finale of 'We Are the World'.

But before that, Phil had visited the aeroplane's cockpit. 'I was supposed to do a live broadcast from Concorde,' he recalled. But the technology failed. All the BBC picked up from the flight was a torrent of static and crackle. Forty years later, cleaned-up audio reveals both a portentous foreboding and tentative uncertainty about the reunion that Collins was jetting into: 'I'm playing with Robert Plant, Jimmy Page and John Paul Jones in the, er, I was going to say Zeppelin band, but it's not that, it's just the guys who were in the band playing old Zep songs. I saw their first-ever concert at the Marquee. I'm an old fan. I'm well versed in the Zeppelin stuff.' Jimmy Page was about to vehemently disagree.

CHAPTER 13

BACK IN THE USSR

Flying to America was the easy part. Travel in the other direction meant penetrating the Iron Curtain. This was a period of heightened Cold War tension between the Western world and the Soviet bloc. The nuclear arms race was continuing unabated and the superpower rivalry was being fought out in proxy wars in Afghanistan, Nicaragua, Angola, Mozambique and Ethiopia.

But there were early signs of diplomatic openings. Only a few months before, Mikhail Gorbachev, a reformer, had become general secretary of the Communist Party of the Soviet Union. Live Aid had sought to prise open the Iron Curtain a little more by sending Richard Lukens to Moscow. Lukens was one of a group of communication enthusiasts who had opened up an experimental TV link between the US and the Soviet Union three years earlier. The goal of the US/USSR Space-Bridge was to foster mutual understanding between ordinary Americans and Russians at a time of high geopolitical tensions.

Five weeks before the Live Aid concert, Lukens had boarded a jet to Moscow with three requests from Bob Geldof: Bob wanted the Russians to broadcast the Live Aid concert over the state radio and television network, Gosteleradio; he asked General Secretary Gorbachev to tape a one-minute message to endorse the concert; and he wanted the Russian authorities to allow two of the country's rock bands – Autograph and Time Machine – to appear, live via satellite, during the broadcast.

At 15.55, London time, on Live Aid day, another chink appeared in the Iron Curtain when the international satellite feed presented Autograph playing two numbers – 'Vertigo' and 'We Need Peace' – live from a studio in Moscow.

It was not without its problems. For the first two minutes of the Russian prog-rock band's performance, the global audience saw a propaganda film of happy workers picking cherries in Bulgaria. At first, Wembley assumed this was the video for a song, but when people on screen started interviewing other people with a microphone, they realised they'd got the wrong video feed and got on the phone to Moscow to get the correct one patched in.

Geldof was disappointed in two other respects. Gorbachev didn't send his one-minute message. The broadcast was not fed to the TV sets of the Russian people and was apparently seen only by the 150 teenagers in the Moscow studio. And Time Machine were nowhere to be seen, perhaps unsurprisingly since the band – hugely popular in the USSR – had a more rebellious reputation which often saw them incorporating subtle criticism of Soviet life in their lyrics. Recently, it had had one of its songs publicly denounced by the Soviet authorities as 'depressive and ideologically unsound'.

Yet for all that, Live Aid was witnessing another historic moment – for both Russian rock and East–West relations: a global link-up across the Iron Curtain. The youth of the world for a few moments caught a glimpse beyond the grey monolithic image of the Soviet Union and saw young people like themselves, albeit with a few incongruous members of the KGB among the crowd in the studio. Fewer than five years later, the Berlin Wall would come down.

⁂

As if to prove that technical hitches were not exclusive to the Communist bloc, at 4 p.m. Bryan Ferry came on stage at Wembley with Pink Floyd's David Gilmour on guitar.

'I have terrible memories of it all going wrong,' lamented Ferry. 'I'd put together an all-star band and the set was fraught with problems. Poor David, his guitar wasn't working for the first couple of songs. With his first hit, the drummer put his stick through the drum skin. And then my microphone wasn't working, which for a singer is a bit of a handicap. A roadie ran on with another mic, so then I was holding two mics taped together and I wasn't really sure which one to sing into.'

Still, for all that, he concluded 'it was a great day, though'. Ferry was not alone in thinking that. So many of the artists who performed felt something they found hard to put into words. 'There was a difference to the day that few can still explain,' said Geldof. 'It was more than a great joy. It was a sense of something other – as if the promise of rock 'n' roll had finally been realised.'

It is unlikely that Cat Stevens would have said the same. As Bryan Ferry was performing, there was a squawk from Pete Smith's walkie-talkie.

'We have Yusuf Islam here, with his brother,' said the doorkeeper using the name the singer had adopted since he converted to Islam. 'They are not on any of our lists.'

'Send them up, please,' Pete said. He had been plotting this, without telling anybody. He had kept a couple of spare passes for them, but no one, apart from Andrew Zweck, the production manager, knew they might be coming.

Pete showed them to a table in the middle of the dressing room village plaza and sent for Harvey and Bob. He said to them: 'We have a few minutes during the next revolve, immediately after Bryan Ferry's set, for Yusuf to play a song with his acoustic guitar, front centre stage, just as Elvis Costello had just done, so effectively. It would be a surprise, even to the BBC.'

Bob wanted to know what he would sing. Yusuf replied that he would sing an Islamic children's song. That was no good, said Bob. The fundamental principle of Live Aid was that only top-selling artists could play. He could do a top Cat Stevens hit – 'Morning Has Broken', 'Wide World' or 'The First Cut is the Deepest'. This was the global jukebox. The singer refused; that was a world he had left behind. Sorry, said Bob. The singer departed. A chastened Pete Smith was left to cope with the realisation that he had seriously overstepped his authority.

❊

The moment was approaching when the live link-up with Philadelphia would begin. Harvey Goldsmith had selected Paul Young, then a huge success in the US, to be the handover artist. The technical auguries were not good. Young had had to play his set, which included a duet with Alison Moyet, while listening through his monitor to a roadie soundchecking

U2's drum kit. To make matters worse, the segue between Wembley and Philadelphia had not been rehearsed.

'I watched Bob Geldof approach Paul Young on stage at 5 p.m.,' Pete Smith later wrote. 'Bob was welcoming Philadelphia to the show. Bryan Adams would be relayed live from America any minute. Paul had not been briefed about this. He clearly thought that Bob was casually joining him for the last verses on stage.'

The precise handling of the handover had only just been worked out by Harvey Goldsmith, Andrew Zweck and Pete Smith, who had been huddled with Bob at stage right. 'There was no way of communicating with Paul mid-song. The BBC had no route to address the live audience in the JFK Stadium. It had to be done live from the Wembley stage.' Bob Geldof strolled out onto the stage and announced: 'Wembley, will you please welcome America to Live Aid Day? Hello America, welcome to the world. Have a great day. Have as good a day as we're having, and please, please give us as much money as we know you have, like everybody else around the world.'

As Bryan Adams was launching into 'Summer of '69' on the transatlantic link-up from Philadelphia, a meeting was taking place in one of the dressing rooms backstage at Wembley. Bono had been told to sit down by the other members of U2. 'They said, "Let us remind you yet again, we are a group",' recalled Band Aid's lawyer, John Kennedy. '"You are not the lead man and us, the backing band. We are a group." And Bono says, "Why would you even need to say that? Of course, I get that." And the band said, "Okay, but do not treat us as your backing band", yet that was precisely what he went on to do.'

In Philadelphia, Jack Nicholson introduced U2 at Wembley. Despite growing success in the UK and the US, at that point U2 were not the major globe-straddling band that they would later become. Bono felt the need to tell the world that U2 were a band 'from Dublin City, Ireland'. After starting with 'Sunday Bloody Sunday', U2's cry for peace in Ireland, Bono jumped onto a lower stage, having first dragged a television cameraman with him.

During their second number, 'Bad', he repeated the trick, but this time he began beckoning to several young women in the audience, encouraging them to join him on the stage. Venturing further out of sight, he made an even more precipitous 8-foot jump to a platform built for press photographers and security guards. He could now no longer be seen by the rest of U2, who just carried on playing blind. Pointing to a few individuals in the crowd, one woman was dragged out of the throng by the security men to join Bono. The two slow-danced for a few moments before he kissed her and she made her way back to the crowd – an intimate moment with one member of a 72,000-strong audience and a global viewership of more than a billion. It was, said one euphoric pop writer, a moment of connection which forged a powerful subliminal message that 'we were all united on this day'.

That was not how the rest of U2 saw it. Bono had jumped down so far that he was totally out of sight of the other three members of the band. Not knowing what was going on, they kept playing the song's instrumental riff like the musical equivalent, one pop critic later wrote, of a plane circling the airspace near Heathrow, awaiting permission to land. At the side of the stage, U2's manager Paul McGuinness was anxiously quizzing Harvey Goldsmith, but Harvey couldn't see what Bono was doing either. The band on stage began exchanging panicked looks. By the time the song concluded – with their singer safely back on stage – 'Bad' had doubled its original running time to twelve minutes.

In fact, the song had carried on so long that the band ran out of time. Their third number had to be dropped. To make matters worse, the song they didn't play was their biggest hit to date, the crossover single 'Pride (In the Name of Love)'. Bono sheepishly left the stage with a towel slung over his shoulder, studiously avoiding eye contact with his colleagues. As he came off, he was warmly greeted by Bob Geldof, who had seen the whole thing on the television monitors and told him it had been great. But a despondent Bono was convinced he had messed up big time.

The rest of U2 ended the song without him.

'When they came off stage, the rest of the band went mad,' said Harvey Goldsmith. 'They were absolutely furious with Bono.'

Bono's excuse was that the girl with whom he danced was being crushed by the throngs of people pushing forwards. He had seen this and gestured frantically to the stewards to help her. They did not understand what he was saying and so he jumped down to help her himself. Others took a different view. Pete Smith described Bono's actions as 'carefully stage-managed'. And Andrew Zweck, looking back, said: 'I do not think anyone's life was in danger in the front row of Wembley Stadium that day. Down the front, security professionals were doing a great job in crowd management.'

The band were not convinced either. Bono had long made a habit of pulling girls out of the audience and dancing with them. Forty years later, an older and wiser Bono confessed this had been a moment of ambiguity. 'As true as it was that I am looking out for somebody slight in the middle of the crowd,' he said in 2025, 'I'm also very conscious that this is a TV broadcast, not just a show. And the other side of me, the performer in me, is, of course, looking for some kind of moment.'

But it was a moment that happened out of sight of the rest of the band. 'I think it's fair to say there was a bit of a row afterwards,' said Paul McGuinness. 'Bono had done precisely what they had told him beforehand not to do,' recalled John Kennedy. 'We told you do not do this under any circumstances. You ignored us, you treated us with disrespect,' Kennedy remembered. Live Aid was U2's chance to reach a global audience and Bono had ruined everything. The singer went back to Ireland and hid away in his wife's parents' home in Wexford for a few days, in a deep dark mood for having let the band down so terribly on such a momentous day.

'They had got to a point where they really were about to break the band up,' said Harvey. 'The rest of the band said, "It's over. We're splitting,"' said John Kennedy. 'They told their manager Paul McGuinness, "We've had enough. Prepare a press release saying U2 is over. We're splitting up, and moving on to solo projects."' It was a sliding doors moment.

What saved the band was a shrewd piece of procrastination by their manager, who convinced them that it wouldn't be fair to make such an announcement on Live Aid day. As Kennedy recalled, 'He told them, "Live Aid need to get all the press coverage tomorrow. We don't want to be raining on their parade. We can wait 'til Monday to put out a press release."'

Back in Ireland, down in Wexford, Bono visited a sculptor friend who was working on a huge new piece of a figure in mid-air. 'It's called *The Leap*. It's about the leap of faith,' the sculptor, Seamus Furlong, explained. 'That's you.'

'What are you talking about?' asked Bono.

'We saw you at Live Aid. You did a leap, when you went into the crowd. You wanted something more. You made a leap of faith, you got something, you touched it.'

Bono remained disconsolate.

Two days later, Bono got a call from McGuinness. 'You're not going to believe this, but everyone's raving about U2.' The media were unanimous in their opinion that Freddie Mercury and Bono had stolen the show.

The Edge couldn't believe it either. 'It really took us by surprise when people started talking about U2 as one of the noteworthy performances of the day. I thought they were joking. I really thought we were crap,' he said. 'But looking back, Bono's complete determination to make physical contact with the crowd somehow made it even more powerful.'

What could have been the end of U2 turned out to be the making of them. 'It was a great piece of theatre and showmanship, which proved to be a landmark moment in their elevation to stadium-band status,' said Andrew Zweck. 'Commercially, it seemed they blew it because they didn't play their new single,' said Midge Ure, 'but instead they won the hearts of the world.' The week after Live Aid, all four U2 albums were back in the UK charts. Within two years, they were the biggest band in the world.

More than that, the episode took on a symbolic status in the U2 mythology. Twenty years after the concert, the *Sun* tracked down the fan whom Bono had pulled from the crowd. He had saved her life, she told the paper. 'The crowd surged,' Kal Khalique claimed, 'and I was suffocating – then I saw Bono.'

Was this true? It didn't really matter. A myth had been born.

Bono was interviewed soon after his performance by the BBC's Paul Gambaccini. He offered the usual interview platitudes: 'Yeah, a really successful day. You know, the sun is shining. So are the people, so are the bands. I'm so happy to be here.' But his thoughts then took a more political turn.

'The thing that interests me though about this, and I don't know if this is the time or the place, but you see, it's a government's responsibility,' Bono said with earnest directness. 'It is the governments of our countries' responsibility. We give them money in tax … and either they invest in life or they invest in death. For the cost of MX missiles or Star Wars or offensive defence budgets, we could turn those deserts in Africa into fertile land. The technology's with us. It is possible to do it.' Live Aid was more than a fundraising exercise. 'What I hope is this, as a public thing, will affect public opinion, which ultimately will affect the politicians and the policy makers… Change is gonna come.'

It was a strangely prescient interview. In it, nascent and unformed, was the impulse that was to result in Bob and Bono's forty years of campaigning. Backstage at Live Aid, one of the aid agencies working in Ethiopia approached him and offered him a private trip to Ethiopia. He and his wife Ali would live and work, out of the sight of the cameras, in a refugee camp for almost two months from September 1985. Forty years on, Bono looked back on the Live Aid moment: 'It began a journey for all of us. A lot of people on that stage, not least Bob and myself, but many others in the crowd in Philadelphia, in Wembley, on a journey from what you might call charity to what you might call justice.' Live Aid was more than 'a load of rich rock stars tin-cupping it with their audience to help out'. Instead, he said, 'we ended up asking deeper questions'.

⁂

For Bob Geldof, too, pop and politics were about to mix explosively. After Dire Straits at Wembley and the Beach Boys in Philadelphia, the next band up was Queen. Geldof had not invited them to sing on the Band Aid single. He thought they were past it, which was ironic since that was what many people thought about the Boomtown Rats. In the US and UK, Queen had never been darlings of the critics, noted Andrew Zweck. 'They were absolutely not cool. You were embarrassed to say you were a fan of Queen.' The band certainly knew that the Live Aid audience might well not be a Queen audience since the tickets had sold out before they had agreed to appear on the bill. So they were faced with the challenge of how to win over a crowd who had not come for the exclusive purpose of seeing them. 'Every act on that bill knew that it was going to be an amazing stage to be on. They were going to be seen by a lot of people,' said Queen's drummer, Roger Taylor. 'We realised it was potentially an incredible showcase.'

Geldof had, from the outset, billed Live Aid as a 'global jukebox', telling bands that they were to play their biggest hits. Queen now took this literally, carefully curating six of their best numbers into a skilfully abridged medley. Even though the band were musically tight from the ten-month tour they had recently completed, they hired an empty London theatre for five full days to hone their Live Aid slot to perfection. Security was kept tight to keep secret exactly what they were doing. Their management wouldn't even send a set-list to Pete Smith. 'They simply assured us,' he later wrote, 'that they would be within the allotted time slot.'

In the event, Queen's twenty-one-minute set was magical. 'I remember a huge rush of adrenaline as I went on stage and a massive roar from the crowd, and then all of us just pitching in,' recalled guitarist Brian May. 'Looking back, I think we were all a bit over-excited and I remember coming off and thinking it was very scrappy.'

No one else thought that. The band gave what the rest of the music world regarded as a career-defining performance, not least because of the commanding vocals, strutting sexuality and teasing playful humour of Freddie Mercury. The call-and-response game he had played with audiences for more than a decade was at its peak that evening. His a cappella 'Aaaaaay-o' later came to be known as 'The Note Heard Round the World'. Tens of thousands of people raised their arms like a human forest, and clapped and swayed as one, in homage to a master showman.

'Freddie was our secret weapon,' said Brian May. He could connect with the last person at the back of the furthest stand in the largest venue. 'He was able to reach out to everybody in that stadium effortlessly. It was really his night.' The meld of great anthemic choruses was very clever, said Andrew Zweck, 'but the energy and charisma of Freddie at his peak were what were so special.'

Freddie Mercury was, said Roger Daltrey of the Who, 'the best virtuoso rock 'n' roll singer of all time. He could sing anything in any style. He could change his style from line to line and, God, that's an art. And he was brilliant at it.'

No one would have thought beforehand, added Zweck, that – of all the bands there that night – it would be Queen who would 'head and shoulders' steal the show. 'It was for me the greatest twenty-one-minute performance in the history of rock 'n' roll. I can't think of another performance to compare, except perhaps Jimi Hendrix at Woodstock.' In 2005, Queen's Live Aid set was voted the greatest rock gig in history by a panel of music industry experts. Such praise was echoed by many of the big names there that day. Elton John even rushed into Mercury's dressing room after the set and exclaimed: 'You bastards, you stole the show.'

Later, Bob Geldof was to agree. 'Queen were absolutely the best band of the day,' he said. 'They played the best, had the best sound, used their time to the full. They understood the idea exactly, that it was a global jukebox. They just went and smashed one hit after another.'

Yet, at the time, he was consumed by another feeling. Queen had been extraordinary and they were followed by the hilarious, over-the-top Jagger/Bowie 'Dancing in the Street' video, which was exciting the Wembley crowds such that one critic described it as 'quantifiably the moment the planet achieved Peak Eighties'.

But everyone was getting so absorbed in the music that they were forgetting the point of the exercise – to raise large amounts of cash to alleviate the famines in Africa. 'People were starting to give money,' said Harvey Goldsmith, 'but it was only dribbling. The idea of a fundraising telethon was comparatively new. Most of the people watching on television didn't really know what they had to do, much as we kept telling them.'

Bob asked Band Aid's accountant how much had been raised so far and was told that – nearly seven hours into the concert – only £1.2 million had been pledged. That was less than had been raised in Ireland, despite the fact that the UK population was twenty times bigger.

Geldof left the backstage area and ran around the outside of the stadium, his painful back arched as he climbed to the top of the gantry to the glass eyrie overlooking the massed Wembley crowd and the turning stage. At the top, he burst into the BBC presentation box and shouted: 'Right, we're doing an appeal. Now!'

GIVE US YOUR FUCKING MONEY

Among those crowded around a television watching the Live Aid concert on the global broadcast was a group of stable boys near the Curragh in Kildare. So engrossed were they that, at first, they did not notice that the owner of the racehorses they were looking after had entered the stable block.

'What is all this?' enquired Sheikh Mana Al Maktoum, a member of the Dubai royal family, and the founder of a thoroughbred breeding operation that spanned six countries. He was in Kildare to inspect his stable of horses. His enquiry was not censorious but curious. The stable boys told him what Live Aid was about.

Without any fuss, the Sheik phoned his lawyer in Dubai. The lawyer phoned the Live Aid donation line and said he had been instructed to pledge a million pounds to the appeal.

Bob Geldof was delighted. But this single act of generosity only underscored the general sense of alarm that had prompted him to bound up the stairs to the BBC's makeshift Wembley studio when he found out how little money was coming in from the watching public. People were too taken up with the amazing music. They had forgotten the purpose of the day.

He looked into the TV camera and addressed the audience direct. Queen's performance had been followed by the flamboyant Jagger/Bowie video. Geldof bluntly declared: 'Mick and David did that video specifically so that you could give something – and it's not happening enough. You've got to get on the phone and take the money out of your pocket. Don't go to the pub tonight. Please stay in and give us the money. There are people dying *now* so give me the money.'

When the BBC presenter David Hepworth then began to give the mailing address so that people could post in their contributions, Geldof interrupted him in mid-flow and shouted: 'Fuck the address. Let's get the numbers.' The explosion passed into Live Aid mythology as 'Give us your fucking money' – one of the most misremembered misquotes of all time. Regardless of that, it was immensely effective. After his outburst, telephone donations increased to £300 per second.

Simple Minds, in Philadelphia, were followed, just before 8 p.m., by David Bowie in Wembley. Bowie, who had not been on stage since the last night of his Serious Moonlight tour in Hong Kong eighteen months earlier, had hastily assembled a band of ad hoc musicians. They had been allocated five numbers, but Bowie had decided to drop the final number, the *Ziggy Stardust* album opener, 'Five Years'. Instead, after concluding with '"Heroes"' – which he dedicated 'to my son, to all our children, and to the children of the world' – he made an announcement in an unexpectedly low-key voice: 'Lest we forget why we're here, I'd like to introduce a video made by CBC Television. The subject speaks for itself. Please send your money in.'

It was the video which Bob Geldof had not wanted to be shown, not due to time constraints as has been reported, but because he feared it was so shocking that large sections of the global television audience would turn off their televisions. It had been Bowie who insisted that it should be shown.

'I saw the crowd look up at the screens, as David had asked them to, and I saw their faces freeze,' said Bob.

Geldof did not watch the film, which he had seen many times before. Instead, he watched the crowd. 'I saw the youth of the world at the height of their beauty, at the peak of their health – beautiful girls on the shoulders of beautiful boys,' he later said. 'They're smiling and just so in love with that moment, and with Bowie, and then they look up at the screens and you watch their faces crumple...'

What they were watching was the three-minute video edited of heart-wrenching footage from Ethiopia's famine fields edited to fit the Cars' song 'Drive', its poignant refrain, about a lost love, became pitiful when set against the images from Ethiopia. The bizarre juxtaposition of the famine

film and the pop record brought home the purpose of the day – to use music
to right a terrible global wrong.

On the screen a small boy, weakened by starvation, is trying and trying to stand up on his little matchstick legs. As he struggles to rise, it
becomes clear he is totally naked.
Who's gonna tell you when it's too late?

The boy reaches for the hand of his mother, who is lying prone on the
ground. She lifts her arm but is too weak to assist him. He rests his hand
on the head of his little sister for support.
Who's gonna tell you things aren't so great?

The boy's head looks huge compared to his shrunken stick-thin legs.
He waves his skeletal arms for balance. His belly is swollen with the
fluid retention that comes with severe protein deficiency.
You can't go on, thinking nothing's wrong

The child can't support his own weight. He falls to the floor and is
reduced to crawling.
Who's gonna drive you home tonight?

The camera switches to a woman lifting her child, whose bottom is just
flaps of skin. All the fat and muscle has wasted away.
Who's gonna pick you up, when you fall?

The mother puts her child to her empty breast. All the while, she looks
directly into the camera. Her stare is accusatory. She reaches for her
threadbare brown tunic and covers her body.
Who's gonna hang it up when you call?

A sleeping child, her eyes crusted with discharge.
Who's gonna pay attention to your dreams?

A child pulls away from an empty breast. Another opens her mouth in
a silent anguished howl.
Who's gonna plug their ears when you scream?

A shrill scream on the film soundtrack cuts through the music. It pierces the heart of everyone who hears it. A child, so shrunken from lack of macronutrients that his wasted face looks like that of a little old man, drops his huge head into his shrunken hands – and then covers his eyes in a gesture of total defeat.

You can't go on, thinking nothing's wrong

The images continue. A child turns from the camera and hides his face in his mother's tattered clothing. The little silver cross hanging from a string around a mother's neck, a reminder of a dignified past in a terrible present. The racking tubercular cough of a tiny child. A little bowl of grains. The grimace of total agony on the face of a child whose shoulders are twisted in pain.

Who's gonna drive you home tonight?

Towards the end, the camera passes over the face of a despairing father. It then lingers on the half-closed eyes and parched lips of three-year-old Birhan Woldu, on the very edge of death – though, at this point, the world has yet to learn her name. And at the end, the terrible image of a man who is placing a bundle with great tenderness on the floor. It is the body of his dead child, tightly swaddled in old sacking, to wait for burial.

Who's gonna drive you home tonight?

The camera pulled back to reveal the heads of the Wembley crowd watching in silent horror, struck dumb by what they saw. Billy Connolly, in the makeshift BBC studio, was wiping tears from his eyes.

The Live Aid set designer, Jeremy Thom, was among the crowd when the film was shown. 'The atmosphere changed,' he said. 'You could hear a pin drop. It was as if everyone was just in shock at the reality of what this concert was for.'

The Canadian reporter who had given the video to Geldof was reporting for CBC inside the stadium when he saw the images on the big screen. He had had no idea that the public were going to see the tape. 'It had been a real festive atmosphere until then, marijuana being smoked in the crowd – a real party. And then the place went quiet. People couldn't look away from the film. It captured the eye, as well as the heart. Everyone suddenly realised the reason we were all there.'

The man who had put together the video, film editor Colin Dean, was equally taken by surprise. He was listening to Live Aid on the radio as he drove through the English countryside on his way to board a ferry for a holiday in France. Unlike the rest of the radio listeners, he did not need to wonder what was being seen by the TV audience: he had the pictures seared into his brain.

Brian Stewart, the television journalist who had written the original report containing the harrowing images, was also taken unawares. He had left Ethiopia behind and gone to stay with his father in Toronto to 'erase his mind'. He was haunted by that first encounter with the dying Birhan, and with the thousands of others in the northern Ethiopian Highlands. It was a sunny day and Stewart intended to spend it in the garden. He had planned only to watch the start of the concert but, like hundreds of millions of others around the globe, found he was unable to tear himself away from the television set. When Birhan's face appeared on the giant screen, a sudden thought occurred to him. This girl, who he had seen miraculously come back from the dead – what had happened to her? Might she possibly still be alive? A plan began to form in his mind.

The worldwide television audience had a different, more visceral, response. Once the film finished, David Hepworth struggled for words but, with immense presence of mind, declared: 'Pictures like that started this whole thing off. There's not much you can say after seeing that. It makes music sound rather minor. But your contributions to this event can help relieve that kind of thing in future.'

'In the stadium, 80,000 people were just chilled to silence,' said Band Aid trustee John Kennedy. 'There were tears everywhere and it became a turning point for the money coming in.' After the CBC video, 'people realised this was not just entertainment. The money started coming in like an avalanche,' said Harvey Goldsmith. 'That's when the phone lines quite literally collapsed,' added Geldof, who got a phone call from the show's producer in Ireland. 'Bob, we've got old ladies down here. More than a dozen of them. They say they have nothing to give except their wedding rings. They're standing here asking me for soap so they can pull them off their fingers. They're banging on the counter because we won't take them. What should we do?'

'What age are they?' Geldof asked. On being told they were 'quite old', he replied: 'Take the rings and their names and addresses, and give them your phone number. Tell them we'll wait a week. If they change their minds, they can come back anytime and collect them. After that, we'll sell them and send the money to Africa.'

That video did not just change Live Aid, it changed the course of the entire relief effort, said Geldof. It appalled whole nations, moved governments to action and saved countless thousands, if not millions, of lives. And though he did not know it then, his life and the life of the child dying on the screen were to become interwoven for the next forty years.

The impact of the video was not, however, confined to the Live Aid audience. The performers were profoundly affected. After the video was over, David Bowie retired alone to his dressing room. His PR man Bernard Doherty went to the Portakabin to join the singer. 'Usually, after a performance there is some small talk to help the artist wind down,' the PR man said. 'You talk about the crowd being louder than normal, that kind of thing. But this time I walked in and just stood there, and we looked at each other and he burst into tears. I've never seen him do that, before or since.'

As for the man who wrote 'Drive', Ric Ocasek, his song had become so entwined with the video that he was unable to play it for a long time. 'The video had stolen his own song from him,' said Band Aid's lawyer, John Kennedy. After Live Aid – some twelve months after its original release, when it had already been a top-five hit in the UK – the song re-entered the UK charts, with Ocasek insisting on donating the proceeds from the revived sales to the Band Aid Trust.

❧

It was left to the Who to lift the mood after the sobering video. The tensions generated during their shambolic rehearsal were still very much in evidence. 'I watched the Who from the side of the stage,' said Queen's guitarist, Brian May. 'It was obvious they weren't getting on very well with each other. Sparks were flying – it was actually quite exciting.'

Unfortunately, the technology was similarly temperamental. John Entwistle's bass kept cutting out at the start, causing a minute's awkward delay before they could start playing. Then, during their opening number, 'My Generation', just as Roger Daltrey sang the line 'Why don't you all fade away?', the BBC blew a fuse, causing the Wembley stage feed to temporarily fail. The band didn't stop playing, but the broadcast was interrupted, only returning as the last verse of 'Pinball Wizard' was played.

If Status Quo, who started the day, were – as Geldof described them to Prince Charles – 'a cartoon of a rock 'n' roll band', near the end, the Who were the apotheosis.

Pete Townshend would later be critical of his performance, but as he left the stage, he was euphoric enough to enthusiastically embrace Elton John, who was en route to perform as soon as Santana had finished their set over in Philadelphia.

Why did the fuse blow during the Who's performance? 'There was no electricity left in there,' said the production manager Andrew Zweck. 'We had three generators. We couldn't physically find room to park more up. We were at the absolute limit of the power supply. Apart from the technical problems with the Who, we got away with it pretty well.'

Another major disaster, though, was yet to come.

Over in Philadelphia, Eric Clapton stood backstage, chatting to Jimmy Page and Robert Plant. They were all waiting for Phil Collins to arrive from his Concorde flight from London. Phil had promised to play drums for both Clapton and the Led Zeppelin reunion. Madonna was due on stage next.

As she got out of her limousine, her entourage started pressing through the crowds, with her young bodyguards commanding the crowds to 'Move, please, move. Madonna's coming.' They spoke with the zealotry and self-importance of acolytes of the new saviour of pop.

One of them touched Clapton's arm and told him to move over.

'What's this?' Clapton asked incredulously.

'Madonna's coming!' the perplexed crowd-clearer said. He had clearly never before met anyone who lacked such reverence for his boss.

'You must be joking,' said Eric Clapton and stayed firmly where he was.

Back at Wembley, Freddie Mercury, off the leash after Queen's meticulously controlled performance, was behaving badly backstage in the Hard Rock Café. Bono, who was walking by with his wife Ali, was his first target. Mercury pulled the U2 frontman aside and asked: 'Bo-No or Bon-O?'

'It's Bon-O.'

'Come over here with me. We've all been talking, Roger [Daltrey] and Pete [Townshend] and David [Bowie], and we all agree there are no singers anymore. Everyone is shouting these days, but you're a singer.'

Bono later wrote: 'I was up against a wall and he put his hand on the wall and was talking to me like he was chatting up a chick. He had me laughing, but I was shifting nervously at the time, with Ali and myself exchanging glances. I thought, *Wow, this guy's really camp.* I was telling somebody later and he said, "You're surprised? They're called Queen!" But I was really amazed. It hadn't dawned on me.'

Midge Ure had a similar experience. He was sitting backstage chatting with Parfitt and Rossi from Status Quo when he saw Mercury. 'I'd met all the rest of Queen, but Freddie was the invisible man. I went over and shook hands with him. He wouldn't let go of my hand. After he'd been holding my hand for two minutes, he said: "You're that lovely boy from the Boomtown Rats, aren't you?"'

'No,' gasped Midge, 'I'm the lovely boy from Ultravox.'

Freddie's approach to David Bailey was more direct. The photographer had set up a makeshift studio backstage to take a portrait of each Wembley act. As he was getting ready to photograph Queen, 'I got a tap on my shoulder and spun round,' he later recalled. 'Suddenly, there was a big tongue down my throat! It was Freddie.'

�֍

Introducing Elton John, the comedian Billy Connolly made a startling announcement. He had just been told, he informed the Wembley crowd and the wider world, that 95 per cent of all the television sets on the planet were now tuned to Live Aid. No one afterwards was quite sure who told him this – nor whether it could possibly be true – but it was a measure of the exhilaration of the day. What certainly did turn out to be the case was that more people watched Live Aid than saw the first man on the Moon take his giant step for humankind. Making compassion hip, to use Geldof's phrase, was a giant step of a different kind.

At thirty-two minutes, Elton John had the longest set of the day. After the high drama of Queen and the primal passion of the Who, Elton presented a polished pop spectacle which showcased his versatility. His touring band were sharp and his voice was strong, both on his own and in two duets.

Kiki Dee joined him to revive their 1976 duet 'Don't Go Breaking My Heart', and Wembley sang along. But the highlight was a surprise appearance by George Michael, whose powerful version of 'Don't Let the Sun Go Down on Me' was accounted by some critics as one of the highlights of the day.

With his new beard, this felt like George's transition from teen pop star to adult artist, being anointed by Elton along the way, foreshadowing his leap into superstardom. A year later, Wham! would perform at Wembley for their final show, this time with Elton joining them. Live Aid felt like a symbolic passing of the torch between generations of British pop.

At the end of Elton's set, a short shower of rain fell, bringing a moment of relief to the crowd towards the end of a long, hot day. But it may have done more than that.

While Elton was on stage, David Bowie, Pete Townshend, Alison Moyet and Bob Geldof gathered in Paul McCartney's dressing room to rehearse their role as backing singers for the final chorus with the former Beatle. Then, as Madonna took to the stage in Philadelphia, Geldof and Midge Ure herded the rest of the performers together in the Hard Rock Café for a ragged run through of 'Do They Know It's Christmas?', which was to follow McCartney as the finale of the Wembley leg of the Live Aid. At the last minute, Bernard Doherty was sent scrambling to produce fifty photocopies of the lyrics of the song because, as he recalled, 'everyone kind of knew the chorus, but Bob suddenly realised half the acts didn't know the words. It was shambolic. Bob was trying to conduct them, and lead them, and write down who would sing what part.' But the rehearsal was, in any case, brought to a premature end by the crisis which was unfolding on stage.

Paul McCartney had been led to Elton John's white piano by Andrew Zweck. He was only to sing that one song, 'Let It Be', which Geldof had described as a benediction – a blessing on the end of the proceedings.

When I find myself in times of trouble...

There was a grim irony to the words that evening, as it slowly dawned on McCartney that the 80,000 people in Wembley Stadium could not hear him properly.

'He was playing and singing away, thinking he was doing fine,' said Zweck. 'He could hear himself on his monitors. The television broadcast was picking up sound from other microphones near Paul McCartney.

But the crowd in the stadium were getting nothing – and were starting to groan and ask what was going on. After a while, Paul began to sense this too. He could feel there was no oomph in his sound.'

At the side of the stage, Linda McCartney looked at Pete Smith. No words were exchanged, but her eyes spoke volumes. He had promised Paul everything would be fine.

A few people in the crowd booed and whistled. But, thirty seconds in, they could now faintly hear the piano. The crowd began to sing. 'They were singing it for Paul,' Geldof later said. They had come to the rescue. One hundred seconds into the song, the voices of those in the stadium had swelled to fill the void. It felt like a moment that hugely symbolised something central to what was happening that day – in Wembley, Philadelphia and all around the world: an act of great human togetherness.

At the side of the stage Geldof, Bowie, Moyet and Townshend were waiting to come on for the final chorus.

'We've got to go on *now*,' said Townshend. 'We've got to help him.'

But before they could move, the microphone sprang back into life. The crowd roared as McCartney's voice powerfully joined their own massed voices.

'All together,' he shouted and the stadium responded in full throat.

Let it be, let it be-ee…

'Okay, now you,' he said to the people. 'Come on.' The stadium sang as one.

A huge roar went up as Geldof, Townshend, Moyet and Bowie came on to join in the final choruses. It was the emotional climax of the Wembley concert.

⁂

It was only afterwards that the postmortem began. What had gone wrong? In the immediate aftermath, blame was put upon the sudden shower during Elton's performance. The rain must have affected the electrics, people said. Forty years later, Harvey Goldsmith offered a simpler explanation: 'One of the road crew tripped over a cable that came out of the distribution box and suddenly you couldn't hear him. That's what really happened. Everyone was flying around trying to figure out what the problem was, but the problem was really simple. He literally tripped over a cable and it came out of its fix.

The Paul McCartney saga was an accident waiting to happen somewhere during a show with so much change-over.'

Andrew Zweck still hangs his head over what happened. 'I've been forever embarrassed about the fact that Paul McCartney's microphone failed. I've never, never spoken with him about it. But I've never been invited to work with Paul since. Neither has Harvey.'

On the night, the glitch was soon subsumed by the jubilation that followed as the entire nebula of stars crammed onto the stage to sing 'Do They Know It's Christmas?'. At the end of the finale, Geldof was raised triumphantly onto the shoulders of Townshend and McCartney. 'He's a heavy bugger,' said Townshend afterwards. A strict 10 p.m. curfew had been imposed upon the Wembley concert by Brent Council, anxious that the crowds should disperse in time to get the last train home. After ten solid hours of music, Harvey Goldsmith noted with satisfaction, they had only overrun by a single minute.

CHAPTER 15

THIS IS
YOUR WOODSTOCK

Philadelphia was now in charge. The final six hours of Live Aid music came exclusively from the JFK Stadium, where Larry Magid's plan was working perfectly. Mike Mitchell was in the Philadelphia television control room, coordinating the most ambitious international satellite operation that had ever been attempted. Mike Ahern was in charge of getting the acts on and off the stage at the right time. And Larry was overseeing the whole operation from his trailer. Meanwhile, the agonised genius that was the leading US rock impresario, Bill Graham, had allowed himself to be confined to the backstage area for fear that the police would come again to arrest him as they had the night before. So paranoid was he about this possibility that he had a portable toilet installed backstage for his personal use, and his alone. It was the perfect combination: Graham was allowed to feel that he was in charge – and to give everybody else the impression that this was so – without actually being in a position to mess things up.

'In many ways, the American concert was an ongoing struggle from beginning to end,' said Pete Smith. 'There was the dynamic to be sorted out between Bill Graham and the TV companies. Larry Magid had to continually find solutions and to mediate.' Larry's tactic was brilliant, Smith said. 'He gave Bill a job. Bill was to remain on stage and control the artists and the celebrities, coming on and off the platform. He was to be uber-stage manager, in full view of the crowd who recognised him and loved him for the legend that he was, as did the celebrities and most of the artists – if not their managers perhaps. Larry knew that Bill would be more than happy to be the man in view, where the talent was performing. And so sense was thus made out of nonsense.'

At 9 a.m. Eastern Standard Time, the first person out on stage for the official opening was Bill Graham. He introduced Jack Nicholson, who in turn introduced the first act, Joan Baez, who told the crowd: 'Children of the '80s: this is your Woodstock and it's long overdue.' She sang 'Amazing Grace', the hymn written by a repentant slave trader. Bill was out again for the next act, introducing the comedy duo Chevy Chase and Joe Piscopo, who in turn introduced local Philadelphia band, the Hooters. They had been placed on the bill by Larry Magid, despite the opposition of Bob Geldof, who had witheringly asked: 'Who the fuck are the Hooters?' It was a question he came to regret some years later when the Boomtown Rats had to play as support for the Hooters in Berlin.

Then Graham was out again to thank the first of the black acts on the US bill, the Four Tops, who produced a Motown medley of five of their top hits with a full horn section. Bill allowed Chevy Chase to introduce Black Sabbath who, despite the resistance of Harvey Goldsmith, he had squeezed into the running order at the unseasonable hour of 11 a.m.

But Graham was back on the stage to introduce Santana himself. Then he was back to welcome Bette Midler, who introduced Madonna as 'a woman who pulled herself up by her bra straps – and who has been known to let them down occasionally'. It was 95 degrees Fahrenheit when Madonna walked on stage in Philadelphia. 'Some guy screamed from the audience, "Take it off baby!"' recalled Nile Rodgers, who had produced Madonna's breakthrough album, *Like a Virgin*. The man in the crowd was referring to the fact that both *Playboy* and *Penthouse* had just published some of her old nude art photos. Madonna hit back immediately, saying: 'I'm taking shit off today. They might hold it against me ten years from now.' Live Aid, said Rodgers, was what made Madonna globally. 'Now she can conquer the world,' he remarked.

But Bill Graham wasn't finished. He introduced Eric Clapton, Dionne Warwick and finally, Jack Nicholson, whose role it was to introduce Bob Dylan. To some of those on stage, he was the lynchpin. 'Things were moving so fast, rolling them on and run them off,' said Kenny Loggins. 'Bill Graham was in charge of everything and you couldn't fuck around.' But, back in London, Bob Geldof, who was watching the entire American proceedings from Wembley's post-concert party in Legends nightclub, found Bill's constant presence on the stage immensely irritating. 'It drove me fucking mad watching the television,' he said years later, 'and seeing the person who had nearly ruined the whole concert, strutting up and down, shouting at people. But he loved it. He was the star of the day – a man who's out of control.'

Graham certainly appeared out of control when he left the stage to pick a fight with a radio industry tip-sheet publisher named Kal Rudman, who had been on the same transatlantic Concorde as Phil Collins. A radio play kingmaker, Rudman's tip-sheet, *Friday Morning Quarterback*, had a huge influence on whether or not a record would be played on the radio in the US. It could launch careers or keep artists in the charts. What Graham and Rudman were quarrelling about is not known. But Larry Magid was clear about one thing: Bill Graham was once again in a place that he had been told not to be.

'What are you doing off stage, Bill?' asked Magid. 'Get back on stage. This is crazy.' He had to separate the two quarrelling men and say to Graham: 'You come off stage again, Bill, and you're leaving.' Graham went back on stage. 'But it was a crazy incident,' Larry said forty years later. 'And I'm not here demeaning Bill. I really had a lot of affection for him, but it just seemed that this was a troubled time for him.' Bill Graham died in a helicopter crash six years later, returning home from discussing another benefit concert with Huey Lewis & the News. The authorities had advised against flying that night, but Bill Graham, characteristically, had ignored them.

✄

The Concorde G-BOAG, Flight BA195, carrying Phil Collins landed in New York just four and a half hours after he had performed in Wembley Stadium. He was about to become the first person to ever appear live on television twice in one day from both Europe and North America. It had only been done thanks to supersonic flight. Now that Concorde has been decommissioned, and never replaced with anything so fast, it may well be that the record he set that day will never be broken.

Phil Collins said goodbye to his fellow passengers, Kal Rudman and Cher, and took a helicopter from John F. Kennedy International Airport in

New York to John F. Kennedy Stadium in Philadelphia. Arriving at 7 p.m. local time, he rushed first to see his old friend Eric Clapton, for whom he was about to play drums, and then moved swiftly on to Robert Plant's caravan to chat about the set they would be playing together. But as soon as he got there, Plant warned him that 'Jimmy is being belligerent'. Phil also discovered that 'it wasn't so much me playing with my mates Jimmy Page and Robert Plant, but a Zeppelin reunion' with former bass player John Paul Jones also present. The three former members of the band had not played together since the death of their drummer John Bonham five years before. 'I'd always heard that individually these guys were great,' Collins said, 'but together there was this black cloud that appeared.'

Jones had only arrived that day, leaving the trio with just an hour's rehearsal. Phil Collins' own 'rehearsal' had been restricted to listening to Zeppelin songs on the Concorde flight. Jimmy Page immediately began to quiz him on how to play 'Stairway to Heaven'. Collins mimed the drum part, only to have Page shout aggressively: 'No, it doesn't go like that!'. Collins later noted the legendary guitarist was 'as high as a kite'.

There was another complication. Collins had been invited because he had played on singer Robert Plant's first two solo albums. But Plant had also invited Chic drummer Tony Thompson, who was playing at Live Aid with another band, Power Station. Phil tried to smooth the way. 'I talked to him about playing with two drummers – something I'd done quite a lot and it can be a train wreck,' said Collins. He said to Thompson: 'Let's stay out of each other's way and play simple', but 'I really got the impression that he didn't want me to be there.' The atmosphere did not feel auspicious.

After accompanying Clapton on drums at 7.40 p.m. for his allotted twenty minutes, Phil then sat down at the piano on the dot of 8 p.m. for his own solo set. It was an amazingly precise piece of timing. The US network broadcast, showing the last three hours of the concert, had been scheduled to begin with Collins playing the same two songs he had played earlier that same day in Wembley. The US network ABC wanted to start promptly at 8 p.m. Hal Uplinger, the producer of the American broadcasts, knew that the chances of that happening were minimal. They could plan for it, but it involved a transatlantic crossing, a supersonic jet ride, and two helicopter shuttle rides. Timing that exactly at the end of thirteen hours of other acts was almost impossible.

'As the second hand was coming up towards eight o'clock – exactly – Phil Collins sat down at the piano bench and the ABC people absolutely couldn't believe it,' said Uplinger.

'He sat down at the piano ... literally two seconds before the ABC show was to start,' said Live Aid's global executive producer, Mike Mitchell, 'and all of us in the production crew cried. We literally all cried.'

They were overcome by the momentousness of what had been achieved. They had not simply outsmarted time. They had, said Mitchell – crying again four decades later, as he remembered the feeling – all become 'part of something bigger'.

Collins was introduced by Jack Nicholson and Bette Midler together. The pair wondered aloud how one person could play both concerts in one day on opposite sides of the world. 'I'd say that's impossible,' said Nicholson.

'But the truth is,' said Midler, 'that everything is possible. We can beat time. We can beat hunger. If we just pull together.'

The crowd roared.

'Good evening, Philadelphia. Good evening, America. Good evening, London. And good evening, the world,' proclaimed Collins. Turning to the 100,000-strong US crowd, he quipped: 'I was in England this afternoon. Funny old world, innit?'

Starting with 'Against All Odds', the choice of the song suddenly seemed somehow to fulfil the prophecy he had made when he first sang it in Wembley earlier that day.

But the next item on Phil Collins' Live Aid timetable was historic in an altogether less satisfactory way. His foreboding about what was now being billed as a Led Zeppelin reunion proved correct.

'As soon as I got up on stage, I could see it was going to be a weird one,' Collins said. The on-stage monitors were not working properly. Jimmy Page was intoxicated and his guitar was badly tuned. Robert Plant's voice was hoarse and struggled on the high notes. And 'Tony Thompson was just playing whatever he wanted,' Collins added. The performance was a disaster. Critics variously described it as 'a car crash' and 'one of the worst rock reunions of all time'. Plant himself later described the performance as 'a fucking atrocity'.

Jimmy Page, whose speech was slurred in an after-show interview, tried to place the blame squarely on Collins' shoulders. 'One drummer was half-way across the Atlantic and didn't know the stuff. We played "Whole Lotta Love" and he was just there, bashing away cluelessly and grinning.'

'Maybe I didn't know it as well as he'd like me to have done,' Collins later conceded. 'But it wasn't my fault it was crap. The whole thing was a disaster, really. Robert wasn't match-fit with his voice and Jimmy was out of it, dribbling. If I could have walked off, I would have. But then we'd all be talking about why Phil Collins walked off Live Aid – so I just stuck it out ... The essence of the day was about being there and doing the best you can.'

Led Zeppelin were so embarrassed that they blocked re-broadcasts of the performance and refused to allow the footage to be used on the official Live Aid DVD. Page later admitted that the whole thing had been 'a bit of a kamikaze stunt ... when you think of how well everyone else was rehearsed'. Looking back, he told *Rolling Stone* in 2014, that his 'main memories, really, were of total panic'.

❊

Other artists had trouble of a different kind. The immense complexity of coordinating the feeds from the Wembley and Philadelphia concerts – plus feeds from Australia, Japan, the Soviet Union, the Netherlands, Austria, Yugoslavia and West Germany, which all hosted acts – meant that some performances were not broadcast in every country. Crosby, Stills & Nash (and Young) did six songs, but only two of them were broadcast by the BBC – and that was after the Wembley Stadium crowd had dispersed. 'We had live musical acts performing throughout the world coming to Philadelphia from over a dozen places via satellite,' said Hal Uplinger. 'It was a little complicated.'

It was more than that. In the rush to set up the transatlantic feeds, the sound feed from Philadelphia was sent to London via transatlantic cable, while the video feed was via satellite. This meant the two could not be synchronised on British televisions. In the US, the entire broadcast was the responsibility of ABC, even though they only showed the final three hours on the network. ABC broadcast the rest on independent stations through a syndicated outfit, Orbis Communications. There was an entirely separate feed for cable viewers provided by MTV which, unlike the others, broadcast in stereo. To complicate matters further, ABC decided that some of the acts that went out earlier in the day should be recorded, not shown live, and then edited into their three-hour network special. National broadcasters, other than the US and the UK, were allowed to 'drop in' performances from their artists and 'drop out' whatever was going on in the main feeds. On top of all this, though the telecast was run continuously by the BBC, the commercial stations, including ABC and MTV, dropped songs randomly wherever they needed to run adverts.

Everything was fed through one master control truck in the grounds of the stadium in Philadelphia, which, as Hal Uplinger explained, was linked to thirty-five other trucks set in 'an entire field of satellite dishes that controlled our uplinks and downlinks'. All the signals came into Philadelphia by satellite and were then sent back from there to the rest of the world, again by satellite. There were separate trucks for the US feed, the BBC feed, the world feed and the MTV feed, as well as video and sound feeds. It was close to a miracle that nothing else went wrong.

And while there were those – like Crosby, Stills & Nash – who missed out, there were others who benefitted. When David Bowie's management heard that he was to perform in Wembley at 7 p.m. – which would be just 2 p.m. on the East Coast (and even earlier elsewhere in the US) – they protested. 'I remember getting a call from Bowie's office in London, very upset and saying, "Why is he going to be on in the afternoon in America and he's not going to be a part of the ABC network?"' recalled Uplinger. But they changed their tune when he explained that Bowie would be taped to be included in the network special, while someone less famous would be shown on non-network US televisions. 'So what you have is prime-time throughout the world and you are going to be taped for prime-time in the United States.'

Bowie's people did a swift about-turn. 'Don't let anyone change his time,' they said. 'We want to keep it right where it is.'

Uplinger was not above pulling a few strings. There was one helicopter that kept flying back and forth through the beams from the satellite dishes. 'The engineers would see a little blip when that happened. The viewer at home wouldn't see anything, but it drove these engineers crazy,' Uplinger recalled. It was towing a sign 'that said "Eat at Joe's" or some type of thing'.

Uplinger called the airport and got a number for the federal aeronautical authorities, who said: 'They have a right to be in the air and there's nothing I can do about it. They are not breaking the law. We've told the pilot and he just smiles.'

President Ronald Reagan was having an operation that day, but he had sent an official from the White House and another from USAID. Uplinger told them the problem. A phone call was swiftly made to Washington. Moments later, the airport called back. The problem helicopter was grounded.

'Would you like everybody out of the air, sir?'

'No, as long as they stay out of the dishes, it's okay,' the television producer said.

Hal Uplinger had one other interesting reflection about his end of the Live Aid concert. 'We didn't have enough time,' he said. 'Yet the fact that we didn't have the time probably made it possible. There was an urgency to this whole thing – an urgency that had been instilled by Bob Geldof. People were losing their lives. Every day, people were dying.' That urgency, together with the sense of common purpose it instilled, 'touched the spirit of humanity for this higher cause,' he concluded. 'We really came together as one … the broadcasters … and therefore the peoples of the world, together for the first time.'

To fill the occasional gap in broadcasts, the US television team filmed a series of one-minute segments with well-known people talking about hunger: President Carter, Coretta Scott King, Archbishop Tutu, Charlton Heston, Pelé, the head of Sony in Japan… 'There was one spiritual master, a Bulgarian named Omraam Mikhaël Aïvanhov. At the very end of his message he paused, looked into the camera, and said: "This show … will change the world."' At that moment, Hal Uplinger was certain that Live Aid was going to succeed.

CHAPTER 16

UPSTAGING MR JAGGER

For four solid hours after the concert switched over to Philadelphia, there were no black acts. The final two hours of Live Aid's sixteen-hour extravaganza was when the music world's black megastars should have been on stage. Stevie Wonder, Prince, Michael Jackson, Diana Ross, Lionel Richie... They had all been asked to perform. They all had better things to do.

At 9 p.m., Patti LaBelle, Philadelphia's hometown girl, took to the stage. 'My manager said, "Would you like to do Live Aid?" When he said it was in Philly, I said, "Don't ask me silly questions. Who wouldn't want to do that?" If you're a woman or a man, or black or white, you're just there giving your talent. It's just beautiful.'

'She came out and literally blew the console apart,' laughed the man in charge of the Philadelphia sound desk, Dave Skaff. 'Before she went on, we did as much as we could to turn the damn thing down – and she just lit the desk up red! The whole stage was her voice, dialled up through all the monitors. It was like the voice of God was there that day, and it was Patti LaBelle!'

Earlier, a wide-ranging selection of performers had drawn on the rich heritage of black music. BB King, the name as synonymous with the blues, it was said, as Louis Armstrong's once was with jazz, delivered a classic blues performance – patched in from the Netherlands – that reminded everyone where rock got its roots. The Four Tops crammed in five of their greatest Motown hits, while the British singer Billy Ocean – gamely singing live to a backing track while the revolving stage turned – added disco-funk to the tradition.

Other black performers were invited on-stage by white performers. Bo Diddley took to the stage to play with George Thorogood, who concluded his set by bringing on another distinctive black guitarist, the 'Master of the Telecaster', Albert Collins. But perhaps the most moving collaboration of the day came when the prolific songwriters Ashford & Simpson welcomed Teddy Pendergrass, the one-time lead singer of Harold Melvin & the Blue Notes.

It was Teddy's first appearance on stage since a car crash had left him paralysed from the chest down, three years earlier. He never walked again. But he came out onto the Live Aid stage in a wheelchair and delivered a version of 'Reach Out and Touch', which was one of the emotional highlights of the day. Live Aid marked the resumption of a singing career for the Philadelphian native which continued for another two decades. Kool and the Gang, whose Robert 'Kool' Bell, JT Taylor and Dennis Taylor had played on the 'Do They Know It's Christmas?' single, recorded a live video. The legendary performers David Ruffin and Eddie Kendricks came on as guests of Hall and Oates to perform three Temptations classics. And, finally, Tina Turner joined Mick Jagger for a couple of Live Aid Philadelphia's most outrageously memorable numbers.

All in all, there were more than a dozen slots at Live Aid by black performers, which represented around 16 per cent of the total number of performances. Some saw that as a demographically representative percentage since African Americans then made up around 12 per cent of the US population, and with black Britons being just 1 per cent in the UK. But others complained that many of the black performances were truncated or delayed to fit into the broadcast between white artists who were considered the priority. But it was the refusal of the greatest black American superstars to appear which caused the greatest perception of imbalance.

There was, however, one area in which Live Aid broke new ground. The eponymous debut album by the New York hip-hop act Run-D.M.C. had gone gold in 1984 – the first hip-hop album ever to do so. Their second album, *King of Rock*, had been released in January of 1985 and went platinum. Yet, even with such phenomenal sales, pop radio stations were still reluctant to play this new form of music. Live Aid was to change that.

Run-D.M.C.'s white agent, Bill Adler, pointed out an uncomfortable irony.

'Live Aid was conceived by Bob Geldof to help raise money for the poor in Ethiopia and the prospect was huge news in the music business, with this person signing up, and that person signing up,' he said. 'But the line-up was almost nothing but white folks. So I made a phone call and I said, "These guys need to be on the bill."' One of Bill Graham's team turned them down out of hand. It was only when Graham himself heard about it, and registered the fact that these young New Yorkers had a gold and a platinum record, that he rang Adler back and put them on the bill. 'See you in Philadelphia,' he said.

The young rappers from Queens were unimpressed. 'One day Bill Adler says, "You're playing this big thing called Live Aid", but to tell you the truth, I did not know until the last second that I was about to go do something so big and so historic,' said Joseph 'Run' Simmons. 'We drove up to this big place full of people and I'm worried, because I'm saying "How are these hundreds of thousands of people gonna know 'Rock Box' or 'King of Rock' or any of my records?", 'cause I know these people cannot know us. I'd never seen anything like it in my life and I was terrified.'

Darryl 'D.M.C.' McDaniels was no different. They were, he said, 'scared to death' – not least because he knew they were bound to raise some eyebrows by taking to the stage in JFK Stadium without a band. Behind the two MC rappers was just their DJ, Jam Master Jay, behind two turntables.

Bill Adler, who had been a music journalist before he took on Run-D.M.C. as his clients, was apprehensive too. 'Hip-hop at its birth was essentially a black culture,' he said. 'Would music lovers who weren't black, who heard it for the first time, decide that they loved it as well?'

They did.

'When we dropped "King of Rock", I remember looking out at these hundreds of thousands of people and I see hands going up,' said Run. 'The crowd is actually with us, even though they're probably there to see Rod Stewart or whoever … I found that, on that day, our records were reaching more people than I knew.' (Rod Stewart, in the event, did not materialise at Live Aid; without him realising it, his manager turned down the chance to play because he felt Stewart was not being given a slot high enough up the bill.)

Run-D.M.C. came off stage elated. 'I'm like, *Wow, I feel like I'm accepted,*' said D.M.C. 'This says that we are everything we wanted to be.'

'They were the only rappers to perform at Live Aid,' said Adler. 'And they killed it.'

Forty years later, he declared that 'Run-D.M.C.'s performance at Live Aid accelerated the development of hip-hop in that cultural moment and took the genre outside black culture.' The band saw Live Aid as a milestone in pioneering their new-school rap, helping to usher in a golden age for hip-hop. A year later, they celebrated the fact on 'My Adidas', the first single from their bestselling multi-platinum *Raising Hell*:

'*Stepped on stage, at Live Aid, all the people gave, and the poor got paid!*'

❧

The Rolling Stones had been adamant they would not play Live Aid. But when Keith Richards heard that Mick Jagger was doing a solo spot in Philadelphia, just before the finale of Bob Dylan, Keith suddenly reconsidered.

Mick had read in *Rolling Stone* that Tina Turner liked his new single 'State of Shock', so he invited her to sing with him at Live Aid. Turner and her band cancelled a gig in Newfoundland to attend.

She publicly spoke with compassion about the starving peoples in Ethiopia and the rest of the drought-hit belt beneath the Sahara. 'These people are in desperation and that's why I'm here,' she said, but Mick was an added attraction. Tina later confessed to having a crush on Jagger: 'Mick is just naughty. He's like every bad boy you've ever known at school.'

Bill Graham and Larry Magid had offered Jagger a slot near the top of the bill. Only Dylan was above him. But then, on the night, Keith Richards, who had earlier derided the idea of the Rolling Stones performing at Live Aid, stole a march on his lead singer.

Twenty minutes before the sixteen hours of music from Wembley and Philadelphia was brought to a close, Jack Nicholson walked to the front of the stage to introduce the final act of Live Aid. 'Some artists' work speaks for itself. Some artists' work speaks for his generation,' he began. 'It's my deep personal pleasure to present to you one of America's great voices of freedom. It can only mean one man, the transcendent Bob Dylan!' His introduction was, unfortunately, more memorable than the act which followed it.

Dylan walked out onto the stage alone, carrying an acoustic guitar and wearing his harmonica harness around his neck. He looked something of a lonely figure centre-stage before announcing: 'Let me introduce two people who just came along, Keith Richards and Ron Wood.' The audience roared their approval. What more fitting conclusion could there be to a concert in aid of the starving and abandoned than this champion of social justice, the poet who highlighted the plight of the dispossessed and oppressed?

The singer had clearly given a lot of thought to his choice of material. From his huge back catalogue, as his opener he chose the rarely played 'Ballad of Hollis Brown', which tells the story of a farmer from South Dakota who, driven by desperate poverty, kills his wife, five children and then himself.

> *Your children are so hungry / That they don't know how to smile…*
> *If there's anyone that knows / Is there anyone that cares?…*

It was a ballad without a chorus, and a song unfamiliar to many of the audience. The sound was poor and Dylan's delivery nasal. It was hard to make out the words, but at the end they applauded the man, less the song. Dylan looked content. 'Thank you. I thought that was a fitting song for this important occasion.'

So, indeed, was the next number. 'When the Ship Comes In' was a song of liberation. It spoke of the bursting of chains and the sun shining with respect upon every face. The ship's wise men, he sang, 'will remind you once again that the whole world is watching'. Those who oppress the poor will be forced into saying they will pay to make a deal and meet all the demands of the poor, 'but they'll know in their hearts their days are numbered … like Pharaoh's tribe they'll be drowned in the tide'. But, again, it was hard for the crowd to catch all the words. And, besides, they had been hoping for one of his iconic hits.

Worse still, the guitar playing of the three men seemed ragged and uncoordinated. Dylan was strumming rhythmically in his usual idiosyncratic way, but Richards and Wood were playing over him without a clear sense of timing or arrangement. Neither of the two Rolling Stones provided any vocal support or harmonies. It was a mess. They were accused of not having rehearsed, of being drunk or coked-up. Or all three. Verdicts ranged from wayward and shambolic, to 'the biggest disappointment of the evening'. Dylan left the stage with his head down. At the after-show party, he was asked if he had had fun on stage and replied: 'Fun? No, we couldn't hear anything' before adding, 'we had fun rehearsing'. Ronnie Wood later insisted that the three had rehearsed for two days. In his 2007 autobiography, Wood said Dylan turned up at his house on West 78th St in New York to choose songs. Wood had invited Keith Richards along.

'The three of us started rehearsing and got through pretty much the whole Dylan catalogue,' Ronnie said. On the day of Live Aid, Dylan had turned up at West 78th in a truck and told the two Stones to follow in a limo.

'We're on in Philadelphia,' said Dylan. 'Follow me.'

'This better be fucking good,' Keith said to Ronnie. According to Wood, the two guitarists had no idea where they were going.

It was an unlikely tale. Sceptics pointed out it would be impossible to get through Dylan's back catalogue in two days. And how could the two Rolling Stones not know they were rehearsing for Live Aid until the actual day of the concert? Richards would have known full well that, by joining Dylan on stage, he would be up-staging Mick Jagger. The rough and ready perform-ance, doubters declared, suggested there had been no rehearsal at all.

But there *was* a rehearsal. And it was recorded in the studio in Wood's New York house. In his book, he writes: 'On the stairs up to the stage, Bob turned to us and said, 'Let's do "Blowin' in the Wind" … I couldn't believe it because that was the only song of his we hadn't rehearsed.' But the sixteen bootleg recordings of the rehearsal tell a different story. The three musicians practised the song at least twice. They also rehearsed 'When the Ship Comes In' with some lovely guitar riffs that were missing from the Live Aid performance. And there are three rehearsal tapes of 'Ballad of Hollis Brown', again with some inventive backing riffs which they didn't use on the night.

Having heard the sixteen bootleg recordings of the rehearsals, it's clear that Ronnie Wood's story about the two Stones not knowing that they were rehearsing for Live Aid is a piece of rock mythmaking – presumably designed to allow them to deny that they were putting one over on Mick Jagger. Ironically, all of the rehearsals on the tapes are far more imaginative and interesting than the Live Aid performances.

The tapes also contain some revealing conversations. Referring to the controversy when Dylan first went electric, Ronnie jokes to Bob that this time 'you're probably going to get complaints about going back to acoustic'. Dylan laughs. Live Aid, they acknowledge, is 'history-making time'. They discuss how the satellite technology requires strict time-keeping from them. But Richards' earlier scepticism about the cause appears undiminished on the rehearsal tape. 'What the fuck are we doing here anyway? The money's not going to get there. How many Ethiopians are really going to benefit from this? There'll be one truck of wheat actually gets there…' The three of them then go on to sing 'Careless Ethiopians', the reggae classic by Toots & the Maytals: 'Oh you careless Ethiopians have lost your way…'

So, given the care and creativity of the rehearsals, what went wrong on the night? Perhaps there is a clue on the rehearsal tapes, where the trio send out for booze. 'We got Jack…' (presumably Daniels). 'That's too sweet.' 'Rum, vodka…' 'Get half a pint.' 'I gotta drive.' 'Get a pint.' 'Yeah, get a pint.'

If alcohol was consumed in quantities on Live Aid night, that was not the only problem. Dylan & co had difficulty with the sound monitors, which were not working properly. Both Richards and Wood at times were forced to lift their acoustic guitars to their ears to make sure they were in tune. Dylan, who usually appears very in control of his performances, looked visibly annoyed and uncertain throughout. At one point, he shouted out to the audience 'Sound alright out there?', as if he couldn't hear the instruments himself.

But what annoyed Bob Geldof most was that Dylan, at the end of 'Ballad of Hollis Brown', decided to make an appeal for help for American farmers under pressure from the US banks. 'I hope that some of the money that's raised for the people in Africa … maybe they can just take a little bit of it – maybe one or two million, maybe – and use it to pay the mortgages on some of the farms that the farmers here owe to the banks.' Geldof was unconstrained in his criticism of Dylan's American exceptionalism. 'He displayed a complete lack of understanding of the issues raised by Live Aid … Live Aid was about people losing their lives. There is a radical difference between losing your livelihood and losing your life … It was a crass, stupid, and nationalistic thing to say.'

Dylan ended with 'Blowin' in the Wind'.

How many ears must one man have, before he can hear people cry?
How many deaths will it take 'til he knows that too many people
   have died?

'It ought to have been one of the greatest moments of the concert,' said Geldof. 'Unfortunately, the performance was catastrophic.' Dylan broke a string on his guitar. Ronnie Wood took off his own guitar and gave it to Dylan. Left standing on stage without an instrument, Ron began playing air guitar, swinging his arm in wide circles mimicking Pete Townshend – a piece of pantomime which the Live Aid DVD omits. Michael Gray, author of *The Bob Dylan Encyclopaedia*, called it 'the most dishevelled, debilitatingly drunk performance of his career'. As Dylan left the stage, he walked past his manager and just said one word:

'Sorry.'

☆

Fortunately, 'Blowin' in the Wind' was not to be the finale of the Philadelphia concert, as Geldof once expected it to be. Late in the day, Lionel Richie, despite having refused to put together a band and appear on the main show but having seen just how big Live Aid had become, turned up to lead the finale of the USA for Africa single 'We Are the World'.

'The finale was so overwhelming,' he said. 'Every massive artist was there, the audience was there, the campaign was there.' As all the stars of the day gathered together to sing the finale, he thought, *You turn around, behind you there's this sea of artistry. You turn around, in front of you there's a sea of humanity.*

Phil Collins, who had had a long day, was not there. 'By the time I'd finished, it just felt like 5 a.m. to me and I didn't think I could carry on to the finale. So I went back to my hotel in New York and got there just in time to catch the end of the show on TV. Everyone came on to sing "We Are the World" and there, at the back, was Cher, singing along. She'd just turned up!'

Only Keith Richards looked dejected. During the finale, he sat down on the sound monitor that had failed him during the Dylan set. He was at the very front of the stage, in front of all the other performers, but he had his back to the audience and a towel over his shoulder.

He looked totally wasted, while Mick Jagger moved round the stage joining joyously in the final song.

Keith did not have the last laugh after all.

❖

Over in London, Bob Geldof had stayed up until 4 a.m. to watch the climax of the American concert. The whole transatlantic event, he said was, 'the fulfilment of all my dreams'.

He and Harvey Goldsmith could never have imagined a success like this. 'Our target until the week of the show was £1 million,' Harvey said. 'The night before the concert, Bob and I thought we might actually make £5 million. Little did any of us realise just how much would come in.'

At the end of the day, nearly 2 billion people across 110 nations had watched the proceedings and £50 million had been raised towards famine relief in Ethiopia. Within a few weeks, as donations continued to roll in, that figure doubled.

In the days that followed, performer after performer remembered it as one of the greatest days of their lives. 'This may not be a decade noted for charity, but I don't think we were ever any less charitable than we are now,' said Paul McCartney. 'But it needs people like Bob to organise it, to put it together.'

Geldof himself declared that the world now had a new *lingua franca*, 'no longer English, but rock 'n' roll – that's the language in which the planet speaks to itself.' It was, he said, forty years on, a day like no other. 'The rich world had been asked for some cash to help people they would never meet and they had done it. Not just willingly, but with a full-throated roar of solidarity that sounded all around the globe.'

The greatest show on earth had turned out to be the greatest fundraising event in human history. But it was more than that. As Chief Olusegun Obasanjo, the president of Nigeria, put it: 'What Live Aid did, for me, was not so much the amount of money... The most important thing was the amount of global attention. It was a wake-up call.' It awoke the world to Africa, its people, its needs and its extraordinary potential.

CHAPTER 17

CHILDREN OF LIVE AID

The concert was not the end. For a number of people, it was just the beginning. Harvey Goldsmith and the other Band Aid trustees had assumed that they would be getting back to their normal lives within a few weeks. 'Our original intention was literally that, within a month of us doing the concert, we would have distributed all the funds and shut down,' Harvey said. 'But we didn't know what we had unleashed.'

For a few of the key players, a grim normality had reasserted itself. The BBC journalist Michael Buerk, whose original report from Ethiopia had been the catalyst for the whole Band Aid/Live Aid enterprise, was not even at the concert. He was back in South Africa and, on 13 July 1985, he was in one of the grimmer townships to the east of Johannesburg, struggling with the tear gas which the white police were firing at black demonstrators. There would be five more years of violent protests before apartheid was to fall.

Back in Britain, Claire Bertschinger, the Red Cross nurse interviewed by Buerk in that seminal BBC report, was about to begin treatment for post-traumatic stress disorder. She had sat on the sofa at her parents' home watching the Live Aid concerts in a state of bewilderment. She had returned to the UK only a month before after a year in the famine fields. It had taken a grim toll on her, both mentally and physically.

'My brother had tried to get me tickets. But I didn't want to go. I'd never been to a rock concert. It seemed so surreal that Michael Buerk's interview with me had been one of the catalysts for all this,' she told me. She sat, watching the television with the terrace doors open, looking out over the green fields of England, feeling numb. 'I felt as if I just landed on the planet and was trying to make sense of what I saw. The music felt disconnected from my life. Then Birhan appeared on the screen in the stadium with her father pleading for her life. It was the only thing that felt real. Tears poured down my cheeks. Suddenly I felt terrible pain and I broke down completely at the memories of all I had witnessed and lived through. I switched the television off.'

⁂

But those who had not experienced the reality on the ground were having their own moment of transformation. Something changed inside many of those who watched the television that day. Among them were two junior Labour backbench MPs, Tony Blair and Gordon Brown, future prime minister and chancellor of the exchequer, in which jobs they shifted UK policy on Africa so that it focused on the relief of poverty. Later, they would persuade the world's eight most powerful nations in the G8 to wipe away the debts of the continent's poorest nations.

Such was the emotional power of the collective experience that Gordon Brown later said Live Aid was the single most important public event in the lives of two entire generations. Thanks to Live Aid, Brown said, 'millions more people are understanding just how closely and irrevocably bound together are the fortunes of the richest persons in the richest country to the fate of the poorest persons in the poorest country of the world'. Strangers who may never meet, and who may never know each other at first hand, were being brought together as neighbours – 'by shared needs, mutual interests, common purposes and our linked destinies'.

Tony Blair was to cite the same inspiration two decades later when he launched the report of his ground-breaking Commission for Africa. Spurred by the kind of images which had been shown on the screen at Wembley, he said: 'I fear my own conscience on Africa. I fear the judgement of future generations, where history properly calculates the gravity of the suffering. I fear them asking: "But how could wealthy people – so aware of such suffering, so capable of acting – simply turn away to busy themselves with other things?"' Geldof later christened him 'the Live Aid prime minister'.

This new generation of leaders extended beyond the UK. Two American politicians later revealed they had watched Live Aid: the governor of

Arkansas, Bill Clinton, and a Texas oil man called George W. Bush. Each, when they became US president, were to pursue policies influenced by Live Aid, with Clinton focusing on debt relief for Africa's poorest nations and Bush launching an initiative on AIDS which was to save 26 million lives. Several top European leaders, including the German Chancellor Gerhard Schröder, also watched the concert and later implemented policies on international development that were influenced by it.

Politicians in the generation below them were also heavily influenced by their experience of Live Aid. David Cameron had the day off from his privileged education at Eton to watch it on television. So did George Osborne, a fourteen-year-old student at another of England's poshest public schools, Westminster. He would later go on to take charge of the nation's finances under Cameron's Conservative government. Their commitment to the Live Aid cause was such that they explicitly referenced it when they enshrined in law a pledge that the UK would meet the United Nations target of spending 0.7 per cent of its national income – seven pence in every £10 – on aid every year.

And, when the nation's finances got difficult, Cameron insisted – despite opposition within his own party – that the aid budget should be exempted from the swingeing austerity cuts imposed by Chancellor Osborne. 'Look at the response to Live Aid. If we are going to try to get across to the poorest people in the world that we care about their plight and we want them to join one world with the rest of us, we have got to make promises and keep promises.' Osborne did not just do as his boss told him; he was enthusiastic for the strategy. He even abandoned Margaret Thatcher's policy of refusing to waive the VAT purchase tax on the 2014 re-recording of the Band Aid single – and went on social media to reveal that he had promised Bob Geldof that there would be no tax on the Band Aid 30 single so that 'every penny goes to fight Ebola'.

The film-maker Richard Curtis, who was inspired by Live Aid to found the biennial Comic Relief fundraiser, has warned against underestimating what he calls the cultural power of Live Aid: 'Pop musicians are younger than politicians. So they're at their maximum power when they're twenty-three or twenty-five, and politicians when they're forty-five, so the political impact of Live Aid was bound to come later.' Bob Geldof agreed: 'I wouldn't call Blair and Brown my friends,' he said, 'but I do know them pretty well and this whole issue of Africa really does bother them. If they hadn't done anything, I think they'd regard it as a badge of shame.'

It was a sentiment shared by politicians of all backgrounds. 'We had to keep Band Aid non-political if it was to work properly,' said Geldof. 'It was a moral issue. Whether you were of the right or left was irrelevant.' Moreover, it could be fitted into the ideology of any of the mainstream British political parties. To the Conservatives, it manifested the power of the individual. To Labour, it demonstrated the power of collective action. To the Liberal Democrats, it was a celebration of community. In the US, it was to help bridge the gap between Republicans and Democrats. Live Aid transcended local politics because its central issue was both ethical and global.

Most importantly, it appealed directly to the hearts of a whole raft of individuals who were present at Live Aid that day, either in person or through their television set. Many of their names were not yet known, but they were to go on to play major roles in the forty-year-long story of the Live Aid phenomenon. In the garden of his cottage in Oxfordshire, Richard Curtis gathered with friends to watch the concert on television. In 1985, Curtis was known as a writer on the satirical BBC programme *Not the Nine O'Clock News* which starred Rowan Atkinson, Pamela Stephenson, Griff Rhys Jones and Mel Smith. He had co-written the first series of the historical comedy *Blackadder* with Atkinson, but he was far from a household name. He and his friends all agreed that they would chip in £50 each, but only one of them wrote a cheque and sent it off. The others never got round to it after the exhilaration of the day had passed. But Curtis was to go on to raise $1.5 billion in the wake of Live Aid and to play a key part in a political change which was to deliver ten times that amount to Africa.

In Oxford, a twenty-eight-year-old postgraduate named Kevin Watkins was finishing his PhD on Indian history and reading Amartya Sen's seminal academic work on famine. But he allowed himself to be distracted by Live Aid on his TV. 'It was tapping into something that people like me – who look at these issues just from an academic or economics angle – often miss,' he said. 'It was a thing called human connectivity. And when it's tapped into, in a way that has resonance with how people see the world and see their lives, it is a very powerful thing.' Watkins, who went on to become a key figure for the activist community on aid and poor countries' debt, was to have a pivotal role in how Live Aid developed over the next four decades.

So would a young Ugandan-Asian in the crowd at Wembley. Shriti Vadera – now Baroness Vadera – had been schooled in India, where she had begun to think about what kept people poor. At Somerville College, Oxford, where she had read philosophy, politics and economics, she joined the university's Oxfam and Third World First groups, and began to focus on development economics. On the day of Live Aid, when she turned up at Wembley with friends, she was aged twenty-three and in her first year working for Warburg's investment bank. 'My interest was very much in emerging markets when nobody was interested in them,' she recalled. She would go on to advise African governments about 'their debt restructuring and their external balance of payments'. It would lead her to a major behind-the-scenes role in what Bob and Bono were to do over the decades to come. Live Aid, she said, was a revelation, because it showed her that 'more people than me were interested in doing something about global poverty'.

There was another key player watching all day on the television with friends in a student house off the Cowley Road in Oxford. Justin Forsyth was studying catering management at Oxford Polytechnic, where one of his lecturers ran, on the side, a centre for South Africans and Namibians who had been tortured in the struggle against apartheid. Forsyth began to volunteer there and, in the process, was recruited to go out to South Africa to work with uMkhonto weSizwe, the military wing of the African National Congress. 'That gave me a very different perspective.' But though his focus was then more on the anti-apartheid movement, 'Live Aid sparked in me a lifelong commitment to the fight against hunger and poverty – and an understanding about the power of popular culture to move and inspire a mainstream audience to action.' On returning from Africa, he went to work as chief campaigns strategist at Oxfam – the best strategist the aid movement ever had, according to Kevin Watkins, who said Forsyth transformed Oxfam from a voice of protest to a changer of government policy. After Oxfam, he was recruited to work as a special adviser to two prime ministers, Tony Blair and Gordon Brown. Forsyth, too, was to become a key operator in the development of Live Aid strategy inside Geldof's inner circle over the next two decades.

The other two members of this core group were Jamie Drummond and Lucy Matthew, who were both still teenagers when Live Aid happened. Drummond watched the concert at school: 'I was blown away by it and the sense that it was a protest against things that were going on in the world.' It inspired him to go on to study development economics at the School of Oriental and African Studies, where he acquired detailed knowledge of what was then called Third World debt. After working at Christian Aid, he became Geldof's chief number cruncher.

Live Aid was 'a big deal for us at school', recalled Lucy Matthew. Her best friend got a ticket for Wembley – 'and everyone was very jealous' – but Lucy watched the concert at a friend's house because she didn't have a television. 'I knew it was to raise money for Ethiopia, but to be honest, at the age of fifteen, I was much more interested in the fact that the bands plastered all over my bedroom wall were playing in one gig.' Still, it was enough to inspire her to study economics and, after doing a Master's at the LSE, to volunteer to work in a hospital in Zambia at a time when the country was cutting its health services to pay its debts to Western governments. That took her into campaign work with Christian Aid and, eventually, to become Bono's chief of staff on his activism on AIDS, aid and debt.

Over the months and years that followed, this group of nine individuals, directly inspired by the Live Aid concerts, were to meet clandestinely at Shriti Vadera's mews terrace, down a cobblestone cul-de-sac in Kensington. There, between them, they shaped not only the strategy of a global activist campaign, but the political policies of eight of the world's most powerful governments.

⁂

Long before that came to pass, it was evident that Live Aid had been a watershed moment. That was true in music *and* in politics.

'Before Live Aid, music was an also-ran in mainstream newspapers,' said Harvey Goldsmith. 'There were music magazines – *Melody Maker*, *New Musical Express* and, in America, *Variety* – but the only time you ever read about rock stars in the press was either because they were getting divorced or busted for drugs. Live Aid changed the whole culture because suddenly the national press, particularly in England, realised that pop stars sold papers.' That had its downside, he believed, because it built a whole cult of celebrity. 'But it also empowered people. For the first time, the public could feel they were part of making something happen.' For many music fans, 13 July 1985 was the day that music changed the world.

Not everyone agreed. One of the hosts of the BBC coverage, the DJ Andy Kershaw, was heavily critical. 'Musically, Live Aid was entirely predictable and boring – another parade of the same old rock aristocracy in a concert for Africa, organised by someone who – while advertising his concern for, and sympathy with, the continent – didn't see fit to celebrate or dignify the place by including on the Live Aid bill a single African performer.' Kershaw described the event as 'smug in its assumption that a bunch of largely lamentable rock and pop floozies was capable of making a difference, without tackling simultaneously underlying problems'.

But such a contrarian reaction was, at the time, an exception. Immediately after the concert, the response from both press and public alike was overwhelmingly positive. Live Aid was applauded for the quality of the performances, the huge sums it raised for the starving, and the massive feat of organisation and collaboration it had required. Criticism was minimal – certainly in those early days – and the overall tone was celebratory. Conversations were sparked about global inequality and humanitarian responsibility. Only a few voices were raised to suggest that the Live Aid model defused, drained or stifled more radical forms of protest or political mobilisation, though, as the years passed, those voices grew louder.

Looking back, forty years later, it is easy to forget what a technological feat was involved in putting the show together in an era when there was no internet, no emails, no mobile phones and very few fax machines. The laboriously punched ticker-tape of the telex was the standard form of written international communication. In many countries, international phone calls still had to be booked, sometimes hours in advance, through the operator. Computers were outside the reach or salary of most ordinary people. It seemed a challenge bordering on the impossible to broadcast the first absolutely live, all-day, multi-artist, two-continent, simultaneous concert to the whole world. Yet the innovations which Live Aid ushered in presaged the technological revolution that was to follow in global communications.

Live Aid established the global 'mega-event' as a cultural form. It also changed the template for giving. 'Twenty years ago, charity was something the Women's Institute did,' said Midge Ure. Bob Geldof made it fashionable to really care about people in a country thousands of miles away, people that most of us would never meet.

Michael Buerk is a hard-nosed and unsentimental commentator. It is easy to forget, he said, that in the 1980s, most voters had voted for Margaret Thatcher and Ronald Reagan but, despite that, they seemed to be uneasy about the retreat of welfare and post-war consensus. 'Market-driven individualism might work better with the grain of human nature. It might make most of us more prosperous. But it sometimes made us feel selfish. There was something obscene about us piling up mountains of food we could not eat, while millions of others starved to death, a few hours flying time away.'

The Live Aid concert was the biggest shared event in human history. The billions of people who watched it 'were not just watching the greatest assembly of rock musicians ever gathered together,' said Buerk. 'They were sharing in a worldwide act of human solidarity. There was a sense of everybody being involved, of rules being waived, willing it all to be a success.' It was pop's greatest moment when a concert wrapped half the globe in a euphoric sense of goodwill. 'Something very special happened that year. It might not have solved much in the long term, but it made a difference then. We felt, we cared, we tried and we saved millions of lives. Maybe the memory of what we did then will one day lead us to a fairer and better organised world where famine is described by historians, not reporters.'

That day in July 1985 was a harbinger of political change. The fall of the Berlin Wall, the revolt in Tiananmen Square, the end of apartheid and peace in Northern Ireland all soon followed. Something new was in the air and Live Aid was an early sign of it.

But political change requires hard work. Live Aid had been the biggest charitable event the world had ever seen. Yet Bob Geldof was now to learn a swift lesson. He had raised more money on 13 July 1985 than had ever before been raised at a single event – around £77 million on the day. As the weeks, months and years passed, the money would keep coming in from merchandising, record sales, DVDs, streaming and licences granted to broadcasters and film-makers who wanted to use footage of the concert. By the fortieth anniversary of Live Aid in 2025, a staggering total of £146 million had been raised.

But Geldof was shocked to learn soon afterwards this huge sum was the same amount that African nations were obliged to pay to rich countries *every week* in repayments on old debts.

Live Aid had not sorted Africa's problems. It had addressed the symptoms but not the structures that were the root of the problem. It had asked: what can we do about Africa's poverty? But it had failed to ask: what keeps Africa so poor? Addressing those problems – and pressurising the world's politicians to bring forward solutions to them – was a task which was to occupy Bob and Bono for the next forty years.

CHAPTER 18

SACKS AND TRUCKS AND ROCK 'N' ROLL

Bob Geldof spent the day after Live Aid in bed. But, on the Monday morning, he went down to the Picasso café in the King's Road for his usual coffee and was astonished to see queues of people standing outside every bank and post office. These were the people who had rung in to pledge money on Saturday but had been unable to get through, so busy were the 300 phone lines the BBC had dedicated to fundraising. He was moved by what he saw.

'How much are you giving?' one man, who had pledged £5, asked the woman in front of him in the queue outside the building society.

'£20,' replied his neighbour.

'Me too,' revised the first man, increasing his donation to keep up.

That same day, Geldof got the news that the Live Aid concert had raised about £4 million in the UK. Then came the news that Ireland alone had raised £5 million. The figures seemed to change hourly. Money kept coming in, donation after donation. By the end of the day, direct contributions from the British public rose to £18 million. The amounts were such that members of both the British and Norwegian parliaments announced they would be nominating Bob Geldof for the Nobel Peace Prize.

Live Aid's chartered accountant, Phil Rusted, was shell-shocked. 'We were hoping to clear £1 million,' he told reporters. Geldof always knew it would be more than that. He had raised $10 million in corporate sponsorship even before the concert began. Indeed, he had already spent £1 million of it.

Two days after the Live Aid concert, the UK minister for overseas development, Timothy Raison, flew out to Ethiopia. Emergency food drops by the RAF's Hercules transport planes were due to finish at the end of September. Geldof had pleaded with Margaret Thatcher over their late-night whisky for a change of mind on this. A few days later, Raison was in the House of Commons announcing a change of plan: the aircraft would remain in Addis Ababa until the end of the year.

The whisky had warmed her heart perhaps.

Rain was now falling in many parts of Ethiopia. Some crops had been planted. Livestock was beginning to recover. But rains were only intermittent in the famine areas. It was essential, he told MPs, that the relief effort was maintained into 1986. But the big problem was a shortage of trucks to transport the food aid.

The staff of Band Aid knew this already. In the days leading up to the concert, news had been reaching them that food was building up in the ports in Ethiopia and Sudan. Then came news of famine in Darfur and Kordofan, Sudan's traditional breadbasket. Farmers had suffered a total crop failure. A million people were on the move and malnutrition was up fivefold. Kevin Jenden had returned to London from Sudan a few days before the concert. In one of the interviews between the music acts, he had told the television audience that hundreds of thousands of tonnes of grain was sitting in Port Sudan, waiting to be trucked to the West or smuggled through the back door into Ethiopia. Far more trucks were needed to transport it.

What he didn't tell the television audience was that the relief effort in Sudan was being stymied by a cartel of lorry owners who were forcing aid agencies to compete with one another. They had massively inflated the price of transporting food to the starving. 'It was ransom money,' said Harvey Goldsmith. To break that cartel, Band Aid decided they should buy their own trucks. Even before the concert, Geldof had earmarked £1 million of the Live Aid sponsorship money to buy a fleet of lorries.

'We had to set up a trucking corporation in a desert,' said Geldof. Band Aid discovered forty trucks and sixty trailers in a compound which had been abandoned by a mining company, Geosource, which was under contract to Chevron Oil. It had been involved in oil exploration, but had been forced to reduce its operations dramatically because of the civil war in the south of Sudan. The trucks came with a compound, oil storage facilities, Land

Rovers, forklifts, cranes and a quarter of a million pounds worth of brand-new spare parts.

'It would have cost $5.5 million new, but we negotiated, bartered, squeezed, pinched and pushed and basically got it for $1 million,' Jenden said. He arranged for fuel for the trucks to be imported from Saudi Arabia on one of the ships Band Aid had chartered. The fleet of vehicles would be operated in conjunction with Save the Children. It would be the first coordinated radio-linked transport distribution network in the country.

But it would take some time to get the fleet operational. Some of the trucks had to be cannibalised into spare parts to get the others running. In the meantime, Geldof wondered if there was a quicker way to smash the lorry drivers' cartel. Band Aid staff made enquiries in Port Sudan and discovered, to their amazement, that the cartel was operating under the aegis of the US government official aid agency, USAID.

Harvey Goldsmith contacted a lawyer he knew in Washington.

'You'll need to come over here,' the lawyer said. 'I'll tell you who to talk to.'

By extraordinary coincidence, Geldof had recently been invited to Washington to receive a congressional honour – to receive two, in fact. Just before the concert, the US government had declared 13 July 1985 to be Live Aid Day. The document authorising this was the most signed bill ever to go through Congress. Even President Reagan signed it, although he was laid up following an operation. After the concerts in London and Philadelphia, the Arts Caucus of the US Congress decided to make an award to the man behind it all. So did the Black Congressional Caucus who, later that year, awarded him their prestigious 1985 Chairman's Award – the first time a white man had received one. Geldof decided to take Kevin Jenden and Harvey Goldsmith with him. As well as all the glad-handing, there would be serious business to be done.

Even Bob Geldof, a man not intimidated by much, was overawed when he arrived at the seat of American power on 23 July 1985. Congressmen and Congresswomen and their staff came out to line the corridors as Geldof and co walked through the marble halls and underneath the great Dome of Congress.

They applauded and wanted to be photographed with the 'Live Aid Man'.

'They didn't look at us, of course,' said Geldof. 'They shook hands with their heads twisted round so they could smile at the television cameras.' Geldof was presented with his Arts Caucus scroll amid much handshaking.

Lunch was laid on in the Speaker's dining room. Tip O'Neill, the 47th Speaker of the United States House of Representatives, was a proud Irish American. A huge avuncular man – with a red face, bulbous nose, bushy white eyebrows and shock of white hair – he looked to Geldof like a man he might have seen in an Irish country bar. 'I thought I heard the accent,' Tip said. Turning to the press, he put his arm around Bob and said: 'We very much admire this young man and any laws we may have to pass to smooth his path, and any red tape we may have to cut … we're going to do.' Whether he meant it or not was irrelevant, Bob thought. He said it and it's on camera.

Over lunch, Geldof talked to politicians who had been sent to Congress from rural areas with big farming communities. They, and their constituents, were caught up in the same vicious circle as the farmers in Europe. Basically, there were too many farmers for US needs. But they represented a big voting lobby and so the government, as in Europe, paid out large amounts in subsidies to American agriculture. When agri-business got in on the act, the result was vast overproduction – and massive amounts of money spent on food storage or even destroying food. Geldof tried to persuade the politicians that the interests of American farmers coincided with those of Africans in need.

'It's not just a moral requirement that you should give more aid to Africa, it is also a sound economic one. It makes no sense for you to mouth platitudes about how Africa needs to stand on its own feet and then in the next breath announce a $50 million increase in internal agricultural subsidies.'

He talked so much, he didn't get chance to finish his soup.

An appointment to meet Vice-President George Bush Sr in the White House followed. Harvey Goldsmith had been told by a friend that visitors to the Oval Office were offered a souvenir pen. 'But he told me they also do really nice cufflinks. His friend had said, "Don't take the pen. Ask for the cufflinks." So we were in this line-up having our photograph taken and Vice-President Bush said, "It's our honour to give you a little souvenir of the White House."'

One of Bush's assistants gave Bob a pen and was about to give Harvey one too when the impresario piped up. 'I understand you've got great cuff-links...' Bush turned to his secretary and said: 'Can you get Mr Goldsmith a set of cufflinks?' They came with a vice-presidential scarf pin.

'Bob was livid,' Harvey gloated. 'He went on at me for about half an hour.' Geldof, like some gluttonous tourist, snaffled a load of 'Welcome Aboard Air Force One' cigarettes by way of compensation.

❖

But things turned serious when they got to the offices of USAID. There they were shown into a large room with a horseshoe-shaped table and maps of the world on the walls. It was like a wartime operation room with clocks showing the time in different parts of the world.

One said Zulu Time and had stopped at 06:35. 'I kept staring at it, wondering what Zulu Time was, but I never found out,' said Harvey. Zulu Time is, in fact, the armed services term for the time at zero degrees longitude, Greenwich Mean Time. It is used to coordinate military activities across several time zones where all the operatives needed to be synchronised. Its presence revealed the close coordination between USAID and the US State department and the Pentagon which, Geldof was to learn, had a significant influence on the famine in Ethiopia.

The USAID officials began to introduce themselves, but Geldof cut through the formalities.

'We've got something we'd like to discuss in detail with you.'

Kevin Jenden produced a copy of the contract Band Aid had obtained in Port Sudan. It covered the distribution of American food aid in Sudan.

'This is what USAID has been doing in Khartoum,' began Geldof. 'The way your trucking operation has been set up, whether you know it or not, means you're maintaining a cartel which has trebled the price of distributing food in the past three months. As a result, at the request of the agencies, we've had to embark on the purchase of a fleet of lorries in what is essentially a cartel-busting operation which has cost us a fortune and it shouldn't really be our job.'

Geldof passed across a copy of one of my articles from *The Times*. 'The press are beginning to sniff at this thing. You may not have realised it, but your policy seems to be entirely wrong here.'

Suddenly, the USAID officials began to talk very differently. They embarked on a detailed discussion of the policy options in the area where both Band Aid and USAID were involved. The Washington officials were clearly troubled, so much so that they took Geldof, Goldsmith and Jenden upstairs to meet the political head of the organisation, Peter McPherson.

'We think you should talk to these guys. They have some points worth listening to,' one of the officials – a general – told him. McPherson looked at the contract which Kevin Jenden had produced.

'You do understand the implications of this clause here?' said Kevin, beginning his detailed analysis.

By the end, McPherson seemed genuinely concerned. 'I think we've got to look into this,' he said. Within a few weeks, the trucking cartel in Sudan was dismantled.

But there was something more. Geldof suggested that USAID should match the funding, on a dollar-for-dollar basis, of some Band Aid projects. The American agency was the biggest single aid donor in the world. That would double the spending power of the donations the American and British public had made at Live Aid.

USAID decided that they were happy to work with Band Aid. In part, this was because they were keen to be seen to support a cause that US voters had responded to so emphatically. But it also gave Washington plausible deniability; it could back projects through Band Aid without being seen to be involved. 'We could put together joint projects where they didn't have to be involved at all physically and where we could use our apolitical stand as a bargaining tool to gain concessions,' said Geldof. 'This happened and it worked.'

Nowhere was this truer than in the secret cross-border operation set up to feed the rebel areas in Ethiopia, where more than a million people were starving. Band Aid's objectives here were clear-cut. The huge amounts of food aid now being shipped to Ethiopia were not reaching the hungry people who lived behind the rebel lines. The cross-border operation was the way to reach them. But the motives of the Reagan administration were a good deal more murky.

At the height of the famine, food was reaching Ethiopia in two ways. The first was via the channel through which the bulk of the world's food aid was sent to the Marxist regime in Addis Ababa. But this was distributed only at the government-run feeding centres along the main roads. These were avoided by people in rebel areas, for fear government soldiers would forcibly resettle them to the south of the country. In February 1985, I revealed in *The Times* a confidential report by the Ethiopian government which confirmed that 'more than three-quarters of the people in the famine-stricken province of Tigray are failing to receive food aid'.

A second operation was run by two rebel groups, in Tigray and Eritrea. This smuggled grain from the east of Sudan across the Ethiopian border to people behind rebel lines. The food was provided by a consortium of aid agencies, who largely kept their identities hidden for fear of irritating the regime in Addis. Band Aid joined in with this third group, which operated under the obscure name: the Emergency Relief Desk.

Band Aid knew the Americans had mixed motives here. As early as May 1984, a top-secret US government report showed that the White House was well aware that a deadly famine was looming in both guerrilla- and government-held territory. Ronald Reagan repeatedly assured the American public that 'a starving child knows no politics'. Yet he set up an Ethiopian famine task force which was political in the extreme; its members included CIA operatives, top generals and Defense Department officials, as well as representatives of USAID and the Department of Agriculture. Headed by a retired general, it was to play a critical role in determining who ate and who starved in the Horn of Africa.

Early in 1985, Vice-President George H.W. Bush had flown into the Sudanese capital, accompanied by USAID boss Peter McPherson and two US private aid agencies that had played key roles in supporting the Contra rebels, which Washington backed against the socialist government in Nicaragua. Bush and McPherson held private discussions with Sudanese officials and proposed that the leading American aid agency, CARE, should build a $100 million road into the rebel-held areas and give them as many as 500 trucks. Again, I leaked details of this in *The Times*, which Bob Geldof read. The rebels in Tigray and Eritrea looked set to become Ronald Reagan's Contras in the Horn of Africa.

But the Reagan administration had a change of heart. A later secret study by a top CIA operative came out strongly against the US supporting the rebels. The guerrillas were anti-Soviet, and anti-Mengistu, but they were hard-line Marxists of a different kind. USAID did not, in the end, give the support it had promised to the cross-border operation, which remained grossly under-supplied throughout 1985.

Band Aid stepped into the breach. It could not match the kind of funding the US government had promised – and then withheld – but it smuggled grain, vehicles, water trailers, blankets, dried milk, sugar, vegetable oil and medical supplies across the Ethiopian/Sudanese border into Tigray throughout the whole year. Band Aid's work there was to continue for the next six years, spending $11.8 million to get food and medicine to those suffering in the forgotten famine.

But while that was going on behind the scenes, Band Aid had a much more public task getting food across the 1,250 miles of desert wastelands from the Red Sea to the arid savannah of Darfur and Kordofan. The United Nations Children's Fund, UNICEF, was reporting that as many as 6 million Sudanese were seriously affected by drought there, with more than 2 million people having left their homes in search of food. Many were to die needlessly, but many others were saved by the activities of aid agencies, including Band Aid. The Geosource fleet of lorries it had bought before the Live Aid concert was now operational, but more were needed to carry grain on the 32-hour journey to Sudan's far-off border with Chad.

Things were improving in Ethiopia now. In September 1985 Band Aid bought another fifty-four trucks, most of them from Kuwait, and shipped them to the Ethiopian port of Assab, where Band Aid also paid for improvements to the dock's unloading capacity. More than half the trucks for the Ethiopian food distribution operation had now been supplied by Band Aid. By the end of November, they arrived in the famine region of Wollo, carrying more than 1,000 tonnes of grain. The fleet was operated by the UN World Food Programme but financed by Band Aid over six years at a cost of $9 million.

The operation was not without problems. After the fifty-four trucks had been unloaded at Assab, the Ethiopian military boarded the Band Aid ship and seized a 65-tonne truck loaded with food intended for the rebel-held area of Tigray. The ship was supposed to go on to Port Sudan to unload it there for transportation across the border, direct into the rebel-held area. Band Aid had to send a replacement, but the next time the ship took care to call at Sudan before travelling on to Ethiopia.

The Band Aid trucking operation in Sudan was subjected to the scrutiny of BBC Television's investigative documentary series, *Panorama*, in September 1985. The programme asked critical questions of the Band Aid decision to buy the second-hand Geosource fleet. Were these trucks repairable? The film showed pictures of lorries with broken axles at the side of the road.

'They had obviously concluded that our trucks were useless, that they weren't operating and that we'd wasted our money,' said Band Aid's lawyer John Kennedy. 'But there was simply nothing in the programme with any credibility.'

Band Aid now had assembled a fleet of 154 trucks. The Geosource trucks had been standing idle for eighteen months, but Band Aid mechanics had made almost all of them serviceable, with just a few that were beyond repair being cannibalised for spare parts. They had imported tyres for the vehicles. Convoys of trucks filled with grain were continually making the 500-mile journey from Port Sudan to Khartoum, and from there 800 miles more out west to the famine areas in Darfur.

'The *Panorama* film showed a few trucks stopped, with engineers and mechanics getting sand out of the carburettors,' said Kennedy. 'But the idea that vehicles broke down from time to time in the sand in the desert was not a very compelling story.'

Bob Geldof was robust in his defence of the Band Aid project. The trucks had cost a fifth of what would have been required to send new vehicles from Europe. The initiative eliminated the problem of building a compound, which alone would have cost a million dollars. It eliminated Band Aid's spare parts problem. And it did away with the need to wait for months while Sudan's bureaucracy got round to giving agreement for the import of trucks that were in perfect mechanical order.

Film of trucks with broken axles suggested that the Band Aid project was 'a cock-up', the BBC reporter said. Geldof was dismissive. 'When you see pictures of broken axles, you think "Oh my God, they've bought a complete turkey,"' he told *Panorama*. But broken axles are endemic in Africa. 'The trucks that everybody said wouldn't work, we have over 50 per cent of them working now. We've broken up the cartel at Port Sudan that was preventing the flow of food to the West. We have a free shipping service and we have a direct line from London through the shipping service and through our trucks, right out to the West. That to me is not a cock-up. That to me is pretty well thought-out.' The cost of transporting food had fallen. Where before aid agencies had had to compete with each other and pay inflated prices, now food and essential medical supplies could move more efficiently inside Sudan and the huge stockpiles at the docks had been reduced.

Still, suggested the *Panorama* reporter, Band Aid had had its fingers burned with the Geosource project. Geldof was scornful in reply: 'I don't know any people who've gone into Africa who haven't had their fingers burned one way or the other, and the people who had their fingers most burned are the ones who were dying.'

Band Aid was developing ways of working that some aid professionals decried as amateurish and unsophisticated. Buying second-hand trucks went against the acquisition protocols established by mainstream aid agencies.

But Band Aid, said Midge Ure, had a 'gung-ho attitude, which meant we suggested a lot of stuff that regular charities couldn't – or wouldn't – do'.

In the case of the Sudanese lorry fleet, the Band Aid maverick approach was a huge success. In the first two years, Band Aid bought $43 million worth of food and medical supplies, and transported them from Europe to Africa. 'Rank amateurs can grasp things quickly,' it turns out, said Geldof.

The unsophisticated approach, it seems, can produce results. But then hunger is a rather unsophisticated experience.

CHAPTER 19

ACROSS AFRICA TO SPEND THE MONEY

Not everyone was convinced that Bob Geldof knew what he was doing. In the months after Live Aid, disquiet grew among the professional aid agencies at the dismissive attitude he repeatedly expressed towards them. It was as if, faced with the terrible situation in Ethiopia, he assumed that all those involved – governments, the United Nations, the European Economic Community and voluntary agencies – must each be in some way to blame. In these early months, aid agencies grew frustrated, declaring that it was, as one put it, 'ludicrous for Geldof and his group of amateurs to set up a network of complex programmes from scratch'. One popular newspaper wrote a headline asking: 'IS IT TIME FOR SAINT BOB TO CALL IN THE EXPERTS?' The British government privately sounded out agencies for their views on Band Aid and found them unfavourable. Seasoned aid workers couldn't, at that point, work out whether Geldof's 'red tape cutting, rock 'n' roll attitude' was suspect or something to be envied.

Bob knew he had a lot to learn because, the more he learned, the more he discovered what he did not know. Three months after the concert, he and Kevin Jenden embarked on a two-week tour across the Sahel, the belt of land which stretches from west to east across Africa, just below the Sahara. Their aim was to see how Band Aid money had been spent in Ethiopia and Sudan, and to identify funding priorities for the rest of the famine-hit region.

'You can read all the reports, but unless you talk to people who actually work there and who know exactly what's going on, you don't really get a feel for the place. And in the countries that we haven't been to before, that's the priority,' Geldof said as he boarded a private jet which had been provided free to Band Aid by British Aerospace. Bob asked me – having read my reports now from Sudan as well as Ethiopia in *The Times* – if I would accompany him on the trip to decide how to spend the £100+ million that Live Aid had raised. He was looking for independent advice. His only plan, at the outset, was to arrive in each country, call all the aid agencies together and ask them to set aside their interagency rivalries to come up with a common plan on how the money should be spent in each African nation.

But if the agencies had doubts, they were pretty much on their own. Geldof was now one of the most famous people in the world. An opinion poll in the UK said he was 'the person most people would like to meet'. In Australia, another poll voted him 'the man in the world with the most credibility'. Newspapers straightforwardly referred to him as St Bob. His newfound fame meant that, wherever we arrived in Africa, he was greeted as a global celebrity. He was presented with guards of honour to inspect. Troops of dancers and singers came out to perform for him. Government officials greeted him with long and tedious speeches, which he found immensely irritating and frustrating. He began to develop what he called Prince Charles syndrome. 'I knew I had to meet many of the leaders of these countries because now I was "an international figure", as stupid as that was,' he said – a realisation which only marginally curbed his propensity to pepper every sentence with four-letter words. There was very little that was saintly about his vocabulary.

'Why are we seeing *him*?' he said, pointing to a line on the itinerary drawn up by the Red Cross, which had helped organise Geldof's visit to our first destination on the trip, Mali.

Bob was pointing to a line which said: 'A courtesy visit to the Minister of Sports, Arts and Culture'.

'We're here to find out about famine, we're not making a state visit. Cut that out.'

'I can't cut that out,' said the man from the Red Cross. 'He's a minister. You've got to understand there's protocol involved here. I can't ring up a minister and say, "Good morning. Mr Geldof thinks meeting you is boring so we've cut you out."'

'Fucking protocol...'

Mali is at the western end of the Sahel. At the airport in Bamako, there was a reception committee from the Ministry of Protocol, numerous government officials, members of the Red Cross and the British Honorary Consul. There was also a cloud of grasshoppers; one of the insects became entangled in Bob's long hair. A plague of grasshoppers had wiped out 90 per cent of the crop in north-west Mali, he was told. From there, we went straight to the Amitié Hotel, where all the local representatives of the international aid agencies were gathered. Someone else was there too – the French minister for co-operation. He had arrived from Paris and decided to gatecrash the meeting. The minister basked in the television lights and made a speech about how the French government had made sure that the famine in Mali was not as bad as in Ethiopia. Geldof immediately went for the jugular:

'What I don't understand about you people in the European Economic Community is why you don't open your silos and send the grain to where it's needed most.'

'I think you do not understand the issues of agricultural policy. It's a difficult and complicated subject,' the minister said.

'It is not an agricultural problem, it's a moral problem, Minister,' said Geldof. 'Why did the EC pay £10 million for a report on how to get rid of two million tonnes of butter?'

The minister perspired gently, perhaps not only from the African heat.

Geldof and Jenden had allocated $1 million dollars for Mali. There were thirty different international aid agencies present. Many of them confessed afterwards that they felt hostile to Geldof when the meeting began. They had been summoned away from their projects to meet a rock 'n' roll singer who knew nothing about the country and its problems. 'It is aid theatre,' one said scornfully.

Geldof was well aware of this. His opening remarks at the meeting, and all the others that followed in other countries, took the line: 'Look, I don't know the best way to spend the money. I need you to tell me. All I ask is that you reach a consensus about the best way to do it.'

It was in Mali that Geldof first heard the term 'desertification'. We travelled north to see the problem first-hand in the city of Timbuktu – a place which for hundreds of years had been a synonym for the most remote place on earth – and found that its ancient mud palaces were now being overtaken by the sands of the Sahara.

From the thirteenth century onwards, this forbidden city had carried on an impenetrable existence in the heart of Africa. But to its inhabitants and to those merchants able to converge on this crossroads of the ancient caravan routes, the town on the fringes of the desert was a haven from the unyielding harshness of the Sahara, a place of rich grazing for cattle and camels, a university town, a revered centre of worship and a marketplace of both commercial and cultural exchange.

During the previous two decades, however, the desert had been reclaiming Timbuktu. There had been drought there for the past fifteen years. For the past four, it had been increasingly severe. And, that year, the area had had only half as much rain as in the previous year. The sands were moving south. Every year, the encroachment continued so that the desert had swept around the town and now surrounded it entirely. Huge dunes of sand were creeping onwards, thousands of tons at the rate of twenty miles a year. As Geldof arrived, a fine, white dust was falling, almost imperceptibly, from the heavens. Some days, the sun was blotted out for days on end. There was an apocalyptic quality to living with the earth above your head for so long.

Deserts, Bob was told by local ecologists, feed upon themselves and grow. Bare soil and stone reflect more solar radiation back into the atmosphere than grass and trees do. The increased reflectivity keeps the air hotter, disperses clouds and reduces rain. Without rain, the grasses on the edges of the desert wither. Overgrazing, and felling trees for fuel, make things worse. Without vegetation, the wind throws more soil into the air. Increased evaporation lowers the moisture content of the earth and further suppresses rain. It was a vicious circle.

The strangulation of Timbuktu had, paradoxically, doubled its population. Most of the merchants who once dominated the place had moved south. But almost 150,000 nomads had moved down from the desert and settled in the town. North of the river, they said, the land is finished. They were moving onto land already occupied by farmers. We visited a settlement built nearby by UNICEF for a group of Tuareg pastoralists who had lost all their cattle and camels. 'What we have seen is the death of a traditional way of life,' said Geldof. 'The possibility of them ever being able to return to it seems pretty remote.' It was his first indication that something more permanent was wrong in sub-Saharan Africa. His encounter with the advancing desert foreshadowed what he would later come to see as climate change resulting from global warming.

❊

Bob Geldof spent the next two weeks striding around Africa like an arche-typal Western Everyman. He was inappropriately dressed and shod. He got headaches from dehydration; he took no hat and wouldn't drink enough water. He developed a septic toe – an injury he made worse by impromptu self-surgery in a filthy hotel in Chad. But he asked questions which the professionals had forgotten how to ask. 'I ask the questions which the people who gave the money would ask. If professionals say they are naïve or ill-informed, fair enough – just so long as they can give a good answer.' He had the same attitude towards the heads of state he met. Protocol men – who were quick to put an end to unpalatable queries from journalists by shouting 'No more questions, no more questions' – found they were unable to do the same to the honoured guest with millions of pounds in the back pocket of his pink trousers.

'Do you torture people as Amnesty International says?' he demanded baldly of Thomas Sankara, the president of Burkina Faso.

'How can you justify requesting 400,000 tons of food aid for Darfur next year when your harvest elsewhere should bring in a million-ton surplus?' he asked General Swar al-Dahab, the military leader of Sudan.

'Is it true that your president once personally strangled two of his pol-itical opponents while they were awaiting execution in the condemned cell?' he asked a cabinet minister in Chad. When the minister's moder-ately fluent English proved unequal to the task, the lead singer of the Boomtown Rats seized him by the throat and started to throttle him by way of demonstration.

There was something wilfully gauche about his behaviour. In these early days, he was like a deliberately naughty schoolboy seeing how far he could push things. When he eventually met the president of Chad, Hissène Habré, he did not ask whether he strangled his enemies but opened the conversation by saying:

'Hello. You've got grey hair. It's brown in the pictures. Do you dye it for the photos?'

Coolly, Habré replied that grey hair was the lot of any ruler of Chad. Had Geldof not been surrounded by television cameras, he might have gone the same way as the 40,000 people Habré was found guilty of killing when he appeared before an international tribunal three decades later. But here, as in all his interactions with political leaders, Geldof was naïvely fearless.

Often the answers, from all sources, were more complex than Geldof wanted to hear. He would then stop listening and embark on one of his tirades about 'moral imperatives' – a phrase he picked up from the German philosopher Immanuel Kant. Geldof, who is almost entirely self-taught, reads widely on an eclectic range of subjects, from history to music to politics.

Sometimes Bob responded to complexities by trampling all over them, but out in the field, his sense of moral indignation was powerful. In Burkina Faso, he discovered an old man dying in a hut in a village. He turned his fire on a government official standing in a storeroom with piles of USAID sorghum grain towering above his head.

'What I am saying is this: why is that old man dying of hunger in the village over there when there is all this food here?'

The official was sweating profusely beneath the scrutiny of the BBC television crew which accompanied us. He wiped his brow and took a quick breath before launching on a long and complex explanation of their system of distribution.

'I'm not interested in the bloody system,' Geldof shouted. 'Why has he no food? Why is he starving to death?'

The UN worker who had organised the trip looked embarrassed. He would have to work with the local government officials after Geldof had gone. 'He's just walked all over local etiquette here,' the frustrated UN worker said. He had just explained to Geldof that he was not being invited into one particular village because the head man had no hospitality to offer in his house. Not realising that, in this circumstance, the house and village were synonymous, Geldof said 'Okay' and walked straight in anyway. Aid workers accused him of being a famine tourist, but he later countered belligerently: 'If I hadn't gone in, we wouldn't have found the dying old man – and he wouldn't have got any help.'

During our journey across the Sahel, Geldof had, overall, been optimistic. In Mali, Burkina Faso and Niger, there was suffering and appalling deprivation, but there was also hope that conditions would improve. International aid, and Band Aid's contribution to it, could assist towards the long-term development of the local people and their economies in a way which, Bob hoped, might ensure that the horrors of the 1984–85 drought did not occur again. Even in the ravaged wastes around Timbuktu, we had seen a rice paddy irrigation project that could be used to keep the population of that city alive. By comparison, though, Chad was a nightmare.

Geldof arrived in the capital N'Djamena to find the city's buildings pockmarked with bullets and its streets filled with beggars whose legs had been blown off by landmines. The north of the country had been occupied by Libya, whose ruler, President Gaddafi, was also supporting rebels against the government of Chad. Just the night before, a Libyan warplane had flown over the capital, causing widespread panic as Gaddafi had bombed N'Djamena previously.

The southern part of Chad was filled with troops from France, defending the regime of Hissène Habré, who had taken over in 1982 through a military coup backed by Paris and Washington. To maintain his grip on power, Habré was running a repressive regime that tortured and killed his political opponents. Chad was already among the poorest countries in the world, even before the economy was devastated by two decades of conflict. It was heavily reliant on foreign aid and heavily in debt. Roads, schools and healthcare were virtually non-existent outside the capital.

'How can you plan long term when you've got two civil wars, Libya, drought, disease and no money?' Geldof asked. It was a question to which there was no answer.

It was all part of a steep learning curve for him. In addition to drought, famine and desertification, Geldof was now discovering that much of Africa was dogged by war. Famine was not a natural phenomenon. It was the mismanagement of drought, of land management, of government and of spending priorities. It was no coincidence, he came to realise, that the African countries suffering most from famine were all embroiled in bitter civil wars. Peace is a prerequisite of prosperity. Spending should be on grain, not guns. The irony was, he was told, the soils of Chad were so fertile that – given a degree of mechanisation, better strains of seeds, fertilisers, insecticides, and sensible soil and water conservation measures – the country could grow enough to feed not just all the people of Chad but the entire Sahel region, and still have a grain surplus to export.

We visited the hospital in N'Djamena. It was the best medical centre in Chad, he was told. That was not saying much in a country where most people have no doctors or medicine. The conditions were appalling. It was so overcrowded that the children who had been admitted with extreme malnutrition slept two or three in a bed. Others slept on the floor beneath the beds or out in the corridor. There was a crust of blood on the floor and no running water – except for a brown viscous liquid that flowed down the side of one ward. It was a sewer, running from a lavatory.

As Geldof left the hospital, dusk was falling and the power supply had failed once again.

There were tears in Kevin Jenden's eyes.

'What this sums up is the disaster of underdevelopment even without the famine,' Jenden said. 'For Christ's sake, this is the national hospital!' He was not without knowledge of how such places should be. In the mid-1970s, he spent some time in Ethiopia as an architect with the Red Cross, designing medical buildings. As the pair left the hospital, a diplomat for the US Embassy came to meet them with the news from Washington that they had been awarded the Presidential World Without Hunger Award. President Ronald Reagan wanted to speak to them both personally on the phone later that day.

'Well, okay, that's very nice,' said Geldof. 'But I'm not sure how we can take the call.' This time he was not being impolite. 'It's just that what we have seen today has been so shocking. I've seen that kind of suffering before but, I suppose, after those optimistic reports we heard from the government, I didn't expect to see kids in that condition. They were starving, in the best hospital in the capital city. Sometimes the enormity of this problem is shattering.' The US Embassy tried several times to connect with the White House without success. In the end, Bob recorded a piece to camera to be sent to the US president.

'It's not that me and Kevin aren't flattered by this award. It's just that in this context, here in Chad, it seems so irrelevant.' President Reagan should triple US international aid and he could then give himself the award, he suggested. Then, in an unaccustomed attack of diplomacy, Bob asked the man behind the camera:

'That doesn't sound churlish, does it?'

'No, it's okay,' said the BBC man.

When the World Without Hunger Award was being presented in Washington the next day, 17 October, Geldof was already in mid-air, heading for Sudan. He had decided to spend the cash that Band Aid had allocated to Chad to build a bridge to allow relief aid, grain and medicine to enter Chad from neighbouring Cameroon.

In Sudan, there was better news. Geldof and Jenden found that the millions Band Aid had pumped into the region before the Live Aid concert had made a real impact. The head of UNICEF's emergency operations in the country, Egil Hagen, talked them through the fast-moving distribution of medical supplies that the Band Aid money had facilitated. Without it, hundreds of people would have died.

'When cholera broke out in eastern Sudan in June, we had to intervene quickly. Band Aid sent three million doses of antibiotics and intravenous fluid and we had them into the camps within days,' he said.

'In one camp, full of refugees from Ethiopia, Wad Sharifi, there were 1,733 cases of cholera. There were thirty-two deaths and these would have turned into hundreds if the medicine had not arrived quickly.'

Band Aid had built a school and a clinic in a shanty town called the Devil's Horn, in Port Sudan, where 60,000 people lived in houses built on a rubbish dump. Band Aid's money had also been used to take food to the isolated tribes in the Red Sea hills. And Band Aid was the only agency flying supplies into Boonja in rebel-held southern Sudan. Most significantly, it was one of the few Western agencies moving shipments of food and medicine illegally across the border from Sudan into the rebel-held areas of Ethiopia.

The impact was such that the government of Sudan decided to present Geldof with a medal. But before it was presented, Bob paid a visit to the local hospital to get some treatment on his big toe, which had been growing steadily more infected throughout the trip. He emerged with a huge bandage on it, but fortunately was still able to get his foot into a pair of sneakers before we travelled to the presidential palace where he was to be given his medal.

Bob might have changed his footwear, but he was still wearing a pink shirt and baggy blue trousers. When we arrived, the chief of protocol took one look at us and walked straight up to the only person in the group wearing a jacket and tie.

'Mr Geldof,' he said. 'We wish to welcome you to Khartoum, and the president will present you with an honour.'

'I am not Mr Geldof,' I said. In those days, as the official representative of *The Times* of London, I did my best to look respectable to meet presidents. Unlike Bob. 'That's him over there,' I said.

The chief of protocol looked nervously at the dishevelled Geldof, but the president, General Swar al-Dahab, was relaxed enough when he entered the room bearing an impressive blue-and-gold medal made by Spinks of London. It was the Order of the Two Niles (Second Class).

'Where are the earrings?' Geldof quipped. The president simply smiled. Perhaps he had heard about Bob on the African leaders' grapevine.

'I wonder what the Order of the Two Niles (First Class) looks like and what you have to do to get it,' Geldof said afterwards. We did not know it at the time but, he later discovered, to get first class you had to be Harry Belafonte.

The president and the pop star sat down together on the sofa.

'Could you do us a favour?' asked Geldof.

'Yes, what is it, Bob?' said the president.

'Have a word with Libya for us, General. Would you ask your friend Colonel Gaddafi what he's doing about the famine victims and the displaced people in northern Chad. Hissène Habré says that they live in a ghetto up there, without any sort of food or medical relief.'

'I will certainly raise that with the Libyans,' said the smiling president.

❖

When Geldof landed in Ethiopia, he was greeted with great warmth by Berhane Deressa, the deputy commissioner of Ethiopia's Relief and Rehabilitation organisation. The two engaged in friendly teasing.

'Bob, I've got your programme for you,' said Deressa.

'So you're trying to programme me already are you, you Marxist bastard?' said Geldof. In response, Berhane called Bob a 'running dog of imperialism'. The two of them laughed.

But there was no such warmth for me.

'Vallely cannot enter the country,' said the officials from Internal Security, who had been waiting at the steps of the aircraft for me.

This was not entirely a surprise. The last time I was in Ethiopia, I had been expelled as 'an enemy of the revolution' after publishing pieces in *The Times* on the inadequacies of the Marxist regime's handling of the famine.

'You will stay at the airport. You will not leave this room until you get on the first plane in the morning.'

Geldof spoke up. 'I don't want to cause any trouble,' he told the officials, 'and I must stress I'm not threatening to pull any Band Aid money out of Ethiopia. But Vallely has been on the trip with us through Africa and that's how it's going to stay. If he goes in the morning, then so do I and I won't come back. This is not an idle threat. We have our own plane and we will all leave on it in the morning.'

He then gave them a lecture on the freedom of the press. 'I'm only here,' he said, 'because I've read the kind of things that Vallely and other journalists have written about Ethiopia.'

The officials retired in confusion. There was, it later emerged, a battle between the Internal Security people, who keenly desired to throw me out, and the Relief and Rehabilitation Commission, who could see the damage it would do to their image abroad, among donors and donor countries, if Geldof left next morning in a blaze of bad publicity. The famine relief officials won the day. I was allowed to stay, but as a non-person without a visa or an entry stamp on my passport.

That night, we all slept better than we had done in two weeks. Addis Ababa is almost 8,000 feet above sea level. The air was cool, thin and pure. It was a blessed relief after the heat of the lowland desert countries. The next morning, Geldof and Jenden had their first major meeting of the day with the forty-seven different foreign aid agencies then working in Ethiopia. Geldof began with the same message he had delivered in every other country: 'Look, we've allocated several million for Ethiopia. I don't know your world, so you decide what to do with it. Set aside your rivalries and agree together.' In other countries, he had added: 'We will come back in two hours and if you have agreed on something, then that will be Band Aid here.' But, in Addis Ababa, he stayed throughout the meeting.

Geldof was already familiar with some of the issues there, from his visit after Band Aid in January when he had forged an alliance with his fellow Irishman, Brother Gus O'Keefe, who ran the Christian Relief and Development Association. The CRDA was the independent umbrella body that coordinated the work of all the non-governmental organisations working in Ethiopia. Also present was the Oxfam field officer, Hugh Goyder, one of the senior agency people who were immensely sceptical about Geldof when he had arrived in Ethiopia in January.

Since then, however, aid agency staff had come to see that there were advantages as well as disadvantages to the Geldof approach. Goyder knew that his boss, Oxfam director Guy Stringer, had written to Geldof, praising his 'superb initiative, brilliantly carried through' and stating that Oxfam was at Band Aid's service. The large US aid agency, CARE, had come on board too. Its New York headquarters had sent an urgent telex to its field offices ahead of Geldof's Africa tour, alerting its staff to this new 'VIP donor organisation' and requesting they 'extend all courtesies' to Geldof. Head offices back home had briefed aid workers in the field to build personal relationships with the Band Aid team, if only because they were keen to get a share of the Live Aid cash.

'My opinion of Bob Geldof changed at the first meeting,' said Goyder. 'Before I met him, what I'd heard was he had a very loud mouth and a propensity to swear. And, secondly, that he was fairly critical of us in the established relief agencies. But once one met him, I found he had a good propensity to listen and to learn. And he was interested in what people were saying.'

Geldof, who could be rude and arrogant with presidents and prime ministers, demonstrated a degree of humility in his dealings with the aid agencies. 'I was well aware that I needed to learn from the experienced people who'd been through hell, who lived in hell, who knew that the people they were helping would probably die,' Bob said. 'And they would look at me and think, "Who the hell is he, swanning in here?".'

The pop star listened and learned. 'The good thing about Band Aid,' Goyder said years later, was that 'it never went operational, which might've been tempting for it. It didn't bring in its own teams of people. They had the Band Aid logo on trucks, but these trucks were then given to people like Oxfam or Save the Children to deploy, which was the best way of doing it.'

One of the early marks of Geldof's growing sophistication in his under-standing of aid came in his discussions about the way that aid was being distributed. Aid workers had become concerned at a marked shift in food distribution patterns over the previous six months. Individual donor countries had stopped passing grain and medicines through the govern-ment's Relief and Rehabilitation Commission (RRC). Instead, they were sending it through the growing number of voluntary agencies whose head-quarters were based in the West. The result was uneven and unsatisfactory distribution of emergency food. Individual Western agencies sent the food to the areas in which they operated. These were often located in places chosen by historic accident or fashion, which left serious gaps in the distri-bution. Previously, the RRC had been the body with the overview, but now it was receiving only half of the food aid it needed to fill the gaps.

Geldof quickly realised that this re-apportioning of resources was the result of a conscious political decision by Western governments – and, in particular, the United States, which was providing more than a third of all the country's food aid. The West was anxious to be seen to help the victims of famine, but equally anxious to avoid bolstering the pro-Soviet regime of Colonel Mengistu and his Marxist Workers Party. To use the voluntary agencies seemed the obvious solution. But, on the ground, it was clear this was causing a major problem.

'Eritrea and Tigray seem to be the "in" places as far as US opinion is concerned,' Bob was told by one aid worker based in the northern highlands of Wollo. 'Hence all the American agencies, with all their massive food sup-plies, are there. In Eritrea today, they have food surpluses. Here in Wollo, we have a chronic famine still.'

The facts to back up this analysis were provided to Geldof by Hugh Goyder of Oxfam, David Alexander of Save the Children and Peter Searle of World Vision.

'If things do not change quickly,' said Searle, 'in six months a lot more children will start dying.'

The irony was, Geldof learned, that the RRC was considered, by even those who opposed the Ethiopian regime, to be the most effective famine relief organisation in the whole of Africa. It pre-dated the current Marxist regime, having been at work for more than a decade, since the famine of 1974 which brought the downfall of Emperor Haile Selassie. It had a staff of 17,000, more than 400 field stations, an effective monitoring procedure and an early-warning system whose predictions had been consistently verified by events. It had the strategic overview lacked by individual agencies.

But the RRC was now receiving only 50 per cent of the grain it needed – and so was distributing only half rations, with alarming irregularity, in areas of great need.

There was no point in Band Aid bringing in expensive supplementary foods for extremely malnourished children if there was no basic diet to supplement. Geldof discovered that, at one Oxfam medical centre, patients were being restored to health by intensive feeding, only to return home to an inadequate RRC ration, leading to their readmission to the clinic several months later.

'Foreign donor governments have developed a lack of confidence in us,' Geldof was told by Berhane Deressa.

'When you consider some of the policies of this Marxist government, it is hardly surprising,' Geldof riposted.

Yet, while it was understandable for Western governments to prefer their donations to go through a private charity, they needed to think more deeply about whether that meant they were spending money in a way that was counterproductive. At least a third of the Live Aid money would therefore be spent through the RRC, Geldof said, although its use would be carefully monitored. And he would put pressure on Western governments to do the same when he went to lobby for the additional million tonnes of grain Ethiopia currently needed to keep 5.8 million hungry people alive. The US had already pledged 300,000 tonnes. When he left Ethiopia, Geldof would travel to Strasbourg to ask for 250,000 tonnes from the European Economic Community. Later that week, he would travel to Australia for a meeting with Prime Minister Bob Hawke, before moving on to Canada to meet Prime Minister Brian Mulrooney. From each man, he would request another quarter of a million tonnes.

Before he left Ethiopia, though, Geldof decided he would like to revisit the refugee camp at Korem, the place where the BBC had filmed the report which had galvanised him into action the year before. This time, we flew by helicopter. Even from the air, the differences were apparent. A year before, there had been around 85,000 people there. Now there was a chequerboard of bare patches where once there had been tents. The place was perhaps half its former size. As the helicopter landed, it was surrounded by a massive crowd of excited children. To say that they looked healthy would be misleading. By European standards, they were scrawny and undernourished. But their upper arms were fleshy and their thighs were strong; these were the classic measures by which aid workers had foretold the imminence of death only six months before.

Yet, one year after the BBC film, and despite the improved health of the people, there was still something disturbing about the place. There were no longer more than 100 people dying every day, but where Korem had once been shocking, it was now depressing. The residents who remained seemed to have been seized by a listless dependence. There was a hopeless air of sullen permanence about the place. The inhabitants had developed the apathy of people whose lives had lost all natural rhythm and sense of purpose. It felt a sump of human degradation.

'No human being should be forced to live in circumstances like this,' Geldof said dejectedly. 'It is not enough for us to have kept them alive if this is how we condemn them to live. We have helped save their lives. Now we must give them a life worth living.'

❈

Two weeks after he had set out on his journey across Africa, Bob Geldof arrived back in Europe with lessons learned and new resolutions set. Famine, he now knew, was not merely the result of drought. It was caused by desertification, war, Africa's colonial legacy, clashes between nomads and farmers, poor government policies, the imbalance between its urban and rural populations, the growth of an unproductive civil service class and the politics of aid. He had a lot to think about.

Some of the responses which were required were, he knew, straightforward and simple. Within days of being back in the UK, he appeared on the BBC's leading chat show and told the host, Terry Wogan, how struck he had been by the creativity of the starving children.

'Out in Western Sudan, the little chaps had never seen a plane before. And suddenly they saw the planes bringing in food and they made these sort of reed aeroplanes.' Sending food was not enough. The spirit needed to be nourished too. 'It would be nice if we could send them some toys for Christmas ... because the kids there have got nothing ... and if we could do it through your show, it'd be great. And if you're going to buy dollies, try to get little black dolls, if you would, please.'

But far bigger changes were needed elsewhere. Two days later, he travelled to the plush European Parliament building in Strasbourg with the dust of the African famine belt still on his shoes.

With his long hair and open-necked shirt, he presented the greatest contrast possible to the sober-suited bureaucrats and Euro-MPs. But he was clearly as well-briefed as they were on the Lomé Convention – the basis of Europe's aid to the developing world – and the Common Agricultural Policy, which subsidised over-production by Europe's farmers. The resulting grain mountains and milk lakes were 'a preposterous outrage' and 'the crowning idiocy' of European politics.

'This place needs a laxative,' he observed, with the same bluntness he had used on Africa's leaders, this time delivering an impassioned and articulate plea for greater and more efficient aid distribution. Most specifically, he demanded the creation of an emergency taskforce to supervise the better distribution of Europe's food aid.

One of the chief bureaucrats who was in Geldof's crosshairs, Willy De Clercq, the European commissioner of external relations, launched into a lengthy defence of the system of subsidising Europe's farmers to produce more than the continent could consume. As to Geldof's suggestion that an aid task force was needed, Europe already had one, he said.

'It obviously doesn't work then,' Bob said, looking thunderous. 'There is a crisis in Africa, but there is also a crisis of morality in Europe epitomised by this building.'

As if to placate him, he was awarded a special gold medal by the European Parliament to mark the achievement of Live Aid. Geldof was deeply unimpressed.

'I'll put it on a gold chain and use it if I do any pop concerts in Las Vegas,' he said witheringly.

His mission to speak truth to power had only just begun.

CHAPTER 20

A LONG-RUNNING
FEUD BEGINS

Something else happened in Ethiopia in October 1985 which was to haunt Bob Geldof for a decade, or longer. Soon after arriving in Addis Ababa, he had a meeting with representatives from all of the forty-seven voluntary organisations that were working on getting food to the starving. After they had briefed him on their work, he had a series of follow-up questions. One of these concerned the Ethiopian government's controversial plan to move hundreds of thousands of peasant farmers from the drought-hit regions in the north of Ethiopia to the underpopulated fertile land in the forests to the southwest of the country.

Geldof then produced a copy of the *Wall Street Journal*, which contained a report from a US human rights organisation called Cultural Survival. Its researchers had recently visited six refugee camps that had sprung up in Sudan, just across the border from Ethiopia. There, they had interviewed nearly 250 individuals who had escaped from Ethiopian resettlement camps and fled across the border.

The refugees told terrible stories of how they had been forced into Soviet aeroplanes and Ethiopian army trucks against their will and dumped in inhospitable forests 800 miles from their homes. Many people had died on the overcrowded journey. Others perished when the highland farmers encountered lowland diseases like malaria and tsetse fly for the first time. Extrapolating from their interviews, Cultural Survival claimed that between 50,000 and 100,000 people must have died in the resettlement process.

'Is this true?' asked Geldof, waving the newspaper.

'I've read it and I don't believe it,' said an Irish priest, Father Jack Finucane, who ran the relief operation for the Irish aid agency Concern.

He had visited the areas himself, he said, and had seen no sign of the horrors the report described. There had been problems, but nothing on that scale.

Someone in the room listened with disbelief to the priest's words. Michel Fiszbin, from the French medical group Médecins Sans Frontières, had attended another meeting exactly one month before where Finucane had addressed Western ambassadors about the same subject. Then he had told a very different story. The meeting for the diplomats had been a private one at the Hilton Hotel in Addis. No press were present. More significantly, neither were any of the government officials who now flanked Geldof.

A month earlier, Father Finucane had said that half a million people had been transported so far in the resettlement programme in 'horrible conditions'. He added that 'out of 77 resettled areas, only two or three' could be said to be a success. Worst of all, he estimated that between 15 and 20 per cent of the settlers may have died on the journey or during the first three months in the resettlement areas. Fiszbin had noted these figures and sent them on to MSF headquarters in Paris. Half a million people had been moved so far so, using Finucane's guesstimate, that meant between 75,000 and 100,000 people had died. The figure was close to the claims made by Cultural Survival.

One of the journalists present, David Blundy of the *Sunday Times*, contacted Concern's head office in Dublin. Staff there confirmed that 'Finucane's investigation of villages in the resettlement area showed that, in some cases, 25 per cent of the people died'. So when was the Irish priest telling the truth? When he spoke to the ambassadors? Or a month later when he spoke in front of the press?

Forty years later, it is pretty clear what Father Finucane was up to. Speaking to the ambassadors, he had emphasised the bad side of what was happening in the resettlement areas to encourage Western donors to fund projects to improve life there. Speaking to the press, he played down the horrors for fear that media reports would put the Western public off giving. His motives were honourable, but he set running a bitter feud between Médecins Sans Frontières and Band Aid which was to carry on for almost thirty years.

✣

The idea of moving farmers away from the arid unproductive landscape of the northern highlands had been around long before the Marxist regime took control of Ethiopia. The region had long been routinely hit by droughts. It was also subject to massive erosion by the winds and sudden downpours when the rains did come. Storms would wash the good soil from the high plateau and down the rivers, away from the land on which millions of subsistence farmers depended for survival.

As far back as the 1950s, there were spontaneous migrations of people from the northern plateaux to the south and west. As many as a million people moved. In 1971, the World Bank recommended a resettlement programme. In 1973, the aid department of the United States government did the same. That same decade, the UN Food and Agriculture Organization conducted a massive twenty-volume study which strongly recommended a resettlement policy. So did the UN Environment Programme. By 1982, there were more than 100 resettlement centres cultivated by 120,000 farmers who had migrated from the north.

But in 1984, ten years after Ethiopia's Marxist revolution, its government decided to increase resettlement dramatically. Mengistu announced his intention to resettle 1.5 million people to the south and southwest, where arable land was plentiful. This was a huge number of people, though it was a relatively small proportion of Ethiopia's 42 million population. The target was over-ambitious. In the event, around 600,000 people were moved in three phases: in 1984, 1985 and 1987.

But although the government was unquestionably correct about the environmental collapse in the northern highlands, Mengistu had a nefarious additional motive. He wanted to move farmers from their individual plots of land to collectivised farms and villages where peasants would be more easily controlled by officials of his newly-established Workers' Party of Ethiopia.

More than that he thought, it would also be a way of depriving rebel forces of their natural support base. 'Mengistu wanted to get rid of peoples who were protecting the rebels,' recalled Ethiopia's relief commissioner, Dawit Wolde Giorgis, who was part of the dictator's inner circle before he defected to the United States. Others claimed it was not so simple. One of Africa's foremost historians, Gebru Tareke, after an extensive study of resettlement records, noted that 80 per cent of those resettled were from Wollo and Shewa – outside the rebel areas. Only 15 per cent were from the principal rebel territory of Tigray. So if the resettlement's primary aim was to depopulate the rebel hinterland, it was extremely poorly targeted.

For many outsiders, things were seen as more black and white. Washington had supported resettlement before Ethiopia's socialist revolution, but now that the country was an ally of the Soviet Union, it took the opposite view. The head of USAID, Peter McPherson, described it as a 'reckless and brutal programme'. The Cultural Survival report was music to McPherson's ears.

Reporting from Ethiopia in the early part of 1985, I encountered a more complicated picture. And mine were the reports which Bob Geldof was reading. Certainly, in the early months, there were significant numbers of farmers volunteering for resettlement. Farming had become impossible for many in the highlands. In January, a party of European diplomats and senior relief workers were, for the first time, allowed into resettlement areas where 160,000 men, women and children had been resettled two months earlier.

'There seemed no attempt to steer us away from any particular settlement,' one aid worker told me. 'We were favourably impressed. The people seemed pleased with their new homes. But some of the larger settlements – we saw one of about 1,200 people – seemed a much more dicey business.'

The aid workers had serious doubts about Mengistu's claim that the settlers would be self-sufficient within one year. 'There is no chance of that,' one said, 'and there is no prospect of that happening for several years, for they will need enormous back-up on a scale the government cannot afford.' One of the party, Brother Gus O'Keefe, who coordinated the work of all the aid agencies in Ethiopia, drew the conclusion that Western donors should fund voluntary agencies to work in the resettlement areas to help find solutions to these problems.

The BBC's East Africa correspondent, Mike Wooldridge, was collecting the same mixed reports as I was. 'Was everybody being coerced? No, I don't necessarily think so. I think some people thought anything was better than where they were and would give it a try,' he recalled forty years later. 'Other people much preferred to be fed and helped where they were, still up in the north.'

But that was not what Mengistu wanted. In February and March, resettlement at gunpoint increased. Other pressures were applied. Food aid was withheld from refugee camps, while two cooked meals a day were being provided at resettlement transit camps half a mile away. Aid workers were forbidden from distributing blankets, clothing and tents for fear that famine victims would 'get too comfortable'.

As the year progressed, it became clear that many, if not most, of the resettlers were being coerced into relocating. When I travelled to the Sudanese camps where Cultural Survival had interviewed escapees from Ethiopian resettlement, I recorded similar heartbreaking stories. But, as the eminent Africa journalist Colin Legum noted, only those who were dissatisfied with resettlement would make the effort to escape to Sudan. 'Because all those interviewed were refugees from resettlement camps, it is possible that they are keen on presenting only the worst side of the picture,' Legum wrote. Those who stayed behind might tell a different story.

Yet the Cultural Survival report was cited by Médecins Sans Frontières as incontrovertible evidence of abuse. Its surmises became facts. It also became the basis of a series of increasingly wild claims. Its author, Jason Clay, compared Mengistu to Pol Pot and the Khmer Rouge. Dr Rony Brauman, president of MSF France, attacked aid agencies working in resettlement areas as 'accomplices of genocide'. One US diplomat went so far as to make comparisons with the behaviour of the Nazis at Auschwitz.

Such emotive language was roundly condemned by Alula Pankhurst, one of the few anthropologists who actually conducted rigorous and extensive fieldwork inside the resettlement areas. Reports that resettlement was entirely voluntary – or entirely forced – were equally misleading, he said. Jason Clay travelled to London to persuade the main aid agencies of his view. 'In England, nobody would speak to me directly,' Clay complained. 'Ten times I asked for meetings with the head of Save the Children. He wouldn't even talk to me on the phone. Oxfam was even worse.'

⁂

The battle lines were now drawn. As Bob Geldof and Harvey Goldsmith were making the final preparations for Live Aid, aid agencies were internally debating how to respond the Mengistu's resettlement scheme. Should they criticise the behaviour of the Ethiopian government publicly and refuse to work in resettlement areas? Or should they make their complaints in private and work to make life a little better for the people who had been uprooted from their home and moved hundreds of miles to a strange new land? A rift began to develop in the aid community, which was to resolve itself into an angry confrontation between Médecins Sans Frontières and Band Aid.

It was clear which side Washington was on.

US officials were meeting with members of the European Commission to solidify opposition to resettlement. The EC was persuaded to cut its aid to Ethiopia. Peter McPherson told the World Food Programme that he would axe its funding – unless it stopped sending food to resettlement areas. He told aid agencies he would withhold US cash if they did not fall into line.

By contrast, Ethiopian churches and overseas Christian charities began working in resettlement zones to improve conditions there.

This was the political maelstrom into which Bob Geldof stepped when he landed in Addis Ababa for the second time in October 1985. From the outset, he made clear to the minister of the interior, Berhane Biyuh, that he totally disapproved of forced resettlement. But Geldof was politically savvy enough to understand that, whatever Band Aid's view, resettlement was happening and would continue to happen. The key question was how Band Aid should react.

Contrary to press reports at the time, Geldof had not arrived in Ethiopia in a state of ignorance. Nine days before he landed, another Irish priest had arrived in Addis. Father Aengus Finucane was Jack Finucane's brother – and boss. Aengus, who headed up the entire Concern operation in Dublin, had travelled to two resettlement areas where Concern had already signed up to work. The Irish charity boss told Geldof that he had been allowed to move freely, and without supervision, in seven new villages.

He had written a report which was passed to Geldof. The Canadian government, the report revealed, had secretly broken ranks with other Western governments on resettlement. It had already agreed to give a grant of $750,000 to Concern to work in a new settlement at Jarso. The Irish charity was the first voluntary agency to have entered into formal contract with the government of Ethiopia to undertake a major programme in the new resettlement areas of Wellega. It had signed the contract that month.

The confidential report, unpublished until now, began by setting out Concern's reservations over coercion. 'Few of the people are here by totally free choice any more than were the Irish on the ships to America in our own famine time,' it said.

Concern did not approve of the coercion used by government but concluded: 'Our commitment is to the poor and the weak. Concern recognises the importance of being with the poor,' it said, drawing on Ireland's distinctly Catholic ethos. The charity had agreed to provide financial and technical assistance for the comprehensive development of the seven villages. It would construct health facilities, stores, flour mills, water supplies, access roads, agricultural inputs, engage in water and soil conservation, and would train farmers. It was asking Band Aid to help finance the work.

Bob Geldof and Kevin Jenden had discussed the proposal with their panel of development experts before they left London. Now, in Addis, Geldof declared that Band Aid would consider 'on their merits' project proposals for the resettlement areas. The Irish charity boss had been tipped off about that in advance. What surprised him was 'the chorus of support coming from agencies which, a year ago, and much more recently, were strongly opposed to the whole resettlement concept,' Gus Finucane said.

The tide was turning and it was the charity field officers on the ground who were leading the change. Father Jack Finucane seized the opportunity to declare that Western governments should stop being squeamish about resettlement and channel money into improving life for the peasants who had been transported there. Michel Fiszbin of Médecins Sans Frontières was outraged. He told the press that Finucane had said the opposite a month before and gave them the figures. Concern hit back, saying it broke a confidence to repeat what had been said in a private meeting.

'That was the start of hostilities,' said Dr Brigitte Vasset, medical coordinator of the MSF operation in Korem.

Within days, MSF's indignation was redoubled. On 28 October, its medical staff in Korem watched a group of armed militia force 600 of the camp's occupants into trucks and drive them off to be resettled. So brutal was it that 10,000 other peasants fled Korem, fearing they would be next. It was the final straw for the horrified MSF president, Rony Bauman, who received permission from his board of directors to speak out publicly against the Mengistu regime. The following day, he publicly threatened that Médecins Sans Frontières would pull out of Ethiopia if the government's behaviour continued.

Geldof now publicly took the opposing view. People in resettlement areas were suffering and they needed Band Aid's help. 'If we had been in existence during the Second World War, and we heard that people were dying in concentration camps, would we refuse to give them food and aid in those camps? Of course not,' Geldof asserted. 'The same principle applies here. I may not agree with resettlement, but the government is going ahead with it whether we agree or not. People are in need and we're here to help save lives. If we can do that in resettlement areas, then so be it.'

Rony Brauman hit back. Geldof was providing cover for President Mengistu to pursue an ideological project. It was resettlement that was killing people now, not famine.

Geldof was as vehement in his reply. 'I'll shake hands with the devil, on my left and on my right, to get to the people we are meant to help.'

❧

The United Nations weighed in on Geldof's side. Kurt Jansson, the head of UN operations in Ethiopia, acknowledged there were problems with resettlement. It had been poorly planned and executed haphazardly, yet it was necessary. Critics who compared resettlement to Pol Pot's murderous effort to depopulate Kampuchean cities had no idea what they were talking about, said Jansson, who had actually served as the UN relief coordinator in Kampuchea immediately after the Pol Pot era. Mengistu's timetable for resettlement was overly ambitious, but there was 'little doubt' that mass migrations were needed.

But Médecins Sans Frontières was now set upon a course of confrontation and began to make statements to the press. It told the *Sunday Times* in London that at least 50,000 people had been killed in population transfers. It gave *Libération* in Paris a dossier which claimed that 'one of the most massive violations of human rights' was 'being carried out with funds and gifts from international aid'. It now asserted that 100,000 people were already dead and as many as 300,000 were likely to perish. In response, the deputy commissioner of the Relief and Rehabilitation Commission, Berhane Deressa, announced, 'MSF is conducting a defamation campaign. Its aims are political rather than humanitarian.' MSF persisted. At the beginning of December, the Ethiopian government expelled the thirty staff of MSF France, froze its bank accounts and grounded its aircraft.

MSF staff hoped for backing from other agencies. It did not come. Berhane Deressa circulated a carefully constructed dossier about the organisation and its claims. It was extremely critical of Rony Brauman and Michel Fiszbin, while praising the work of MSF medics in the camps. 'It articulated,' reported *Libération*, 'a series of balanced arguments to which MSF in Ethiopia has difficulty responding.' And it drew attention to the links between MSF and its recently established anti-communist think-tank, Liberté Sans Frontières, whose founders had extreme-left backgrounds. For several months, this had been causing deep divisions within the MSF family. Most damagingly, the dossier pointed out that MSF's figure of deaths was not extrapolated from hard facts gathered by its medics in the field. Rather, it was MSF's projection from the guesstimates made by Cultural Survival. The figures were totally unverifiable. Worst of all, said Deressa, 'MSF has never asked to visit the resettlement camps and verify its claims.'

A series of inaccurate MSF 'facts' were to bedevil Band Aid for decades. None of the dozens of voluntary agencies working in Ethiopia at the time seriously disputed the fact that population transfers were carried on in atrocious conditions. All agreed that many people were coerced, families were separated and people were sent who were unfit to travel.

But, even now, there is no clear picture about how many people died. MSF maintained it could be as many as 300,000. Cultural Survival said between 50,000 and 100,000. The Red Cross estimated 50,000. The highly respected Ethiopian historian Gebru Tareke, who conducted in-depth research on the resettlement records in the years after the famine, reckoned 33,000. Dawit Wolde Giorgis, Ethiopia's relief commissioner, claimed, after he defected to the United States, that 20,000 died.

For Bob Geldof, the wide variation in these figures only cast further doubt on the integrity of the MSF position. And they did not alter his view that Band Aid's pledge to relieve suffering in Ethiopia applied as much in the resettlement areas as it did everywhere else.

His view was shared by almost every other organisation working on the famine – in Ethiopia, France, the UK and the US. All condemned MSF for abandoning the needy. British aid organisations held an emergency meeting in London to discuss the crisis and concluded that MSF had taken their protest too far. It was essential to keep the issue in perspective, Oxfam said, since the resettlement programme was affecting only about 5 per cent of the population. The United Nations described MSF's account as 'an extraordinary version of events that, when investigated, turned out to be highly exaggerated and unreliable in facts'. Even the French ambassador distanced himself from his compatriots.

What was perhaps most damning was that the two other branches of Médecins Sans Frontières operating in Ethiopia failed to back Rony Brauman and MSF France. MSF Belgium and MSF Holland both insisted on staying. 'None of our people said that we should leave,' said Dr Philippe Laurent, director of MSF Belgium. 'Out of forty-seven NGOs working in Ethiopia, not a single one agrees with him,' Laurent said of Brauman.

By the time of the Live Aid concert, MSF's internal dispute had become so bitter that the French medics took their Belgian counterparts to court to stop them using the name Médecins Sans Frontières. The judge ruled against the French. 'MSF Belgium was like a bunch of Boy Scouts. All they wanted to do was practise medicine,' said MSF France's Claude Malhuret scornfully. By contrast, MSF France's Brauman declared: 'We are a human rights organisation, not just doctors giving tetanus shots.' MSF Belgium hit back, saying that MSF France had deliberately exaggerated events in Ethiopia in order to justify the existence of its anti-communist sister organisation, Liberté Sans Frontières. The behaviour of the Ethiopian authorities was no worse than the authorities in Sudan or Chad, said Laurent, but they were not the ideological opponents of Brauman and his friends.

Whoever was right, it was clear that the creation of Liberté Sans Frontières distracted MSF from its urgent famine response. It brought Cold War politics down into the voluntary sphere. Liberté Sans Frontières 'threw a spanner in the works of the peaceful NGOs in early 1985,' wrote Laurence Binet, the historian of the Médecins Sans Frontières movement.

All this might have remained an internal matter, but all the global publicity around Live Aid made Brauman switch the focus of his indignation to Band Aid. 'By July, I was worried that all the money Geldof and Live Aid were generating was providing cover for President Mengistu to pursue his ideological project of resettlement,' Brauman later said. His anger only grew. In November, the week before Brauman's final confrontation with the Mengistu government, Band Aid began working inside the resettlement areas.

❧

Bob Geldof was convinced, as we left Ethiopia in October 1985, that it was Band Aid's duty to work wherever people were starving in Ethiopia. It would fund famine relief in government-controlled areas, behind rebel lines through the cross-border operation and now in resettlement areas. Concern's work, he had decided, was not only as essential in itself. It was important as a way of persuading other donor agencies to work in resettled communities.

Geldof was pushing at an open door. Over the days following MSF's expulsion, a series of key players began publicly to back the idea of working in resettlement areas. The UN's Food and Agriculture Organization and the EEC's development committee came out in support. And the UN's new head of emergency operations, Michael Priestley – after visits to resettlement areas in Gojjam, Illubabor, Wellega and Keffa – wrote that some of the achievements there 'with very limited resources have been truly remarkable'. The Ethiopian government 'should build on these successes'.

The voluntary agencies working in Ethiopia agreed; forty-six of them put out a statement insisting that they could do more for the poor by working in the new settlements than by boycotting them. They underscored the unreliability of the Cultural Survival/MSF guestimates of how many people had died – and pointed out that it was also impossible to say how many of those who died in resettlement areas would have died from starvation, had they stayed at home. MSF's high-minded stance would result in some donors cutting aid in the year to come. They ended by saying: 'As humanitarian agencies, our first concern must be to assist the people of Ethiopia, wherever they are.'

The president of MSF France was antagonised rather than cowed by the increasing marginalisation of his organisation. With condemnation of MSF now virtually universal, Rony Brauman turned his anger on the most high-profile of his critics: Bob Geldof.

The following month, January 1986, Brauman travelled to the United States in an attempt to find sympathy there. He held a press conference in Washington DC, alongside the researchers from Cultural Survival, to repeat the claim that resettlement would kill 300,000 people. Band Aid was firmly in their crosshairs. Their allegations got onto the front page of the *New York Times* and produced a headline in the *Wall Street Journal* which read: 'LIVE AID DIGS GRAVES IN ETHIOPIA'. Again, Brauman repeated his accusation: 'Aid is doing more harm than good.' But, in the absence of any actual evidence beyond MSF's assertions, the story was a one-day wonder. It was dismissed by the UN aid coordinator in Ethiopia, Michael Priestley, who countered: 'There is no way to determine how many people actually died, because there is no data on which to work. It is impossible to come up with any figure.'

Two months later, Father Jack Finucane announced that he had visited thirty-five resettlement camps and adjudged that there was 'a good chance these people will eventually become self-sufficient, perhaps in four years'.

His announcement came as Band Aid's project evaluator, John James, approved a proposal to extend its backing of Concern's work to an even bigger resettlement site in Ketto, providing wells, irrigation and anti-erosion terracing. Band Aid offered to donate half of the $3.3 million cost, if Concern raised the rest. With Band Aid as its partner, Concern had no difficulty raising the remainder. It signed the Ketto project agreement with the RRC on 21 May and work commenced in August.

Over the following five years, Band Aid provided stores, clinics, schools, mills, agricultural tools, oxen, beehives, nurseries, drugs and medical equipment in Ketto and Jarso. An evaluation in 2004 found that all the villages in the region had 'for the most part become self-sufficient and many are producing a reasonable surplus every year'.

※

All this seemed only to provoke Rony Bauman to further outrage. In June 1986, he again visited the United States for an event organised by the music magazine *Spin*, published by Bob Guccione Jr, who had previously worked at *Penthouse*. The press conference was to publicise an article which the magazine claimed was an exposé of the misappropriation of Live Aid funds. Alongside Brauman sat the same two anthropologists, Jason Clay and Bonnie Holcomb of Cultural Survival. There was nothing new in their allegations, but they were regurgitated with new vehemence.

The article in *Spin* – headlined 'LIVE AID: THE TERRIBLE TRUTH' – produced no evidence beyond the old assertions. Again, it was based only on the claims of MSF and Jason Clay without quoting any Ethiopians. The allegations were printed and reprinted in 1986, 2015, 2020 and 2021 under headlines like 'Live Aid – the Terrible Truth', 'Sympathy for the Devil',

'The Real Stories Behind Live Aid' and 'The Dark Legacy of "Do They Know It's Christmas?"'. When Guccione reprinted the article in 2015, he talked about having seen footage of Bob Geldof bearhugging and playfully punching Mengistu on the arm 'as he literally handed over the funding for this slaughter'. *Spin* have never printed photographs of this supposed interaction. No video or photo libraries have a record of any such footage and *Spin* have never produced any. In fact, Geldof only met Mengistu once and there was neither filming nor photographs permitted during the meeting. Kenny Lennox, the *Daily Star* photographer who was present throughout the meeting, has testified that he was not permitted to take any photos. Nor were there official photographers or film crews present. Yet the unsubstantiated accusations still circulate on the internet today – and Geldof's critics find them convenient sticks with which to beat him. Geldof did not grace Brauman's unsubstantiated allegations with a detailed reply. He merely issued a statement lamenting the fact that Médecins Sans Frontières appeared to have 'allowed itself to be used as pawns ... to aid the flagging circulation of a pop magazine'.

Rony Brauman was still not finished. In October, he wrote what he described as a 'hard-hitting' article which 'reveals the shocking truth' about Live Aid. It appeared in the *Reader's Digest*, hardly a byword for hard-hitting investigative journalism. Brauman later boasted that, after it was published, fundraising for three of biggest US charities collapsed. It seemed an odd boast for a humanitarian. 'I really tore into Geldof,' he said afterwards. 'I wanted it to end up in court. You see what state of mind you can get into! I wasn't afraid of a court case, I wanted it!'

Whatever Brauman's state of mind, Geldof decided not to rise to the bait. He left it to Peter Davies, head of a coalition of US development agencies, to reply. Brauman's assertions were founded on hearsay and had been criticised by every American voluntary agency and church group working in Ethiopia, he told the *Washington Post*. 'It is clearly a polemic on which no wise government should now base its policy toward Ethiopia.'

The debate is not over. On the fortieth anniversary of Live Aid, Brauman told a television documentary that he still 'was really angry' with Band Aid and Geldof. Had they spoken out, like MSF did, 'I think the forced relocation would have stopped immediately'. Geldof 'bears a heavy responsibility' for the continuation of 'the murderous resettlement' process.

That is a deeply unrealistic judgement, according to Gayle Smith. In 1985, she ran the operation to smuggle food across the border from Sudan to people starving behind rebel lines in Tigray – an operation which Band Aid part-funded. Later, under President Barack Obama, she rose to become head of the US government's entire aid operation. 'Bob couldn't have stopped it even if the whole international community had spoken out,' she said. 'The alternatives were to let them die – or to feed them. Basically, he couldn't win. Whatever he did, he would have been criticised for, by somebody. In hindsight I think Band Aid did pretty well. They ended up providing assistance on both sides of the frontline in an active war – which not everybody did.'

It was not quite the end of the story. In 1987, Band Aid again met with officials from the United Nations and Ethiopian government to plan a resumption of resettlement. Again, Band Aid, in the shape of its executive director, Penny Jenden, asserted its disapproval of forced resettlement and set down parameters under which it would cooperate with a further movement of peoples. It did the same again in 1999, under a new Ethiopian government.

As for Mengistu, his regime fell in 1991 when rebels from Tigray captured Addis Ababa and the dictator fled to Zimbabwe. The following year, he was put on trial, *in absentia*, in Ethiopia for 'crimes against humanity'. Rony Brauman and Brigitte Vasset received a letter inviting them to testify for the prosecution against the tyrant they had condemned in such strong terms in 1985 and thereafter.

They refused to participate. The purpose of publicly denouncing the crimes of the Ethiopian government in 1985, MSF official records stated, was not so much to influence the actual course of events in the field as 'to discharge MSF from the situation of being an accomplice to these acts'. And as for the controversial think-tank Liberté Sans Frontières, which had so politicised aid to the starving, it was dissolved on 28 April 1989, just four years after starting all this trouble.

Forty years on, Bob Geldof was unrestrained in his verdict on MSF France: 'They cut and ran. Their job was to look after the people they said they would take care of – and they abandoned them. You're either in politics, or you're there to help the people you say you will help. That's it.' Band Aid trustee Lord Grade, looking back, turned the focus on Band Aid: 'It's the innocent people that we're there to help,' he said. 'We're not there to change the politics. We're there to help the victims of politics.'

CHAPTER 21

DOING SOMETHING FUNNY FOR MONEY

B ob Geldof's critics routinely levelled the accusation against him that the whole Live Aid enterprise was a massive exercise in self-promotion. It was all designed to revive his flagging career as a rock star. If that was his intention, it did not succeed. The year after Live Aid, Harvey Goldsmith tried to promote a solo tour by Geldof. It totally failed. The British public had supported him wholeheartedly as St Bob. But as a musician, they were not interested.

Harvey had booked twenty venues up and down the country. The ticket sales were abysmal – between 20–25 per cent of capacity. It quickly became evident the tour was going to fail. Everyone would lose money. There was no one more famous in the whole country than Bob Geldof and yet they didn't want to know him as a musician. One of Harvey's staff then had to make a series of difficult phone calls to all the venues they had booked and ask if they would refund part of the deposit which had paid to hire the halls.

Because it was Bob, a lot of them didn't charge the full rate. But £35,000 had been spent on advertising.

'Give Bob a call and tell him that it's all over,' Harvey said to one of his staff. 'He'll know anyway because we've been sending him the sales figures. Call him and tell him we'll go 50/50 on the costs.'

'No, surely, Harvey, you should be the one calling him,' his assistant replied.

'No, no, you call him,' Goldsmith instructed his employee.

The hapless employee rang. 'Harvey thinks we should split the advertising costs,' he told the unhappy singer.

'Are you seriously saying Harvey told you to call and ask me to put my hand in my pocket for this fiasco? Tell Harvey to stuff it.'

Live Aid didn't do a thing for Bob Geldof's career, said Live Aid's production manager, Andrew Zweck. 'He would've much preferred to be a successful musician and songwriter rather than St Bob. But the truth is that he's struggled ever since. It elevated his status as a punk-rock statesman, but he's just never been accepted as a musician.'

Bob's fellow Boomtown Rat, Pete Briquette, goes further, saying that Live Aid actually 'damaged his musical career. People see his music as an addendum.' Band Aid trustee, John Kennedy, regards that as admirable: 'Having written "Do They Know It's Christmas?", he didn't then just walk away. Forty years later, he's still working hard at it.'

Midge Ure agrees. 'My career was unscathed by Live Aid. I didn't have to play St Midge. I was allowed to slip out of the back door into my day job and be a pop star again. But Bob had become something else entirely – a spokesman for unruly youth, a pseudo-politician, a living conscience.' Unlike Bob, Midge finished his solo album and went on tour. When he was headlining at Wembley Arena in December that year – following 'If I Was', a number-one single in September – Geldof sent him a massive bunch of flowers with the message: 'Congratulations. I wish to fuck I was you.'

Bob Geldof's ambiguous status testified to something else. Band Aid and Live Aid did not just raise more money than had ever been raised for a single cause in modern history, they also changed something in the way people in the late twentieth century thought about both charity and politics. People started to get personally involved in a new way in causes dear to them, and – for a generation, at any rate – began to expect politicians to share those values.

Live Aid became something exemplary. Band Aid-style records to raise money for Ethiopia were launched in more than twenty-five countries around the world. But Live Aid spawned much more than that.

The year after Live Aid, 20 million sportsmen and women, and ordinary members of the public, in 277 cities, from London to Melbourne, set out to run ten kilometres over designated courses to raise money for Africa.

Sport Aid's 'Race Against Time' was the biggest mass-participation sport event ever organised. Omer Khalifa, a champion middle-distance runner from Sudan, signalled the start by lighting a torch from the embers of a fire in a Sudanese refugee camp. He then carried the flame through twelve European capital cities, where he was greeted by presidents, princes, prime ministers and the Pope. Even a convicted armed robber ran, round and round the exercise yard at Dartmoor jail, paced by two prison warders. Tears for Fears re-recorded their hit 'Everybody Wants to Rule the World' as 'Everybody Wants to Run the World' as the event's theme song. Sport Aid alone raised $100 million for the hungry.

Only in the United States was the outcome disappointing. There, Sport Aid clashed with the East to West Coast human chain, Hands Across America, organised by Ken Kragen. Among those who participated in the Kragen event were Michael Jackson, Lionel Richie, Diana Ross, Gregory Hines, Oprah Winfrey, Bill Cosby and Whoopi Goldberg – many of the people Ken Kragen had not pressed to appear at Live Aid for fear that they would then have had enough and turn down appearing for his own fundraiser. In doing so, he deprived Live Aid of some of the world's most prominent black acts.

Other distinct groups wanted their communities to do their bit. The pop artist Peter Blake, who designed the artwork for the Band Aid single as well as the Beatles' celebrated *Sgt. Pepper* cover, decided to approach his fellow artists to follow in the footsteps of the musicians. 'I felt that the artists hadn't done their share,' he said. Some 104 of the artists he approached for Visual Aid submitted their artwork by the deadline, including David Hockney, Frank Bowling, Patrick Caulfield, Richard Hamilton, Patrick Hughes, R.B. Kitaj, Eduardo Paolozzi and Bridget Riley.

Two of the biggest names in contemporary art were missing. Blake decided that Lucian Freud was too grand to ask – only to be told afterwards that Freud would have been pleased to be included. He did though write to the other great figure in contemporary painting, Francis Bacon, but his assistants failed to pass on the request. Later, when they encountered one another in the Colony Club in London's Mayfair, Bacon said to Brad Faine, the master printer who organised Visual Aid with Blake: 'You silly boy, you should have come here and found me.'

One hundred of the individual artists' offerings were printed in a grid, their positioning determined randomly by Faine pulling their names out of a hat, with four of the most emblematic images in the margin. Each silkscreen print in the limited edition of 500 was signed by all the artists, who gathered in groups of twenty-five at the Royal Academy for the signing. Once the first 100 of the prints had been sold – for £350 each – Geldof suggested opening up the rest to bids in an auction, an idea unprecedented for the fine art community.

The fashion industry was also moved to come together. In a world normally riven by jealous rivalries, top fashion houses came together to show off their gowns at a one-off event at a packed Royal Albert Hall in London, and again the following night at the Palladium in New York. 'Getting the fashion icons in the same room on the same fashion show had never happened, ever,' said promoter Harvey Goldsmith. 'To get Giorgio Armani, Versace, Chanel and all of these iconic brands to do a fashion show together was unheard of. But they came together for Fashion Aid.' The idea was conceived by Fameed Khalique, a fashion student from North East London Polytechnic, as a part of his degree course. He took the idea to Geldof, who made it happen.

The resulting extravaganza featured 125 models, 120 dressers, sixty make-up artists and thirty-five hairdressers, as well as a host of celebrities – actors Michael Caine, Jane Seymour and Anjelica Huston, models Jerry Hall and Grace Jones, singers Freddie Mercury, Kate Bush, Boy George, George Michael, Madonna and Ringo Starr, together with Spandau Ballet and Madness – setting off fantastical outfits by designers Jasper Conran, Wendy Dagworthy, Jean Muir, Zandra Rhodes, Katharine Hamnett, Calvin Klein, Giorgio Armani, Issey Miyake and Yves Saint Laurent.

At the climax, Freddie Mercury and Jane Seymour came down the catwalk dressed as bride and groom to the celebrated Toccata from Widor's Symphony No. 5 – he bare-chested beneath an epauletted military uniform, she in a white lace dress tied up with bows, with an extravagant flower crown of lilies and lily of the valley. Both outfits were designed by David and Elizabeth Emanuel, who had created Princess Diana's wedding gown. The UK and US events raised $3 million between them.

Such was the spirit of the times that every community threw itself into making a contribution. Hear 'n Aid was a supergroup of forty heavy metal/ hard rock musicians, including members of Judas Priest, Mötley Crüe,

Twisted Sister, Blue Oyster Cult and the parody band Spinal Tap (who performed in character) raised more than $3 million. Bhangra musicians from Birmingham and Southall staged Asian Live Aid in the Birmingham Odeon, with turbaned Sikhs sashaying through the sari-clad audience in front of a Live Aid logo in which the guitar had been replaced by a sitar.

Every community made its distinctive contribution. At the Donmar Warehouse in London, big-name actors – including Hayley Mills, Jonathan Pryce and Michael Palin – staged a twelve-hour-long Actors' Aid improvisation with a poster designed by the master satirical cartoonist Ralph Steadman. In Covent Garden, street performers got together for Busk Aid, with singers, acrobats and even a fire-eater taking part. Delia Smith's *Food Aid Cookery Book* raised half a million pounds for Band Aid.

Live Aid fever spread contagiously across the UK. The Grimsby and Cleethorpes Live Aid gig featured two dozen local bands in a whole-day event introduced by the local MP, Austin Mitchell. At the finale in Cleethorpes' Winter Gardens – 'All You Need is Love', with a full brass section – the town's mayor was at the front of the stage, swaying in his mayoral chains of office. Above the stage, a banner read 'One World for Africa'. Telford Ice Rink presented a Country & Western Live Aid, all Stetsons and fringed buckskin jackets.

Live Aid in Aberdeen was rock 'n' roll in kilts, fly plaid and *Braveheart* helmets, while in Burnley, a seven-hour Live Aid marathon took place in the town's leisure centre, with forays out onto the streets by Morris dancers in clogs. Magnanimously, as if to finally signal the end of the Wars of the Roses, the Yorkshire Bank Live Aid account number was flashed on screens throughout the Lancashire town and collecting tins did the rounds all day, most of which were full by the end of the evening.

Valley Aid in south Wales stood as a testament to both the collective efforts of a local community coming together to demonstrate international solidarity – and also an extraordinary ability to have a great time despite the mist, rain and low cloud which lingered in the steep valleys, keeping the audience permanently soaked.

More politically, in Wiltshire a group of fifty Live Aid supporters tried to stop a delivery of barley to a Common Market grain store, proclaiming that they wanted it sent to Ethiopia via nearby RAF Lyneham rather than join an EEC grain mountain.

❖

Such responses were spontaneous expressions of empathy and action from individuals and communities. But Geldof wanted to involve the next generation more directly. School Aid was launched at Haverstock School, a comprehensive in Chalk Farm, north London, in July 1985. It encouraged children to spend their pocket money on a bag of flour, sugar or lentils to bring to school and place in sacks. These were then taken to the local railway station and delivered free of charge by British Rail's Red Star service to Tilbury Docks, where Band Aid ships transported them to Ethiopia.

'You get a tangible sense of achievement,' said Geldof, watching pupils at the school fill the sacks. 'In fact, it's the ultimate sense of achievement because there are people walking around who would otherwise be dead – and all because you spent your pocket money one afternoon on a bag of flour.'

Television companies went to school after school to film children – from London to Shropshire to Manchester – bringing in bags of sugar, flour and split peas. They delivered them with heart-rendingly simple statements like: 'There are people dying when we've got plenty to eat and they've got nothing.'

In Sheffield, children donated a tonne of grain to the famine appeal. One school in the city, Myers Grove, won a national competition to raise the most amount of money for Live Aid. Their reward was a free gig by synth-pop star Howard Jones. He arrived at the school in a massive tour bus and played two gigs, one in the afternoon and one in the evening.

Some £3 million worth of aid was raised by schoolchildren in this way. But more than that, Band Aid provided schools with videos and information packs to offer new perspectives on Africa and dispel some of the old colonial clichés about the continent. They showed that charity was only part of the answer; the rich world had to change its policies on unfair trade, debt and aid which were holding Africa back. But what was most important was the sense of active involvement this created. The aim was to empower a whole new generation and make them feel they could make a difference in the world.

Richard Curtis knew how to harness and develop that feeling among the general public. Directly inspired by Live Aid, he decided that his fellow comedy writers and comedians needed to make their own contribution. The result was Comic Relief, an annual telethon on BBC Television, which has to date raised more than £1.6 billion. More importantly, it has inspired generations of adults and children to become personally involved in the tragedies of people who they will never meet.

Curtis had first become involved in 1985 when, at a dinner party in Clapham, a friend called Jane Tewson, who ran a homelessness charity, told him she had been invited to travel to Ethiopia or Sudan to see how she could apply her expertise in the famine-hit region. Curtis said to her: 'If you want someone to go with you, so you've got someone to laugh with at night, I'll come.'

It was a casual remark that started a lifelong commitment to working with Bob Geldof and Bono on campaigns to combat poverty in Africa. 'We went to a meeting at Save the Children. There was a guy from Oxfam there who said, "It seems a bit of a waste sending the two of you to the same country. Why don't you go to Ethiopia, Richard, and Jane will go to Sudan?" So, suddenly, literally having intended just to be a nice friend, I was launched into a month-long trip to Ethiopia with no plans or organisation or anything.' He took a camera with him but, soon after he arrived, it broke.

He returned from Ethiopia 'very traumatised' and determined to do something to help. It was a life-changing experience. Comic Relief was launched live on BBC One on Christmas Day 1985 on Noel Edmonds' *Live, Live Christmas Breakfast Show*. Many of Britain's top comedians appeared, including Rowan Atkinson, Billy Connolly, John Cleese, Lenny Henry and Dawn French. The television audience gave generously. They watched families all around the UK as they sent Christmas greetings via a pioneering satellite link-up with their relatives working as relief workers in Sahawa refugee camp in the east of Sudan. Helen Fielding, later the author of the *Bridget Jones* books and films, and then a BBC television researcher, presented part of the show from a camp full of Ethiopian refugees who had crossed into Sudan in search of food.

In contrast to the footage shown at Live Aid, the scenes in the camp were joyful and uplifting, showing what a difference six months of emergency aid had made. Where once ninety people were dying every day, the grim death toll had reduced to less than one. Once listless and malnourished children were seen singing and dancing.

'The really wonderful thing about the camp here is that it's such a success story,' Fielding told television viewers via the first-ever live satellite link from Sudan. 'It's full of happy children. Life is starting up again. They're well-fed, it's organised and the people here are passing on their knowledge to the Tigrayan refugees so they don't have to rely totally on the relief workers.'

The Save the Children camp administrator interrupted to add: 'It should be emphasised that this is thanks to all of the people who gave us money to do this.'

Fielding told the television viewers: 'The point is that if you send money, it achieves results.'

This opening broadcast established many of the hallmarks of Comic Relief – the need to offer signs of optimism, to show poor people helping themselves rather than being totally dependent and to show the difference made by even small donations.

The following year, Richard Curtis brought together a collection of pop stars, comedians and celebrities – Rowan Atkinson, Frank Bruno, Kate Bush, Billy Connolly, Angus Deayton, Ben Elton, Dawn French, Howard Goodall, Lenny Henry, Howard Jones, Jennifer Saunders – for a series of Comic Relief fundraisers at the Shaftesbury Theatre in London's West End. It included a sketch in which Bob Geldof and Midge Ure attempted to explain the concept of charity to an uncomprehending bank manager, played by Stephen Fry. The Young Ones appeared with Cliff Richard to sing his 1950s hit single 'Living Doll' – the first Comic Relief charity record, which was then number one in the UK top forty. After the show, the cast repaired to the home of comedian Lenny Henry. There, after a certain amount of drink had been taken, they all agreed they'd like to do it again – on television. 'The next thing we knew, Richard had figured out a deal with the BBC and suddenly we were on telly,' Henry told me.

Curtis had been pushing at an open door. The controller of BBC One, Michael Grade, was of course a Band Aid trustee. 'When the producer came to me with the idea for Comic Relief, it was to do little bits and pieces between programmes,' Lord Grade recalled. 'I said, "If you're going to do it, let's do it properly. I'll give you the whole night if you can find the material and the people to do it."' Having agreed, Grade promptly 'left the BBC with no record of where the money was to come from, but by then,' said Curtis, 'I was already sitting in a room and starting to make it.'

Comic Relief swiftly came up with the idea of selling plastic clowns' red noses as a fundraising gimmick. It became the enduring symbol of the organisation. The first Red Nose Day telethon was held in February 1988. Lenny Henry went to Ethiopia and 150 other celebrities and comedians participated. The evening attracted 30 million television viewers and raised £15 million. The sums increased, year by year. Initially, Comic Relief alternated with Sport Relief, an initiative to bring the sporting community into the fundraising. Having run every other year since then, in 2021 Red Nose Day became an annual event. Comic Relief, as Bono put it, has kept 'the injustice of life in the poorest countries in the minds of people in one of the richest'.

Comic Relief added an important dimension to the Live Aid legacy in several ways. It spoke the language of the living room. When Lenny Henry went to Ethiopia, he held up a goat and told the television camera: '£3 will buy a goat for this family' – only to be told by the farmer that the animal was not a goat but a sheep. Lenny's incompetence humanised the business of charitable giving while portraying people in Africa as equals rather than objects of pity.

In another village, he talked to a lively old man in his nineties. 'We'd funded something in the village and he was really grateful. He said to me, through an interpreter: "Thank you, guys, so much for coming here and helping us." And then he says, "And if ever you need us, just say the word and we'll come and help you sort things out at your end." And I thought, *That's amazing. We've been seeing you as a victim, but actually you're just a bloke that this has happened to, and you're saying, "When you need us, we're ready."*' It's a human thing – an instinctual thing to help. And we must whatever happens hold on to that. Because if we lose that then we're lost.'

Comic Relief added both a new perspective and a new enthusiasm. It adopted the Band Aid maxim that every single penny donated by the public must be spent on charitable projects. It called this the Golden Pound Principle, insisting that all operating costs, such as staff salaries, are covered by corporate sponsors or by interest on money waiting to be distributed. The organisation was also anxious to move beyond responding to a crisis and instead to start talking about long-term development. It began to make short films to run between the comedy, showing how aid could make a lasting difference.

'For the first couple of Red Nose Days, a third of the international money went to Oxfam and a third went to Save the Children,' says Kevin Cahill who was, for twenty years, Comic Relief's chief executive. From early on, the organisation decided to apportion a smaller part of its funds to UK projects in order to forestall the criticism that charity should begin at home. It focused on neglected parts of the domestic agenda, such as street homelessness, domestic violence and disability. Oxfam and Save the Children initially shaped Comic Relief spending policies; 'then, over the years, we developed our own process so we can be fully accountable for the money the public have given us – and trust us to spend well'.

Part of that process is Comic Relief's determination to fund projects that are user-led. Home or abroad, right from the outset, 'when we were funding work on disability, there was a requirement that the board of management of any disability charity should be 51 per cent-plus disabled people. That was radical, way back then, because it was saying that the people who know best what disabled people need are disabled people, not non-disabled people. Over the years, we've moved overwhelmingly towards funding African-led organisations. And where there was a white person running the project, we needed to know that, in three years' time, it would evolve so there was a local person running it.'

From the start, there was more to Comic Relief than fundraising. It was about allowing people to realise, said Curtis, that 'there is something you personally can do to help people living tough lives – and it needn't be miserable, helping other people – and that would eventually be as valuable as any money that they gave to Comic Relief'. The organisation's slogan, 'Do something funny for money', turned everyone into a lord of misrule. 'The charity landscape didn't have anything like it going on – raising money by kids saying to their teachers, "Shave your beard off or spray your hair red, and we'll collect money for you to do it". Comic Relief, as our slogan had it, "put the fun into fundraising",' said Cahill. 'You don't have to be angst-y and guilt-ridden to give money and to try to help people change their lives.'

One of the distinctive things about Comic Relief, which was an extension of the Live Aid way of working, was that it did not merely ask people to dip into their pockets. It asked them to do something, to give their time too. That created a greater sense of commitment.

'It's been half of my life,' said Sir Lenny Henry, looking back forty years later. 'We were just this bunch of young people thinking *Let's have a go at this*. There was a lot of passion, a lot of determination. I think that our youth had a lot to do with the energy of it.' Richard Curtis likes to quote the anthropologist Mary Mead, who said: 'Never doubt that a small group of committed people can change the world. It's the only thing that ever has.'

⁎⁙⁎

The day after the Live Aid concert, members of the Norwegian and the British parliaments announced they would be nominating Bob Geldof for the Nobel Peace Prize.

In a letter of nomination to the Norwegian Nobel Committee, which awards the Peace Prize, the parliamentarian Sissel Rønbeck wrote: 'He has engaged millions across the continents, and power-blocs, in a concrete effort for peace and development. He has mobilised the grown-ups of the future to realise the motto for the United Nation's international youth year: Participation, Development and Peace.'

It was only the start. In June 1986, it was announced that Geldof was to be awarded a knighthood, apparently on the recommendation of the foreign secretary, Geoffrey Howe. Unusually, the ceremony was rushed forward so he received the award little more than a month later. Attired in an unfamiliar black tailcoat, he turned up at Buckingham Palace to be presented with the insignia of the Knight Commander of the British Empire by the Queen.

'This is a small token for the work you have done,' said Her Majesty.

'Believe me, it was harder work getting into this,' riposted Geldof, indicating his morning suit, collar and tie, his hair still untamed and dishevelled.

'Yes, I can see that,' replied the monarch, drily.

Because he was an Irish citizen, he did not have to kneel or be dubbed with a sword as her subjects were. In theory, he was henceforth to be Bob Geldof KBE, but the British press immediately opted for Sir Bob.

Outside in the palace courtyard, he described it as 'the nicest knighthood I've ever seen'.

'I'm not getting it for some outstanding service to the state. Or any great artistic achievement,' he explained. 'I'm getting it because millions of people decided to do this thing.' Addressing the public via the television cameras, he said of the knighthood: 'If you helped at all, it must belong to you because that's what it's for. It sounds corny, but I can't put it any other way. It is a shared thing.' He showed off the ribboned medal and insignia, before adding sardonically: 'But I'm the one who gets to take it home.'

Soon after, Garret FitzGerald, the Irish taoiseach, announced he too would put Geldof's name forward for the Nobel Peace Prize, breaking Ireland's policy of never nominating candidates: 'His personal magnetism, powers of persuasion and the high esteem in which he is held by his fellow musicians have helped to make the Third World and its problems appear more real and important in the developed world.' He instructed Ireland's diplomats to seek support from other nations for the nomination. They did. But, embarrassingly, the Irish government missed the deadline to submit the official nomination.

Still, all this official recognition began to give Geldof access to international figures at the highest level. He received an invitation to lunch from the president of France, François Mitterrand, at the Élysée Palace. There, Geldof displayed his usual irreverence, taking one look at the emerald-green damask upholstery of the chairs in the Napoleon III sitting room and telling Mitterrand: 'You have the same taste as Nancy Reagan.' The president threw up his hands in resignation and then blamed Napoleon III. When they moved to the dining room, which had been restyled in the 1970s, he declared it to look like the lair of the head of SMERSH in a James Bond film.

With Madame Danielle Mitterrand to his left and the president directly across the wide round table, they began talking about Africa. The famine was getting worse in western Sudan. There were stocks of food aid in Port Sudan, but no money to move it.

'We will move it,' said the president, nodding to an official, who immediately took notes.

'There are French food stocks in the port at Djibouti, but there is no train to take it to Ethiopia.'

'How much is there?' asked the president

'About 30,000 tonnes.'

'Send the air force,' said Mitterrand. The official made notes.

There was one more thing. The aid agencies knew that there were military satellites that showed detailed geographical and agricultural pictures of the famine regions. Monitoring them would help with the prediction of imminent famine. But the Americans and the Russians would not make them available. Could they have pictures from the French military satellites?

Mitterrand summoned a general.

'Do we have a satellite over Africa?'

'No,' said the general. Geldof looked sceptical. He knew France was about to launch a new SPOT satellite. The acronym stood for Satellites Pour l'Observation de la Terre.

By the end of the meeting, Geldof had permission to access the satellite photographs. He also had an undertaking to move food in Sudan. And the president had promised to pay for the freight expenses of Action École – the French version of School Aid. It had mushroomed because it became a symbol of rebellion for schoolkids after teachers refused to become involved in it.

During the course of the lunch, Bob had mentioned that his daughter was called Fifi. After they had finished eating, Mitterrand took him to a small anteroom. It was exactly as Napoleon had left it. The abdication papers he signed were there on a small table. The ink on his signature was smeared with tears. Mitterrand gestured to a lilac chaise longue.

'In the nineteenth century, a previous president enjoyed some rather vigorous amorous activity on that very couch – and expired in the arms of his paramour, a certain Madame Fifi. I am sure your Madame Thatcheurre has nothing like this, non?'

He was in a good mood for a man whose lunch had cost him $10 million.

'I wondered why it couldn't always be so easy,' said Geldof afterwards. 'But then you don't always have an ideologically sympathetic man in power, with one eye on the upcoming election.' Still, Bob concluded, 'Mitterrand was one of those lucky people who can instigate action by the flick of his fingers and is not afraid or ashamed to use that power.'

It was a lesson Geldof was to apply in his dealings with a host of prime ministers and presidents in the future.

✂

And with popes.

Bob Geldof was at home in his flat in Battersea one night watching *Dynasty* on the television, when the phone rang.

'Is that Bob Geldof?' asked an Irish voice, an elderly voice, calling from some distance away. She introduced herself as a Catholic nun.

'Now would you be related to the Mr Geldof who used to sell towels to my father in Ballygombeen?' Bob's father had been a travelling salesman, journeying all across Ireland for many years.

'Yes, Sister, that's my dad.'

'Oh, a lovely man. We used to look forward to his visits. He became a great friend of my father.'

'That's lovely, Sister. What's this about?'

'I'm calling from the Vatican. Would you be available to speak to the Holy Father in thirty minutes?'

Fuck! The Pope?! thought Geldof, rather inappropriately.

It was 1989. Famine had returned to Ethiopia and Sudan. Food aid was needed once more. And it needed moving to the inaccessible regions. But on the international front, there was new movement. In the Soviet Union, a new, more open leader had taken power, Mikhail Gorbachev. He spoke of *glasnost* and *perestroika*. It encouraged Russians to a new freedom of speech on political issues and spoke of modernising the Soviet economy. On 1 December, Gorbachev was meeting Pope John Paul II at the Vatican – an historic meeting, the first between a Soviet leader and a pope. The next day, he had a summit with the American president, George H.W. Bush, on a naval warship in the Mediterranean.

'I had had this whizbang idea,' Geldof recalled of a plan he'd floated. A few months earlier, he had called the leader of the Catholic Church in England, Cardinal Basil Hume, and asked him to put it to the Pope.

'It will make the new *perestroika* thing tangible and real with proper value,' the pop singer said to the cardinal. 'My plan is to get the Pope to ask Gorby and Bush to use Soviet Antonov planes based in Ethiopia to carry US grain to wherever it's needed. It would be a great symbol of a different world.'

'Hmmm,' said the English cardinal. 'I'll try, but don't hold your breath.'

Months had passed. And then came the phone call from the Irish nun.

Pope John Paul II came on the line. 'He talked with a translator,' Geldof recalled. 'He spoke in a thick Italianish/Polish English with the translator supplying the occasional words. He said he liked the idea and he'd try, but couldn't promise anything. He ended by saying that God blessed me.' Geldof was stunned. 'That was a pretty cool end to the conversation,' he said.

Whether the American grain was ever carried in the Russian planes is unclear. Their encounter on 2 December became known as the Seasick Summit because the weather off the coast of Malta was so rough that many of its meetings had to be rescheduled. But, certainly, they agreed to work together at their next meeting in Washington, the following June, when they jointly pressurised the Ethiopian government to clear the blocked port at Massawa. It was one of the last things which Ethiopia's dictator, Colonel Mengistu, did before he was overthrown.

✳

There was one other legacy of Live Aid, although it was not to become clear until more than a decade later.

Before he went on stage at Live Aid, Bono was approached by a senior aid worker from the aid agency World Vision. One of its founders had been the American evangelist Billy Graham and the organisation had a hunch that Bono, who had been a member of a charismatic Christian house group in the 1970s, would be sympathetic to its request. Would he like to come to see their work in Ethiopia first-hand? Yes, he said, so long as there was no publicity. And he didn't want to just tour around. He wanted to work in a refugee camp, with his wife Ali.

Several months after the Live Aid paraphernalia had been cleared from Wembley Stadium, Bono and Ali took a plane to Ethiopia. He had grown a beard in the hope of hiding his identity. 'We received word that we were to take great pains to keep his visit a secret,' said World Vision staffer Steve Reynolds. 'I didn't know what all the fuss was about, since several celebrities (and wannabes) had passed through our office already that year, most of them wanting only to be seen.'

When he heard that Bono and Ali wanted to work at a feeding centre that catered to thousands of people each day, he was deeply sceptical. 'I knew what the conditions were like in these camps, the local food that was served, the sleeping quarters and the rest. I remember thinking, *Well, they are certainly in for a shock.*'

Bono had half-anticipated that. When Reynolds picked him up at the airport, he seemed uncomfortable. 'I detected a hint of fear in his eyes,' the aid worker thought.

World Vision took them to several remote camps, including Ibnat, a tent city of about 60,000 people. Looking round, a phrase came to Bono's mind: 'where the streets have no name'. The tour concluded at a feeding centre in Adjibar, in southern Wollo, where the couple were to live and work for a month. 'I was certain they wouldn't last a week,' Reynolds said.

At Adjibar, they were catapulted into caring for a group of orphans. The young Irish couple did not know what had hit them. 'People would leave their children in rags, some would be alive, some wouldn't,' Bono recalled. 'For a couple of kids from the suburbs, it was a very overwhelming experience.'

It left an indelible mark on the singer. 'We saw the everydayness of despair,' he later said. It was not just the bloated stomachs of extreme malnutrition and poverty. 'The grieving was operatic.' He recalled the Irish word 'keening' – a noise made by the bereaved which was 'blood-curdling'. He spoke of 'the slow slaughter of obscenity of famine in our world of plenty'. Later, he wrote: 'In the desert, we meet God. In parched times, in fire and flood, we discover who we are.'

But it was a time of joy as well as sadness. Bono and Ali spent a month working with the World Vision staff, who used music and role play to teach basic survival skills to the children at the orphanage. Bono and Ali joined in with energy and creativity, helping develop music and drama to encourage the children to eat vegetables – or wash their hands to stop the spread of disease in the camps. 'There was a song I wrote about not eating seeds, because they used to eat the seeds they were given to plant,' said Bono. The children in the camp warmed to the two *ferenji* – as they called all foreigners – though they developed a particular name for Bono: 'The Girl with the Beard'.

The night before Bono and Ali flew back to Ireland, the World Vision staff threw a party. 'We sang songs and traded stories,' Steve Reynolds recalled. 'Bono mimicked himself as we listened to "Do They Know It's Christmas?". It was a time of celebration after much sadness and heartbreak.

For those of us working in Ethiopia, it was a healing and uplifting moment – one we would all treasure.' On the day they left the orphanage, a man approached the couple and handed them his baby.

'Would you take my son with you?'

He knew, in Ireland, that his son would live, and that in Ethiopia, his son might die. 'Well, I turned him down,' Bono later said. 'It was a funny kind of sick feeling, but I turned him down. And it's a feeling I can't ever quite forget. And in that moment, I started this journey.'

A few months later, Bono and Ali went to visit Central America. 'I'd become interested in liberation theology, a fusion of politically left principles with biblical ideas.' In El Salvador, his political prejudices were turned upside down. 'The good guys may turn out to be the communists,' he began to suspect. And the West had been supporting 'the bad guys' keeping them down. After meeting families whose children had gone missing, he wrote the lyrics for 'Mothers of the Disappeared'.

As they parted, Steve Reynolds – a man who had said Bono would not last a week – noted that 'something in him had changed'.

'You promise that you'll never forget … but you do,' Bono said, forty years on. 'You get back to your life, to being in the band. But something in the back of my mind told me there's something here I don't fully understand – but that I will, at some point in my life, be able to help those people.'

He thought back to the father who wanted to give his baby to Bono and Ali. 'I remember the look in that man's eye, what it took for a grown man to make that request. He's handing me his son. That's a very hard thing to walk away from. But there's part of me that didn't say no. And when I get a call ten years later from Jamie Drummond at Jubilee 2000 – a campaign to drop the debts of the poorest countries to the richest – I'm back there, immediately.'

❊

Back in London, Bob Geldof went into the Band Aid office to discuss, yet again, how Band Aid should best be wound down. 'For the past year, Band Aid had been the be-all and end-all of my life. Every hour of the waking day, seven days a week, had been consumed by it,' he recalled. 'I knew that, if I did not set a limit, it would take over my entire life.'

'It'll have to be wound up by the end of 1986,' Bob told Penny Jenden, who had taken over from her husband Kevin as Band Aid's director.

'But what about the projects? They need monitoring,' said Penny.

'Are you seriously suggesting we hang around for fifteen years? Some of our projects are that long-term.'

'But the money is still coming in.'

'The money will carry on coming in for years,' said Geldof. 'At the end of the year, we'll hand over to a standing committee made up of representatives from all the agencies.'

It never happened.

CHAPTER 22

FROM CHARITY
TO JUSTICE

The year after the Live Aid concert, Geldof and I had worked together on his autobiography, *Is That It?*. He was only thirty-five when it came out, but he already had a story to tell which was full of more incidents than that of plenty of people twice his age. The same year, he left the Boomtown Rats and launched a solo career with his album, *Deep in the Heart of Nowhere*.

The record got to number one in Ireland and Norway, but only to number twenty-five in the UK and number eighty-two in the US. Over the next couple of years, Geldof had desultory gigs across Europe, in the US, in New Zealand and in Australia. In 1988, he was making money, unconventional as ever, by filming adverts for drinking milk alongside his dog, Growler. In 1989, with news of famine once more in Ethiopia, he was shepherding together a new generation of pop stars – including Kylie Minogue and Jason Donovan, to Bros and Cliff Richard, under the producer Pete Waterman – to remake 'Do They Know It's Christmas?' under the branding Band Aid II. As with its predecessor, the single became that year's Christmas number one, remaining at the top for three weeks.

⁜

While Bob Geldof returned to the business of trying to revive a career in pop music, I returned to Africa to report for *The Times*. Geldof and I had visited half a dozen countries together. Now I was reporting from half a dozen more in sub-Saharan Africa. The more I visited, the more I was struck by the common factors which underlay their struggles.

It was not just drought, famine and war that they had in common. They were all struggling under massive debts owed to Western banks and financial institutions like the International Monetary Fund and the World Bank.

These debts had not been incurred by the ordinary people and yet they were suffering to repay them. Money had been loaned during the Cold War to any corrupt ruler who signed up to back the West. Banks, which were awash with money after the massive oil price hikes in the 1970s, had lent it out irresponsibly without checking whether the borrowers were able to repay.

The IMF and World Bank had strong-armed African governments to slash their spending on health and education to redirect their meagre income towards repaying the loans. In banking jargon, these iniquitous demands were called Structural Adjustment Programs. For decades, poor countries spent four times more repaying debts than they did on health and education combined.

Yet the brutal fact was that these debts could never be repaid. Poor African countries earned their living by selling what they could farm or mine, but the prices for these raw materials had plunged on the international markets. For every £1 rich nations gave in aid, poor nations had to pay back £3 in debt repayments. The interest on these debts mounted faster than they could be repaid. They were, in effect, unpayable. And yet the attempts to repay them were falling upon the shoulders of the world's poorest people, whose clinics and schools were being closed to pay rich bankers.

Sitting one night in a guesthouse in the copper belt in Zambia, piecing together what I had found about the common factors in one sub-Saharan African country after another, I came to a dramatic realisation. Debt was not just an economic issue. It was an ethical one. Debt was both economically unsustainable and morally unacceptable. The poor world did not need charity. It needed justice.

When I got back to England, I began to write a book: *Bad Samaritans – First World Ethics and Third World Debt*. One line in it stung Geldof. He admitted as much in a lecture to the Bar Human Rights Committee in St Paul's Cathedral. He told the packed assembly that 'in his book *Bad*

Samaritans of 1990, Paul Vallely wrote correctly: "For all his skill as a populist, Bob Geldof could not shift the agenda from one of charity to one
of justice.'"

In private, he was more direct. 'That, you fucker, was the spur for me
to change tack. When you said I was not gonna change the political or
economic landscape, I said: "Fuck off, Vallely". And I began to try to do it.'

It set him on a course which was to consume him for the next four
decades.

❧

Over the previous two years, Geldof had swiftly developed a detailed understanding of the politics of aid. Now he began to read about the complexities
of debt and the convolutions of fair and unfair trade. Two new notions
presented themselves to him. One was from the Bible; the other was from
the world of international banking law.

In an attempt to urge the churches to take up the issue, *Bad Samaritans*
had made reference to the biblical idea of Jubilee. The books of Leviticus
and Deuteronomy had urged the people of Israel to adopt a series of rules
which ensured that the poor were, from time to time, allowed a fresh start.
All debts were to be cancelled every seventh year, the sabbath year. Every
forty-nine years – a sabbath of sabbath years – was proclaimed a jubilee and
all slaves were to be freed. It was a mechanism to secure justice for the poor,
rather than leaving them to the mercy of the charitable impulses of the rich.

The Bible set out some clear ethical principles. Loans should be handled
in a way that respects the dignity of the borrower. Unjust social structures
which marginalise the poor should be challenged. Debt that could never
be fully paid should be written off. Austerity programmes, which actively
discriminate against the very poorest, were immoral. These was not just
my reading. The Vatican declared that 'debt servicing cannot be met at the
price of the asphyxiation of a country's economy'.

The second concept was from banking. More than fifty years earlier,
bankers had acknowledged the notion of 'odious debt'. A debt was odious
if it was incurred without the consent of the people, if it didn't benefit the
population and if the lenders were aware (or should have been aware) of
those facts. The notion had been accepted as an international political reality a number of times in the twentieth century.

Geldof began to mull on both these ideas.

�֎

The idea of debt relief was not new. But, until now, it had been handled only in a piecemeal manner. Rich nations, calling themselves the Paris Club, met regularly to renegotiate the debts of African nations who could not pay. At first, they did this mainly by extending the repayment period. But, in 1988, they agreed to actually *reduce* the debt – in return for economic reforms. The detail of these negotiations was fearsomely complicated. But three of Bob Geldof's future allies got the measure of them.

Shriti Vadera was just six years out of university, having studied politics, philosophy and economics at Oxford. She had been born in Uganda, to Gujarati parents. Her family had owned a small tea plantation, but fled to India in 1972 when Idi Amin expelled all the Asians from Uganda. Born in Africa, and educated in India, she had developed an interest in poverty issues. On leaving Oxford, she had gone into the City. In 1990, she was working for the investment banker Warburg, where she gave advice to African governments, and most particularly Uganda, on debt restructuring.

The second key figure was Kevin Watkins, a brilliant development economist who was then head of policy at Oxfam. He had decided that it was time for the aid world to turn the spotlight on to the debt issue. Watkins wanted to use Uganda as a test case since, he said, 'the Ugandans were the blue-eyed boys of the IMF/World Bank reform programme at the time'. Both institutions used highly complex criteria to determine who received debt relief and who didn't. By contrast, Watkins said the yardstick should be that no poor country should be forced to spend more on repaying its debt than it was spending on hospitals and schools – an idea that the IMF at the time vehemently opposed. 'But the detail was all very technical.'

Shriti Vadera was one of the few people who understood all that detail. Watkins went to see her. 'Oxfam was engaged with very limited resources in a street fight with the IMF and parts of the World Bank, with their vast technical resources. It was an uneven battle and Shriti gave us the nitty-gritty to cut through when the IMF deployed spurious arguments against debt reduction,' Watkins said.

The pair – who were to become two of the key influences behind the Live 8 crusade for the next twenty years – swiftly developed a mutual respect. 'One thing you learned very quickly working with Shriti was that she acted out of deep moral conviction, backed by an extraordinary intellect and commitment to evidence-based argument,' said Watkins. For her part, Shriti reciprocated: 'Kevin was very much the thought-leader for the whole NGO community.'

The two began to meet regularly. Oxfam were working their way through the small concessions the Paris Club was making. 'We were nudging them,' Watkins recalled, 'and they would respond with some tiny incremental change. Basically, they just lengthened the time over which countries were allowed to pay.'

Something more radical was needed, said Shriti. The Paris Club only dealt with what was called bilateral debt, the debt owed by one country to another. Change was needed at a higher level – on the money owed to the IMF and World Bank, which was called multilateral debt. 'We've got to get the rules changed there,' Shriti told Watkins.

Shriti wrote what became the first paper from a debtor country, Uganda, on why the IMF and World Bank had got it all wrong. Together, she and Watkins went off and lobbied Gordon Brown, the Labour shadow chancellor, who had long been concerned about the debt burden of poor countries. 'At the meetings, it would be the likes of Oxfam, Christian Aid and Save the Children,' Shriti recalled, 'and me as the banker to tell you why this is financially literate.' She threw herself into this new alliance with enthusiasm, researching, publishing and speaking at events. By the end of the decade, she had become a member of Oxfam's board and a full-time adviser to Gordon Brown, who was then chancellor of the exchequer.

But already by the end of 1993, the direction of travel was clear. Kevin Watkins had written a report for Oxfam, *Africa Make or Break*, with the subheading *The Failure of IMF/World Bank Policies*. He now focused on persuading influential publications, such as the *Financial Times* and the *Economist*, to shift the focus of their coverage of debt from a very technical approach to one of 'how many kids could you get into school?'.

The third member of the trio who were to steer the policy of Live Aid over the next three decades was Justin Forsyth. After working in the anti-apartheid movement, he joined Oxfam and, in 1994, was sent to Washington DC. There, he lobbied the IMF, the World Bank and the United Nations to change their policies on how to fight global poverty.

Much of this involved painstakingly detailed paperwork, but it also had its cloak-and-dagger moments. One was reminiscent of the Deep Throat scenario from the Watergate scandal.

'I used to meet this amazing woman, Nawal Kamel, in a car park,' Justin said. 'She was the head of the section of the World Bank that was responsible for debt. She used to leak me documents, which would end up on the front page of the *Financial Times*. What she was doing was in clear defiance of the official World Bank line, but it revealed to us there was ambition inside the Bank for proper debt cancellation.'

Nawal Kamel passionately believed that the world's poorest countries needed to have their debts cancelled – not reduced. But her superiors in the World Bank did not agree. They thought it would cause chaos in the markets, so they blocked her plan. At one point, her bosses were so rattled by the leaks that they hired a private investigator to follow her. It stalled her career in the institution's ranks until a new World Bank president, James Wolfensohn, took over in June 1995.

'She's the hidden hero of the whole debt cancellation campaign,' Justin Forsyth said, three decades later. She was not alone. Shriti Vadera, Kevin Watkins and Justin Forsyth were also key behind-the-scenes figures in bringing about a political and economic change, via Live 8, which was to dwarf the achievement of the Band Aid single and the Live Aid concerts.

Bad Samaritans was not alone in applying the biblical idea of Jubilee to the burden of unpayable debt which was weighing down Africa's poorest people. In the same year that the book was published, Martin Dent, a former colonial civil servant, now a politics lecturer at Keele University, conceived the idea of launching Jubilee 2000, a campaign for debt relief.

Together with a retired senior UK diplomat, Bill Peters, the pair – both Christians who laid great emphasis upon the biblical principle of Jubilee – set up a lobby group to get Britain's churches on board. But it soon began to draw wider support – from aid agencies, trade unions, political parties and bodies as disparate as the Mothers' Union and the British Medical Association. What made Jubilee 2000 different from previous debt initiatives was that it called for a definitive one-off cancellation of unpayable debt, rather than merely reducing or rescheduling debt interest. Africa should not be asked to starve its children to pay its debts.

✂

Bob Geldof was only half-aware of all this, but he was unable to give proper attention to it because of the turmoil in his private life. In January 1995, his wife Paula moved out of the family home, taking their three daughters with her. Geldof was devastated. The separation almost drove him to suicide. 'When she left me, I was destroyed. I didn't understand why: never saw it coming. The grief was universes of grief. My head was crowded with loss.' At his lowest point, he made a list of reasons to live and reasons not to. 'There was only one item in the list for why I should continue: it just said, "The children".'

In addition to that private anguish, the breakup of his marriage subjected Geldof to a new kind of celebrity. After the glitter of the pop world and the beatification of the work that brought him his knighthood and the respect of millions, there now came the highly public parading of the disintegration of his marriage.

For weeks, he had some forty tabloid journalists outside the house. 'They were in blacked-out vans, on motorbikes tailing me, following me on foot.' It was like something out of Kafka. 'You don't know what it's about or what you're supposed to have done,' he told me at the time. 'It seems so preposterous. You start to behave like you're in a movie, jumping into cabs and then jumping out the other side immediately and taking one going in the opposite direction. You're asked the most outrageous and hurtful things in front of your children.' I remember thinking that it felt like he was under siege in his own home.

His tone was resigned rather than embittered. 'It's a condition of life. I've been in people's faces in this country for twenty years. I've accepted it, there isn't anything you can do about it, so to resist it is to completely frustrate yourself. I can't, in this instance, object. Unfortunately for me, I do realise it's a great tabloid story.

'I don't read any of it at all, I really don't. It would be too much misery. If you were to construct a biography from the tabloids, you would create something I wouldn't recognise. But my actual life has been like a soap opera. I await with trepidation the next success or the next catastrophic failure.'

All of this had a sharp impact on Geldof's desire and ability to create. His old Rats colleague, Pete Briquette, set up a little 24-track studio in the basement of Geldof's home, but Bob could not bring himself to use it. 'It just sits there and glares at me accusingly and I have to leave the room.' Throughout all this, the problems of Africa's debt burden were far from his mind as he coped with the anguish in his private life, the crowd of cameramen constantly outside his home and the hurtful process of the proceedings of the divorce court.

A month after Paula walked out, the BBC approached Bob with a proposal to mark the tenth anniversary of Live Aid. They wanted to re-run six hours of music from the 1985 concerts, interspersed with new interviews. They would be screened by the BBC in the UK and on VH1 and MuchMusic in the United States. They wanted Bob to go back to Ethiopia to see how things were ten years on.

Geldof was not interested. 'I was going through a long dark night of the soul,' he told me. 'I didn't want to go anywhere. I just wanted to sit and own the grief and absorb it.'

Five BBC executives came round to try to persuade him. Going to Ethiopia would give him a sense of purpose, they said. Geldof was not convinced. Among the BBC delegation was a young freelance film-maker named John Maguire.

When the BBC mandarins had left, Maguire set out a vision for ten short films which would not be news updates but rather meditative little essays depicting Africa as a continent of luminous life rather than dark deprivation. Maguire wanted to transfer the techniques he had learned making natural history films to the project.

'I wanted to shoot them all at forty frames a second, so that they'd have a certain grace and elegance – dignified films rather than famine films.'

Geldof was intrigued, but his personal trauma had rendered him uncharacteristically inarticulate. The loss of his wife and children was strangely echoing the loss of his mother in his childhood. He had grown up without a family and now the one he had created had been snatched away.

'I can't find the words,' he told Maguire.

'That's fine. We can do it without you speaking,' the young director said to Geldof's astonishment. Maguire had spent two years in an order of monks which practised the virtue of silence. 'We can make that work.'

Perhaps just as significantly, Maguire had recently been through a relationship breakup. The two would have much to talk about.

'I don't really want to go,' Geldof told him. 'But it offers a practical means of getting out of the country and away from all the paparazzi.'

In April, the two of them found themselves in Ethiopia for a month. 'Bob's mood was one of tortured relief,' recalled Maguire. 'It allowed him to hit the pause button and also to look back from a distance and reflect and consider, and to be in a completely different environment. It was one that he was familiar with, but he wasn't familiar with being there in that emotional state. It gave him something else to think about. It was a distraction.'

Geldof returned to Korem, the epicentre of the famine in 1984–85, and found it a bustling little African market town full of happy, healthy-looking children. He visited several projects which Band Aid had funded, providing clean water, building an orphanage and establishing a nursery to grow yams.

The films ranged from a reflection about the Queen of Sheba and Ethiopia's historical and mythologised past to another about how today's satellite technology could protect the country against another famine. But they were films about the past and the present which did not move outside his familiar world of charity and venture out onto the territory of justice.

'He was totally engaged with being there,' said Maguire. 'It suited his life at that moment. Ethiopia was clearly something that had remained very close to his heart.' But when the films were screened, Geldof did not watch them as part of the Live Aid re-run. 'I've no interest in my own past at all. I'm too preoccupied with the monstrous present and with a tentative future which I do not particularly relish.'

The monstrous present continued for Bob on his return from Ethiopia. In May 1996, Paula Yates finalised her divorce from him. The public proceedings were unbearable, he said. But his ordeal was far from over. The courts had awarded primary custody of his daughters to their mother. Bob was only allowed to see the children every other weekend, despite previously spending 'every single day' with them. Geldof called the decision a 'disgrace'.

Bob's energies were now diverted into a new cause: public advocacy for family law reform, particularly concerning the rights of fathers in custody disputes. The court's gender typecasting, he said, amounted to 'state-sanctioned kidnapping'. 'All I wanted was to see my kids 50 per cent of the time. The courts prevented that as much as possible.' Geldof argued that the custody decision prevented him from adequately caring for and protecting his children – an argument which was vindicated in 1998 when he was awarded primary custody of his three daughters.

Those close to Geldof knew what a toll this was taking on him. 'Bob kept this immense dignity throughout the entire process,' Midge Ure later said. 'He remained very controlled, not getting into public slanging matches or screaming and shouting from the rooftops. He just kept control – for his girls.'

✹

While Bob Geldof was embroiled in this private agony, the campaign for debt relief for poor countries moved up a gear. The scheme cooked up by 'the hidden hero of debt cancellation', Nawal Kamel – the one which had been roundly rejected by her World Bank bosses – had come into effect, thanks to the new president, James Wolfensohn. Following extensive lobbying by development agencies and other NGOs, it set out to ensure that no poor country faced an unmanageable debt burden. Called the Heavily Indebted Poor Countries (HIPC) Initiative, it reduced the amount due to be paid in repayments or offered low-interest loans to help poor nations pay rich ones.

It was a significant step forward. But it still required poor countries to reform their economies in ways which put the needs of foreign importers before those of poor Africans. And it failed to address one of the key yardsticks of the call for global debt justice: that poor people should not suffer to pay for debts incurred by discredited dictators.

All this may have fallen from Geldof's radar during his visit to Ethiopia to mark the tenth anniversary of Live Aid, but Jamie Drummond was frustrated by the shortcomings of latest debt relief plan. As a teenager, Drummond had been inspired by Live Aid in 1985 to study development economics. He was now working for Christian Aid. In 1995, he persuaded a BBC *Newsround* team to report on Ethiopia ten years on.

'A fact that I came across in Ethiopia blew my mind,' he recalled. 'That year, Ethiopia was supposed to spend $400 million repaying debts to the IMF and the World Bank, while its budget for health and education was just $150 million.' Worst of all, the $400 million repayment was mainly paying off interest. The actual debt remained the same.

'How is it,' Drummond asked, 'that we live in a world where poor people in a new young democracy are expected to repay the debts of departed dictators?'

Drummond decided to ring the only well-connected person he knew.

As a boy, his family spent every holiday in the west of Ireland and one of their neighbours there was Chris Blackwell, the boss of Island Records. Through Blackwell, Drummond got a number for Bono's company, Principle Management, in Dublin.

He rang the number. And rang it again.

He rang repeatedly over the next two years, sending documents and leaving messages for Bono with what he later described as 'the embarrassing frequency of a stalker'.

He rang so unrelentingly that a colleague in the Christian Aid office, called Kevin, began making regular prank calls to Drummond, pretending to be Bono. Then, one day, the phone rang and a voice said:

'Hi Jamie. Thanks for all the Jubilee stuff you've been incessantly sending us. Isn't your proposal for the debt cancellation for the year 2000 impossible now because of the Southeast Asian financial crisis?'

Was it Kevin? Or was it Bono?

'I thought, *That's not something Kevin would say. Maybe this really is Bono.*'

It *was* Bono. Fortunately, Drummond gave him a proper answer. It was the start of a thirty-year partnership on behalf of the world's poorest people. 'Jamie's explanation was like a calling,' Bono later said.

U2 had always been a political band. In their early years, they played gigs in support of the anti-apartheid movement. They had been closely aligned with Amnesty. In 1992 had done a 'Stop Sellafield' gig for Greenpeace to protest against the proposed building of a second nuclear power plant. In 1997, the band called leaders from the opposing sides in Northern Ireland onto the stage in celebration of the Good Friday peace agreement. Jamie Drummond also knew that the band had been members of a Christian house church in Dublin in their early days. The biblical principle of Jubilee would resonate with them, if only he could draw their attention to it. After two years, he had succeeded.

❊

The pieces in the jigsaw were beginning to fit together. In May 1997, a Labour government was elected in the UK. The new prime minister, Tony Blair, immediately announced Britain's aid ministry would become a full cabinet-ranking department, headed for the first time by a secretary of state, Clare Short. Eliminating world poverty was to become its stated aim.

Aid would no longer be used to boost Britain's trade or foreign policy ambitions – as it had been under the Conservative government when aid had been used to bribe foreign governments to buy British ships, planes and missiles. The new chancellor, Gordon Brown, announced that debt relief was to be high on the new government's agenda. Within the first week, Clare Short called Bob Geldof into her new Department for International Development and asked if he could launch a Live Aid-style movement around debt relief.

'It's too esoteric,' he told her. 'This is opaque economics. How do you create a popular movement around that? I don't understand it. How can I sell it? It's just too boring.'

The new secretary of state was disappointed and frustrated. The two never really collaborated thereafter.

But, elsewhere, things were beginning to move. The following year, Jubilee 2000 spread its campaign to the United States, opening an office in Washington, where it tapped into a coalition of forty Catholic and Protestant church organisations that had been lobbying the IMF and the World Bank for several years. In the British government's aid department, a senior civil servant, Myles Wickstead – who, ten years later, was to develop a key relationship with Geldof – had just completed a seminal white paper defining Labour's new approach to overseas aid. It put the eradication of extreme poverty as the clear primary and legal objective of Tony Blair's foreign policy. In the UK in May 1998, a human chain of 70,000 demonstrators was organised by Jubilee 2000 to encircle the leaders of the world's richest nations at the G8 summit in Birmingham. They forced the eight world leaders to promise to extend debt relief to more countries. What the campaign could not yet do was persuade Bob and Bono to take part.

The campaigners determined on one last push. Just before Christmas, Jamie Drummond and Adrian Lovett of Jubilee 2000 flew to Dublin to meet Bono, who was taking a break from U2's exhausting ninety-three-gig tour to promote the album *Pop*. Drummond had had numerous phone conversations with Bono, but this was to be their first face-to-face. A lot was riding on the meeting. They knew that if they could persuade Bono to join the campaign, he would quickly elevate their profile.

The two campaigners were only expecting to meet the singer. But when they got to U2's offices at Principle Management in Dublin docks, they found themselves sat around a long boardroom table with Bono, plus the rest of the band, along with their formidable manager, Paul McGuinness, and their communications strategist, Sheila Roche. It was a lunchtime meeting and what the campaigners did not realise was that the whole U2 crew were there because they were waiting for the meeting to be over so that they could start their office Christmas party.

'I'll never forget the look on Sheila's face,' said Drummond later. 'She was waiting to start the Christmas holiday and suddenly Bono's saying he'd like to find a way of supporting Jubilee 2000 in its aim of cancelling Third World debt by the end of next year. She'd just done a world tour. She was absolutely exhausted. And she looked incredibly pissed off.'

Bono had read all the material Jubilee 2000 had sent him. He was interested, but the rest of U2 were not so engaged. 'I got the sense,' said Lovett, 'that he needed us to show the rest of the band, and the people around them, that we weren't crazy and that he would be in good hands if he was going to work with us. The others weren't hostile or resistant, but they sat with their arms metaphorically folded as if to say, "Okay, convince us."'

But Bono had invited somebody else to the meeting: Bob Geldof was there on speakerphone.

'Do I know you?' he asked Lovett and Drummond fairly aggressively before warning Bono that 'you have to be really careful with these fucking NGOs'.

But the two campaigners gave Geldof pause for thought. All the money he had raised by doing Live Aid would only be enough to pay Africa's debt repayments for three days. Charitable giving was not the solution. Something had to be done about the structural injustices that were built into the flows of finance between the rich world and the poor world. The meeting ended with Bono clearly eager to get involved and the rest of the band and his management prepared for him to do so. Geldof, on the speakerphone, was yet to be convinced.

Back in London, the two campaigners reported back to the head of Jubilee 2000, the economist Ann Pettifor, who was not entirely enthusiastic. 'We don't want celebrities coming in here and thinking grandly that they're here to rescue poor black Africans suffering from drought,' she said, 'because this is nothing to do with drought. It's a man-made financial system that is the root of the problem.'

But two things then happened. Bono rang Pettifor to quiz her about the idea of Jubilee. 'I told him that, in everyday language, jubilees are about grandmother's fiftieth wedding anniversary, but that in the Bible, a Jubilee was something entirely different. He was enthralled. Then, when I started talking about bilateral debt and multilateral debt, he said, "Why don't you come to Dublin and explain it?".' She flew over to Bono's home for Sunday lunch and talked it all through with the singer and his wife, Ali.

After she returned, Pettifor was sitting in the tiny Jubilee 2000 office, telling Adrian and Jamie how it had gone, when the door was flung open. It was Bob Geldof.

'Right, explain all this fucking debt stuff to me,' he said.

Things were falling into place. In Washington DC, Gayle Smith – who had worked with Band Aid on the cross-border operation to smuggle food to the starving behind Ethiopia's battlelines – had become special assistant on Africa to President Bill Clinton. Not long afterwards, Shriti Vadera left her investment bank and joined the Treasury to work for Gordon Brown. Then, Justin Forsyth would quit Oxfam for 10 Downing Street to become Tony Blair's special adviser on Africa.

The team was assembling.

CHAPTER 23

PUNKS, POPE AND
PRESIDENT

Bono asked for a couple of minutes at the BRIT Awards. It would be a
good place to launch the Drop the Debt campaign onto the wider world.
But the man who ran the awards had a better idea. Richard Constant, chair
of the British Phonographic Industry, decided to award Drop the Debt
with the 1999 Freddie Mercury Award 'for outstanding charitable work'.
Bono would collect the prize on behalf of the Jubilee 2000 campaign. But
then he, too, had a better idea. He would hand it on to a true champion.

'Look at this, ladies and gentlemen,' said the awards' presenter, Johnny
Vaughan. Behind him, a series of slogans flashed up on the screen:

Live Aid raised $200 million

Africa repays that in debt every week

For every £1 we give in aid, £9 is paid back

DROP THE DEBT

Military spending costs you £316 a year

Cancelling Third World debt would cost you £12 a year

And could save 7 million lives every year.

DROP THE DEBT

Bono took to the stage and addressed the host of celebrities gathered
for the British music industry's annual awards. 'Since Live Aid with

Bob Geldof, there hasn't been a coordinated attempt to do something about poverty,' he began. 'Here's the idea. They don't want our money. We don't have to send in our money. We've just got to stop asking starving people to give back the money our governments lent them – plus interest. That's kind of it. Sounds good, but the banks won't cancel the debts unless the politicians tell the banks to do that. And the politicians won't tell the banks unless we tell them to do that. So that's why I'm here. Are you with me?'

The audience were. They roared their approval. Then, to crown the moment, he leapt down from the stage, as he had once done at Live Aid, and pushed his way through to a table at which sat the boxing legend Muhammad Ali, who had taken on the role of international ambassador for the Jubilee 2000 campaign. The crowd began to chant the name of the former world heavyweight champion turned philanthropist who had fed 22 million people around the world from his own pocket. It was another Bono *coup de théâtre*, which filled television screens and newspapers around the world the next day. The call for Western governments to cancel poor countries' debts by the turn of the new millennium had been heard by the wider world.

It had been a carefully stage-managed move by Jamie Drummond. 'The celebrity stuff made the media interested, which meant the politicians could not ignore it any longer,' Drummond said. The following day, the chancellor Gordon Brown publicly endorsed the cause. The *Financial Times* declared 'the case for appropriate and radical action is compelling'. The involvement of Muhammad Ali, who toured the streets of Brixton in an open-topped car the next day, cheered by crowds of thousands, alerted the African American community across the Atlantic to the campaign.

Bob Geldof had been wrong about the idea that debt cancellation was opaque and esoteric. 'The general public could see immediately that debt is a justice issue,' said Laurie Lee, a junior civil servant in the new Department for International Development, who was to go on to become Tony Blair's private secretary on African affairs. 'They feel that there's something inherently wrong about an extremely poor country paying more to us in interest than we are giving them in aid.'

✵

Bob Geldof was being pragmatic, rather than magnanimous, when he said to Bono: 'You are now the biggest band in the world. You've got the numbers. You've got the imprimatur of Live Aid because you did it. It makes sense for you to take the lead in America.' Bono agreed to spearhead the campaign for debt cancellation in the United States and began by educating himself on the subject. He was able to start at the top.

Bobby Shriver was an American attorney and a member of the Kennedy family. He had been a friend of Bono since U2 had contributed a track to a charity record made by his mother, Eunice Kennedy Shriver – sister of the late president John F. Kennedy – a decade earlier. Bobby was immensely well-connected in Democrat circles in Washington DC. He was also, said Bono, 'a political strategist of the highest order'. So was his mother. Eunice advised the Irish singer to 'get to understand every side of this'.

Shriver set up a meeting with Bono and the liberal economist Jeffrey Sachs from Harvard, who gave the rock star a crash course in economic policy. Bono spent so much time with him that, he later said, at times it felt like he was moving in with Sachs and his wife, Sonia. 'They didn't just suffer my stupid questions but encouraged them.' Bono proved as adept at grasping complex arguments as he was at memorising song lyrics.

Following Eunice's advice, Bono organised a lunch with Sachs, to which he also invited the conservative economist Robert J. Barro. 'This was to become our model for twenty years,' Bono said, 'trying to get the left and the right on board before they took up entrenched positions.' Talking to the opposition also sharpened his debating skills. Barro was sceptical, but thought that cancelling debt was an option if it could be tied to tackling corruption and bad government in Africa.

More meetings followed. 'I just kept asking the same question: Who's Elvis here?' Bono recalled. 'I needed to know who was the person at the top of the ladder.' Shriver set up a meeting with James Wolfensohn, the head of the World Bank, who was broadly sympathetic despite being scolded by Geldof, who was also present. Next came David Rockefeller, a towering figure in global finance and philanthropy, who was emblematic of the influence of the US banking elite. Then Paul Volcker, the tough former chairman of the US Federal Reserve and one of the architects of Reaganomics, who 'laughed out loud' at Bono's pitch, but then introduced the singer to a key contact in Japan before later coming out 'cautiously' in support of Bono's idea of tying debt relief to poverty reduction efforts.

When he was offered a fifteen-minute meeting with Stephen Schwarzman, the founder of the world's largest asset manager, Blackstone – which controls $1.17 trillion – he took Ann Pettifor with him, in case he was asked awkward questions. Schwarzman apparently only does fifteen-minute meetings. Pettifor remembers that, in the taxi on the way to the encounter, and knowing her propensity to talk at length, Bono said to her: 'When we get in there, Ann, shut up. I don't want you to say anything. This is my meeting.' She duly complied. Bono was moving closer to the seat of power. He and Pettifor had a meeting with Timothy Geithner, the undersecretary for international affairs in Clinton's Treasury. He now felt ready to ask the president to cancel the $6 billion debt that the poorest African nations owed the US.

Shriver arranged a meeting for Bono in the West Wing of the White House with Gene Sperling, Clinton's chief economic adviser. 'No one expected the meeting to be very substantive,' said a Treasury official who was present, Sheryl Sandberg, who later became chief operating officer at Facebook. But she and Sperling were taken aback when Bono began talking about capital markets and debt instruments. He had more than mastered the detail, but he also disarmed them with his intuitive eloquence. He 'reached right in' and grabbed them emotionally, Sperling said.

Bob Geldof wasn't surprised when he heard. 'Every time you go into these meetings, you're surrounded by civil servants who know their stuff, even if the protagonist doesn't. So you have to be *au fait* with the issues,' he said. 'For months, we'd had high-level tutorials from some of the world's top Nobel Prize-winning economists – Jeff Sachs, Amartya Sen, Joe Stiglitz, Paul Collier – until we completely knew this boring shit backwards. Bono's an exceptionally clever man, and he's also a paddy, so he's very verbal.' The US Treasury secretary, Larry Summers, was similarly impressed. After briefly meeting Bono, he said to President Clinton: 'You know that guy who wore jeans to the White House and only had one name? Boy, is he smart. Do you know anything about him?'

Clinton did. Seven years earlier, when he was on the campaign trail to become president in 1992, he had met Bono in a hotel in Chicago, where U2 were staying on the Zoo TV tour. After 3 a.m., when a copious amount of drink had been consumed at the after-show party, Bono had sent a message to Clinton's room that he should join them. Clinton's Secret Service escort refused to pass the message on until the following morning.

'I'd love to have seen them. Where are they now?'

The politician found their room. Bono and The Edge, U2's guitarist, had been up most of the night, writing a song. The place was a mess. Pizza boxes and beer cans were everywhere. Bono was only wearing a robe from the bathroom. He put on the first thing he could find, a crushed velvet suit that he had been wearing the night before.

'When Clinton walked in, it was rock 'n' roll Babylon,' said Bono. 'The faces of the people with him were like, "Why would we bring our guy here?". But Bill just burst out laughing.'

'Why would you want to be president?' asked Larry, the U2 drummer.

'Well, you know, I don't know if the president of the United States can be the one person to turn it all around, but I know one thing: no one else can.'

Bono was impressed. Clinton, he decided, was 'pretty cool'. Still, he told him, the band were not going to endorse him because 'that wasn't what we did'. Also, if he got in, they would be on his back for the next four years because that was the proper relationship between pop stars and politicians.

Seven years later, would he remember that line?

❊

On 16 March 1999, Bono walked through the cream oak doors of the Oval Office looking like a cat burglar. He was wearing a black T-shirt and black combat pants, having removed his black cashmere coat. 'I'd bought a posh coat, but it was too hot to wear, so I'm sitting there looking like a roadie, in black combat gear.' The president's secretary shot him a bemused look. Maybe the big black Prada boots weren't respectful enough, Bono thought, though 'they were pretty swanky where I come from', he later said.

He handed Clinton a volume of poetry by W.B. Yeats. The inscription he had written read: 'Bill, this guy wrote some good lyrics, too.'

The president placed it on his desk. The Resolute Desk, it was called. He too could play the one-upmanship game. 'This desk was sent by Queen Victoria,' he said. 'But President Kennedy liked to remind people it was Irish oak.'

Bono began his pitch, telling Clinton that the rich countries held the keys that could unlock the doors of a prison of poverty for the poor world. It was a moral issue, but it was also a long-term one. In fifty years, the strategic importance of Africa would be clear, with twice the population of China and a third of the planet's youth. Now was the time to get serious about writing off the historic and unpayable debts of the poorest countries – and 1 January 2000 could be the symbolic date to allow them to restart their own clocks. 'The turn of a millennium, Mr President. What a moment to be leader of the free world.'

'Tell me more about this Millennium idea,' Clinton said, leaning forward. 'We're already doing debt relief – with the World Bank.'

'With respect, Mr President, the World Bank process looks dead in the water – and they're the words of its own president, Jim Wolfensohn. What we're talking about is bigger, demanding the richest countries mark the Millennium by announcing a new start for the poorest countries … abolishing the "economic slavery" caused by old Cold War debts.'

'Go on.'

'Economic slavery – it's a spiritual concept, Mr President.' It was drawn from the injustice of the rich world exploiting the poor world for hundreds of years. 'Redemption, I've discovered, is an economic term.'

Bono had found the right line to engage the president. 'Clinton started unpacking the idea with the enthusiasm of a child at Christmas,' said the singer. 'A child from the South who had grown up in the era of social segregation, Bill understood racial injustice. He was a master of political symbolism. A few more questions and he sent me down the corridor of the West Wing with instructions to speak to some of his closest advisers, the people who could get things done.'

The following day, Clinton told a conference of African government officials from forty-six nations that he intended to propose a plan to forgive $70 billion in debt, in return for economic reforms, at the G8 summit in Cologne in June. It was one more step forward.

❉

When Bill Clinton talked about 'the people who could get things done', he was speaking above all about Larry Summers, who had just taken over as US Treasury secretary when Bono met him. He clearly was only seeing the musician because he had been instructed to do so; he had told his aides he was not prepared to waste precious time meeting a rock star with one name who sang with a group named after a spy plane. He arrived with his number two, Sheryl Sandberg, and his speechwriter, Stephanie Flanders, who would later become the BBC's economics editor.

Bono began his pitch. Summers drummed his fingers impatiently. Bono began to get nervous, thinking he was not doing the arguments justice. Summers told the rock star that the idea of 100 per cent total debt cancellation was impossible.

'It's not just up to us,' he told Bono dismissively. The finance ministers of other nations would also have to agree the same thing.

Bono looked Summers directly in the eye. 'You know what,' he told Summers, 'I have been all over the world. I've met with all the finance ministers. They've all said, "If I can get Larry Summers, this can get done." So don't tell me this can't get done because I know it can.'

It was, Sandberg later said, 'a really important moment. I think we were all inspired and motivated.'

Summers left the room with his two aides, leaving Bono thinking that he'd messed up.

Shortly afterwards, Sandberg returned. 'That couldn't have gone better. The secretary is in.'

But if the Democrat administration was on board, that was only part of the story. Now Bono had to convince the US Congress.

❈

Persuading Democrats, even a Democrat president, was one thing. But US spending plans had to be approved by the Congress, which was controlled by conservative Republicans. Bobby Shriver told Bono: 'We need Republicans [but] I'm a Kennedy and you're a rock star. We'll be lucky if they return one phone call.' Fortunately, Shriver did know one Republican: his brother-in-law, Arnold Schwarzenegger, the future Republican governor of California.

'Go and see John Kasich from Ohio,' Schwarzenegger told Bono. 'He has a heart as well as a brain.' The movie star rang the politician to ask if he would see the rock star.

Congressman Kasich was chair of the House Budget Committee. He was a fiscal conservative with an economic view of the world which Bono did not expect to share. 'I was about to make friends with people I'd always presumed were the enemy,' Bono later said, 'and to fall out with people I thought would be friends.' He was about to discover 'that the left does not have a monopoly on compassion for people living in poverty'. There were 'compassionate conservatives just as affronted' by poor people struggling under a non-payable burden of debt.

How was he to approach them? He rehearsed what he was going to say in front of Eunice Shriver, who had helped write speeches for her brother JFK. In the event, Congressman Kasich threw Bono with his first question: 'Which is your favourite: *OK Computer* or *The Bends*? I was a *Bends* man, but I'm changing.' Kasich was talking Radiohead albums. The congressman, it turned out, was a rock aficionado.

But they swiftly got beyond talking music. Kasich had become increasingly worried that US wealth and power were provoking resentment among poorer nations. Debt relief, he explained, 'was kind of an answer to what I'd been groping for'. It emboldened him to fight for the cause Bono was espousing when it came to the debate in the House of Representatives.

'We blow more money than this in Washington just leaving the lights on at night,' he fulminated, 'so to spend less than $1 billion to help people improve their economies and help people dying before our eyes is just the right thing to do.' The singer had stiffened his resolve. 'Very quickly, you get beyond rock star,' Kasich recalled of Bono's conversations with senior Republicans. 'Bono knew what he was talking about.'

Not all Bono's stereotypes were shattered over the weeks and months he spent on Capitol Hill. The chair of the Appropriation Subcommittee on Foreign Operations, Republican congressman Sonny Callahan, did not buy the Jubilee 2000 line.

'This money on debt relief is going down a rat hole,' he said with an unmitigated bluntness, which was all the more curious for the fact that he would not look Bono in the eye. Instead, he looked over the singer's head as though he were talking to people at the back of the room. He spoke about him in the third person and he could not even get his name right. 'I'm just gonna say it straight: *Bonio* here may have priests in the pulpit working for him, may even have the Pope in Rome, but I'm standing up for the taxpayer.

This money is going down a rat hole. People buying goddamn Gulfstream jets like they're Nike sneakers.'

But other Republicans were more open to changing their views.

When a debt relief bill was sent to the House Panel on Financial Services, its chairman, Republican congressman Spencer Bachus, was visited by four members of a church in his congressional district in Alabama. They knew that their congressman could sabotage the bill or help carry it through Congress. There was a religious duty to vote for debt relief, they told him.

The congressman's aides looked sceptical, but Bachus listened. He went home and talked to his wife about it. When the debate began in Congress, he declared that voting for it was a moral imperative. It would cost every American just $1.20 a year – 'the cost of an ice cream cone' – to help poor countries prevent the deaths of children. This choice would follow lawmakers forever, he said, adding: 'We will not only live with it in this life, but we will live with it in the next.' A fellow Republican called it 'one of the most moving statements I have ever heard'.

Bachus went on to join Bono and Jeffrey Sachs at a key meeting to promote debt cancellation just ahead of the annual IMF and World Bank meeting in Washington that year. The idea that there was a religious duty to assist the poor was one, Bono realised, that could have great purchase in the United States. It was a tactic which Bono was to deploy with great effect.

❊

In June 1999, the leaders of the world's eight major industrial democracies met again at the G8 summit in Cologne. This time, Bob Geldof and Bono joined 40,000 demonstrators as they threw a human chain around the meeting. Geldof made a dramatic entry, arriving late on a motorbike which zigzagged through the traffic to join Bono and The Edge, Thom Yorke from Radiohead, the Senegalese musician Youssou N'Dour and Cardinal Joachim Meisner, Archbishop of Cologne.

On a signal, the protesters blew whistles and banged drums, while church bells were rung throughout the city. Demonstrators paraded a golden calf – the biblical symbol of the worship of riches – outside the summit. The musicians handed a petition, signed by almost 20 million activists from all over the world, to the German chancellor, Gerhard Schröder, as the crowd joined hands in a four-mile human chain. The demonstrators' demand was for 100 per cent debt cancellation.

A private meeting had been arranged between Bob, Bono and Tony Blair by the prime minister's communications strategist, Alastair Campbell. New Labour had started to wonder if there might be mutual advantage in working with the rock stars.

But then news filtered out that the summit was only going to agree the 70 per cent which Bill Clinton had announced in Washington the day after he met Bono in March. Bono was so indignant that he told a journalist that he would be boycotting the meeting.

Alastair Campbell heard and rang Geldof. 'It would be seen as total grandstanding not to turn up when the media were already there waiting,' he told Bob.

In the event, it was Geldof who lost his rag at the meeting and started shouting at Blair. 'Fuck it, why haven't you cancelled these debts yet? What are you doing?'

Blair looked shaken. Half-laughing, he turned to Bono and asked: 'So how... how are the *Greatest Hits* selling?'

But the PM then gave a serious answer. 'We'd love to do more, but we can't because of the United States. And the United States can't do more because of the US Congress. Go and talk to the Americans.'

That meant Bono. Bob Geldof and the Boomtown Rats had never made it in the States, whereas U2 were one of the biggest bands in the US, which gave Bono access at the highest levels. He had lobbied a few Republicans, but there were 223 of them in the House of Representatives and fifty-five in the Senate, meaning they held the majority in both houses. Jamie Drummond decided he was going to have to move to Washington. Congress was a massive job.

Tony Blair and Alastair Campbell adjudged the encounter a success. 'We had a very good meeting,' Campbell wrote of Bob and Bono in his diary that night. 'I like them both. They were really funny but also incredibly committed, and they knew what they were on about. They had facts at their fingertips. There was no way this was just a spray-on cause to help their rock-star image.'

Blair had said, at one point, that he was pushing as hard as he could, but that different countries had such different agendas it was like looking at Mount Everest. Bono replied: 'When you see Everest, Tony, you don't look at it. You fucking climb it.'

The meeting provided a revealing insight into the way Bob and Bono worked together. Outsiders had a rather stereotyped view of this. Bono was the charmer and Bob the belligerent, it was said. Bono was the quintessential fixer – the ultimate persuasive networker – where Geldof was more of an anti-diplomat, a provocateur, a shock-jock.

Bob often played into this. He once described the pair of them as 'the Laurel and Hardy of Third World debt' and said they 'play soft cop/hard cop because in the end I always lose my patience and he's always eminently reasonable'. Bono wants to give the world a great big hug, he summarised, 'and I want to punch its fucking lights out. But we arrive at the same point, ultimately.'

The reality, as the meeting with Blair showed, was more complicated: both rock stars were capable of controlled displays of anger, but both had a keen eye for strategic advantage. In private, both impressed the world's most senior politicians and their advisers with their grasp of the realities of global geopolitics.

The two men were close friends, as likely to discuss music as the debt crisis when they were together. Certainly – in these early years – Bono saw Bob as his emotional and intellectual godfather, whose analysis he solicited before making any major move in international politics. Privately, Bob once told me: 'Bono is the point man. He's got far more fame than me, particularly in the States where celebrity equals access. And he's a really smart person.'

Passing judgement on the Cologne G8 at a concluding press conference, they were measured in their verdicts. This time, Geldof played soft cop, criticising the outcome as a 'half measure' and asking the politicians 'to go with their consciences and do more', while Bono played hard cop, announcing: 'It's obscene to think that in a country like Nigeria they have a life expectancy of forty-seven years, and they spend more on servicing their debt than they do on health and education.'

Privately, their strategist, Jamie Drummond, took a longer view. Germany had been quite sceptical about debt relief, so it was good to have got Schröder involved and to have brought to bear the pressure of the Catholic and Protestant churches which were politically powerful in Germany. For all that, he pointed out, the G8's claim – that the summit would halve the debt of Third World nations – was exaggerated. The real figure was closer to a third. And, five years later, only fourteen countries had received any of the promised debt relief.

'It's too little, I'm afraid,' said Jubilee 2000's director, Ann Pettifor. 'It's really depressing. These countries owe $370 billion. In Birmingham [in 1998], the G8 promised to cancel $25 billion. That moved up to $50 billion. Yesterday, it moved up again to $70 billion. That is the achievement of this campaign, but it's still far from dealing with the fundamental problems of debt.'

Something else was needed.

※

It would take a big push to get world leaders to agree to write off 100 per cent of the debt. Who was the biggest global figure whose endorsement they could seek?

'Pope John Paul II,' said Ann Pettifor.

There was no doubt that he supported the idea. In 1994, he had published a papal encyclical *Tertio Millennio Adveniente* ('Towards the Third Millennium') which, though it concerned itself primarily with spiritual renewal, made an explicit call for 'reducing substantially, if not cancelling outright, the international debt which seriously threatens the future of many nations'. But would he come out and explicitly endorse the Jubilee 2000 call for one-off total cancellation?

'What we needed,' said Jamie Drummond, 'was a major media moment just before the annual meetings of the IMF and the World Bank.' A call was put in to the Vatican. There, Monsignor Diarmuid Martin – the cleric deputed by the Pope to lobby the Fund and the Bank on debt relief – immediately saw the potency of such a gesture. Providentially, the pontiff was free to see a Jubilee 2000 delegation on 23 September 1999 – exactly 100 days before the Millennium. The symbolism of a countdown was perfect.

But who should go? Bob and Bono, obviously, because they would generate wide international media interest. 'But we wanted it to be very much a serious Jubilee 2000 event, not just a "pop stars meet the pope" photo-op,' said Lucy Matthew, one of the campaign's prime movers who later became Bono's chief of staff.

So the party also included musicians Quincy Jones and Willie Colón; activists Laura Vargas of Jubilee 2000 Peru, Julian Filochowski of CAFOD and Randall Robinson of TransAfrica; and economists Jeffrey Sachs, Ann Pettifor and Adebayo Adedeji – at which point the delegation was told by a Vatican official, 'Enough … this is not rent-a-pope.'

'Everyone was very excited beforehand,' said Lucy Matthew. 'It was a mixture of slight school-trip giddiness at the fact that they were meeting the Pope, but also a sense that this was a really big moment and a profound opportunity.'

The meeting took place in the Pope's summer palace at Castel Gandolfo in the hills above Rome. Quincy Jones kept making jokes to cover his nervousness. The Renaissance paintings were 'so totally hip-hop', while the papal oxblood shoes were 'some pimp loafers'. Geldof got the giggles at Quincy's corner-of-the-mouth comments.

But the mood changed when Pope John Paul II entered the room on a walking frame. 'He was fighting with his own frailty to be with us,' Bono observed.

There was no doubting the solemnity of the Pope's message. He asked why progress was so slow in resolving the debt problem and expressed impatience with the protracted negotiations. 'It is the poor that pay the cost of indecision and delay,' he chastised. 'The Catholic Church looks at the situation with great concern … because she has a moral vision of what the good of individuals and of the human family demands … The law of profit alone cannot be applied to that which is essential for the fight against hunger, disease and poverty.'

Afterwards, there was an exchange of gifts. The Pope gave each member of the delegation a white rosary, while Geldof reciprocated with a Jubilee 2000 symbol – three metal zeros hung from a number 2, like a section cut from the chains of debt. Bono presented a volume of poems by Seamus Heaney and told the pontiff that he was not just a holy man but also a showman.

The Pope looked at Bono's blue-tinted sunglasses. Catching the glance, Bono offered them to him and, as if to fulfil the showman epithet, the pontiff took the shades in his palsied fingers and put them on with a mischievous grin.

The photographers snapped furiously, but the Vatican confiscated the photographs and they were only seen after the John Paul II's death.

'I'm pretty sure that was the most surreal moment of my waking life,' the singer said afterwards.

But despite the jollity as they departed, the Pope's words had given an intellectual charge to the Jubilee 2000 campaign more urgent and more radical than any of the delegation had expected. 'This is a day that will go down in history,' Ann Pettifor said. 'The Pope has given his endorsement and blessing to the passion and commitment of millions of Jubilee 2000 campaigners around the world. It is now up to the world's leaders to rise to the Pope's call and moral leadership.'

They flew to Washington the following day. When they got off the plane, Bono and Jeffrey Sachs went straight to a meeting entitled 'Alternative Approaches to Debt Relief', where one of the other speakers was Bono's new Republican ally, Congressman Spencer Bachus. Professor Sachs read out to the meeting a letter written the day before by the Pope in support of the Jubilee 2000 campaign. In the Bible, the Pope wrote, the Jubilee was the time when the entire community was called upon to restore the original harmony which God had given to human relations. At the Jubilee, the burdens which oppressed and excluded the weakest members of society were to be removed. Then all would share in the hope of a new beginning. As 1999 turned into 2000, that must mean debt relief for the poor. Today's world had need of a Jubilee experience.

On the Sunday, Bono called the White House to ask the president's chief economic adviser if he could come to see him in his office in the West Wing. The IMF and World Bank annual meetings were in just two days' time, so Gene Sperling was working on Sunday.

Sperling told Bono that he had recently been invited to the presidential cabin on Air Force One to find President Clinton waving a letter. It had been written by Bono.

'Gene, can you give me one good reason why we can't get this debt stuff sorted out?' the president had demanded. 'I mean, really? Just explain to me why we can't do the right thing here?'

Now, back in his own office, it was Sperling's turn to ask an awkward question – of Bono.

'If we do this, who will back us? Who will follow the lead of the US?' the economic adviser asked the pop singer. Answering his own question, he said: 'What about Michel Camdessus at the IMF? I'm not sure he agrees with how you guys want to do this.'

'I met him yesterday actually,' said Bono casually. 'He was not the devil I thought he would be. I'd imagined him in a big office instructing a bunch of postgrads on how to push sovereign states around with Structural Adjustment Programs. He's a Catholic so I pulled out my rosary beads.' They were the ones the Pope had given him the day before, in exchange for his designer sunglasses.

Sperling was not sure whether or not to believe him. 'So what had happened with Camdessus?'

'He pulled up his jacket sleeve and, around his wrist, he wore beads of his own – Buddhist prayer beads given to him by the Dalai Lama. He's a humble man. Nothing like the Lucifer I was expecting.'

'Humble?' laughed Sperling, 'Or just humbler than you?'

'Listen,' he continued. 'The president really wants to do more to help more. It's just that I'm not sure we can get it into the budget this year, but we're trying to figure something out.'

Bono, sensing the brush-off, replied: 'Gene, we are in September of the year 1999 and in the public mind – and the mind of the Pope – the whole argument hangs on the Millennium. Miss this budget cycle and we miss the moment.'

The conversation ended with them arguing about whether debt cancellation should be 90 per cent, as the US Treasury wanted, or 100 per cent, as the Jubilee campaigners demanded. Ninety per cent sounds a lot, Bono said, but paying the remaining 10 per cent would still take too much money away from schools and hospitals.

'It has to feel like history,' Bono declared as he was leaving. 'Incrementalism leaves the audience in a snooze. Cancelling 90 per cent is not a melody line. You can't sing about two-thirds of something.' Bono may have been spending long arduous days looking at statistics, but he had not forgotten the lessons he had learned in making music: every hit needs a strong melody line.

After Bono left, Sperling picked up the phone and called a Treasury official.

'I want to insert something on debt relief into the speech that the president will be giving at the World Bank.'

Two days later, in the presidential limo on the way to the World Bank meeting, Gene Sperling and Larry Summers spoke to Bill Clinton and recommended that he call for 100 per cent cancellation of the debts that thirty-three impoverished countries owed to the United States.

It was not a long car ride. 'I mean, you could walk it,' said Bono afterwards.

When he got to the meeting, Clinton announced that the United States would go beyond previous commitments and cancel 100 per cent of debts, provided the debtor nations put the savings into health, education and poverty reduction.

But it turned out to be only the first of many hurdles.

CHAPTER 24

BONO IN AMERICA

No one would say it, but Bill Clinton's recent sexual liaison with Monica Lewinsky threw a long shadow over Bob and Bono's campaign to write off the debts owed by the world's poorest people. The Democrat president held the executive authority, but the Republican Congress controlled the purse strings. In that balance of power, the president had been weakened by scandal. Yet his sexual impropriety had also fuelled within Clinton a desire to show repentance for what he had only recently admitted was an inappropriate relationship with a White House intern. That sense of remorse had been nurtured by his confessor, the fiery Baptist minister and social activist Tony Campolo. The preacher had stressed to Clinton that easing the financial burden of the world's poorest people was a matter of unusual moral importance. Campolo was also a spiritual adviser to Bono.

All this emphasised the importance to Bono of dealing direct with the evangelical Christians who were immensely influential in the Republican Party. They must be confronted with the challenge that debt relief was something which should appeal to their moral and religious conscience – and which should override their instinct for confrontation with a Democrat president.

In 1999, Bono now set out to woo right-wing US Republicans. He asked Congressman Kasich – the Radiohead fan – to introduce him to the key players.

As Kasich took Bono around Capitol Hill in June 1999, staffers poured out of their offices, hoping to get a photo. Bono was more interested in the details of the foreign aid spending bill, which did not provide enough money for debt relief. Passion and moral conviction were essential to an effective campaign, he knew, but he also had to be able in command of the economic complexities if he was to persuade those who held the key to the purse strings of the world's most powerful, and potentially most generous, nation.

The singer travelled back and forth to Washington, to the constant irritation of his band who were trying to record a new album in Dublin and the south of France. It was supposed to be finished by the end of the year, but Bono's commitment to the cause of the poor was now getting in the way of their music. U2 were recording a song which they could not get quite right. Ironically enough it was called 'Love and Peace or Else'. Getting it finished was so problematic that, in the end, it did not appear on their next album, but on the one after. It was being produced by the great pioneering guru of pop music, Brian Eno. He had grown so frustrated that he told the studio they were to put through no further phone calls on the occasions that the band were recording together.

'Phone call for Bono,' said the switchboard, when they rang through.

'I said "No calls!"' shouted Eno. 'Who the hell is it?' he enquired tetchily.

'It's the Pope,' said the switchboard.

❖

Though it was now almost four years since Bob's wife had left him, he still found himself unable to take solace in the music which had once been the greatest pleasure of his life. After the acrimony of the divorce and grinding courtroom battle, Geldof had found himself paralysed with a deep depression. Friends came round to make him eat. But he wasn't sleeping. He wasn't even getting up. His doctor put him on medication, but he didn't like the way it made him feel and threw it away after a month. He could not write or record music; he could not even listen to it.

When the Boomtown Rats bass guitarist Pete Briquette – who had set up recording equipment in Bob's house – found that his friend would not use it, he went round to work there on his own recordings. 'His way of helping was to move in,' Bob recalled. 'He stayed there for a long, long time, just doing his own work down in my basement. And when I was forced to move from house to house, he would be there with his gear and follow. And bit by bit, it was him doing his own thing that made me listen to music again. I sort of became alert one day to what he was doing.'

Both with the Rats, and with Geldof's solo records, Pete Briquette had been Bob's most long-standing collaborator. Now, four years after Paula had left Bob, it was Pete who coaxed him into playing again. Over an eighteen-month period, Bob began to write again, intensely personal fragments of songs – about the emotional devastation he experienced at Paula's leaving.

Over the year that Bono spent lobbying the US Congress, Geldof set out to salve his intense personal grief by producing what turned out to be an album full of songs about the trauma of the years in which he lived without the love of his life and his children. 'Inside Your Head' was a howl of rage, the final line of which – one reviewer was to say – 'freezes the blood'.

For six years, Bob had maintained a dignified silence about the whole bleak affair. But the catharsis he underwent writing the songs was clear when the album, which he called *Sex, Age & Death*, came out a year later. It was not true, however, that it was intended as a kind of posthumous vengeance. Paula Yates was still alive when it was recorded. 'It's not anger at the specific people involved,' he told me when the record was released. 'It's just anger that this happened at all, and in the way it did.'

❊

While Bob Geldof was in his deep despond, Bono persisted in his siege of the US Congress. In July 2000, the House of Representatives passed a bill raising spending on debt relief from $90 million to $133 million. But Bono was not rejoicing. The sum was far lower than the $240 million that President Bill Clinton had asked Congress to authorise. Opponents to paying the full amount included Sonny Callahan, the Republican who had told Bono that all aid went down a rat hole. The Jubilee 2000 campaigners knew that this reduced amount would not allow the US to take a lead at the next meeting of the G8 at Okinawa at the end of the month. So no one was surprised at the failure of the G8 to make any progress in Japan.

Undaunted, the Irishman turned up at the United Nations headquarters in New York at the start of September 2000. There, 149 heads of state and other high officials from more than forty different countries were attending the UN Millennium summit. Bono teamed up with the president of Nigeria, Olusegun Obasanjo, to hand a petition of 21 million signatures – from 155 different countries – to the UN secretary-general, Kofi Annan. It called on the world's wealthiest countries to cancel the debts of poor nations. Having done it, Bono felt that, despite the vast numbers and the celebrity endorsement, there was little to show for all their efforts.

But something important came out of the encounter. President Obasanjo, he discovered, was a Christian, and not just a Christian but a Baptist. Some of the most powerful lobby groups in the United States were the Southern Baptist churches of the conservative Bible Belt. Armed with this knowledge, the US wing of Jubilee 2000 hit upon the idea of asking the Nigerian president to write a long letter to all the Baptist churches across the American South, explaining the biblical principles behind debt cancellation. In August 2000, Obasanjo wrote to the churches of the Southern Baptist Convention:

> The imposition of suffering upon the poor is an offence to God's holiness. We enter a new millennium, not in a spirit of new beginnings. A millstone of debt grinds our country and its people into endless poverty. Nigeria borrowed $5 billion from Western creditors in 1978. Since then, we have paid back $16 billion. It may also surprise you to know that we still owe $31 billion! This is largely due to compound interest and interest rate fluctuation. The Prophet Isaiah railed against this form of economics … Dear brothers and sisters in Christ, you have the power and influence, in your Congress, to right this wrong – by writing the debts off.

Framing the issue of debt in religious terms changed everything. Members of Congress began to get mail, phone calls and visits in their districts in small but significant numbers. All at once, Bono realised that the Bible was the key to gain access to whole swathes of strongly evangelical Republican politicians who would be compelled by this Old Testament theme. That said, he probably wouldn't have got through the doors of the arch-conservatives had he not been given the credibility of an introduction by John Kasich.

By the end of September 2000, Bono had discussed debt with several key fiscal conservative senators. Undoubtedly the most significant of the conservative Republicans he encountered was Senator Jesse Helms, the conservative head of the Senate Foreign Relations Committee.

Helms was not just a conservative. He was an extreme reactionary. Throughout his political career, he had been a vociferous opponent of the civil rights movement, filibustering against making Martin Luther King's birthday a national holiday. King was a practitioner of 'action-oriented Marxism', he said, whose principles were 'not compatible with the concepts of this country'. When a caller to a TV phone-in praised him for 'everything you've done to help keep down the n****rs', Helms replied, 'Thank you.' He opposed any kind of progressive legislation on social programmes, arts funding, abortion and gay rights. Homosexuals were 'weak, morally sick wretches' who caught AIDS 'as a result of deliberate, disgusting, revolting conduct'. Violence in the US was linked to Satan's involvement in the music industry. He once cornered a political opponent in an elevator and told a friend who was with him at the time: 'Watch me make her cry. I'm going to make her cry. I'm going to sing "Dixie" until she cries' – which he reportedly preceded then to do. He did not seem a man who was likely to take much notice of an Irish rock star who was pleading for kindness and empathy for Africans.

Yet anyone who thought that Helms was an impossible nut to crack completely misunderstood Bono's extraordinary capacity to get alongside an opponent, to see the situation from their point of view and then to slowly turn his argument around so that it made sense from the other person's standpoint. With the conservative evangelicals of the American Bible Belt, his secret weapon was religion.

Bono is a deeply committed Christian. As a young man in Dublin, he – along with The Edge and, to a lesser extent, U2's drummer Larry Mullen – had been part of a group of evangelical Christians known as the Shalom Fellowship. Indeed, they had only left when tensions arose as they were working on their second album, *October*, with the leaders of their church telling the band that their music was incompatible with their faith. Faced with the choice, they'd committed to their music. But although their Christianity was no longer institutionalised in a church, it remained a profound influence on the band who continued to pray together before going on stage.

At the meeting with Helms, the politician was taken aback when the pop star suggested they pray together. Before he had entered Helms' office,

Bono had made a conscious effort to put out of his mind that he was one of the characters behind U2's withering song 'Bullet the Blue Sky' about a Cold War warrior pressing for US intervention in Central America in the 1980s. Helms, too, had had to suspend judgement before the meeting began. 'When I was first told that Bono wanted to meet with me to talk about boosting US aid to Africa, I didn't know who he was,' he said afterwards. He was only persuaded by his Senate staff, who certainly did know who Bono was.

But then the singer not only started with a prayer, he dived straight into talking about the Old Testament Book of Leviticus. 'He's a religious man, so I told him about the biblical origin of the idea of Jubilee.' Then he addressed the subject of foreign aid, a concept Helms had been very tough about in the past. 'I told him that there are 2,003 verses of scripture that pertain to the poor and that Jesus speaks of judgement only once – and it's not about being gay or sexual morality, but about poverty.'

Finally, he moved on to talk about HIV/AIDS, which was then heavily stigmatised by the Christian right as being a disease of gay men and drug users. Bono pointed out that millions of innocent children had been orphaned in Africa because of AIDS. Many of them had, in addition, been infected with the virus themselves while in their mothers' wombs. Bono had taken along to the meeting Senator Bill Frist, another staunch Republican but one who had been a surgeon before he became a politician and who now travelled to Africa during his vacations to give medical care to the poor. Frist pointed out to Helms that mother-to-child transmission of AIDS could be prevented with a single dose of a new medicine. AIDS, concluded Bono, was the plague of today – as leprosy had been in the time of Christ and Jesus had shown exemplary care of lepers.

'Jesus had touched the outcasts, the untouchables of his day, those with leprosy. They were the ones he sought out to welcome and heal. Today it is those suffering with AIDS,' Bono said. 'This is not a conservative or liberal issue, but it's an issue impacting children. There are 10 million orphans created by this disease. We can prevent 10 million more children from losing their parents, and from contracting the disease themselves.'

By the time Bono had finished, Helms had tears in his eyes. For all his reactionary views on other topics, the senator had been a staunch supporter of assistance for children globally for many years, backing vaccination programmes to combat polio and measles, and supporting legislation to fight child trafficking and champion international adoption. He was, now, Bono said, 'genuinely moved by the story of the continent of Africa'.

'America needs to do more,' he told the singer.

At the end of the meeting, Jesse Helms, the iconic conservative, was so moved that he got up from behind his imposing desk and walked round to stand in front of the Irish singer. He touched Bono's head.

'Son, I want to bless you. Let me put my hands on you.'

Afterwards, he said: 'I knew as soon as I met Bono that he was genuine. He had his facts in hand and didn't have any agenda other than doing all he could to help people in desperate need. He has a depth that I didn't expect. He is led by the Lord to do something about starving people in Africa.'

Inevitably, Helms had his caveats. He insisted that Bono should involve the international community and the private sector so that the cost of the campaign against HIV/AIDS would not be borne by 'just Americans'. But his was a genuine conversion. He went on to announce in the *Washington Post* that he was ashamed to have done so little during his Senate career to fight the worldwide spread of AIDS. And he became co-author of a bill authorising the US to contribute $600 million to international efforts to fight the disease. He even became a fan of U2, attending concerts, said one aide, 'like they were revival meetings'.

Washington insiders, on the left and the right, were taken aback. 'The senator is very much a fan of Bono,' said one of his senior staffers, failing to disguise his incredulity.

Bono's liberal friends, including bandmate The Edge, were appalled. Edge told U2's frontman that he was 'stretching the patience of the band and of our audience'.

But Bono and Geldof were unrepentant. 'People go on about us supping with the devil,' Geldof said with exasperation at the time, 'but what's the point in supping with God? He's already on the side of the angels. If the devil wants to make the lives of the world's poorest people more bearable, then I say: "Pull up a chair to the table."'

Bono was more direct in dismissing the critics. 'We grow up with this rather juvenile idea that people who are not like us don't get it – the suits don't get it – but it doesn't make sense anymore. Sometimes the enemy is your own indifference. And if you accept that and that there are people within the walls of government who went there for the right reasons, these are people who are going to listen to reason. It's far more glamorous being on the barricades with a handkerchief around your nose than standing with a briefcase and a bowler hat arguing with someone on the other side of the barricade.' But there came a time, he said, when 'it felt like agitprop had to grow up a bit'.

⁂

Paula Yates's funeral was held on Saturday 23 September 2000 at St Mary Magdalene Church in Davington, near Faversham in Kent. It was where her marriage to Bob Geldof had been blessed and where their three daughters were christened. Now he was there to grieve with them and their little sister Tiger. Two months later the courts awarded Bob custody of the four-year-old so that she could live with her three sisters and he and his new partner, the French actress Jeanne Marine. Some years later, he adopted her.

During the service Bono sang 'Blue Skies', accompanied by Jools Holland, Paula's co-presenter on *The Tube*, at the piano. Shortly after the funeral, Bono flew to Prague for the annual meetings of the World Bank and IMF.

It was going to be a difficult meeting. When Bono met the new head of the IMF, Horst Köhler, the German said:

'Ah, Bono. You get rich and now you find the conscience.'

'I think I had a conscience before I was rich,' the singer shot back.

And his wit was to the fore at the press conference with World Bank president James Wolfensohn.

'You'll have to excuse my shyness,' Bono began. 'I'm not used to speaking to crowds of less than 70,000 people.'

He called Wolfensohn 'the Elvis of economics' for his debt relief initiatives, but said he didn't go far enough. Wolfensohn said he greatly admired the singer, but could not go '100 per cent up the mountain with him' to turn debt relief into debt cancellation. Their mutual appreciation society was not delivering. A third of all debts of the world's poorest countries were owed to these two multilateral institutions. Rich nations were still, in effect, asking, 'How much can the poor afford to pay?', while the correct question was 'Should they owe this at all?'

The debate then pivoted towards the question of whether the World
Bank and the IMF were actually promoting globalisation or merely seeking
to live with its consequences. This was not an issue that was central to the
concerns of Bob and Bono. But it was very much at the heart of the anxieties
of the protesters, who that day suspended themselves from a nearby bridge
– and were threatening to close down the whole meeting the following day.

On the sidelines of the meeting, Bono had an important encounter
with George Soros, the billionaire financier and philanthropist. Soros was
a generous funder of groups that promoted human rights, democracy, a
free press, and open government around the world. But he was decidedly
not anti-globalisation. He supported global economic integration and free
markets, but with strong controls on unfettered capitalism to avoid instability and protect vulnerable populations.

He and Bono clicked. 'He was super-impressed and massively open to
our agenda,' recalled Jamie Drummond. 'In contrast to what had happened
at Seattle, we weren't anti-all-globalisation. We didn't think the solution
was to close down the World Trade Organization and stop trade. What we
wanted was fairer trade, and a more level playing field, and efforts on debt
and aid when there's an emergency. We wanted an ethical globalisation.
And George really liked the ideas we were proposing.'

Within a year, Soros was to become a major funder of the organisation
that Bono and Geldof were to set up to devise, develop and deliver the
strategy behind their campaigning for the next twenty-five years.

⁂

In late September 2000, President Bill Clinton invited an unlikely crew to
the White House to discuss debt relief. There were members of Congress
from both sides of the political divide. The tele-evangelist Pat Robertson
was there, along with religious leaders from the Catholic, Episcopal and
Jewish communities. Someone from the aid agency World Vision came,
as did business leaders from Merck, Motorola, Caterpillar and Goldman
Sachs – companies which had all earlier that month signed up to support
the debt relief push. And Bono from U2, signifying his alternative status
with a black leather jacket and a single earring.

This eclectic and disparate group had been brought together because
the president had hit yet another barrier on the road to debt cancellation.

The UK chancellor, Gordon Brown, who was also the chair of the IMF's International Monetary and Financial Committee, had thought up a way of raising the cash so that the Fund could afford more debt relief – without having to ask its members for more money. It could sell off some of the gold held in the IMF reserves, revalue it and immediately buy it back in such a way that it generated profit, which could be used for debt relief. All it required was a change in the rules.

But although Jesse Helms and Spencer Bachus were now leading an extraordinary coalition of liberal Democrats and conservative Republicans, they had not mustered a sufficient number to get the House and the Senate to approve the $435 million debt package that President Clinton had pledged the US would deliver.

The problem was that the chairman of the Senate Banking Committee, the Republican senator Phil Gramm, didn't want to do it – not without reforms at the IMF and the World Bank, which he insisted wasted taxpayer billions propping up corrupt dictatorships and failed economies.

President Clinton's collection of strange bedfellows had been brought together in an attempt to find a way around the roadblock. Each now did their bit. Pat Robertson went on television and told his 1 million daily viewers that they should 'let Senator Gramm know that this is a good initiative'. Bono threatened to bring U2 to the US to play the hometowns of members of Congress who opposed debt relief and urge young people to vote them out of office. Bobby Shriver was impressed. 'People thought, "These guys are crazy", but they also knew we were dead serious. Bono was like, "I'm ready to go to war on this." That's a good quality to have in Washington.'

Then, on 11 October 2000, the Republican presidential candidate George W. Bush announced – as part of his platform to promote himself as a 'compassionate conservative' – that he too now backed debt relief. During a presidential debate with Al Gore, he was asked whether US wealth and power brought with it special obligations? 'Yes, it does,' replied Bush. 'Take, for example, Third World debt. I think we ought to be forgiving Third World debt under certain conditions.' He issued caveats about the need for reform in the developing world, about the need to combat corruption, and about swapping debt to protect valuable rainforest. But he was clear that 'we do have an obligation'.

By 18 October, resistance inside Congress had been overwhelmed. Even those who were not convinced by the arguments caved in, such was the combined pressure from celebrity campaigners, religious leaders, aid agencies, development groups, street demonstrators and parish activists. 'The debt relief issue is now a speeding train,' said Senator Sonny Callahan. 'We've got the Pope and every missionary in the world involved in this thing, and they persuaded just about everyone here that this is the noble thing to do.' He himself did not agree. He was, after all, the chair of a subcommittee that had earlier approved only $69 million of the $435 million requested. 'I remain sceptical,' he declared. But he recognised irresistible political pressure when he saw it. If debt relief was a speeding train, he had no intention of standing in front of it.

Nor did Phil Gramm. 'I don't like the bill. I'm afraid the benefits will be squandered or stolen by the same leadership elite that squandered or stole them before,' he said. But he also announced that he would not attempt to block passage of the bill in the Senate, recognising that debt relief had become a priority for Republicans as well as Democrats.

On 25 October 2000, the US Congress voted by a wide margin to approve the full $435 million for the US contribution to international debt relief. On 6 November – the day before Americans went out to vote for their next president – Bill Clinton signed the measure into law, saying: 'It's not often we have a chance to do something that economists tell us is a financial imperative and religious leaders say is a moral imperative.'

Revealingly, the Democrat president singled out Congressman John Kasich – a Republican – as the man responsible for creating the cross-party consensus that had made it all possible. In turn, Kasich turned the spotlight on Bono. 'I don't think celebrities have a big impact over the long haul in Washington, because they come in, have their pictures taken and leave,' he said. 'But I bet the other members of U2 wanted to toss him out of the band because he was so focused on this the last year. If you want to move government, you have to be in it for the long haul, and Bono was.'

Debt forgiveness had now become a touchstone for the moral health of the rich world.

CHAPTER 25

VLADIMIR PUTIN'S SMILE

And with that, it was all over. For three years, Geldof and Bono had yoked their advocacy for Africa to the work of Jubilee 2000. But that organisation had built in obsolescence. Its aim was to campaign for the abolition of all Third World debt by the end of the old Millennium. When the calendar changed from 31 December 2000 to 1 January 2001, its lifespan was, constitutionally, over – but the job was only three-quarters done.

It had been a significant success. Under the leadership of the campaigning economist Ann Pettifor, it had brought together 24 million people and achieved billions in debt relief. But it had focused largely on bilateral debt – money owed directly by a poor government to a rich one. Multilateral debt – money owed to institutions like the IMF or World Bank – remained.

Most economists recognised many African nations would never be able to pay them off. Debt cancellation, not debt relief or rescheduling, was what was needed. And the money saved must be invested in health, education and other measures that would relive poverty. If Geldof and Bono were on a journey from charity to justice, they had not arrived yet at their final destination.

How was the legacy of Live Aid to be continued now?

Bob Geldof had two sets of thoughts, public and private. And they didn't align.

In public, he spoke at a rally in Trafalgar Square to celebrate the achievements of Jubilee 2000. It was entitled 'The World Will Never Be the Same Again'. Geldof paid tribute to the moral force of ordinary people, especially in the faith communities, who had carried the campaign at ground level. He thanked campaigners from all walks of life for their commitment to justice. Thanks to them, billions in debt relief had been promised. But it had not yet been delivered. Jubilee 2000 had changed the conversation around debt and poverty, but he warned the crowds against complacency.

He had a similar two-pronged message for the politicians. He praised Gordon Brown, who had taken an 'immense' step in freeing forty-one of the world's poorest countries from their debt repayments to the UK. He had achieved something that would last beyond his lifetime. But Geldof delivered a moral challenge to world leaders: 'you cannot walk away now'.

In private, Geldof feared that they would indeed now walk away. Bob was characteristically frustrated and impatient with the closure of Jubilee 2000. 'It was a good organisation,' he told me. 'Ann Pettifor was really good. So to create a structure and then blow it up was ridiculous. How could you throw away an organisation like that when the job wasn't done? I couldn't understand all that firepower going to waste.'

Bob and Bono knew they were going to have to plough their own furrow. Early in January, Bono set off on a trip across rural Uganda, accompanying Senator Bill Frist, the doctor-politician who spent his vacations from the US Congress giving medical care to poor communities in Africa. At the end of the month, Geldof and Bono accepted an invitation, together with their partners Jeanne and Ali, from Tony Blair to dinner at his country residence, Chequers. It was a bizarre gathering. Among the other dinner guests were the racing driver Jackie Stewart and the cricket umpire Dickie Bird who, on being introduced to Bono, asked him if he had had any hits.

The two campaigners did not waste the opportunity. Blair later told his communications chief Alastair Campbell that the pair were 'a good double act and deadly serious on the policy front'. They did their hard cop/soft cop routine, with Geldof raging at the injustices served on Africa by the West and Bono asking politely what we're all going to do about it. What they discovered, Geldof found, was that as far as Blair was concerned, 'we were pushing at an open door'.

So what should be the next step? Three of the key players in Jubilee 2000 shared Geldof's sense that they could not give up now. Jamie Drummond, Adrian Lovett and Lucy Matthew took one of the Jubilee slogans, 'Drop the Debt', and set up an ad hoc lobby group with that name. 'We were halfway through the cycle of G8 meetings,' recalled Lucy. 'We couldn't just give up at that point.' Another aid agency offered them free office space near London's Borough Market. What should they focus on? The UK and Europe, as Bob Geldof had been doing? Or the United States, where Bono had made some headway?

⁂

Things had changed in the US. The Democrats had lost the presidential election and a Republican was in the White House. He had been inaugurated on the same day as Bob and Bono's dinner at Chequers. On 21 January 2001, when George W. Bush became the forty-third president of the United States, all of Geldof and Bono's contacts in the Clinton administration were replaced. 'A lot of the development community was of the view that there was absolutely no point in trying to engage with the Republicans,' recalled Lucy Matthew. 'They thought it was better to sit it out and regroup and plan what we would do when the Democrats were back in power. The assumption was the Republicans would just slash the aid budget. There was real scepticism about whether there was any possibility of getting them to do anything.'

But Bono's experience over the previous year, building a bipartisan coalition in Congress, pointed in the opposite direction. 'America was obviously the massive global power,' said Lucy, 'so we knew we really had to try. But when we began to approach Republicans, a lot of them were not remotely interested in seeing us.'

Bob and Bono flew to the US to get the advice of Harry Belafonte, who had been a civil rights activist for decades before he had phoned Geldof to kickstart the US equivalent of the Band Aid single. After regaling them with stories about his affair with Marilyn Monroe, and Marlon Brando's sexual exploits when they were actors in training, he told them an oblique tale about his early days marching for civil rights with Martin Luther King. Bobby Kennedy had just been made attorney general and King's colleagues were all badmouthing him: 'There's nothin' good about this man. He's an Irish redneck. Got no time for the black man's struggle.'

Dr King let them rant and then cut them short.

'Gentlemen, I'm releasing you into the world to find one positive thing to say about Bobby Kennedy, because that one positive thing will be the door through which our movement will have to pass.'

Belafonte pressed the same approach. Geldof and Bono now had to find the door through which *their* movement could pass.

It was, Bono said later, 'a lightbulb moment for me and a conviction that's informed my life as a campaigner ever since. A simple but profound idea: that you don't have to agree on everything if the one thing you do agree on is important enough.'

It was something Geldof had already intuitively understood. 'There was very little about Margaret Thatcher's policy that I agreed with,' he said. 'I understood what she was trying to do, but I didn't approve of her methods. But when you have been given a limited amount of time with a politician, you have to stay on point, regardless of that person's other policies or character.' Over the years that followed, he was to work closely with the Labour government, but when the leader of the opposition, David Cameron, asked Geldof to advise a Conservative Party policy group on global poverty, he said yes. Gordon Brown, the Labour chancellor, was so upset that Bob recalled he rang and said: 'When did you become a traitor to me?' Geldof was unmoved and replied that he would do anything which would push the policy agenda forward and help build consensus across the political parties: 'Gordon, of course, wouldn't accept that.'

When U2 flew out to the US in March 2001 to begin their three-month Elevation tour, Bono couldn't get to see President Bush. But Bobby Shriver did manage to get him a meeting with the new secretary of state, former general Colin Powell. Bono took him a present – a signed note from George C. Marshall, another military man turned Secretary of State, who'd been the author of the Marshall Plan, an American aid package that put Europe back on its feet after the Second World War.

'You still find people my parents' age who talk about the Marshall Plan,' he said. That was when Europe felt the grace of the US, he added, and now Africa is in need of that grace. Could this generation of Americans do something that people would be proud of in decades to come? 'It turned out Powell was very interested in our campaign to get universal treatment for people with AIDS in Africa,' said Lucy Matthew. 'He had already decided that AIDS was much more than a health pandemic. He saw it as a strategic issue.' So many diseases in Africa killed mainly children and the elderly, but AIDS was taking out the working population and middle-class professionals.

It was, he said, a weapon of mass destruction. It had the potential to destabilise the entire continent.

Without direct access to Bush and the rest of the administration hierarchy, Bono was reduced to public statements once more. Throughout the Elevation tour, he invited fans to email the president and his Treasury secretary, Paul O'Neill, to tell them to finish the job of Third World debt cancellation.

'During the three months of the U2 tour, over a million children will die from Third World debt and 100,000 people will be infected with HIV/AIDS in Africa,' Bono said. 'Deeper debt cancellation could stop this madness. We're calling on George Bush and Paul O'Neill to take leadership on this issue and direct the IMF and the World Bank to cancel the debts which kill. The people of Miami, Atlanta, Houston and wherever we go can help us deliver this message to the Bush administration.'

He then gave out the email addresses of Bush, O'Neill and a dozen top decision-makers at the IMF and World Bank.

The pressure worked. Later that spring, he secured a meeting with George Bush's national security adviser, Condoleezza Rice. When Bono's advisers had originally tried to fix a meeting with her, Dr Rice's advisers passed on the request only very reluctantly. But they were amazed to find that Rice, a classically trained pianist, was more enthusiastic: 'I'm a huge fan of U2. I would love to meet Bono.'

Bono arrived with a very substantive policy agenda. 'Six thousand Africans are dying every day, but they don't have to,' he said. 'There is a treatment and we just have to get it affordable and accessible for these people.'

'I'll never forget him walking into the office and looking at me suspiciously and saying, "What you really need to do is something about AIDS",' Rice later said. 'President Bush, when he was Governor Bush, told me the heart of America had to show through our foreign policy. We had to have a foreign policy that brought compassion to its centre, something which will knock people's socks off. It had to be a big number. More importantly, it had to make sure American taxpayer dollars were not going to be wasted.'

Bono's AIDS initiative fitted hand in glove with the Bush administration's policy ambitions.

But President Bush's money man, Paul O'Neill, was less easy to impress. He was reluctant to meet the pop star. 'He just wants to use me and I don't have time for this,' O'Neill said. But he was eventually persuaded by Bobby Shriver to have a short meeting with the singer. He pencilled in just thirty minutes and startled Bono by opening with an anti-aid diatribe.

'Have you ever been to Africa?' he asked Bono.

'Quite a few times, Mr Secretary.'

'Well, I worked all over the place there. If you think this administration will give you an extra dime to waste on some of the most corrupt countries in the world, you're crazier than I already think you are... These tin-pot dictators rob and steal from their own people. You know, we don't even believe the accounts of our own government aid agency about how they spend the money we pour into these countries, so why would we believe you?'

'All countries have corruption at different stages of development, including Ireland,' began Bono.

Bobby Shriver took up the baton. 'New leaders are emerging in Africa with more principled positions than just being our friend or enemy in the Cold War.'

'Nonsense. Absolute nonsense. You're reading the wrong newspapers,' retorted O'Neill.

Despite all the disagreement, the meeting extended itself to ninety minutes. Afterwards, the Treasury secretary grudgingly admitted that Bono understood economic theory and the impact of colonialism.

As he was leaving, Bono propped open the door with his foot and turned to O'Neill.

'If I could show you ten African countries moving in the direction of good governance and accountability, would you reconsider?'

'If you could show me five, I'm happy to talk more,' the politician replied, 'but I don't think we'll be seeing each other again. Thank you, Mr Bono, good day.'

⁂

While Bono was trying doors in the US, Bob was busy in Africa. He took his daughters, and their little sister Tiger who was just four, to South Africa on a safari to Kruger National Park to see the wildlife. While there, they flew to Johannesburg to meet Nelson Mandela at his home, where the great man sat Tiger on his knee. Mandela had stepped down as president of South Africa two years before, but was still active on the international stage, brokering a peace deal in Burundi and waging war on HIV/AIDS – an issue he felt he had neglected during his time as president. Geldof wanted to get him to add his voice to the campaign for debt cancellation.

The two men exchanged information. Geldof gave Mandela a new report from the global accountancy firm Chantrey Vellacott, which proved that the World Bank and the IMF could easily afford to cancel 100 per cent of the debts owed by the poorest countries. Mandela told Bob of the clear linkage between Africa's debt problem and the continent's inability to cope with the AIDS pandemic, which had now infected 20 per cent of the South African population. Zambia was now losing two-thirds of its trainee teachers to AIDS each year, devastating the country's shaky education system.

'His head turned down, and that familiar voice began to shake as he spoke,' Geldof recalled. This was a man who had not been broken or embittered by imprisonment, 'but who now sat silent, for a moment beyond words at the monstrous enormity of what faced his continent'.

Two days later, South Africa's president Thabo Mbeki showed Geldof the Millennium Action Plan, drawn up by him and other African leaders, which they would be taking to the next G8 summit.* In broad, bold and blunt language, it demanded deeper debt cancellation.

※

The summit meetings of the world's eight most powerful nations, the G8, had by now become the focal point for the campaign for debt cancellation. The next G8 summit was to be in Genoa in July. After the failure of the summit in Cologne, all hopes now rested on the meeting in Italy. It was to be President George W. Bush's debut on the international stage.

Tensions were high, for two reasons. Bob and Bono knew about one of them. They only found out about the second after the event.

Violent street demonstrations by anti-globalisation protesters had overshadowed the World Trade Organization's 1999 meeting in Seattle.

---

* The G8 was the G7 group of the world's most powerful governments, plus Russia. But Russia, with weaker economy, was not included in the G7 finance ministers' meetings, hence the confusing references to both the G7 and G8 which follow.

A month before Genoa, live rounds had been fired by police at demonstrators in the Swedish city of Gothenburg, where European Union leaders were meeting. Three protesters were taken to hospital with gunshot wounds and a dozen police officers were injured in street battles which raged for several hours. There had only been 1,500 protesters there. In Genoa, it was predicted that between 100,000 and 250,000 people would be on the street – a mix of anti-globalists, anarchists, environmentalists and Drop the Debt campaigners.

The anti-globalisation movement was billing Genoa as their biggest protest yet. 'We are going to start a great battle,' said the website of one of 700 protest groups. A minority had pledged to use violence. The Italian government had drafted in 15,000 police and troops – including paratroopers and specialists in germ and chemical warfare – to protect the summit in the Palazzo Ducale, the city's mediaeval palace.

A 'Red Zone' in the city centre was cordoned off with barricades and steel doors. The sewers were sealed. Neighbouring highways, train stations and the airport were closed five days ahead of the arrival of the world leaders. A battery of ground-to-air missiles, with a range of nine miles and an altitude of 5,000 feet, were installed at the airport. The Italian government was accused of an over-reaction bordering on hysteria.

Geldof and Bono had accreditation for the Red Zone. Convinced that all the security was excessive, Bob left the zone to mingle with the demonstrators. 'You get a sense of being hyper-protected and privileged inside these zones. I wanted to get a feel for what was going on outside,' he said. He wandered around, taking photographs of the protesters. 'It wasn't menacing at all. More a carnival atmosphere. Everyone dressed up, not in the anarchist masks, but in all kinds of silly outfits. There was a phalanx of cops but they were just loafing about. It all felt quite benign.'

It did not remain so.

By the end of the hot July day, dozens were hospitalised following clashes with the police. The security forces raided the headquarters of activist groups and inflicted beatings on anyone there. Then one protester, who was in the act of throwing a fire extinguisher at a police van, was shot dead. Cars went up in flames. Tear gas was freely used. Things got so out of hand that Lucy Matthew and the other Drop the Debt organisers decided to cancel the march by debt campaigners who had arrived from all over Europe.

'It was quite scary and precarious,' Matthew said. 'There were anarchists dressed in black, with their faces covered, running round. Protesters were being smashed by police on horses. We felt awful cancelling because all these people had travelled an awfully long way to be there – and it was an important moment in terms of debt cancellation moving to the next stage – but we felt we had no choice.'

Geldof and Bono were furious. 'The violence isn't helping us,' Bono told the media. This was the first time in the history of the G8 that African leaders had been invited to join the debate. 'Of all the days to destroy, they destroyed one where there was some actual dialogue happening between the G8 and leaders of developing nations.' Anger was understandable, he said, but not violence. 'It's okay to bang your fist on the table, but it's not okay to put your fist in the face of an opponent, whether they are protesters or police.'

※

There was another reason, it transpired, for the hyper-vigilance of the Italian security forces. On 13 June, only a month before the summit, Egyptian intelligence services had intercepted a tape sent by the Islamist terrorist Osama bin Laden to his al-Qaeda followers. It spoke of a plan to crash a plane full of explosives into the Genoa summit to assassinate President Bush and the other G8 heads of state. The Egyptians had passed the intelligence on to the French secret service, who passed on the warning to their US counterparts.

Just ten days before the world leaders arrived in Genoa, the head of the CIA, George Tenet, had met with the US national security adviser, Condoleezza Rice. The intercepts were genuine al-Qaeda communications, he told her. 'It's my sixth sense, but I feel it coming,' Tenet told Richard Clarke, Dr Rice's counter-terrorism director. 'This is going to be the big one.' Rice listened but was unconvinced. The US defence secretary, Donald Rumsfeld, even went so far as to suggest that the tape could be a grand deception designed to measure US responses and gauge its defences. President Bush had said he 'didn't want to swat at flies'. Interestingly, the 10 July meeting between Tenet and Rice went unmentioned in the various reports into the attacks in which al-Qaeda flew passenger airliners into the Twin Towers and the Pentagon just two months later.

Whatever the American calculations, the Italian security services were not so sanguine. They briefed Italy's deputy prime minister, Gianfranco Fini, that they were expecting a small civilian aircraft, with the range to fly from dozens of European airports, to be the suicide plane, not a passenger jet.

When they installed a missile defence system at Genoa's airport – and enforced a no-fly zone – the Italian authorities were publicly mocked. But they felt privately – if sickeningly – vindicated two months later when the attacks materialised on 9/11. 'In the end,' said Jamie Drummond, 'it turned out not to be Genoa but New York.'

Just before the summit, the Italian government decided to move all the world leaders from the hotels that had been designated for them. Instead, they were all housed on a 58,600-tonne cruise ship, the *European Vision*, which was moored in Genoa's old port and which the military deemed easier to keep secure. Twelve helicopters and four reconnaissance aircraft patrolled overhead constantly, while warships and mini submarines prowled the bay to protect the ship. President Bush did not join the other G8 leaders on the cruise ship, but slept overnight on an American aircraft carrier on the open Mediterranean.

The high security produced its moments of levity. One morning, Bono and Jamie Drummond were sitting having a coffee on the quayside by the leaders' cruise liner with Condoleezza Rice. They were pitching to her the idea of a Marshall Plan for Africa, much as Bono had tried to sell to Colin Powell the year before. They were brimming with ideas: about a new fund to combat AIDS, TB and malaria, and about how to take the debt cancellation process further.

Suddenly, out of the water, came a man in a wetsuit. 'He walked right up to us in his flippers and stared at us,' recalled Jamie.

'Are you Bono?' said the frogman.

'I am.'

'I'd ask for your autograph, but I can't really get out of my gear,' the diver said, dripping puddles before them.

The frogman then stared at the national security adviser, not realising she was his ultimate boss, and said to her: 'Are you the woman off the TV?'

Condoleezza Rice looked back at him and said: 'Well, kind of.'

Entirely satisfied, the navy diver jumped back into the docks to swim around the cruise ship again, checking to see that no enemy had attached an explosive mine below the water level.

Geldof, who had missed the meeting on his excursion to see the demonstrations, quipped on his return: 'It would have been good if he'd unzipped his suit, exposed his tuxedo and produced a box of chocolates for the lady.' The reason he and Bono did not feel out of place at events like this, he said, was because of 'the huge amount of theatre involved – it's the world that rock musicians live in'.

But there was substance behind the theatre. 'There were several results of that conversation after the frogman departed,' Jamie Drummond revealed. 'Privately, we got the extraordinary pledge from the Bush government that it would work toward 100 per cent debt cancellation.' Another was that Drummond would be seconded for several months to Washington to help draught the parameters of a massive new initiative which the Bush administration was cooking up. As if to complete the paradoxical juxtaposition of the serious and the absurd, when he got to the US capital, he didn't have an office, so he worked out of a photocopy shop.

Bob and Bono had, by now, become used to the access they had to the British prime minister. But, at Genoa, they got access to all the G8 leaders for the first time, even Vladimir Putin. Blair was keen to use the G8 to try to bring Russia into the fold of civilised nations and had brought Geldof and Bono onto the cruise ship to exchange information about progress.

'Come and meet Vladimir,' Blair said as the singers were leaving the vessel. In 2001, Blair's foreign policy was all about trying to bring Russia out of the cold.

'These are pop singers,' he said to Putin. 'They are doing great work on Africa. The African Marshall Plan. They are here talking about the debt issue.'

Putin replied with a straight face. 'I want to congratulate you on the work you have done for the Third World and when you have finished that, I hope you can work on the Russian debt.'

Bob and Bono laughed. Debt was a complicated business in Russia, they knew. Putin had inherited the debts which the Soviet Union had made to client states in the developing world during the Cold War. But, on the other side of the scales, Russia was also in significant debt to the West from money borrowed after the collapse of the Soviet Union. So Russia was both a creditor and a debtor. But it was a shareholder in the IMF and World Bank, and had a vote on debt cancellation issues.

'Debt is very simple,' added Putin, who could speak more English than he made out. 'If people owe me money, they pay me.'

Blair looked bewildered and turned to the translator, but Bob and Bono picked up the mafia allusion immediately.

'Oh, we're working on that,' said Bono, laughing. 'We're finding out where everyone lives…'

'That's next,' said Geldof, joining in the mirth. At this, Putin hugged them, making clear that was enough of that, then turned to Tony Blair and said, with a sudden asperity, 'Let's go inside.'

For all the public jollity, Geldof wrote in his notebook later that day: 'Putin – cold, cynical, calculating.'

Was Genoa a success? Not much progress was made on extending debt relief; the G8 merely affirmed their intention to press on with what had been agreed at Cologne. But there were victories of other kinds.

For the first time, the Live Aid activists had met face-to-face with world leaders. Blair had told them beforehand that, although much of the work was done in advance by officials and finance ministers, when the G8 leaders looked into one another's eyes, 'anything is possible'. Having met directly with Chancellor Gerhard Schröder of Germany, Prime Minister Jean Chrétien of Canada and the European Union president Romano Prodi, Geldof and Bono realised that the G8 was the best place for them to pursue a fairer political and economic deal for the world's poor. There had been another breakthrough; for the first time, the leaders of the rich world had invited African leaders to the summit. They had come and presented their Millennium Africa Plan and the G8 leaders had given a commitment to respond in detail to it at the next G8 in Canada.

More than that, the G8 had responded to lobbying by the World Health Organization and other bodies, and committed to launching a new fund to fight AIDS, TB and malaria. It had pledged what campaigners thought was an outrageously inadequate amount of money – just $1.3 billion to fight the three most deadly diseases in forty-eight countries south of the Sahara. But it was a start.

✂

With Jubilee 2000 now defunct as a vehicle to fight for the world's poor, how were Bob and Bono to go forward? If they were going to focus the struggle on the G8, they would need to change their style of lobbying and advocacy. A few days after the summit in Genoa, U2 were playing in the Netherlands. Three of the key people who had made Jubilee 2000 and Drop the Debt work so well – Jamie Drummond, Lucy Matthew and Adrian Lovett – flew out to Amsterdam to have lunch with Bono.

The U2 frontman was adamant that he did not want this highly effective little team disbanded. 'It dawned on me that I loved being part of this new band,' he said. 'I didn't want to let go of my new comrades.'

Adrian had just been offered a job as head of policy at Oxfam. His wife was expecting a baby and he decided to opt for salaried stability. But Jamie and Lucy were eager to continue in support of Bob and Bono. 'We not only liked the idea of working together, but we also had a strategy we believed in,' Bono wrote later. It consisted 'of not playing the left off the right or the cool off the uncool'. Instead, they would inhabit 'a space where it didn't feel like we had much company, a space critics might dismiss as a compromised middle, but which I imagined as a radical centre'. Rather than piggybacking onto an existing development agency, Bono asked them if they would like to start something new. Jamie and Lucy were enthusiastic. The singer announced that Bobby Shriver's mother, Eunice, had agreed to give some start-up money to get the new body off the ground, and so would he.

At the end of August 2001, they all met in Bono's home outside Dublin the morning after U2 played a homecoming gig at Slane Castle. Bob Geldof had been invited to the meeting, along with Bono's US fixer Bobby Shriver and U2's manager, Paul McGuinness. There were two others. Dr Paul Zeitz was an American physician and epidemiologist who was setting up something called the Global AIDS Alliance. And Scott Hatch was a right-wing lobbyist whom Bono thought could help the new group win over Republicans in the US Congress to approve the massive initiative on AIDS which he had set his sights upon.

They kicked around a number of ideas. Earlier in the year, Bobby Shriver had proposed the new entity ought to be something like a talent agency, offering services to rock musicians and movie stars who wanted to get involved in campaigning issues. Bono saw the AIDS crisis as a major focus of the new body. Jamie wanted to focus on aid and trade as well as debt.

It was Geldof who pulled it all together. 'What we need is some sort of think-tank, where people are writing research papers that we can use to lobby,' he said. This made sense to the others. One of Lucy's favourite mantras was: 'Celebrity gets you access, but once you've got access, you won't last long if you haven't got something to say.' Geldof told the group that they all had to play to their strengths. 'I said to Bono, "U2 are the biggest band in the world, you've got the numbers." I said to Lucy and Jamie, "You've got what it takes to write some deeply analytical policy papers."' And then we can lobby based on empirical facts. It's now time to get really serious.'

'What do we call this new body?' asked Bono.

'It's obvious. Debt. AIDS. Trade. Africa – DATA. Data is scientific, it's empirical, it's hard facts – and that's what we need if we are to convince the people in power.'

'And it's Democracy, Accountability, Transparency in Africa,' said Jamie.

'So it works from the other side,' said Lucy.

It was exactly what they needed, as Bono put it, 'to barge our way into the corridors of power'.

CHAPTER 26

IN THE SHADOW OF
THE TWIN TOWERS

Jamie Drummond was sending a fax to the United States from Oxfam's office in Oxford when the first plane hit. After the summit in Bono's Dublin home, he had been given the task of drawing up a proposal to find funders for Bono and Bob's new think-tank, DATA. While the fax was chugging through, Drummond turned to look at a nearby television. He could scarcely believe his eyes. The first of two jetliners pierced the side of the twin towers of the World Trade Center. There was a flash of flame. This was the strike by the Islamist terrorists commanded by Osama bin Laden which Bob Geldof and Bono had been warned would happen in Genoa in July. Instead, it was happening two months later in New York.

Everything would now change. For nine months, Bono and Geldof had been making headway to woo the new Republican administration in the US. Their aim had been to persuade George W. Bush to complete the job started by Bill Clinton on debt cancellation. One look at the thick smoke billowing out of the tallest skyscrapers in the world told Drummond, even before the second plane hit the other tower, that the Bush government would now have entirely different priorities. Africa and world poverty would be off the agenda. He and his fellow campaigners would have to find other avenues of influence.

In the middle of January the following year, Bono travelled to Malawi with the Harvard economist, Jeffrey Sachs. They were to address a meeting of the leaders of the sixteen countries in southern Africa. The politicians had cash-strapped budgets, but Bono and Sachs wanted to present them with findings from the World Health Organization which showed that increasing spending on healthcare would bring them serious economic benefits. When they got to Malawi, though, Bono found he was the one who learned the biggest lesson.

In a hospital in Lilongwe, he met an Irish nun, Sister Anne Carr, who was a nurse with the Medical Missionaries of Mary. She had spent her life working in maternity units or mobile clinics in remote villages. In a hospital crowded with three times as many patients as it was built to hold, Bono passed a line of women in the corridor waiting to be admitted to a consulting room. There, they would learn from a healthcare worker that they were HIV positive and that there was no treatment for their condition. They must prepare to die.

Had they been unfortunate enough to have contracted AIDS in the US or Europe, they would have been given drugs which would save their lives. But, five years after these had been developed in the West, they had not reached Africa. They were too expensive. And it was not just the weak and vulnerable who were dying. Nurses, doctors, teachers, farmers, accountants and lawyers were being killed off, Bono learned. Cheap generic versions of the anti-retroviral AIDS drugs could be manufactured, but the giant international pharmaceutical companies would not permit it.

The singer entered a classroom where a group of women were being told 'The rules of preparing to die':

- Find a family who will care for your children.
- Prepare a memory book for them, full of love.
- Educate those in your community who do not have HIV.
- Embrace and pray for those who do.
- Look after each other.

The women showed the singer and the economist the boxes they were preparing for their children. They were filled with photos, mementos, family history, letters for future occasions, advice and messages of undying love.

There were a few anti-retrovirals available, but nowhere near enough to go around. The doctor placed three of them in Bono's hand. 'I felt the gelatinous surface that contained life or death,' he later recalled, 'and the showman/salesman in me knew that we had the visual props to win the argument – an argument about justice rather than charity.'

He put the three pills carefully in his pocket. In a few weeks, he would drop them into the hand of the new president of the United States.

⁂

Back in New York, Bono decided he should try to enlist the support of the world's biggest media mogul. Bobby Shriver arranged for him to meet Rupert Murdoch in the News Corp headquarters in midtown Manhattan, around the corner from the newly Disneyfied Times Square. In the meeting, Murdoch was flanked by the head of Fox News and the editor of the *New York Post*.

Murdoch listened to Bono's pitch and said he accepted that AIDS was destroying the lives of millions of people in Africa – but then gave his verdict.

'If you're asking can News Corp involve itself in campaigning to influence the president of the United States on the issue of HIV/AIDS, the answer is no. A definite and non-negotiable no. But if the president of the United States takes up an historic AIDS initiative of the kind you're arguing for, then we here in this building will come on like the tide.'

No sooner were they out of the door than Bobby Shriver was on the phone to Bush's senior adviser, Karl Rove.

'Hey Karl, here's a surprise: Rupert Murdoch has told us that if your guy goes big on the AIDS emergency, he'll be all over it with his support. Come on, man, you can do this.'

⁂

The richest man in the world invited Bono for lunch. The singer began fantasising about what kind of fantastic wine might be on offer. Bono was a big red wine man, as was Geldof. Bill Gates was staying at the Waldorf Astoria in New York, so it was sure to be a slap-up meal. In the event, Gates wanted a Big Mac with fries. The Irishman hoped that this was a reflection of his personal taste, not his level of generosity. He had come to see Gates to ask for money to fund DATA.

After 9/11, the World Economic Forum, which normally took place at Davos in Switzerland, moved to New York in solidarity with the city. It was held at the Waldorf, which is why Gates was there. He had been persuaded to meet the rock star, but he was very sceptical. But that February morning, the two of them had appeared on a panel with the US Treasury secretary Paul O'Neill to discuss the best ways to build public support for aid and development.

'I was kind of amazed that he actually knew what he was talking about,' the multi-billionaire said afterwards. 'He had a real commitment to making things happen. It was phenomenal. After that, we've been big partners in crime.' Gates gave him $1 million to set up DATA with an office in Washington.

That afternoon, they held a press conference. Bono told the media: 'We have an agenda which we're calling the DATA Agenda: Debt, AIDS and Trade for Africa, in return for Democracy, Accountability and Transparency in Africa.' The singer described it as 'kind of a Marshall Plan for Africa'. That was a good analogy, particularly after September 11, he added. 'The United States invested in Europe after the Second World War as a bulwark against Sovietism. And it had debt cancellation as part of it, and trade, etc.' At the moment, Africa was in the same kind of position, vulnerable to extremists and ideologies. 'I think it would be very smart for the West to invest in preventing the fires rather than putting them out, which is a lot more expensive.'

He was echoing what he knew to be the fears of the Bush administration. The nests of terrorists who had brought the attacks on the World Trade Center, and also on the Pentagon in Washington, could easily spread from the Middle East to Africa.

Bill Gates warned the media that his donation was only enough to kickstart a solution. 'Private philanthropy is no substitute for governmental action here,' Gates said. 'The scale of the problem and the need to engage, government-to-government, is just way too great.' But if governments stepped up, so would philanthropists.

DATA had found a new line of attack. While in New York, Bono went to meet activists at the protest centre which had been set up to lobby the world leaders. He knew that access to top politicians depended upon him being seen as the representative of a large-scale protest movement. It was important to be seen as an outsider as well as, now, an insider. But he and Geldof had created a new vehicle to lobby at the highest level for the world's poorest people.

With Bill Gates on board, two other billionaires followed. Gates's friend George Soros and the software entrepreneur Edward W. Scott both chipped in $1 million each to get DATA fully organised and staffed. When Geldof and Bono assembled the first DATA board meeting, it was held at George Soros' house in London.

Geldof was happy to let Bono take the lead in the US. Bono, who had once regarded Bob as a kind of uncle figure, had very much come into his own. Bob knew he did not have the celebrity in the US to command the access and the leverage which Bono did.

'Lobbies in America only work with two things,' said Geldof. 'A lot of money and a lot of people power behind you. If you have both, you have access. People power combined with money terrifies the US Congress.'

More than that, said Lucy Matthew, Bono was 'a very natural, skilled and gifted political strategist'. Perhaps it was, she added, because he was such a good chess player. He was a chess champion as a child, playing tournaments and studying the grandmasters at the age of twelve. 'Bono likes strategic things.'

Perhaps so. But early on he got one thing very wrong about the Bush administration. The deaths of nearly 3,000 people on 11 September 2001 did not knock poverty in Africa off the White House radar. Instead, it moved the topic up the agenda, most particularly after Washington discovered that Osama bin Laden had spent many years in Sudan.

'At the outset we thought, *This is all over now. All they're going to do now is deal with 9/11*,' said Jamie Drummond, the man who was now DATA's chief strategist. 'But a couple of months after the attacks they began to say, "No, no, actually just keep talking to us. Keep talking."'

DATA's agenda on AIDS and extreme poverty fitted with Bush's compassionate conservatism.

'I guess they also saw Africa as needing attention from a security point of view, given what they were now calling the global war on terror.' Bono put it the other way around. He quoted General James 'Mad Dog' Mattis: 'If you want to cut the aid budget, then buy me more bullets.' Aid could be an adjunct of the strategy against bin Laden. Above all, Africa needed good government, to keep terrorism out.

One morning, while in New York for Davos, Jamie Drummond received a phone call from Gary Edson, Bush's deputy national security adviser.

'Jamie, I'd like you to move to Washington to work with me for several months on an initiative for Africa. We're interested in your ideas.'

They were the ideas Drummond had outlined to Condoleezza Rice by the dockside when the frogman had appeared out of the water.

This was the opening which DATA had been waiting for. Drummond moved from London to Washington and stayed there for three months. 'At first, I could hardly believe it. Little old me, in and out of the White House.'

But Drummond had a good brain for statistics and strategy. In a series of closed-door meetings, he worked closely with Edson, who was acting as George Bush's 'sherpa' – his personal representative to prepare the way for the G8 summit in Canada.

Edson was 'fiercely intelligent', Drummond found. His reputation in the West Wing was of a spiky operator – or, in the words of another observer, 'brainy and impatient ... a spicy jalapeno pepper in the midst of the smooth cream cheese of the White House'. He was highly rated by his boss, Condoleezza Rice, who described him as one of the best policy engineers she'd ever known – 'one of those rare individuals who can take an idea from inception to implementation'.

Through Edson, Jamie – and, by extension, Bono and Geldof – came into close contact with Dr Rice, Bush's special adviser on Africa, Jendayi Frazer and the president's chief of staff, Josh Bolten. Together, they drafted the parameters of an aid programme that would give hundreds of millions of pounds in new grants to those African countries willing to improve their governance and economic management.

It was a radical rethink of how foreign aid was delivered. Instead of blank cheques, countries would receive aid if they cracked down on corruption and invested more in health and education. It was separate from all previous initiatives. It was new money. George Bush called it the Millennium Challenge Account and said it was 'aid for results' rather than 'aid to fix failure'.

It fitted Bob and Bono's agenda of more effective aid, along with George Bush's election manifesto of 'compassionate conservatism'.

Above all, it fitted the White House's new strategy on the War on Terror.

✂

Bono had flown to Los Angeles for the Grammys at the end of February 2001. U2 had won four awards, including Record of the Year and Best Rock Album for *All That You Can't Leave Behind*. He flew home via Washington DC, where he had lunch with Condoleezza Rice. The pair got on instantly. 'Condi was an academic, a sophisticated thinker, a concert-level pianist and a fluent Russian speaker,' he wrote later. 'She seemed to possess religious faith, but she was not happy-clappy. Hers was not a dancing-in-the-aisles kind of church.'

When she worked out in the early mornings, sometimes next to the president in the West Wing basement gym, she told Bono it might be rock 'n' roll music in her ears.

'Like who?'

'Led Zeppelin is one of my favourites.'

Bono was not surprised, 'because nothing was surprising about this woman who was tougher than the rest, this hawkish presence in the White House, moving effortlessly from Chopin's nocturnes to "Whole Lotta Love".'

'The president has given me permission to try to understand what you're doing,' she said. She took the brief seriously. On numerous occasions, she let Bono, Bobby Shriver, Jamie Drummond and Lucy Matthew enter her office. 'Meetings ended up with the contents of Jamie and Lucy's backpacks spread all over Dr Rice's desk while she pored over Christian Aid or Oxfam analytics,' Bono said. 'It was inspiring that Dr Rice was open to any relevant information. She asked us hard questions about whether these numbers added up. When they did, she kept asking us back.' A genuinely collaborative relationship developed between the rock singer and the national security adviser.

But although she was signed up to increases in aid – which she clearly saw as linked to the question of national security – Bono felt he was not making any progress on getting extra funding to tackle Africa's AIDS epidemic. The issue came to a head on 13 March 2002 when the Bush administration sought to call in a favour from Bono in return: his public endorsement. The campaigner was asked if he would appear alongside President Bush the next day at the Inter-American Development Bank to announce the Millennium Challenge Account.

'It'd be great to have a person who would not normally be identified with the president's development agenda as a part of it,' Rice told him.

Bono realised that he now had bargaining power.

But for Bono – and DATA – it was also very awkward. It would be deeply uncool for a rock star to do a photo op with a pugilistic president who, having recently invaded Afghanistan, was now sabre-rattling about a war in Iraq. As Bono put it, 'with his cowboy rhetoric and added swagger, George W. was now even alienating conservative moderates. Publicly, I had kept out of the news on Iraq. For an Irish big mouth, this had been almost impossible, but I forced myself to button it. Now I could already hear the booing from my own band, from our fans as well as our critics. Where's your white flag of non-violence now?'

It was an extremely delicate moment. The money was a big deal. And DATA liked the fact that African governments would only get it if they adopted policies which were friendly to the poor. But there was to be no extra cash for AIDS drugs for Africa. More aid would not work if the AIDS crisis was not addressed.

'It was a challenge, to say the least, to have to say to the president of the United States that $5 billion for Africa was not enough,' said Jamie Drummond. Bono would be paying a very large price – in terms of reputational damage – and the feeling was that in return they needed something more. DATA's top advisers in Washington felt the same. Mort Halperin, who had served in the Johnson, Nixon and Clinton administrations – and who was a senior adviser to DATA's billionaire backer, George Soros – told Bono not to appear in a photograph with Bush on those terms.

DATA rang Condoleezza Rice's office and said Bono would appear if President Bush also committed to 'an historic AIDS initiative'. The word came back that the White House could not do this.

Condoleezza Rice, who never lost her cool, lost her cool.

'She's *really* pissed,' Bobby Shriver told Bono.

Bono decided to go to see Rice in person. He went to the White House and was hurried through security and into the West Wing. 'Condi closed the door behind me for what I immediately felt was going to be one of the most critical conversations of my life,' Bono said.

'Bono, I'm a relationship person, relationships are everything to me, and if you do not turn up for the president tomorrow, you embarrass us. The Millennium Challenge Account is $5 billion of new money. If that's not enough for you, I sense our relationship is coming to an end.'

Bono argued back.

'Bono, we will get to the AIDS problem. Just not yet. You have to believe me. Any real relationship requires trust.'

'You are committing to an AIDS initiative?'

'Yes.'

'An historic one?'

Pause. 'Yes.'

Bono reached out to shake her hand.

'Okay, I'll be there tomorrow.'

Bono left the White House and returned to the DATA office. His advisers – there in person, or on the conference-call speakerphone – went mad with him. Jamie Drummond and Lucy Matthew told him he was naïve. Jamie was most rattled about the impact on DATA's reputation among the left, where most AIDS activists were to be found. 'I was concerned that there was no definition around what constituted a historic AIDS initiative,' said Lucy. 'I thought, *They will do something, but what magnitude will it be?* That was my concern.'

The moment revealed the importance of personal relationships to Bono. 'He's a very loyal person. Most people would not have taken that as a promise they could rely on. He risked an awful lot because of that personal connection with Condi and her promise that she would keep her word.'

George Soros was blunter. Making reference to the biblical passage in Genesis in which Esau sells his birthright for 'a mess of pottage' (a bowl of lentil stew), Soros said with disgust: 'Bono, you have sold out for a plate of lentils.'

❊

The following day was the first time that Bono had met George W. Bush face to face. He wanted to set a particular tone to the encounter. He rode to the White House in a Chevy suburban with a Bible on his lap. He was searching for a verse and couldn't find it. He was running late for his appointment with the most important man on the planet, but he told the driver to circle the White House until he found the passage in the Gospel of Matthew.

When he entered the Oval Office, Bono presented the president with a gift, an old Irish Bible. As he handed it over, Bush was clearly touched. The start of their conversation was entirely about religion. Bono pointed out that the only place in the Bible to speak directly of judgement is in Matthew 25, where a warning is given to those who have ignored the hungry, thirsty, naked, sick and imprisoned: 'Truly, I say to you, whatever you did to the least of my brothers and sisters, you did it to me.'

'You're right,' Bush told Bono. They fell to talking about which sin was the most grievous. 'The sin of omission perhaps,' said Bush.

Bono spoke, as he had with Jesse Helms, of how the great plague of Jesus's time was leprosy, but today it was AIDS. He produced the three small anti-retroviral pills he had been given in the hospital in Malawi. 'With a few pills, you can save millions of lives,' the singer told him.

He dropped the three tablets into Bush's hand.

'Mr President, paint these pills red, white and blue if you have to, but in Africa, these pills will be the best advert ever for the United States of America.'

Later, Bush wrote in his autobiography that he was wary of do-gooder rock stars until this point: 'I was sceptical of celebrities who seemed to adopt the cause of the moment as a way to advance their careers.' But Bono quickly dispelled the notion that he was a self-promoter. 'He knew our budgets, understood the facts and had well-informed views about the challenges in Africa.'

As the two men headed out to the presidential motorcade, Bono recalled Martin Luther King's advice about the need to find a door through which a movement might pass. *Have we found that door?* he wondered.

By the roadside, crowds waved at the president. Bush waved back.

'You're pretty popular around here,' Bono said.

'Yep, it wasn't always that way. When I came here first, people used to wave at me with one finger.'

Bono laughed. He thought Bush was funny.

But many others did not. The Edge was horrified and the other members of U2 were decidedly unnerved. Bass player Adam Clayton later wryly observed: 'I'm in a band with Bono … for that alone I deserve an access-all-areas pass through the pearly gates.'

Bono felt under siege from both sides. He knew that many of the politicians in Washington regarded him as 'a pest' or 'a stone in the shoe'. Now old friends in the music world were scathing. Some even stopped speaking to him.

The singer simply shrugged. 'It is much easier and hipper for me to be on the barricadese – it looks better on the resumé of a rock 'n' roll star. But I can do better by just getting into the White House and talking to a man who I believe listens, wants to listen, on these subjects.'

'This is an emergency – normal rules don't apply,' Bono added. 'There are no easy good or bad guys. Do you think an African mother cares if the drugs keeping her child alive are thanks to a Democrat or a Republican? I don't think that mother gives a damn about where that 20-cent pill comes from, so why should we? It can lead to some uncomfortable bedfellows, but sometimes less sleep means you are more awake.'

❊

He had planted a seed with the president. He had extracted an undertaking from the national security adviser. But Bono had still not convinced the money man. He had left the office of the Treasury secretary Paul O'Neill a year earlier, having been issued with the challenge of finding five well-governed African countries before O'Neill would discuss the issue of debt cancellation.

Bono found six – or, rather, Jamie Drummond did. As a result, O'Neill accepted Bono's challenge and, at the end of May, the pair of them set off on an eleven-day tour of sub-Saharan Africa, including Ghana, Uganda, Ethiopia and South Africa.

O'Neill, who was formerly the head of the world's largest aluminium firm, Alcoa, seemed to have little in common with the Irish rock star. The media dubbed them The Odd Couple. The idea, said O'Neill, was 'for the two of us to see life through each other's eyes'. He would get a set of blue wraparound glasses, he quipped, and find a grey wig for Bono.

Before they set out, Bono had asked local organisations to set up meetings with sex workers, doctors, AIDS educators and activists. O'Neill had got the Treasury to fix visits to the Stock Exchange and a Ford car manufacturing plant.

As the days passed, the perspectives of the two men flipped. O'Neill and his team of monetary theorists were plainly shaken by the stories of heartbreak that the AIDS pandemic placed in their path, while Bono began to appreciate the role of domestic industry, commerce and especially public infrastructure in bringing people out of extreme poverty. O'Neill – who had brought along his wife Nancy and their daughter Julie – ended up spending longer than planned, talking to nurses, doctors and patients in clinics and hospitals. Bono began to pay more attention to economic data.

There was one important shift of focus. Washington, thanks in large part to Senator Jesse Helms, had begun to think about what could be done to prevent the transmission of HIV to children in the wombs of mothers with AIDS.

'It was a much safer place for them to be politically,' said Lucy Matthew, who accompanied Bono on the trip. Even those who were judgemental about adults with AIDS, she said, were clear that something needed to be done about transmission to innocent children.

But visiting a clinic in Soweto, O'Neill discovered that although the US was funding drugs to prevent transmission in the womb, there was no money for anti-retroviral drugs to save the life of the mother herself. 'He was really shocked that all this effort was going into making sure that kids weren't born with HIV, but they were basically being born to be orphans because their mothers were going to die,' Matthew said. 'We left the continent starting to believe that the Bush White House might make a serious move on AIDS in Africa.'

At the end of the trip, O'Neill told the press: 'I can't begin to describe all of the emotional moments during this trip. But they confirmed three things for me.

'First, a truth we've always known: all people everywhere can do great things when they are given the tools and incentives for success.

'Second, that with leadership – honest, accountable and committed to progress – everything is possible. Without leadership, nothing is possible.

'And, finally, that in the right environment – focused on growth, enterprise and human development – aid works. Knowing that it can work, we have a moral imperative to demand as much. Assistance should make a real difference in people's lives.'

The road to Johannesburg had been, for Paul O'Neill, a road to Damascus.

Back in Washington, his assistants, Tony Fratto and Bobby Pittman, began to work closely with Bono's DATA team. They now held regular clandestine meetings – coats off, ties down, sleeves rolled up – in the cigar tavern Shelly's Back Room in DC. Here, among the soft lighting and overstuffed armchairs, they would share information, coordinate actions and discuss with Jamie Drummond how to seduce right-wing members of Congress to their cause.

❖

A month later, the White House announced that President Bush was making $500 million available to prevent mother-to-child transmission of HIV. A million women a year would receive the treatment. Senator Jesse Helms had been as good as his word and had lobbied the president personally. Announcing the package to reporters in the White House rose garden, President Bush said: 'As we see what works, we will make more funding available.'

The team at DATA were pleased, but this huge sum was not, in their view, an initiative of 'historic' proportions. Historic meant billions, not millions. Bono contacted Condoleezza Rice, who kept telling him 'be patient, be patient'.

But patience was running thin in the DATA office. Bono was alarmed to read a newspaper article in which the head of the US government's official aid organisation, USAID, was dismissing the idea of anti-retroviral drugs for Africa. Africans didn't understand Western time, he said, and couldn't be trusted to take their medication reliably. Bono was incensed. His concern intensified when Bobby Shriver got a call from the White House claiming that the top AIDS expert, Dr Anthony Fauci, the head of the National Institute of Infectious Diseases, had put the brakes on the idea of President Bush doing 'something big and bold'.

'Apparently, his advice is to take it step by step,' the White House official told Shriver.

Bono decided to act. He accepted an invitation to appear on the most popular US daytime TV show with Oprah Winfrey. After talking about music, fatherhood, fame and the reputation of the US in the rest of the world, they moved on to the topic of AIDS. Why, she asked, should her 10 million viewers care about AIDS in Africa when they have worries of their own at home?

Bono went for the jugular: 'I don't think you have to explain to any mother that the life of a child in Africa has the same value as her child.'

The studio audience applauded vehemently in agreement. The dots between the US and Africa had been connected.

But there was one more thing to do. Bono and Lucy and Jamie went to Washington and turned up at Dr Fauci's redbrick home in Georgetown.

'What exactly are your concerns?' they asked him.

It turned out they were not quite as the White House leaks had made out. He was not at all happy to hear that his name was being used to block an ambitious initiative. Providing universal access to anti-retrovirals, he said, was 'our moral duty, and we can make it possible'. He and the DATA team agreed to work together.

As the trio left his home, the doctor said to them: 'You guys turn up the heat and I'll turn up the cold science.'

If there were people in the White House who were having second thoughts about financing an historic initiative on AIDS, then Bono and his fellow campaigners would have to go over their heads – direct to the people.

They had heard cynics on Capitol Hill shrugging and saying, 'Americans just don't care about this kind of thing'. 'So we decided to show them they were wrong,' said Lucy Matthew. 'We fixed on a tour of the Midwest designed to show politicians in Washington that ordinary Americans did care about people on another continent living and dying with AIDS.'

On World Aids Day, 1 December 2002, Bono launched his Heart of America tour. Over the next seven days, he made stops in Nebraska, Iowa, Illinois, Indiana, Ohio and Kentucky, culminating with a final event in Nashville, Tennessee. 'We did seven states in seven days,' Matthew said. 'We went to universities, theatres, town halls, schools, truck stops, churches, the local editorial boards of the *Indianapolis Star*, *Chicago Tribune* and *Nebraska Journal*, almost as if we were organising a campaign for a political candidate.'

At the first meeting, in Nebraska, Warren Buffett – who was at the time the second-richest man in the world – turned up. Bono was putting a postcard on every seat with the name of the local congressman on it to make it easy for people to contact their political representatives. Buffett offered Bono some advice: 'Don't appeal to the conscience of America. Appeal to its greatness and I think you'll get the job done.'

Bono took the hint. At every meeting – after telling the crowds how half a million mothers in Africa would pass HIV to their children through childbirth or in their breast milk – he talked of compassionate conservatism and encouraged their audiences to write to their Republican senators. In Iowa, Bono said: 'I'm told you can grow anything here. We're here to grow a movement.' More than 10,000 people phoned the White House over the seven days.

On the platform, he was joined by celebrities like the actor Ashley Judd and the comedian Chris Rock, who spoke passionately of the situation. But the star of the roadshow was Agnes Nyamayarwo, a nurse from Uganda, who described her life as an activist after losing her husband to AIDS and being tested positive for HIV herself ten years earlier. She spoke differently from the other speakers and touched the hearts of the audiences.

'Agnes brought the reality of AIDS in Africa into the hearts of policy-makers,' Bono later said. 'She didn't just change minds, she changed history.'

❖

A full nine months after Condoleezza Rice had made her promise to Bono, he got a phone call from her at his home in Ireland. It was Tuesday 28 January 2003.

'Watch the State of the Union address on the television. You are going to be pleased. I'm very proud of the president. You will have all you're looking for. We are announcing it at the State of the Union.'

'How much?' asked Bono.

'I can't tell you yet. They are still hashing it out.'

Five minutes later, the phone rang again. It was Josh Bolten.

'It's $15 billion over the next five years. It's new money. It's unprecedented.'

At the appointed hour, Bono turned on the television in Dublin. He watched President George W. Bush, across the other side of the Atlantic, walk out into the chamber to address the US Congress and announce that he was launching PEPFAR – the President's Emergency Plan for AIDS Relief.

Since then, over the past twenty-two years, through PEPFAR the United States has spent $110 billion in the fight against AIDS.

It is the largest health intervention to fight a single disease in human history. As of the start of 2025, it has saved more than 26 million lives.

CHAPTER 27

A NEW BLUEPRINT FOR AFRICA

'It's happening again,' Bob Geldof exploded. 'Almost twenty years after Live Aid and things are no better. In some ways, they're getting worse. What happened to all the early-warning systems we put in? What happened to the improvements in EU aid? They're double-counting again. None of it is working. And there are all these new forces at play which nobody properly understands.'

'Calm down, Bob,' said the prime minister, 'and come and see me when you get back.'

Bob Geldof was in Ethiopia and Tony Blair was at a meeting of world leaders at the G8 summit at Evian in France. Geldof had just returned to Addis Ababa after a tour of the new famine regions. It was 2003. What he had seen there had chilling echoes of the 1984 famine that had pushed him to action with Band Aid and then Live Aid.

'It was the contrast which prompted me to immediate action,' Bob said, looking back twenty years later. 'I knew the leaders of the rich economies were meeting in the idyllic spa at Evian, sipping their cool water, while in Ethiopia, kids were once again dying of thirst and malnutrition. I was angry that nothing seemed to have changed. That's why I got on the phone right away to Tony Blair.'

Yet it was not true that nothing had changed. The situation on the ground was bad. And yet, this time, there was no war to blame. There was no Marxist dictator in power pursuing crazy agricultural policies. The Ethiopians had elected a democratic government with a very competent prime minister. 'I knew I could not go back to the public with the exact same story,' Geldof said. Charity was not the answer. The world had to address the structural economic problems which kept Africa permanently teetering on the brink of crisis. He had a plan and he knew it needed endorsement at the highest political level.

It was a measure of the impact which Bob Geldof and Live Aid had made that the prime minister took his call in the middle of a summit of world leaders. 'I wouldn't have reacted in that way with anyone,' Tony Blair later said. 'But it was him – with his track record, his commitment, his knowledge, his dedication, and therefore it made sense.'

❄

Geldof and Bono had gone in for a breakfast meeting at 10 Downing Street a month before the Evian summit. They wanted to lobby Blair to push the other rich world leaders into action on Africa's AIDS pandemic. The prime minister had been receptive to the idea. He had been looking ahead. In two years' time, the UK would be chair of both the European Union and the G8, which would be having its British summit in Scotland at the celebrated Gleneagles Hotel and golf course. Being chair of both organisations in the same year would give Blair a moment of unique international influence. He was already thinking of placing two subjects at the heart of the agenda: the education of girls, and the scourge of AIDS in Africa. These were topics that he knew would align with the priorities of George Bush.

Blair and his chancellor, Gordon Brown, were both children of Live Aid. The 1985 concert – when they were both backbench MPs largely unknown to the public – had been a formative influence upon them both. Gordon Brown was the son of a Christian minister who remembered missionaries from Africa coming to his father's church. He now saw the burdensome debts of poor countries as a moral – as well as an economic – challenge. He wanted a far more ambitious agenda than just tackling AIDS and girls' education. 'We particularly didn't want just two specific areas,' said Brown's adviser, Shriti Vadera, 'because what then happens is that you can divert your resources to those two measures and forget about the rest.'

Earlier in the year, Brown had had a brainwave on how to get rich nations to massively increase aid to poor ones. He called it the International Finance Facility. Its basic idea was that wealthy governments would make long-term pledges of what they would give in aid over the next twenty years. Bonds would then be issued – backed by these pledges – on the international money markets. The cash from the bonds could be spent upfront on vaccinating children, educating them and building the infrastructure – roads, railways, ports, airports, power stations, electricity grids and clean water supplies – needed to promote economic growth. It was called front-loading aid. Geldof endorsed the idea in various leading European newspapers as 'smart and cute'.

But in May that year, Bob's attention was diverted from high finance to something more dramatically immediate. The UN children's organisation, UNICEF, was getting reports of drought, flood, malnutrition and disease creating a severe emergency in Ethiopia, which was still one of the five poorest countries in the world. The average Ethiopian had an annual income of only $100 a year. Now another drought was threatening to push them over the edge. UNICEF estimated that 14 million people were at risk of starvation once more. Children were growing up chronically stunted. They were dying from preventable diseases.

By coincidence, Bob's sister Lynn was a journalist with UNICEF. She contacted her brother and asked if he would be willing to go back to Ethiopia. Bob undertook a five-day tour of the emergency areas.

The problems were the same and yet different. The rains had failed again, so had the crops. The climatic conditions were repeating themselves. But the fighting was over and money was not being wasted on arms. Local officials were no longer indifferent or hostile to the lot of the ordinary people. Although around 60,000 children were badly malnourished, the feeding centres were not like they were in the 1980s. 'There's no kids lying in pools of diarrhoea and vomit with flies everywhere,' Bob noted. 'They have a good programme to control the flow of children coming in from the country. They understand nutrition a lot better. They're getting children back to health a lot quicker. It is us, not them, who are not doing our bit to avoid catastrophe.'

He could also see drastic improvements in the way Ethiopia was run. In 1985, the country was under the thumb of a repressive Stalinist regime that was fighting the longest war of the twentieth century. 'The task in 1985 was to keep people alive and wait for the political moment to pass,' Geldof reflected. 'It passed. Now they have a pragmatic decent government and blossoming businesses. I met a local businessman who gives 20 per cent of his profits to food relief. There has been a real change. It feels very positive.'

But this time, in contrast to his first visits twenty years earlier, Bob knew a lot more about the structural factors that kept Ethiopia poor. Geldof's potency as a lobbyist now resided in more than celebrity outrage. He had developed a powerful command of the complexity of the issues that underlay African poverty. 'What's different?' he asked, rhetorically. 'I'll tell you what is different. The Four Horsemen of the Apocalypse that are galloping across the plains of Ethiopia are Debt, Aid, Trade and AIDS.'

Measuring Ethiopia's debts against the goods it produced every year revealed it to be one of the poorest countries in the world. It had qualified for debt relief, but not yet been given it. It had a large trade deficit: it exported cheap raw materials and imported expensive finished products. There was a structured unfairness to the world's trading system. To correct this, Geldof knew, required trade reform, aid increases and debt cancellation all at the same time. This time he made a beeline for the local representatives of the IMF and World Bank. He had known nothing of them when he had visited in 1985, before and after Live Aid. 'We had,' he observed drily, 'full and frank discussions, to say the least.' Geldof was never overawed by the powerful.

In 2003, he knew better what questions to ask on aid too. Why had Ethiopia only two-thirds of the food aid it needed to get through the next three months? Why was the European Union only delivering cereals and failing to provide the blended food and vegetable oil it had promised – which made up the vital supplementary food for malnourished children? Why was the EU claiming it had sent 44 per cent of the food it had pledged when in fact it had sent only 28 per cent?

'It's a blatant outright lie,' he told Blair. 'It's clear on the ground that the EU has been double counting and re-announcing things. They're really massaging the figures.' Where in 1985 Geldof was fuelled largely by outrage, twenty years later, he understood the mechanics and the economics.

In Ethiopia, he encountered the problems of unfair trade at first hand. In the southern province of Sidamo, he met farmers producing the country's only real cash crop – coffee. Keffa in Ethiopia was the birthplace of the coffee plant. There had been no famine here in the 1980s. There was drought, but no hunger, because people were rich enough to buy food after selling their coffee.

But globalisation had brought about a collapse in the price of the crop. It had plummeted 70 per cent in the previous four years as coffee from Vietnam flooded the market.

'Yet there is a solution,' he said. Rich nations place import tariffs on coffee. These increase with every stage of coffee processing to discourage Africans from doing anything except export the raw beans. France had proposed a cut in the tariffs, but the US was refusing to discuss it. 'This is unfair trade and the G8 need to discuss it at Evian,' Geldof insisted to Blair.

There was one other great contrast between now and 1985. Then, Geldof had gone out of his way to make sure that no photographer could take a picture of the white pop star with a black baby. 'They are not props for media images,' he said at the time.

But, twenty years on, AIDS had weakened medical systems and the ability of families to cope in their everyday lives. Geldof visited an AIDS clinic in the south of the country.

'It was one shitty little hospital to treat an area of a million people, with just one doctor – a brilliant man – who had started doing random HIV tests. He's discovered that 14 per cent of the population is positive – double the official estimate.'

The doctor was holding a baby, which he passed to Geldof. Bob took the child and held it tenderly. It was one of a million AIDS orphans in Ethiopia.

All this was what fuelled his rage in that phone call to Tony Blair. Debt, aid, trade and AIDS: if the international community was serious about breaking the cycle of famine – which had first taken him to Ethiopia in 1984 and was being repeated now in 2003 – it had to address all of these at the same time: 'The G8 must not get away with doing nothing. Tony Blair mustn't leave Evian empty-handed.'

But if Bob Geldof had become more sure-footed on questions of policy, his loose lips continued to generate PR problems for the strategists of DATA. Lucy Matthew had accompanied Bob on the trip to keep a beady eye on the impact Geldof's messaging might have on DATA's strategy on the eve of the Evian G8. She briefed him carefully for an interview with a *Guardian* journalist, Rory Carroll, in Addis Ababa.

'We wanted to give George Bush credit for what he had done by setting aside the massive sum of $15 billion for the fight against AIDS,' she said. 'The idea was to use his good example to put pressure on other countries to step up funding through the Global Fund.' The Global Fund to Fight AIDS Tuberculosis and Malaria had been proposed by the UN secretary-general, Kofi Annan, in 2001 and had gained support from Bill Gates and George Bush with contributions from the UK, France and Japan, but other G8 countries had yet to contribute significant sums.

The interview was taking place in a vehicle moving from one feeding centre to another. When they stopped at a checkpoint, Lucy got out to smooth their passage. When she returned, the interview continued uncontroversially – or so she thought.

The next morning, her phone was filled with alarming voice messages asking what was going on.

'Bob has been bigging up Bush,' one said.

It was only two months since Bush, supported by Blair, had controversially invaded Iraq to overthrow Saddam Hussein. Bono had called the move 'sincerely wrong'.

'Bob has just totally dissed Clinton,' said another.

Lucy went to the journalist.

'Oh my God, Rory! What have you written?'

Rory showed her the piece. Geldof hadn't just praised Bush, he'd done it by running down his predecessor Bill Clinton, and in fairly graphic terms. 'Clinton was a good guy, but he did fuck-all,' Bob was quoted as saying. 'You'll think I'm off my trolley when I say this, but the Bush administration is the most radical – in a positive sense – in its approach to Africa since Kennedy.' The neo-conservatives and religious right-wingers who surrounded Bush were proving unexpectedly receptive to appeals for help, he said. 'You can get the weirdest politicians on your side.'

By contrast, Bill Clinton had not helped Africa much as president, despite his high-profile visits and apparent empathy with the downtrodden. 'Clinton talked the talk and did diddly squat, whereas Bush doesn't talk, but does deliver,' added Lord Waheed Alli, the Labour peer and co-founder of Geldof's television production company Ten Alps, who was accompanying Geldof on the UNICEF trip.

Lucy was horrified.

'When did he say all this?'

'When you got out of the car,' replied the journalist.

'Oh my God. Bob is so polemical, so black and white. Obviously, Clinton didn't do "fuck-all for Africa". He signed America's 100 per cent debt relief into law!'

Lucy sought out Bob. 'I understand why you said it, but it wasn't entirely accurate. I think you should write a letter of apology.'

'Why? Bush *did* do more than Clinton did.'

'That is not the same as saying Clinton did fuck-all. You should write and apologise.'

Bill Clinton was, unsurprisingly, offended – and wrote to Geldof to tell him so. Before Bob could reply, the former president arrived in London for a party thrown by the philanthropist Lynn Forester de Rothschild. By coincidence, Bob had been invited too. Geldof thought about raising the subject at the gathering, but couldn't get to Clinton, who was, 'as ever, holding three dozen beautiful women in thrall'.

Eventually, the apology was written. It began: 'Oh dear. I hate pissing off heroes…'. It went on to take a dubious swipe at the English journalist who had 'reduced to a neat soundbite' Bob's nuanced explanation of the complexities of the relationship between a Democrat president and a Republican Congress. After this, Bob proceeded on a long paean of praise for the former president's many achievements. Lucy made sure that it got to Clinton personally.

It was not an isolated example of Geldof's ability to simultaneously insult and charm. Bob's relationship with the new regime in Ethiopia became positively warm. Hearty laughter was heard from a private meeting between Geldof and the new prime minister, Meles Zenawi, whose rebel troops had overthrown the dictator Mengistu. It turned out, when Bob emerged, that Meles had kept referring to Geldof as Crazy Irish. Bob responded by calling him Enver, since Meles had, in his early days, been an admirer of the Albanian dictator Enver Hoxha, who was an anti-Soviet, anti-Chinese Marxist. Albania was so self-reliant under his rule that no bananas were allowed to be imported. The schoolboy nicknames produced endless mirth in the pair.

Meles, who became head of state once the Tigrayan rebels overthrew Mengistu, swiftly abandoned Marxist rhetoric once in power. Instead, he embraced what he called 'revolutionary democracy', a vague but more prag-matic technocratic form of governance. In its early days, Geldof saw it as a hopeful model for a new kind of African democracy.

⁂

Before Geldof could meet up with Tony Blair, in September 2003 the prime minister received a letter from Oxfam on behalf of all Britain's development agencies. They were thinking ahead to 2005 too. The letter informed Blair that they had got together and decided to organise something big ahead of the UK presidency of the G8. They hoped the PM was also planning to use it to do something 'bold and ambitious'. Blair wrote back to say he was planning something on girls' education.

The agencies were underwhelmed. 'I remember we all thought that girls' education was a hugely important thing,' said Adrian Lovett, who was now at Oxfam and coordinating the NGOs' collective plans, 'but it was a subset of the broader agenda that we wanted him to take on.'

Blair was coming under pressure – first from Gordon Brown and now from the development agencies – to do something bigger. It was Bob Geldof who told him what that should be.

Geldof went to Downing Street to see him. 'Africa is fucked,' said Bob, by way of an opening.

Geldof had been thinking for several months about the Brandt Report, which had been written in 1980 by a group of eminent retired politicians led by the former German chancellor, Willy Brandt. Called *North-South: A Programme for Survival*, it had offered a new blueprint for relations between the rich world and the developing world. 'Trouble was, it had been written by people who were now out of power.' It just became a wish list.

'What we need is a new report, a twenty-first-century version – but one written by people who are in power and who have a chance of implementing it this time. Not the Brandt Report, but the Blair Report.'

Geldof wanted input from leading intellectuals from a variety of backgrounds.

'The UK presidency of the G8 will coincide with the twentieth anni-versary of Live Aid. It's the perfect time to have a fresh look at the world and work out ways to narrow the widening gap between Africa and the rich nations.'

The report would work out how Africa needed to change – but also what the West could do to facilitate that change. Rich nations needed to remove the handicaps they had placed upon the poor world that inhibited its development.

Blair and Geldof talked for half an hour. Then he called in his communications chief Alastair Campbell, together with a bevy of special advisers and civil servants. Geldof went through his pitch again.

'We just don't need to do this, Bob,' said Alastair.

He and Blair had too much else on their minds. The invasion of Iraq was unravelling. No Weapons of Mass Destruction had been found. Public suspicion was growing that the case for war had been 'sexed up'. The government weapons inspector, Dr David Kelly, had been found dead. Blair had ordered a public inquiry into the whole affair as opinion polls showed that public trust in him had plummeted. He and Alastair Campbell had a lot else on their plate.

'What good will another report do?'

Geldof turned the tables. 'Is Africa on the agenda for the Gleneagles G8?'

'It hasn't been finally decided.'

'This new report could be a template,' Bob said. 'You set up a commission of top people from Africa and the West. The commission agrees their conclusions and writes the report. The UK makes it policy and you bring it to the other world leaders at our G8. And Britain has this worldwide success for fuck-all money.'

The prime minister turned to a civil servant.

'How much could this cost?'

'Five or six million pounds.'

'Right,' said Blair. 'We'll do it.'

There was some low-volume grumbling in the room, before Blair said: 'None of the other G8 leaders will want to do this. I know, I've often talked to them about Africa. They are simply not interested. They need to be pushed.'

Looking back, Blair's senior special adviser, Liz Lloyd, reflected that 'Tony thought Bob was a serious guy, so he took him seriously. Tony saw him as a valuable ally potentially.'

Blair looked resolute. 'So, Bob, I'll do the politics, but you have to do the public. We need them, to get an agreement. I can't afford a failure.'

'Right, I'll do the public,' said Geldof.

'Don't let me down,' said Blair.

'I won't. But don't *you* let *us* down.'

※

Geldof had been preaching to the converted. Blair had been interested in doing something special for Africa since he was at university, where he was influenced by an Anglican priest, Peter Thompson, who introduced him to communitarian socialism. Live Aid in 1985 consolidated his concern for Africa. At the Labour Party conference in 1995, he announced that his socialism was defined by a moral purpose that extended to the whole human race.

When his New Labour party took power in 1997, Britain's aid budget was in a parlous state. It had been cut and cut, year after year, under previous Conservative governments. Blair changed all that. He created a separate development department and brought the aid minister into the cabinet. He commissioned the first white paper on development for a quarter of a century – with the title *Eliminating World Poverty: Making Globalisation Work for the Poor* – and then personally wrote the introduction to it. He steadily increased the aid budget. After making two visits to South Africa in 1999, he was so shocked by the poverty that he and his wife Cherie began privately to sponsor a child in an HIV orphanage in Cape Town.

That same year, Blair delivered a lecture in Chicago, which laid the template for his foreign policy. In it, he set out the case for states to intervene in other countries to prevent humanitarian disasters or gross oppression. The international community should not stand idly by, he said. 'But armies can't build democracies,' said Laurie Lee, who was to become Blair's special adviser on Africa. Massive increases in aid were also required.

The terrorist assaults on the United States on 11 September 2001 reinforced this notion in Tony Blair's mind. A week after the traumatic attack, he had been due to host talks at Chequers with six reform-minded African leaders. No 10 aides expected it to be cancelled. 'I remember thinking, *Is all this going to be put on the back burner?*' said Liz Lloyd, one of Blair's most trusted aides. 'For me, one of the first tests of his seriousness on the issue was that he insisted that meeting still went ahead. Even with the context of 9/11, there was a real appetite from the prime minister to progress this agenda.'

A month after 9/11, Blair told the Labour Party conference that Africa was 'a scar on the conscience of the world' – but a scar which could be healed if the world as a community focused upon it.

Yet he could not make the hoped-for breakthrough with the rich nations. At the G8 meeting in Kananaskis in Canada in 2002, he had pressed for an ambitious set of proposals, but had been thwarted by the US and Japan. A deal of sorts had been done – $1 billion in extra debt relief to make up for falling commodity prices – but campaigners were scathing. 'It looked fairly promising until a month ago,' said Geldof at the time. 'But in the past two weeks, it has all unravelled into this meaningless conference.' Oxfam's campaigns director, Justin Forsyth, organised for little bags of nuts to be handed out to journalists at the press centre. The bags bore the words: 'Peanuts for Africa'. That was all Oxfam deemed the G8 to have produced. Blair was so irritated with this jape that he instructed a senior diplomat to ring Forsyth to chastise him.

But it had got him noticed. Within a couple of years, Blair had brought him into Downing Street as his primary special adviser on Africa.

A significant change now occurred in the prime minister's thinking. In a speech to a joint session of the US Congress in July 2003, Blair linked economic development in Africa with the drive for global security, which was at the top of the agenda for President Bush. It was quintessential Blair. He was driven by a strong sense of moral commitment to the poorest people on the planet, yet he was also the archetypal political pragmatist. His decision to work with Geldof reflected both those motivations.

Bob was soon back on the phone to Blair, adding a new prescient line of argument. Unless rich nations found a way to enable Africans to make a living at home, Geldof warned with considerable foresight, 'they will come to our shores, resulting in massive social upheaval'.

A week later, he continued the pressure, writing to Blair and urging swift progress so that a really comprehensive report could be published in good time before the Gleneagles summit. 'I know I'm pushy, and I know you're up to your neck, but something short of the normal seven-week delay response would be welcome (do you use Royal Mail?). Seriously though, this must be implemented almost immediately.

'I do think this needs to be a direct commission from you personally – your vision, your authority, your weight. This can't be a UK government document or – God help us – a G8 document. The report will, however, intellectually underpin that particular shindig.' It would offer a vision which was 'a holistic, coherent – rather than piecemeal – rescue plan for the beleaguered billion of Africa'. That vision would be 'beyond politics, and beyond bureaucracy'. Borrowing Blair's own words, Geldof concluded: 'As you rightly said, Africa is not politics, it's a passion.'

But Geldof posed a number of problems for the prime minister. The idea of a commission was a huge undertaking and there was a risk it might come to conclusions with which the UK government did not agree. Also, Geldof was strongly opposed to the idea that the new commission should have two co-chairs, one from Africa and one from the rich world. The report must have Tony Blair's name on it, said Bob, to give it authority, since its primary audience was the US.

This was particularly 'tricky', Liz Lloyd wrote in a note to Blair. Geldof 'is scathing about the ability and worthiness of virtually all African leaders … he therefore does not want an African co-chair.' But the commission would need 'prominent African involvement', so she suggested that Blair 'talk carefully' to the South African president, Thabo Mbeki, to secure his support.

Other Downing Street officials also urged caution. If the plan failed, then Geldof and Bono would pour 'opprobrium' down on Blair's head, one warned. The Americans would only take the report seriously if there were people on the commission whose names they recognised, said another.

Moreover, Downing Street aides expressed concern at Geldof's idea that the commission could be chaired by Blair and yet also somehow be 'independent' of the UK government. 'If this document is going to have your name and be sold by you,' Liz Lloyd wrote to Blair, then Geldof must accept 'that we have the final editing role'.

Blair listened, but then overrode the objections. 'Bob can be rather unreasonable in his persistence, actually manic about it,' he later reflected. 'However, he has two enormous saving graces: he is smart and he is brave. He is smart enough to know when to stop short of provoking catastrophe or making an unreasonable demand non-negotiable. He's brave because he isn't one of your fair-weather "now you're not popular I don't want to associate with you" types, of which the arts world is inordinately full. He and Bono are both genuinely committed, properly knowledgeable and ultimately care more about getting things done than about protecting their egos.'

Geldof – who was about to set off for South Africa to perform and speak at a concert hosted by Nelson Mandela – had a power which could not be ignored, and which, Blair hoped, could be harnessed. He was in for a bumpier ride than he anticipated.

CHAPTER 28

THE ODD COUPLE

Gordon Brown got in first. The wheels had been turning slowly in 10 Downing Street on Bob Geldof's idea of a Commission for Africa. Ten days before Tony Blair announced the launch of the commission, the prime minister's ally – and great political rival – called a meeting of all the leading aid agencies in the country, also inviting Bob and Bono, as well as Richard Curtis of Comic Relief.

As he got closer to the levers of power, Geldof took care to avoid seeming to take sides in the rivalry between Blair and Brown. The relationship between the two Labour politicians had become tense and increasingly bitter. A decade earlier, they had struck a deal over which of them should stand for election as prime minister. The pact was that Blair would be PM first, and Brown his chancellor. But then Blair would step down and make way for Brown to succeed him.

By February 2004, Brown had been waiting nearly seven years to succeed his old friend. But Blair, despite being weakened politically by his disastrous decision to join the invasion of Iraq, was still refusing to set a timetable for when he would step down. Brown remained loyal in public, but was more openly staking out his own agenda and building his support base within the party. Geldof and his fellow campaigners knew they had to tread warily.

Brown went public about the meeting with all the aid agencies in a newspaper article in which he paid tribute to Live Aid – 'an event that marked for many the moment when the world woke up to the enormous challenge of tackling poverty'. On the surface, it had been called to discuss how the world could make better progress towards the UN's Millennium Development Goals to alleviate global poverty. What Brown didn't tell the agencies was that he already had a plan.

'We did something reasonably naughty,' said his adviser, Shriti Vadera. They had drawn up an ambitious programme – 'not just health and education and debt relief, but also trade and budgetary and financial stability, which were the key drivers of development'. Now Brown aimed to make the aid agencies think that they had thought of the plan he had come up with. 'A politician can't just randomly stand up and announce something without the public having some awareness of why it was needed,' Shriti said. His plan was to get the agencies to lobby him to do the things that he already wanted to do.

To fix this, Shriti – in consultation with Kevin Watkins and Justin Forsyth at Oxfam, and Lucy Matthew and Jamie Drummond from DATA – handpicked the individuals who chaired the meeting's break-out groups. At the end of the day, the gathering had agreed upon the outcome which the chancellor of the exchequer desired: debt relief, improved aid and trade reform. 'We pre-cooked it,' said Shriti. It was now impossible for Blair to restrict Britain's G8 agenda to girls' education and HIV in Africa, as he had originally planned. 'Tony now had to buy in to the more ambitious agenda.'

❖

Ten days later, on 24 February 2004, Tony Blair announced that he was setting up a Commission for Africa. It would have 17 members,* the majority

---

*   The members of the Commission for Africa were:

1. Tony Blair (Chair) – Prime Minister of the United Kingdom
2. Fola Adeola – Chairman of the FATE Foundation (Nigeria)
3. K.Y. Amoako – Executive Secretary of the Economic Commission for Africa and Under-Secretary-General of the United Nations (Ghana)
4. Nancy Kassebaum Baker – former Senator (United States)
5. Hilary Benn – Secretary of State for International Development (United Kingdom)
6. Gordon Brown – Chancellor of the Exchequer of the United Kingdom
7. Michel Camdessus – Africa Personal Representative (France)
8. Bob Geldof – Musician and founder of Live Aid (Ireland)
9. Ralph Goodale – Finance Minister (Canada)
10. Ji Peiding – Member of the Standing Committee of the National People's Congress and its Foreign Affairs Committee (China)
11. William S. Kalema – Chairman of the board of the Uganda Investment Authority (Uganda)

of them from Africa, but Blair alone would chair it, as Geldof had forcefully requested. The members were drawn from a mix of men and women from the worlds of government, business and the development sector. They included two prime ministers, a president and two finance ministers. To underscore its independence Blair invited Geldof to become a commissioner too. They did not quite know what they were letting themselves in for – though neither did he.

Blair chose leaders with the political will and technocratic competence to create the kind of economic change that benefitted the poorest people. They were to go for a 'hand up, not handout' model of development.

There were several ambiguities at the heart of the Commission for Africa. Geldof had insisted that the commission had to be independent and yet he had wanted its members to be active players at the highest level. That would cause tensions. Blair saw the commission as a vehicle to put Africa at the top of the agenda for the UK's simultaneous presidencies of the G8 and the EU.

Geldof and Blair shared a moral agenda, but without any clear idea initially of how this might best be achieved. The commission set no specific targets at the outset. It wasn't even clear whether its recommendations should be addressed primarily to African leaders or those of the rich world. It had no terms of reference – its way of working was made up as it went along.

As a result, some Western leaders suspected that the Commission for Africa was a Trojan horse designed to push them into commitments they might not welcome. By contrast, governments within Africa feared it might be yet another attempt by the West to impose an external agenda on the continent, undermining the mechanisms and strategies Africans were setting up for themselves under the African Union.

---

12. Trevor Manuel – Minister of Finance (South Africa)
13. Benjamin Mkapa – President of Tanzania
14. Linah Mohohlo – Governor of the Bank of Botswana
15. Tidjane Thiam – Group Strategy and Development Director Aviva PLC (Côte d'Ivoire)
16. Anna Tibaijuka – Director of UN-HABITAT and Under-Secretary-General of the United Nations (Tanzania)
17. Meles Zenawi – Prime Minister of Ethiopia

Development specialists were suspicious too. Blair's new private secretary for Africa – a young civil servant from Hull named Laurie Lee – had arrived in Downing Street from the Department for International Development. He brought with him some of the suspicion from his old department.

We know all this stuff, he thought. *We don't need another commission to tell us what to do.* 'But when I got to No 10, I realised that what Tony Blair was doing turned out to be rather clever.'

What Blair did not know, as he launched the Commission for Africa, was that Gordon Brown's right-hand woman, Shriti Vadera, was engaged on a commission of a different kind. After the chancellor's meeting with all the agencies in the Treasury, she invited Bob and Bono, and Richard Curtis and his partner, Emma Freud, to dinner at her home in Holland Park, together with Oxfam's two top strategists, Justin Forsyth and Kevin Watkins and the key movers behind DATA, Jamie Drummond and Lucy Matthew. Another attender was Jo Leadbeater, head of advocacy at Oxfam who later, as Jo Cox, became a Labour MP. The group were to become the key behind-the-scenes coordinators of a new movement which was to bring millions of people onto the streets, not just in the UK but all around the world.

From the outset, they knew that the following year, 2005, offered an unprecedented opportunity for action. So many events and influences would be aligned. The realisation of that struck Richard Curtis as he sat listening to Jim Wolfensohn at Gordon Brown's February aid agency meeting at the Treasury. *It's twenty years since Live Aid*, he thought. *We've got a supportive Labour government. We've got the UK chairing the G8. And we've got an interested World Bank.* When the meeting divided into its break-out groups, 'that's when the conversations began'. Not long afterwards, he decided to set aside work on his latest film and dedicate a whole year to nothing but campaigning for the movement which would come to be known as Make Poverty History.

At their first meeting in Shriti's mews cottage in Holland Park, the group discussed their goals for the year ahead. All were agreed that the agenda had to be expanded beyond HIV and girls' education. 'We all wanted a much bigger moment,' said Shriti. 'We could perhaps have got $5 billion for an HIV initiative and another $5 billion for educating girls. But everyone wanted something more ambitious and holistic.'

Over the year that followed, they came together for dinner most months. The discussion expanded as the individual members, from their contrasting perspectives, shared information about what the campaign strategies and tactics would be. They began coordinating their activities.

'Lucy would say, "We're going with Bono to Paris next week. Is there anything we should be watching out for?",' Shriti recalled. 'There was a little group of us that knew which ones were being targeted, in which order and what was the problem in each country.' They began to build a portfolio of shared information on the concerns and campaign points in different G8 nations.

The dinners helped bind them together. This sense of unity became even more important as they moved into separate institutions. 'I was still in Oxfam, but Justin moved to Downing Street and Shriti was in the Treasury,' said Kevin Watkins. Jamie was working with Bob, while Lucy became chief-of-staff to Bono on his activism. 'It was tactical,' recalled Geldof. 'We talked about how far could we take things and in which direction. But it was also about staying in touch with the innermost circle. It grew into simple friendship.'

The atmosphere of trust that was built extended to Shriti's boss. 'Extraordinarily, you would find Gordon ringing you, rather than you ringing Gordon to lobby him,' Kevin remembered.

They did not agree on everything. She and Bob had a massive argument about it once in Sheekey's fish restaurant in the West End.

'Why are you so obsessed with trade when Africa doesn't really do much of it?' demanded Geldof. 'More importantly, it's not even on the G8 agenda. It's a matter for the World Trade Organization.'

'Africa will only get wealthy when it does start to trade more,' Shriti replied.

The argument became so heated that the other diners in the elegant wood-panelled restaurant were turning around to look. Justin's girlfriend told them both to calm down, stop talking to each other, and turn to talk to somebody else. The atmosphere only shifted when Shriti turned to the man next to her.

'I'm sorry, I don't think we've met. Who are you, and what do you do?' she asked.

'I'm Matt Damon. I'm an actor.'

Everyone round the table burst out laughing.

Clearly, Shriti had been spending too long looking at spreadsheets.

❧

Over at the Commission for Africa, a secretariat had been created to assist the new commissioners. Its head was Myles Wickstead, the man who had overseen the writing of Tony Blair's pioneering manifesto for a new approach to overseas aid. It was a revolutionary document. It shifted British aid from its traditional role of promoting British trade and industry abroad and refocused it to become entirely poverty-focused.

Bob had met him before when Wickstead was British ambassador to Ethiopia. For such a distinguished man, Wickstead wore his achievements with modest amiability. The two warmed to each other immediately. Now, in February 2004, Myles was assembling a team of forty civil servants to do the commission's research. And already he was having to fight off various UK government departments who wanted to meddle in the commission's work. 'I spent a lot of time saying, "This is an independent commission and we are not going to be told what our report will say",' Wickstead recalled.

So he was alarmed, two months later, when a senior Treasury official was made the commission's director of policy and research. Sir Nicholas Stern, a former chief economist at the World Bank, was head of the Government Economic Service at the UK Treasury. He was a civil servant, not a political appointee, but he worked under Gordon Brown. Now, in April 2004, he was asked to lead the writing of the report of the Commission for Africa.

'There was some concern about how the work on the commission was going,' Stern said. 'Casting around, asking a variety of people what they thought should be done, is fine as part of the process. But it doesn't give you a coherent overall strategy. I was asked if I would take over the lead, giving it a structured analytical evidence-based approach.'

Sure-footed as he was as an academic economist, Nick Stern was a novice when it came to the world of pop celebrity. Soon after being asked to take on the task, he received a call from Geldof, who suggested meeting the following morning at the Picasso Café in the King's Road. 'This was slightly contrary to my puritan ethic. I don't normally go to cafés in the middle of the morning,' Stern recalled. After fifteen minutes of nervous preliminaries, the economist began to disagree with Geldof. 'At that point, I felt I had started to pass the test and, as the conversation ran on, felt a real kindredness of spirit. I realised he was a very smart man, who knew rather a lot, and who had thought carefully about development, and he recognised that I was not some kind of neoliberal maniac from the World Bank.'

After they had been talking for about an hour, another Picasso regular, Charlie Watts, came in. Bob leapt up to greet him and admire the Rolling Stones drummer's rather elegant Italian jacket. 'He then introduced me to Charlie as a friend of his, and I felt that I really had passed the test,' said Nick. 'I hadn't realised, when I got up that morning, I was going to meet one of my teenage heroes.' Unsure of what to say to Watts, the economist blurted out: 'Last time I saw you, Charlie, was more than forty years ago – on Eel Pie Island – and it cost me five shillings.' The Rolling Stone looked at Stern for what felt an age and then, utterly deadpan, replied, 'I don't remember you', at which point the economist dissolved into nervous laughter.

But if Stern had passed the initial test with Geldof, things were rather different at the secretariat of the Commission for Africa. The arrival of the high-powered Treasury mandarin did not go down well with the existing team.

'Suddenly, Nick Stern was there, completely unbeknownst to any of the rest of us,' said Wickstead. 'He had been parachuted in by the Treasury – effectively by Gordon Brown.' The former ambassador had a shrewd idea that all this was an outworking of the bitter rivalry between Brown and Blair.

Wickstead went straight to 10 Downing Street and spoke to the prime minister's principal private secretary, Ivan Rogers, and declared: 'I am not going to put up with people being parachuted in without my prior knowledge. This is just not right. And I will step down and do it with a lot of fuss if this continues to go on.'

What Wickstead did not know at the time was that a new crisis point had been reached in the breakdown of the relationship between the prime minister and the chancellor. The month before, shortly after the Budget on 17 March 2004, Blair told Brown he was intending to make a public announcement within the next few weeks concerning his retirement in the autumn. The two men had discussed the matter more than once. Brown, unexpectedly, felt it would be against the interests of the Labour Party to pre-announce his decision to go because it would spark a damaging six-month leadership contest. But, by April, Blair had changed his mind after his closest allies persuaded him to stay on. Suddenly he stopped talking about the matter to Brown, who began to suspect that Blair was not going to keep his word. It was around this time that Nick Stern was sent into Blair's Commission for Africa.

Brown had an odd relationship with the commission. He was a full commissioner and yet, over the months that followed, he did not take a prominent role in its workings. Perhaps he did not need to, now that Nick Stern had been brought on board. 'Brown clearly wanted to make sure that, through Nick, he had some sort of input into the commission,' said Wickstead who, after this unhappy start, went on to develop a good working relationship with Stern. 'We had our moments, but we got on very well. We became friends and have stayed in close touch.'

That was a lot more than could be said for their respective political masters.

⁂

Bob Geldof had been in Downing Street many times before, but there was something special this time. He sat down on the left of Tony Blair at a long, polished oak table, around which sat the fifteen other members of the Commission for Africa, which had been called into being at his request. Twenty years earlier, through Live Aid, he had raised the largest amount ever collected for charity in human history. But that was millions. Today was the start, he hoped, of assembling *billions* to give Africa a fresh start.

He and I entered Downing Street together. I was to be his chief adviser on the commission, sitting just behind him at all the meetings. It gave me a ringside seat. 'I was bizarrely excited,' Bob remembered twenty years later. 'I never, I suppose, believed it could ever have got this far.' Outwardly, however, he did not publicly display any inkling of that. It was 4 May 2004 and the first meeting of the Commission for Africa. Tony Blair was upbeat. The commission would not duplicate, replace or undermine existing processes. It would support and encourage African leaders who had begun reform. It would offer a platform from which the UK could, through its presidencies of the G8 and the EU the following year, put Africa high on both agendas.

'This is why the commission has to be a powerful agitator for change,' he said. Then he introduced Bob.

'It was like a repeat of walking into the USA for Africa studio all over again!' said Geldof. 'Except Tony was Quincy and introduced me exactly like Quincy had: "We're all here 'cos of Bob and you all know him, of course..." The idea that they knew me seemed ridiculous. I'm the singer in the Boomtown Rats, for fuck's sake.' But, on the day, Geldof displayed no sign that that was what he was thinking.

Gordon Brown joined in. 'I remember Gordon picking up from Tony. I was just trying not to be the thick, scruffy doofus and maybe afraid of being patronised...' But the meeting was reminded that the following year would be both the twentieth anniversary of Live Aid and the twenty-fifth anniversary of the Brandt Commission. The group felt – to borrow a phrase which Blair had coined while negotiating peace in Northern Ireland a few years earlier – the hand of history upon their shoulders.

'To actually be creating thoughtful and new policy at the absolute top-most level of government national and international – and to be accepted by these extremely serious and often brilliant people, as someone who deserves and has a right to be there... Wow!' Geldof recalled. 'I was a bit embarrassed to be there. I wasn't sure I bore intellectual scrutiny in a room with that massed brain power, knowledge and expertise. Yet I didn't feel out of my depth because I knew precisely what I wanted out of this.'

For all that, Geldof knew that there was a lot of scepticism abroad about the commission. Many within Africa, and beyond, had greeted the idea with a sense of weariness. Similar initiatives had been tried before, and had failed time after time. Some Africans feared the commission was just a front behind which the West would impose another external agenda on the continent and that it would undermine African politicians' own initiatives.

Everyone in the room knew they had this cynicism to combat, but they were up for it. The commissioner from Tanzania, Anna Tibaijuka, said that both Africans and Westerners were responsible for the mess Africa was in – and both needed to act.

Ethiopia's prime minister, Meles Zenawi, looked around the long Downing Street table, at the collection of black and white faces, and told them that the fact the commission was composed of both Africans and non-Africans gave it a better chance of coming up with a package that really worked. Change would be required from African elites as well as Western ones.

✂

One of the first tasks in this inaugural meeting was to allocate areas of work. Geldof was asked to work on the idea of culture and participation. He was less than impressed. Other commissioners had been given economics, conflict and peace-making, health and education, natural resources, food security and good governance. 'I've been palmed off with a nice safe area where I could go and talk about African music,' he said to me. '"No," I said. "I think we can make something really fundamental out of this."'

If the Treasury thought that would keep him quiet, they were wrong. Culture is more than the arts, I told him. It is about shared patterns of identity. It is about how social values are transmitted and individuals are made to be part of a society. Culture explains why 'development' means one thing in our Western vocabulary but another thing entirely in Africa. In Europe and the United States, development is about increasing choice for individuals; in Africa, it is more about increasing human dignity within a community. Culture explains that difference. Culture is how the past interacts with the future. Together, Bob and I turned the whole subject upside down and made culture the basis of the commission's whole report.

Bob decided on a two-pronged approach. He and I would seek out new thinking from top intellectuals in the West, reaching out beyond the usual African experts. And we would travel through eleven different African countries to explore how much the continent had changed since our previous visits. While there, to spread the message back home, Bob would make a series of BBC One documentaries, *Geldof in Africa*, to be broadcast on the twentieth anniversary of Live Aid. It would put pressure on world leaders to implement the commission's recommendations.

Nick Stern was unenthusiastic. 'What are you and Bob going to find in Africa in two months that hasn't been found by people working on Africa all their lives or by the African commissioners who live there?' he asked.

But Geldof was fixed upon his course.

We organised what Bob called New Thinking seminars in London, Paris, Berlin, Rome and New York. 'We want some radical new thinking.

Let's get original thinkers in their own field and bring them together with some Africa experts to see if there's any lateral thinking they can do on Africa.'

The people we invited were told in advance to 'think outside the box'. But the box was not just the orthodox economics of the IMF, World Bank and Western bankers. It was also the standard aid agency critique of that. Participants were asked: 'What are the main obstacle to progress – inside Africa and in the West? What do Africans need to do? And what can rich countries do to change their policies which discriminate against Africa's development?' Geldof met individuals and groups from forty-nine different countries in Africa, and from every G8 country, plus China, and India. We received nearly 500 formal submissions.

What was missing were the views of Africans who now lived outside Africa. A seminar was organised with members of the African diaspora at Cumberland Lodge in Windsor Great Park. It turned out to feature what diplomats like to call a 'full and frank exchange of views'. The evening began with Bob asking for the views of the UK's African community, but it ended in a shouting match that nearly descended into a fistfight. It was recorded in the official Commission for Africa minutes thus:

> Mr Geldof's choice of words, comments and approach in address-
> ing the Africans present offended several of the participants and
> was deemed as unacceptable by the participants, some of whom
> expressed their displeasure to him after his speech.

What the diplomat who wrote the minutes omitted was that – after Bob had offered the meeting the chance to feed their ideas into the commission – some of the Africans accused Geldof 'like Livingstone before him' of representing 'the cultural arm of global capitalism'. His brand of humanitarianism served only to 'suppress African voices and aid the exploitation of the continent'.

Bob got angry. He responded that he had, for twenty years, been working with Africans and that Band Aid was giving money daily for African health and education. By contrast, most of the diaspora lived comfortable lives in Britain. They enjoyed expressing self-righteous indignation about colonialism and capitalism, but did little for their home countries. 'Why are only 6 per cent of diaspora remittances used for investment back home?' he asked, before finishing with a stinging peroration.

'Just look at you, sitting on your fat arses, while children in your countries starve.'

Interestingly, not all the Africans present were hostile. 'Geldof, with all his outbursts and outlandish ways, has been the only commissioner actively seeking engagement of Africans in the work of the commission,' wrote Tajudeen Abdul-Raheem, general-secretary of the Pan African Movement 'He has a track record of speaking truth to power internationally on global poverty, debt and suffering. He often rubs people the wrong way … but Africans in the Diaspora must learn not to throw the baby away with the bath water. They must work in concert with African groups in Africa.'

Nor were Geldof's fellow commissioners, Tony Blair and Gordon Brown, immune from his barbs. Two months after the inauguration of the commission, Bob was at a press conference in parliament where he turned his fire on the PM and chancellor. He told a meeting of thirty MPs and faith leaders that launching the commission was all well and good, but asked why didn't Brown 'put our money where his mouth is' and increase UK aid to the 0.7 per cent of our national income which the United Nations recommended every industrialised country should do.

'I'm sick of sitting with Tony and Gordon and hearing of grandiose schemes and guff about African scars,' he declared. 'If they really want to get rid of the scars and give the African Commission real credibility, then they must increase British aid to 0.7 per cent.'

No one, it seemed, was safe from Bob's moral indignation.

Three weeks later, Gordon Brown committed the Labour government to reach 0.7 per cent by 2013.

❊

In August 2004, Geldof was leaked a document with the title *Commission for Africa: Emerging Conclusions*. What was this? Whose conclusions could they be? As he began to read, it became clear. The paper claimed it was based on the first meeting of the Commission for Africa, with additional intensive discussions with individual commissioners, academics, think-tanks, private sector and NGOs. It had been sent to the prime minister.

Geldof was outraged. No one had had any discussion with him.

'This is utterly premature,' stormed Bob. 'No one can tell us what to think!'

The document was unsigned, but it was clear who was its author. Geldof rattled off a fierce letter to Nick Stern.

'Preparing conclusions at this stage seems to go beyond the role of civil servants,' he wrote. 'If I have got this wrong, please inform me so I may tender my resignation.'

'I remember Bob being really, really cross about it,' recalled Myles Wickstead. 'And he got a few of the other commissioners behind him on that, probably rightly as well.' Stern had acted prematurely. 'And it would have been better if he'd called it something other than *Emerging Conclusions*.'

Geldof began to worry that he and the other commissioners would simply get pulled along in Nick Stern's slipstream. Several anxieties now coalesced in Bob's mind. He had long ago feared that the commission's report would be 'dry and dull and full of impenetrable development jargon' if it were written by civil servants. Now he feared for its independence from the UK government and for the credibility it would have in the wider world. A few days later, he came to me and said: 'Vallely, you are going to have to write this report. I've got Blair's okay on this. We want something that's accessible to the general reader.'

CHAPTER 29

THE GIRL WHO CAME BACK FROM THE DEAD

There was a loud bang at the side of the road. The Land Rover veered off. Before Bob Geldof had time to think, all the doors of the vehicle were wrenched open by men in combat gear, wearing balaclavas. They pulled him by the hair and the arm into a ditch at the side of the road, screaming like wild men all the time. Guns were pointed in his face. He and the rest of the film crew were made to kneel with their hands on their heads.

The next thing they knew, they had been roughly hooded before being frogmarched down the road and into a building. They could not see where they were; they could only hear echoes from bare concrete and a tin roof. They were there for what seemed like hours, with their hands tied behind the chairs on which they sat. Then, one by one, the crew were taken out of the building. Geldof could hear muffled conversations outside and then a gunshot. Every time the same. Then they came for him.

The hood was jerked from his head. As he blinked his eyes against the sudden light, he saw a man in army fatigues pointing a pistol straight at his face.

'Your friends are all dead.'

'Well, that's a problem for you,' Geldof said.

The man with the gun stood silent.

'Our job is to interview your boss. We have got permission. It took us a long time. We've got the permits. Go and look in the car. You'll see we've got written permission from your commander to come and interview him.

It'll be first interview he's ever done. We are the BBC. And you are in deep fucking shit, mate, you know? Go and check the permits. My name is Bob. Check them out. My name is Bob Geldof. It's on the permit… Bob.'

Geldof talked on and on and on, without drawing breath.

'Look, this is a mistake. It's not your fault. You're just doing your job. But we have to be there by 5 p.m. this afternoon. If we're not there, you are in trouble.'

'Shut up.'

'Okay.'

Geldof shut up. For a few minutes.

Then he said: 'Honestly, if I was you, I'd check. I'm just giving you advice because I'm sure like me, you've got children. And from what I know about your boss, he doesn't take disobedience kindly. And what'll happen to your kids? What'll happen to my kids? You know, I've got a little girl. How many kids have you got?'

Bob was burbling on, but it wasn't random. He was recalling the advice he had been given about what to do if he were ever kidnapped. Tell them your name. Keep saying it. Mention your children as soon as you can. Ask them their name. Ask about their kids. Build a human relationship so that you are not just an anonymous figure in a deadly game.

There was one other piece of advice: never turn your back on a gun. It is much harder to shoot someone in the face than in the back of the head.

Geldof's film director, John Maguire, forgot that advice. He turned round when the gunman told him to. And the man in the balaclava pulled the trigger. The rest of the film crew made the same mistake.

The soldier was joined by two others.

'You're going to see the commander,' they told Geldof and took him into another room.

'About fucking time,' Geldof said. 'You made the right decision because I wouldn't fancy your chances if the commander doesn't get this interview.'

But when they got there, they told him to stand against the bare wall. All three of them cocked their handguns.

'You are never going to meet the commander. We don't believe a word of this. Turn around.'

Bob refused. Instead, he railed at the three men.

'How dare you? How fucking dare you? How dare you point a gun at me? Put those fucking guns down. When the commander hears about this, you are all fucking dead!'

He was in full flight now, ranting on for three or four minutes. At the end, one of the men dropped his gun to his side and spoke.

'Okay, mate. Off you go. You passed.'

Geldof had been kidnapped by former members of the SAS. It was a training exercise at the end of a week's residential course on how to survive in a hostile environment. Bob hadn't wanted to go on it. But when the BBC's insurers saw the list of places that he was to visit, they insisted. The trip had a dual purpose. He was making a series of six programmes on Africa for BBC One to mark the Live Aid anniversary, but he also wanted to examine his own preconceptions about Africa by testing them against the reality on the ground. In more than one place along the journey, he was to be grateful for the lessons the SAS training had taught him.

Our first stop was Somaliland. It seemed the safest place to start. To the south was Somalia, a failed state plagued by feuding warlords. But Somaliland, which had declared independence from its feral southern neighbour in 1991, was a place of relative peace and stability. When we landed in the capital, Hargeisa, an official asked us about our filming schedule.

'We want to go to the coast, to film at the spot where one morning, some 100,000 years ago, a group of early humans broke camp and set off walking north,' said John Maguire. In those days, he explained, there was no sea. What is now the continent of Africa was joined to the rest of the world by the Arabian peninsula. 'From that group, those first few individuals – the group may have been as small as fifty men, women and children – everyone in the rest of the world is descended.'

'Very interesting,' said the official, very uninterested. 'But first you will film an interview with the president.'

Geldof was, by now, too used to African protocol to protest.

'Let's get that out of the way and get off,' said Bob.

'Now we will give you a feast,' the president said, generously, at the end of the interview.

We left his carpeted air-conditioned rooms and went out into the sticky Hargeisa night. There were tables set out in the yard. At the front was a row of velour-clad sofas. 'It is a Somalia tradition before eating,' explained a luminary from the Ministry of Culture, 'to sing a song to welcome an honoured guest. The tradition is that the performers improvise the lyrics as they go along.'

Onto a flimsy podium came a group of disengaged-looking musicians. They rambled up to their instruments and looked at Geldof. 'Oh fuck,' Bob thought, 'they're going to ask me to sing.' To his relief, they didn't. Instead, three women singers stepped onto the stage.

'Bob Geel-duf,' they sang. 'Welcome! Welcome! Welcome!'

Bob smiled in appreciation and stole a surreptitious glance at his watch. The improvisation carried on for fifteen minutes without any real sense of variation and, rather disconcertingly, ended in a fit of giggles from the performers.

It was only later that he found that his name was intrinsically amusing. 'In Somali, *geel* means camel and *duf* means looter,' said the translator. 'Welcome Mr Geel-duf, most honourable camel-looter.'

The following day, we set out for Puntland, the northernmost region of Somalia, which, six years earlier, had declared itself an autonomous region, nominally part of the Somali federal government, but with its own government and security forces. There, Geldof encountered first-hand an example of how skewed Africa's trade was with the rest of the world.

The man in charge of the port of Bossaso had trained in Grimsby. Yahye Abdulla Mohammed showed us round the bustling quayside. There were dhows from India, from which teams of sweating stevedores were man-handling sacks of flour, cases of tomato paste and huge bundles of clothing in the mid-morning heat. There were tramp ships from Dubai, from which ancient cranes were winching television sets and fridges. There were dusty bulk-carriers from Oman carrying cement and other construction materials. There was a tanker with diesel oil from Iran. There was even a ship carrying sugar from Brazil. Elsewhere on the dockside were stacked huge piles of other imported goods: rice, palm oil, ginger, garlic.

'So what do you export from here?' Bob asked the man from Grimsby Technical College.

'Livestock,' Yahye said. Then he thought and augmented his one-word answer. 'And frankincense. To Saudi and the Emirates.'

There, in that one little port, is the story of Africa's problems with trade.

'It imports everything. And exports fuck-all,' as Geldof succinctly put it. 'Why is Africa poor? Because it does not trade enough. Look at the history of the world over the last century and you'll see that it is trade that usually drives economic growth.' That was the story in Europe and the US, then Japan, then Singapore and the other East Asian tiger economies, and more recently, India and China. 'Trade is what has transformed other countries which were once classed as underdeveloped. Two decades ago, 70 per cent of the goods exported from developing countries, particularly in Asia, were raw materials. Today, 80 per cent of exports from those countries are in manufactured goods.'

But not in Africa. 'The last twenty years, by contrast, have seen Africa's share of world trade fall from around 6 per cent to just 2 per cent, often because of all the trade walls that we have erected against them. Africa has been left behind. And the task of catching up gets harder every day.'

Back in the 1960s, as the world's former colonies began to become independent, the place everyone worried about was Asia. It had a huge population and big problems. The people of Africa were poor, too, but they had vast riches in the form of gold, diamonds, copper and ground so fertile that plants seemed to grow overnight wherever you dropped a seed the day before. Africans earned double what Asians did. Africa would be all right.

Forty years on and things were decidedly not all right. 'Today, Africa is the poorest region in the world,' I told Bob. 'Half of the population live on less than one dollar a day. Life expectancy is actually falling. People live, on average, to the age of just forty-six. In India and Bangladesh, by contrast, that figure is now a staggering seventeen years higher.'

Why had Africa fallen so far behind? Set a map of Africa's railways alongside those of India and you see why. India's railways join up the subcontinent; Africa's merely link the mines and plantations to the ports. On the Indian sub-continent, an effective colonial administrative system was established. But Africa emerged from the colonial era with far weaker admin systems. By the 1970s, south Asia was expanding, building roads, railways and ports, educating its workforce and building up manufacturing industry. But Africa stuck to exporting minerals and crops, for which world prices were falling.

Until Africa built its ability to produce more goods, and better infrastructure to cut the cost of trading, it would remain in an economic ditch,

Geldof thought. Rich nations were not helping here. They were hindering Africa's economic development by slapping import tariffs on African goods as they entered rich countries' markets. Without that, Africa would continue to rely on crops like cocoa, the price of which had fallen by 70 per cent in the previous two decades, or coffee, which was down 64 per cent, or cotton, down 47 per cent.

'Unless that changes, ports like Bossaso will continue to have a list of exports as long as your arm and a list of imports that can be written on the back of a postage stamp,' Geldof expostulated. 'And if that imbalance continues – with all the poverty and hardship that implies – we should not be surprised one day to see not just Yahye Abdulla Mohammed but his entire people turning up in Grimsby.'

❖

Back in Britain, Bono was fighting the same fight at a different level. The prime minister had invited him to address the Labour Party conference at the end of September 2004. Blair and Brown saw him as someone who could help rally public support and energise civil society around their development agenda. Bono's presence, they thought, would give it an international platform.

But the U2 frontman had not immediately accepted the invitation. 'We knew that, despite the Commission for Africa, there was still talk in Number 10 of limiting the G8 agenda at Gleneagles to girls' education and AIDS,' said Bono's chief of staff, Lucy Matthew, 'towards those with micro initiatives. We wanted something bigger on Africa.'

The prime minister's head of events, Kate Garvey, handled the arrangements for the speech with Bono's staff at DATA. 'They were incredibly impressive, committed, tough,' she recalled. 'They were negotiating the whole time. "Bono will say this if you promise to do that." And they really went to the wire with it. In Downing Street, we took them really seriously. We could see the value they put behind Bono's image and endorsement, and they were not going to give it without extracting something from us. It was very clever advocacy.'

The content of the speech did, indeed, go down to the wire. The DATA strategists were still writing it late in the evening, the night before Bono was due to speak. They needed the singer to sign off on it and he was nowhere to be found. He had gone for a drink in the prime minister's room.

'Lucy was pulling her hair out,' said another key member of the DATA staff, Zita Lloyd. '"He was meant to be here half an hour ago."' So Zita set out to find the errant rock star. Navigating the corridors, she found the prime minister's room, guarded by two police officers.

'I work with Bono,' she told them. 'I've come to fetch him because he's been too long and we need him.'

The two policemen exchanged a glance. 'I think they were having a bit of a chuckle at me,' Zita recalled.

'Just go in and get him,' one of them said. 'Just open the door.'

Zita turned the handle and put her head round the door.

'There was Tony Blair, in his pyjamas, just chilling out in his room, hanging out with Bono, having a drink at the end of a long day. Bono looked up and saw me and gave me a look. I thought, *Oh no I've really done the wrong here thing here. The cops have really set me up.* So I just sort of looked at Bono, gave him a look as if to say "Come on, hurry up" and withdrew quickly.'

As she closed the door, she could see the policeman laughing.

'I was no doubt blushing madly, having seen the prime minister in his pyjamas.'

The following day, Bono wooed the Labour conference with his characteristic mix of humour, flattery and coercion. 'I've come because Prime Minister Blair asked me,' he began. 'He might well regret it.'

First, he made the moral case for helping Africa on a massive scale. 'Africa makes a fool of our idea of justice. It makes a farce of our idea of equality. It mocks our pieties, it doubts our concern, it questions our commitment. Deep down, if we really accepted that Africans were equal to us, we would all do more to put the fire out.'

Then he made the muscular case. 'The war against terror is bound up in the war against poverty – I didn't say that, Colin Powell said that. And when a military man from the right starts talking like that, maybe we should listen. Africa is not the frontline on the war against terror, but it could be soon. Justice is the surest way to get to peace.'

Then he turned his attention to the prime minister and chancellor of the exchequer.

'I want to say a few words about two remarkable men. Like a lot of great partners, they didn't always get along as the years passed. They didn't always agree. They drifted apart. They did incredible things on their own, as individuals. But they did their best work as a pair. I love them both: John Lennon and Paul McCartney.

'I'm also fond of Tony Blair and Gordon Brown. They are kind of the John and Paul of the global development stage, in my opinion. But the point is, Lennon and McCartney changed my interior world – Blair and Brown can change the real world.'

One journalist in the room noted that Blair and Brown grinned away like autograph-hunting schoolboys as the U2 man made this point. But Bono was about to use the conference to hold them to account.

'I've met people whose lives will depend on the decisions taken by these two great men. They have great ideas. And the promises they have already made will save hundreds of thousands of lives – if they follow through...

'Don't let them forget who they are. Promise me that, conference.'

He ended with a reprimand to Blair over the invasion of Iraq, but neatly turned it into a call for common purpose. 'I know that on certain issues this room is already divided. I know many people – and I include myself – were very unhappy about the war in Iraq. Still are. But ending extreme poverty, disease and despair – this is one thing everybody can agree on... I don't care if you are Old Labour or New Labour, what is your party about if it's not about this, if it's not about equality, about justice, the right to make a living, the right to go on living?

'We have the cash, we have the drugs, we have the science – but do we have the will? Do we have the will to make poverty history? Some say we can't afford to. I say we can't afford not to.'

The speech was a tour de force. The conference loved it. The media worldwide reported it. And it pushed Africa back to the top of the political agenda, exactly as Blair and Brown wanted.

It is a 2,000-mile journey from the Mediterranean, down the Nile to Gojjam in the remote western highlands of Ethiopia. There, the river plunges down a waterfall 150 feet high and 1,000 feet wide in the rainy season. The vast gush sends water vapour so high into the air that the Blue Nile Falls are known in Amharic as Tis Abay – the Great Smoke. It's a difficult place to get to and not many tourists make it there.

Bob Geldof stood looking across at the mighty falls, having lofty thoughts, when a small boy approached.

'He wants to know where you are from,' said the translator.

'England,' said Bob.

'Ah,' said the small boy. 'David Beckham.'

The same thing happened the time that Geldof travelled to Mali and ventured out far into the Sahara to the ancient city of Timbuktu, a place so remote it was once a byword for the ends of the earth. David Beckham had got there before him too.

'England? David Beckham. He miss goal Euro 2000.'

'Yes, we know that, thank you very much.'

The entire continent was gripped by the footballer. He was one of the biggest brands in Africa, the marketing men said: Coca-Cola, the BBC and David Beckham. Satellite dishes pointed straight up at the Equator. 'There's no pissing about trying to angle it,' Geldof said. 'Boosh, up it goes, point straight up at the sky, thank you very much. Arsenal vs Man Utd live.' That was what they had been watching in Lalibela, the cradle of Ethiopian Christianity, when Bob arrived there.

It was a testament to the technological revolution via which Africa had leapfrogged straight into the wireless era. Dusty little towns, which had no school or clinic, had thriving internet shops and cafés. The use of mobile phones had increased in Africa far faster than anywhere else in the world. Some 75 per cent of all telephones in Africa were mobile. Pre-paid phone cards had become a form of electronic currency. Cellphones were used to collect healthcare data or, by one farmer we met, to discover whether he would get a better price for his tomatoes in the market to the south or the one to the north. The mobile phone was creating virtual infrastructures and raising the possibility of dramatic transformations in African society, economies and politics. Where 20 per cent of a population have access to cellphones and text messaging, dictatorial or totalitarian regimes find it hard to retain power.

Still, it was ruining Bob's stereotypes of African mystique and isolation. Despairing that there wasn't anywhere in Africa that they hadn't heard of David Beckham, he tried a new tack.

'Where are you from?' asked another small boy.

'Ireland,' replied Bob.

'Ah,' said the child. 'Roy Keane!'

⁂

The night before Tony Blair was due to fly to Ethiopia, on Tuesday 5 October 2004, a COBRA meeting was held. COBRA is shorthand for the senior UK government committee that is convened in one of the Cabinet Office Briefing Rooms during moments of national emergency. The intelligence services had received reports that Islamic extremists in Somalia were plotting to fire a missile at the prime minister's plane as it came in to land at Addis Ababa, where Blair would be attending the second meeting of the Commission for Africa at the headquarters of the African Union. Senior members of the secret service, military officials, close protection officers and senior civil servants gathered to assess the level of danger.

'Everyone was sitting round, all these civil servants, weighing up how reliable was the intel, how risky this was and what could be done to reduce the dangers,' recalled Laurie Lee, the prime minister's private secretary on African affairs. 'I was sitting next to one of the close protection officers from Number 10 who turned to me and said, "You know, we are the only two in this room who're actually gonna be sitting on this plane" as everybody else talked about how much risk they were willing to take with it.'

The decision was made that the flight would go ahead, but that the plane would 'land dark' as they called it. 'So, basically, you turn off all the lights on the plane, so it's not obvious that it's got a great big British Airways Union Jack on the tail fin,' said Lee, who had only arrived in Downing Street a few months earlier. 'It was an interesting introduction to the sort of security that happens around world leaders.'

In the event, the plane landed without incident and the commission assembled at the headquarters of the African Union. Located on Roosevelt Street, it had been built by the China State Construction Engineering Corporation as a gift from the Chinese government on the site of an old prison used during the Italian occupation of Ethiopia. It felt like a symbol of Africa's past, present and future.

In an impassioned forty-minute public speech in the Africa Hall before the commission's meeting, Blair announced that Africa would be central to his chairmanship of the G8 in 2005, which he described as 'a year of decision for Africa'. In a nod to George Bush's War on Terror, and acknowledging that al-Qaeda had bases in Africa, he declared 'poverty and instability lead to weak states'. Two of the biggest threats to progress in Africa were disease and conflict. That progress must be led by Africans, but it needed the assistance of the rich world. In defence of his commitment to Africa, Blair ended: 'I know that however difficult politics is, there is at least one noble cause worth fighting for, and it is here, on this continent... Two groups of human beings recognising what they have in common – and what they could share in common.'

When the commission's private session began, Bob Geldof – looking unusually respectable in a blue pinstripe suit, purple checked shirt and tie, and black trainers – presented a paper to his fellow commissioners. It argued that reflecting on Africa's culture should not be seen as some bolt-on afterthought to the commission's working. It should, rather, be seen as integral to the process of working out why some things have worked, and others failed, in African initiatives over the past two decades.

'If we ask the big question "What is development for?", we get very different answers in different places. The terms of the debate carry very different meanings in different cultures. Ideas which are not premised on the culture of Africa won't work.'

He had begun to look at Africa differently, he said, as he had travelled through the continent in recent months. 'In the West, people assume development is a progress from tradition to modernity,' Bob said. 'If the commission thinks this, we will fail.'

Last month in war-torn Somalia, he told his fellow commissioners, he had come across a doctor using half-traditional, half-Western methods. He was replacing shattered limbs by implanting camel bones into the legs of men and goat bones into the heads of children – sterilised with a mixture of camel's milk and frankincense – and then treated with antibiotics.

'Amazingly, it worked,' said Geldof. 'Tradition and modernity were not opposites, or a starting and a finishing point, but something which fused to make a singular African solution.'

What was true in medicine was true for wider society. Why, he asked, is Somalia a place of violent warlord anarchy and Somaliland a place of modest but ordered prosperity?

For centuries, Somalia had been a place of feuding clans. These clans policed themselves using the Tol, a phrase which literally means 'my clan come to me'. When a Somali was in trouble, he would shout 'Tol, Tol' and the members of his tribal group would fly to his aid. Contrary-wise, a victim of a crime did not seek redress from the wrongdoer, but from his Tol. If a man steals a camel, his clansmen will say: 'Where did you get that?' They then tell him, 'Well, take it back or else his clan will come to us and demand that we all pay compensation.'

In war-torn Somalia, the Tol had collapsed. But in Somaliland, it had been retained to maintain order between the area's five rival clans. More than that, it had actually been elevated to the status of the second chamber of parliament. 'It is not a system which any bright young Harvard politics graduate would have thought of inventing,' Geldof told his fellow commissioners, 'but there was no doubt that it was an effective system of peer-group pressure. Adding it alongside the "one-person-one-vote" first chamber of parliament created an odd mix of African and Western systems of government. But it works. The challenge is to find such hybrids for the rest of Africa.'

When the commission came to write its report, said the Ugandan commissioner, William Kalema, it should include such imaginative material and draw on traditional African forms of cultural communication, such as fables.

'We want a bestseller,' said the Ugandan commissioner, looking at me.

Until the lions have spoken, the only history will be that of the hunters. The lions were now about to speak.

✳

There was one more thing before they left Ethiopia. An enterprising journalist from the *Sun*, Oliver Harvey, had decided to mark the tenth anniversary of Live Aid by trying to track down the girl whose photograph had stunned the 1985 Wembley concert into silence. Might she still be alive? Providentially, she had survived and Harvey found her. Would Blair and Geldof like to meet her after the commission meeting?

After the meeting, and the subsequent press conference, the pair were led into an anteroom with creaky wooden sofas covered in white throws. After a couple of minutes, an interconnecting door was opened and in walked Birhan Woldu. This was the three-year-old who had been given only minutes to live on the screen at Live Aid. Now aged twenty-four, she looked like a princess, with her hair styled in Tigrayan braids that cascaded in curls over a plain white dress with a panel embroidered from neck to hem. The two men were shocked into open-mouthed silence. She gave a shy smile and extended an elegant hand to the prime minister.

The *Sun* reporter passed Tony Blair a photograph of Birhan as she had been discovered by the CBC team back in 1984 – emaciated and dehydrated, with her eyes half-closed and her parched lips wide open. But he did not need to see it. He was one of the Live Aid generation whose memories were seared with the images seen on the Wembley screen back in 1985. It had been the single most memorable image at the concert. Blair's eyes filled with tears as the translator told him Birhan was now studying plant science studies at university and dreamed of being a nurse.

This one single individual brought home to the British prime minister the reality of what aid and development meant. Here, before him, was the miraculous proof that aid saves lives. Ethiopia's narrative need not be one of endless tragedy and failure.

'I remember her coming in,' Blair said twenty years later. 'She had a great presence about her.'

'I gave Tony Blair a Lalibela cross as a gift,' she later said. 'He encouraged me to be strong and said he would place the gift in his office to remember me always. I felt as if I had a protector, someone who would support me. It gave me a unique sense of reassurance.'

Blair was visibly emotional. He told the famine survivor that he would treasure it and put it above his fireplace when he returned to London.

'It was a very moving meeting,' he recalled later. 'In politics, you don't often get many moments where you think, *Well, that was good. We did that.* She brought home to me that the whole thing that we were trying to do was important. Many people didn't survive, weren't surviving, but her being there was a representation of the fact it *was* possible to do something.'

The encounter filled him with determination that he would make Gleneagles a meaningful summit – a place where 'we were going to try to do huge things on Africa'.

⁂

But events now took a dark turn. Bob Geldof and I were sitting in the hotel bar, discussing the events of the day, when he received a message asking him to go to see Tony Blair. Bob went down the corridor, where he met the prime minister and his aides who were clearly in a rush.

'I've got to go back to London,' Blair told Geldof.

'You can't,' said Bob. 'What about tomorrow?' There was a final session of the commission the following day at which Geldof and other commissioners wanted to express anxiety about the way British civil servants were communicating with them.

Blair looked solemnly at Geldof.

His office had just received a secret communication which said that fears were growing that the British engineer Ken Bigley had been killed by his terrorist kidnappers in Iraq.

Bob was utterly shocked. Moments ago, he had been irritated about the truncation of the commission meeting. Now he was aghast and appalled. 'I was filled with an aching sympathy for the man. He was in deep, deep pain. You could see the anguish,' said Bob as soon as Blair had gone.

Geldof knew that Ken Bigley had been abducted three weeks earlier along with two American colleagues, who had both then been executed. A week before the Addis meeting, Bigley appeared in a video pleading for his life. Directly appealing to Blair, he begged the prime minister to help secure his release, saying: 'I need you to help me now, Mr Blair, because you are the only person on God's earth who can help me.' The kidnappers had said he would only be released in exchange for women being held by the US and UK in prisons in Iraq.

What Geldof did not know then was that, four days earlier, a man had approached the British Embassy in Baghdad, offering to pass messages directly between the Blair government and the kidnappers. The British foreign secretary Jack Straw had then flown to Iraq and exchanged messages with the captors in an attempt to dissuade them from carrying out their threats to kill Ken Bigley. All the messages, which emphasised that there were no Iraqi women in British custody, had been approved by Blair. Ken Bigley's family in Liverpool and his wife in Thailand were kept fully aware of the communications with the intermediary. But the terrorists had refused to drop their demands.

Blair and Geldof stood and looked at one another. Bob spoke first. Reaching out and putting his hand on the prime minister's arm, he said: 'There's nothing you can do.'

Blair stood silent. There were tears in his eyes.

'It's not your fault.' Geldof kept talking, to fill the void. 'They are doing this, not you.'

Blair said nothing and hurried away. He had to get back to London.

The burden of power registered with Geldof in that moment. Just three days before the trip to Addis, Blair had undergone a two-and-a-half-hour operation to correct an irregular heartbeat. Despite that, he had flown to Ethiopia for the second meeting of the Commission for Africa – making a surprise stop in Khartoum to press the Sudanese president to act on the humanitarian crisis in Darfur. All the while, he had been keeping abreast of the communications with the Iraqi terrorists. Now, the enormous weight of all that was evident in his pale face.

At 10.30 p.m., Blair's plane left Bole airport to return to London. If those awful unconfirmed reports turned out to be true, he had to be in Downing Street to respond. After he had gone, Geldof reflected on his words to the PM as he was leaving. 'I said what I had to say, but it in no way comforted him. Tony Blair may have made the wrong decision over invading Iraq, but he is a good man, a very good leader and a very significant prime minister. I don't think there was anything else he could have done to save Ken Bigley.' Then Bob, too, fell silent.

That night had, to Geldof, summed up something quintessential about power. First Birhan, and then Ken Bigley. 'A strange awful night, when so many good things were happening, when he had joy in what he could do with power, where he could feel precisely why he had ever bothered to want this job,' Geldof reflected. 'And then this terrible graphic illustration of the consequences of wielding power.'

It also revealed something about the relationship between Geldof and Blair. 'Tony didn't really talk properly to people he didn't trust,' said his special adviser Justin Forsyth, years later. 'But he and Bob would speak to each other openly and honestly. There was no kind of wall between them, or holding back. Tony did that with very few people in the end. He did it with Bob. He let his guard down and he talked openly. He really trusted him and he trusted Bob's political judgement on where the British public were.'

The next day, the kidnappers released a video of the British hostage being decapitated.

Blair, now speaking from Chequers, told the television cameras: 'I feel desperately sorry for Ken Bigley and his family, who have behaved with extraordinary dignity and courage. I feel utter revulsion at the people who did this, not just the barbaric nature of the killing but the way, frankly, they played the situation in the past few weeks.' At his memorial service in Liverpool's Anglican Cathedral a month later, the prime minister escorted Ken Bigley's eighty-six-year-old mother Lil to her seat.

❖

As soon as he was back in London, Geldof wrote to Blair to set out 'some key thoughts post-Addis'. The commission 'is on course to produce something important and interesting,' he wrote.

Traditionally in international trade negotiations, there is a simple rule. Both sides have to get something out of every deal. If the UK makes a concession, so must Ethiopia. In the jargon, this is called reciprocal liberalisation. This must not be the case for the commission, Geldof told Blair. 'The idea that we have to get something out of any negotiations in which we give something to Africa is morally repugnant,' he wrote. 'It doesn't grow out of any serious economic need.' It was a matter of political ideology. Such an idea should have no part in commission thinking, he insisted.

At the Addis meeting, Geldof had called for aid to Africa to be quadrupled. South Africa's finance minister Trevor Manuel had argued against that. Africa didn't have the 'absorptive capacity' to do that.

'What does that mean?' asked Geldof.

'We haven't got enough engineers, surveyors, road builders, water and sanitation experts, project managers, doctors, teachers and educated administrators to be able to spend that much aid effectively.'

Bob reluctantly accepted the point – for the time being. But, in the letter, he now told Blair: 'We need to build that capacity. In the medium term, Africa can receive as much aid as we are prepared to build the capacity for.'

No 10 took Geldof's input seriously. 'Bob was just a force of nature,' said Blair's senior aide, Kate Garvey. 'He was driving the political agenda inside government, which was incredible.'

A week later, the prime minister sent a handwritten reply. It summed up Tony Blair's approach to politics. A sense of moral purpose was intermingled with an eye for what was politically achievable.

Blair then set out a tactical plan for achieving that. G8 governments should be pushed hard on trade where it was hard for them to publicly resist basic moral arguments about the need to remove unfair barriers to Africa's trade. But G8 leaders should each be allowed to come up with different ways of paying for the extra aid and debt cancellations that the commission would demand. This would allow the report to make some radical demands.

Blair's thinking in all this was visionary, but his tactics were those of practical politics. It was a characteristic combination. Geldof gave it the thumbs-up.

❊

A few weeks later, Geldof was back in Africa, this time in the Democratic Republic of Congo. It was the most dangerous part of his trip, with remnants of Rwandan Hutu militias, local warlords and other rebel factions fighting each other and the national army. Ethnic tensions coupled with competition over land and resources – particularly gold and coltan – fuelled violence. Despite the presence of a UN peacekeeping force, massacres, rape, abductions and looting were endemic. The conflict created one of the world's worst humanitarian crises. Three million people had been killed in the past six years.

Congo was one of the worst places in the world for child soldiers. There were tens of thousands who were active combatants, porters, labourers, spies and sex slaves. They were commonly abducted, indoctrinated, drugged or brutalised to ensure their compliance. Geldof was headed for a project which aimed to demobilise and rehabilitate them.

Ten-year-old girls make good child soldiers, Bob discovered in Kinshasa. The braver and more brutal they were, the more their status rose. They gained respect. They stopped being beaten. They stopped being raped. But once they had been rescued, they had to be taught how to play again. The Commission for Africa report would underscore the importance of international support in strengthening African institutions to protect such children. It would call for greater investment in education and economic opportunities as long-term solutions to reduce the vulnerability of children to recruitment by armed groups.

There was an unspoken tension in the vehicle in which they travelled back to the airport. Kidnappings, ambushes and looting of convoys were common along this road. Everyone in the vehicle fell silent as they entered a section of the road which their translator said was known locally as Snipers' Alley. The driver turned off the headlights.

Geldof's cellphone rang. It was his daughter, Pixie, back in Battersea.

'Can I go on a sleepover tonight, Dad?'

The driver put his foot down. 'Keep your heads down,' he shouted.

'Have you done your homework?' Bob asked, keeping his head down. 'Okay, get it finished and you can go.'

Pixie was fourteen years old – easily old enough to be a child soldier.

CHAPTER 30

BONO AND RICHARD START PLOTTING

A new generation of pop stars now came on board with the Live Aid message. In the run-up to the twentieth anniversary of 'Do They Know It's Christmas?', Midge Ure was besieged with calls from the press asking if Band Aid would be doing a remix of the original song. No, he kept telling them. But news of famine in Darfur and the launch of the Live Aid DVD early in November 2004 only intensified the media interest.

'There was nothing to remix,' said Midge. 'Because we only had twenty-four hours to do the whole thing, it was the barest, most minimalist recording. None of the artists had sung the lyrics all the way through so you couldn't do a remix of the vocal parts.'

Then Bob Geldof rang.

Midge found he was re-doing the song for Christmas 2004.

'For about ten minutes, I thought about re-recording it myself,' Midge recalled. But then it would end up sounding just like the 1984 version. 'Fresh blood was needed. I thought, *Who's the biggest record producer right now?*' Nigel Godrich was the obvious choice. He'd made huge albums with Radiohead and Travis, worked with U2 and R.E.M., and was busy recording in LA with Paul McCartney. Godrich agreed immediately. Bob swiftly roped in Chris Martin from Coldplay and Fran Healy from Travis.

Twenty years after that first landmark recording, they did not restrict themselves to those they could get into a studio together at the same time. Paul McCartney was, this time, determined not to miss out. He agreed to come into the Mayfair studios the day before the main recording to form a supergroup for the day: McCartney on bass, Fran Healy on acoustic guitar and singing the guide vocal, Thom Yorke and Jonny Greenwood from Radiohead on piano and guitar, and Danny Goffey from Supergrass on drums. Where Midge Ure had carefully sequenced the original recording, Nigel Godrich encouraged the musicians to interact. 'The result was very organic,' said Midge. 'It sounds different from the original, it's got a proper live feel to it.'

In 1984, there had been huge time pressure to get the recording done in one day. But Godrich had the luxury of several days' recording, as well as dropping in contributions from elsewhere. Robbie Williams and Dido recorded their parts from Los Angeles and Melbourne respectively. Dizzee Rascal dropped in some counterpoint rap, which he wrote on the spot in the studio. Sugababes and Tom Chaplin from Keane came in the day before the main recording to do their vocals, while Justin and Dan Hawkins arrived to add the twin-guitar sound of the Darkness to the end of the track.

On the day of the recording, 14 November 2004, a galaxy of music stars assembled at Sir George Martin's Air Studio in Hampstead. Among the forty singers were Chris Martin, Will Young, Joss Stone, Natasha Bedingfield, Ms Dynamite, Estelle, Jamelia, Katie Melua, Beverley Knight and Gary Lightbody of Snow Patrol. Damon Albarn was there, but he didn't sing. Instead, he designated himself 'tea boy', wandering in and out of the studio wearing a pink apron and carrying a tray of cups of tea.

Just before they started recording the 'Feed the World' chorus, Bob Geldof gathered all the singers together in front of a screen. He wanted to show the young stars – many of them barely old enough to remember the 1984 reports which had so shocked the world – the heart-wrenching video which had stunned the Live Aid audience into silence twenty years before. He played the chilling edit of famine footage Colin Dean had cut to the Cars song 'Drive'.

'I thought breaking up the recording session to show the video was a bad idea,' confessed Midge Ure. 'I hadn't seen it for twenty years. The footage of that child spending two and a half minutes trying to stand up was as hideous as ever. Everyone had a lump in their throat. Jamelia walked away from the screen because she couldn't bear to watch it. Joss Stone was in floods of tears.'

But, as the video reached the dehydrated features of a three-year-old girl, Geldof stopped the tape. He signalled to the door of a side room and out walked Birhan Woldu, the child whom death could not claim.

'This beautiful and intelligent woman,' Bob told the twenty-first-century Band Aid stars, 'and thousands of others like her, are here today because of what Band Aid did twenty years ago.'

'The same little girl who'd been dying in front of their eyes on the TV screen was standing there, beautiful and sparkling with life,' said Midge. 'She was the living, breathing example of what Band Aid and all the other charities had achieved.'

'I don't think there was a dry eye in the room,' said Natasha Bedingfield. 'Seeing someone who had been so close to death looking so healthy made me realise that doing this really can help people.'

A new generation had taken on the Band Aid mantle. Africa was back at the top of the political agenda.

There was one late arrival in the studio. When all the recording seemed complete, something was bothering Midge Ure. Several versions of the song's most controversial line – 'Well tonight, thank God it's them instead of you' – had been recorded, but none of them made the hairs stand up on the back of the neck the way Bono's original had done in 1984.

Robbie Williams had done a version from LA.

Bono had sent a version down the line from Dublin, 'but it was half-hearted,' said Midge. 'He sang it like he didn't want to do it. It didn't have the same spark as the original. We tried to mix that in, but it sounded wrong.'

Justin Hawkins desperately wanted to sing the line. 'He sang it really well in a Justin way, with a big octave jump and all of that, but to me it sounded jokey.'

So Bob called Bono, who was in Dublin.

'Can you get over here? You have to come and do the line.'

'Next thing I know is that Bono *is* coming after all. He's jumped on his private jet. So we waited and he walked in. He sang it differently, but he sang it properly. He sang it with passion.'

Bono didn't confine his passion to the singing. Someone else had been present at the recording: Richard Curtis, fresh from his triumph

◄ 1999: Bono hands John Paul II his tinted sunglasses for the Pontiff to try on.

▼ The Commission for Africa, seen here at its first meeting in Downing Street in May 2004. Tony Blair made Geldof a member. He did not know what he was letting himself in for.

◤ Perhaps the most powerful ally in Live Aid's struggle for justice was Nelson Mandela. In February 2005, Bob Geldof introduced him to crowds of Make Poverty History supporters at a mass rally in Trafalgar Square calling him 'the unofficial president of the world'.

◢ At the end of a long day's recording of the Band Aid 20 charity single in Air Studio, London, Midge Ure reads the report in the next day's edition of the *Sun* newspaper.

(All images: Getty)

Commission for Africa

The British government was fully behind the Commission for Africa but other world leaders were not. Geldof decided to stage concerts in the world's eight most powerful nations. Live 8 was launched by Bob along with Elton John, Midge Ure, French politician Jack Lang, Harvey Goldsmith, Richard Curtis and Band Aid lawyer John Kennedy in May 2005. (Getty)

Bob Geldof and Paul Vallely board a helicopter in Battersea to fly into Hyde Park for the London Live 8 concert — one of ten simultaneous gigs in Philadelphia, Berlin, Rome, Paris, Tokyo, Ontario, Moscow, Cornwall and Johannesburg. (Paul Vallely)

Bob Geldof and Paul Vallely on the Live 8 stage. (Paul Vallely)

▲ It was twenty years ago today: Paul McCartney and U2 open the Live 8 concert on 2 July 2005 in London's Hyde Park.

▼ Madonna and the twenty-four-year-old student Birhan Woldu, the inspiration for Live Aid 1985, together on stage during Live 8 in 2005. Twenty years before, Birhan had been given ten minutes to live at a famine clinic in Ethiopia.

(Images: Getty)

▲ Just before Robbie Williams took to the Live 8 stage the police threatened to turn off all the power because the show was overrunning. A government minister intervened and Robbie drew the biggest television audience of the Hyde Park concert. (Getty)

▲ Comfortably numb: The reformed Pink Floyd receive the audience's rapturous applause after performing together for the first time in two decades. David Gilmour, Roger Waters, Nick Mason and Rick Wright – reunited but not reconciled… (Getty)

▲ Bob Geldof, three days after the Live 8 concerts, boards a train for Edinburgh to join the Long Walk to Justice. A quarter of a million Make Poverty History supporters were assembling on the eve of Gleneagles to demand a doubling of aid and a cancelling of debt for Africa.

◀ Tony Blair, Bob Geldof and Kenyan Nobel Peace Prize winner Wangari Maathai are upbeat at a press conference the night before the G8 Gleneagles summit on 6 July 2005. The delegation from Live 8 and Make Poverty History were lobbying for the ninety recommendations of the Commission for Africa to be implemented in full.

(Images: Getty)

▲ Bono and Bob meet with George and Laura Bush. The US president had been deeply moved when Birhan stepped out with Madonna on the Live 8 stage. The singers pushed him to give more for girls' education and anti-AIDS drugs for all of Africa.

▶ The German chancellor was jovial when Bob and Bono lobbied him. But he did not commit to what they wanted. So Bono told Gerhard Schröder that he would denounce him from the stage at U2's Berlin gig two days later – or praise him if he delivered...

(Images: Getty)

◀ Through his interpreter, Bob and Bono ask French president, Jacques Chirac, to stop unfairly subsidising French farmers to export at prices that ruin the market for African farmers. (Getty)

▶ Behind the scenes at Gleneagles, UN secretary-general Kofi Annan advises Bob and Bono as they start to worry their demands might not be delivered. When the results are announced he declares Gleneagles 'the greatest summit for Africa ever'. (Getty)

◀ The G8 signed the cheque, but would they pay out? For the next five years Geldof and Bono relentlessly pursued world leaders to make sure they delivered on their Gleneagles promises. Bob lobbies George Bush at the G8 summit in Heiligendamm in 2007. (Getty)

◤ Forty years on, a West End musical about Live Aid is produced. Bob Geldof and Midge Ure return to Wembley Stadium in May 2025 to launch *Just For One Day: The Live Aid Musical*. (Getty)

▲ On the fortieth anniversary of the Live Aid concert a gala performance is held. John Kennedy, Midge Ure, Harvey Goldsmith and Bob Geldof appear on stage after the show at the Shaftesbury Theatre on 13 July 2025. Brian May tells the audience: 'This is not just a musical. This is the continuation of a project for humanity'. (Getty)

▶ Official Band Aid and Live Aid memorabilia on display at the Live Aid 40 exhibition at the British Music Experience in August 2025. After forty years locked in a storage time-capsule, the original merchandise was sold, with profits going to the Band Aid Trust. (Private)

Who would have thought it? Bob Geldof at Heathrow Airport in December 1984. Forty years on, Live Aid remains a defining moment in musical and humanitarian history. It was, says Harvey Goldsmith, 'a bold, chaotic, and surprising endeavour that united the world for a cause greater than ourselves'. Its legacy lives yet. (Getty)

as the writer and director of *Love Actually*, with the second *Bridget Jones* film completed but not yet released. On his wrist he wore a prototype of the white band that would soon become the emblem of the Make Poverty History movement. That year alone, he had raised £73 million through Comic Relief. But, like Bob and Bono, he had come to the conclusion that charity was not enough. Massive political change was needed for Africa to make the major economic and social breakthrough it required.

Richard invited Bono back to his home in Notting Hill. There, in the first-floor drawing room, the two men agreed that the meeting of world leaders at the G8 Gleneagles summit could prove the nodal point in their twenty years of campaigning for Africa. But to prod the politicians into action required a mass mobilisation of the public.

Live Aid was the model to which they both kept returning. Bob Geldof's extraordinary power to galvanise people to act was clear. The release of the Live Aid DVD was a reminder of this, as was the way he had just handled a new generation of pop stars in the Band Aid 20 recording, and the way he had cajoled Tony Blair into starting the Commission for Africa.

'We need another Band Aid single,' they said to one another. 'Or another Live Aid concert.'

Both had said it individually to Bob.

Both had been told, in no uncertain terms, that he was not interested.

'Live Aid 2 will just be a pale shadow of the original,' Bob said. 'It just won't work.'

Geldof thought that political change could be prompted through the work of the commission. Pressure could be applied to the G8, once the report was written, through a series of high-profile political lobbies. He had conceived the idea of what he was calling Intellectual Live Aid, a debate on Africa connecting the leading global thinkers with speakers like Nelson Mandela in venues like the Royal Albert Hall, linked together around the world.

'A concert will have more leverage,' said Bono and Richard Curtis.

'Well, you fucking do it,' replied Geldof. 'No one's stopping you.'

❊

The three men continued to plough separate furrows. Richard Curtis, who was taking a year off to focus on Africa, went off to talk to aid agencies, non-governmental organisations and other campaigners about the idea that became Make Poverty History. Bono flew off to the US for the opening of Bill Clinton's memorial library. And Geldof continued with his New Thinking seminars.

The next two seminars revealed to Geldof how difficult it was going to be to get agreement among the different G8 countries. The French and the Americans had very different views, with the French placing much greater emphasis on the role of the state than did the US. But that was not all.

The Paris Seminar in the Hôtel de Lassay suggested that France and the UK needed to take the lead in the debate on Africa. Both countries had historical and colonial links to Africa. Both had a particular responsibility for the poor state of the EU aid budget in Africa. But both had a strong post-colonial conviction that priorities in the continent must now be defined by Africans, not Europeans.

In Paris, Geldof fulminated against the unfairness of the EU's Common Agricultural Policy, which dishonourably subsidised rich European farmers to compete with poor African ones. After the seminar, France's member of the commission, Michel Camdessus, a former head of the IMF, took me to one side and reprimanded me for passing notes to Geldof during Bob's diatribe about unethical subsidies.

'There is no way that the Common Agricultural Policy is going to be up for revision by the Commission for Africa,' he told me. 'For Bob to keep raising it is politically unrealistic. It just makes him look naïve and lowers the credibility of everything else he is saying. So stop passing him notes encouraging him.'

'The notes were not about that,' I replied. 'And, anyway, Bob doesn't need encouragement from me on this. He's fully across the detail of how devastating European farm subsidies are to farmers in the poor world. He doesn't need me to tell him.'

Immediately afterwards, we flew to New York for the seminar there the next day. A wide range of thinkers had assembled at the US Council for Foreign Relations and yet they offered a distinctly American consensus. Impassioned speeches about moral imperatives would cut little ice with the

Bush administration. Geldof should only debate with Bush on the grounds of US national interest. Praising US leadership on issues like HIV/AIDS would be far more effective.

As if to prove the point, that same week Bono visited the US for the opening of the Bill Clinton Memorial Library in the former president's home town of Little Rock in Arkansas. The opening was attended by four US presidents – George Bush senior, Jimmy Carter, Bill Clinton and George Bush junior. Bono went out of his way to speak of something positive that each of them had done for Africa before serenading them – unplugged and in the pouring rain amid a sea of colourful umbrellas and cagoules. He and The Edge sang 'The Hands That Built America'. You could see the collective presidency preening itself.

It was peak Bono, a characteristic blend of charm and ethical blackmail. He approached the recently re-elected president, George W. Bush, and said: 'After 9/11, we were told America would have no time for the world's poor. America would be taken up with its own problems of safety. And it's true these are dangerous times, but America has not drawn the blinds and double-locked the doors.

'In fact, you have doubled aid to Africa. You have tripled funding for global health. Mr President, your emergency plan for AIDS relief and support for the Global Fund have put 700,000 people onto life-saving anti-retroviral drugs and provided 8 million bed nets to protect children from malaria.'

Bono had an absolutely natural gift for politicking, said Tony Blair. 'He was great with people, very smart and an inspirational speaker. I knew Bono would be an important person to get to see George. Bono could have been a president or prime minister standing on his head. I knew he would work George well, and with none of the prissy disdain of most of his ilk.'

�֍

Bob was in Africa again. This time, his BBC TV series took him from Tanzania and the East African Rift Valley – the supposed birthplace of humankind – to the Slave Coast of Benin and Ghana. There, he encountered The Forgetting Tree, around which those bound for slavery in Louisiana walked in chains seven times – first to forget their land, then their village, their people, their wife, their sons, their daughters and finally, their very name.

Six months on the ground in Africa – from September 2004 to February 2005 – changed Geldof's view of the continent he had so graphically described to Tony Blair as 'fucked' before the Commission for Africa was launched. Revealingly, in his work with the commission, he had encountered two different versions of Africa.

'Here's an oddity,' Geldof observed at the time. 'Go to visit experts on Africa all across the West – as I have done extensively in recent months – and you find one common denominator. Whether it is development economists, scholars, policymakers or professional Africa-watchers, you encounter a kind of despair. The problems Africa faces are intractable – drought, famine, hunger, disease, ignorance, witchcraft, corruption, bad government, bureaucracy, war, AIDS, death… Afro-pessimism, they call it.'

But travel through Africa and you find the opposite of all that. 'Among the people of this shimmering continent, there is no despair. Rather, there is a sense of flux, and of opportunity. There is dynamism in the air, and change. Africa today is very different from the place I first visited twenty years ago at the time of Live Aid.'

In recent years, change had swept like a tide across the continent. Cities were bustling and a new class of entrepreneurs was in evidence. 'After nearly forty years of stagnation, almost half of all African countries had recently had economic growth of more than 5 per cent,' Geldof told anyone who would listen in 2005, 'far better than most Western countries achieved.'

The changes went far beyond the economy. 'When I was first in Africa in 1985, there were about twenty wars going on across the continent. Today, there are just four. Then, half African countries were run by dictators. Today, more than two-thirds had had multi-party elections.' Some were freer and fairer than others. 'But there had been several examples of peaceful changes of government, even if creeps like Mugabe clung on and even one-time good guys like Museveni in Uganda had outstayed their welcome. But, elsewhere, a new generation of political leaders is showing a new commitment to the common good of their peoples.'

A solid middle class was growing, bringing political stability through the ability of educated classes to hold governments to account. Things were beginning to change all across Africa.

❊

Back in London, civil servants on the Commission for Africa in November 2004 produced what they called a 'consultation document'. It was, in effect, the Treasury's idea of what the commission's final report should say.

Geldof received the document with some alarm. While still in Africa, he wrote to the other commissioners expressing disquiet over the way the secretariat's civil servants had drawn up the document and distributed it. The document contained 'the seeds of some real radicalism', but it had 'several notable omissions,' Bob said. It portrayed culture as 'a bolt-on' rather than the fundamental underpinning of 'our whole approach'.

The way the document had been prepared did not bode well. Bob wrote to the other commissioners on 22 November: 'I was very concerned that a full three weeks were spent batting the document about within British government departments to get a text approved and then only three days were allowed for the Africa Commissioners to express their views. I do not want to appear to carp, but it was unhelpful that the final session of the Addis meeting was cancelled.' It was entirely understandable that Tony Blair had to leave early (because of the execution of Ken Bigley), 'but there was no reason why that final session should not have been chaired by another commissioner, for which the head of the secretariat and the director of policy ought to have remained. This is a concern that was voiced to me by several other commissioners who had issues to raise at that final session.'

The fear was growing in Bob that the civil servants were having too great a voice in determining what the commission's conclusions might be. 'It must not be seen to be a tool of the British government,' he said. And if the report was to be read by the general public, it had to have the voice of a single author and not read like it had been written by a committee.

'You are going to have to be the one to write this,' he said to me.

Bob was now so worried about the dead hand of the civil service falling across the commission and its report that he paid a visit to Alastair Campbell, Tony Blair's now former director of communications and strategy. According to Campbell's diary entry for Wednesday 5 January 2005, Geldof 'swore massively but was intelligent and political'. He continued: 'He and Vallely were full of stories of non-joined-up stuff in government and I told him it was one of the reasons I left.'

Geldof told Campbell he was really worried about two things: 'the fact nobody was in charge of overall presentational strategy, and the fact that Gordon Brown was basically laying out the store before the store was built.' Campbell's diary recorded that 'Geldof said Brown could blow it. I advised him to have a very frank word and say he would not be forgiven if this became part of the TB-GB gameplay. I said he might take it from him. Bob had a very direct way of speaking, and enormous passion, and clearly got really frustrated at the way politics had got hijacked by personality stuff.'

The next day, following Campbell's advice, Geldof arranged a meeting with Brown, with myself and Nick Stern in attendance. In fairly plain language, Bob expressed his anxiety about what he saw as attempts to manipulate the commission's agenda into a pre-set outcome. He insisted that he wanted me to write the report. It would be based on the research of Stern's civil servants, 'but Vallely must write it, so it will be actually readable by the ordinary person in the street'. Otherwise, he said, he would have to resign from the commission on the grounds that it was not sufficiently independent of the UK government. 'No Vallely, no Geldof,' he said. I was quite taken aback by the bluntness with which he spoke to the chancellor of the exchequer, but Brown didn't get riled and things went more smoothly from that point on.

A couple of days later, Bob met with Blair to make clear that he expected the commission's recommendations to become the agenda for Britain's Gleneagles G8 summit. Rather than resenting this, Tony Blair seemed positively to welcome the pressure.

'I could see that Tony was energised,' recalled his aide, Kate Garvey. 'It helped bolster what he wanted.'

Blair wanted to feel some public pressure. A few days later, he told Richard Curtis: 'If we're gonna do this, I need to feel the heat.' The PM needed it to be demonstrated that a large sector of the public saw this as a priority issue, Garvey said.

Meanwhile, Gordon Brown was running along parallel tracks. That month, he made a week-long visit to Africa, taking in the biggest shanty town in Kenya, an HIV/AIDS orphanage in Tanzania and a women's credit union in Mozambique. This was very different from his usual practice, noted the BBC's political correspondent, Mark Mardell, who travelled with him. The chancellor, he reported, 'believes it is time for the world to see a new Gordon Brown'.

It was not a new Gordon Brown. He had been working on issues of poverty in Africa for decades. 'He had a deep commitment which went beyond an intellectual dimension,' said Nick Stern. 'It was a moral imperative and it was very important to him. The fact that many people called the Commission for Africa the Blair Commission irked him. There was a view that somehow Tony was, as it were, muscling in on Gordon's territory.'

Making public his interest in Africa was part of Brown's way of responding to Blair's refusal to give him a central role in shaping the upcoming 2005 election campaign.

The mistrust between the two men was deepening and, at that point, Treasury insiders suspected that Gordon was ready to blow the whole thing up.

⁜

On 1 March 2005, less than two weeks before the publication of the commission's final report, Bob Geldof wrote to Tony Blair and laid down some red lines. Without them, he said, 'I feel I cannot put my name to this report'.

On debt, sub-Saharan African countries needed 100 per cent of their debts cancelled – and that meant cancelling the whole debt, not just the interest on the debt. Geldof also wanted a condemnation of the way IMF and World Bank economic policies had hurt Africa's poor. 'Evidence shows that in the 1980s and 1990s [they] took far too little account of how these policies would potentially impact the poor in Africa.'

On aid, Geldof insisted that the report must state that 'rich nations should commit to a timetable for giving 0.7 per cent of their annual income in aid'.

On trade, it must reject the way rich nations make their aid conditional on African nations giving concessions on imports from the industrialised world. This undermines the power of democracies in Africa. 'If they are to be accountable to their own citizens, African governments have to be allowed the space to make their own decisions,' Geldof said. 'The report will be rejected by the activists if we do not prominently highlight some of their very real concerns about who makes the decisions in African economies.' On corruption, Western firms who pay bribes should be refused export credits.

The report must insist that politicians put poor people first when drawing up policies. 'I will not be able to defend signing a document that does not acknowledge that the absolute poorest people in the world should not have to pay for health and education,' he told the PM.

Finally, the report should emphasise that its recommendations were not a shopping list from which African nations and rich donor nations could pick and choose. 'These problems are interlocking ... Africa requires a comprehensive "big push" on all these fronts at once.'

All that said, Geldof had learned that he had to compromise. Politics is indeed the art of the possible, he learned. He had backed down when the South African finance minister Trevor Manuel said that Africa did not have enough engineers and other trained specialists to handle a quadrupling of aid. Bob had learned that he could not win every battle.

Tony Blair's role in all this was revealing. He allowed Gordon Brown to lead on the substantial deal on debt cancellation; Brown, for whom Africa was a visceral moral issue, had spent more than a year manoeuvring his fellow finance ministers into a big debt cancellation deal. And Blair left Hilary Benn, the development secretary, to handle the development details. But it was the prime minister who set the parameters of the commission's considerable achievement by his choice of commissioners. It was he who understood how to balance the visionary with the politically achievable. Perhaps most significantly, Blair happily endorsed Geldof's insistence on rejecting the old idea that aid should come with strings attached. Instead, aid should be agreed between donor and recipient as equal partners.

Africa had to do the right thing; not because donor nations told it to, but because there was a growing realisation on the continent that Africa could not keep avoiding the tough decisions. Similarly, the West had to do the right thing. It had to stop hindering Africa's development and start to assist that development far more effectively – not as its half of the bargain for Africa's compliance, but because it was self-evidently the right thing to do.

In the end, Blair and his staff did not interfere with the shaping of the report, which was done in collaboration by me, Nick Stern and Myles Wickstead from the input of the commissioners, most of whom were

Africans. The Penguin edition of the report was written by me in the single authorial voice the commission had requested.

Geldof kept fighting his corner to the very end. Blair, who was a consummate chairman in the commission sessions, stayed out of the final processes of internal negotiation. At least six people threatened to walk out at various points. But negotiations only went down to the wire with Bob, who represented the activist viewpoint, and the French commissioner Michel Camdessus, who represented the economic orthodoxy of the IMF, of which he was a former managing director.

The two of them continued arguing past the deadline. The final bargaining session lasted more than two hours. Caught between them was Tony Blair's private secretary, Laurie Lee. 'I remember juggling three phone lines one evening at No 10,' he recalled. 'I had Bob Geldof on one line insisting that the commission must recommend 100 per cent debt cancellation for Africa. I had Camdessus on another line saying he would not agree to that. And Myles Wickstead was on the third line, literally at the printers, waiting for the green light to print the report.

'Having listened carefully, and multiple times to both of them, I finally came up with three words that I hoped would work,' said Laurie.

'I said to Camdessus, "I understand why you don't want to give debt relief to countries that don't want it, but presumably you agree that we should give it to all the countries that do want it."'

'I suppose so,' he said.

Laurie switched to Geldof's line. 'I understand why you want to give debt relief to all African countries, but presumably you don't want to force it on any country that doesn't want it.'

'No, of course not,' said Bob.

Laurie gave Myles the green light for the printers. In the final report, the Commission for Africa recommended that 'for poor countries in sub-Saharan Africa *which need it*, the objective must be 100 per cent debt cancellation as soon as possible'.

It was a triumph of diplomatic negotiation.

※

The Commission for Africa's final report was published on 11 March 2005. It was entitled *Our Common Interest* in recognition of the fact that helping

Africa was in the collective self-interest of the national security and economic interests of the rich world. Despite all the endless redrafting and compromises, its ninety detailed recommendations constituted a package that was both bold and radical.

It let no one off the hook. Africa was made to bear its share of the blame and responsibility for the solutions. African leaders were required to crack down on corruption, become more answerable to their people, put in place more open budgets and processes, create a better investment climate, remove the barriers to trade between African nations and scrap the fees that poor people pay for schools and healthcare.

The list of requirements on the rich world was just as demanding: doubling aid, cutting subsidies and tariffs, and cancelling debt.

Other proposals were both imaginative and exacting: making the IMF and World Bank more answerable; compelling Western banks to report on dodgy dealings by African leaders; and controlling the flow of small arms to Africa from G8 and EU countries. The second half of the report drew up a detailed plan of how this could be done.

For me, there was the singular satisfaction that I had sneaked into the report the phrase: 'There is more to this than the kindness of strangers. It is about a journey from charity to justice' – the phrase from my 1990 book, *Bad Samaritans*, which had originally stung Geldof into political action, and which was to become the slogan above the Live 8 stage.

The report was generally well-received. The Harvard economist Jeffrey Sachs called it a 'masterful display of diagnosis and politics', while the former UN general-secretary Kofi Annan described it as 'an important contribution to the continuing search for effective solutions to the continent's problems'. The *Political Quarterly* declared it 'one of the most thorough and rigorous analyses of Africa's problems ever undertaken ... both authoritative and remarkably readable'. And the *Financial Times* added: 'If we act on these recommendations, there is a good chance of a better life for hundreds of millions.'

Bob Geldof was happy with the end result. 'It was a fine piece of work,' he said, looking back. 'One of the key things was that it looked at the problem through African eyes rather than the usual Western ones.' But what pleased him most was that, at the press conference for the launch of the report, wearing my journalist's hat, I asked Tony Blair a question.

'Prime Minister, will this be the British policy for the summit you will be hosting for the G8?'

'We haven't fixed that yet,' Blair replied.

'Yes, it will,' interjected Geldof.

'Gosh, well, if Bob's going to make the policy, I guess that's what it is,' said Blair.

'Unbelievable,' said Bob afterwards. 'From the Band Aid Christmas record and the Live Aid concert, it had taken twenty years, but eventually the boys and girls with the guitars got to write the policy.'

CHAPTER 31

MAKING POVERTY HISTORY

They are known as 'media buyers'. They are key people in the advertising business whose job it is to do deals with television companies and other media outlets to buy advertising space and airtime on behalf of clients. In February 2005, Richard Curtis had invited 150 of them to a party. They were some of the best deal-makers in the business.

There was food and drink and entertainment. The comedian Ruby Wax softened them up with a characteristically smart and acerbic routine. The singers Beverley Knight and Katie Melua serenaded them. And then Bob Geldof stood up to tell them that they had been invited so that they could donate free advertising space to the Make Poverty History campaign. The media buyers had worked that out from the invitation. But after he had made a very moving speech about Africa, and shown some footage from his latest visit to Ethiopia, Geldof pulled one of his characteristic stunts.

'Hands up anyone in the room who is not willing to double the amount of free media space they've offered?'

No one raised their hands.

Peter Souter, boss of the UK's largest advertising agency, Abbott Mead Vickers (AMV), chuckled. 'It was classic Bob – making people who were already doing something good feel that they had to do more. For somebody who's a pop star, he is a brilliant marketeer.'

Souter and his team had organised the evening after being approached by Richard Curtis, who had asked them if they would do the advertising for a new idea he had had. He wanted to launch a big campaign to eliminate poverty in Africa.

'The world's eight most powerful men will be gathering in a hotel in Scotland next year,' the Comic Relief boss told Souter. 'We want to create a massive campaign to put pressure on them to take action on poverty. Tony Blair has told me that if we can apply the heat, we could get an extra £100 million for Africa. Will you do the advertising?'

'Sure,' said Souter. 'What's the budget?'

'Zero. There is no budget.'

'That's interesting,' said Souter.

❊

After the Live Aid concert in 1985, the key players had gone their separate ways: Bob Geldof had concentrated on change in the UK, persuading Tony Blair to launch the Commission for Africa; Bono had focused on promoting change in the United States, working with presidents Bill Clinton and then George Bush; Richard Curtis, through Comic Relief, had raised a total of £337 million for Africa.

But 2005 was to bring them together in their biggest common enterprise. And not just them, but a coalition which grew to more than 500 other organisations – aid agencies, activist groups, churches and faith bodies, trade unions, universities and schools, and grassroots political parties. By the end, it corralled 38 million people to back it. It was later to be described by Tony Blair as 'the most extraordinary civic society campaign I have ever come across'.

❊

At first, the new movement had no name. The idea of a massive public campaign to bring pressure on the G8 summit at Gleneagles had been germinating for more than a year. But a group of aid agencies had met in May 2004 at the unlikely venue of the Mothers' Union offices in Westminster. There, they set up a steering group to work out a structure and constitution for a campaigning coalition on trade, aid and debt. But a row broke out about whether to include climate change. Those against said it distracted from central concerns about poverty and that climate change was too hard to explain to the public. At this point, the representative from Greenpeace walked out. 'In those days, many in the NGO community felt that climate change and development were in competition,' said Shriti Vadera. 'It was only in later years that everyone came to understand that the two issues were integrated.'

Among those present was Richard Curtis who now committed himself to working with the coalition.

But early on, the new coalition made a tactical error. They were determined to avoid the mistake they felt had been made with Jubilee 2000 a few years earlier. Then, one strong central figure, the economist Ann Pettifor, drove the policy of the Drop the Debt movement in a way that left many of its members feeling dragged along in her slipstream. To avoid this, the new grouping set up a 'coalition coordination team'. But this created a different problem. The committee was to prove overly bureaucratic and slow at decision-making. And it lacked a high-profile individual to be its spokesperson, which was to cause big problems.

Richard Curtis quietly took matters into his own hands. He persuaded Peter Souter to put Britain's leading advertising agency at the service of the new coalition free of charge.

'The first big challenge was to come up with a name, a slogan, the visuals and some events,' Curtis said. When that didn't seem to be happening inside the coalition, Curtis turned to Souter.

Since he would be working with no budget, Souter asked for volunteers. His staff were happy to give the lie to the notion that there was no such thing as a free launch.

Bridget Angear stepped forward. She was one of the agency's top planners. A planner's job is to conceptualise the campaign, to work out who is the target and how they should be reached. 'Bridget is one of the cleverest people I've ever worked with,' said Souter, 'and certainly the best planner.' She went away with another AMV planner, Tom Johnstone, and brainstormed.

They looked at what had happened at previous G8 summits and concluded that if all the aid agencies had been ignored before, then they could easily be ignored again. Appealing to the world's leaders directly hadn't worked previously and it seemed unlikely to work this time. They needed a different model.

'Okay, the target is eight people – the leaders of the G8,' she told her boss. 'But to influence those eight leaders, we have to get through to the people they rely on to stay in power: the voting public.' That meant reaching millions of people in eight different countries.

'We don't have a budget for mass communications, so our plan is to use people to deliver our message. We need people to be more than just supporters, we need them to be campaigners. The trouble is that all the different NGOs have different campaign messages. They need a single message. Something that will clearly tell the G8 to Eliminate Poverty.'

The coalition needed a brand that was quickly recognisable and instantly understandable. It needed a clear and very simple name. One of AMV's best copywriters, Mary Wear, went off and came back with a list. Richard Curtis and his partner and script-editor Emma Freud went into the agency's office on Marylebone Road to look at it.

'That's the one,' said Emma. She was pointing to Make Poverty History.

'It has a very English rhythm,' mused Richard. 'How will it translate into other languages?'

'It doesn't need to translate,' said Souter. 'It's like an airline slogan. All airlines speak English.'

Curtis and Souter now had to sell the idea to the disparate members of the coalition.

'Richard and I went to pitch Make Poverty History to 141 different NGOs,' recalled Souter. 'There, all in the same room, was everyone from rabid communists to dyed-in-the-hair Tories. A combination of Richard's brilliance, charm and passion – and the basic strength of the title, Make Poverty History – persuaded them all to sign on. In the end, that name was the highest common denominator. It's really hard to argue against the desire to end poverty.'

What nobody noticed at the time, but which was to later prove very significant, was that Souter and AMV saw their client as Comic Relief and not Make Poverty History. Before the meeting, Comic Relief had taken care to copyright the name Make Poverty History so that Curtis could control who used it and on what terms.

Make Poverty History set up a 'Policy and Lobbying Working Group' and work proceeded on a series of launches.

'The secret,' said the ad-man Souter, 'is launch, launch and launch again.'

In September 2004, Make Poverty History was launched to the British media. In the same month, at a meeting in Johannesburg, 100 international NGOs and networks, trade unions, religious groups and other civil society bodies issued what they called the Johannesburg Declaration. It announced the Global Call to Action Against Poverty (GCAP) – a call to action that shared Make Poverty History's key demands. But, in addition, it called for more 'democratic, transparent and accountable' forms of government in the developing world. GCAP was to be officially launched on 27 January 2005 at the World Social Forum in Brazil. It saw Make Poverty History as its UK arm.

Throughout the first half of 2005 Make Poverty History launches continued apace. In November, fifty-seven MPs attended a parliamentary launch with a group of Comic Relief celebrities including Lenny Henry, Dawn French, Kirsty Young and June Sarpong. Between them, Richard Curtis and AMV had come up with a campaign symbol. They had borrowed the idea from the yellow cancer-awareness bracelets popularised earlier that year by Nike and the Lance Armstrong Foundation.

The symbol of Make Poverty History would be a white band with the MPH name printed on it.

'We believed it would be important to turn these words into something more tangible,' said Angear, the lead AMV planner. 'Because people were to be our media, we decided we needed something to "dress" them with. People wear black armbands to mourn death. Our idea was to create a white band to symbolise its prevention: a sign of hope that positive change really could be achieved.'

And it needed to appeal to a new younger generation. Every significant societal development since the 1960s, the ad agency staff noted, had been credited to the Baby Boomers. But now they needed to appeal to later generations. Generations X and Y were routinely characterised as apathetic in comparison with their predecessors. Make Poverty History needed to give Gen X and Gen Y a cause to rally behind.

The white band would be the political fashion accessory of these young people. 'They didn't need to sign up to give a tenner a month,' said Tom Johnstone of AMV. Simply wearing the white band was enough. 'It was with people when they had a shower in the morning and was on display to everyone throughout the day from when they bought a sandwich to when they were reading the paper on the train home. The white bands allowed us to go one stage further than people simply supporting the cause. They were showing the world around them their support. They were campaigners.'

The white band had its own separate launch. In November, the supermodel Claudia Schiffer – the first celebrity to wear the wristband – wore one to meet Gordon Brown. Heavily pregnant with her second child, she told the chancellor: 'If I was living in parts of Africa, I'd have a one-in-five chance of dying when my baby is born. And my child would have a one-in-five chance of dying before his or her fifth birthday. If the campaign works, then something will at last be done about these terrible statistics. As a mother, I'm asking you to support this campaign.'

At the recording of the Band Aid 2004 single on 14 November, Richard Curtis, Bono and Chris Martin all wore the white band on their wrists. 'We believed that a few of the right sort of people showing their support for Make Poverty History could create desire amongst the general public to want to be part of it,' said Angear.

Throughout November and December, campaigners prepared for the official launch of Make Poverty History on 1 January 2005. A specially commissioned report – *Make History: A Challenge to the British Prime Minister in 2005* – was printed to be issued to the media on 28 December.

Make Poverty History now had 160 member organisations. It was to launch on New Year's Day. But then disaster struck.

❧

On Boxing Day, 26 December 2004, an immense undersea earthquake off the coast of Sumatra triggered a tsunami which sent massive walls of water hurtling across the Indian Ocean. They devastated the coastal areas as colossal waves reached the land. Some 220,000 people were killed in fourteen countries. Millions more were displaced from their homes in Indonesia, Thailand, Sri Lanka, India and the Maldives. It was one of the largest disasters, in terms of loss of life, in modern history.

The international response was unprecedented. There was a huge global surge of aid from governments and private individuals to provide rescue missions, food, clean water, shelter and medical care. The attention of the UK aid agencies was diverted from Make Poverty History and into immediate humanitarian assistance. Many in the coalition feared that their launch plans would be overshadowed by the terrible emergency.

But the opposite happened. The tsunami led to a swift outpouring of compassion among the general public, which only served to heighten awareness of global poverty.

Make Poverty History was launched officially on 1 January 2005 on BBC Television with a special edition of Richard Curtis's sitcom, *The Vicar of Dibley*. Watched by 10 million people, it showed the comic actor Dawn French as the eponymous vicar asking her parishioners to write to the prime minister to denounce world poverty. In the *Guardian*, George Monbiot wrote:

> There has never been a moment like it on British television. *The Vicar of Dibley*, one of our gentler sitcoms, was bouncing along with its usual bonhomie on New Year's Day when it suddenly hit us with a scene from another world. Two young African children were sobbing and trying to comfort each other after their mother had died of AIDS. How on earth, I wondered, would the show make us laugh after that? It made no attempt to do so. One by one, the characters, famous for their parochial boorishness, stood in front of the camera wearing the white armbands which signalled their support for the Make Poverty History campaign. You would have to have been hewn from stone not to cry.

Two years later, a BBC report complained that the episode should never have been shown as it was in breach of the corporation's impartiality guidelines. But, by then, it was far too late. The programme had contained a Make Poverty History campaign video that lasted nearly a minute and a half. And at the end of the episode, Dawn French had logged on to the MPH website with the address on display to 10 million viewers.

Curtis was unapologetic. His fictional vicar would have been aged twenty at the time of Live Aid, he said, 'so it seemed a very apt idea for an episode of *Vicar of Dibley* to centre around her trying to mark the anniversary of a day which changed her world. I believe she'd still be totally up in arms about the horrific statistics twenty years on – one child dying every three seconds, unnecessarily, as a result of extreme poverty.'

A fortnight after the broadcast, Dawn French led 600 real women vicars and priests to the gates of Downing Street to sing hymns, swap jokes and wave their white wristbands at the passing traffic. Tony Blair came out to have his photograph taken with them. A few days later, the white band was adopted by the Global Call to Action Against Poverty when it was launched at the World Social Forum in Brazil at the end of January. Two days after that was the launch of the Churches' Make Poverty History campaign at Bloomsbury Baptist Church in London. 'Launch, launch, and launch again,' as Peter Souter had advocated.

The major launch of Make Poverty History came when Nelson Mandela, who had been invited to London by Gordon Brown for the G7 finance ministers' meeting, appeared in Trafalgar Square, wrapped up against the February weather in a heavy overcoat and fur hat.

Some 22,000 people turned out to see him.

The square was packed.

Bob Geldof introduced him, to the huge cheers of the crowd, as 'the unofficial president of the world'.

The eighty-five-year-old looked frail but spoke with a steady confidence. Although Oxfam had organised the event, he spoke beneath a gigantic banner which read Make Poverty History. He began by namechecking the organisation and also the Global Campaign for Action Against Poverty. He then said: 'I can never thank the people of Britain enough for their support through those days of the struggle against apartheid. Many stood in solidarity with us, just a few yards from this spot.'

People in the crowd felt he was speaking to them personally. Across the road was the South African High Commission, outside which many of the people present had campaigned against apartheid for more than a decade.

Mandela then made a direct link between the past and the present. 'Like slavery and apartheid, poverty is not natural. It is man-made and it can be overcome and eradicated by the actions of human beings. And overcoming poverty is not a gesture of charity. It is an act of justice. It is the protection of a fundamental human right, the right to dignity and a decent life.'

Addressing the world's politicians, he said, 'I say to all those leaders: do not look the other way; do not hesitate. Recognise that the world is hungry for action, not words. Act with courage and vision.'

His speech was the work of many hands. Shriti Vadera and Adrian Lovett had had input to ensure that its points of policy aligned with those of both the coalition and the UK Treasury, while John Samuel from the Mandela Foundation framed it in a South African perspective. And the pen of Richard Curtis was in evidence too, most memorably in Mandela's departing words to the activists in Trafalgar Square:

'Sometimes it falls upon a generation to be great. You can be that great generation. Let your greatness blossom.'

The speech, one onlooker said, was a masterclass in how you motivate an entire movement. Those present would never forget his words for they called to 'the deepest part of our shared humanity'.

Mandela's speech brought a gear change to the MPH campaign. By the following month, the majority of British MPs had signed a parliamentary motion in support of Make Poverty History. On Red Nose Day, 11 March 2005, Comic Relief celebrated its twentieth anniversary and that night ran a series of MPH films that managed to get around the BBC's strict editorial guidelines forbidding anything that could be seen as political activity.

That same day, the Commission for Africa report was published and Martin Drewry, head of campaigns at Christian Aid, claimed that pressure from MPH was part of the reason for the report's insistence that African countries should not be forced to remove their tariffs on imported Western goods.

In March, Oxfam ordered millions more white wristbands and the BBC bought a made-for-television rom-com movie from Richard Curtis, *The Girl in the Café*, starring Kelly Macdonald and Bill Nighy, about the naïve young girlfriend of a senior civil servant who causes havoc at an international summit on Third World debt by speaking the truth. Laurie Lee, Tony Blair's private secretary on Africa, noted with pleasure that the protagonist had been given the same name as him.

March was also the month when all the free television advertising that Bob Geldof blagged was used to deliver one of the stand-out moments of the campaign. Peter Souter's ad agency had been asked to come up with something special because the MPH ad would air simultaneously on seventy-seven commercial TV channels at 8.58 p.m. on 31 March 2005. The ad industry called it a 'road block' because whichever channel you switched to, you would see the same thing. There was no way round it.

It was the first time that an ad 'road block' had ever been successfully put in place. There were later erroneous reports that the first draft for the ad – because it was an awareness-raiser, not a fundraiser – was to be entitled 'Don't Give Us Your Fucking Money'. In reality, the unused ad was one which used CGI to depict a child going from healthy to dead in thirty seconds. 'There was a big debate in the coalition about whether we should use that,' said Adrian Lovett. In the end, they didn't.

Anyway, the Abbott Mead Vickers team had a more sophisticated idea.

The great Make Poverty History visual signifier was a sequence of top celebrities, each of them clicking their fingers every three seconds – the rate at which, in 2005, a child in the developing world was dying from extreme poverty. The ads were shot in stark black and white, and the famous faces included Brad Pitt, George Clooney, Cameron Diaz, Kanye West, Kylie Minogue, Hugh Grant, P Diddy, Kate Moss, Colin Firth, Claudia Schiffer, Justin Timberlake, Emma Thompson and Bryan Adams, as well as Bono and Geldof. Different versions were made for different countries, with versions also created by campaigners in India and Africa.

Over the months that followed, the ads were seen, heard or read by millions of people on television and radio, in cinemas and in print. All the ads were in space donated without charge by the media. Ironically, in September that year, the UK media regulator Ofcom ruled the click ads were directed 'towards a political end' and banned them from TV and radio – even though not a single complaint had been made about them by viewers. But, by then, they had done their job.

�֍

Momentum continued to build. In April, the largest number of people ever to assemble for an overnight protest in Whitehall gathered to attend a 'Wake Up To Trade Justice' vigil. At the end of the month, Britain's political parties, which were fighting a general election campaign, called a truce on 27 April – World Poverty Day – during which the leader of each party made a speech in support of Make Poverty History. 'That was the moment when it was depoliticised,' adjudged Peter Souter. 'It wasn't left, it wasn't right, it wasn't middle. It was just correct. It was just the right thing to do.'

Within only six months, more than 7 million people in the UK were wearing the ubiquitous Make Poverty History wristbands. And they were not just wearing the white band. Some half a million of them had signed up to the MPH database, which became key to mobilising public support. In the years that followed, the compilation of email lists and the use of the internet, for spreading the word and for lobbying politicians, became a standard tool for campaigning organisations. But, in 2005, this was a pioneering strategy. It was one of the internet's first mass-activist campaigns.

'It was important for us to target young audiences,' said Glen Tarman, who oversaw MPH communications. 'This was the first generation who was digitally native. It offered them a chance for their voices to be heard. When people see they're part of something bigger, they want to get involved.' It happened two years before smartphones and social media were commonplace, but 8 million people signed the MPH trade-aid-debt petitions that were handed in to the prime minister at 10 Downing Street.

'There were so many signatures they arrived on scores of CD-ROMs inside a large black case,' recalled Tony Blair's private secretary, Laurie Lee. 'We kept it in our office until the summit to remind us of the public expectations on our shoulders.'

By now, more than 500 organisations had joined the Make Poverty History coalition. Recognition of the MPH brand among the general public had jumped in six months from zero to 88 per cent, a figure higher than Coca-Cola in June 2005 according to Millward Brown, the leading global research agency specialising in advertising effectiveness. Newspapers ran stories entreating the public to visit the MPH website and sign the petition. The *Daily Mirror* hired an open-top double-decker bus to tour the country promoting its extensive MPH coverage. Vans were driven around the Houses of Parliament to protest about what Bono was now calling 'stupid poverty'. Geldof offered his own contribution by endorsing an initiative called 'Every Gig a Live Aid', to which touring musicians signed up, pledging to dedicate a few minutes of every show to talking about Make Poverty History and encouraging fans to sign up. Bono wrote to all the record companies, asking them to encourage their artists to join. Artists as diverse as U2, Keane, Kylie, Snow Patrol, Simply Red, Paul Oakenfold, Spiritualized, Razorlight, Girls Aloud, McFly, Damon Albarn and Bloc Party came on board, while Glastonbury, the Isle of Wight and V Festival all agreed to the call-out for justice – not charity – for the world's poor.

But for all this, Bob Geldof was not happy. At one interminable Make Poverty History coordinating committee meeting, the discussion focused on what to do on the eve of the G8 summit at Gleneagles in July. 'Their answer was a march in Edinburgh on the Saturday before the summit,' Geldof recalled. 'I said, "What good will a fucking march do? They'll take no notice. A million people went onto the streets to march against the war in Iraq and they just ignored it completely." A march was just so English and polite. It had no bite.'

The unhappiness was reciprocated. The minutes of one MPH meeting deputed Adrian Lovett to go to DATA to see if its strategists could do something about 'getting Bob Geldof on message'. Lucy Matthew at DATA laughed. 'He's got a very uncompromising personality,' was her simple response.

The most skilful diplomat at DATA was Zita Lloyd, so much so that the others called her 'The Bob Wrangler'. Zita was fastidiously diplomatic as ever. 'There are always tensions in coalitions. Bob can be abrupt and abrasive, but he also knew that we had to collaborate. But there's a sort of belligerence about his attitude that "I want this to happen, so why won't you just make it happen?".'

At this point, she said, 'he was getting a bit frustrated that the momentum wasn't growing enough and that Make Poverty History wasn't getting enough traction. And that as much as we loved the Commission for Africa, that just didn't cut through with the general public.'

Geldof was more direct. 'The Make Poverty History people like to think they're radical, but they're very safe. A march is the lowest common denominator,' he told me. 'The wild radicals will go on it with their wild radical placards, and the mainstream people will politely sing "We Shall Overcome". These guys are letting the ball drop in my view. How are you helping Blair get the deal over the line with the other G8 leaders with a protest march in Edinburgh – an hour's drive away from Gleneagles? It isn't going to work, it never fucking works. I'm out.'

Bob decided he had a better idea – and he was going to do it on his own.

CHAPTER 32

WHAT CHANGED BOB'S MIND

'It's the twentieth anniversary of Live Aid this year,' observed Michael Grade, who by now was the chairman of the BBC but still a member of the Band Aid Trust. 'Is there any pressure to celebrate with another concert?' he asked his fellow trustees when they gathered for a meeting on 25 January 2005. The question was met with a resounding 'no'. One after another, the trustees gave their reasons. It would be hard to match the original 1985 occasion. It would detract from the main issue of 2005, which was to persuade world leaders at the next G8 to write off Africa's debts. 'The purpose of the trust should now be to push for change, as opposed to fundraising,' said Bob Geldof. 'Any event should be left for someone else to organise.'

But that was not to prove the end of the matter.

Geldof had spent six months working on the Commission for Africa. His focus now was to persuade the wider world to implement the recommendations the commission was on course to make. To do so, he had dreamed up that idea which he called Intellectual Live Aid. It would bring the world's top thinkers together in a series of meetings to draw the attention of the global media to the issue. His aim was to change the way that opinion-formers thought about Africa.

But many of his fellow activists had other ideas. The four strategists of DATA, the think-tank Geldof had helped set up, took the same view as Bono and Richard Curtis. They thought that another concert, Son of Live Aid, was needed to galvanise the public and pressurise the politicians.

For months, Jamie Drummond, Lucy Matthew, Olly Boston and Zita Lloyd all pestered Bob to organise another concert. But Geldof was adamant in refusing them too.

He had public, and private, reasons for doing so.

Live Aid had been 'almost perfect in what it achieved,' Geldof said. 'I can't see how anything could possibly be better than that glorious day twenty years ago. We can never recapture that. A second concert would be a mere imitation.' He accused the others of a failure of imagination. 'Think of something new,' he responded.

What he did not tell them was that he was afraid of a repeat of the impact that the massive effort of Live Aid had had upon him. 'Career-wise, it broke up my band,' he later told me. 'And it seriously impacted my family life and emotional life. Something shifted, although it only really came to a head a couple of years later.' He did not say so, but he was clearly thinking about the breakup of his marriage to Paula Yates and the temporary loss of his children. He now had a new partner, the French actress Jeanne Marine, and had taken Paula's daughter, Tiger, into his home to grow up with her sisters. 'I was afraid of that being repeated now I was with Jeanne, and Tiger was still very young, and the girls were teenagers. This just monopolises all your life, you know?'

Bono and Curtis kept trying, in vain, to persuade him. But Geldof kept refusing. 'He told us, "It won't shift the needle as effectively as Live Aid did",' recalled Curtis. 'And he didn't want to sign up to a million meetings with a million other people.'

Bono decided to take matters into his own hands. He called Paul McCartney and Chris Martin – who had made his own trip to Africa and filmed a video to show audiences before Coldplay concerts. Bono asked if they would be up for performing at another massive global event. Both agreed. Bono rang Bob and told him. Bob still refused. 'Bono was definitely as keen as I was, and as humble in the face of Bob's power in this context,' Richard said. Both knew that they would not have been able to do it half so well without Geldof's unrelenting drive.

Bob was, in any case, otherwise engaged. He and John Maguire had finished filming their *Geldof in Africa* series for BBC One and were in the editing suite writing the scripts for the six programmes. And he was getting bad news about the fate of the Commission for Africa. Its final report would not be out until 11 March, but the consultation document drawn up by civil servants in November was circulating. And responses from other governments were decidedly mixed.

There were some wins. European Union ministers had agreed a virtual doubling of EU aid by 2010. The US and French governments had indicated they were prepared to significantly increase their aid budgets though with differing timelines, conditions and methods of payment. But both the US and Canada refused to sign up to the International Finance Facility, claiming there was no mechanism to ensure that these new aid funds would be well spent. The US wanted to act alone, not collectively. The Germans and the Italians said they had no money. And the Japanese seemed immovable. The Commission for Africa's plan – for a 'big push' on aid, debt and trade all at once – was not getting backing.

'Bob had continuing faith that if the Africa Commission put together a plan that was rigorous and robust, then Tony Blair could just sort of sell it to the G8,' said Olly Buston of DATA. 'I think that was naïve, in view of the politics. There was huge public support in the UK, where Make Poverty History felt massive. But it was nothing anywhere else in the world. And the only thing we really had was pop.'

Geldof's colleagues in DATA were as anxious as Bono and Richard Curtis that he should do another big concert around the anniversary of Live Aid. 'I remember me and Lucy having a screaming match with him outside the Treasury at one point,' said Olly. 'He just kept saying, "I'm not fucking doing it. I'm not fucking doing it", because he knew it would be a nightmare.'

'Bono was really convinced from his interactions with the UK government that, without something really big and gripping, Blair and Brown – whatever the scale of their ambition – would just not be able to deliver the other countries,' Lucy Matthew recalled. As the days and weeks went by, Geldof became steadily more depressed. Had all the efforts of the Commission for Africa been in vain? 'This is the best chance for Africa for a generation,' he kept saying. 'We can't afford to blow it.' The Commission for Africa report carried a section called 'Broken Promises'. Bob now feared there was going to be a repeat. Gleneagles was creeping steadily closer – and the deal on Africa felt like it was being blocked at every turn.

✽

In the editing suite, Bob kept getting calls from Bono and, then, from Paul McCartney. He became more and more irritated with the interruptions, but Bono persisted.

'I've got an idea I want to come to see you about.'

'Okay,' said Bob wearily.

When Bono arrived, his idea changed everything.

'Okay. So, Live Aid, the twentieth anniversary. The concert opens with Paul McCartney, backed by U2, dressed in the uniforms off the cover of *Sgt. Pepper's Lonely Hearts Club Band*. McCartney sings: "It was twenty years ago today..."'

Bono could see Geldof's face begin to change.

'Bob, you are Sgt. Pepper, you taught us how to play... and all that shit.'

'Stop it, please,' Geldof said to the younger man. 'It's me, you know. Spare me.'

'I'm fucking serious,' said Bono, quite agitated, as if he realised this was his last shot. 'Paul is up for it...'

Geldof was silent.

'It was genius,' he said later. 'A moment in pop history. It was your Sgt. Pepper's sleeve animated. I needed to see it happen.'

'You wanker,' he said to Bono. 'How can anyone say no to that?'

But, as so often, Bob transformed the idea he had been given into something far bigger. The following day, he marched into the DATA office. 'I've had an idea,' he announced. 'Not Live Aid 2, but Live 8. Simultaneous concerts in London, Paris, Berlin, Rome, New York, Toronto, Tokyo, Moscow – one in each G8 country – at the end of which we ask everyone to get up and begin to walk to Gleneagles to lobby the G8.' Not *The Long Walk to Freedom*, as Nelson Mandela had entitled his autobiography, 'but a Long Walk to Justice'. Instead of being a repeat of the greatest charitable event the world had ever seen, it would be the biggest political lobby in global history. 'We'll tell people: "We don't want your money. We want your voice."'

For that, he needed a bigger venue. 'Let's get Hyde Park,' he said.

So Zita found herself trawling around, trying to find the right person to speak to at the Royal Parks Department. 'Then he sent Lucy and me to talk to Harvey Goldsmith,' she recalled. 'I think we were sent in to soften him up. Bob didn't want to talk to Harvey first himself in case there were explosions.'

A meeting followed in Richard Curtis's film production offices in Notting Hill. Present were Geldof, Bono, Midge Ure, Harvey Goldsmith, John Kennedy and Curtis himself. 'We didn't want to take the lead,' said Harvey. 'We decided to see whether artists wanted to do anything.'

Geldof began calling his friends in the music world to see if there was a general appetite to take part. Once he had a list containing the names Paul McCartney, U2, Coldplay, Sting and Madonna, he knew that everyone else would follow. 'Actually, I didn't have Madonna and Sting on the list,' he admitted later, 'but I knew they wouldn't say no!'

A few days later, Geldof, Kennedy and Curtis turned up at the Park offices in the Ranger's Lodge in the middle of Hyde Park. 'When we entered the room, there were about sixty people there,' recalled Kennedy, the Band Aid lawyer. 'Bob, Richard and I sat at a trestle table. It was more like a town hall meeting than a friendly chat.' Kennedy had no idea who all these people were, but it soon became apparent that they were from the fire brigade, the police, the ambulance service, London Transport, the parks maintenance department and the managers who ran Hyde Park. 'This motley crew were all united with one message: it was absolutely impossible to put on a concert in Hyde Park of the scale that was envisaged – let alone in the very few weeks to the suggested date. It just wasn't realistic or safe. They were loud, forceful, passionate and convincing.'

But they had reckoned without Geldof. 'Make no mistake, this concert is happening. This meeting is not about *whether* it happens – just about *how* it happens.'

The meeting was not productive.

Various dates were mooted, but there was only one date Geldof wanted: 2 July, the Saturday before the G8 summit. That was completely impossible, he was told. Hyde Park was already booked that day by the Prince's Trust and Capital Radio for their annual Party in the Park concert. The meeting broke up with everyone present convinced that the Live 8 concert would not happen. Everyone except Bob Geldof.

As soon as he left the meeting, Geldof began lobbying Downing Street to pressurise the bosses of everyone who had been present in the Ranger's Lodge. First stop for him and Kennedy were the offices of the Prince's Trust in Regent's Park. Charles Dunstone was the chairman of the organisation's trading arm. He was surprisingly sympathetic and said that the trust would stand aside as long as Live 8 would cover the costs he would incur by cancelling the Party in the Park.

How much?' asked Bob.

'At this point, £350,000.'

'Deal,' said Geldof.

Kennedy gulped. Live 8 hadn't got going, hadn't raised a penny to cover its expenses and it was already £350,000 in debt.

Geldof was playing his cards close to his chest. In public, as late as the middle of May, he was still talking about the twentieth anniversary of the 1985 concert being marked by Intellectual Live Aid. But, behind the scenes, he was working on Live 8. Intellectual Live Aid was a big idea which continued to lumber down the runway, but just never got off the ground.

Back in the television edit suite, while John Maguire was matching up his elegant *Geldof in Africa* footage to Bob's spare scripts, Geldof was doodling a new version of the Live Aid guitar-shaped logo. This time, the elongated neck of the guitar twisted itself into a figure eight.

※

Over at Number 10 Downing Street, work on preparing for the Gleneagles summit had come to a temporary halt. Tony Blair had called a general election. The government was coming to the end of its five-year term. Despite the controversy over the Iraq war, Labour remained ahead in the polls. The economy was relatively strong, with low inflation, low unemployment and sustained growth. Labour had delivered on key domestic promises on education and health, including reducing NHS waiting times. But tensions between Blair and Brown continued to simmer. Tony had still not given Gordon a date on which he might take over as prime minister. Blair hoped a fresh electoral mandate would strengthen his authority and allow him to control the timing of his departure on his own terms.

For all the strain between them, Brown and Blair were working well on Bob Geldof's Africa agenda, with the chancellor having spent many months lobbying on the debt issue with his fellow G7 finance ministers (Russia wasn't included because of its weaker economy). But the two men were undoubtedly kept in step on Africa by the fact that Brown's economic adviser, Shriti Vadera, was a good friend of Blair's Africa adviser, Justin Forsyth. They had worked closely together since they were both at Oxfam five years before. Both were close allies of Geldof, with whom they had been having private dinners at Shriti's home for more than a year, and both fervently agreed with their two bosses that this was the year for the UK to be as ambitious as possible on Africa.

'Gordon and Tony really complemented each other,' said Forsyth, 'and in their best moments they were the best double act in the world.' Not for nothing had Bono called them the Lennon and McCartney of global development. Many of the politicians around both men were very tribal in their allegiances, 'but because Shriti and I were really good friends, we could make sure that everything worked. Shriti worked immensely hard at it and, though occasionally she annoyed the Downing Street people, she made sure that the overall package was delivered.'

Usually before every G8 meeting, each world leader would appoint a personal representative called a sherpa (because they prepared the way to the summit). Ordinarily, these sherpas met regularly beforehand to hammer out an agreement. All that the eight most powerful people in the world then had to do was turn up, drink fine wine, chat about the latest pressing international situation and smile for the television cameras. But Blair and Brown had decided to do it differently. They wanted to leave the final agreement to the summit itself, in the belief that they would be able to press the other leaders to do a better deal for Africa.

'They basically told us: "Aim high. Don't blink first. Keep the key bits to the last moment. Use all the pressure from Make Poverty History and Live 8..." That was the strategy really,' Justin recalled.

But to do that, they had to convince the civil service. 'We were pushing the rest of Whitehall very hard in a way that was quite unusual for a G8,' said Blair's private secretary, Laurie Lee. 'The idea that so many of the big issues would still be open at the beginning of the summit was broadly unheard of.'

The problem was that senior civil servants didn't like this idea. They thought Blair and Brown were annoying the UK's allies unnecessarily by proposing an unrealistic package. After the election was called, and the politicians went out on the campaign trail, the civil servants immediately tried to water down Blair's demands to the rest of the G8. The package which

Geldof and the others on the Commission for Africa had agreed was now under threat from within.

Blair and Brown had foreseen this, so they had left Forsyth and Vadera behind in Downing Street to keep an eye on the Whitehall mandarins. 'I was told to stay behind and guard the ambition,' said Forsyth. 'I'd been brought in from Oxfam, in effect to be a link with Bob, with Bono, and everyone on the outside. The strategy was to use all the pressure from Make Poverty History to get people across the line. And, internally, to give Tony advice about which bits of the NGO world he could ignore because, whatever he did, they would never be satisfied. Political advice, not civil service or technical advice.'

He was also told to be on the lookout for sneaky tactics from the civil servants who, in effect, ran the country during the election campaign.

One morning, Justin was called to a meeting at the Foreign Office. He had a shrewd idea what would be on the agenda. He rang Shriti.

'You've got to come,' he said.

'It sounds really boring. Do I really need to come? Because there are other things that are pressing.'

'I really need you to come to this meeting. It'll be obvious when you come because they're going to try to erode the G8 agenda.'

Justin was right. 'They thought that the ambition that we had of doubling aid, cancelling debt – and universal access to education and AIDS treatment, and the International Finance Facility that Gordon wanted – all of that was madly ambitious,' he recalled. 'So they just thought, *Right, while they're all out fighting an election, let's cut some of this stuff out and have a more realistic negotiating position with our G8 partners.*'

'You can't do this,' Justin told them. 'Your political instructions from the prime minister and the chancellor of the exchequer have been set down. You can't just change our negotiating mandate. If we don't get the doubling of aid, and the debt cancellation and the universal access, this isn't going to work as a package. It needs to be a package.'

The civil servants looked set to plough on regardless. 'They thought that, because there were no ministers around, they could just do what they wanted,' said Shriti. 'Justin was the good cop and I was always bad cop, needless to say. I just threw my toys out of the pram and said, "I'm not having this. Justin and I are going to write the paper for the incoming chancellor and prime minister, whoever that might be. And it's going to say exactly the opposite of what you are saying."' Which is what she did.

Blair and Brown were re-elected, as everybody – including the wayward civil servants – knew they would be. On his return, Blair doubled down on his original approach. 'I was going to take the risks of failure rather than let fear of failure diminish the scale of [my] ambition,' Blair said. 'And I wasn't going to waste a moment or set my sights low.' It was a sentiment with which Geldof heartily agreed.

❊

By the time Blair and Brown had won the election, Geldof had enough stars on his list that he felt confident the Live 8 show would succeed. Indeed, he had too many but he was constantly trying to add more, to the despair of Harvey Goldsmith. 'One day in my office, we had the most furious row. Basically, Bob came and said, "We gotta add the Killers",' Harvey said. The band's single 'Mr Brightside' had charted in both the UK and the US.

'My kids are all complaining that all the only acts on the Live 8 bill are old farts,' said Bob.

'We cannot have one more act on this show because we are already going to overrun,' said Harvey.

Geldof was unyielding, as ever. The Killers were added.

On 8 May, Bob rang the Live Aid publicist Bernard Doherty, who was helping to run a VE Day concert in Trafalgar Square. He told him about his Live 8 plan.

'You are in, mate, whether you fucking like it or not,' said Geldof. 'And I'm not paying you.'

Next, he rang the artist Peter Blake, who had created the collage on the front of the 'Do They Know It's Christmas?' single. Blake worked quickly and came up with an image of the leaders of the G8 sitting, in their suits, with a map of the world behind them and, in front, a table loaded with cakes and party jellies. Looking on was the same skeletal child who appeared, like the silenced voice of conscience, on Blake's original 1985 Live Aid poster.

Geldof was thrilled, but he had one further request. Could Blake remove the politicians' suits and make them wear the uniforms from the *Sgt. Pepper* album cover which Blake had designed back in the day?

The artist got angry. 'Absolutely not.'

'I thought it was a ludicrous suggestion,' Blake said afterwards. 'It would look ridiculous. Anyway, I really didn't want to repeat the *Sgt. Pepper* idea because people often think it's the only thing I did.'

Geldof explained that McCartney and Bono wanted to open the concert with the opening line from *Sgt. Pepper*. 'And these G8 leaders are all Beatles fans. The prime minister of Japan has a Beatle haircut, literally. Putin is a big Beatles fan. They are all extremely vain and will love it if they think they are being associated with their idols.'

'No, I really don't want to…'

But, later, the line resonated with Peter Blake too – 'It was twenty years ago today.' He began to think, *What's going on now? Where have we got to?* Blake thought of 'the serial figure of the African child' with his back to the viewer 'who becomes us, becomes me, becomes Bob, becomes the world watching'.

His reluctance to put the politicians in Sgt. Pepper jackets was, he concluded, 'only to do with my relationship with the album'. (He was still sore about the meagre fee he had been paid for the cover of the multi-million selling album.) Once he set that aside 'and thought about what Bob was trying to do, I saw the point'. The politicians duly appeared in ironic homage to the iconic album.

But if things were falling into place for Geldof, the same could not be said of the Band Aid lawyer, John Kennedy. On 10 May, he felt impelled to write a letter to Bob and Harvey explaining to them that they were currently trading while insolvent. This meant that, as trustees, they were now personally liable for the debts which were being incurred – and that their personal assets, including their homes, were now at risk.

Bob did not read the letter. He was getting fed up of these legal and financial communications from Kennedy. So much so that he rang Kennedy's secretary, Lesley, and asked her to stop sending them.

'I just bin them without reading them so you might as well not bother.'

Her boss then immediately wrote to Geldof, who was chair of the Band Aid trustees, to say that he had to keep writing the letters, even if Bob binned them.

I imagine these envelopes are distinctive, so when you get them, you can put them straight in the bin without reading them if you choose to do so. If you have trouble identifying the envelopes, we could even write on the front of every one HEADING FOR THE BIN.

One day, you will complain there is something you don't know about and whilst I know you hate e-mail, it is great at keeping a load of people informed.

best wishes

John

The flood of letters, as Kennedy pointed out, were essential to the lawyer because Geldof would not use email. Always something of a Luddite and technophobe, he was a very late adopter of technology. Having masterminded the whole of the 1985 transatlantic Live Aid concerts with no more equipment than a telephone – and a landline at that – Bob felt no need to join the twenty-first century by getting an email address. He now wanted to organise Live 8 using only his Nokia 6210 phone, which he called 'the Stratocaster of mobile phones'. He never put this to his ear and only used the loudspeaker, very occasionally resorting to texts full of indecipherable spelling mistakes. All other communications had to be emailed to Zita, who printed them out and biked them round to Geldof's flat in Battersea – which was why he was getting as many as six separate letters a day from Band Aid's lawyer and moneyman.

To add to Kennedy's high anxiety, Geldof now decided that the concerts should be free. 'The expenses were clearly going to be somewhere over £8 million,' the Band Aid lawyer told Bob and Harvey. 'We haven't got a sponsor. If we go bankrupt, the three of us will be responsible. The only comfort I take from this is you two are richer than me. So hopefully you'll pick up more of the bills than I will.'

Bob was unperturbed. The money would sort itself out. It always did. When the Metropolitan Police said they would be charging £5 million for policing the Hyde Park event, Bob just approached a couple of billionaires he met at a party on a boat on the River Danube and got them to sign a pledge that they would pay it if Live 8 couldn't. As to the letter warning that they were trading insolvently, Geldof opened it fifteen years later when, bored during a COVID lockdown, he decided to go through the contents of his attic.

Long before that, however, EMI had paid £5 million for the rights to the Live 8 DVD and Nokia and AOL came in with sponsorship deals for similar amounts. On 15 May, the BBC came on board, paying another £2 million. In the end, Live 8, though not a fundraising event, was to make a £12 million profit, which went into the Band Aid funds.

So how should they start to bring the other G8 leaders round to the agenda which Geldof and his fellows on the Africa Commission had agreed? Blair, Brown, Bob and Bono were of one mind. If they could get the US completely on board, the other countries would follow. They would not want to stand out as difficult. 'Don't worry, I'll bring them round,' Blair told his Gleneagles sherpa, Sir Michael Jay, who had taken on the role in February in addition to his job as permanent under-secretary at the Foreign Office. 'I knew that if George agreed,' Blair said later, 'no one else would disagree.'

Shortly after the election, the British foreign secretary, Jack Straw, visited Washington. He knew that George Bush was broadly sympathetic to what Blair wanted. The two had forged a really close personal friendship after Blair had controversially decided to back the US president over the invasion of Iraq. But Bush and his White House aides had objections to the way it was being proposed. 'America's position was broadly, "We don't want to do this through a multilateral process,"' said Laurie Lee. '"We don't want other people telling us what to do."' Washington would decide the how and when by itself.

President Bush received Straw with a mixture of jocularity and defensiveness. 'I know the Gleneagles summit is all about kicking American ass,' he quipped, to which Straw replied: 'Sometimes, Mr President, you present your ass to be kicked.' But he went on to reassure Bush that the UK was not trying isolate the US publicly as some US advisers suspected. The president ended with the reassurance: 'We'll play our part and I'll make it okay for Tony.'

Blair's top aides in Downing Street were unsurprised to hear that. A video meeting between Blair and Bush was held every week in the bunker of the basement of No 10. It was a top-level affair. Those present, in addition to the two leaders, included Vice President Dick Cheney and Blair's chief of staff, Jonathan Powell. One of the others always in attendance was Justin Forsyth, Blair's Africa adviser. His presence signified the importance which the prime minister attached to the issue of Africa.

'We'd always get there a little early before Tony, who was always run-ning late. And Bush was always running late too,' said Forsyth. 'So we'd be sitting there with Dick Cheney. It wasn't a meeting of minds,' he added, with considerable understatement. So much so that Jonathan Powell used to say, before the camera was switched on, 'Let's see who can make Dick Cheney smile…'

Cheney was routinely focused on hard security issues, on Iraq or global terrorist threats. Blair would always have Africa as number two or three on the agenda. 'Tony would be saying, "George, I really need your support on this bit of the Africa plan" and Dick Cheney would be looking at him as if he was completely mad.'

This was, to Justin Forsyth, evidence of the genuine importance of Africa to Blair. 'At this level of politics, you have to make a calculation as to how much political capital you are willing to spend to get the result you want. Well, Tony Blair, in his weekly meeting with George Bush, kept rais-ing Africa, so Bush knew it was important to him.'

And Downing Street knew how important Africa was to Bush. He had shown a massive commitment in launching his $15 billion President's Emergency Plan for AIDS Relief just two years earlier. 'His passion for Africa was almost religious and there were a lot of people around him in the White House we knew shared that passion,' said Forsyth.

'Bush felt like you could tackle AIDS, or debt, or aid – but to try to do all of it in one go was ridiculous,' Forsyth recalled. By contrast, 'Tony believed that it was really important to have measures on education and conflict and governance as well as on aid, trade and debt. Actually, he believed that doing just one of them was counterproductive because Africa needed a comprehensive package of support. He wanted to change the narrative about Africa.'

It was all very well for Bush to say, 'I'll make it okay for Tony', but how he would do so was unclear. The need for Live 8 was growing ever more evident.

❧

A few days later, Midge Ure got an email from John Kennedy.

'Bob wants you to do the Scottish event,' it said.

'*What* Scottish event?' asked Midge.

Bob rang him. 'Concerts in Rome, Paris, Berlin, New York and London,' he said briskly. 'It will end with a long walk for justice. Everyone will end up in Edinburgh for a rally.' On the actual eve of the G8, there would be a concert in Murrayfield. 'Will you organise it?' Bob asked and, without pausing to wait for an answer, added: 'One final thing. Don't tell anybody that we're doing it. I'm denying everything. George Washington I'm not. I will lie until we're ready to announce.'

After a brief panic, Midge contacted three people: Tom Hunter, Chris Gorman and Graham Pullen. 'Tom and Chris were the money men. Chris Gorman was a Newcastle lad and multi-millionaire who took six weeks off his business,' Midge recalled. 'Twenty years ago, Tom Hunter sold trainers from the back of a Transit van. Today, he travels in a Rolls-Royce that's so flash, it makes FAB1 look like a Dinky toy. Tom told me that he wanted to get involved because, twenty years earlier, all he knew of the world was selling trainers. When Band Aid 20 and the Live 8 DVD came out, he donated pound for pound what they made, up to £7 million. Once they came on board, they guaranteed the money to put on the concert.'

Graham Pullen, a former manager of Edinburgh Playhouse who was now a major concert promoter, told Midge to focus on getting the artists. Pullen would deal with everything else – the stage, the lights, the sound, the security and even the Red Cross. The special magic of Band Aid, which from the outset had prompted everyone to give their services for free, was undiminished. Tom Hunter even offered to pay to re-lay all the Murrayfield turf after the concert.

In the US, Bono broke off from U2's Vertigo tour for a private meeting in Washington with Condoleezza Rice, who had just been promoted to US secretary of state. George Bush needed to come on board with the Africa agenda, he told her, otherwise Bono would tell U2 audiences at every concert to ring the president. He would give out the switchboard number from the stage, he said.

'I'll get 10,000 fans a night to call the White House,' he said.

Dr Rice was unimpressed. 'We can take the calls,' she simply replied.

'Right,' said Geldof, when he heard. 'We've got to do something so fucking *big* that even *they* can't ignore it.'

Bob's final roll of the dice was to embark upon a campaign to entice the world's most eminent figures to participate in Live 8. He could not have aimed higher. He wrote to Pope Benedict XVI, the Dalai Lama and Nelson Mandela, asking them to turn up in Edinburgh for the rally.

'You don't imagine they will actually come, do you?' I asked him.

'Doesn't matter,' he said. 'I'll be able to say tomorrow that they've been invited.'

At a press conference in London the following day, 31 May 2005, Geldof announced them, along with Paul McCartney, Coldplay, Madonna, Mariah Carey, Robbie Williams, R.E.M., Dido, Scissor Sisters, Keane and Stereophonics.

In Philadelphia, Stevie Wonder, Will Smith, Jay-Z and Bon Jovi would be on stage.

The line-up at Unter den Linden in Berlin would include Brian Wilson, Lauryn Hill, A-ha and Crosby, Stills & Nash.

Outside Paris, at Versailles, those on stage would include Jamiroquai, Craig David, Youssou N'Dour and Yannick Noah.

At the Circus Maximus in Rome, Duran Duran and Faith Hill would appear.

More than a thousand artists would perform across the eight venues to pressure the leaders of the world's richest G8 nations into taking action on African poverty. And, having announced he had invited the Pope, the Dalai Lama and Nelson Mandela, it would be 'the greatest show on earth'.

But Geldof and Richard Curtis also hoped that it would be much more, they said. 'This is not Live Aid 2,' said Bob. 'These concerts are the start point for the Long Walk to Justice, the one way we can all make our voices heard in unison.' Politics is numbers, he added. 'Tony Blair will go to a five-star hotel on a golf course next month and say to seven other guys, "I come with the largest democratic mandate ever collected in the history of this planet."'

Some 70 million people have died of AIDS in Africa, explained Curtis on behalf of Make Poverty History. 'We've got our own private holocaust going on now.' If 50,000 people a day died in Europe, leaders would 'find the money to solve that particular problem as they walked from the front door at Gleneagles to the reception'.

Tickets for the Hyde Park concert were to be allocated by a text message competition beginning a week later with text messages costing £1.50. Two million people applied. Live 8 looked set to be watched by even more people than had seen Live Aid.

———◆

CHAPTER 33

MAKING PIGS FLY

'Gosh, Bob.' That was all Tony Blair could say. Geldof had gone into Downing Street to tell the prime minister of his plans to get huge numbers of people out on to the streets in the capital city of every G8 nation.

It was a madly ambitious notion, one which dwarfed all previous plans. Geldof spoke of the eight concerts, of the big-name veterans and the new generation of artists who had signed up, of his plan to get Pink Floyd to set aside their twenty-year feud and re-form. He might even bring back the Spice Girls. 'The only person we haven't got is Elvis,' he said.

That was only the start. Geldof was planning massive fleets of trains and boats and planes to move activists to march upon Edinburgh ahead of the summit. He'd asked Richard Branson to provide free transatlantic planes to bring marchers from the US and trains to move them within the UK. John Travolta, who was a pilot, would lead a fleet of jets from Hollywood. He had asked the around-the-world yachtswoman, Dame Ellen MacArthur, to head a cross-channel flotilla of little boats to bring marchers from France, an operation he described as 'Dunkirk in reverse'. On and on he went. The plan was to get a million people to Edinburgh.

Tony Blair laughed as Geldof outlined more and more of the wheezes he had dreamed up.

'Gosh, Bob.'

Later, however, he was more articulate. 'What can I say about Bob? He can drive you completely nuts. He can talk forever. He can speak to world leaders like they were errant school kids. Personally, I didn't mind that – but I was the exception, believe me.'

Others had no trouble in speaking their minds. Edinburgh's police chief immediately criticised Geldof for encouraging such a large crowd to assemble in the Scottish capital with so little notice and no consultation with local authorities about how to accommodate so many people. But Bob was not bothered, just as he was unconcerned when the cross-channel flotilla didn't materialise.

'Won't it be embarrassing,' I asked him, 'if a million people don't turn up in Edinburgh after you've made this announcement?'

'Not at all,' he replied laconically. 'Just announcing it has the desired effect, even if people don't turn up.'

In any case, he had victories to cover any reverses. Two days after the press conference, Gordon Brown announced that VAT would be waived on the cost of the Hyde Park concert. Geldof had no need to fight a battle, as he had had with Margaret Thatcher. Gordon even did the sums for Bob, estimating that his VAT exemption would save Live 8 half a million pounds. And, at the same time, the chancellor publicly supported Geldof's call for rally in Scotland on the eve of the G8.

✂

Although Gordon Brown had worked extremely hard to get the G7 finance ministers to the brink of an international agreement to cancel huge swathes of developing world debt, Tony Blair knew that there was still one last push needed to get President Bush over the line. A week after the press conference to launch Live 8, the prime minister set off for the United States.

He flew into Washington late at night through a massive storm. 'We were flying through lightning,' recalled his Africa secretary, Laurie Lee. 'It was scary stuff.' He hoped this was not an augury of things to come. A big meeting of finance ministers was happening in London the following week. Blair's main goal was to help Brown get the debt deal done then so they could use the last month before Gleneagles to negotiate everything else.

'The US were happy to agree on the debt relief, but they didn't want to pay for it,' said Lee. 'They wanted the money to come out of IMF and World Bank funds. Gordon argued that the G7 needed to provide the money for the debt relief, otherwise the fund and the bank would be starved of funds to make future loans to developing nations.'

That's fine by us, said Washington. The IMF and World Bank could just cancel the debts and become smaller institutions with less money. *No problem*, the Bush administration thought. *Big problem*, thought Gordon.

Bush and Blair had a private dinner, just one-to-one. Blair went in armed with two arguments. One, a perennial theme of Geldof's, was that things were getting better in Africa so more aid would be building on success, not compensating for failure. The other was that Africans were increasingly seeing the importance of good governance and anti-corruption initiatives. Later that night, Blair spoke to his confidant, Alastair Campbell, who recorded in his diary that the prime minister seemed to have made real progress on debt, aid and Africa. 'Bush was ready to wipe out $15 billion worth of debt and join in big style with the general trend of huge increases in aid,' Blair told Campbell, though the PM noted that 'Bush was a bit sore that [the US] gave so much and yet still got seen as mean and difficult'. He was also 'sick of being lectured' by European and African leaders. On the plane home, Blair briefed his aides on his private talks with Bush. He was optimistic things were going in the right direction.

❖

There was quite a backstory to all this. Rewind six months, to February and the day Bob Geldof introduced Nelson Mandela to the Make Poverty History crowds in Trafalgar Square.

Mandela had gone from that rally to meet the G7 finance ministers at the invitation of Gordon Brown. Before their dinner at Lancaster House the following day, Mandela gave a short but intensely moving speech. In it he praised the politicians sat before him for the new 'resolve of the developed world to make war on poverty in the developing world'. He told the finance ministers that Africa needed a big package now rather than individual initiatives dribbled out over the years. Debt should be scrapped now. So should the subsidies and tariffs given to rich Western farmers, which penalised the exports of poor nations.

This was the very package for which Geldof had lobbied in the Commission for Africa and which Brown had been pressing on his fellow finance ministers for the past two years. The Mandela magic worked on everyone – 'though it possibly didn't work on the Germans', one of those present archly observed. Germany's socialist chancellor, Gerhard Schröder, had developed a deep antipathy to Tony Blair after the invasion of Iraq.

The recommendation of the Commission for Africa was for a doubling of aid, to $50 billion a year every year for the next ten years. At the February meeting, Brown had secured agreement on $43 billion of the $50 billion. 'Gordon had done most of the heavy lifting on both aid and debt,' recalled his aide, Shriti Vadera. But various sticking points remained. One was over the debts of Nigeria, which was an oil-rich country and therefore should not get any debt restructuring, the Germans said. When agreement was not forthcoming, Brown forced the ministers to carry on talking all night. 'Nobody was allowed to leave the room until they committed,' said Shriti.

At one point, the tetchy German finance minister told Brown to stop getting members of Christian Aid to send postcards and emails to him protesting about the lack of progress.

'I know they're from you, Gordon, because one of them came from your mother.'

Gordon laughed. 'We needed all the pressure we could bring to bear,' said Shriti. In the end, the debt deal that Brown secured went further than the agreement between Bush and Blair in Washington earlier that week.

But the big problem with the February meeting of the finance ministers was that the US Treasury secretary, John Snow, did not turn up. A US government website said he had 'a bad chest cold', but it wasn't bad enough to prevent him appearing in an online Q&A session with members of the American public. As a result, the $7 billion from the US had not materialised – and Gordon Brown was counting on it to take the $43 billion up to the required $50 billion to double aid.

What was really going on became evident when the phone rang in the middle of the Lancaster House meeting. It was Blair asking to speak to Brown. He had just had Bush on the phone. The Americans had not turned up because Bush had decided that the whole Commission for Africa package was 'too much to commit to'.

'He's happy to do HIV/AIDS. That's what he's interested in. That's what he wants to do,' said Blair. 'He doesn't want to do all this debt relief and doubling aid. He just wants his money to go on HIV and that's it.'

Gordon Brown was alarmed. 'That leaves us $7 billion short,' he told the prime minister.

'Gordon, I think you need to back off. The Americans are getting really wound up.'

'But, Tony, what is the point? What's the bloody point of being in government if we're not gonna do this? You've got to do this.'

The rest of the room went silent. Everybody was listening.

'Look, Bush is telling me we need to back off. Gordon, you've got to back off because I've got this guy on the phone, you know, ringing me three times a day, telling me to back off.'

'Well, just tell him to fuck off,' said Gordon and put the phone down.

All of this explains why it was essential for Blair to go to Washington to see Bush in person before the next G7 finance ministers meeting on 11 June. There was a clear sense in both Downing Street and the Treasury that Bush wanted to give something to his friend Blair rather than the more prickly Brown.

⁂

Having been criticised at Live Aid for not having enough black acts, twenty years later, Bob Geldof found himself being attacked for not having enough African acts. This time there were plenty of big-name black artists on the various Live 8 stages, including Stevie Wonder, Jay-Z, Kanye West, Destiny's Child, Alicia Keys, Snoop Dogg, Mary J. Blige, Will Smith and Patti LaBelle. But two weeks after the Live 8 concerts were announced, Damon Albarn – the Blur and Gorillaz frontman, who had collaborated with musicians in Mali – declared that the list of artists in the London concert was 'too Anglo-Saxon'. The Senegalese musician Baaba Maal called it patronising. Live 8 was 'a noble idea', but 'if you want to get the message to the poor, you have to use their language, which is their own music,' he said. 'It will be Africans who are going to make this work,' which was ironically the very conclusion hammered home by Geldof at the Commission for Africa.

Geldof responded with the same defence he had deployed at Live Aid. The concerts were about attracting the biggest audiences possible and that meant using the artists who sold the most records, regardless of their ethnicity. 'It is academic what the colour of the artist is,' he said. 'It is who sells records.' He was supported by the Grammy-winning singer from Benin, Angélique Kidjo, who asked: 'Why are we having this controversy? If there were not big stars, there would not be the attention of the media. What is important is that we all work together against poverty.'

But now, in the twenty-first century, the zeitgeist had shifted and Bob's defence sounded rather old-fashioned. Representation was a widely accepted concern. Geldof's attitude betrayed 'a deep disregard and disrespect for African musicians,' one critic told him.

Bob maintained his robust defence in words. 'My job isn't to promote African music,' he said. 'We are not doing an arts festival, we are trying to fill stadiums and arenas and get millions on the streets. This is about politics.' Yet, for all that, the Live 8 organisers swiftly added three black artists to the Hyde Park line-up: the British R&B singer Ms Dynamite, the US rapper Snoop Dogg and the Senegalese musician Youssou N'Dour. And Geldof extended an invitation to help Albarn organise a parallel concert with African artists in Regent's Park, but heard nothing back.

Peter Gabriel, the co-founder of the world music festival WOMAD stepped forward. He had been approached by Midge Ure about artists for the Murrayfield concert. Now he offered to organise a ninth Live 8 concert – Africa Calling. 'I talked at some length with Bob about this,' Gabriel said. 'I understand his criteria of trying to keep the largest audience around the world switched on and looking at issues about Africa through the artists selling the most records. I would have done it a different way – I think it's important to be seen to be allowing the voices of Africa to be heard directly.'

Africa Calling would be held in Cornwall on the same day as the other Live 8 concerts. Its African acts would include Youssou N'Dour, Angélique Kidjo, Mariza, Salif Keita, Thomas Mapfumo and Maryam Mursal. The DJ Andy Kershaw condemned it as 'musical apartheid', but Damon Albarn was pleased. His criticisms, he said, had in some degree been addressed. 'That's really good … Live 8 will make a difference – it's already created a debate that we're all involved in. Everybody's working to the same end.'

❊

Bob Geldof was in the studios at Abbey Road when the plan came about for a *tenth* Live 8 concert. It came in the form of a message from Nelson Mandela. Around three weeks before the concerts were to be staged,

Mandela was told about Live 8 by the chairman of his foundation, John Samuel.

'How can it be that this whole thing is focused on Africa, and not one single concert is happening in Africa?' the great man asked.

Samuel contacted Kumi Naidoo, the chair of the Global Campaign for Action on Poverty, who was based in South Africa. Kumi travelled to the UK to meet Geldof, only to be given the usual line about Africans not having sold enough records. But the message from Nelson Mandela was a potent one. Kumi said the World Alliance for Citizen Participation, of which he was secretary-general, would be happy to help organise the African leg of the concerts in Johannesburg. Geldof agreed to release some of the money which had been raised from corporate sponsors.

'It was a modest amount compared to what was spent on any of the other concerts, but it enabled us to pull together a team of performers,' Kumi said. 'But basically, Bob delivered on our requests. It was very last minute, and it would have been better if they had included African artists earlier, but, in the event, Nelson Mandela came to the Johannesburg concert and film of the speech he made was shown at the other Live 8 concerts and on pretty much every news bulletin all around the world.'

⁂

Within a few days of the Live 8 tickets being allocated to the public, a number of ticket holders – whose entrepreneurial instincts outweighed their ethical ones – put the free tickets up for sale on eBay at extortionate prices of up to £600 per ticket. 'Would really help to pay off student debts,' said one of the more shame-faced sellers, asking £300 apiece. Another offered to swap a pair for men's quarter-final tickets on Wimbledon's centre court. Geldof was outraged, calling it 'profiteering from the poor'. But eBay was unrepentant. The sales were perfectly legal, it insisted.

Kate Garvey, who had left her job in Downing Street after running Tony Blair's successful election campaign, was now helping out on Make Poverty History in Richard Curtis's Portobello Studios office. Bob's response offered her an instructive insight into the difference between working in government and in the activist sector.

'I'd gone from being gamekeeper to poacher,' she laughed. 'In Downing Street, there were lots of hoops you'd have to go through to do anything.

But Bob just says, "This is a fucking disgrace" and marches out to an ITV television crew who were filming outside and tells them what he thinks. We soon get a call from the head of eBay, who wants to speak to Bob.'

But, by this time, other television crews have turned up outside. 'I say, because I've got my old Number 10 head on, "Right, why don't you speak to the chap from eBay? He's surely going to capitulate and do what you want. Then we can gather the media, you can go outside and you can announce that you've sorted it.'

'Fuck that,' said Geldof, marching outside to the cameras.

So Bob went out and told the public that eBay were 'electronic pimps' for selling tickets to free concerts. The public should all boycott the use of eBay and conduct a campaign of cyber-terrorism by lodging ridiculous bids of millions for the tickets.

The media lapped it up. 'So he builds it and builds it,' said Kate. 'And all the while the guy from eBay is waiting to speak to him. So when Bob finally speaks to him, he capitulates immediately and then Bob calls all the media back to tell them. It was genius. He just got all-day live news, it was brilliant.'

Later that day, eBay formally announced they were blocking the selling-on of Live 8 tickets 'because of the concerns of our customers'.

❊

Events began to move apace. By now, Bob was based permanently in Portobello Studios, having hijacked Richard Curtis's entire office staff for the running of Live 8. 'He spent all day marching around the offices, wearing a hideous pink jumper, and shouting into his mobile phone,' Curtis recalled.

Two weeks before the concert, when the Gleneagles deal was still $7 billion short, the phone rang in Curtis's office. It was Paul Wolfowitz, the man who had provided George Bush with the intellectual rationale for invading Iraq. Wolfowitz had been moved on: he was now head of the World Bank.

Wolfowitz was ringing to tell the Live Aid campaigners what they should say to persuade Bush to cough up the final $7 billion. Bono was due to meet the US president in a couple of days, but, first, U2 had a gig in Manchester on 15 June as part of their Vertigo tour. Backstage, as the rest of the band prepared to go on at the Etihad Stadium, I briefed Bono with the intelligence which Wolfowitz had passed on.

'It's not generally known but one of Bush's daughters, Barbara, has been working clandestinely in an AIDS hospital in Africa,' I told him. She had visited a clinic in Botswana in 2003 when her father went to launch his PEPFAR initiative. She had been shocked, she said, to see literally thousands of people lining the streets, waiting for drugs that were plentifully available back home in the United States.

'After graduating from Yale last year, she returned to Africa to intern at a paediatric AIDS initiative there, working to give psychological support to HIV positive children. Wolfowitz says that the president's other daughter, and his wife Laura, are big advocates of teaching girls to read. He says you should press Bush for the money, saying it is needed for AIDS and girls' education.' Two days later, Bono met Bush and pushed the right buttons. Bush agreed to come up with the final $7 billion.

Between them, Blair and Brown, with assistance from Bob and Bono, had pulled it off. The next finance ministers' meeting agreed to double aid and find an extra $22 billion of debt relief for eighteen of the poorest countries. 'Gordon Brown deserves enormous credit for that because he did all the legwork for many years to get to that point,' said Blair's Africa secretary, Laurie Lee. 'And Blair played a key role by getting Bush to agree it, after which all the other countries knew they had to fall in line. But the idea that all of this had to be done as a complete package came from Bob and the Commission for Africa. It was the Bible, the roadmap, the intellectual framework for the whole achievement.' And Bono had given it the final push.

Together, they could achieve things which separately they could not.

Reports were coming in that there would be provision for more than a million people at Philadelphia. But there could only be 300,000 in Hyde Park.

'Why can't we have more?' asked Bob. 'The park is massive.'

'It is about health and safety,' came the reply from the Royal Parks Department

'Bollocks,' said Bob.

He arranged to meet the senior civil servant in charge of Hyde Park. John Kennedy went with him. The Band Aid lawyer got to the parks office first and was chatting informally over a cup of tea 'with the lovely parks lady' before the meeting started.

'To be perfectly honest, Mr Kennedy,' said the woman from the Royal Parks, 'this is going to be a very short meeting.'

When Geldof arrived, he outlined his plans: 300,000 people in the ticketed area – plus another 200,000 watching on giant screens in another part of the park. 'That's half a million. That at least sounds respectable.'

The lovely parks lady was very polite. 'I understand your ambitions, Mr Geldof, but it is not safe to have 200,000 people in that field. We are not able to deal with 300,000 there and 200,000 here. This just can't happen.'

The argument went back and forth for a while before Geldof produced yet another Bob Bluff.

From his pocket, he produced a scrappy piece of paper and showed it not to the woman from the Royal Parks, but to John Kennedy.

'Kennedy, do you know what this number is?'

'I have no idea, Bob.'

'That number is a direct line to the chairman of the International Olympic Committee. At the moment, the International Olympic Committee is thinking about whether to award the Olympics to Paris or to London.'

Kennedy was thinking, *Where on earth is this going?*

'What do you think he would say if I called him up and said London is not even capable of putting on a concert for 500,000 people? What chance have they got of putting on the Olympics?'

Kennedy looked at Geldof. *I can't believe you just said this*, he thought to himself. 'I'm thinking, *Please don't do this*.'

The woman from the Royal Parks summoned up the bravura to push back: 'Mr Geldof, I don't like your tactics, but I will discuss this with my colleagues.' She left the room.

On the way back to Kennedy's office, the incredulous lawyer challenged Geldof: 'Would you *really* have used that number?'

'I knew I'd never have to.'

Live 8 got the screens for the extra 200,000 people.

Bob Geldof was on a train passing through East Croydon, not exactly a rock star destination, when his phone rang. It was David Gilmour.

'Bob, there's no point. Get off the train.'

'No, I'm coming anyway.'

The headline was too easy. 'Pigs might fly', said several newspapers when the rumour broke that Geldof was trying to get Pink Floyd to reunite to play Live 8. The band had splintered acrimoniously two decades before, with Gilmour and Roger Waters locked in a bitter feud ever since.

That hadn't deterred Geldof. He had rung Gilmour. It had been more than ten years since the band had played live together.

'David, will you put Pink Floyd back together to play Live 8?'

'No. I'm in the middle of my solo album.'

'I'll come down to explain.' When Gilmour heard Geldof was on the train, he tried to turn him back, without success.

Bob travelled down to Gilmour's farm in the Sussex countryside, armed with a number of arguments.

'First, the way things ended, you never said a proper goodbye to your fans – and they deserve a thank you for buying you this amazing fucking farmhouse.

'Second, if you guys get together, you'll attract minimum of 30 million additional fans and they'll be the kind of fans who wouldn't turn out to watch anyone else on the bill. If you don't play, we'll lose them and that will be a body blow.'

Gilmour's wife, the novelist Polly Samson, leaned back against the farmhouse Aga, holding a mug of tea and regarding Geldof rather quizzically.

'And, third, we'll never get this chance again. Everything is aligned: the twentieth anniversary of Live Aid, a sympathetic government chairing the G8 in this country, the Make Poverty History campaign, and all of these G8 leaders are of the generation that they will be Floyd fans – they'll all own a copy of *The Dark Side of the Moon*. Except Jacques Chirac – he's more Charles Aznavour...'

Gilmour listened in silence. 'He explained the whole thing to me in detail, which made me feel a bit guiltier,' the guitarist later said, 'but I was hanging on to my selfishness.'

'You've got enough great people,' he told Bob. 'You don't need us.'

'No, we need you.'

'I don't know, I...'

'Don't say no. Drive me to the station while you think about it.'

'But you know I'm going to say no.'

'Don't say no. Just promise me you'll think about it.'

Gilmour took him to the station and, as he left, gave him a sad little half-smile which said no without the need for words.

On the train back, Bob was angry – with himself as much as Gilmour. 'I'd given him my whole shtick and it had just bounced off that Floydian veneer of imperturbability,' he reflected.

As soon as he got off the train, Bob rang Nick Mason, Pink Floyd's drummer and the longest-serving member of the band. Nick was happy to play Live 8. 'Ring David and persuade him,' Bob said to Nick.

But Nick didn't want to do that. 'I thought David would become more entrenched if I called him up,' Mason told me. 'I told Bob to talk to Roger, because the only person who could get Dave to do it would be Roger.'

Nick then texted Roger: 'You might get a call from Bob.'

Geldof rang Waters. The two were on good terms. Bob had played the lead role in the movie Waters had written, dramatising the Pink Floyd album, *The Wall*. In 1985, Waters had written a song, 'The Tide Is Turning', about Live Aid. 'On Saturday night, the airwaves were full of compassion and light with a million candles burning,' he had sung.

'Roger was really pretty interested in doing it,' recalled Nick. 'He thought it was a good idea.' But bizarrely – perhaps because he knew that David had said no – Waters couldn't bring himself to actually say he would do it.

Eventually, Geldof said to him: 'Look, Roger, I think you want to do this, but you can't bring yourself to utter the word yes. So, I'm gonna sit here and say nothing for thirty seconds and if, in that time, you don't say no, then I'll take it you're doing it.' Which is what happened.

'It was as if,' Bob later reflected, 'he wanted to be able to blame somebody else for him agreeing to it.'

Then, very briskly, he said to Geldof: 'Can I have David's number?' After twenty years of not speaking, he didn't have it. Bob gave it to him.

Waters made the call. 'My mobile rang,' said Gilmour, 'and it was, "Hi, this is Roger. How about it?" It was … surprising.'

What changed Gilmour's mind? 'Roger said to Dave, "We should do this,"' recalled Nick, the band's go-between. 'And David felt, yes, we should. Or perhaps he felt it would be sort of unfortunate if he was the one person who stopped it happening. For me, the big thing was that – however great the arguments or disagreements in the past – people came together for the right reason.'

Announcing the Pink Floyd reunion, Gilmour posted on his website: 'I want to do everything I can to persuade the G8 leaders to make huge commitments to the relief of poverty and increased aid to the Third World. It's crazy that America gives such a paltry percentage of its GNP to the starving nations. Any squabbles Roger and the band have had in the past are so petty in this context, and if re-forming for this concert will help focus attention, then it's going to be worthwhile.'

Three days of rehearsals began in Black Island Studios in Acton, west London, at the end of June. It was, Waters later said, 'like putting on an old shoe'. But not for everyone. He felt put out that the others didn't want to take on board some new ideas he had. 'It made for an uncomfortable atmosphere,' recalled Tim Renwick, who played as an additional guitarist with them at Live 8. 'He did not seem to credit the fact that most of the musicians and crew had worked together on and off for seventeen years without him being there.' Eventually, Gilmour said to him: 'Look, we're doing four numbers and, at the end of the day, people are expecting to hear the hits exactly the way they sounded in the old days.'

The night before Live 8, with just half an hour before Hyde Park was due to close its gates, the reunited band walked out onto the Live 8 stage and played their four numbers. A couple of dozen workers in hi-vis jackets, putting up the barrier at the front of the stage, stopped, stared and applauded. They had just witnessed the first Pink Floyd performance with the reunited line-up for two decades.

After they finished, the four members of the band and their wives went out for dinner at the Ivy.

❋

Over at Lancaster House, the mansion on The Mall which houses the British government's wine cellars, a drama of a different kind was unfolding. The G8 sherpas were holding yet another meeting to try to agree the decisions for their leaders to sign off at Gleneagles.

The Live 8 concert had already had a significant impact upon the proceedings. Whenever details were released of another concert in one of the G8 countries, attitudes shifted noticeably in the negotiations. As Live 8 began to get huge media coverage in each country, its sherpa began talking about things that weren't on their agenda before. The tone of the debate changed. Finally, even Russia joined in. Vladimir Putin agreed that a concert could take place in front of the Kremlin. When Live 8 administrators asked if any further permissions were needed, they were told that there would be no red tape in Red Square. Indeed, Putin asked, would they like him to instruct any particular Russian bands that should appear?

'Er, I think it's supposed to be the pop stars putting pressure on the politicians, not the other way round,' Emma Freud told the Kremlin. The Pet Shop Boys had been in touch to say they'd like to do the concert in Moscow, along with several Russian bands who had said they would play.

At the sherpa meeting, the deal on debt was done. On aid, commitments had been made, but financing mechanisms were still under negotiation.

And there was a lack of progress in other areas. The British sherpa, Sir Michael Jay, had been told by Tony Blair to keep the bar high and not make early compromises. 'This was the opposite of the normal way of working,' said Justin Forsyth, 'and the sherpas of other countries were becoming increasingly anxious that they wouldn't have a deal ready in time for their bosses.' Blair told his team: 'I'd rather have no deal than a bad deal.'

The way the meetings worked was that discussion centred around a draft text in which everything that had not been agreed was surrounded by square brackets. 'This text was hugely in square brackets,' said Forsyth. Blair was gambling that he would be able to push his fellow leaders much further at the last minute at Gleneagles. Despite the pleas of the other seven sherpas, Jay remained unmovable. It was, said Laurie Lee, very unusual to hold up agreeing a G8 communiqué until so late in the day. If it hadn't been for Live 8 and Make Poverty History, 'I don't think the rest of the G8 would've tolerated that. They'd have just rebelled.' Things were going pretty close to the wire.

But Blair was determined to hold out. Negotiators were told not to agree to the deletion of any of the square-brackets material. 'Most of the important stuff is still in there, even if it is in brackets,' one of the negotiators told me. 'We've been told, "Whatever you do, don't agree to removing any of it. Leave it in brackets and let the PM take it to the table." He's probably the best negotiator of all of them.'

❋

After Geldof's triumph with Pink Floyd, the folk in Harvey Goldsmith's office began to dream about a reunion of the remaining Beatles. 'Paul McCartney was talking with Ringo Starr about doing something together and we were having discussions about how to deal with this,' Harvey recalled. 'Paul and Ringo were talking of doing a little set, and bringing on Dhani Harrison – George's son who is a good musician in his own right – but the plan got leaked to the papers and the idea got scotched.'

The leak was the final straw for the promoter. 'All the time we were sorting out artists, I kept reading it in the *Daily Mail* or the *Mirror* or the *Sun*,' Harvey said. 'And I'm going, *There's something wrong here. There's somebody leaking information.*'

He looked around the office. It contained quite a few additional people now, well beyond his usual staff, and he began to form a shrewd idea of who might be the culprit. So, he sprang a trap. 'One day, I announced to the office that my wife, Diana, was coming in to manage a special project. Next day, I sat Diana next to the person I suspected.' At a moment when only she and Harvey and the suspect were in the office, Diana looked up excitedly and shouted:

'Yes! The Spice Girls are getting back together for Live 8. They are gonna do the show!'

'Lo and behold, the next day, the front page of the *Daily Mirror* was "SPICE GIRLS REUNION AT LIVE 8",' said Harvey. 'I knew exactly who it was. I chucked her out of the office and said, "You're not coming back".'

The Spice Girls, of course, were never reforming, and nor did they.

✳

'Okay, send it now,' said the text. It was from Mick Jagger.

Bob Geldof went over to the fax machine and fed the paper through.

If the Beatles reunion was not to happen, there was still one '60s mega-group within Geldof's reach. The Rolling Stones had not played at Live Aid because Mick Jagger and Keith Richards were having one of their spectacular fallouts. But Mick was keen they should play Live 8 as the Stones, rather than as individuals.

'We're recording in France,' Jagger told Geldof. 'Best if you write to Keith directly. But wait 'til I give you the nod before you send it.'

Sometime later, Bob got a text: 'We're sitting down for dinner. OK, send it now.'

Pause.

'He's got the letter now. He's reading it.'

Sitting in his flat in Battersea, Geldof had an image of Keith Richards having dinner in some chateau in the Loire, reading the request. 'Keith gets this fucking note, reads it and then completely ignores it, saying nothing to any of the others.'

The following day, Bob contacted the Stones manager, Joyce Smyth.

'They can't come anyway,' she said. 'They've gotta stay out of the country for tax reasons.'

'Okay. But if they *didn't* have tax reasons, would they come?'

'Well, yeah, I expect so. Mick wants to do it.'

'If I can get them a tax break, will they come?'

'Oh Bob, don't be ridiculous.'

But ridiculous was not a word in the Geldof vocabulary. He rang Shriti Videra, Gordon Brown's right-hand woman.

'The Rolling Stones, it's fucking huge,' he told her. 'But they can't come because of a tax thing. Can you get them an exemption?'

The conversation went back and forth as Shriti herself went back and forth to the chancellor of the exchequer.

'They're not getting paid, Shriti,' Bob said. 'It's a charitable thing. They're huge. It's in the political interests of the country to get them on the bill.'

A few days later, the Treasury granted the Rolling Stones a 24-hour tax break. They would be playing in Hyde Park, but for tax purposes they would not officially be in the country.

Keith Richards seemed snookered. But he would not give in. 'They just can't do it,' the Stones manager said when she came back to Bob.

'After all that effort...,' said Bob. Even Geldof was defeated sometimes.

But that was not that. A few days before Live 8, Bob got back to his flat at one o'clock in the morning after a long day in Richard Curtis's office. He had not eaten for hours. His partner Jeanne prepared a late-night bowl of pasta. Just as he started to eat, the phone rang.

'Bob, it's Pete.'

'*It's Pete Townshend!*', Geldof mouthed to Jeanne. Even after all these years, he still could not fully fathom the enormity of getting a phone call from someone who had once been a poster on his teenage bedroom wall.

'Hi Pete,' Bob said, trying to sound blasé.

'Mick just called me and he's asked me to put a band together. Is there a slot for us?'

'Are you kidding? Mick Jagger and Pete Townshend? Of course, there's a fucking slot for you. Who else are you going to get?'

'I don't know, but I'll put something together. I've got some rehearsal rooms already. Mick's really excited.'

A few mouthfuls of pasta later and the phone rang again. It was Barrie Marshall, tour manager for Paul McCartney.

'Hi Bob, it's Barrie. Listen, Paul has just heard from Pete that he's putting a band together with Mick...'

'Yeah.'

'Paul's just wondering where are they going to be on the bill.'

'Oh, fuck me, man. It's just early days, I don't know.'

'Yeah, but, you know, Paul's finishing the show, isn't he?'

'Yeah, of course he is.'

'Okay, I'll pass that on. Good luck with everything. It's great what you're doing.'

Back to the pasta. The phone rang again.

'Bob, it's Pete. Paul's been on. So where, um, you know, where are me and Mick going to be on the bill?'

'Well, Paul's finishing the thing, and you know, the Floyd are reforming, that's fucking huge.'

'Yeah, it's great. So, are we going on before Paul or after? Mick wants to know.'

'Oh Pete, like, it's one-thirty in the morning, man, I've had a hard day. You know, you've just sprung this on me. Obviously, this is one of the great rock 'n' roll moments, you know, it's gonna be fucking amazing...'

'Yeah, but, you know, Paul's really worried about it.'

'I'll speak to Paul tomorrow.'

Back with his pasta, Bob's head was awhirl. Did Mick plus Pete think that together they were bigger than Paul? Could they think a Rolling Stone plus a member of the Who trumped a Beatle? He knew Keith Richards thought so.

Bob had heard that Keith had once hurled a newspaper across the room after it called the Beatles the greatest rock band in history. 'Rock band? They were a fucking shit pop band,' the Stones iconic guitarist had shouted. But Bob had promised Paul that he would open and close the show. Nothing could usurp that. All this was suddenly playing around in Geldof's head.

The phone rang.

'Hi Bob, it's Paul. I hear Mick and Pete's doing something. So, Barrie just said, like, that, you know, we're still going on last.'

'Abso-fucking-lutely. You're Paul, you go on last. You start the day with Sgt. Pepper and you end the day.'

Pasta. Phone.

'Hi Bob, it's Pete. Paul's been on. He says he's on last.'

'Yes, the vibe is he starts the gig and he ends it.'

'But where will we be?'

'Oh, for fuck's sake. Look, okay, what if Paul ends with "Hey Jude" and then he stands up from the piano and he says, "We started today with *Sgt. Pepper's Lonely Hearts Club Band*, so, ladies and gentlemen, may I introduce to you … the act you've known for all these years"? On guitar Pete Townshend, on vocals Mick Jagger, on piano Elton John, on bass Paul McCartney, on drums Nick Mason or Ringo Starr or whoever. You know, you all become the greatest ever rock 'n' roll band in all history.'

'Yeah, but I don't know if those guys will play.'

'I'll fucking ask them to play. Can you just work out what you're going to do with Mick? Fucking hell, you know, I'm trying to have my dinner. It's two in the fucking morning.'

'Okay. I'll speak to Mick.'

No time for pasta. Phone.

'Hi Bob, it's Paul again.'

'Paul, how come everyone's awake at two in the morning?'

'Yeah. I've just spoken to Pete. He says that they're coming on after me.'

'No, I said, to float the idea – but obviously I'd have to put it past you first – what if we hear "Hey Jude" and the world is singing it with you, and then you say, "I am Billy Shears" and you go into *Sgt. Pepper* again with Pete and Mick and whoever…'.

'Yeah, but I'm finishing the show, aren't I?'

'Yes, you are, Paul…'

'Thanks. Great. This is good, Bob.'

The phone rang one last time.

'Bob, it's Pete. I've had Paul on. You can't fuck with a Beatle.'

Pete, it seemed, had changed his mind – or had it changed.

'Pete, I'm not fucking with a Beatle. This was your idea, remember? I was just trying to suggest a way of keeping everyone happy.'

But not everybody could be kept happy. Some things were just not possible, even for Bob Geldof. And that was the end of the greatest band in history.

❖

The day before the Live 8 concert, the G8 sherpas were having another preparatory meeting. It was a warm day and the windows were open. Through them, the political representatives could hear the sound of the Live 8 rehearsals and soundchecks wafting across Green Park.

'By now, the sherpas were viscerally feeling the pressure,' said Justin Forsyth, one of the senior negotiators. 'They could hear the preparation for the concerts. They knew that the Make Poverty History marches went beyond the normal activists. This was a much bigger thing. The media across the world were telling them that this was mobilising middle England, middle America and ordinary people all across the industrialised world.'

At the end of the meeting, vital matters were left unresolved. The language on universal access to AIDS drugs had not been agreed by the Americans. And the US, Germany and Japan continued to resist the plan to include a firm commitment to boost aid by $50 billion in the summit communiqué. 'But,' recalled Forsyth, 'we pointed to the voices we could hear a mile away in Hyde Park to show why we would not compromise and why – unheard of for a G8 summit – were leaving major parts of the communiqué to be finalised in Gleneagles itself.' To bring the meeting to a close, Sir Michael Jay told the representatives that, unusually, they had all been asked to go to Downing Street for a drink with the prime minister.

When they got there, they were not ushered into one of the formal rooms in No 10 but were taken upstairs to the prime minister's flat. There, Tony Blair, relaxed and wearing jeans, welcomed them into his home. It was a masterstroke; it was not the head of government who spoke to them, but rather the private man. 'He was brilliant, passionate and clear about the bottom lines of what was needed from the G8,' recalled Justin Forsyth.

That was not all. There was someone else in the room – Bono. The singer had arrived half an hour before the sherpas to be briefed by Forsyth on the three key points to make: the need to reach the $50 billion aid target; the importance of funding specific 'deliverables', such as education; and the need for the G8 to send a strong message on trade to the World Trade Organization meeting in Hong Kong in December.

'Bono was brilliant with the sherpas,' Jay recalled. 'He is a subtler, more feline figure than Bob Geldof, who was a pretty straightforward sock-it-to-them sort of figure.'

'First, I tried to get them to laugh,' Bono later said. 'Then I tried to inspire them by asking them to think how proud their grandchildren would be if they did the right thing.' He spoke to the eight men about previous summits and concluded: 'This is the big one.' If they did the right thing, they could remember it for the rest of their lives: 'This is your chance to make history.'

Jay was impressed. 'They all loved it. They got his autograph to take home to show their children. It was the sort of thing which is not supposed to happen in diplomacy, but it can make a real difference, this parallel diplomacy. Blair was very good at getting that. And Bob and Bono were very good at delivering it. They enabled Blair to present the whole thing as being not just him asking for this, but the whole wider community. It was a clever move by Blair to have Bob and Bono working on it too.'

Or, to invert that thought, it was a clever move by Geldof and Bono to harness the government to work at their agenda.

Blair saw it in more nakedly political terms. Bob and Bono had gone to each nation and tried 'to frighten the pants off the leadership by demonstrating the breadth of public support for action on Africa. It was done cleverly, with them always giving enough praise to the leaders to encourage them. With Bob and Bono at the helm, there would be a sensible debate. If we delivered, they'd say we delivered. If not, they would condemn us. Fair enough.'

CHAPTER 34

IT WAS TWENTY YEARS AGO TODAY

Bono was very pleased with his new satin frock coat. He hadn't just ordered one for himself. He'd got Sgt. Pepper suits in different pastel shades for the rest of the band. Wearing them to open Live 8 would turn U2 into a homage to the Beatles' most celebrated album cover.

'You can't wear them,' Paul McCartney stated, baldly, when he saw them on the eve of the Live 8 concert. 'No one except the Beatles can wear Sgt. Pepper outfits.' After several days being subjected to his very exacting standards during rehearsals, Bono and the rest of U2 had learned the Pete Townshend lesson that you did not argue with a Beatle. The outfits are still in storage, unworn, Bob Geldof says, in the U2 warehouse in Dublin.

The next day, U2 gathered, as was the band's custom, in a quiet place before they went on stage. 'We're in our dressing room, we close the door, have this prayer thing,' Bono explained. 'Our tour manager, Dennis Sheehan, God rest his soul, knows nobody can come in in that moment. It's a private moment.'

This time, however, there was a loud banging on the door.

'Don't answer the door,' Bono said. 'Finish the prayer.'

When they went outside, Bono asked Dennis: 'What was that at the door?'

'Oh, um, that was Sir Paul McCartney.'

'Paul McCartney, oh God,' said Bono and ran out to find the great man. 'Paul, so sorry…'

'What were you doing?'

'We just have little prayer moments, you know?'

'Why didn't you ask me? I mean, if you'd asked me, I'd have loved to be part of that. Have it again, with me.'

The five of them went down in a huddle, like a football team before kick-off, at the bottom of the steps to the stage.

Whatever the prayer was, it left them all smiling.

�֍

The area at the side of the stage in Hyde Park was a glorious array of colour. Waiting to go on first were a dozen trumpeters of the Coldstream Guards. Their red tunics, white belts, silver trumpets and gleaming black bearskin hats made McCartney and U2 look dowdy in their pop-regulation denim. Behind them, four French horn players, who evidently hadn't been given the McCartney message, had got away with dressing like the Beatles from the *Sgt. Pepper* cover. A medley of 1985 Live Aid tunes blared from the speakers at the 300,000 crowd before the huge stage.

'There's a million already in Rome at the Circus Maximus,' Geldof shouted, although it turned out that, in the translation from the Italian, an extra zero had got stuck upon the early figure. 'They're pouring into the Palace of Versailles. Tokyo is in full swing. Good luck.'

McCartney stood, suddenly grim-faced, lips pursed with concentration, as the military trumpeters marched onto the stage to blow the opening fanfare.

'Ten seconds,' someone shouted.

'Here we go,' said Macca, punching fists with each member of U2 in turn.

'Ladies and gentlemen, it's two o'clock. This is Live 8, the greatest rock show in the history of the world,' boomed the voice of Jonathan Ross across the park and across the globe.

As McCartney belted out 'It was twenty years ago today', it did not, for once, sound like a rock music fiction. Bob Geldof stood at the side of the stage and watched with tears glistening in his eyes.

Nor did the emotional temperature drop when McCartney departed after the opening number and U2 took over. A cloud of 200 white doves were released and flew off across the stage as the band performed 'It's a Beautiful Day'.

'This is our moment,' declaimed Bono. 'This is our time. This is our chance to stand up for what's right.

'We're not looking for charity. We're looking for justice. We can't fix every problem. But the ones we can fix, we must…'

'It's all downhill now!' laughed Geldof in the wings. He was so elated that he even hugged Harvey Goldsmith.

❖

Geldof had arrived by helicopter earlier in the day. When he landed, he was besieged by journalists pointing microphones as he strode towards the backstage area. He spoke to them, but without ever letting up on his relentless pace.

'Are you nervous?'

'No,' he lied. An hour earlier, as we waited for the chopper at the Battersea Heliport, he had written in the visitors' book: 'I'm nervous!'

'How big an audience are you hoping for?'

'We're aiming for a TV audience of 5 billion, though ultimately we're playing to an audience of just eight.'

'How will you measure success?'

'By whether those eight men at Gleneagles do what the Commission for Africa has asked for on aid, trade and debt.'

'Will today really make a difference?' asked a US journalist.

'It will be the greatest cultural event in the history of the world,' said Bob with characteristic modesty. 'This will be a bigger broadcast than the Superbowl, the World Cup, even than the Olympics – and here, nations won't compete, they will cooperate. All the promise of rock 'n' roll is made concrete today. The answer is no longer blowing in the wind. There *is* nothing you can do that can't be done. All you *do* need is love.'

The big screen in the artists' area was already showing scenes from the first Live 8 concert to open. In Tokyo, a forest of arms were waving, fingers pointing, clutching sunflowers and wearing the white wristbands of *Hottokenai Sekai no Mazushisa*, the Japanese equivalent of Make Poverty History. From the start of the concert in Japan to the end of the Canadian concert, Live 8 would run continuously for almost twenty hours.

Milling around backstage at Hyde Park was an extraordinary collection of international figures, from Kofi Annan, the secretary-general of the

United Nations, to Brad Pitt, Bill Gates to Elton John, David Beckham to Robbie Williams, Ian McKellen to Madonna, Roger Daltrey to Posh Spice. The rapper Snoop Dogg walked through the crowd flanked by bodyguards the size of mini mountains. The stars had not arrived just before they were due on stage. They all wanted to be there from the beginning. No one, it seemed, was not famous.

�֍

Bob's fourteen-year-old daughter Pixie arrived. She was hoping to meet her latest crush, Pete Doherty, formerly of the Libertines, who already looked rather the worse for wear and it wasn't even 3 p.m. He was wearing a bandsman's bumfreezer jacket and peaked cap. Excess being the watchword of youth, he wore both belt *and* braces.

Doherty shambled towards us. He had found his disposable camera and was prepared to lower his cool for long enough to ask if he could have his photo taken with Bob.

Geldof introduced Pixie. 'She's in love with you,' he said, in the embarrassing way only a father can manage. Pixie seemed suddenly to find something very interesting to look at on the floor. She kept the 'I love Pete' henna slogan on her wrist well out of sight.

Geldof found Bill Gates in conversation with Roger Waters. 'You don't have to say this exactly,' he said, handing the philanthropist a speech. 'It's just a guide in case you wanted one.' Gates grinned and began to read it. His lips began moving as he learned his lines. His cue card had Dido's name spelled phonetically – Dye-doh – just to avoid any misplaced transatlantic emphases.

As he left the stage with Coldplay and collaborator Richard Ashcroft, Chris Martin introduced a short film about Africa to the crowd: 'It's probably the most important film you will see today. Just watch it. And if the BBC don't show it, they aren't doing their job properly.'

In fact, the film was *not* being seen by British TV viewers. The broadcasters had cut away in favour of some celebrity interview with Jonathan Ross for fear that showing it would be thought to compromise their political impartiality. Indeed, the BBC blocked most of the between-act films made by Richard Curtis for the Make Poverty History campaign. Television viewers in other parts of the world saw a more holistic show that explained far more fully the political injustices which had led more than a thousand artists to appear at the Live 8 concerts.

'It was a big shock to us to find the stance that the BBC were taking,' said the Band Aid lawyer, John Kennedy. 'They had been so instrumental in making Live Aid happen and they knew exactly what we were trying to do. Richard Curtis had made some fantastic short films illustrating the background issues on aid, trade and debt. We couldn't understand how the BBC could be against the idea of making poverty history – where was the Make Poverty Permanent party with which the broadcasters were seeking balance?'

Curtis himself, who had a relationship with the BBC to maintain, was more diplomatic. 'The BBC had seen the films and had reserved the right to show them, or not, according to their editorial feeling at the moment,' he said. 'I think that, at the final moment, whoever was calling the shots must have got an instruction that there was enough quite strong political and emotional content in the show already. But I don't actually know what happened on the day.'

By 3 p.m., when Elton John went on stage, the show was running ten minutes late. Harvey Goldsmith had estimated that the London concert would end at 10.16 p.m. – forty-five minutes after the time the Royal Parks authorities wanted the final sounds to die away. It was already running even further behind. Harvey began to get agitated.

Half an hour later, Bob Geldof made his first appearance on the Live 8 stage. A huge roar went up. 'Thanks for coming. It would have been crap if no one had showed up,' he told the crowd. He went on to introduce the next person to appear on stage: 'He is one of the great businessmen of our time and certainly the greatest philanthropist of our age. He says our plan is the right plan, it's the only plan. Ladies and gentlemen, one of our biggest supporters, Bill Gates.'

The plan Bob spoke about was the comprehensive package of more than ninety recommendations made by the Commission for Africa. 'I believe that if you show people the problems and you show them the solutions, they will be moved to act,' Gates told the crowd. Whether they were the words he was given, or remarks of his own, he began to be cheered. 'Success depends on knowing what works and bringing resources to the problem. We know what to do. We can do this and, when we do it, it will be the best thing that humanity has ever done.'

Word was filtering through to the artists that the BBC was blocking the
Make Poverty History films. Singers now began to beef up the introductions to their songs, knowing these could not be cut.

Dido, who duetted with the Senegalese singer Youssou N'Dour,
addressed the G8 leaders directly: 'There are millions and millions of voices
asking you to do the right thing and we will be waiting.'

Ms. Dynamite spoke to the British public: 'We as a nation have robbed,
killed, tortured and stolen from the Third World for centuries,' she said.
'If there is a debt to be paid then, surely, we are the ones that owe it,' she
added as she launched into Bob Marley's 'Redemption Song'.

'No more broken promises,' shouted Johnny Borrell of Razorlight. 'All
you need is love – John Lennon said that. Music can change the world –
Bono said that. Sign the fucking petition – I said that.'

Harvey was looking at the clock again. 'Bob,' he said, 'we're running
twenty minutes behind now. You're not thinking of playing, are you?'

Geldof was not down on the running order. There was no time, said
Harvey. If he sang, it would somehow diminish his role as a lobbyist at
Gleneagles, argued Richard Curtis. But Harvey had heard a rumour.
Geldof, a man who has learned from his contact with politicians that say-
ing nothing is preferable to lying, said nothing. But Bob had told the rest
of his band to turn up and be ready backstage. Just in case.

By late afternoon, nerves were beginning to jangle backstage. Brad Pitt
was now in the wings.

'Is there an autocue?'

'It's down there,' I told him.

'Is that it? Down there. It's tiny. Isn't there a big one out there?' he
asked, pointing towards the crowd in the hope that there would be one of
those transparent screens that politicians use so they can read their speeches
and look, apparently, straight into the eyes of their audience.

'Nope. That's it.'

'Are you sure?'

'Come on,' said his make-up lady. I'll help you learn it.' And off they
went.

It was approaching 5 p.m., the time when there was due to be a live
link-up between London and Philadelphia. At the backstage control desk
sat Lorna Dickinson, the executive producer for the BBC responsible for

the worldwide broadcast. Beside her sat Richard Curtis, controlling the Make Poverty History messages that flashed up above the stage throughout the day. And Mitch Johnson, the DJ known in the trade as 'the Voice of God', who was announcing each act across the Hyde Park PA system as they came on stage.

Across the way, Harvey Goldsmith stood at his desk; he was too tense to sit, particularly as the schedule slipped further and further behind. The Royal Parks might never allow him to do a show here again, he thought. His anxiety moved through the gears from agitated to annoyed to rather angry.

'We're running late, I said,' bawled Harvey. 'We're running later and later.'

Harvey started shouting at the Voice of God: 'Go!'

'Harvey, I'm waiting for a cue from the BBC,' said Mitch.

'Go!'

Next, he shouted at Lorna from the BBC.

'I've lost all talkback,' she replied calmly, pressing buttons that ought to have got her through to the rest of the BBC operation in various locations elsewhere on the huge site.

'Philadelphia is going live at 5 p.m.,' she said to Harvey. 'Make sure that Keane are off stage by 5 p.m.'

The veins in Harvey's temple started to bulge. It was he who was trying to get people off and everybody else who was buggering about wasting time, he fumed.

'Will Smith ready to go live at 5.'

'Stand by for voiceover.'

'Okay,' said Lorna. 'The crowds in each country are, consecutively, going to say hello to each other. This is something that has never been done in broadcasting ever before. Rome, Paris, Berlin, Ontario, Johannesburg, London, Philadelphia... If there's going to be a bloomer, it will be now. This is the global bloomer moment...'

Lorna jabbed one of her buttons. 'London calling Philadelphia... And Philadelphia isn't answering.'

'One minute, ten seconds to go,' shouted a technician.

'Oh God, there's no sound.'

Over in the US, the rap star and actor Will Smith began to speak. At least his lips were moving. Perhaps he was miming.

'There's no bloody sound!'

Harvey had done his bit. He got Keane off the stage on time and Geldof was already walking out. 'There are over three billion people watching you right this minute,' Bob told the crowd, who roared in delight. 'I want you to say hello to Paris and Rome and Berlin and Tokyo and Toronto and Johannesburg and right this second, in 84 degrees in Philadelphia, one million people are on the streets – your brothers and sisters on this weekend of independence in America. Let's make it a weekend of *inter*dependence.

'Will you please say hello to Philadelphia?

'Welcome America to Live 8.'

Over in Philadelphia, Will Smith walked out. Smith celebrated this notion of international solidarity by wearing a T-shirt bearing the legend 46664 – the prison number of Nelson Mandela on Robben Island during his two decades of incarceration as South Africa, waiting to be liberated from apartheid.

Behind him in a large frame was the actual American Declaration of Independence. Before him was assembled a staggering 1 million people all along the Benjamin Franklin Parkway.

'Philadelphia, shout out and say hi to Hyde Park in London.'

The world could hear him as he spoke. The heart-stopping terrible silence backstage at Hyde Park ended. Lorna from the BBC clapped in relief as the sound was restored to her monitor.

Smith then set off a chain reaction. The Hyde Park crowd roared greetings to the Circus Maximus in Rome, then Rome shouted out to the Brandenburg Gate in Berlin, Berlin to the Palace of Versailles outside Paris, Versailles to Ontario, and Ontario back to Philadelphia.

But then came a message that stilled the crowd in every country.

'And the reason that millions of you have tuned in is because every three seconds, in one of the poorest countries in the world, a child dies from extreme poverty. Dies of hunger or malaria or TB. Dies for lack of drugs that we here – in Philly, and you in Berlin, and you in Moscow – can buy at a pharmacy.

'Every three seconds someone else is dead.'

The eerie echo of a woman's aghast voice could be heard immediately after he spoke: 'Someone else is dead.'

Will Smith clicked his fingers in a slow rhythm to mark the timing of each death.

'Just like that. Every three seconds somebody's son, somebody's daughter, someone's future is gone.

'Dead.

'With a stroke of a pen,' he concluded, 'eight men can make a difference and end the misery of millions of people.'

The television screens showed fingers clicking in Paris, Ontario, London, Rome and Berlin. Smith was visibly moved as the thousands in the crowd held their hands aloft and clicked their fingers every three seconds. At the side of the stage in London, there were tears in the eyes of Lorna Dickinson.

'That was the moment everyone has been waiting for,' she said, turning her attention back to the broadcasting technology and blinking back her tears at the stark encounter with the remorseless ticking of the clock of death. 'That has never happened before. It was technologically amazing – a global moment in which different parts of the world talked to one another. How can we ignore Africa when its people can talk directly to us?'

※

For Harvey Goldsmith, a different clock was ticking. He had just received another message from the Royal Parks office reminding him of the end time. Yet, for all his worries about late-running, he knew in his heart of hearts that there was no way he was keeping Bob Geldof off the stage at Live 8. As Travis came off, Bob and his band were waiting in the wings. Travis had given Bob the nod that he could use their equipment.

The crowd in Hyde Park roared. 'I know it's cheeky,' he grinned, half-embarrassed, 'but I just had to play on this stage.' He sang just one song. Inevitably, it was the Boomtown Rats' biggest hit, their 1979 number one 'I Don't Like Mondays'. Inevitably, because it is his song that's best known across the world. Inevitably, because of its most famous line:

The lesson today is how to die.

It was the line that had stopped the show at Live Aid in 1985. A song written years before, after reading in a newspaper about a school massacre in the United States, had become charged with new meaning. A new, even more terrible meaning.

That day in 1985, he had stopped on that line, his fist in the air, and allowed the world to think. And now, in 2005, in a different place, in a different world, he did the same thing again.

There was still a pregnancy in the pause. But it was different from before, and it was a different man who stood there with his fist in the air. It was not just that the unlined face and the long brown hair had given way to features in which the years had etched their passing, or that the tangle of hair was now grizzled and on its way to being fully grey.

The difference was there in his eyes. In 1985, they had been filled with an uncomprehending horror, as well as a determination that something had to be done. This time, the horror had gone and in its place was the knowingness of a man who has learned that justice is harder than charity, but more essential. They were the eyes of a man who now saw further than he did before.

'Thanks for letting me do that,' he said at the end of the song.

Annie Lennox was up next. Brad Pitt was to introduce her. But first there was the small matter of his speech. 'Come on,' said the make-up lady, 'I know it as well as you do now. I'll say it with you from back here.' He stepped forward. Even for a Hollywood star, 300,000 upturned faces can be intimidating.

For all his earlier nerves, he gave a fine speech. He spoke of how, on his first trip to Africa, a young mother with AIDS had grabbed his arm and said: 'Please bring us the drugs, please help.' He had been startled at the time and the shock seemed to have remained with him. Today, he wanted to pass on that message to the Live 8 crowds. 'Let us be outraged, let us be loud, let us be bold,' he ended.

The crowd cheered wildly as he left the stage and Annie Lennox arrived. As she began, with a performance of 'Why' played solo at the piano, behind her ran a film made on her last trip to Africa. A caption flashed up: 'Everyone in this film has AIDS or HIV, apart from Annie Lennox. Many of them are now dead.' It was time to take action, she told the crowd, 'for all the nations where poverty and despair are a way of life'.

As Annie left the stage, Harvey glanced between his schedule and the clock. He was now a full thirty minutes behind. Another message arrived from the Royal Parks. He was not sure what more he could do.

His production team were achieving little short of miracles, working with immense speed and intensity – but without panic – to turn around the acts. 'Do you realise how long it normally takes to turn around these acts – some of them the biggest names in the world?' he said. 'About an hour. My guys are doing it in just four or five minutes.'

Harvey stormed over to the control desk. He pointed at Lorna from the BBC and Mitch the announcer. 'We're over half an hour late now. I can't do it this way. I gotta run to my own time. You're fired!'

Lorna ignored him.

Harvey turned to Mitch: 'You're fired!'

'You can't fire me,' said Mitch, 'You're not paying me. I'm working for free.'

Just before 8 p.m., Geldof stepped back onto the stage. 'Some of you were here twenty years ago, some of you were not even born. I want to show you why we started this long, long, long walk to justice. I want to show you, just in case you forgot, why we did this. Just watch this film.'

On the giant screen behind him began to play the video from the 1984 Ethiopian famine that had silenced the crowd at Live Aid in 1985. Again, the music of the Cars offered up its surreal, incongruous counterpoint. Again, the film ended on the face of a single child, a dying child. Again, the image stopped the world.

The audience in Hyde Park stood stock-still. They were visibly shocked, their eyes wide with horror, their jaws dropped with disbelief. As the television cameras panned along the lines of the crowd, the stunned silence was universal.

Then Geldof spoke again. Those in the crowd who had been reading cynical newspaper stories about how aid to Africa was a waste of time might be wondering, he said, why we should even try to do anything.

'I'll tell you why. See this little girl?' He gestured to the face frozen in time on the giant screens. 'She had ten minutes to live twenty years ago. And because we did a concert in this city and in Philadelphia, and all of you came, because we did that, last week she did her agricultural exams in the school she goes to in the northern Ethiopian highlands and she is here tonight. This little girl – Birhan. Here is this beautiful woman.'

A striking young woman strode onto the stage, beaming, with a smile which lit up the whole world.

She had the characteristic bearing of all the women of the Abyssinian highlands: noble, upright, confident, aristocratic. Her hair was plaited in cornrows across the crown of her head and then exploded in a glorious burst behind her. She wore a plain white dress, embroidered with blue Ethiopian crosses and covered in a *shamma*, a fine linen shawl. She looked like a princess.

The child had been snatched from the grasp of death and had become this fine young woman. It was a resurrection.

In that moment everything was different for the crowds around the world at Live 8. They had been bludgeoned with facts, but here was the person, Birhan Woldu, a twenty-four-year-old woman who made flesh those statistics. Each one of the children who die needlessly somewhere – every three seconds – is a Birhan, confident, beautiful, intelligent, brimming with possibility and potential. Here was the enormity of one life saved. Now do the multiplication.

Birhan, unfazed by the 200,000 people before her, addressed the crowd. 'Hello from Africa. We Africans love you very much,' she said in her native Tigrinya. 'It is a great honour to be here to stand on the Live 8 stage. We love you very much. Thank you.'

'Don't let them tell you that this stuff doesn't work,' Geldof told the crowd. 'It works – you work – very well indeed.'

Moving 'from one immensely strong woman to another', Geldof introduced Madonna, the only person on the bill whose name and reputation had penetrated Birhan's home village in the remote Ethiopian highlands. She had not heard of Paul McCartney or U2 or Elton John, but she knew about Madonna and had asked if she could speak to the world from the same stage as her.

It was a deeply emotional moment for both women. The pair hugged with huge intensity.

The Queen of Pop, the ultimate professional, was momentarily overcome. She raised Birhan's hand in hers – two hands, black and white – in a gesture of equality and solidarity, and held it aloft. It was a triumph of the human spirit, a uniting of the First World and the Third.

Of course, it was not Live Aid which had saved Birhan. She had been drawn back from the brink of death by the loving vigilance of her father, the skill of the nurse who rehydrated her, the devotion of the Irish nuns who ran the feeding camp in which she was filmed, the dedication of the Ethiopian men and women who worked there, and the aid that funded that Catholic feeding centre. And all that had happened months before the 1985 concert took place. But Birhan's survival was a testament to the fact that the compassion of ordinary people – combined with the efforts of those they sought to help – could change the world.

Birhan was living proof that aid worked.

Madonna continued to grasp Birhan's hand as she began her first song, 'Like a Prayer'. And beside the singer the young Ethiopian woman stood, like the answer to a prayer. She was a reminder of what the world loses each time a child dies of starvation, and an implicit reprimand to those who refuse to act to prevent millions of lives being wiped away by poverty every year. Her father Woldu had told her that God had spared them from the famine for a reason. 'I think today was the reason,' Birhan said solemnly.

'Was I okay?' Madonna asked Geldof as she left the stage, looking genuinely concerned that he might say she wasn't. But he didn't. She had been okay, he laughed.

As she moved off to her dressing room, she encountered Ricky Gervais, who was still lurking around after introducing R.E.M. and performing his exquisitely embarrassing dance routine from *The Office*. She told him he was her most favourite comedian in the world, said she worshipped him and told him she would clean his floors for him. His reply was to look at her blankly, and say mischievously: 'Who are you?'

The cynics in the press, whom Geldof lambasted with withering scorn in introducing Birhan, had suggested that the younger bands agreed to play Live 8 simply because it was a great way of putting themselves in front of the biggest audience the world has ever seen. 'Cynicism says more about the cynic than it does about people who find the idea of doing nothing intolerable,' said Fran Healy from Travis. 'I've been to Africa and there's not a day goes by now without me thinking of the people I met there and what I can do. All the bands here today know why we're here and know the issues. We have had to have a crash course in what it has taken Bob Geldof twenty years to learn. But the lesson is that if enough people get involved, anything can happen.'

By 8 p.m., when the Killers took to the stage, the show was running nearly an hour behind. But now a difficulty of a different kind presented itself. Nelson Mandela had appeared on stage and addressed the crowds at the Live 8 concert in Johannesburg. 'There's a problem editing the Mandela material,' one of the Make Poverty History Team announced, as he rushed over from the BBC mobile edit suite to find Richard Curtis. 'He's come in at eight-and-a-half minutes and they've edited it down to a minute and a half – but by dropping the reference to what the G8 must do.'

Curtis left the desk for the edit. Mandela was speaking more slowly the older he got and talking to a big audience in a large public space had slowed his delivery even further. His middle section – on aid, trade and debt – was uneditable. The BBC editor had done the best he could. But there was one line that could be put back: 'While there is poverty there can be no freedom.' George Bush would like that. Mandela ended with a paragraph which he now often repeated: 'Sometimes it falls upon a generation to be great. You can be that great generation. Let your greatness blossom.' Richard Curtis quietly smiled to himself but said nothing.

✶

Backstage, so many hangers-on were now traipsing in and out that a shift system had been introduced to keep visitors away from the three-foot margin Harvey had carved out for himself in the wings. Once a set was finished, the freeloaders were bundled out unceremoniously.

There was something odd watching from the wings. It was like seeing the concert down the wrong end of a telescope. The acts were performing only a few yards away and, sideways on, they seemed small and insignificant in the flesh. It was as if it were distance, and the frame of the screen, which gave the sense of scale, grandeur and history to the proceedings. Strikingly, throughout most of the concert, Bob Geldof stood with his back to the acts, watching them on the BBC's TV monitors.

Sting was out on stage now, singing 'Every Breath You Take'. Those paying close attention noticed that he had altered the words to sing: 'Every game you play, till election day, every bond you break, every step you take, we'll be watching you.' Behind him flashed the pictures of the G8 leaders he was addressing.

It was coming up to 10 p.m., half an hour before the Royal Parks authorities had insisted that the show must finish. Officials had been bombarding Geldof's phone all day with dire warnings demanding the concert must finish on time, but Bob hadn't looked at his phone since he arrived. But Harvey Goldsmith was getting the messages. Now he was approached by the Parks police, who informed him that they would be cutting off the power so that the huge crowd could disperse before London's public transport system closed for the night. 'I had to deal with a platoon of policemen marching towards the stage about fifteen minutes before the official curfew time. They were literally coming to switch the power off. And there were a quarter of a million people out in the audience.'

If the power were switched off without Robbie Williams, Pink Floyd and Paul McCartney performing, there could have been a riot. Band Aid's lawyer John Kennedy tracked down the leading PR man Matthew Freud – brother of Emma Freud and son-in-law of Rupert Murdoch – who was in the VIP section at the front of the crowd. Freud had brought along as his guest the culture secretary, Tessa Jowell, whose department was responsible for the Royal Parks. One word to the police from her and the threat to cut the power evaporated. Harvey Goldsmith could breathe easily at last.

As darkness fell, an additional magic seemed to descend on the place. David Beckham sauntered out onto the stage to introduce Robbie Williams. The England football captain gazed around like a man stumbling across something remarkable in a clearing in a forest. He grinned boyishly, absorbing the applause for being Beckham, and showed no inclination to leave. It was as if he were in thrall to the 300,000 faces peering at him through the gloaming.

Robbie Williams looked like a man who didn't want to come off either. He gave a barnstorming performance which began with Queen's 'We Will Rock You', which he later said was intended 'to bring a bit of Freddie back from the original Live Aid'. He continued with three of his biggest hits. After 'Let Me Entertain You' and 'Feel', he ended with his anthem 'Angels'. It was a shop window for his showmanship – bending down to kiss a succession of female fans in the front row – in a performance all the more remarkable for the fact that he had not been on a stage for more than two years. Few were surprised to learn later that his spot drew the biggest UK television audience.

The Who tore through their set with the righteous indignation of a group half their age. Townshend and Daltrey were joined on stage by Pino Palladino in place of the late John Entwistle with Zak Starkey drumming instead of Kenney Jones. Their set was short but ferocious – just two songs. 'Who Are You' was crisp and driving, delivered with a ferocity that belied their years, while 'Won't Get Fooled Again' was transformed into an anthem of scepticism towards authority and empty promises. It felt they were delivering a direct call for action to those gathered in Gleneagles.

At the side of the stage, the band's manager Bill Curbishley complained to Harvey and the BBC about 'too many wide shots'. To placate him, Harvey picked up a phone. 'Get me the studio,' he shouted. What he didn't tell the band's manager was that that phone hadn't been working all day.

As they left the stage, Townshend and Daltrey in turn embraced Geldof briefly and disappeared into the darkness.

❄

From out of the darkness, dots of light appeared above the stage. They slowly turned into moons and, with no announcement, the wide, spacey sound of Pink Floyd's first number, 'Breathe', floated across the cool night air.

The tempo had changed. On stage, the band cautiously traded passing glances at each other while eyes glistened among those watching at the side of the stage.

'I never thought I'd see this day,' said Geldof, in a voice tinged with a quiet ecstasy.

Under the slogan 'No More Excuses', the band played 'Breathe' and then 'Money'. That night, the irony of the lyrics seemed directed at the G8: 'I'm all right, Jack / Keep your hands off my stack'.

The slightly cerebral edge Floyd had in the old days was softened, perhaps by the purpose of the day, perhaps by the act of reconnection. David Gilmour did not make eye contact with Roger Waters in the way he did with drummer Nick Mason, but there was an echo of the old chemistry between the two antagonists when they played 'Wish You Were Here', which Waters dedicated to the band's lost genius, Syd Barrett. They were not perhaps reconciled, but they had suspended hostilities to join in something bigger.

'It's actually quite emotional, standing up here with these three guys after all these years,' Waters said. 'Standing to be counted with the rest of you. Anyway, we're doing this for everybody who's not here and particularly of course for Syd.' At the close of their final song, 'Comfortably Numb', Gilmour prepared to leave stage, but an ebullient Waters gestured to him to join a group embrace. Gilmour, smiling for the first time, put his arm around Waters, and Waters did the same – his other arm round Nick Mason, who placed his around keyboard player Richard Wright.

'Pigs have flown' read a banner in the crowd.

Geldof hugged them all as they left and made their way down the steep stairs from the stage. Later, some of the magnificent old grey hairs could even be seen, touchingly, exchanging phone numbers.

'The other bands all know why they're here,' Nick Mason told me. 'But, for us, there is the additional dimension. For Pink Floyd to reform after not playing for twenty years was something special,' he said, quiet understatement being the English way. 'For me, the big thing was that – however great the arguments or disagreements – people came together for the right reason.'

'It was terrific fun,' Waters said later. 'Quite moving. It was good to have that chance to let bygones be bygones, if only for a few days. Dave sent me an email afterwards saying, "I am so glad you made that phone call. It was fun, wasn't it?" And I said, "Yeah, it was. It's all good. There's nothing bad about it."'

Finally, nine and a half hours after he opened the extraordinary day, Paul McCartney returned to the Live 8 stage with his own band to close the show.

'I remember you lot from this morning,' he joshed to the audience and launched into a set of rocking Beatles standards, beginning with 'Get Back'. His second number was to feature a guest appearance by George Michael, but McCartney forgot to announce it and started the number without him. George ran out, provoking a collective gasp from the audience to duet on 'Baby You Can Drive My Car'.

'From wherever you are to Edinburgh' read the legend above the stage as the concert closed with a mass rendition of the refrain from 'Hey Jude'. Most of the day's performers – Geldof included – joined McCartney on stage to sing the much-loved tune. And, this time, his mic worked throughout.

It was not long before midnight. The concert had lasted ten hours. But the full Live 8 event had lasted even longer, beginning in Tokyo at 6 a.m. and ending in Barrie, Ontario, nineteen hours later.

It had been, said Bob Geldof, one amazing day.

All at once, it was finished, an hour and a half later than planned. The darkness was still and the adrenaline began to fade. Hyde Park was silent. Live 8 was over. Musicians, technicians and activists drifted aimlessly into the night. The backstage bar had run out of booze. The after-show party in Regent Street seemed too wearyingly far away.

Bob Geldof and Richard Curtis sat in a production office with the remnants of a bottle of wine. Mariah Carey stuck her head round the door. 'Anyone want to go clubbing?'

'I don't think so, love,' said Bob. He smiled and thanked her for everything. 'Are you not going to get changed before you go?' said Geldof, the father of four daughters, instinctively. She was still wearing the two-sizes-too-small black number laced tightly at the sides that she had worn during the show.

'Well, I do have my blue dress, but that's kinda more revealing,' she smiled sweetly.

'Okay,' laughed Bob. 'Off you go.'

'There's one place with some booze left,' someone arrived and said.

'Where?'

'Paul McCartney's dressing room. He's invited us over.'

The former Beatle was still high after his performance in front of the biggest audience the world had ever seen. 'I just don't think it is possible,' said McCartney, 'that the politicians can ignore the will of the people that has been displayed today.'

Geldof took a glass of red wine. But even the company of a childhood hero could not tempt him for long. 'I'm all in,' he said, with a triumphant weariness. 'I think I'll just go home.'

'Give us a ring if you need me in another twenty years,' shouted McCartney.

'I don't think so,' called back Geldof, over his shoulder. 'Somehow I don't think so.'

CHAPTER 35

THE CRACKS BEGIN
TO APPEAR

Not everyone agreed with Bob Geldof that Live 8 had been 'one amazing day'. Indeed, there were some activists within Make Poverty History who declared that the overall impact of Live 8 had been negative. A few even went so far as to claim that the concert in Hyde Park had undone much of the good work that had been done by anti-poverty activists up and down the UK across years of campaigning. Live 8 in London had overshadowed a rally by a quarter of a million Make Poverty History demonstrators in Edinburgh.

That, at any rate, was the claim by John Hilary, the executive director of War on Want, one of the more radical aid agencies in the Make Poverty History coalition. 'The celebrity-charged Live 8 concerts took away the great majority of the media coverage we had hoped to achieve for the Edinburgh demonstration and its political aims,' he complained. The challenge to the G8 had been completely subsumed in the glitz and glamour of a pop event. 'Geldof's arrogance is simply in a different league,' he later wrote. 'To suggest that he alone was responsible for creating a mass movement on global poverty is a direct insult to the millions of people around the world who have worked steadfastly for debt cancellation, trade justice, women's rights, workers' rights and environmental sustainability over decades.'

There were at least two problems with this critique. The first is the assumption that the Edinburgh rally would have been splashed across the front pages if the world's pop stars had been busy elsewhere that day. The popular press would almost certainly have turned to a different subject entirely for their front-page headlines, consigning the Edinburgh rally to the inside pages. 'The idea that if Bono were not at Live 8 there would be trade policy on the front page of a German tabloid is ridiculous,' said another key MPH figure, Kirsty McNeill of the Stop AIDS Campaign. The second problem is the allegation that Geldof suggested that he alone was responsible for Make Poverty History. Geldof made no such claim. Indeed, he routinely distanced himself from involvement with the MPH campaign out of a temperamental inability to being told what to do and say by anyone.

Yet the complaints came as no surprise to those who worked with Geldof. 'There was a load of resistance within Make Poverty History to us vaulting in and doing a Live 8 concert,' said Zita Lloyd from DATA. 'Some people thought, *This is great, let's go*. Others were like, *No, you are treading on our toes, you bigwigs throwing your weight around*. So there was a lot of negotiation and diplomacy needed.'

Adrian Lovett, the campaigns director at Oxfam, who chaired the first MPH meeting, agreed that bringing Live 8 into a coalition which already contained a wide spectrum of views was 'a nightmare'. There were more tensions in the campaign about the use of celebrities – and about the role of Geldof in particular – than in 'any other campaign I've known,' he said. 'It was a hairy ride at times.'

Yet for all that, after the massive success of Live 8, it was 'astonishing' that anyone in the campaign would say they would rather the concerts hadn't happened, Lovett continued. 'Live 8 explicitly directed the world's attention towards a political rally in Scotland that would otherwise have gone largely unnoticed.' The independent evaluation commissioned by Make Poverty History at the end of the campaign concluded that celebrities were a key part of the effectiveness of the coalition. And yet, said Lovett, the 'extraordinary and wrong' idea that the overall impact of Live 8 was negative 'was a widely held view in our sector'.

There had been tensions inside the Make Poverty History coalition from the outset. When the advertising agency boss, Peter Souter, had been brought in early on by Richard Curtis, he noticed them immediately. He characterised the two camps as 'the marketeers versus the puritans', and swiftly detected two things. There was an imbalance of power within the coalition. Its Messages, Actions and Communications Working Group (a classic NGO name and construct) lacked people with marketing expertise. And there was, among the puritans, an automatic suspicion of him as a businessman. Shrewdly, the ad-man decided that Curtis and Comic Relief would be his client rather than Make Poverty History. He could see the trouble coming.

Part of the problem was that MPH was deliberately set up as a loose coalition in order to prevent a repeat of what had happened with Jubilee 2000. There, a formidable director, Ann Pettifor, ran everything centrally, leaving some in the coalition feeling they were marginalised in decision-making. This time, the aid agencies were determined to keep control. To do so, they set up a coordination team with sixteen members in which nobody really had the final say. As a result, MPH lacked an obvious leader and decision-making was far from swift. This was to become a serious problem.

For a start, the coordination team did not always coordinate very well. A month before the Live 8 concert, an embarrassing situation arose over the white Make Poverty History wristbands. The *Daily Telegraph* ran a story revealing that Christian Aid had bought half a million wristbands from a disreputable sweatshop with illegal hours and bad conditions in China. It turned out that Oxfam had discovered months before that the workers were being paid as little as nine pence an hour and switched its orders to a different factory – but failed to tell the other MPH charities.

But the main problem was that the marketeers and puritans wanted very different approaches. This was summed up in the first academic study undertaken of MPH by the academic Nicolas Sireau. His *Make Poverty History: Political Communication in Action* identified two separate areas of expertise in the coalition: campaigning and marketing. These two specialisms often existed within a single aid agency. Oxfam, for example, had a campaigning section and also a professional fundraising staff who used a wide variety of marketing and branding techniques. Yet, Sireau found, there was little sign of the agencies' professional fundraising staff being involved in Make Poverty History. The division in the coalition was between, on the one hand, campaigners and, on the other, those with creative and advertising skills, such as Comic Relief and its advertising agency, AMV.

'The campaigners wanted more hard-hitting, complex messages that focused on the structural causes of poverty,' said Sireau. 'The marketeers, arguing that advertising works best when it is simple, wanted messages that were softer, easier to understand, promoted the MPH brand and created a general awareness of the issue.'

That was not all. There were two other fault-lines in MPH. The campaigners were also divided, between radicals and moderates, and outsiders and insiders. The radicals came from the far left, were highly critical of contemporary capitalism and globalisation, and were looking for systemic or revolutionary transformation. The moderates wanted significant change on debt, aid and trade, but thought that this could be achieved gradually, one step at a time.

Among the moderates, there was a further division between outsiders and insiders. The outsiders thought they could best bring change by putting public pressure on politicians through demonstrations and criticism in the media. The insiders – the smallest but perhaps the most powerful faction within MPH – were working closely with Tony Blair and Gordon Brown's aides on the detail of the changes which could be delivered. Bob and Bono were, in Sireau's classification, moderate insiders. John Hilary of War on Want was one of the most extreme examples of a radical outsider.

All these fault-lines were, it turned out, an earthquake waiting to happen.

'Coalitions are always difficult,' said Lucy Matthew. 'Jubilee 2000 was really difficult. It was brilliant, but it's harder than you think for NGOs to work together. There's always a tension. It happens in any organisation. It happened within DATA when there were only four of us,' she laughed. 'Policy by its nature is complex and contingent on lots of different things. But when you have some really creative people like Richard and Bob and Bono – who think differently to traditional NGO folk like me, and come up with mad ideas, some of which are brilliant, some of which are not – it's not easy to fit neatly into a policy framework.'

The initial solution was to keep the coalition's demands very simple. 'There were no substantial policy disagreements because we kept the policy ask at a very top-line level: debt cancellation, more and better aid, and trade justice,' said Kumi Naidoo, chair of the Global Call to Action Against Poverty, the umbrella body for MPH's sister organisations around the world. 'We didn't put in figures because there was no general agreement on what we should be asking for.' But beneath the top-line agreement, there were differences in what the member organisations meant by the debt, aid and trade demands.

So the disagreement shifted to easier territory: the role of Geldof and other big names. Many in the coalition – which had now grown from 205 to 540 member organisations – felt that the use of celebrities went hand in hand with the oversimplification of the campaign's political messaging. Others were more visceral. 'I just found it slightly distasteful,' said one campaigner. 'People who are incredibly rich talking about the poor and the dying.' But most were delighted to have the celebrities on board, seeing them as an excellent way of reaching a wide range of the general public, such as when actor Ewan McGregor played the part of a Make Poverty History worker in a cinema ad for Orange mobile phones. Even then, some radicals criticised Orange for not attempting to air explanations for the deeper causes of poverty.

'Activists often talk about getting people up the ladder of engagement, and then promptly forget that most people climb ladders from the ground,' said Kirsty McNeill of the Stop AIDS Campaign and a member of the MPH coordinating committee. 'It isn't good enough to throw bodies at the top rung and hope that some will cling on. You need to encourage people onto the first rung by making the climb seem both easy and worth it… Live 8 didn't end the conversation but it did, in one day, start a lot of people out on a journey.' In this, celebrities were vital in attracting ordinary members of the public. Yet both Live 8 and getting the MPH launch written into the script of *The Vicar of Dibley* 'caused arguments that seem bizarre in retrospect,' she said.

'When Richard Curtis offered to mention the campaign in the New Year special of his much-loved sitcom, our instinctive response was not to send some thank-you flowers, but to work out which committee should vet the script.

'If we wouldn't let Richard Curtis write our policy report, we probably shouldn't have asked to write his show. One of the campaign's biggest failings is that, in working with incredible talents from the creative industries, we tried to make them more like us – not us more like them. I wish we'd been more appreciative at the time of what a difference it made to have some of Britain's biggest creative brains on board.'

Next, there were rows about the choice of celebrities. 'Nelson Mandela is the one celebrity I'll make an exception for,' declared one MPH activist. 'His integrity is just immeasurable.' But was integrity top of the list of celebrity desiderata? What about fame? Or expertise? 'Bob and Bono are not celebrities in the usual sense,' argued another. 'They have been campaigning in this field for two decades.' By contrast, 'some of the people criticising them had been working on this cause for only two years,' said Kirsty McNeill. 'You can't disqualify Bob because he is an expert who happens to be famous.'

What brought all these divisions to a head was an article in the *New Statesman* just before Live 8. It was clearly based on briefings by radical outsiders who felt they were losing control to Bob Geldof and the moderate insiders. It claimed that fears were growing inside Make Poverty History that one of its dominant members, Oxfam, had become too close to the Labour government and that the coalition's ambitious demands were being diluted as a result. The relationship between Oxfam and government ministers had become 'far too cosy'.

Oxfam had 'incredible access' to ministers and, as a result, the policies of the two had become virtually indistinguishable, the article claimed. Oxfam was backing Gordon Brown's proposed International Finance Facility to raise extra cash to increase aid. By contrast, radical outsiders like the World Development Movement saw it as a 'spend now, pay later' mechanism which was a threat to future aid levels. And when Brown announced that the government would lift the aid budget to 0.7 per cent of national income by 2013, Oxfam applauded – while the radicals asked why it could not be done more quickly.

This closeness on policy, the *New Statesman* alleged, was as a result of 'the revolving door' through which key individuals moved between Oxfam and the Labour government. Shriti Vadera, who advised Brown on international development, was, the article noted, an Oxfam trustee. Justin Forsyth was director of policy and campaigns at Oxfam before joining Downing Street to advise Blair on Africa and development. When Oxfam advertised for Forsyth's successor, two of the four candidates called for interview were either current or former special advisers, and Vadera was on the interview panel. The radical outsiders smelled some kind of conspiracy.

All of that looked at events down the wrong end of the telescope, according to Bob Geldof and the moderate insiders. The journey from Live Aid to Live 8, from 1985 to 2005, was not just one from charity to justice. It was also one from a world in which the UK's Conservative government was essentially hostile to aid and development to one in which New Labour politicians were actively sympathetic to those issues. What was different now was that those in power were receptive to the suggestion.

'Blair and Brown, like Cameron and Osborne after them, were children of Live Aid,' Geldof said. 'There was something about the Live Aid experience which affected them profoundly and permanently.' It was not that the Labour government tried to hijack Make Poverty History. Rather, 'Blair and Brown wanted to associate themselves publicly with the campaign and take on its discourse – because they recognised that there was a confluence between our values and theirs,' added Bob. 'It was a common agenda – we just had different roles. He would do the politics and I would do the public. And that's what happened.'

Yet it was the sea change in the political mood between 1985 and 2005 which made Live 8 possible. 'We'd had seventeen years of arguing with the Conservatives, which was like arguing with a brick wall,' said Kevin Watkins, who for decades shaped thinking on development policy at Oxfam, the United Nations Development Programme and Save the Children. Suddenly, Labour was doing much of what he had been demanding for decades. 'Gordon Brown would be ringing me, rather than the other way round, telling me, "Look, you guys need to be making more noise." We had the chancellor of the exchequer lobbying Oxfam to turn up the heat!'

The moderate insiders saw all this as a sign that the centre of power at last shared their concerns about global poverty. The radical outsiders saw it as a threat to their campaign's independence. Forsyth noted in his diary that the radicals' conspiracy theory was merely 'the usual stuff by infantile leftists'. The tensions created by this divergence began to worsen dramatically the day after the Live 8 concerts.

It need not have happened. To Ann Pettifor, who watched Make Poverty

History from the sidelines, the conflict was unnecessary. 'You need both sides,' she said. 'You need your high-profile celebrities, you need your experts, you need your thinkers, you need your campaigners, you need the people who are willing to chain themselves to railings, etc. To be an effective campaign, you need it all.'

Kirsty McNeill, who after Live 8 went on to become a special adviser to Brown as prime minister, took a similar view. 'The public might have been piling on the pressure, but in the end, the deal was done by governments. The leaders had the power to do the right thing. We had the power to make them. Both sides played their part.'

And it took one thing more, said Kevin Watkins. Make Poverty History may have been a coalition, but it was part of a still-wider one. 'The politicians, the celebrities, the NGOs, the activists from the churches, faith groups, trade unions, and all the rest – all that was held together by the genius of Justin Forsyth,' Watkins said. 'Bob Geldof is a magnificent driving force, but maybe not an instinctive coalition-builder. That was where Justin excelled. I could do the research and the policy-facing side of things, but Justin was brilliant in seeing how to fuse all the different elements together – the popular campaigning, the high-level advocacy, the policy analysis. Justin was the best strategist the NGO movement ever had. He was light years ahead of everyone.'

⁂

Inside MPH, however, it was Adrian Lovett who did his best to hold together the competing sides in what he called 'the inside/outside strategy'. He was, however, unable to broker a compromise over the event that would lead the coalition to split wide open.

Bob Geldof had fixed the date for his Live 8 concerts without consulting Make Poverty History. The MPH coordination team had decided months before to organise that big march around Edinburgh on the same day. Both had chosen the Saturday before the Gleneagles G8.

It was Lovett's thankless job to try to reconcile the two events. At first, he tried to persuade the MPH team to move their march to the Sunday, the day after Geldof's concerts. 'My dream was that we could make a sequence of all of this campaigning activity,' he recalled. 'First, the big global moment of music with Live 8. Then they'd all get on overnight coaches and travel to Edinburgh and turn up bleary-eyed on Sunday morning in the Meadows in Edinburgh to join the Make Poverty History marchers already assembled there. And we'd set up a stage and do some event there and then all march on again to Gleneagles the next day.'

His plan was thrown by the fact that the rest of the MPH planners wouldn't budge on their insistence on keeping the rally on the Saturday. In part, this was for practical reasons. Fewer trains run on Sundays. But there was also a petulant element within the organisers who insisted that they had chosen their date first so it should be Geldof who moved. Given the logistics of eight concerts in eight different countries, there was zero chance of that. Then there was Bob.

'Fuck that,' he said.

'So, in the end, we tried to make a virtue of the concerts and the rally being simultaneous,' said Lovett. 'I remember going on stage in Edinburgh and, at three o'clock, introducing a live feed of Live 8 from London.' In the end, even some among the radical outsiders conceded the success of the interaction. 'Live 8 elevated the thing to stratospheric levels,' said Martin Drewry, the head of campaigns at Christian Aid. Glen Tarman of the Trade Justice Movement concurred: 'Without the public figures, without celebrity endorsement, without the unusual organisations sitting alongside each other, without the Mandela moments, without this kind of spread, we wouldn't have got anywhere at all.'

Once Live 8 was announced, media interest in Make Poverty History increased exponentially, so much so that MPH's media coordinator Catherine Cullen complained: 'Sky News would phone me and I would have to turn down interviews saying, "We've already been on your channel five times today. What else could we possibly say that's new?"'

But there was one divide which even Adrian Lovett could not bridge. The radical outsiders and moderate insiders wanted to interact with G8 governments in diametrically opposed ways. The moderate insiders – like Oxfam, Save the Children and CAFOD – felt that they would achieve more change if they praised politicians occasionally when they had taken a step towards fulfilling a campaign demand. 'The moderates wanted to encourage politicians by playing on their egos,' as Nicolas Sireau put it, 'to make them feel good about themselves and present them as heroes of the poor, which would encourage them to take more action.' By contrast, the radical outsiders habitually adopted an adversarial and oppositional stance, portraying the politicians critically, 'pointing out their double standards and hypocrisy in order to shame them into action'.

War on Want and the World Development Movement were classic radical outsiders. 'We need to emphasise the differences between us and the government,' said Peter Hardstaff, head of policy for the World Development Movement. 'There is a real need for us collectively to explain where the UK government is doing good things and where there are real differences.'

Christian Aid and Action Aid sat uneasily, halfway between. 'Oxfam has clearly invested more in that insider-track lobbying approach and that brings both pros and cons,' said Martin Drewry. 'Because Oxfam has more direct lobbying contact, it might have to be less critical, less frequently – but when it is critical, it stings more. But I would have to say that a number of organisations wish Oxfam would be more radical and critical of the government.'

Bob Geldof had long ago decided that the moderate insider approach was more fruitful. Richard Curtis was struck by the psychology of all this: 'Around a quarter of the MPH people appeared to believe that the way to make people passionate about issues was through anger and failure. They thought that if people could see how many things were going wrong, it would make them angry and make them want to do more. By contrast, I believe – and Bob does too – that people are motivated better when you show them success and progress. That is what drives them on to campaign for more to happen. Make Poverty History had a measure of anger in it, but it also had its measure of positivity. That is why Bob felt it really shifted the needle.'

The temperament of the moderate insider leans towards optimism, whereas that of the radical outsider appears usually to presuppose the worst. Certainly, that's how it came across to Tony Blair. Campaigning NGOs, he said, have learned to play the modern media game. 'As it's all about impact, they shout louder and louder to get heard. Balance is not in the vocabulary. It's all "outrage", "betrayal", "crisis". They also have their own tightly defined dogma and conventional wisdom which, if you challenge them, they defend fiercely – not usually on their merits, but by abusing your motives for challenging them.'

⁎

There was one other factor that accelerated the disintegration of the Make Poverty History coalition. The campaign's determination, in its early days, not to become dominated by a single powerful individual or agency led to the creation of its cumbersome coordination committee. Decisions were arrived at after lengthy debate. Its determination to be democratic meant that it had no obvious leader.

Faced with this leadership vacuum, the media decided that Bob Geldof was the obvious figurehead for the campaign. Geldof, as ever, took no account of technical niceties and simply spoke to the press unfiltered, in his usual manner. Though he never claimed that he was speaking on behalf of Make Poverty History, many inside the coalition – particularly the radical outsiders – became frustrated and annoyed. Complaints were made that he was saying things which were not MPH policy.

Live 8 messaging became so confused with Make Poverty History messaging that even people who were very close to the campaign couldn't see a difference, lamented Steve Tibbett, director of policy and campaigns at Action Aid. Senior members of the coalition tried regularly to engage in contact with Geldof and the staff at DATA to influence his messaging. 'We had a whole coordination team in constant dialogue with Bob in an attempt to influence the messages coming out of Live 8,' one insider said. Bob, as ever, had no patience with committees or protocol. He continued to instantly capture the attention of the media and the public. Inevitably, said Adrian Lovett, 'journalists who describe things in broad brush strokes were going to get confused'.

In the few days between Live 8 and Gleneagles, the temperature began to rise inside MPH. One of those who spurned the concerts to go on the rally in Edinburgh summed up the fury: 'I was really angry about the way the rally was kind of sabotaged by Live 8. I was disappointed in other people's reactions. All they focused on was Live 8. That's all they were talking about. "Have you got the tickets to Live 8?" And when I said I was heading to Edinburgh, they kind of looked at me like I was completely mad, from another planet. So I was annoyed at the way Live 8 just really swamped, totally eclipsed, what I felt was the more important thing.'

Kumi Naidoo, of the Global Call to Action Against Poverty, was also becoming concerned at the gap between the demands of Live 8 and the demands of GCAP. When Richard Curtis was asked about Live 8's demands, he replied: 'We have a blueprint and it's called the Commission for Africa.' That was not how Kumi saw it: 'Bono and Geldof were focused on Africa. But GCAP was focused on global poverty.'

Still, partnership with Geldof and Live 8 was a price worth paying, he insisted – at that point, at any rate. When members of GCAP or MPH raised concerns about the influence of the celebrities, he tried to calm their fears. 'I had to manage them. I had to say, "Folks, listen, I am concerned about it, but given the media realities that we live with, they are amplifying our core demands. We can reflect on all this after Gleneagles and figure out how we continue to work. But, right now, let's not upset the apple cart because we've got real momentum in the public square."'

But that uneasy sense of common purpose was not to last. Just a few days after the Live 8 concerts, Make Poverty History was to implode.

CHAPTER 36

PLAYING POKER
AT GLENEAGLES

Tony Blair was disappointed. While Bob Geldof and his constellation of stars were preparing for Live 8, the prime minister was having to get ready to board a flight for Singapore. Bob had promised to make sure he got a tape of the concert, but Blair had really wanted to be there. Instead, he had decided upon a mad dash to east Asia, where the International Olympic Committee were meeting to decide which city would host the next Olympic Games. The IOC was choosing between Moscow, New York, Madrid, Paris and London. Everyone told him it was a waste of time and that he should stay to prepare for the G8. But Blair had fixed his mind on giving the UK the best chance of winning the Games.

As Live 8 was getting underway in Hyde Park, Blair was with his Gleneagles team in Downing Street. He was beginning to lose patience with the lack of progress in persuading the Americans to agree to sign up to providing AIDS treatment to everyone in Africa. He wanted to take over control of the negotiations himself.

'If we push too hard, we'll isolate the Americans,' Sir Michael Jay warned him.

'I'm prepared to do that,' Blair said with uncharacteristic impatience and put a call through to the White House.

It was a difficult conversation. The weather did not help. Lightning flashed overhead as they spoke and the phone line went dead several times. Bush couldn't understand why Blair was placing such emphasis on the need for 'universal access' for AIDS medicines. He felt that Blair was painting himself into a political corner and it would all end badly for his British ally. But Blair felt that, ultimately, he could count on Bush. 'Personal relationships matter' in politics, he insisted. 'If you like a leader, you try to help them, even if it stretches your interest.' His instinct was that the US president would yet go further.

'Push Bush on AIDS' were his final words to his team before he left for the airport.

Laurie Lee did not need telling. He brought to mind a phone call he had had a couple of weeks earlier with his counterpart in the White House, John Simon. 'The call went on for literally three hours,' Laurie told me. 'My colleagues in the foreign policy team went home one by one. But I was not going to put the phone down until I made some progress. Eventually, I resorted to borrowing one of Bono's tactics and appealing to the US sense of ambition, urging them to see it as this administration's moon shot! I said that if we went for universal access, we might at least achieve 90 per cent and that would be amazing. But if we only went for 50 per cent, we'd be lucky to achieve 40 per cent. Eventually, John said their "experts" didn't think it was possible, but he'd ask them again.'

The negotiations were to carry on until the very last minute, throughout President Bush's flight to Scotland.

✻

While Tony Blair was busy in Singapore, Bob Geldof was marshalling his troops for Gleneagles. Richard Branson had donated a series of trains to take protesters to Edinburgh. On the Tuesday after Live 8, Bob boarded one of those trains with the Hollywood stars Susan Sarandon and Tim Robbins, who had both undertaken to appear at the final Live 8 concert at Murrayfield on the eve of the G8 summit. On the journey, Bob outlined the details of plans for the next few days and I briefed them on the recommendations of the Commission for Africa, which we hoped would form the basis of the Gleneagles agreement by the end of the week.

In Edinburgh, we set up headquarters in the Balmoral, the grand railway hotel next to Waverley station. There, we were joined by Bono, George Clooney, Youssou N'Dour, Jamie Drummond, Lucy Matthew and the rest of the DATA crew. Calls were coming in from activists all around Europe with inside information on what different politicians were agreeing to and what they were baulking at. Plans were being made on which star would tackle which politician. Clooney was asked to get alongside the head of the World Bank, Paul Wolfowitz, and get him to press George Bush to finance the World Bank's programme to provide free public education.

An hour up the road at Gleneagles, a five-star golfing hotel in the rolling hills of lowland Scotland, the civil servants had arrived early. Blair's top negotiating team – Sir Michael Jay, Justin Forsyth and Laurie Lee – had set up the No 10 office in two cramped rooms filled with computers and masses of papers next to the prime minister's suite. Not long before they left London, the BBC in the UK and HBO in the US had broadcast the Richard Curtis made-for television rom-com called *The Girl in the Café*. The film, about a civil servant called Lawrence working on the upcoming G8 Summit, dramatised the conflict between political pragmatism and compassionate idealism at the centre of the Live 8 movement. It, too, had a cliff-hanger ending. Justin Forsyth sent a copy of the film to each of the G8 sherpas, screened it in Whitehall and gave a copy to Tony Blair to watch over the weekend. It felt like the stakes were getting high.

Blair's top civil service team had arrived at Gleneagles on the Monday for a final pre-summit meeting of the sherpas. They had had dinner in one of the grand dining rooms, where the polished table was set with silver candelabra. At the end of the meal, when they should have been settling down to enjoy some relaxing Scottish whiskies in the soft candlelight, the negotiations were still not concluded. They were a long way from a deal. At this point, Sir Michael Jay embarked upon a speech which was unusually ardent for a senior Foreign Office mandarin. He appealed to his fellow sherpas to think about how their children and grandchildren might be affected if they all failed to lead the G8 to an important agreement.

'What I was saying was, "Look, Tony Blair's not doing this for himself. These are subjects which matter to the future and we need to show that the G8 are interested in them",' Jay recalled. 'I was making a rather passionate speech and was waving the draft of the unfinished text around, trying to make them think this really mattered, and I held it too close to the candle and it burst into flames.'

All the sherpas immediately burst out laughing. After an aide had rushed the burning document out of the room, the US sherpa, Faryar Shirzad, laughed: 'If you could just set light to the climate change communiqué as well, we'd be done.'

But the deadlock in the negotiations was no laughing matter. On the day before Live 8, the sherpas had met and argued and haggled until two in the morning without success.

'This was the hardest meeting in my life,' Forsyth wrote in his diary before he finally went to bed. 'Michael [Jay] desperately wanted to do a deal on Africa and in my view gave too much away on the second-tier issues like education and conflict. But he was in a tough place. Only France and the EU were supportive and everyone else against.' George Bush had announced that he would double US aid to Africa two days before Live 8 – and went to Philadelphia, site of the US concert, to do it. But on many of the other points in the Gleneagles deal – on AIDS medicines, education and export subsidies – the American sherpa continued to be obstructive. Along with the German, Italian, Japanese and sometimes Canadian sherpas, he tried to water the text down, again and again.

The negotiations were going to the wire. Right up to the last minute, Blair's team were unsure as to whether they would succeed. But they kept on trying, so much so that Laurie Lee carried on negotiating with John Simon over the phone throughout the flight of Air Force One, right up until Bush's plane landed at Glasgow, the aircraft being too heavy for the runway at Edinburgh. He and John Simon had talked so long as Air Force One flew to Scotland that Laurie had drained three batteries on his Nokia 3310. Fortunately, the sophistication of the communications link between Gleneagles, via the Downing Street switchboard, to the US presidential plane could keep the line open while batteries were switched. Tony Blair was insisting that George Bush should sign up to giving the poor world universal access to AIDS medicines. Universal access was the recommendation of Bob Geldof and the Commission for Africa. Blair had pretty much convinced Bush on this, but the president's people said this was a technical impossibility, fearing it would undermine the achievement of Bush's $15 billion President's Emergency Plan for AIDS Relief (PEPFAR). 'If you insist on universal access, you're gonna turn it from a success into a failure,' Simon said.

Blair's Africa secretary persisted.

'Look, Laurie,' said Simon from Air Force One, 'if you can get a technical person to tell you this can be done, we'll run with it, but my technical people say universal access can't be done.'

When the Americans arrived at Gleneagles, Laurie took his White House counterpart to the hotel bar. 'There, we hammered out the final text,' said Laurie. It spoke of 'as close as possible to universal access to treatment for all those who need it by 2010'. It was a classic diplomatic compromise, but Laurie knew the NGOs and press would distil that into 'universal access by 2010'. That, said Laurie, 'would be the pressure we needed over the next five years to hold the G8's feet to the fire; 2005 became a turning point on AIDS.'

After Gleneagles, the number of people on treatment globally began to rise – and deaths from AIDS finally began to fall for the first time. Fifteen years later, 75 per cent of people worldwide who know they are HIV positive are accessing treatment. Deaths have fallen by two-thirds.

✳

Over in Singapore, things were going better than expected for Tony Blair. There had been three rounds of voting for the Olympics. Moscow had been knocked out. So had New York. So had Madrid. Just London and Paris were left.

The French president Jacques Chirac was there, doing some very heavyweight lobbying. 'The French were runaway favourites,' Blair conceded. But the UK had a formidable team which included Princess Anne, David Beckham, Sebastian Coe, the culture minister Tessa Jowell and the mayor of London, Ken Livingstone. After an exhausting round of one-on-one meetings with a fair proportion of the 115 voters, the prime minister left late on the evening of Tuesday 5 July, before the final vote, to take a plane to Gleneagles. President Chirac, by contrast, remained behind to carry on lobbying. The London contingent were not overly alarmed about this – they thought that the French president's final speech had a touch of arrogance about it.

Blair had been intending to do some preparation for the G8 when he got on board the chartered Boeing 777, but, overcome with jet lag and exhaustion, he soon fell asleep, landing in Scotland early on the morning of Wednesday 6 July. 'He was exhausted but wired,' recalled Justin Forsyth. 'We briefed him, sitting outside in the gardens, running him through the key arguments and tactics.' The prime minister was very clear on the bottom lines as he went to greet the first of the foreign leaders arriving in Gleneagles. He was now seized with the conviction that defeat for London on the Olympics would be a real dampener on the atmosphere surrounding the G8.

At 7.49 a.m. in Singapore, 12.49 p.m. in Britain, the switchboard at No 10 called the PM's chief of staff Jonathan Powell, because Tony Blair never had a mobile phone. Powell passed his phone to Blair. 'I think this will be the news we didn't want to hear,' he said. But Powell was overly pessimistic. 'We've won!' the jubilant switchboard operator shouted into the PM's ear. 'Tony did a little jig around Jonathan,' recalled Justin Forsyth. 'We had won the Olympics against all odds. And thanks – many of the team back in Singapore said – to Tony's mad dash. It had been a huge risk to go to Singapore but it had paid off.' Blair himself recalled that, after his little dance around Powell, he hugged him: 'Jonathan is not a natural hugger, but he was there and he got hugged.' Civil service restraint was set aside and joy was unconfined. It had been a close victory, by just four votes, but a victory nonetheless.

Over in the Balmoral hotel in Edinburgh, Bob and Bono heard the news from the television in the bedroom suite that had become their campaign HQ. Kirsty McNeill, of the Stop AIDS Campaign, had just entered the room to brief the pair on some of the technical details of the policy work on AIDS treatments, on which they would need to speak knowledgeably in negotiations.

'Just as I was about to begin, the news came on the television that London had won the Olympics. There was huge and instant joy from everyone,' Kirsty said. 'But the thing that struck me about Bob was how quickly focused he became on what this news meant.'

'This is really important for the big picture,' he said. He had an intuitive understanding that this was not just about sport, the Olympics was a moment when the world comes together. And it was coming together in the UK when the world's eyes were already on the country. He had an immediate understanding of the figurative meaning of this Olympic victory.

'Okay, let's get back to the details and how we can use the Olympics to leverage this.'

McNeill was very impressed by the way Geldof 'immediately saw the importance of the announcement to what we were doing'. The news lifted everybody. Now anything seemed possible.

✳

George Bush had arrived at Gleneagles on the Wednesday afternoon. He had stopped off on the way in Denmark, where he had said something rather revealing. Bush was regarded as an inveterate climate change denier, but asked about global warming, this time he said that he recognised 'that the surface of the Earth is warmer and that an increase in greenhouse gases is contributing to the problem'. The United States were still going to refuse to sign up to the Kyoto agreement to contain targets for emissions, though. It was impossible for them to do that, he said, while so many developing countries were not party to the agreement. The US would lose too many jobs that way. Still, this was a significant shift.

On 30 June, Bush had announced that the US would indeed be doubling aid to Africa. Laurie Lee and John Simon had reached an agreement of sorts on funding for AIDS treatment. Now, here was a little movement on climate change. John Simon was clear that a lot of this was to do with Bush's personal relationship with the British prime minister. 'It never would have happened with any other leader apart from Blair,' Simon said. Bush's slight concession was, Blair hoped, a step in the right direction.

To get a bit of exercise at the end of the day, the president had gone out for an evening ride on his mountain bike. He was going so fast that when he passed a group of British policemen – and raised his hand from the handlebars to wave and say 'Thanks, you guys, for coming' – he lost control of the machine and crashed into one of the Scottish bobbies, who had to be taken to hospital. 'It could only happen to George,' said Blair.

The last of the world leaders to arrive was the French president, Jacques Chirac, who touched down from his failed Olympic bid in Singapore at around 5.30 p.m. Blair greeted him as sympathetically as he could.

'I felt genuinely sorry for him. No, I really did. He had lost the referendum on the EU treaty, a terrible blow, and I'm sure a deeply felt personal rebuff from his own people. Now this.'

It was more than that. Chirac had failed to secure the Olympics first as mayor of Paris, secondly as prime minister, and finally, now as president.

More significantly, worried Justin Forsyth, 'We still hadn't got three or four Gleneagles outcomes and Tony was worried that Chirac would be so pissed off with us that he wouldn't want to help us get across the line.'

For once, Blair was less political. 'Whatever else you may say about Jacques, he has courage and he is a pro. He was immensely gracious, congratulating me personally as well as the country, wishing me all the best and doing so with dignity and sincerity. In defeat, he was rather magnificent.'

✣

In the early evening, Bob Geldof, Bono and Richard Curtis flew to Gleneagles by helicopter to meet the world leaders.

Kumi Naidoo was supposed to go with them, but in the first sign of the widening divide between the celebrities and the global campaigners, he pulled out at the last minute.

'Tony Blair had invited me,' explained Kumi, 'but I said, "That's ridiculous. How can you have a delegation with no women in it?" So I gave up my seat in the helicopter and insisted they should take Wangari Maathai.' Wangari Maathai was a Kenyan social, environmental and political activist who founded the Green Belt Movement, which focused on the planting of trees, environmental conservation and women's rights. The previous year, she had become the first African woman to win the Nobel Peace Prize.

'Even so,' complained Kumi, 'if you look at the footage of the press conference, there was not really sufficient effort to treat her as an equal or give her more voice, given that she was the only person from Africa there.'

Before the press conference, the two rock stars had a private session with George Bush. It was supposed to last just a quarter of an hour, but was extended to forty minutes. What they found surprised them. Bush was quite passionate, Justin Forsyth recalled. He told the pair that he had watched the Live 8 broadcasts. 'The most moving moment, he said, was when Birhan came out,' Forsyth said.

'It clearly reminded him that when politicians negotiate in the rarefied atmosphere of a place like Gleneagles there are individuals like her who live or die by their decisions,' Geldof said afterwards. The two Irish musicians were unprepared for the level of engagement with Africa which the president demonstrated. 'His two daughters have been working there and his wife, Laura – who was at the meeting – is about to tour Africa,'

Bob told the press afterwards. 'And she is particularly concerned with the education of girls.'

Girls are far less likely than boys to go to school in Africa, in part because of cultural gender biases. But it is also for reasons which aid could rectify, as Geldof explained. 'Bush was clearly struck by the fact that many girls will not go to school merely because they lack separate toilet facilities.' And that those who do go often lose a quarter of their schooling because, when they have a menstrual period, they are kept at home for a week every month because school has no proper toilet facilities. Plus, 'free school meals have also been shown to create a powerful incentive for parents to send girls to school'.

Bono pressed the president to add further to the increases in aid to Africa which Washington pledged in the run-up to Live 8 – but which Bob and Bono had been told was still short of what was needed to raise the additional $25 billion a year recommended by the Commission for Africa. The US keeps talking about amounts and percentages of spending, noted Bono. But the singer wanted Bush to say: *Malaria just can't be allowed. We're going to get rid of malaria.* 'That was how the president talked about terrorism,' Bono said afterwards. 'He should talk about malaria in the same way.'

On trade, the pair also secured a commitment from the US leader to fix a date to end the way rich countries subsidise their farmers' agricultural exports to Africa, undercutting the prices at which African farmers need to sell to scrape a living. Bush said he would be happy to agree a date to be included in the summit's closing communiqué, provided European leaders did the same. He probably knew full well that the French would never agree to that.

After seeing Bush, Bob and Bono had a shorter meeting with Gerhard Schröder, the other leader seen as standing in the way of the Blair deal. Chancellor Schröder told the two musicians that he would stick to his commitment to increase aid to 0.56 per cent of Germany's national income by 2010, but he was unclear as to how he intended to raise the money.

Bono told Schröder that the following night he had a concert in Berlin. 'If you keep your word on this, I will praise you from the stage, which is a very uncool thing for a rock star to do,' he said. 'But if you don't, I will denounce you at our gig just ahead of the German elections.' Schröder was reluctant. The German leader was antagonistic towards Blair for a number of reasons. He had not forgiven him for joining the invasion of Iraq. Schröder, a socialist, thought Blair was not a proper man of the left. He was irritated by the fact that there had been no German on the Commission for Africa. He was sufficiently intemperate to have previously been overheard saying privately to George Bush:

'Blair is being a real pain in the arse about this Africa stuff, isn't he?'

'Yeah,' replied Bush, 'I wish he'd give it a rest.'

Bad blood with Schröder was seen as the primary reason why the Germans moved so slowly. Personal relationships were key at a body like the G8, which was originally conceived as a fireside chat between leaders. 'France was a fantastic ally throughout the whole G8 process,' said Laurie Lee. 'France had a history of commitment to Africa and development, so Blair was working with the grain.' But Blair and Chirac also had good personal chemistry.

At the press conference that followed the meetings – which was attended by George Clooney, Youssou N'Dour and the Beninese actor Djimon Hounsou – Geldof told Blair that the 38 million people who had signed the Live 8 petition constituted the 'biggest mandate in history'. If the prime minister encountered objections from other world leaders, he should remind them of that – and of the 50,000 people dying daily because they were too poor to live.

In return, Blair paid tribute to the anti-poverty campaign led by Bob, describing it as 'the most extraordinary civic society campaign I have ever come across'. Poverty would not be made history overnight, but a successful G8 would 'allow us to claim plausibly that we can do it in the coming years'.

Back in his hotel in Edinburgh, Kumi Naidoo, chair of the Global Campaign against Poverty, was watching what he saw as this mutual back-scratching by Bob and Blair – and feeling increasingly unhappy at what he was seeing.

※

Bob and Bono took a helicopter from Gleneagles straight to Murrayfield rugby stadium. The final Live 8 eve-of-summit concert had begun with Lenny Henry rallying the crowd with the call: 'Tonight sees us take the final steps on the long walk to justice.' The music kicked off with the Scottish band, the Proclaimers, singing their old hit '500 Miles' with lyrics suitably

altered to reflect the journey from London to Edinburgh. Six of the acts
on the bill were Scottish, including Wet Wet Wet, Travis, Texas, Annie
Lennox and Midge Ure, though other artists made genuflections to the
location, with pianist Jamie Cullum draping a Saltire over his piano before
accompanying Natasha Bedingfield on a cover of 'All You Need is Love'.

After sets by McFly and Sugababes, Bono came out onto the stage,
carrying an unlikely looking object – a briefcase, which he put down by the
side of the microphone like a man coming home from the office.

'So, I just came back from the most famous golf course in the world
at Gleneagles.

'I hope you don't mind,' he said, leaning into the microphone as if to
speak confidentiality to the stadium's 60,000 crowd, 'but I gave them your
permission to spend your money … ending extreme poverty in our lifetime.
They wanted to know where did I get the authority to say that and I held
up this box.' He raised the little case for the audience to see.

'In this box are the signatures of the 38 million people who are ready
to go to work on this issue – and that's just the Live 8 campaign. When you
add to that 157 million people who signed up for Global Action Against
Poverty in seventy-five countries, I would call that permission to spend your
money. That's the most powerful mandate in the history of mandates.' The
crowd roared its approval.

Then Bono introduced Nelson Mandela. The audience hushed as he told
the presidents and prime ministers gathered at Gleneagles: 'Do not look the
other way. Overcoming poverty is not a gesture of charity. It is an act of
justice. It is the protection of a fundamental human right, the right to dignity and a decent life. History and the generations to come will judge our
leaders by the decisions they make in the coming weeks. It is easy to make
promises but never go to action… We want action… Not to do this would
be a crime against humanity.'

Following a succession of Hollywood A-listers, from Susan Sarandon to
George Clooney, Geldof took the stage. He hailed the Murrayfield assembly as 'the gathering of the clans'.

'From all over the world, from all over Scotland, from all over the UK.
We told them we'd come,' he said to the cheers of the crowd.

'We came.'

The crowd cheered louder. He announced that he would be singing an old Scottish folk song, but in fact offered up one of his own, a scathing celebration of apathy called 'The Great Song of Indifference'.

But there was certainly no apathy – rather a quiet ferocity – about the way that Germany's most famous rock star Herbert Grönemeyer and the supermodel Claudia Schiffer delivered their public message to the German chancellor, who had now arrived up the road in Gleneagles.

'Gerhard Schröder – we're watching you. You made history by saying no to the war in Iraq. Now you can make history by saying no to poverty.'

With 150 artists and eighty one-minute changeovers, this final Live 8 concert was another logistical triumph. Moreover, Fran Healy told BBC Radio Scotland, all the performers there had agreed the atmosphere in Murrayfield was even more electric than at Hyde Park.

Before a finale from James Brown, in one of his last major appearances before his death in 2006, Bob Geldof and Bono walked out onto the stage with Midge Ure.

Those eight men out at Gleneagles, Geldof told the crowd, have no idea what was going on here in Murrayfield tonight. They have no idea what is really going on anywhere outside the little bubble of security in which they were trapped at their luxury golf course. 'But we swear to you that we will make them feel every ounce of emotion and noise that you have generated in this stadium here tonight,' he shouted above the roar of the crowd. 'We swear!'

'They hear you now. They hear you now.'

The noise rose to a crescendo.

'Tell me, how can these eight men refuse us now…?'

Turning to directly address the politicians of the G8, Bob warned: 'Should you fail, we will not be cynical, we will bide our time and when you come to us and ask for your approval at the ballot box, we will tell you to fuck off!'

Speaking directly to the eight men, Bono added: 'We beseech you. Don't let this be politics as usual. Don't look for compromises. Do more than is expected, not the least you can get away with.

'Our job is to write songs. You eight men, your job is to write history. Write us a chapter we can all be proud of.'

Midge concluded by asking the multitude to sing their unofficial national anthem, 'Flower of Scotland'. Midge, Bono and Geldof stood with their hands raised – Midge smiling proudly, Bono's chin set with grim determination and Bob's face filled with a sense of uplifted wonder, as they each took in the scene.

The massed voices started separately, but swiftly found a common time. From the throng, two lines sounded clear: 'Send them homeward, to think again.'

✳

Over at Gleneagles, things appeared to be moving in the right direction for Tony Blair. The summit was to officially begin with a dinner hosted by the Queen. Beforehand, Blair and Bush had a quiet drink together, with their wives, Cherie and Laura. 'I could see he was going to help,' Blair later said. 'George had moved some way ... but not as far as I wanted. He had constantly refused to say he would commit the US to being part of a deal on climate change. And although he had been really forward on Africa, and had a really impressive record on funding action on HIV/AIDS, we were asking big numbers – $50 billion extra over the coming years – and filling in details of how it will be spent. Instead of an agreeable but general set of discussions, we were putting real figures, real commitments and real deliverables on the table.

'Bush was nervous,' Blair observed, 'and I was absolutely aware that although others were going along, they were doing so in the belief that George would save them by volunteering to be the party pooper. I also knew that if he agreed, no one else would disagree. I was putting real pressure on – to be honest, quite a bit above and beyond what the other leaders thought was desirable or necessary. Without George's backing, indeed, it would've been impossible. Even with it, there were limits and I was significantly outside them.'

What Bob and Bono had learned, and what Blair had long known, was that US governments had a predictable tactic at G8 summits. Their style was to be really difficult, make it look as though they were prepared to crash the summit, argue over every last word and then come in at the end, making everyone feel grateful that they've even shown up.

'It doesn't win many friends,' said Blair, 'but they know everyone hides in their slipstream. If they cave, no one will do their fighting for them, so they fight for themselves.'

The tactic would cause anxious moments, Blair knew that. 'I knew if push really came to shove, I could probably square George, but we were going for both climate change and Africa, and he might just think one was enough, whereas I wanted both.'

Bush was wary. He knew that from the moment he conceded, he was on a travelator that might take him where he did not want to go. But on the other hand, the friendship between the two men was real, as both Bob and Bono came to understand. Both rock stars would privately admit – unpopular as it would have been in more liberal music circles – that they both rather liked the man they came to call George. In private, he was warm, self-deprecatory, smart and funny.

Certainly, the friendship between Blair and Bush was real and based on what the former called 'a really good personal chemistry'. When close friends would ask in private what he really thought of Bush, Blair would shock them by saying he really liked him. The feeling was mutual. And Bush knew how important Africa was to Blair.

'I don't want to be the skunk at the picnic,' the president had previously told the prime minister.

The dinner that the Queen hosted for the G8 leaders that evening was cooked by the Scottish chef Andrew Fairlie, who had trained in France and who, the following year, was awarded a second Michelin star. What the Queen didn't know was that a few days earlier – presumably in an attempt to outdo London in the Olympics vote – President Chirac had been very rude about British cooking. 'You can't trust people who cook as badly as that,' he had said.

As the politicians were served the Fairlie signature starter – locally sourced langoustine, smoked over whisky barrel chips – the Japanese prime minister, Junichiro Koizumi, said loudly in his faltering English: 'Hey, Jacques, excellent British food, don't you think?'

There were peals of laughter round the table. The Queen looked politely puzzled.

The same thing happened when the main course was served – fillet of Scottish lamb with local peas and beans, aubergine caviar and Parmesan polenta.

Jacques Chirac looked at Koizumi acidly, but was forced to join in the joke, while protesting to the Queen that he had never actually said what it was alleged he had said.

'Said what?' asked the Queen.

She was the only one who had not heard the story, Blair revealed, 'thus necessitating the whole thing being explained again, much to everyone's amusement – especially Koizumi's, who realised he was on to a rich vein and exploited it mercilessly, punctuating each course with raucous comments about the brilliance of the cooking'.

By the time the Queen, a lover of chocolate, was presented with a pudding called 'textures of chocolate' accompanied by a 1990 Château Climens, Chirac was thoroughly chastened. When the chef was brought in to be presented to the Queen at the end of dinner, the French president could only stand up and congratulate him.

❖

Bob Geldof's tactics rubbed off in the most unlikely places. Sir Michael Jay – now Baron Jay of Ewelme GCMG – was one of Whitehall's grandest civil servants. While Tony Blair was out wining and dining, his sherpa embarked upon what was, for an eminent diplomat, a rather unorthodox manoeuvre.

In the run-up to Live Aid years before, Geldof had perfected the Bob Bluff. This involved him telling Elton John that Dire Straits had agreed to play when they hadn't, and telling Dire Straits that Elton was on board when he wasn't yet. Or telling every major record retailer that their rivals had all agreed to distribute 'Do They Know It's Christmas?' for free, when they hadn't. It all ended with everyone agreeing to do what Geldof wanted before they had a chance to check with each other.

On the eve of Gleneagles, Tony Blair's private secretary for Africa, Laurie Lee, knew that something similar was needed at the highest diplomatic level.

The problem was this. Individual members of the G8 were prepared to give an indication of how much they might spend in the future in the areas the G8 was discussing. But they didn't want all the money to go into some giant pot labelled G8 funds. If that happened – and some nations did not fulfil their promises – the rest of them would be held responsible for raising the missing cash.

The G8 just didn't do this sort of thing. 'This is not a pledging conference,' one of the sherpas told Sir Michael Jay.

This was not what Tony Blair wanted. The Commission for Africa had recommended that aid should be doubled and he wanted the G8 to commit to that. But that was precisely what the other nations did not want to do.

So Laurie Lee contacted his old boss Richard Manning, a former Whitehall mandarin who now chaired the international body responsible for collecting and analysing global statistics on aid, the OECD.

'Can you do me a favour, Richard?' Laurie asked. 'If I pass you the figures for what we think the individual G8 nations will promise to give at Gleneagles, can you do a forecast of what aid would be in five years' time if the G8 deliver everything they have promised?' It was an unorthodox thing to ask, but Manning agreed. Bingo! The forecast was the figure Tony Blair wanted – $50 billion extra, every year, by 2010.

Very clever, thought Laurie, 'but we knew it was going a bit further than everyone wanted to go.'

That night, while all their bosses were still sipping the Château Climens with the Queen – and while Bob and Bono and George Clooney were buttering up the president of the World Bank at the Murrayfield after-show party – Sir Michael Jay and Laurie Lee did a quiet tour of the bedrooms of the other sherpas. In his hand, Laurie clutched what was now the OECD's official estimate of what global aid figures would be in 2010 on the assumption that every G8 leader kept his promises.

In a diplomatic variation of the Bob Bluff, Sir Michael told each sherpa: 'Okay, so we've got everyone's individual totals. They add up to 50 billion and so we're going to say in the communiqué it adds up to 50 billion. All right?'

'Is everyone else okay with this?' each sherpa asked, with varying degrees of scepticism.

'Oh yes,' said the dynamic duo, showing each sherpa the official OECD estimate. 'I think Michael and I both thought we were walking a bit of a tightrope,' said Laurie Lee. 'We were crossing our fingers that we were going to get round all these bedrooms before they all started talking to each other. What we were saying was true: that everyone had made these commitments and this is what they added up to. But it was unorthodox by G8 standards, that's for sure.'

It was an unusual ploy for such a fastidiously correct diplomat, but in conjunction with the groundwork that had been laid by Blair's political team, it worked with almost everyone – except the Germans. Partly this was a legacy of the country's inter-war economic trauma, which left it with a strong preference for balanced budgets and fiscal discipline. Partly it was because of Schröder's strong personal dislike of Tony Blair. The Germans continued to play hardball. Even so, at the end of the night, Jay and Lee put the OECD 'doubling aid' figure into the communiqué as a starting point for the morning. 'We knew we had got our big headline,' said Laurie. 'And that would be the headline target the world could hold the G8 accountable to – for the next five years.'

They reported back to Tony Blair. The PM knew that he still had to outflank the German chancellor, but he now felt reasonably confident about the morning.

But, the following day, his quiet confidence was to be shattered.

CHAPTER 37

DOING THE DEAL

B ob and Bono and the rest of the celebrity delegation were still in their beds in the Balmoral hotel in Edinburgh, but an hour up the road at Gleneagles, Tony Blair and George Bush had already finished breakfast. It was a morning of bright sunshine, a sunglasses-and-shirt-sleeves morning. The two politicians had taken breakfast outside on the terrace. Having waved away various aides, they ate alone. By 7.30 a.m., they were out for a stroll in the gardens. *George is more or less there on Africa*, thought Blair as they walked. The rolling hills of the Perthshire countryside were bathed in morning sunlight. Things were looking good. The prime minister was optimistic that the G8 leaders would reach a deal on at least one of the two topics he had chosen for the British presidency.

They were in high spirits when they went for their early morning press conference. George Bush opened by declaring: 'It's a beautiful day for a bike ride… So was yesterday, I thought.' The press corps all laughed.

Three minutes before the end of the press conference, three bombs went off 400 miles away on the London Underground, killing dozens of people on their way to work in the morning rush hour. The explosions injured more than 700 others. Three British-born Islamic fundamentalist suicide bombers had blown themselves up simultaneously at different points on the Tube.

Unaware of all this, Tony Blair entered a reception room overlooking the handsome lawns ready to greet the leaders of five major developing countries – Brazil, China, India, Mexico and South Africa – who had been invited to join the G8 leaders to discuss the impact on the global economy of climate change. First to arrive was Chinese president Hu Jintao, who congratulated the British prime minister on his successful 2012 Olympic bid; Blair reciprocated by saying he was sure the 2008 Beijing Olympics would be spectacular. As the PM welcomed his Indian counterpart, Manmohan Singh, news came through to his aides of a 'power surge' on the Underground.

Leading the newly arrived politicians to the main conference room, Blair immediately suspected that the 'power surge' was in fact terrorism designed to wreck the international summit. Nonetheless, he decided to proceed with the formal opening ceremony. But everyone present was aware that something serious was unfolding in London. Blair tried to keep them to the agenda, with each delivering an opening statement.

At 9.15 a.m., London Underground's network control centre realised that they were dealing with multiple explosions. A Code Amber alert was issued. The entire railway network was instantly shut down. All trains were to terminate at the next station. All passengers were to be evacuated.

In Gleneagles, Tony Blair's chief of staff, Jonathan Powell, entered the sacrosanct G8 leaders-only meeting. He passed the PM a note. It looks like terrorism, Blair was told. At 9.47 a.m., a fourth suicide bomber, having failed to detonate his bomb underground with the others, blew himself up on a number 30 bus. This was clearly a coordinated assault of the kind which al-Qaeda had inflicted on the city of Madrid the year before, just days before the Spanish general election.

In the Balmoral, Bob Geldof watched the horrifying events unfold on the television in his hotel room. As he watched, he was being filmed by another television crew who had come to do a routine interview. Their footage captured his speechless bewilderment. He watched the screen and threw his hands in the air and silently shook his head – he had no words.

When he found them, they lacked eloquence but not force. 'We're fucked. It's over,' he said to me as we stood in the foyer of the hotel waiting for Bono to arrive. The two Irish musicians threw their arms around one another. On the table, a single lily filled the morning air with its funereal scent. They stood ashen-faced, both avoiding putting into words what they were thinking: that these fanatical bombers had done more than kill fifty-two people and irrevocably change the lives of hundreds of the injured and their families. They had also put paid to the chance of saving tens of millions of lives in Africa at a G8 summit on which campaigners had worked tirelessly for more than a year. 'We knew that, in the face of this terrible outrage, we couldn't and mustn't complain about all those years of work for nothing,' Bob later reflected. 'But that was part of what filled me with such great personal rage.' At the time, they just stared at each other in a state of confusion.

'What are we going to do now?' said Bono.

Everything was thrown into confusion. It was the same at the Gleneagles media centre, where Adrian Lovett of Oxfam had just arrived. 'I remember all the oxygen was immediately sucked out of the place,' he said.

Back in Edinburgh, Geldof, for once, felt lost. Bono had flown to Germany to re-join U2 for a gig in Berlin that night – the one at which he had threatened to praise or denounce Schröder. After it, he would fly back to Edinburgh for the final day of the G8 when it would be announced whether or not the deal for Africa had been done. The bombs made everyone pessimistic. 'We had this whole day of different activities planned,' said Zita Lloyd from DATA, 'various photo-ops and campaigning moments that we were going to be appearing at.'

They were all cancelled. 'We didn't know what to do with ourselves that morning,' said Zita. She and Bob, and Richard Curtis and Emma Freud, wandered out aimlessly and ended up in the National Gallery in Edinburgh. 'There was a Francis Bacon exhibition on. It was very dark,' said Zita. 'It kind of fitted the mood, which was very strange.' Eventually, in a rather desultory manner, Geldof decided to go to Gleneagles. On the way, he was thinking about the paintings. 'How apt Bacon was,' he thought, for he offered 'the perfect physical visualisation of the tortured human mind and its awful horror.'

✼

Tony Blair had no time for such reflection. At 11 a.m., he suspended the G8 meeting to hold talks with the heads of MI5 and MI6, and counter-terrorism police in London. The flags outside the hotel had been lowered to half-mast. Security at Gleneagles, already tight, was immediately tightened. George Bush left for the presidential suite to hold a ten-minute secure video conference with national security advisers and homeland security chiefs in

Washington. When Blair returned to the garden room, the other world leaders crowded round him to find out what was happening.

'I was in a genuine quandary as to whether to leave the summit,' he said. This was the biggest conference of his premiership. Was it his duty to stay and chair it? Or to leave and take control of the response to the attacks? 'In hindsight, it was obvious I should return to London,' he later said. 'It didn't seem like it then.'

It was an extraordinary moment, even for a diplomat as experienced as Sir Michael Jay. 'There you had eight world leaders round the table having to decide in real time how they were going to react to a really serious terrorist attack.'

Jacques Chirac and George Bush spoke first.

'You have to go back,' said the French president. 'The British people will expect it.'

'Get down to London,' said the US president. 'We can handle it on our own up here. Get down to London and do your job.'

The Italian prime minister had a different suggestion.

'Let's all go to London with you,' said Silvio Berlusconi.

But Bush gave that idea short shrift. It would be a massive security operation to transfer seven other world leaders to the capital, he said. And who knew what danger might be lying in wait there?

'We stay here. You go, Tony.'

The moment brought an eerie echo to Bush of the moment he had been given the news about 9/11 – and the lessons that had taught him. 'You need to go soon, but not immediately. You need to know exactly what is going to happen first, before you get on that plane.'

'But who will take over here?'

Chirac gestured towards Sir Michael Jay: 'Your guy here is really good. Why don't we have him?' the French president suggested. Bush concurred.

Jay wrote a note on his tablet, which the Gleneagles logistics room could read in real time. They watched as he tapped out:

'Prime Minister addressed meeting.

'Prime Minister informs meeting of events in London.

'Prime Minister informs meeting he will be leaving to go to London and will return.

'Prime Minister informs meeting that G8 sherpa will take over chairing of meeting.'

Then, over in the logistics room, the staff watched as a singled word appeared in capital letters:

'HELP.'

At 11.25 a.m., the G8 session was officially suspended. In the media centre, just a few hundred yards away, journalists could see a visibly shaken Tony Blair on their plasma screens. The prime minister and his aides quickly prepared a statement and, at noon, he appeared live on television to address the nation. He looked grim but determined as he announced his intention to leave Gleneagles 'within the next couple of hours' to return to London to talk directly to police chiefs and ministers.

'It is particularly barbaric that this has happened on the day when people are meeting to try to help the problems of poverty in Africa and the long-term problems of climate change and the environment.' But it was the will of all the G8 leaders, who all 'have some experience of the effects of terrorism', that they should 'continue to discuss the issues that we were going to discuss and reach the conclusions which we were going to reach'. Otherwise, the terrorists would have won. He would return to Gleneagles that night, he said.

Privately, he told his team that the summit timetable would need reshuffling. Thursday was supposed to be the day to discuss climate change. Blair worried insufficient progress would be made in his absence. He told his team to announce there would be no climate change communiqué that afternoon as had originally been planned. Before he left, he wanted to see Bob Geldof, who was in the small bedroom he and the other campaigners had been given to use as a base at the back of the hotel. 'He came into our room and told us he had to go to London,' said Geldof. 'For me, there were shades of that time at the Commission for Africa meeting in Addis Ababa when he had to leave early to go back to London because of the killing of Ken Bigley. Again, he looked anguished. Again, it seemed too crass, too selfish, too inappropriate to say anything other than "Of course, prime minister".'

At 1 p.m., Tony Blair went back out in front of the live television cameras. A small stage had been hastily set up. On it stood the presidents and prime ministers of the G8, along with the leaders of the additional five countries invited for the climate change talks. Some of them had differed sharply with Blair over the war in Iraq, but today they came together in international solidarity.

'We are united in our resolve to confront and defeat this terrorism that is not an attack on one nation but on all nations and on civilised people everywhere,' a solemn Blair told the television audience. 'The war on terrorism goes on,' said President Bush to the cameras as Blair crossed the eighteenth hole of the Gleneagles golf course to a waiting Chinook military helicopter. 'If the ambition of the terrorists was to prevent us from carrying out our work, then they failed,' said President Chirac.

※

Day Two at Gleneagles was supposed to be given over to climate change. It was not a topic at the top of Geldof's agenda. In 2005, the heating of the planet was not taken anywhere near as seriously as it was to be in the decades that followed. It was never part of the preoccupations of Bob, Band Aid or, indeed, of Make Poverty History.

Yet, at G8 summits, much of the key business gets done outside of the formal meetings. The official sessions on Day Two – in the morning, over lunch and in the afternoon – all focused on the relationship between the global economy and climate change. Some limited agreement was reached on developing clean energy, but the G8 set no binding targets or timelines on the emissions of greenhouse gases. There was some support for better climate monitoring systems in Africa, but George Bush was reluctant to put much American money into it. But, away from the conference table, conversations and lobbying on Africa continued in Blair's absence.

※

Contrary to Geldof's fears that the terrorist outrage would scupper the Gleneagles deal, G8 leaders now voiced their determination to back Blair rather than quibble over details. Canada, Italy and Japan all agreed to double aid to Africa saying, in the words of the Japanese prime minister, Junichiro Koizumi, that doing this was sending out 'a strong message that we shall continue our fight against terrorism'.

By the time Blair's twin-rotor Chinook, with its heavy military escort, clattered down onto the Gleneagles golf course that evening, only Germany was refusing to agree to the doubling of aid to Africa. 'We had got down to the wire with Germany and they were not moving,' said Justin Forsyth.

Blair was 'tired but focused' said Forsyth who, along with Sir Michael Jay, quickly briefed the prime minister on events during his absence. Jay was buzzing after making a great success of chairing the meeting with the world leaders. 'You're going to have to talk to Schröder,' he told the PM. Blair had missed dinner but, despite being very hungry, went straight to the hotel bar, where the other seven heads of government were gathered with their wives. There, he briefed the world leaders on the latest counter-terrorist intelligence and ended with an impassioned plea. 'He spoke of how what had happened was an attack on all of us and on democracy itself,' said Forsyth, 'and how our best response in our defence of democracy was to agree this deal for Africa that demonstrated our democratic values. It was very powerful and very moving.'

The others agreed. 'It was clear that the consequence of the terrorism on the leaders was to bring out the best in them,' Blair later reflected. 'They reacted brilliantly and with total solidarity. There was an implicit collective decision to support the G8 agenda and get a result. The African numbers came together.'

The only person that didn't want to go along with that was Gerhard Schröder. He was saying he wanted to exempt Germany from the communiqué. Blair decided he had to confront Schröder himself – but not in front of the others. He waited until the German got up to go to the bathroom and followed him. 'He literally got Schröder up against the wall in the men's toilets,' said Justin Forsyth, 'and told him he was going to wreck the whole conference and the prospects of progress. "We're gonna do this deal, Gerhard, aren't we?" And, at that moment, I think Schröder gave in.'

As Blair was administering his strong-arm tactic in the men's room, Bono was on stage in Berlin, in the gigantic arena built by Albert Speer for the 1936 Olympics, calling out the German chancellor as he had said he would. Bono told the crowd he had just come from Scotland, where Schröder had not agreed to make Germany's contribution to doubling annual aid to Africa. 'So we do not applaud the chancellor. But if he can deliver this by 4 p.m., your chancellor, in my mind, will be a hero. You have one more night to make sure that he does this.'

Perhaps that was what did it. Or perhaps it was the Murrayfield lobbying of Herbert Grönemeyer, Germany's answer to Bruce Springsteen. Or perhaps it was the ferocity of the look in Tony Blair's eyes in the gents at Gleneagles. Whichever, the next day, Germany agreed to double aid to Africa. Success, they say, has many fathers.

⁂

Richard Curtis had a message from Geldof and Bono for Kumi Naidoo. By the end of Thursday, everyone had acquired a draft of tomorrow's final communiqué. It was still only a draft. Tony Blair's private secretary for Africa, Laurie Lee, would be up all night writing the final *final* version – and he knew full well there would be changes on Friday morning before the final final *final* version was ready to be issued to the press. But the draft was enough for everyone to begin to form their verdicts on what to say to the public when the communiqué was released the next day. The fear was growing that Kumi was going to say something out of line with the others.

Bob and Bono asked the politest member of their group to ring him. 'Richard Curtis calls me,' said Kumi, 'and says Geldof and Bono are saying, "Can you, in your response, pay tribute to the leadership role that Tony Blair and Gordon Brown have taken in getting this deal together?".' Alarm bells rang. Kumi had for some time become apprehensive about the close relationship between the pop stars and the politicians.

'I'd once gone to meet Tony Blair in Downing Street together with Bob and Bono and the Make Poverty History team,' Kumi said, 'and I got really concerned because when we walked in there, Tony Blair says, "Welcome, guys. How are we doing? Are we getting Berlusconi to shift? Are we getting any movement with Bush?" And he was creating this impression that the UK government and Make Poverty History and GCAP were completely aligned.' That was not the case, Kumi insisted. 'I got anxious to see the proximity between Make Poverty History and the UK government. They were all too pally-pally.'

Bob defended his proximity to world leaders: 'Like it or not, the agents of change in our world are the politicians. The rest of us are always outside the tent pissing in. They stay inside their tent, pissing back out at you. This is futile. My solution is to get inside the tent and piss in there.'

But the request from Richard Curtis only deepened Kumi's anxiety.

He told Curtis that he could not personally decide to praise Blair and Brown. Only the global coalition could make that decision. 'Our job is not to evaluate the G8 presidency. Our job is to evaluate what the G8 put on the table. And when we unpack it, we still see massive amounts can be mobilised overnight for war in Iraq, but money for development won't come in full 'til 2010.' That was five years away and gave the politicians plenty of time to wriggle out of the promises they were making.

The stage was set for a massive public bust-up between Geldof and Kumi in front of the world's television cameras the next day.

❖

The Africans only arrived on Day Three. On the Friday morning, seven heads of government – from Nigeria, Ghana, Senegal, Algeria, Ethiopia, Tanzania and South Africa – arrived in Gleneagles to join the discussion. But before that, the G8 leaders gathered on their own to go through the final draft of the communiqué produced overnight by Laurie Lee. It included more than fifty of the ninety recommendations of the Commission for Africa. There were so many similarities between the two documents that a comparison between them ran to some twenty-five pages.

'We weren't negotiating on *what* had to be done,' Lee said. 'The only real question for the G8 was *whether* it had the political will, and if it would provide the funds necessary to do what we all knew needed to be done.' Gordon Brown had virtually tied up the debt deal ahead of the summit. Now, with the German chancellor finally on board, the aid deal was done. The US had swung in behind the idea of making AIDS medicines universally available. So much had been agreed that, by the time the African leaders joined them, there was more time to discuss Tony Blair's idea that aid to Africa was – with the increasing threat of fundamentalist terrorism – an issue of global security rather than just international development.

Behind the scenes, Bob and Bono had been given free rein to wander the corridors of Gleneagles. They had meetings on the side with everyone from Chirac to Kofi Annan, in their bedroom office or in the coffee lounge.

During the early afternoon, the Live 8 campaigners began seeing leaks of the communiqué. It was drawing ever closer to what they had both been tirelessly advocating for many years.

Oh, my God, this is really happening, Bono thought.

But there was still something missing. Debt cancellation was done. Aid was to be doubled. Yet Make Poverty History had also demanded action to make trade fairer. Bob and Bono knew that was never going to happen at Gleneagles. The G8 was not the right forum for progress on trade. That would have to wait until the meeting of the World Trade Organization in Hong Kong in six months' time.

But, with everything else going so well by the Friday morning, in the plenary session Blair decided to try to reach an agreement on reducing the export subsidies that governments paid to farmers in Europe and the US.

'Blair pushed really hard on it,' said Forsyth. 'He thought a G8 agreement on trade subsidies send a strong signal to the negotiators in Hong Kong.'

To everyone's surprise, the idea was backed by Jacques Chirac. Perhaps he was feeling the pressure of Geldof's lobbying earlier in the day. Or perhaps it was just gamesmanship because instinctively he knew that the deal would be scuppered by the EU representative, José Manuel Barroso – which is exactly what happened. Export subsidies should be ended, everybody piously nodded, but there was no agreement on a date by which this should happen. The only concession the G8 made on trade was to declare that African economies would no longer be forced to open up their markets to Western goods – another virtuous aspiration.

There was one final victory. The Americans had flatly refused to back Gordon Brown's idea of an International Finance Facility to front-load spending on aid. But Brown's assistant, Shriti Vadera, had the brainwave of using the mechanism to fund the vaccination of children. Each country would add up what it planned to spend over the next five years immunising children – and then spend it all in the first year.

It made sense to everyone except the Germans – a spend-now-pay-later scheme which offended the German sense of fiscal rectitude.

Okay, said Sir Michael Jay, the rest of us will do it without you.

No, insisted the German sherpa, it has to be removed from the communiqué.

A stand-up row ensued between Jay and his German counterpart, but the Brits held firm. The Germans opted out, but everyone else joined in. It raised $6 billion and vaccinated 100 million children.

Millions of lives would be saved as a result of the UK's innovative thinking.

❋

The television cameras lined up for the last act of the official summit. On the steps of the hotel, the G8 leaders, along with the five African heads of government, came out for the photocall. Once more, Tony Blair set events in the context of the terrorist bombs, which many had feared would wreck Gleneagles. Instead, they only increased the determination of the politicians that the summit must not fail.

'The purpose of terrorism is not only to kill and maim the innocent. It is to overwhelm the dignity of democracy. So we offer today this contrast with the politics of terror,' he said, speaking of the start of a new dialogue on climate change and concrete action for Africa. 'It isn't all everyone wanted, but it is progress – real and achievable progress.' It would not bring an end to poverty, he added, but it offered the hope that it could be ended. The meeting had been, said Olusegun Obasanjo, president of the Africa Union and president of Nigeria, 'a great success'.

In a final act of theatre, Blair asked each of the leaders to step forward and sign the communiqué – something not generally done at the end of a G8 summit but which he thought would give their promises 'added resonance and credibility'. It would lock them into a commitment.

As a departing gift, Bob Geldof had arranged for a different kind of reminder of their pledges. Each world leader was a given a signed print of Peter Blake's Live 8 poster showing them all in Sgt. Pepper uniforms. Geldof had been correct: they were all Beatles fans. Even Jacques Chirac seemed pleased to be given one. Still in signing mood, they all autographed the posters for one another as they got ready to leave.

As the helicopters clattered the leaders off to the airport, over the fifty-two-mile fence that had been erected around Gleneagles and its grounds, what did they leave behind?

The headlines on aid and debt were clear, but you had to dig down into them to understand what the outcome on the ground would be.

A total of $41.9 billion was cancelled for nineteen of the world's poorest countries. That meant that fourteen African countries no longer had to make whopping regular interest payments to big international banks. It was like a homeowner suddenly being told that they no longer had to pay their mortgage each month. The cash that was instantly released could now be spent on new hospitals and medical supply chains, new schools and universities, new mobile and fibre optics networks, new roads and railways, new homes, new clean water, sanitation and irrigation systems.

The promise to double aid every year for the next five years – from $25 billion to $50 billion a year – was the biggest aid deal in Africa's history. It would mean 20 million more children would go to school. It would provide anti-AIDS drugs to 9 million Africans within the next five years, while doubling research spending on the disease. Some 600,000 children would not die of malaria and 85 per cent of the vulnerable population would have access to insecticide-impregnated bed nets, mosquito sprays and drug treatments by 2015. Polio would finally be totally eradicated in Africa. Five million more orphans would be cared for.

These were not merely numbers. Each one of those children could grow up to be like Birhan Woldu, that luminous young Ethiopian woman, who walked onto the Live 8 stage a confident twenty-four-year-old agricultural student just six days before the G8 signed their document.

And, importantly, the Gleneagles communiqué committed the rich nations to change. They undertook to restrict the weapons trade in small arms. They would clamp down on Western companies who pay bribes. They would freeze money in Western banks deposited by corrupt African leaders – and return looted cash to its rightful owners. They would support African governments in becoming more accountable to their people with a peer review mechanism to make good governments a model for their weaker neighbours. The G8 also agreed to train and equip 20,000 more African soldiers as peacekeepers.

Looking back on the six days surrounding Gleneagles – the Olympics announcement, the terrorist bombings, closing the G8 deal on Africa – Tony Blair wrote in his memoirs five years later that they were 'the most extraordinary turbulence I had lived through in my time in politics'. Twenty years on, he reflected more deeply on that week. Pausing momentarily as he felt for the exact words, he said: 'It was probably one of the last moments of truly global solidarity that I can remember.'

At the time, Bob Geldof was more direct. 'This has been, without doubt,' he said, 'the greatest G8 summit there has ever been for Africa.' He would soon be outraged to discover that others were to describe it as 'a disaster for the world's poor'.

CHAPTER 38

THE END OF
THE BEGINNING

As Tony Blair went out onto the steps at the Gleneagles Hotel to present the outcome of the world leaders' summit to the waiting television cameras, Bob Geldof and Bono were already huddled together, poring over the detail in their advance copy of the text. The two musicians were elated. 'We've pulled this off,' Bono whispered to Bob. Geldof was already comparing the G8's recommendations against those of the Commission for Africa. This was the template by which he would judge the success of the Gleneagles Africa deal.

But Bob was in for a rude awakening. As he and Bono were making their way from the hotel to the Gleneagles media centre, the Make Poverty History coordinating team were meeting to produce their own assessment. It was much more lukewarm. Then came the verdict from Kumi Naidoo of the Global Call for Action Against Poverty. He had been asked the day before to pay tribute to Blair and Brown in his response. Instead, what he delivered was downright hostile.

The Make Poverty History verdict was that 'the UK government have demonstrated leadership' and 'important steps have been taken – steps that will bring hope to millions', but that this was not enough. As they unpacked the detail, they tried to have it both ways throughout. Cancelling 100 per cent of debt was 'a positive step', but not the 'giant leap that was called for'. The aid increase 'will save lives', but was 'too little, too late'. On trade, the G8 had offered 'warm words, but little in terms of concrete commitments'. The extra money for AIDS drugs was 'one of the summit's successes', but more money was needed, and sooner. There was language in the communiqué on 'letting African countries set their own trade policies', but what was needed was 'action not words'. In every category, the MPH judgement was 'good, but not good enough'. It was a classic example of a statement produced by a committee.

By contrast, Kumi Naidoo's GCAP verdict thundered. 'The people roared and the G8 whispered,' it began. Having read it, Blair's Africa adviser, Justin Forsyth, sought out its author and confronted him at the side of the stage on which their press conference was due to take place. The two men had been friends for twenty years, working together in the anti-apartheid movement, and so spoke honestly to one another.

'This press release is a fucking disgrace,' said the man from No 10. 'How could you come up with such a horrible statement?'

'I'm not accountable to you,' the man from South Africa replied. 'I'm accountable to a broad global movement and you have to be respectful of that.'

'You're a bastard,' shouted Bob Geldof, clearly not respectful at all.

'You don't understand the political complexity of what we did, how hard we fought and how hard we pushed,' said Justin. 'You are taking a completely unfair position.'

Kumi shrugged. 'Our job here is not to evaluate the G8 presidency. We're evaluating what the G8 has put on the table. You don't get marks for effort.'

The two friends jostled. Someone pushed them behind the stage, to get away from the cameras. Geldof told Kumi he would never speak to him again. Justin and Kumi had to be kept apart backstage.

Adrian Lovett, who was about to chair a press conference with the three men, looked in a state of shock.

Kumi turned to Bono. 'Perhaps it would be better if we had separate press conferences. You guys can do your own. We'll get a smaller attendance, but that won't matter.'

'No,' said Bono. 'We need to go up together. That's the way we can damage-control it.'

At the press conference, Adrian decided it would be prudent to ask Kirsty McNeill, from the MPH coordinating committee, to speak first. 'Kirsty did a very thoughtful and, frankly, slightly boring, but very deliberate analysis of what was good in the Gleneagles deal, and what wasn't so

good and so on,' recalled Adrian. 'It was just right considering she was trying to reflect the various views of the coalition she was representing – and
she cleverly stayed away from a sort of blanket overall verdict.'

Next up was Kumi Naidoo, wearing a brown, open-necked African
shirt. He looked nervous. He still hadn't recovered from his shouting match
with Justin and Bob. 'Our reading is that the G8 has listened,' he said in a
cool, measured voice, 'but that the G8 response has not been a roar but a
whisper.' The promise to deliver more aid by 2010 'is like waiting five years
before responding to the tsunami'.

Bono's reply was oblique. He said he wanted to establish some context.
'We jumped up and down when Live Aid raised $200 *million*,' he told the
assembled media. 'I remember, we thought we'd cracked it. And now, just
stop for a second, we're talking about an extra $25 *billion*.' He paused for a
moment to let it sink in. The G8 had promised a hundred times more than
Live Aid had raised. Kumi took a drink of water and looked down. To ease
the tension, Bono ended with a joke: 'So if an Irish rock star is allowed to
quote Winston Churchill, I wouldn't say this is the end of extreme poverty,
but it is the beginning of the end.' Kirsty clapped. Kumi did not. He was
waiting, apprehensively, to see what Geldof would say.

Geldof got to his feet with the Commission for Africa report in his
hand. His tone was celebratory, but his message was emphatic. 'This has
been the most important summit there ever has been for Africa,' he told the
post-summit press conference. 'No equivocations. Africa and the poor of
that continent have got more from the last three days than they have ever
got at any previous summit...'

'Was this a success?' he asked rhetorically and did not wait for any
answer other than his own.

'Ten out of ten on aid.

'Eight out of ten on debt.

'On trade, the Commission for Africa says that this must be negotiated
at the Hong Kong round. It was never meant to be negotiated at the summit. However, please refer to paragraph 31 for language that even Kumi
would have liked to write himself:'

It is up to developing countries themselves and their governments
to take the lead on development. They need to decide, plan and

sequence their economic policies to fit with their own development strategies, for which they should be accountable to all their people.

Fine words. But they could, Kumi knew, be taken to mean anything or nothing.

For Bob, their meaning was self-evident. 'It is quite clear that this summit uniquely has decided that enforced liberalisation must no longer take place. That is a serious, excellent result on trade. Today is a great day.'

Had he left it at that, things might have been smoothed over inside Make Poverty History. But he did not.

'Let me take up Make Poverty History's quote, "The people roared and the G8 whispered."'

There was controlled fury in his face now. The lives of 10 million people would be saved by the Gleneagles deal, he said.

'When did 10 million people – alive – become a whisper? Up to now, we've heard them screaming.' Bob's anger was barely contained now. 'When were 10 million lives ever a whisper? It is a disgrace to suggest that.'

Kumi scratched his nose and looked down at the table.

'Perspective, please,' said Bob.

As he returned to his seat, Kirsty and Bono applauded. Kumi did not.

'I think I'm going to walk out,' Kumi whispered to Bono.

'No, no,' said Bono urgently. 'I'm going to pass it back onto you.' Having clapped Bob, he now patted Kumi on the back. Bono, ever the peacemaker, now tried to find a way to square the circle.

'A mountain has been climbed,' he said, 'only to reveal higher peaks, for sure, on the other side of it – but it's worth just stopping for a second and looking back down the valley to see where we've all come from.' Adrian Lovett, chairing the fractious meeting, was relieved. 'It was a classic bit of Bono imagery,' Adrian said. 'I breathed a sigh of relief when he said that. It captured beautifully both the sense of remarkable achievement, and of unfinished business. I think it really helped. That was the end of the campaign.'

Geldof was less forbearing. 'Typical Bono,' he said. 'He's a very clever man and he's a beautiful speaker. He's a real friend and I love him deeply. But he's always trying to find a way to keep everybody happy and, frankly, at times you must be judgemental. And this was one of them.'

But Bono was intent on mending fences, as Kumi found. 'Immediately after the bust-up, Bono came up to me,' Kumi recalled. 'He said, "Every movement needs a mad general and Bob is our guy for that, but we are very clear that we are here to support the global movement." And he arranged that we would all meet up two months later at the UN in New York to rebuild the bridges.'

❖

But there were some bridges which could not be rebuilt. While the Make Poverty History coordinating committee was deliberating over its carefully balanced verdict, impatient journalists had turned to other sources for comment. Always eager to build conflict into any story, the media inevitably lapped up the views of the radical outsiders.

The World Development Movement decried the G8 package as 'an insult to the hundreds of thousands of campaigners' – interestingly, a verdict in which they put the campaigners first, only subsequently calling the deal a 'disaster for the world's poor'.

War on Want condemned the aid increases as less than 20 per cent of what was required.

Christian Aid acknowledged that there were 'some nuggets on debt', but declared: 'This will not make poverty history. It is a vastly disappointing result. Millions of campaigners all over the world have been led to the top of the mountain, shown the view and now we are being frogmarched down again.'

But most of the development agencies tried to have it both ways.

Save the Children hailed the agreement as 'one step forward', but said the 'giant leap to make child poverty history is yet to come'.

Oxfam said that 'no previous G8 summit has done as much for development, particularly in Africa'. The outcome 'represents an important and welcome increase in aid levels after many years of scandalous decline'. Yet though it was 'a serious step forward', it still fell 'far short' of what was needed. It would give millions more children the chance to go to school, and provide life-saving medicines for millions, but if the $25 billion aid increase had kicked in immediately – instead of rising gradually over the five years to come – 'it could have lifted 300 million out of poverty in the next five years'. On trade, the G8 had 'failed to substantially move forwards on creating a more just world trade system'.

Yet even where praise was fulsome, there were caveats. On debt, Oxfam conceded that 'for years, governments and the international financial institutions have resisted campaigners' calls for 100 per cent cancellation of these debts, arguing that it was neither necessary nor feasible. Now the pressure of public campaigning has forced them to reconsider, setting an extremely important precedent.'

At the end of that paean or praise, though, Oxfam added: 'However, there is much further to go.'

All of this double-edged language immensely irritated Bob Geldof. 'Blair has done much, much more than we asked him to do. This endless whingeing drives me nuts.'

The mainstream media took a far more balanced view. Tony Blair 'appeared to have scored a victory', wrote the *Guardian*'s economic and diplomatic editors, Larry Elliot and Patrick Wintour. They had never seen anything like it, they told Justin Forsyth afterwards. 'They really couldn't understand why the NGOs weren't happier,' Justin wrote in his diary that night.

Others outside the process were far more upbeat. The UN secretary-general, Kofi Annan, described it as a 'Rubicon-crossing moment' and 'the greatest summit for Africa ever'. The leading academic expert John Kirton, director of the G8 Research Project at the University of Toronto, said Gleneagles was 'a summit of historic significance'. The Harvard economist, Jeffrey Sachs, described it as 'an important, if incomplete, boost to the development prospects of the poorest countries'. Kevin Watkins, by now director of the UN Development Programme's Human Development Report, called it 'a major breakthrough on debt'. For Bill Gates, it had the potential to become 'the best thing that humanity has ever done'.

The response of African leaders was totally positive. The Nigerian president, Olusegun Obasanjo, described the summit as a 'momentous meeting' and 'a great success'. Gleneagles marked 'an historic new step in fundamentally redefining the relationship between Africa and the countries of the North,' said the South African president, Thabo Mbeki, singling out Geldof and Bono for their work in mobilising 'the masses of the people globally, to take up the cause of the poor of our continent'. Meles Zenawi, prime minister of Ethiopia and a member of Blair's Commission for Africa, said the G8 had created 'a new paradigm' which 'no matter what happens in terms of the specifics, creates the right framework for pro-poor growth in this country, as well as on the continent'. All this reinforced the insistence of both Bob Geldof and Tony Blair that 'the only people that will change Africa ultimately are Africans'.

❧

So why had the fault lines inside Make Poverty History now become fractures? There were several factors. To many MPH members, the problem was Geldof and Bono. Kumi Naidoo was by now complaining of what he called 'celebocracy' – rule by celebrities. Bob and Bono had 'too much control', said the radical outsiders. 'The campaign has been too superficial,' argued Christian Aid's Ghanaian head of policy, Charles Abugre. 'There were millions watching, but what was the analysis? What was the message?'

Oddly, however, there were no complaints when celebrities like Bianca Jagger joined in on the other side. Mick Jagger's ex attacked Bob and Bono for 'sleeping with the enemy' by getting too close to New Labour politicians. She declared that she felt 'betrayed by their moral ambiguity and sound-bite propaganda, which has obscured and watered down the real issues'. Betrayal is an interesting word. It suggests an act of treachery among a group with a common cause. But the truth was that the Live 8 activists and the global campaigners had different agendas from the outset. Confusingly, they used the same words, but meant different things by them.

For a start, Bob and Bono – since the days of Band Aid, Live Aid, the Commission for Africa and most recently, Live 8 – had been exclusively focused on the poor of Africa. By contrast, the Global Call to Action against Poverty, though led by a South African, Kumi Naidoo, had a far wider focus that included Asia, Latin America and other parts of the world. 'The demands of Geldof and Bono were not those of Make Poverty History,' said Kumi. 'They were those of the Commission for Africa.' Bob and Bono agreed completely with his analysis, but no one else did.

Then there was the question of trade. The rallying cry of MPH was 'Debt, Aid and Trade'. Though Geldof and Bono privately pushed hard with leaders like Chirac and Bush for an end to agricultural export subsidies in the run-up to Gleneagles, both knew that the G8 was not the right forum for reforms to secure greater trade justice. Using the 'Debt, Aid and Trade' slogan above the Live 8 stage may well have set up expectations among some campaigners which were impossible to fulfil. But more profoundly, not everyone in the MPH movement meant the same thing when they talked about 'trade justice'.

'A lot of these guys would pitch up at meetings and accuse Oxfam of backing a neo-liberal trade agenda that was going to harm developing countries,' recalled Kevin Watkins, who was formerly Oxfam's head of policy. 'That was just nonsense. What we actually argued for was something very different. We called for an end to the European and US farm subsidies that were destroying markets for African farmers. We wanted rich countries to let in more of Africa's exports. And we called for reform of trade rules that were driving up the costs of essential imports, like HIV/AIDS medicines. What we didn't buy was the implausible argument that protectionism in Africa automatically helped the poor when in fact many of its benefits went into the pockets of elites.'

Geldof had no time for the leftist ideology of Oxfam's critics. Bob was wrongly supposed by many to be a leftist because he was an activist. But he was not, though nor was he on the right. His politics were rooted in a combination of morality and pragmatism. 'Walking around Trafalgar Square, singing "We Shall Overcome" is a waste of time. You won't overcome anything,' he said in summary of his approach. 'You can be an instrument of change but you must have a plan and be prepared to act upon it.' He was deeply impatient with ideological leftists. He could not, however, be bothered to argue with them – he just ignored them and carried on doing his own thing.

There was something else. Geldof's work with the Commission for Africa had enabled him to see, close up, the workings of government, national and international. Far from having 'got too close to the government and got burnt', as John Coventry of War on Want put it, Geldof had come to understand that politics was the art of the possible. After two decades as the quintessential campaigner, he knew that protesting was the easier option. 'There's a moral purity to those who stand on the sidelines and shout,' said Bob. 'But they get fuck-all done.'

Over the past year, working with him inside the Commission for Africa, I had seen him learn from the French that the Common Agricultural Policy would never be fixed by the commission. I had seen him accept, initially reluctantly, the South African finance minister's explanation of why it was unrealistic to demand that aid be quadrupled in one go. I had watched him discover that you could get big bucks from the Americans – but only if you asked them for money for things which interested them. Together, he and I had learned, above all, that given the way the G8 works, you have to have the patience to work incrementally.

Geldof has ceased to ask for the ideal and settled for the politically possible, one critic sniped. But Bob and Bono both now embraced that remark as a compliment.

'Look, you can take a totally oppositional stance to everything and there are various reasons you might do that,' Geldof told me. 'Or you can use the platforms that people give you. Gleneagles was a monstrous win. Together, you and I, through the Commission for Africa, lassoed the economic and political structures of the world and pulled them in our direction. And we found one guy, one politician, Tony Blair, who said, "Okay, I'll come with you on this one." Blair went way out on a limb. He used every ounce of political credibility to get it done. We know that, because we were in there and we saw. So I've no time at all for the wankers who whinge but never get anything done themselves.'

The final fault line lay in the psychology the two sides adopted. Bob and Bono adopted a 'glass half full' strategy, said Sir Nigel Sheinwald, the Downing Street foreign policy supremo. By contrast, the NGO voices always saw the glass as half empty. So the agencies looked at the $50 billion aid deal and complained that some of it had been pledged previously, that only $20 billion of it was 'new money'. Geldof looked at it differently: by 2010, there was going to be $25 billion more aid every year than there had been in 2004 – so that was a big win.

These differing dispositions inclined Geldof and Bono to praise politicians when they had achieved something and then urge them on to do more. By contrast, the public rhetoric of the NGOs centred around protest and condemnation. 'Bob was motivated, both temperamentally and strategically, to claim victory. He saw that as the right thing to do,' said Laurie Lee.

'We've marched the whole fucking world up the hill and we have to give them the win that they've fought so hard for,' Bob told him. 'The NGOs, on the other hand, took the view that if it wasn't perfect, it must be shit. We haven't made poverty history, so it's a failure.'

None of this came as a surprise to Tony Blair himself. As he walked across the grass to the Gleneagles Hotel after giving his final press conference, his aide Justin Forsyth told him some of the aid agencies were calling the Gleneagles deal 'a disaster for the world's poor'.

The prime minister shrugged.

'That's what NGOs do. I didn't expect anything different,' he said. 'This is a big victory. We've got everything we really wanted. Bob and Bono were pleased. This will be judged by the test of time.'

He seemed genuinely relaxed, Forsyth said. 'By that point in his life, he just wanted to do something that he felt was right, at scale. He didn't have to win another election.'

Geldof and Bono were heading off into Edinburgh for a celebration dinner with Richard Curtis, Emma Freud and the DATA team. Laurie Lee skipped the celebration and headed off to Perth airport to catch a plane back to his pregnant fiancée. Dazed and overwhelmed as the adrenaline fell away, he rang his brother from the departure lounge. 'I remember crying down the phone, asking him what more we were supposed to have done. He kindly pointed out that most people would think the outcome was extraordinary.' He turned out to be right. The newspapers the next day certainly did. The major promises made by the G8 at Gleneagles on aid, debt and HIV treatment were far more than any G8 had ever promised before – and they were delivered. Eventually.

Back in No 10, Laurie and Justin looked at the little black case Bono had carried onto the stage at Murrayfield. Inside were row after row of CD-ROMs containing the signatures of the 38 million people who had signed the MPH petition. The two aides were frustrated that millions of people in the UK had just achieved something amazing and now some of the charities were telling them that they had failed. Laurie and Justin sent a note to the PM suggesting that No 10 write to everyone on the CDs to say, 'Thank you. You actually did an amazing job and we couldn't have done this without you.' Blair said no. He thought that some NGOs had so poisoned the minds of their supporters that it was a waste of time.

At the end of the following year, Make Poverty History disbanded. The majority of the campaign's 540 members insisted that the coalition had only agreed to come together while the UK held the presidency of the G8 and European Union. In reality, the tensions within the coalition had proved too great.

Ironically, Bob and Bono's organisation, DATA, was one of the few members who voted to keep it going. 'I remember being in a room with all of the NGOs deciding what should happen and being one of the very few voices that said it should just keep going,' said DATA's European director, Olly Buston. The database of millions of supporters it had compiled was alone reason enough to continue.

'It's just criminal to destroy this,' said Buston. 'Make Poverty History has huge value in terms of name recognition. And that database would probably cost you seven million quid to build up.'

Laurie Lee also thought the decision to destroy the database a real mistake. 'They argued that the agreement from the outset was that Make Poverty History would have a limited life,' he said. 'That was the deal to get everyone to buy into it at the start of the year, so they stuck to the deal.' Instead, 'the charities should have built on MPH because it had been so effective'.

The split had another, more venal cause. Every charity had the names of its supporters on the database. No one wanted the names of their donors to be handed over to their rivals for fear they might divert donations from their charity to another. 'They were all worried about other agencies stealing their market,' said Buston. On the surface, there were debates around the suggestion that Make Poverty History had been a bad name because it had set an aim which was impossible to achieve. But, in the end, 'it was driven by competitiveness over lists of supporters'.

Justin Forsyth saw another reason for the demise of the coalition. 'The NGOs got it very wrong, both in terms of tactics and honesty,' he wrote in his diaries just after Gleneagles. 'Sadly, this will ensure they have less impact, not more. It was a real failure of leadership. To say that a $50 billion aid deal is "a vastly disappointing result" is ridiculous. The media reaction reflects this. Nearly all the journalists I talk to felt the NGOs had been far too negative. Just as Make Poverty History climaxed, and had more impact than it had ever dreamed of, it managed to raise real questions about its credibility. Very sad.'

Twenty years later, Forsyth reflected on the opportunity the aid agencies had lost. 'The NGO assessment was not just wrong. It was also massively counter-productive,' he said. 'If they had declared victory – even partial victory – they would have had huge power to take the movement to the next stage and to press for even more – on trade, aid, education and other issues. But by declaring failure, they took the wind out of the sails of the movement and lost their power. A terrible tactical blunder.'

❊

'Where's the editor?' asked Geldof.

'He's in his glass office on the sixth floor, painting a horse.'

'Doing a painting … of a horse?'

'No, painting an actual life-size horse.'

Bob Geldof was in Berlin to edit Germany's biggest-selling newspaper, *Bild*. After Gleneagles, he and Bono switched the focus from mass mobilisation to a more targeted lobbying of individual world leaders. The UN summit two months after Gleneagles failed to maintain the momentum of the Scottish summit. And the World Trade Organization meeting in December once again put the interests of the rich world ahead of the poor world when it came to trade negotiations. But, on 6 January 2006, the IMF cancelled all the debts owed to it by nineteen of the world's poorest countries. The two musicians now had to make sure that the other promises made at Gleneagles were kept.

'We have to make sure they don't just sign the cheque, but that they pay out on it,' Bono said. 'You can kick arse when politicians don't do what they promised.' And that is what they proceeded to do. The two Irish musicians were now working as furiously as ever, but behind the scenes engaging with finance ministers and politicians at quite a junior level – 'where the real legwork was done' – in addition to lobbying heads of state. One of their techniques to keep the pressure on was to offer to edit a newspaper for the day in the capital city of the host nation.

It was 2007 and the G8 was being held at the seaside resort of Heiligendamm in Germany. But when the editor of *Bild*, a red-meat German tabloid, handed over his paper to Bob, he thought he'd better stay in the building, just in case. 'When we went up to the sixth floor to see him,' said Olly Buston. 'He had a giant papier-mâché horse which he was painting white. We were never told why.'

'You're the editor,' he said to Bob. 'Don't disturb me. Do what you want!'

He did. The paper's usual saucy front-page picture was replaced by one of an emaciated child with the headline 'End this! Now!'. Bob ran pieces by

George Bush (reiterating his commitment to fighting AIDS in Africa) and by George Clooney, highlighting the violence in Sudan's Darfur region. He even took over the sports pages, running a photo montage of an African dream football team, led by Chelsea's Ivory Coast striker, Didier Drogba.

Bob's key contribution was to go to interview Germany's new chancellor, Angela Merkel. He extracted from her a story which made the news all across Germany – of the day she cried when a political ally turned against her. 'She cries!' ran the headlines.

More significant was another headline: 'Merkel succumbed to Bob Geldof's charm and chastisement'. It ran over the announcement that Germany would give an extra €750 million in aid every year for the next four years. She also used Geldof and Bono as a back-door channel to sound out the position of President Nicolas Sarkozy of France on African issues. 'The amazing thing about the Germans is that when they say they'll do something, they do it,' said Buston. 'All the money came through, year after year.'

More problematic, as ever, were the Italians. Berlusconi, who had signed for Italy at Gleneagles, was gone and there was a new prime minister, Romano Prodi. The two men could not have been more different: Berlusconi, the maverick populist, and Prodi, the conventional technocrat. But they had one thing in common: their governments had no money.

'We were very friendly with Prodi. He was a nice man,' said Bob. 'But we made it clear that we were going to have to criticise him in public because Italy was so behind with its Gleneagles payments. Geldof and Bono went to see him in the tiny room the Germans had given him in the hotel complex at Heiligendamm.

'Bono and I were sitting on the single bed in this really shit little room and telling him what we were going to say about him,' Bob said. 'U2 had a couple of gigs in Milan coming up and Bono said he was going to have to diss him from the stage.' Prodi turned to his tall adviser, who was standing at the end of the bed.

'Can't we do something?' he asked.

'We really can't,' said Mr Tall.

'Come in here,' said the Italian prime minister, pulling his aide into the en suite toilet. Bob and Bono could hear frantic whispering and, after a while, the two Italians re-emerged with some sums scribbled on a piece of toilet paper.

Geldof looked at it. It said €30 million. But it was nowhere near enough. Bob stuck the paper in his back pocket and they left. Italy would be condemned for falling short on its commitments.

Things had got no better by 2009 when it was Italy's turn to host the G8 and Berlusconi was back in power. This time, Geldof had agreed to edit *La Stampa* ahead of the summit. The paper's editor published an advert in advance saying the Geldof edition would present Africa as far more than a place of problems. It would offer contributions from Archbishop Desmond Tutu, Kofi Annan, Carla Bruni, Sophia Loren, Naomi Campbell and the AS Roma footballer, Francesco Totti – all urging Italy to take a global leadership role on the vibrant continent on its doorstep. Bono would reinforce the message at U2 concerts, where Archbishop Tutu would address the crowd.

The problem came when Geldof went off to interview Berlusconi. The G8 had so far delivered only a third of the aid boost promised at Gleneagles. Bob and Bono's organisation, DATA – which had now merged with a US million-member activist organisation, ONE – had decided to push the G8 for an extra $5 billion for agricultural aid in Africa.

Bob went in to see Berlusconi.

'Italy has cut its aid to Africa by over half a billion dollars in the past year. How can you lead the G8? Where is your credibility?'

Italy's prime minster looked shame-faced.

Bob produced a photo of the Gleneagles communiqué which Berlusconi had signed. 'Here we have the signature of a country and the honour of a man,' Geldof said. It was like a boxing match. Berlusconi clenched his fists. Geldof waved his arms.

'I'm sorry, we made a mistake,' the Italian said. 'You are right. When one commits to something, it has to be maintained. We are behind and we have to put this right.'

Berlusconi proposed a new timetable for Italy to increase its overseas aid by 2015 – five years after the Gleneagles deadline.

'Apologies and timetables don't deliver food to the hungry or medicines to the sick,' thundered Geldof on the front page of *La Stampa* that evening. Bob labelled Berlusconi 'Mr Three Per Cent', saying that he had delivered only 3 per cent of the aid which he had personally promised at Gleneagles.

The paper's editor was not so relaxed as the editor of *Bild*. 'At 1 a.m., he rushed in from his bed to try to stop the presses,' said Geldof. 'But the staff said they would walk out if he did. They said it was their job to follow the instructions of the editor.'

'Bob Geldof is the editor today, not you,' one sub-editor boldly asserted. The presses rolled.

✳

Bob Geldof had been pestering Tony Blair to set up an official body to act as a watchdog to monitor the pledges made to Africa at Gleneagles. Towards the end of 2005, he rang the prime minister and reminded him that the Commission for Africa had recommended such a body, but nothing had happened.

'We need a group of high-powered statesmen and women from Africa and the West to hold the leaders to their promises. To lead it, we need a figure with post-political authority – someone like Bill Clinton.'

Blair agreed. But nothing happened. Bob kept asking.

Eventually, in 2007, Blair rang and said to Geldof: 'Okay, we're setting up the Africa Progress Panel and I've got Kofi Annan to chair it.'

This was not what Geldof wanted. Other members were to include the former US Treasury secretary, Robert Rubin; the former first lady of Mozambique and South Africa, Graça Machel; the former president of Nigeria, Olusegun Obasanjo; the anti-corruption expert Peter Eigen of Transparency International; and three former members of the Commission for Africa. Bob was unimpressed. 'Fucking grey hairs! We are back to Brandt,' he grumbled, harking back to the Brandt Report on North–South relations produced by retired politicians in the 1970s.

But Bob was wrong. 'I learned so much. They were fucking brilliant,' he reflected later. 'I thought I had access but this was uber-access. Kofi was amazing. He got us wherever he wanted – and all silently, beneath the radar. Kofi used to take me along as the bad cop because he was so quiet and so reasonable.'

The only place that didn't work was with Angela Merkel.

'Perhaps Bob would like to say a word,' Kofi said at one point.

'I'm sure Bob would like to say a word,' said Merkel, dryly.

Geldof launched straight in as Band Aid Bob.

'There's no need to speak to me like that,' said the politician the Germans came to call Mutti (Mummy).

What Geldof was coming to find was that, as long as he did not abuse their trust by disclosing in public what they said in private, the world's top leaders would speak as plainly to him as he did to them. He was not becoming friends with them, but he was moving to a new level of intimacy. He was not, to quote Bianca Jagger, sleeping with the enemy, but he was being allowed to speak truth to power. 'Kofi gave me that entrée and free rein,' he said. 'As a pop star, you have no power, but once you are in, so long as they trust you, they will listen.'

Once, at the United Nations, Geldof was with the British delegation who had been trying, without success, to get a one-to-one meeting with Merkel. Suddenly, the German chancellor swept into the hall surrounded by her security detail. As the Brits were trying politely to catch her eye, she saw Geldof, rushed across the room, put her arm around his neck and kissed him, leaving the British diplomats behind, looking bewildered.

❖

Something similar happened with George Bush. *Time* magazine asked Geldof to interview Bush about his policy on Africa and the president invited Bob to fly across the continent with him in the presidential plane, Air Force One. It was clear from the conversation that Bush was as interested in finding out what makes Geldof tick as the other way round. The two men talked about Africa and why the US press was not interested in Bush's considerable achievements there. They talked about evil, with the president pushing Geldof to open up about the war in Iraq. 'I don't want to go there,' he told the president; there was no point in them falling out.

They developed such a chemistry that, six months later, when Geldof was visiting elsewhere in the White House, Bush called him in to the Oval Office to chat. The president was waiting for the outcome of a vote in Congress which could save or sink the economy during the 2008 global financial crisis. 'This sucker's going down,' said the president, referring to the world economy. He had to be present in the Oval Office at a time of national emergency, much as Tony Blair had had to return to Downing Street when Ken Bigley was executed, but he had nothing to do but wait. Bush shut down the phones and he and Geldof spoke for over an hour. The only interruptions were butlers in dicky bows coming in and out with coffee from time to time.

It was not the first time that Bush had shared confidences with Geldof.

At Heiligendamm, he had privately told Bob and Bono about a visit he had made to West Point, the academy that trains officers for the US Army. At the time, the president was trying to overhaul US immigration policy to give legal status and a path to citizenship to the 12 million illegal immigrants residing in the country.

'How is the Migrant Bill going?' Bob had asked, not realising that the proposal had been killed by the US Senate.

'It's dead. Geldof. Don't.'

The president's wife, Laura, who was present, added simply: 'It's a disgrace.'

Bush despairingly told Geldof of how, the day before, he had been at West Point, where the Latino army sergeant, who had presented the colours to him as commander-in-chief, was not allowed to apply for American citizenship – because he had originally entered the country without papers.

'Twelve million people, that's all it is, out of 350 million people, who are working in our country, contributing to the economy,' Bush said.

'It was amazing that he would say all that to us,' Geldof had told me at the time. 'But he had learned to trust us.'

Now, with the global economy teetering on the brink, Bush was confiding in Geldof once again. After ninety minutes in the Oval Office, Bob thought he might have stayed too long.

'Shouldn't I be going?' he said, but the president wanted to keep him.

'Do you have to go?'

'Well, no. Not really.'

'Can you stay another half-hour? They should be out by then.'

'Of course.'

'It was the weirdest amazing thing,' Bob told me afterwards, 'to be there in America's imperial palace, in the Oval Office with this guy who might be about to lose the world if his officials could not persuade Congress to bail out the collapsing global economy.'

The president seemed overcome by the apocalyptic moment. 'It was like he just offloaded to me – about the banks going down, about the world economy, about war, Iraq, about being an alcoholic. And he too was very teary.' The president spoke at length about the Taliban, who were holed up somewhere in Waziristan where the US couldn't get at them.

'Then he just said: "War, how do you avoid it?". He was on a roll so I just shut up and listened,' Bob said. 'And he said: "Do you know something? I was at Gettysburg last week, for the first time – unbelievable. I've been president for eight years and it was the first time I was in Gettysburg."' He had visited the site of the bloodiest battle in the American Civil War, where there had been a total of 56,000 casualties, on both sides. He had taken with him the celebrated Gettysburg Address, the speech Abraham Lincoln made when he dedicated the site as the burial place of those who fell.

'Fifty-six thousand boys. It was so moving, this patch of grass … I had the speech, I read it.'

Tears began to form in George Bush's eyes.

'War is a terrible thing, Geldof.'

'I know, Mr President.'

The two men just sat and looked at one another.

'Do you want a drink?' asked the president. Bob was surprised. He knew Bush was a reformed alcoholic. 'What you drink?'

'Wine,' Geldof said.

'Is that it?'

'Scotch, sometimes late at night. What about yourself?'

'Well, it *was* vodka for breakfast, vodka for elevenses, vodka for lunch, vodka for afternoon tea, vodka for dinner, and then a nightcap of vodka.' He laughed.

Before drink, of any description, could arrive, the news came that the Congress had voted.

'This is the first time I've spoken of this,' Bob told me all these years later. 'Why did they talk like that, Bush – and Blair when Ken Bigley was executed? Why did they talk so openly to us? Perhaps because we never blabbed. We did diss them in public when they deserved it. And we bigged them up when they had done something good. But we never blabbed. They trusted us. That allowed us to tell them the truth. And they listened.'

❄

What came of all that? Twenty years on, what is the verdict on the 2005 Gleneagles deal which Live 8 and Make Poverty History made possible?

Certainly, the deal was not delivered by 2010, as the G8 had promised. The global financial crisis of 2007–08 sent aid clattering down the list of priorities of many governments. Despite it, though, the UK and

Germany delivered on their very big Gleneagles pledges. The USA and Canada over-delivered on their smaller promises. France increased its aid, but didn't fully deliver on its very big commitment. Japan increased a little. Official OECD data suggests the Gleneagles promises on global aid were eventually achieved in real terms six years late, in 2016. But aid to Africa, even at the high point, was just $17 billion extra a year – $8 billion less than the $25 billion which the G8 promised.

So did Gleneagles fail to deliver? Despite the financial crisis that triggered a decade of austerity in rich countries, by 2011 aid to Africa was 4 per cent higher than before Gleneagles – a $12 billion increase. According to the IMF, spending on health, education, nutrition and other poverty measures all rose. What was clear beyond doubt was that, following Gleneagles, the deaths of children in poor countries more than halved. The number of women who died in childbirth plummeted. So did AIDS deaths in Africa, falling from 2 million a year to 630,000. Polio was eradicated in 2020. The statistics on extreme poverty all showed a significant decline. In some countries, like Ethiopia and Ghana, acute poverty was halved. Gleneagles played a key role in that.

'The Gleneagles summit of 2005 is rightly remembered as a high point for the G8,' wrote Kofi Annan in 2013. 'The fact that 21 million more children are in school than at the time of Gleneagles, and 5.4 million more people are on anti-Aids drugs, is a cause for celebration and for the G8 to continue their supporting role.' That figure is even higher in 2025. Fifty million more children are now in school. 'It made a difference to the lives of millions of people,' said Kevin Watkins. 'And it put global poverty reduction on the map in a way that would have seemed inconceivable when I started working for Oxfam in 1992.'

Some, like Kumi Naidoo, have still not changed their initial judgement. 'I think the one-line response of "the people roared and the G8 whispered" still stands,' he said. 'After historic numbers of people came out on the streets, the G8 could have done a lot more than it did. Let's just be blunt about it. We have a system of exploitation that is firmly kept in place with doublespeak and false promises. If they could find almost a trillion dollars for an illegal unjust war in Iraq, why couldn't they find more to combat global poverty? We need substantially bold and structural and systemic change.'

But Kirsty McNeill, of the Make Poverty History coordinating committee, who sat on the platform with Kumi during his big Gleneagles bust-up with Geldof, disagrees. Looking back, she says, Bob's assessment of '10 out of 10 for aid, and 8 out of 10 for debt is, on reflection, a fairer one than the global coalition's assertion that "the G8 has whispered".'

The man who chaired that press conference, Adrian Lovett, is also more positive: 'Gleneagles delivered meaningful, substantial policy decisions which improved the lives of some of the people who have the toughest lives on the planet. Forty million children went to school because of Gleneagles, who would otherwise not have been in school. Kofi Annan said at the time that it was the greatest summit ever for Africa and I can't think of one since then that's been better.'

One of those who worked most closely with Geldof and Bono at DATA, which was later renamed ONE, is Olly Buston – who now gives strategic advice to the foundations of Melinda Gates, Elton John and Jamie Oliver. He believes that the wider development movement now sees the 2005 summit rather differently: 'I think in hindsight, given the massive cuts to aid in recent years, most of the NGOs who expressed reservations at the time would now see things a bit differently. Gleneagles was a massive high point, it was an extraordinary moment.'

The summit did more than raise money, according to his colleague, Jamie Drummond. 'In terms of material outcomes, Gleneagles helped lock in debt relief and grow smart strategic aid. Millions of lives have been saved, communities sustained and economies prospered' – and it would have achieved a lot more but for the global financial crisis. But Gleneagles and Make Poverty History were important for what it taught campaigners like him about how to build a cultural and social movement.

Drummond – who now works at Sharing Strategies building partnerships between philanthropies, think-tanks, international organisations and campaign groups – says one of the great breakthroughs of, first, the Commission for Africa and then the Gleneagles agreement, was that it pioneered a new idea: the idea that rich nations and African nations needed a new relationship with one another – 'a mutually accountable partnership' that took steps to 'strengthen democracy, accountability and transparency' among African governments.

Gleneagles was, in that, a beginning not an end. But then, to quote Bono: 'The battle against poverty is a marathon, not a sprint.'

CHAPTER 39

DID GELDOF GET IT WRONG?

B ob Geldof's good qualities are the same as his bad qualities. You just use different words to describe them. To his many admirers, he is passionate, articulate, tenacious, uncompromising, combative, demanding, convinced that he is right, and very charismatic. To his critics, he is bulldozing, gobby, obstinate, inflexible, belligerent, controlling, arrogant and immensely irritating. The qualities which have made Geldof such a driving force for change over the past forty years – and so widely respected among the general population – have also, in certain quarters, provoked hostility towards him and the Live Aid phenomenon over those four decades. It is rather revealing to look back to see why.

Certainly, many of those who were in Ethiopia when he first launched Band Aid were immensely suspicious. Michael Buerk, the BBC journalist whose reports galvanised Geldof into action, accused him of being 'an attention-seeking, pirouetting pop star'. Claire Bertschinger, the Red Cross nurse filmed in the first reports from the famine camps, called Bob 'a bastard, making money out of starving kids'.

Their reactions were entirely understandable to me. Anyone who had direct contact with the skeletal, staring children I encountered in Ethiopia was, I know, unable to explain to themselves the terrible dissonance between our pampered world and the trauma of theirs. The nearest the rest of the population seemed to get to that was watching the video David Bowie introduced at Live Aid. The music somehow put Us into the film alongside the horrific images of Them. Two worlds clashed. We ceased to be spectators and instead became participants in the grotesque juxtaposition of their life and ours. They were starving in our living rooms.

But the initial reactions of both Buerk and Bertschinger were turned upside down when they discovered what Geldof was actually doing.

Equally understandable was the indignation of those Ethiopians who came into contact with 'Do They Know It's Christmas?'. *Of course we know it's Christmas*, they said. Ethiopians have been celebrating Christmas since the fourth century, long before Christian missionaries arrived in Britain or Ireland, said the head of Ethiopia's Relief and Rehabilitation Commission, Dawit Wolde Giorgis. Geldof did not say so in Ethiopia, but back in the UK, he pointed out that the lyrics of the song were directed to rich Westerners, not poor Ethiopians. At Christmas, people in the West have plenty to eat and drink, and give one another presents. Asking 'Do They Know It's Christmas?' is a figurative way of saying starving Ethiopians have neither food nor drink nor presents. 'It's so bleeding obvious that only a fool, or someone trying to score a point, would take the lyric literally,' Geldof said at the time.

'Scoring a point' was at the heart of the criticisms in 1984–85. The music press did its best to adopt its usual tone of fashionable sneering. The largest-selling paper, the *NME*, said 'Do They Know It's Christmas?' was 'rotten'. *Melody Maker* bemoaned its 'uncomfortably generalised sentimentality … righteous pleading and pompous indignation'. And *Record Mirror* complained of 'cringingly embarrassing lyrics about snow in the desert', before admitted that anyone who didn't buy it 'deserves to choke on their turkey'.

Though the lyrics were later condemned for being filled with patronising stereotypical descriptions of Africa, that was not the focus of the early criticisms of Band Aid and Live Aid. They were essentially to do with music. Critics saw Live Aid as the death of the punk ethic and the revival of the rock dinosaurs who punks – of whom Geldof was a late incarnation – were supposed to have overthrown. 'The pastel shades of corporate pop were now back in control with a whole host of pop stars, old and new, celebrating the mullet mundane,' said the music journalist John Robb, also the frontman of the post-punk band, the Membranes. Why didn't Geldof invite the Clash, the Stranglers or ask the Sex Pistols to reform?

The DJ Andy Kershaw, who was one of the breathless hosts of the BBC's Live Aid coverage, afterwards decried the concert for failing to confront the fundamental causes of the famine. Geldof had, in 1985, never intended to do that. That came later for Bob. Those early criticisms seemed more motivated by musical disagreements and dislike of Geldof personally. It was only later that ideological differences began to emerge.

The political criticism began with the complaints that there were not enough black acts on the bill in both London and, to a lesser extent, in Philadelphia. This was framed by activists as the result of a white paternalist mindset. The reality was more complex. To Geldof, the prime criterion for performing at Live Aid was record sales, not representation. The bigger the artists, the bigger the audience, the bigger the sum raised. But he had invited all the world's top black artists and they had refused to appear, partly because both the US promoters, Bill Graham and Ken Kragen, appeared to discourage them in different ways. There was also, for reasons Bob and Harvey Goldsmith could never fathom, but which Pete Smith detected, a clear block vote against Live Aid by the black artists and some resistance from one of the big US television networks. Eventually, a third US promoter, Larry Magid, pulled in a half a dozen serious black artists for the Philadelphia bill, though that was not enough for critics determined to remain fixed in their disapproval.

A year later, in 1986, condemnation of Live Aid began to be framed in specifically socio-political terms. Chumbawamba, an anarchist post-punk band from Leeds, released an album called *Pictures of Starving Children Sell Records*, which lumped Live Aid in with apartheid, the exploitation of multinational companies and cultural imperialism. The Irish rock star was, apparently, whitewashing Britain's colonial past. But even by the time of Live 8, in 2005, much of the criticism of Geldof remained personal rather than political.

Andy Kershaw was again at the forefront of the attacks. It was now twenty years since he had been a Live Aid presenter and appeared to look back on his earlier involvement as an unhappy compromise with the world of mainstream pop. The Band Aid chairman became the chief focus of his ire. 'Geldof appears not to be interested in Africa's strengths, only in an Africa on its knees,' Kershaw fulminated, clearly not having read Bob's contribution to the Commission for Africa, which celebrated the precise opposite. 'I am coming, reluctantly, to the conclusion that Live 8 is as much to do with Geldof showing off his ability to push around presidents and prime ministers,' was his clincher.

He was not alone. Other critics accused Live Aid of being a catwalk on which a set of ageing musical has-beens had used Africa to revive their flailing careers. In evidence, they pointed to the chart of post-Live 8 record sales issued by HMV. At the top, Pink Floyd's best-of *Echoes* album had increased sales by 1,343 per cent, although the critics failed to point out that guitarist David Gilmour announced that the band would donate the profits from the increased sales to charity. And 100 per cent of the revenue from digital downloads of Paul McCartney's Live 8 performances were passed on to the Band Aid Trust. Nor did detractors note that sales of the Libertines album *Up the Bracket* fell by 35 per cent following Pete Doherty's shambolic performance on the Live 8 stage.

Larry Magid, the man who had made both the Live Aid and Live 8 shows work at the Philadelphia end, was dismissive of the critique that performers were motivated by self-promotion. 'I don't accept that. After Led Zeppelin reformed, they broke up again. Same with Pink Floyd.' Gilmour and Waters later revealed they were offered £150 million for a tour of the US – which they turned down. 'All this had little to do with self-interest.'

⁂

By 2006, criticisms had opened up on another personal front. Eyebrows were raised that year in Ireland at U2's decision to move part of its multi-million-pound operation from Dublin to Amsterdam. In the Netherlands, the tax rate on royalty earnings was only a few per cent, compared to the 12.5 per cent rate for corporate tax in Ireland. It was just a business decision, said the band's manager, Paul McGuinness. But that was not how politicians, or fans, saw it. It was inconsistent for Bono to lecture the Irish government on the necessity of giving aid when U2 'are not prepared to contribute to the exchequer on a fair basis along with the bulk of Irish taxpayers,' said the finance spokesman of the Irish Labour Party, Joan Burton. Inconsistent was not the word the fans used. They spoke of hypocrisy. Bono and Geldof have been 'practically canonised for Live Aid' where they should have been 'harangued over their tax arrangements', some critics said.

Geldof was robust in his response. 'I pay all my taxes,' he said. As an Irish citizen, he was entitled to escape UK taxes on his earnings abroad, but the money from the British TV production companies he owned 'all come into the UK and I pay tax on it', he told one journalist in 2012. But Bono was more chastened. 'Maybe we went too far when we moved one of our companies to Holland to save tax,' he finally admitted in 2022. 'We argued if Ireland could brand itself as tax-competitive, so could our band. We dug our heels in. Looking back, I can see our stubborn streak at play.' There were some arguments, he said, that 'just by being in them you've already lost'.

That said, some journalists gleefully pursue scandal where there is none. 'There were a couple of reporters who thought they'd got the scoop of a lifetime,' said the Band Aid lawyer, John Kennedy. They discovered that the songwriting royalties body, the Performing Rights Society, was making payments to Geldof and Midge Ure for 'Do They Know It's Christmas?'. 'They were convinced they were onto something.'

The PRS is responsible for collecting money for songs played on radio, TV and in stores. 'It insists a songwriter has an inalienable right to receive these monies so that they couldn't sell them to bad managers or other shysters,' said John Kennedy, who went to the PRS and asked for an exception for Band Aid. But the PRS said 'no exceptions'. 'So they paid the money to Bob and Midge each year and Bob and Midge then paid the money into the Band Aid Trust.' The money went to the composers on the last day of November and got paid into the trust on the first day of December. The reporters had found the Band Aid accounts and added two and two to make five. 'Bob and Midge had to go on the radio to deny it because Bob was absolutely adamant that if you don't nail something like this, it will just be perpetuated.'

But what the Band Aid trustees found over the decades is that sometimes, even if you do nail a lie, it perpetuates itself anyway. Thanks to the internet the past is always present. Even when it has been withdrawn and an apology issued.

⁂

Perhaps the most sustained piece of hostility against Geldof came from the US music magazine *Spin*, which in 1986 published what it called an exposé on Live Aid's actions in Ethiopia. The level of sophistication of the critique can be judged by the words with which the magazine's owner, Bob Guccione, opened the attack: 'One night at dinner in late 1985, a friend talked about Ethiopia being in a civil war. Neither I nor anyone else at the table had heard that…' But the truth, he boasted, was 'so easy to discover that an editorial assistant barely out of college did so in a matter of hours at the library'.

The *Spin* report was a classic conspiracy theory. The reporter did not travel to Ethiopia or interview a single Ethiopian. His article, headlined 'LIVE AID: THE TERRIBLE TRUTH', was a farrago of overwrought non-sense with claims that Live Aid hurt more people than it helped. It did not examine alternative accounts from mainstream academics, diplomats, jour-nalists and aid agencies who had actually visited contested areas in person. It did not interrogate the figures it was given by Médecins Sans Frontières.

Geldof replied a month later. He had been under no illusions as to Mengistu's callous disregard for the lives of the people of Ethiopia, he said. But the choice was clear: to stay to help the starving or to make high-flown moral statements and walk away from those in need. The answer to Band Aid was clear. *Spin* derided his response and reprinted its allegations in 2015, 2020 and 2021. The magazine's dubious allegations are routinely repeated on the internet to this day.

✳

But if the reckless allegations could be easily dismissed, more disturbing assertions were to follow from a more reputable quarter. David Rieff had written a respected book called *A Bed for the Night: Humanitarianism in Crisis*. Drawing on first-hand reporting from war zones around the world – including Bosnia, Rwanda, Kosovo, Afghanistan and Sudan – Rieff called aid workers 'the last noble profession', but contrasted their virtuous ambitions with their actual ability to alleviate suffering. Then he turned his attention to Ethiopia – a country of which he had no on-the-ground experience.

On the eve of Live 8 in 2005, Rieff published an essay in *Prospect* maga-zine with the coverline 'The Failure of Live Aid'. In it, he claimed that Live Aid did harm as well as good. Indeed, it 'may have done more harm than good' by Bob Geldof's 'unwitting support of a Stalinist-style resettlement project' in Ethiopia. Or, as Rieff more pompously put it, Bob had fallen victim to 'a narcissistic conflation of the sincerity of good intentions and the effects of those intentions'. In an essay littered with factual errors and ill-informed assertions, he said that Geldof and Oxfam had no awareness of the 'political dimension to the famine' – a clear untruth.

Rieff's problem became clear when the armchair essayist revealed his sources. He relied on the work of Alex de Waal, a social anthropologist and author of a 1989 book, *Famine That Kills: Darfur, Sudan*, who wrote influentially on the use of starvation as a weapon of war. In 1991, de Waal extensively catalogued the human rights violations under the Mengistu regime, but most authoritative scholars agree that de Waal overestimated the number of people who died in resettlement and underestimated the number who died overall in the famine. More than a million people perished in the famine, most authorities believe, whereas de Waal offers a figure as low as 400,000. Rieff also quotes Médecins Sans Frontières uncritically in his essay and adds his own outlandish comparison to Nazi Germany.

Rieff and other critics also ignore the fact that those who died in the malarial resettlement areas might anyway have starved in the empty highlands. Michael Buerk reckons that at least a million people's lives were saved by international aid. Famine was a far greater killer than resettlement. It's hard not to dismiss Rieff's essay as both statistically and morally unbalanced.

✲

The British ambassador to Ethiopia during this period, the late Sir Brian Barder, saw a good deal of what happened at first hand, travelling all over the country. 'I have little doubt that Rieff's allegations about the numbers of people who died as a result of resettlement are seriously exaggerated,' he wrote. Life in the resettlement areas was harsh in part because Western aid donors refused to assist there. Band Aid was one of the first to change that. 'Rieff speculates that it's sometimes better to do nothing than to act,' said Barder. 'Many Ethiopians alive today would take a different view.' Rieff's endorsement of de Waal's 'astonishing assertion that "the relief effort may have contributed to as many deaths" as the number of lives it saved deserves to be treated with incredulous contempt'.

✲

In March 2010 came one of the most damaging attacks on Geldof and Live Aid. A number of BBC programmes and websites ran stories claiming that large amounts of money raised by Band Aid and Live Aid for Ethiopian famine relief had been 'siphoned off by rebel groups to buy weapons'. Some $95 million was said to have gone astray. Midge Ure read it on the BBC website and immediately phoned the Band Aid lawyer, John Kennedy. As the story zipped around the world, it became ever more dramatic – and incorrect – with each iteration. By the time it got to Australia a few hours later, ABC News was proclaiming that 'an investigation by the BBC has found just 5 per cent of the money raised by Live Aid and Band Aid actually made it to the victims of famine in Ethiopia'.

It was all untrue. It had grown from an extraordinarily sloppy piece of journalism. After a nine-month investigation, the BBC World Service's normally well-respected Africa editor, Martin Plaut, claimed to have found evidence that millions raised for starving Ethiopians had been used to buy weapons by rebels in Tigray. His producer used clips from Geldof and music from 'Do They Know It's Christmas?' as background to the report.

The story was riddled with problems. The allegations were made by two men who had been sent into exile by the Tigray People's Liberation Front (TPLF) and who bore a grudge against its leader, Meles Zenawi, who was now prime minister of Ethiopia. They both had a track record of trying to discredit him and these new accusations came at a time when they might do maximum damage to Meles, just before a general election. That alone should have raised the BBC's suspicions. 'It was all about internal Ethiopian politics,' said Gayle Smith, who monitored the Band Aid trucks behind the rebel lines in Tigray in the 1980s.

But the BBC failed to alert its listeners to the unreliability of the source, who claimed that 95 per cent of famine funds were misappropriated. He had actually left the TPLF before the start of the clandestine operation to import food across the border from Sudan, which brought the large influx of aid money. On top of that, the BBC said its story was supported by a secret report from the CIA, which transpired to have been written three months before Live Aid even happened. A US diplomat, whom the BBC said backed the story, turned out to have been quoted in a misleading way.

The BBC's internal news-sharing system knew none of this. It heard the World Service programme, absorbed the Band Aid music and put two and two together. Within hours, incorrect, unfair and misleading reports claiming that 'millions of pounds raised by Band Aid and Live Aid had been diverted to buy arms' were on a succession of BBC television and radio bulletins, current affairs programmes and websites, and soon spread all across the world.

'It was a villainous piece of journalism, idiotic or duplicitous,' said the Band Aid trustee and former BBC chairman, Lord Michael Grade. 'There's no question in my mind that they succumbed to the temptation to sex-up the story by dragging in Bob Geldof and Live Aid.'

The Band Aid Trust immediately put in an official complaint. The cre-
dentials, credibility and veracity of the BBC's witnesses were seriously open
to question and the CIA report did not say what the programme claimed.
All the key allegations centred on a time before Band Aid had spent any
money in Tigray. 'The BBC's misleading and unfair coverage,' said Geldof,
'has the potential to be extremely damaging to public faith, not only in Band
Aid but also other charitable campaigns and people's willingness to donate
their cash to disaster funds.'

Yet instead of backtracking, a BBC editor leapt to the defence of the
programme with an online article that spoke of 'compelling evidence',
'uncomfortable facts', 'systematic diversion' and 'credible voices'. Three
months later, the BBC director-general, Mark Thompson, was still maintaining that the programme was 'robust and excellent journalism'. But a
full eight months later, the BBC's Editorial Complaints Unit said the exact
opposite – and upheld Band Aid's key complaints.

Out of the blue, one day in October, Lord Grade got an email from
his former colleagues at the BBC. 'It said: "We are publishing the following apology tonight",' he recalled. He smelled a rat. 'We hadn't agreed the
wording of the apology, nor had we agreed the date it should go out.'

But then it dawned on him. There was a massive news story that day.
The bulletins were filled with dramatic reports of the rescue of thirty-three
miners who had been trapped for sixty-nine days inside a mine in Chile.
An escape tunnel had finally been drilled through to them and they were
about to be raised to the surface of the earth in a capsule slowly lowered
and lifted by a giant crane. This huge global story was going to dominate
the news. The BBC's apology to Band Aid would get lost.

'I immediately emailed back and said, "First of all, we have not agreed
the wording of this apology. We don't accept it. Furthermore, I know
exactly what you are up to – you think this is a good day to bury bad news."
And, of course, as soon as they got that email, they withdrew,' he laughed,
'because one thing they know about me is that I've got a big mouth on the
platform and, as a former chairman of the BBC, I could have made that
very embarrassing for them.'

A month later, on 4 November 2010, the BBC broadcast a comprehensive retraction of the allegations it had made a full eight months previously.
It stated:

Last March, in reports about aid money donated to Ethiopia in the mid-1980s, a number of BBC programmes and online items implied or stated that large amounts of money raised by Band Aid and Live Aid for famine relief in Ethiopia had been diverted by a rebel group to buy weapons. Following a complaint from the Band Aid Trust, the BBC has investigated these statements and concluded that there was no evidence for them and they should not have been broadcast. The BBC wishes to apologise unreservedly to the Band Aid Trust for the misleading and unfair impression which was created.

It was an unprecedented apology – the first ever simultaneously broadcast every BBC outlet on TV, radio and online.

The repeated hostility to the work of Band Aid was mystifying to the one-time British ambassador to Ethiopia, Brian Barder. 'The strange campaign to discredit the Ethiopian relief effort and all who took part in it (especially perhaps Bob Geldof and Live Aid) continues relentlessly in recurring television programmes and articles in the press,' he wrote. 'It seems to be some sort of hangover from the vitriolic dispute over the resettlement programme in 1985–86 between a highly ideological wing of Médecins Sans Frontières and the rest of the NGOs working in Ethiopia.'

The former diplomat was bewildered by it. The Ethiopian dictator, Mengistu, had been overthrown two decades earlier and the faintest whiff of communism had long vanished into the thin Ethiopian air. And, yet, a group of fixated ideologues seemed intent on continuing to recall how they put 'their ideological purity' before the moral imperative to feed the starving. Alas, he said, it seems we must expect many more manifestations of 'this disagreeable crusade' against all the good things done by so many good people in Ethiopia, including very many brave Ethiopians. 'Ultimately, they may indeed succeed in re-writing the history books. That would, I believe, be an enormous pity and a great injustice.'

❦

Some of the hostility to Live Aid comes from individuals who take exception to Bob Geldof's personality. He has been an extraordinary figure on the landscape of the late twentieth/early twenty-first century, but he has undoubtedly rubbed some people up the wrong way. Others bridled at the idea that anyone rich and famous could speak on behalf of the poor and needy without some ulterior motive – personal aggrandisement, public approbation, boosting record sales, gaining tax breaks or some other hidden self-serving motivation. Someone rich telling governments to give taxpayers' money to the poor somehow smacks of hypocrisy, a sentiment which tax-avoidance schemes like Bono's only reinforce.

When it comes to the hostility shown towards Live Aid, there is a psychological dimension at work too. Scorn is seen as the smarter option. It can even portray itself as a superior moral position, seeing through the illusions the foolish fall for. Distrust is a good defence against being duped. Scepticism reduces the risk of being taken advantage of – financially, emotionally or socially – but it easily crosses over into cynicism. The humanitarian impulse relies on empathy, solidarity and hope, which cynics see as the virtues of the foolish. Cynicism also provides an ostensibly respectable excuse for not putting your hand in your pocket to help those down on their luck. As Richard Curtis has observed, Cynics Nose Day has never raised a penny; there will always be reasons to say no. Pessimism protects where empathy exposes. It offers certainty where empathy offers only possibility. Cynicism is the cheap way out.

But cynicism also takes refuge in shifting ideologies and political fashions. Intellectuals like to think their political purity is both more sophisticated and virtuous than naïve giving. But they delude themselves. Cynicism is corrosive. It shrinks the moral horizon.

In 2014, Adele, One Direction, Ed Sheeran, Sam Smith and others recorded a new version of 'Do They Know It's Christmas?' to raise money for the victims of the Ebola epidemic in west Africa. The lyrics were changed to fit the new crisis, but they provoked the same old criticisms, now more vehemently expressed. In the UK, the *Guardian* attacked the lyrics without listening to the new version. Half the things they complained about had already been changed. The paper printed an apology a few days later, but a tiny one in comparison with their front-page story.

Something else emerged. An internet search on many of the most vehement critics revealed that, until their attack on Band Aid, they had written nothing about either Ebola or Africa for months, if ever. Bad faith was at the heart of this backlash. But the British public saw through it. Band Aid 30 outsold all the rest of that Christmas's top five singles put together.

⁂

White saviour syndrome had surged into the public consciousness two years earlier with the posting of what was then the most viral video of all time. In a short documentary called *Kony 2012*, a film-maker, Jason Russell, told his five-year-old son about the abduction of tens of thousands of children by the brutal Ugandan warlord Joseph Kony, leader of the Lord's Resistance Army. 'We felt if people in the Western world knew about this atrocity, it'd stop in days,' said Russell.

When Oprah Winfrey retweeted Russell's post, its views rose from 66,000 to 9 million. Then Justin Bieber, Rihanna and Kim Kardashian shared it too. Within a week, the video had hit 100 million – a record on YouTube at the time – and Joseph Kony had become the target of a global civilian manhunt. But then, the Nigerian American novelist Teju Cole attacked the film, saying it was an example of 'the fastest growth industry in the US': white saviour syndrome.

The white saviour, said Cole, believes the world exists simply to satisfy the needs – including, importantly, the *sentimental* needs – of white people (and Oprah). The white saviour transmutes the banality of evil into the banality of sentimentality. The world is nothing but a problem to be solved by enthusiasm. Being a white saviour is not about justice, it is about having a big emotional experience that validates your privilege. Africa provides a space onto which white egos can conveniently be projected, said Cole.

It was only a matter of time before this was applied to Live Aid. But no one expected the pejorative phrase to be attached to the organisation by one of the charities to which it regularly gave large grants. In January 2023, the chief executive of Christian Aid, Patrick Watt, launched an extraordinary attack on Band Aid, saying that it 'reinforced deeply troubling tropes about helpless Africans and white saviours'. What made it all the more surprising was that Christian Aid had just accepted a sizeable grant from Band Aid.

Patrick Watt's article appeared in the *Sunday Express*. It began with a sideswipe at 'Do They Know It's Christmas?', describing the money-raising song as 'plaintive wailing'. Then, to add injury to insult, it complained that Band Aid's 'white saviour' attitudes had 'shaped for the worse' how the general public thought about hunger, poverty and aid.

The 1984 hit single, Watt conceded, had made it more difficult for the British public to ignore one of the gravest famines of modern times – and 'spurred a huge outpouring of humanitarian concern'. But, the article continued, 'east Africa faces the most severe hunger crisis in a generation' brought about by five failed rainy seasons, conflict, debt and spiralling food and energy costs. 'Around 36 million people are going hungry, and the region risks a lost generation of children permanently affected by chronic malnutrition,' wrote Watts, who is white. But Band Aid was now not the solution. The British government should reverse its aid cuts and pay up.

'Almost forty years on from Band Aid and over a decade since the last major famine in east Africa,' Watt ended with a flourish, 'it is time to consign the clanging chimes of doom to history.'

The article had originally been written for the *Guardian*, but the paper declined to publish it. So the Christian Aid comms team had offered it to the *Sunday Express*, whose editors knew a good rumpus when they saw one. They snapped it up.

'What is going on?' asked John Kennedy, Band Aid's lawyer and the trustee who, along with Harvey Goldsmith, signed the cheques for the projects the trustees decided to support. Kennedy consulted his records. The Band Aid Trust had given Christian Aid large grants on fifteen occasions over the previous seventeen years. Only a few months earlier, it had been given £373,000 – one of Band Aid's biggest grants.

'When I got hold of the actual newspaper, I discovered that the story hadn't come from an aid worker who had been caught out by an interviewer,' Kennedy said. 'It was a piece prepared by the chief executive of Christian Aid. And when he complained about the agony of everybody having to listen to the plaintive wailing of the Band Aid song each Christmas, I thought, *This is not someone making a strong political comment. This is just nasty.*'

Kennedy read on. Christian Aid was darkly insisting that 'Band Aid cast a long shadow'. It was time to 'move to a more hopeful and accurate depiction of the challenge of extreme hunger'. It was, said Watt, 'time to tear off the band aid'.

The lawyer raised the matter at the next trustees' meeting. 'Everyone was of the same mind, so we wrote to Christian Aid and said, "We seem to be incompatible in our positions."' Over at Christian Aid, its board members debated how to respond. Should they acknowledge they had made a mistake, make a public apology and try to heal their long-term relationship with Band Aid? Or should they decide that Watt was right, accept that their relationship with Band Aid was irreparably damaged and pay back the £373,000?

Archbishop John Sentamu, chair of the Christian Aid board, rang Geldof.

'Can't we meet up and sort this all out just between the two of us?'

'It's gone too far for that,' said Bob. 'The Band Aid Trust has made an official complaint.'

'Did Band Aid want Patrick Watt sacked?' they were asked.

Privately, the Band Aid trustees thought that if a chief executive had lost the organisation more than a quarter of a million pounds in the current financial climate, it might be best if he stepped down. If he knew about the donation and still wrote what he did, his judgement was poor; if he didn't know, he was incompetent.

'That's for Christian Aid to decide, not us,' Kennedy said.

Christian Aid sent the money back. Watt kept his job. His organisation has received no further grants from Band Aid since.

❊

'White saviour' now became a cudgel that Bob Geldof's critics could use to bash him. Yet he continued to insist that an artist's record sales, regardless of their colour, had been the correct criterion for deciding who was on the Live Aid and Live 8 line-ups. 'Would it have altered the politics of the G8 to have genius African musicians on? Would it have forced the G8 to do what we wanted? No! If there had been a black British artist of the stature of Stormzy back then, I'd have been on my knees begging. But there simply wasn't.' Yet many of those close to him increasingly told Bob he was wrong. Representation was an issue too.

'There could have been a greater diversity of artists showcased at the events,' said Kirsty McNeill, who had shared a platform with Bob at Gleneagles and who was now a Labour MP. That said, she added: 'I think in the '80s, he had a very human impulse. People were starving in a world of plenty. Bob responded by laying his hands on the tools at his disposal – the musicians he knew. I think we can all spend a lot of time trying to tear things and people down. It's more my style to say, "Thank you for doing what you felt called to do. Here's another thing that you could do".'

Geldof's chief development analyst, Jamie Drummond, was blunter: 'I think we all consistently disagreed with Bob on this. It was clear that there should have been more African representation in Live 8. The great African musician, Youssou N'Dour, did perform. He was also an incredibly important voice in the campaign and he was able to articulate nuanced points in a way that it was very hard for Irish rock stars to do. I wish his voice had been heard more. I think Bob missed a trick and keeps missing that trick.'

Bono was even more blunt. 'We did our best to make it more involving of African acts and failed. We fucked up.'

Some in the younger generation had also come to that conclusion. For the fortieth anniversary of Band Aid in 2024, Geldof commissioned producer Trevor Horn to create a new mix of 'Do They Know It's Christmas?'. It melded together voices from the different recordings across the generations. The result had Ed Sheeran from the 2014 version singing alongside Robbie Williams from 2004 and Boy George from 1984, along with Harry Styles, Bono, Sting, Chris Martin, Sam Smith, Sugababes and the late George Michael and Sinéad O'Connor.

But when Ed Sheeran heard he was part of the remix, he publicly expressed his unease at the Band Aid message. 'A decade on and my understanding of the narrative associated with this has changed,' he said. His musical collaborator, the British-Ghanaian Afrobeat and hip hop artist Fuse ODG, was more outspoken. The Band Aid records had been fundraising successes, but 'while they may generate sympathy and donations, they perpetuate damaging stereotypes,' he said. These 'stifle Africa's economic growth, tourism and investment, ultimately costing the continent trillions and destroying its dignity, pride and identity'. They fuelled 'pity rather than partnership'.

Bob Geldof at first dismissed the accusations of white saviour complex which were now flung around without much thought. In reply, he said simply: 'This little pop song has kept millions of people alive. Why would Band Aid scrap it now when it is feeding thousands of children who are dependent on us for a meal? Why not keep doing that? Because of an empty piece of ideological dogma?'

But as the accusations continued, he became more focused in his counterblasts. 'So-called white saviour syndrome is a chimera. It does not exist. It's just a concept. It derives from the vastly discredited deconstructionism of Foucault and Derrida. It is just as much a dogma as Catholicism's original sin or Freud's penis envy. It has no basis in fact. It is an easy win of virtue signalling. And, in reality, it is a piece of racism, inverted racism. Are only black people allowed to react to a famine in Africa? If there was a famine in Italy and I responded, would I be a white saviour? The idea that I am reinforcing old colonial stereotypes is nonsense. I'm Irish. We weren't colonisers, we were colonised.'

One of his proudest possessions is a copy of Nigerian novelist Chinua Achebe's brilliant *Things Fall Apart*. It was given to him by Nelson Mandela, who inscribed in it: 'To a fellow revolutionary in the struggle for humanity.'

'White saviour?' Bob asked aloud, and answered: 'No abstract theory should stop us feeding those in need. There are 600 million hungry people in the world – 300 million are in Africa. We wish it were other, but it is not. We can help some of them. That's what we will continue to do.'

Other key Live Aid figures – Midge Ure, Harvey Goldsmith and John Kennedy – took the same stance. 'Forty years is a long time and people's outlook on things has changed quite considerably,' said Midge. But he then went on to describe a visit he had made to the Zip Zap School of Circus Arts in Cape Town. There, children born with HIV from all walks of life – from South Africa's wealthy elite to children born in the townships – went to learn circus skills. The project sought to embody Nelson Mandela's vision of a Rainbow Nation.

'How do circus skills help kids to integrate with one another?' Midge asked.

'Well, when you're thirty feet off the ground on a trapeze and somebody reaches a hand out to grab you,' came the reply, 'you don't care what colour that hand is.'

That's exactly how Band Aid thought, said Midge. 'The thing that would have been wrong, would have been for us to do nothing.'

The man whose report set Bob Geldof off on Live Aid's forty-year long journey, Michael Buerk, confessed to having had 'white saviour' thoughts back in 1984 when he first heard of the Band Aid enterprise. 'But now I take the opposite view,' he said, speaking on the fortieth anniversary of that first Wembley concert. 'If you're a woman picking through donkey dung trying to find some undigested seeds, if you're one of the children whose eyes are rotting through vitamin deficiency, if you're a guy dying from starvation – whose body is eating itself from inside – if you're one of those people, you're not really that concerned about whether your saviour is white or black. In that single moment in history, I think it's rather obscene to go around talking about white saviours. Any saviour in that context is very, very welcome indeed.'

❧

Just after Live Aid's fortieth anniversary, Bob Geldof was in a hotel in Montreal. His wife Jeanne had ordered breakfast in their room. The phone rang.

'I'm not the normal breakfast waiter,' said the voice at the other end, 'but would you mind if I came in and said hello to your husband?'

There was a knock at the door. The breakfast trolley was pushed in by a small man in a well-worn suit. He wasn't a waiter but a middle manager.

'Hi,' said Bob. 'You look like an Ethiopian.'

'Yes,' said the man. He stood up straight and looked directly at Geldof. He had clearly prepared a little speech he wanted to deliver.

'I wanted to say thank you to you,' the man said, his voice trembling with nervousness. 'I don't know who my parents are. They died in the camp at Korem. I was put into a Band Aid hospital. Band Aid paid to make me better. I was brought up in a Band Aid orphanage and eventually I made my way to Paris, where I studied hospitality. Then I came here to Canada.'

'That's great,' said Bob. 'Congratulations. Are you married?' He knew from his time in Ethiopia that this was an important question to ask.

'Yes,' the man said. He fumbled in his wallet and pulled out a photograph. 'I married an Ethiopian girl here in Canada.'

He produced another photo. 'My two sons, they are aged eight and nine.' They were both wearing Man City football shirts, Bob noticed.

The man put the photographs away and paused.

Suddenly he ran forward, pushed his head into Bob's chest and flung his arms around the singer.

'Thank you for my sons,' the man sobbed. 'Thank you for my life.'

Bob hugged him back.

Even if it was just for that guy, for that one guy, said Bob, these forty years have been worth it.

CHAPTER 40

PASSING THE BATON

Forty years after the release of the original Band Aid single, a musical opened at the Old Vic theatre in London. *Just For One Day* was the story of Live Aid. It wasn't the brainchild of someone who had lived through that momentous event looking back nostalgically upon 1985. The producer of the show, Jamie Wilson, hadn't yet been born on the day of Live Aid.

So what drew someone of a different generation entirely to want to celebrate that now-distant event? 'My dad was a DJ at Streatham Ice Rink and he adored that era,' recalled Wilson. 'He had a homemade video of the concert at Wembley, which he taped off the telly on the day. It wasn't complete – and someone had recorded an episode of *EastEnders* over the middle of it – but when I was eight or nine, I used to rewind and rewind it, particularly to watch Freddie Mercury. But I really didn't know anything about Bob Geldof and Live Aid until I caught COVID during lockdown.'

His career as a theatre producer took off with a series of West End musical hits, including *Sister Act* and *Mrs Doubtfire*. But, in March 2020, when the British government ordered the closure of all theatres to curb the spread of the pandemic, Wilson moved to Mallorca where, waiting for the result of a COVID test, by chance he came across a copy of Geldof's autobiography, *Is That It?*.

'It's an incredible book,' he said. 'When I finished it, I was so caught up with the story that I watched a documentary the BBC did for the twentieth anniversary of Live Aid. What blew me away was the realisation that this was a time when the world came together and united around something.

Real ordinary people had a voice and felt they could make a significant difference. And that Bob Geldof had done all this when his career was at a low.' It was like an antidote to the isolation of COVID.

'Every musical needs a protagonist to root for and Bob is ours. A musical has got to have stakes, and what stakes could be higher than people starving? After the massive achievement of Band Aid, Bob went out to Africa and realised how much more there was to do.' Band Aid had raised £5 million for emergency food within the first month, but when Geldof arrived in Ethiopia, he found that the food was stuck at the ports because there were no trucks. 'There was a new, even bigger problem.' It was a great End-of-Act-One moment.

Wilson contacted Band Aid. There, its lawyer, John Kennedy, laid down the proviso that the trust must get a cut of the profits – 10 per cent of the ticket prices plus a share of the investors' profits. Bob Geldof laid down his own condition: 'It better not be shite.'

The novelist and comedian John O'Farrell was brought in as writer. 'I came up with something set in Ireland in the 1950s, with nuns and priests singing at this little Irish boy, and the stained-glass Virgin Mary coming alive,' said O'Farrell. 'And then it flipped to 1985 when the Boomtown Rats were not as famous as they had been and Paula was on *The Tube* every week. And she was now the famous one and…'

Bob took one look at it and said: 'This *is* fucking shite. It's the Bob and Paula show, it's supposed to be about Live Aid. Get a new writer.'

Instead, Wilson re-briefed O'Farrell. First, the show had to give Jamie's dad the best night he'd ever had in the theatre. 'He doesn't go very often and he doesn't really like musicals. I've always wanted to do something that would appeal to him. And Live Aid is perfect because he loves the story and he loves the music,' Jamie said. 'But it also had to speak to a young twenty-five-year-old who's never heard of Live Aid, so that they understand that when the world comes together, great things can happen.'

O'Farrell had been on a very different journey. 'In 1985, I was a young lefty, fighting Margaret Thatcher,' he recalled. 'It was during the miners' strike and I was sending food parcels to the pit villages. I was a supercilious student activist who saw Live Aid as an easy wrong turning. I didn't buy the Band Aid single. I was insisting that you don't solve poverty with a song.' He rather looked down on the youth of Middle England rushing off to Live

Aid – people who weren't political, kids whose *Daily Mail*-reading mums dropped them off at the station with their packed lunches for the concert in Wembley. 'People like me, who went on marches, turned our noses up at all that cosy stuff.'

By the time of the Live 8 lobby on the G8, however, O'Farrell had changed his tune. 'Looking back, it was clear that Live Aid had been a big shared national experience. Obviously it didn't eliminate poverty. It didn't change injustice in the world. It wasn't even transformative for Ethiopia. But it changed Britain. It had created a new model of charity. With Sport Aid, I "ran the world". And, with Comic Relief, I became involved. It made a real difference to millions of people. Everyone wanted to be a part of it. There was a generational shift and it started with Live Aid.'

But how were they to tell the story of the past in a way that would make sense to the present? How were they to create a modern morality tale?

The show's narrative device saw a young woman, also born long after the Live Aid concert, bumping into Bob Geldof and asking the cantankerous singer what it was all about. After snapping that he's bored with talking about it, the stage Geldof – not unlike his real-life counterpart – then talks about it at considerable length. Ingeniously, it created a contemporary frame for events now forty years in the past. 'We have a young woman of colour in dialogue with Bob,' said O'Farrell. 'She's saying, "Hang on a minute, I've only just really clocked those colonial-era lyrics." And he says, "I wrote it in a hurry. And that's what I felt at the time." She's able to challenge him, so we get both the perspective of then and now.'

O'Farrell also included an insight absent from almost all accounts of the Live Aid phenomenon. The on-stage Geldof character reflects briefly on the famine in Ireland in the 1840s, in which a million people died and 2 million emigrated – and which, as his compatriot Bono has put it, still lingers as a folk memory in the psyche of Ireland today. O'Farrell continued: 'It was saying to the audience: "Famine doesn't just happen to black people. It's happened in these islands. And because of a similar imbalance in power."'

Just For One Day did not only bring the past into conversation with the present. It also offered an aspiration for the future. 'Sometimes there have been moments in history like Live Aid when problems seem overwhelming and someone like Bob comes along and brings people together,' said

O'Farrell. 'He made it seem possible to care about people you will never meet in a country thousands of miles away.'

Inevitably, a few reviewers resorted to the 'white saviour syndrome' trope, anachronistically judging the events of 1985 as though they had taken place in 2025, but the public verdict was more enthusiastic. *Just For One Day* was the fastest-selling show in the history of the Old Vic and transferred to the West End just before the fortieth anniversary of the 1985 concert.

'Looking around the audience, there were loads of people for whom it wasn't an external thing that they were watching,' said O'Farrell. 'It was part of their memory. Everyone wants to put themselves into that story. I've had so much feedback from people telling me what they were doing that day.'

At the fortieth anniversary gala performance of *Just For One Day* on Shaftesbury Avenue on 13 July 2025, Brian May of Queen made a speech from the stage, declaring: 'This is not just a musical. This is the continuation of a project for humanity.'

⁂

After Live 8 in 2005, Bob Geldof cast around to find new ways to bring Africa into the mainstream of the global economy. In the years that followed the historic Gleneagles deal, Bob and Bono relentlessly pursued the world's most powerful leaders, badgering them to keep their promises. But Geldof had the feeling that he needed, again, to move up a gear. What Africa now needed was foreign investment. Africa had 15 per cent of the world's population, yet only 0.1 per cent of the world's publicly traded companies. 'Aid can only get you so far,' Bob said. 'You need companies that are going to create employment and pay taxes, and these businesses should be owned by African people, not just multinational corporations. What Africa needed to develop at scale was investment.'

In 2007, he was invited by an Asian investment bank to a conference in Hong Kong to talk about the attractions of investing in Africa. The man who had invited him was an investment banker called Philip Pritchard, who remembered: 'Bob came and spoke for one and a half hours, without any notes. He was incredibly eloquent, very passionate, obviously very knowledgeable and persuasive on his subject.'

'Why don't you start a private equity fund for Africa?' one of the bankers said to Pritchard. 'Then we can invest through you into Africa.'

'We are Asian specialists,' Philip replied. 'We don't know Africa. We don't understand Africa. It's not our game.'

The banker turned to Geldof. 'Bob, why don't you start a fund? You know your way around Africa. We can invest through you.'

'I may know Africa, but I don't know finance.'

Almost before they knew it, over a beer back in London, Pritchard and Geldof decided to set up a fund together. They called it 8 Miles, which was the narrowest distance between southern Europe and north Africa, the rich and poor worlds. Bob became its chairman. They would invest, Bob decided, in the areas he had found most important to African development – agriculture, education, healthcare, energy and utilities, telecoms and financial services, transport and logistics. 'I've done aid, I've done politics,' said Bob. 'And now I want to do something with the private sector.'

Geldof's contacts through the big international financial institutions swiftly secured $200 million. He was aiming for $1 billion. But his timing was bad. In 2007–08, the global financial system went into spasm when irresponsible lending by deregulated US banks brought the world to the brink of financial meltdown. 'All the investors who had initially said they would support us, one by one, dropped away,' said Pritchard. 'But we had enough money from the big boys to begin to invest.'

They started with a vineyard and winery in Ethiopia. 'I loved it,' said Bob. 'I went down to Addis and visited the vineyards, which were very old and established, but had been neglected. We cleaned up the vineyards, modernised the technology, provided clean water, built a clinic, a school, proper houses and cleaned up the river. We directly and indirectly transformed the lives of over 5,000 people.'

Soon, 8 Miles opened a line to produce alcopops for Addis's burgeoning social scene. Partnering with entrepreneurs all over Africa, and typically putting in between $10 million and $30 million in each business, 8 Miles invested in the biggest biscuit factory in Nigeria, a chemical factory in Cairo, a bank in Uganda and farms in Benin. They bought into the largest chicken farm in Uganda and, at one point, they were the largest private sector employer in Ghana – which made allegations that Geldof knew nothing about Ghana particularly irritating. Geldof's investment arm was employing more than 11,500 people across Africa. 'I've never had a cent out of the whole thing,' Bob said at the time. 'But it's doing something amazing for Africa. I love it.'

But then the problems began. The local currency devalued by more than 50 per cent while 8 Miles were acquiring a 15 per cent stake in the Nigerian cream-cracker maker. 'The chemical plant in Cairo was affected by an Egyptian military coup,' said Bob. 'In the Ugandan bank, we discovered IT fraud and the chicken farm was hit by an outbreak of bird disease and had to shut for four months just as KFC were entering the market.'

But the chemicals factory in Egypt was successfully sold for a return of nearly 50 per cent, and the Addis winery – now making 13 million bottles a day – trebled in value. But then, literally the week before it was due to be sold, the Ethiopian government declared a state of emergency, the buyer withdrew and the business was eventually sold at a discount.

'First-time funds have a notoriously bad track record, unless they get lucky, and unfortunately, Bob wasn't lucky,' said Sir Graham Wrigley, a former partner in a global private equity firm who had quit to study development economics. 'On top of that he tried to do very pioneering stuff in a very difficult market.'

So would Geldof do it again? 'No, I wouldn't. But, then, I wouldn't do Band Aid again. It was interesting and I learned a lot. We provided over 15,000 people with jobs, clinics, schools and homes. I'm really proud of that.' But this was not the way to pass on the baton.

⁕

There was one thing he did do again. And again. And again. Virtually every day, Bob Geldof receives an email from Joe Cannon at Band Aid. (After years of resisting, he had finally capitulated to the digital age.) Cannon began working for Band Aid early on as an accountant, but became such an integral part of the operation that he is trusted as the first filter for applications for Band Aid cash. His messages go to Geldof and his five fellow Band Aid trustees with a recommendation on whether Band Aid should fund a particular project. 'If Brian Epstein was the fifth Beatle, Joe is the seventh member of the Band Aid Trust,' said Bob.

'Let me put your book in perspective,' Bob said to me during one of the countless interviews we did for this history of Live Aid. 'Look at this.' He pointed to one of the projects from one of Joe Cannon's emails.

An organisation in Ethiopia called Project Harar is asking for £15,000 to train midwives to identify those babies with a cleft lip and palate whose condition is so bad that they will need special bottles to enable them to feed. Without those bottles, and a supplementary milk formula, they will become dangerously malnourished. But once they've gained enough weight, they will be able to undergo corrective surgery. The grant will cover the training, specially designed bottles, the milk formula and support and counselling for the parents.

Geldof paused for a moment after reading it aloud. Four long decades after he first watched Michael Buerk's film of the famine in Ethiopia, he is still overcome with emotion at the problems of children in Ethiopia and at the small part he and Band Aid can play in making their lives better. 'This. Is. What. We. Do,' he said, stabbing his finger emphatically at the email. 'This is what it is all about.'

Every year, around £2 million still comes into Band Aid funds from the airplay of the single or from film companies wanting to use clips of the concerts. Every day, literally, requests come in from charities asking for that cash. 'It never stops,' said Bob. 'There's been a dozen emails in the last ten days.'

A total of £141.8 million has poured into the trust's coffers over the years. Around £43 million was spent in the first year, mainly on emergency food aid. After that, the trustees determined to spend 60 per cent of the money on long-term development projects. 'But it's been flexible,' said Joe Cannon. 'It's very much dependent on need. We take each year as it comes. We want to focus on long-term sustainability, but so long as there is a need for emergency intervention, then that's the role Band Aid plays.' The trust's lack of bureaucracy means that Band Aid has been a very nimble organisation. 'We are often first responders.'

'In the early days, it was a nightmare,' said one trustee, Lord Michael Grade. 'The aid agencies were so political in their rivalry with one another, but we cut through the bureaucracy and came to see which agencies were reliable.' The Band Aid trustees have been conservative in their choice of partners. 'We are very focused on the fact that this is the public's money at the end of the day,' said Cannon, whose day job is with the international accountancy firm, EY; he works for Band Aid without pay in his own time. 'So we typically only work with established organisations. They must have a good track record in terms of public profile, accountability and compliance with Charity Commission filings and so on, and they must be very transparent in terms of the budgets they ask us to fund.'

'We don't give to organisations for overheads and administration,' said Harvey Goldsmith. 'We only give to projects. And if they are initiated by a Western NGO, they have to be designed to train the local population to take over.' Nor will Band Aid enter into long-term funding arrangements. It won't pay ongoing annual salary costs. 'And we don't necessarily give all the money. If Band Aid agrees to give part of the money for a project, our reputation often persuades other donors to give as well.'

Over the years, the Band Aid Trust has consistently been given a clean bill of health by the Charity Commission, which has only twice raised issues with the trust. One was to advise it to take out insurance. And, on the other occasion, the commission wrote to John Kennedy expressing concern that he might be a 'dominant trustee' who exercised 'excessive control over the charity's operation'. The Band Aid lawyer replied: 'Really? Have you met Bob Geldof?'

⁂

Band Aid's unique status means it can fund maverick projects which other aid agencies place outside their development guidelines. A classic example of that came in 2009 when, on the twenty-fifth anniversary of the Ethiopian famine, Bob and I returned to its epicentre on the plains of Korem. A quarter of a century later, in the very place where so many people had died, Geldof came face-to-face for the first time with some of the survivors.

'We have just come back to pay our respects,' the singer told a group of men, curious at our arrival. The men thanked him.

'We want you to pass on our thanks to the brothers and sisters outside Ethiopia who helped us,' said Alana Abraham, aged fifty-two, who had arrived at Korem in 1985 with three brothers. He was the only one to survive.

'What I remember of the people was their immense dignity in the face of everything,' Bob told them.

They smiled wanly and thanked him, but it was not how the victims remembered it. 'We were reduced to a sub-human situation,' said

Gebremedhin Alemu, now aged sixty, who had walked 100 kilometres with his wife and six children in search of food aid. 'When someone died, we went to bury him, and by the time we came back, someone else had died.'

'People were buried like animals,' said Haile Melicot, now fifty. 'There was no system. No honour. People were just put into mass graves without anyone knowing who had been buried where. We were so weak that the aid agencies had to pay people to carry the bodies from the camp up here to the burial place.'

'Our respect for you, our brother in hard times, is boundless,' Gebremedhin told Geldof. 'At a time when our dignity was questioned, you came and paid for people with energy to bury our dead.'

This was not what Geldof had expected, but the wave of gratitude was overwhelming and humbling.

'Is there anything else we could do for you?' asked Bob. In reply, the men told him of their lives since, of years of good harvests, of the economic booming of the little town, of plenty and prosperity. 'One farmer even has a minibus,' said Alana Abraham, in awe at the very idea.

But there was one thing they lacked because it was not a priority for the government or aid agencies.

They would like a fence around the mass grave areas to stop animals from trampling on the dignity of the dead.

Band Aid would build one, Geldof said. The joy of the survivors took him utterly by surprise. They shrieked their pleasure, hugged the Irishman and turned around to share the good news with the rest of the crowd.

After we said farewell, Geldof walked away to the church at the other side of the graveyard. There, he stared at the vast plain of Korem, across which large rocks seemed to have been randomly scattered. Each stone marked a communal grave in which between eight and twenty people were buried. The fence would turn them into a massive cemetery.

'If we lose our sense of shared humanity,' he said, 'something withers inside us.'

❧

With the fortieth anniversary of the Live Aid concert, the trustees of Band Aid began thinking about how the organisation should pass on the baton. The same six men had been on the board of the trust for all those years.

Though Bob Geldof was the chair, the six had had equal voices in the decision-making and they were now all in their seventies or eighties. Was it time to wind down the organisation?

'We get constant requests from TV companies and film companies wanting clippage and we charge them a fortune to use it,' said Harvey Goldsmith. 'And that money goes back into the funds, so it's never-ending.' On top of that, there are the royalties, bequests and money from YouTube. 'It's the public's money and somebody will have to keep looking after it,' said Lord Grade. 'We have duties of governance and stewardship.'

Spending £2 million annually is not particularly burdensome, said Kennedy. 'We could capitalise our income stream and spend the capital sum in one year. But as long as we are able personally, I would prefer to keep collecting the income and spending it.' Harvey Goldsmith was more ambiguous. 'Should there be a legacy?' he asked. 'I guess maybe there should. It's something all of the trustees will have to sit down and debate properly.'

Surprisingly, perhaps, it is Geldof who sounds a different note. 'I think we've done our job,' he said. 'Band Aid was meant to last a week. It was supposed to be all over by Christmas in 1984. We set out to do two things. The first was to help those in the poorest parts of the world realise the potential of their life. But the other, which I'd strenuously argue was of equal importance, was to awaken the public to the obscenity of wanton need in a world of overflowing plenty. Both were achieved.'

But he was clearly uneasy at the sense of celebration which surrounded the fortieth anniversary. 'On the day, people kept saying "Happy Live Aid Day, Bob", as though it was a sort of Paddy's Day for England,' Geldof complained. 'What people were celebrating was their own nostalgic view of a time when it seemed possible to be a small cog in an instrument of change. And something that "worked".'

Geldof was not entirely uncomfortable with that. 'On the one hand, they were, rightly, celebrating themselves, and music, which is the joy that has resonated down the years.' But it remained nostalgia. 'At no point did it seize the public imagination as a continuing issue that they needed to address.'

Times have changed. 'The world is a fearsomely dangerous place,' Geldof recently said in an email to his fellow Band Aid trustees, 'and the politics that govern that world have moved inexorably away from the politics we grew up with and were able to manipulate. We are all old men. We have little to say to this anymore, and whatever we have to say is easily dismissed as being from another time. Band Aid's time has been and, if not gone, could go relatively quietly and easily. We never wanted or intended to stick around forever, so I believe it would be elegant to exit the stage quietly, subject to finding a mechanism that would allow for the distributions of the legacy amounts we still receive. I personally would like to bow out. I feel I'm done.'

❧

In one sense, the baton has already been passed. Live Aid and its legacy had a direct impact upon the latter part of the twentieth century, an impact that has continued into the twenty-first. Around 1.9 billion people around the world watched the 1985 concert; nearly 40 per cent of the world population, said *Guinness World Records*. The concert, the largest fundraising event the world had ever seen, was testament to music's power to unite the world. But it was so much more.

'Band Aid tapped into an entire generation who had never donated to charity,' said Midge Ure. 'Charity was something that old people did and we were appealing to the young. Kids today don't think that charity is a fuddy-duddy thing to do. They don't feel that it's uncool to care. I believe that Band Aid is directly responsible for that.' It touches something deeper, according to the doyen of development experts, Kevin Watkins. 'It wasn't a blip of altruism. It was a major movement – an unbelievably powerful demonstration of the empathy which fuels compassion. There is something amazing about the human spirit that drives people to do that. And that's what Live Aid tapped into.'

It was also a vivid demonstration that the individual is not powerless, not least in the person of Geldof himself. 'He was a charismatic leader,' said Andrew Zweck, the production manager for both Live Aid and Live 8. 'He was inspiring, he motivated us. The greatest legacy of Live Aid for me, personally, is the example of how Bob Geldof's leadership demonstrated the power of the individual. The voice and action of just one person started a movement that made a massive difference.'

Geldof gave others the confidence that they could, in their different ways, do the same. Michael Grade's showbiz background meant he knew what was involved in getting a big event together. 'In the end, these things only happen through one person's ability, energy and chutzpah,' he said. 'All the blagging to get people to the studio, to get people to Wembley, all the egos and the managers. It must have been an absolute nightmare. But he was determined to do it.'

The same thing applied in the political arena, said the veteran BBC man, Michael Buerk. 'Geldof, for all his foul-mouthed scruffiness, was and is a man of extraordinary sensitivity, intelligence and drive. He short-circuited governments, officialdom, tyranny. You can argue about how effective it really was in a historical sense, but he made whole nations of ordinary people feel they could make a difference. Articulate and coarse, he was shocking yet wonderful and spoke for everyman. I treasure the moment he walked up to Colonel Mengistu, one of the most evil rulers of modern times, and called him a murdering cunt to his face.'

Bob Geldof is what justice looks like when it runs out of patience. 'He's just impossible to argue with,' said Bono. 'I don't believe any of my activism would have happened without his inspiration.'

Something very special happened in 1985, said Buerk, and some traces of it can still be seen. Live Aid was 'a genuine British cultural moment', said the debt campaigner Adrian Lovett. 'Anyone who was then between the ages of ten and fifty, including at least a couple of prime ministers, experienced it very profoundly at that time.'

Writing in what was perhaps the most thoughtful journal of the era, *Marxism Today*, Martin Jacques and Stuart Hall argued that Live Aid dealt a severe blow to the fortunes of Thatcherism and the prevailing ideology of selfishness. It shifted the political centre of gravity for the decade: 'No other cultural form could have played the political role that rock did in the Band Aid/Live Aid phenomenon.' Through Geldof, politics suddenly found itself in touch with the cultural language which most authentically expressed how young people experience the world. He symbolised the fusion of two worlds usually kept well apart. Perhaps, more significantly, Sport Aid – which called on people to be participants, not just spectators – represented a key moment in the erosion of the Thatcherite worldview.

Live Aid did not just capture the zeitgeist, it created it.

By staging concerts on both sides of the Atlantic, Live Aid also shifted the agenda from the national to the international. And it set out only to raise large amounts of money, subliminally throwing the spotlight onto what Jacques and Hall called 'the underlying economic relationships between the First World and the Third World'. Aid was moved from the realm of charity to the world of politics. The traditional left had long regarded charity as a sop, which eases the conscience but does not tackle the problem at the root. 'Of course, it is true that famine cannot be permanently averted in Africa by charity alone. But this partly misses the point... Politically, the state is not likely to do much unless the people are pushing it.' Through their support for Live Aid, the people were mounting an attack on the current set of national priorities.

Interestingly, Michael Buerk, whose politics were considerably to the right of *Marxism Today*, agreed: 'Market-driven individualism might work better with the grain of human nature, it might make most of us more prosperous, but there was something obscene about us putting up mountains of food we could not eat while millions starved to death, a few hours' flying time away.'

Geldof himself intuitively knew all this. 'Live Aid was to do with charity – that great urge of shared humanness, compassion and sympathy for another hurt person,' he said. 'But it was also profoundly political. When people drop a quid into the box for Oxfam or Comic Relief, it looks like charity. Yet if that simple act is done in enough numbers, it becomes intensely political. That pound in the box is the equivalent of a tick on the ballot.'

Live 8 took this unspoken politics and made it shout out loud. Geldof had participated in a majority-African analysis of the problems of the continent in the Commission for Africa. It came up with a two-sided solution. African governments needed to be more honest and open, more focused on the poor and less corrupt. Rich countries needed to stop loading the dice against Africa and to create a more just economic and political relationship in which partnership must replace the exercise of power. Given all that, it was paradoxical to say the least that Geldof – who on his first visit to Ethiopia had forbidden press photographers from taking photos of the white rock star with black babies – continued to be lambasted for peddling patronising colonial stereotypes. He shrugged it off and, at the launch of Live 8, declared that 'Live Aid joyously, enthusiastically, opened up the avenues of possibility. Finally, Live 8 invites you to walk down them.'

Bob Geldof was to be the Pied Piper.

The ten Live 8 concerts drew even bigger combined audiences than had Live Aid. On the day, Bob announced from the stage that more than 3 billion people were watching. Later, faultfinders suggested that the global audience was only around 2 billion. But it was still the largest the world had ever seen. More significantly, it shifted people's thinking from raising money to thinking about the underlying structures that keep people poor.

But, most dramatically, Live 8 was the moment when politicians realised that they could not ignore the wishes of a general public who had begun to exercise power outside the normal electoral process. Some 38 million people signed the Live 8/Make Poverty History petition. Before Band Aid, Africa was hardly discussed at G7 summits; after Live Aid, it became a recurring focus for the world leaders' meetings.

Yet although Live 8 was the bigger event – both in terms of the global audience, the amount of money it prodded world leaders to give at Gleneagles, and the millions of lives that were saved – it has not left the same mark on public consciousness as that first 1985 concert: Live Aid was a watershed.

⁂

The mood of public and political empathy reached a high-water mark with Gleneagles. In the UK, politicians of all parties now agreed that the government should finally reach the UN target of spending 7 pence out of every pound £10 of our national income on aid. Such was the consensus that the Conservative government of David Cameron enshrined the 0.7 per cent target in law. Extreme poverty across the world declined at its fastest rate in human history. In 1985, 40 per cent of people were living on less than one dollar a day; by 2005, that number had halved. On average, poor people lived five years longer than before. The human condition was now better 'than at any time in history', calculated Bill Gates.

But then, in 2007–08, came the global financial crisis. Greedy bankers, driven by short-term profit, recklessly handed out sub-prime loans to people who couldn't repay when interest rates rose and house prices fell. The whole banking system teetered on the edge of collapse, forcing governments to bail out the bankers. The cost was borne by ordinary taxpayers through public spending cuts. The fallout for poorer people was devastating. Jobs were lost. Homes were repossessed. Austerity measures hit low-income families hardest. Inequality widened. Ironically, the financial elite recovered swiftly – resulting in a collapse of trust in political parties, experts, economists and global institutions. It was the start of a long path that would lead to Donald Trump, Brexit and the far-right rise across Europe. Populists exploited the angry belief that globalisation had enriched elites and abandoned the average voter.

When COVID came, ravaging national economies, and when Putin invaded Ukraine, pushing up defence spending throughout Europe, leaders like Donald Trump and Boris Johnson axed aid budgets. There was little protest from ordinary voters who felt besieged by the turn of events. In the UK, the Conservatives slashed aid spending by a third to its lowest percentage for 100 years. An incoming Labour government cut it further, to just 0.3 per cent of our national earnings. Aid was an easy target for governments as they pitted the poor at home against the poor overseas.

But it was in the United States that the assault on aid was most destructive. In 2025, the Trump administration cut 83 per cent of USAID's programmes and slashed $60 billion from the aid budget. In July, the US Senate, with a casting vote from vice-president J.D. Vance, cut $9 billion from foreign aid funds previously approved for spending by Congress. According to the medical journal, *The Lancet*, as many as 14 million children could die by 2030 as a result of all this. The cuts were overseen by the world's richest man, Elon Musk.

Bob Geldof was withering in his condemnation of 'the thuggery of Musk, Vance and Trump'. At the launch of a series of BBC/CNN documentaries to mark the fortieth anniversary of Live Aid, he attacked them as 'abject fools' and a 'confederacy of dunces'. Elon Musk had recently claimed that no one had died because of the cuts, but Geldof pointed to the famine in South Sudan as just one place where that was demonstrably untrue.

Musk had boasted of having fed the US overseas aid programme 'into the wood chipper'. Geldof was disgusted. 'The strongest nation on Earth, the most powerful man on the planet and the richest individual ever seen in the history of our world cackle over feeding the most vulnerable people in the world into the wood chipper,' he thundered. 'Ladies and gentlemen, there is something seriously fucked up about that.'

So had everything that Live Aid stood for come to naught? Or could that era of compassion and generosity ever reassert itself? Part of Geldof says it can't happen again. 'In 1985, the lingua franca of the world was not English, it was pop music,' he reflected. 'Rock 'n' roll is the most powerful art there has ever been – but it has ceased to be the spine of our culture. That culture has fragmented.' When Geldof watched Michael Buerk's fateful broadcast from the famished fields of Ethiopia on the BBC's *Six O'Clock News*, he was not alone. More than half the television sets in the country were tuned to that same bulletin. Around the world, 425 television stations carried it. Half a billion people saw it.

But that was an analogue world. Today's digital world is atomised. People don't watch the same thing at the same time on a limited number of television channels. The younger generations hardly watch television at all. Streaming, time-shifting, social media, podcasting and smartphones have dissolved shared experience. 'Rock 'n' roll was a gathering technology,' said Geldof. 'Social media is an isolating one.' COVID has only added to the general feeling of powerless and despair.

Together, Live Aid and Live 8, he added, drove something like £50 billion towards the poorest people on the planet. 'But that's not possible now,' he said, 'largely because people are so frightened and exhausted that there isn't the emotional bandwidth to deal with the terror of Ukraine, the horror of Gaza, let alone asking them to pay attention to what's happening in Sudan literally right now.'

And yet, if the obstacles to a resurgence of Live Aid-style empathy seem formidable, it should be remembered that the obstacles to the original in 1984–85 were formidable too. Then, as now, was a time of global indifference and structural impediments. Western governments were preoccupied with Cold War geopolitics, viewing Ethiopia through the lens of East–West rivalry rather than humanitarian need. Economics were dominated by an ideology of individualism. Scepticism about foreign aid was widespread. African crises were seen as distant and inevitable. Economic powers like the IMF saw it as normal for poor countries to cut their health and education spending to pay foreign debts. Poverty in Africa was seen as the result of incompetence, tribalism and corruption, not global injustice. Live Aid overcame all this – and staged a massive awakening of our global conscience.

The righteous indignation which fired all that has not died away in Bob Geldof. He saved his fiercest invective for Elon Musk. 'That ketamine-crazed fool, that sociopath, recently said that the great weakness of Western civilisation is empathy. No, Elon, the glue of civilisation is empathy,' said Geldof in an angry counterblast. Back in 1985, the world celebrated the idea that greed was good. 'Live Aid was a reaction to that. There's no such thing as society? The 13th of July 1985 emphatically said there was. Greed is good? No, greed was exposed as callous and stupid.'

'Live Aid was the first moment when the whole world was able to see, hear, listen and connect,' said Jamie Wilson, the producer of *Just For One Day*. 'It was an extraordinary moment in history that should never be forgotten. We need now to look back at it and celebrate what worked, and learn from the things that have changed. As Bob says in the show, every generation fails in some way – but the vast majority of what Live Aid stood for still stands today.'

Live Aid tells a great story of commitment, leadership, organisation and belief. It led us to a place where we could hear what Abraham Lincoln called 'the better angels of our nature'. 'We were led there by our bands,' said Bob, 'by musicians who sometimes articulate better for us what we want to say than we can manage to say with everyday words, for they speak a language – the language of music – which is understood by all humanity.'

Live 8 was the sum of our longing for universal decency. 'What a glorious, magnificent day, what a defeat of cynicism,' Geldof declared as we stood together watching the TV monitor at the side of the Live 8 stage. 'Four continents, nine countries and their greatest artists, ten cities and their greatest sites, millions physically present and thousands of millions spiritually there, as we watched this one concert, one moment, one idea winding itself around what was truly one world that afternoon.'

Forty years on, he reflected that 'if we ever need another event like it, a new generation will know what must be done and they will not fail. These younger people will say, "We're not gonna do it like they did." And they will be right, because that wouldn't work. But they will find their own cause and think of their own way of doing it. And if that's what we leave behind, that will do for me.'

※

Strange things do happen around Bob Geldof. In 1977, when the Boomtown Rats were trying to make it in the United States, a marketing man at Mercury Records, Mike Bone, had a brilliant idea.

'I came up with the idea of sending out dead rats with promotional copies of the album to radio stations,' Bone said. 'I thought this was in keeping with the band's "fuck it" attitude.' So he contacted a biological supply house in Wisconsin. 'I ordered fifty dead rats to be sent to my office. The rats were double-bagged in formaldehyde, but they still had a laboratory smell about them.'

When Mercury's general manager heard of the wheeze, he marched into Bone's office and instructed him that, under no circumstances, was he to send them to the rock radio stations. So Bone got the boy in the Mercury mail room in East Wacker Drive, Chicago, to send them to a store on Clark Street downtown: 'the record store created a window display using the dead rats and Boomtown Rats album covers and posters.' The stunt was a success only in that one of the Chicago news stations did a segment on how disgusting the window display was: 'The record got not one single play,' Geldof recalled.

What was not recorded was the name of the mail boy who posted out the dead rats from the basement of the record company headquarters. His name was Bob Prevost. He had just completed a degree in mathematics at Villanova University and had taken a vacation job back home in Chicago to fill the gap before entering the Augustine seminary in St Louis, Missouri. 'I've only just heard what happened to him,' Geldof told me, as I was completing this book. 'In May 2025, he was elected pope. He's now Leo XIV.'

Bob works in mysterious ways.

ACKNOWLEDGEMENTS

Writing this book has taken forty years. I'd like to thank all those who have assisted me over that time, either in one-to-one interviews, or in other ways. I'm grateful to Bob Geldof, John Kennedy, Harvey Goldsmith, Michael Grade and Midge Ure – members of the Band Aid Trust, and Joe Cannon, the Trust's moneyman – all of whom were immensely generous with their time.

Thank you to: Adrian Lovett, Alastair Campbell, Alula Pankhurst, Andrew Zweck, Angus Macqueen, Ann Pettifor, Annie Lennox, Barry Winkleman, Ben Jones, Berhane Deressa, Bernard Doherty, Bill Gates, Birhan Woldu, Bono, Brad Pitt, Sir Brian Barder, Bridget Angear, Carole Smith, Dame Claire Bertschinger, Dee Flowers, Dido, Sir Elton John, Emma Freud, Fatima Muhammed, Fran Healy, Gary Lightbody, Gayle Smith, George Clooney, Sir Graham Wrigley, Grant McKee, Br Gus O'Keefe, Hugh Goyder, Ian Johnson, Fr Jack Finucane, Jamie Drummond, Jamie Wilson, Jeanne Marine, Jill Sinclair, Jill Turton, John Maguire, John O'Farrell, Justin Forsyth, Kate Garvey, Kevin Cahill, Kevin Watkins, Kirsty McNeill, Kofi Annan, Kumi Naidoo, Kurt Jansson, Larry Magid, Laurie Lee, Sir Lenny Henry, Baroness Liz Lloyd, Lucy Matthew, Marsha Hunt, Meles Zenawi, Michael Buerk, Lord Michael Grade, Lord Michael Jay, Michael Priestley, Michel Camdessus, Mike Shrimpton, Mike Wooldridge, Ms. Dynamite, Sir Myles Wickstead, Nick Mason, Lord Nick Stern, Sir Nigel Sheinwald, Olly Buston, Paddy Coulter, Sir Paul McCartney, Paula Yates, Pete Briquette, Pete Smith, Peter Souter, Philip Pritchard, Richard Curtis, Baroness Shriti Vadera, Susan Sarandon, Sting, Tim Rice-Oxley, Tim Robbins, Youssou N'Dour and Zita Lloyd. I also drew on the writings of: Barbara Hendrie, Dawit Wolde Giorgis, Gebru Tareke, Laurence Binet, Mark Saunders, Nick Sireau and Oliver Harvey. My thanks to them.

Particular thanks to Justin Forsyth for allowing me access to his private Downing Street diaries.

Thanks to my publisher, Pete Selby, for his long commitment to this book and the interweaving of pop, politics and poverty, which make it unique, as well as sharing his detailed knowledge of the music industry. Thanks to James Lilford for oiling the wheels of the publishing process with such skill. Particular thanks to my agent, Adrian Sington of Kruger Cowne, for his stalwart reassurance throughout the many vicissitudes of this project. And thank you to my eagle-eyed copy-editor Nige Tassell, who rescued me from repetitions as well as grammatical solecisms, and the very sharp typesetter Marie Doherty who spotted omissions as well as errors and did sterling work on the index.

Special thanks to those who read the manuscript as it was nearing completion: Ian Johnson, former vice president for sustainable development at the World Bank, my brother Tony Vallely, who read with an accountant's forensic eye, and to my son, Thomas Vallely, who read with the sceptical eyes of an historian. But above all, my most heartfelt thanks are to my wife and life-partner Christine Morgan, my first and best editor always, without whom this book would not have been possible, nor would so much else.

INDEX

The team at New Modern would like to thank the following individuals:

Nige Tassell for copy-editing

Jane Donovan for proofreading

Marie Doherty for typesetting

Paul Palmer-Edwards for cover design

Amanda Russell for image research

Lizzie Dorney-Kingdom for publicity

Charlotte Rose, Andreina Brezzo and the team
at Simon & Schuster UK for sales and distribution